GLOBAL STUDIES

CHINA

D0139338

TWELFTH EDITION

Dr. Suzanne Ogden
Northeastern University

OTHER BOOKS IN THE GLOBAL STUDIES SERIES
- Africa
- Europe
- Islam and the Muslim World
- India and South Asia
- Japan and the Pacific Rim
- Latin America
- The Middle East
- Russia, the Baltics and Eurasian Republics, and Central/Eastern Europe

 **Contemporary Learning Series**

2460 Kerper Blvd., Dubuque, IA 52001

Visit us on the Internet
http://www.mhcls.com

Staff

Larry Loeppke	*Managing Editor*
Beth Kundert	*Production Manager*
Jill Peter	*Senior Developmental Editor*
Lori Church	*Permissions Coordinator*
Maggie Lytle	*Cover*
Tara McDermott	*Design Specialist*
Jean Smith	*Project Manager*
Sandy Wille	*Project Manager*

Sources for Statistical Reports

U.S. State Department *Background Notes* (2003)
C.I.A. *World Factbook* (2002)
World Bank *World Development Reports* (2002/2003)
UN *Population and Vital Statistics Reports* (2002/2003)
World Statistics in Brief (2002)
The Statesman's Yearbook (2003)
Population Reference Bureau *World Population Data Sheet* (2002)
The World Almanac (2003)
The Economist Intelligence Unit (2003)

Copyright

Cataloging in Publication Data
Main entry under title: Global Studies: China. 12th ed.
      1. Africa—History—1976–. 2. Taiwan—History—1945–.
I. Title:China. II. Ogden, Suzanne, *comp*.
ISBN 978–0–07–337991–3   ISSN 1050–2025
MHID 0–07–337991–3

Compositor: Carlisle Publishing Services

Twelfth Edition

Printed in the United States of America   1234567890QPDQPD987   Printed on Recycled Paper

CHINA

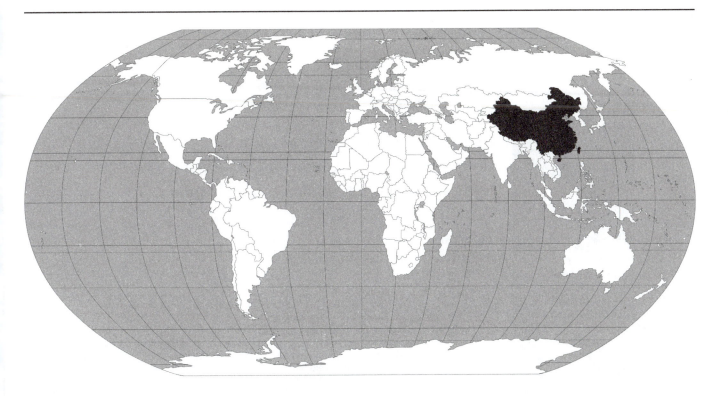

AUTHOR/EDITOR

Dr. Suzanne Ogden

Dr. Suzanne Ogden is a professor in the Political Science Department at Northeastern University, and a research associate at the Fairbank Center for East Asian Studies, Harvard University. She writes primarily about development, democracy, and political culture in China. Her most recent manuscript, *Inklings of Democracy in China,* was published by Harvard University Press in 2002. She is now working on the impact of stakeholder participation in the management of China's river basins on environmental sustainability.

Contents

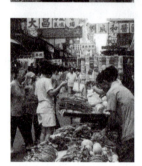

Using *Global Studies: China*

THE GLOBAL STUDIES SERIES

The Global Studies series was created to help readers acquire a basic knowledge and understanding of the regions and countries in the world. Each volume provides a foundation of °information—geographic, cultural, economic, political, historical, artistic, and religious—that will allow readers to better assess the current and future problems within these countries and regions and to comprehend how events there might affect their own well-being. In short, these volumes present the background information necessary to respond to the realities of our global age.

Each of the volumes in the Global Studies series is crafted under the careful direction of an author/editor—an expert in the area under study. The author/editors teach and conduct research and have traveled extensively through the regions about which they are writing.

MAJOR FEATURES OF THE GLOBAL STUDIES SERIES

The Global Studies volumes are organized to provide concise information on the regions and countries within those areas under study. The major sections and features of the books are described here.

Country Reports

Concise reports are written for each of the countries within the region under study. These reports are the heart of each Global Studies volume. *Global Studies: China, Twelfth Edition,* contains 3 country reports: People's Republic of China, Hong Kong, and Taiwan.

The country reports are composed of five standard elements. Each report contains a detailed map that visually positions the country among its neighboring states; a summary of statistical information; a current essay providing important historical, geographical, political, cultural, and economic information; a historical timeline, offering a convenient visual survey of a few key historical events; and four "graphic indicators," with summary statements about the country in terms of development, freedom, health/welfare, and achievements.

A Note on the Statistical Reports

The statistical information provided for each country has been drawn from a wide range of sources. (The most frequently referenced are listed on page ii.) Every effort has been made to provide the most current and accurate information available. However, sometimes the information cited by these sources differs to some extent; and, all too often, the most current information available for some countries is somewhat dated. Aside from these occasional difficulties, the statistical summary of each country is generally quite complete and up to date. Care should be taken, however, in using these statistics (or, for that matter, any published statistics) in making hard comparisons among countries. We have also provided comparable statistics for the United States and Canada, which can be found on pages 12 and 13.

World Press Articles

Within each Global Studies volume is reprinted a number of articles carefully selected by our editorial staff and the author/editor from a broad range of international periodicals and newspapers. The articles have been chosen for currency, interest, and their differing perspectives on the subject countries. There are 33 articles in *Global Studies: China, Twelfth Edition.*

The articles section is preceded by an annotated table of contents. This resource offers a brief summary of each article.

WWW Sites

An extensive annotated list of selected World Wide Web sites can be found on page 10 in this edition of *Global Studies: China.* In addition, the URL addresses for country-specific Web sites are provided on the statistics page of most countries. All of the Web site addresses were correct and operational at press time. Instructors and students alike are urged to refer to those sites often to enhance their understanding of the region and to keep up with current events.

Glossary, Bibliography, Index

At the back of each Global Studies volume, readers will find a glossary of terms and abbreviations, which provides a quick reference to the specialized vocabulary of the area under study and to the standard abbreviations used throughout the volume.

Following the glossary is a bibliography that lists general works, national histories, and current-events publications and periodicals that provide regular coverage on China.

The index at the end of the volume is an accurate reference to the contents of the volume. Readers seeking specific information and citations should consult this standard index.

Currency and Usefulness

Global Studies: China, like the other Global Studies volumes, is intended to provide the most current and useful information available necessary to understand the events that are shaping the cultures of the region today.

This volume is revised on a regular basis. The statistics are updated, regional essays and country reports revised, and world press articles replaced. In order to accomplish this task, we turn to our author/editor, our advisory boards, and—hopefully—to you, the users of this volume. Your comments are more than welcome. If you have an idea that you think will make the next edition more useful, an article or bit of information that will make it more current, or a general comment on its organization, content, or features that you would like to share with us, please send it in for serious consideration.

Selected World Wide Web Sites for *Global Studies: China*

(Some Web sites continually change their structure and content, so the information listed here may not always be available. Check our Web site at: http://www.dushkin.com/online/ —Ed.)

GENERAL SITES

Access Asia
http://www.accessasia.org

Asia Intelligence Home Page
http://www.asiaint.com/

Asia News
http://www.asianews.it/view.php?l=en&art=537

Asia Resources on the World Wide Web
http://www.aasianst.org/wwwchina.htm

Asia Source (Asia Society)
http://www.asiasource.org

Asia Times
http://www.atimes.com/

BBC News, China
http://news.bbc.co.uk/1/hi/in_depth/asia_pacific/2004/china/default.stm

Brookings Institution, Center for Northeast Asian Studies
http://www.brookings.edu/fp/cnaps/center_hp.htm

PEOPLE'S REPUBLIC OF CHINA

Beijing International
http://www.ebeijing.gov.cn/Tour/default.htm

Carnegie Endowment for International Peace: China Program
http://www.ceip.org/files/events/events.asp?pr=16&EventID=674

Center for US-China Policy Studies
http://cuscps.sfsu.edu/

China Business Information Center
http://www.cbiz.cn/

The China Daily
http://www.ceip.org/files/events/events.asp?pr=16&EventID=674

China Development Brief: Index of International NGOS in China
http://www.chinadevelopmentbrief.com/dingo/index.asp

China Digital News
http://www.ceip.org/files/events/events.asp?pr=16&EventID=674

China Elections and Governance
http://chinaelections.org/en/default.asp

China Law and Governance Review
http://chinareview.info/

China Law Home Page
http://www.qis.net/chinalaw/

China's Ministry of Foreign Affairs
http://www.fmprc.gov.cn/eng/wjb/zzjg/ldmzs/gjlb/3488/t17367.htm

China Online
http://www.chinaonline.com

China Related Web Sites
http://orpheus.ucsd.edu/chinesehistory/othersites.html

China Study Group
http://www.chinastudygroup.org/

China's Official Gateway to News & Information
http://www.china.org.cn

Chinese Human Rights Web
http://www.chinesehumanrightsreader.org

Chinese Law in English
http://www.qis.net/chinalaw/lawtran1.htm

Chinese Military Power Research Sites
http://www.comw.org/cmp/links.html

Cold War International History Project
http://wwics.si.edu/index.cfm?topic_id=1409&fuseaction=topics.home

Congressional-Executive Commission on China
http://www.cecc.gov/

CSIS International Security Program
http://www.chinatopnews.com/MainNews/English/

East Turkestan Information Center
http://www.uygur.org/enorg/h_rights/human_r.htm

Foreign Policy in Focus
http://www.fpif.org/index.html

Foreign Policy in Focus Policy Brief Missile Defense & China
http://www.fpif.org/briefs/vol6/v6n03taiwan.html
http://www.uschinaedu.org-Program.asp

Human Rights in China
http://iso.hrichina.org/public/index

Inside China Today—Groups Urge EU to Censure China at UN Over Rights Learn Chinese with Homestay in China
http://www.lotusstudy.com/

Jamestown Foundation
http://www.jamestown.org/

Mainland Affairs Council Malaysia News Center—China News
http://news.newmalaysia.com/world/china/

Modern East-West Encounters
http://www.thescotties.pwp.blueyonder.co.uk/ew-asiapacific.htm

National Committee on U.S. China Relations
http://www.ncuscr.org/

Needham Research Institute, Cambridge, England
http://www.nri.org.uk/

New Malaysia
http://news.newmalaysia.com/world/china/

People's Daily Online
http://english.peopledaily.com.cn/

SCMP.com - Asia's leading English news channel
http://www.scmp.com/

Sinologisches Seminar, Heidelberg University
http://www.sino.uni-heidelberg.de/

SinoWisdom
http://www.sinowisdom.com/main.htm

Status of Population and Family Planning Programme in China by Province
http://www.unescap.org/esid/psis/population/database/chinadata/intro.htm

Tiananmen Square, 1989, The Declassified Story: A National Security Archive Briefing Book
http://www.gwu.edu/~nsarchiv/NSAEBB/NSAEBB16/documents/index.html

The Chairman Smiles - Chinese Posters 1966–1976
http://www.iisg.nl/exhibitions/chairman/chnintro2.html

The China Journal
http://rspas.anu.edu.au/ccc/journal.htm

The Chinese Military Power Page–The Commonwealth Institute
http://www.comw.org/cmp/

U.S. China Education Programs
http://www.fpif.org/briefs/vol6/v6n03taiwan.html

U.S. Embassy
http://www.usembasy-china.org.cn

U.S. International Trade Commission
http://www.usitc.gov/

UCSD Modern Chinese History Site
http://www.usitc.gov/

United Nations: China's Millennium Goals, Progress
http://www.unchina.org/MDGConf/html/reporten.pdf

United Nations Human Development Reports, China
http://hdr.undp.org/

US-China Education and Culture Exchange Center
www.uschinaedu.edu

World Link Education's China Programs
http://www.worldlinkedu.com/?source=overture&OVRAW=List%
20of%20Chinese%20language%20television%20channels&OVKEY=
chinese%20language&OVMTC=advanced

Xinhua Net
http://news.xinhuanet.com/english/

Yahoo! News and Media Newspapers by Region Countries China
http://dir.yahoo.com/News_and_Media/Newspapers/By_Region/
Countries/China/

HONG KONG

Chinese University of Hong Kong
http://www.usc.cuhk.edu.hk/uscen.asp

CIA
http://www.cia.gov/cia/publications/factbook/geos/hk.html

Civic Exchange, Christine Loh's Newsletter
http://www.civic-exchange.org/n_home.htm

Clean the Air
http://www.cleartheair.org.hk/

Hong Kong Special Administrative Region Government Information
http://www.info.gov.hk/eindex.htm

Hong Kong Transition Project, 1982–2007
http://www.hkbu.edu.hk/~hktp/

Shenzhen Government Online
http://english.sz.gov.cn/

South China Morning Post
http://www.scmp.com/

TAIWAN

Mainland Affairs Council
http://www.mac.gov.tw/

My Egov
http://english.www.gov.tw/e-Gov/index.jsp

Taipei Times
http://www.taipeitimes.com/News/

Taipei Yearbook
http://english.taipei.gov.tw/yearbook/index.jsp?recordid=7345

Taiwan Economic and Cultural Representative Office in the U.S.
http://www.tecro.org/

Taiwan Headlines
http://www.taiwanheadlines.gov.tw/mp.asp

Taiwan News
http://www.etaiwannews.com/Taiwan/

See individual country report pages for additional Web sites.

The United States (United States of America)

GEOGRAPHY

Area in Square Miles (Kilometers):
3,717,792 (9,629,091) (about 1/2 the size of Russia)

Capital (Population): Washington, DC (3,997,000)

Environmental Concerns: air and water pollution; limited freshwater resources, desertification; loss of habitat; waste disposal; acid rain

Geographical Features: vast central plain, mountains in the west, hills and low mountains in the east; rugged mountains and broad river valleys in Alaska; volcanic topography in Hawaii

Climate: mostly temperate, but ranging from tropical to arctic

PEOPLE

Population

Total: 298,444,215

Annual Growth Rate: 0.91%

Rural/Urban Population Ratio: 24/76

Major Languages: predominantly English; a sizable Spanish-speaking minority; many others

Ethnic Makeup: 82% white; 13% black; 4% Asian; 1% Amerindian and others

Religions: 56% Protestant; 28% Roman Catholic; 2% Jewish; 4% others; 10% none or unaffiliated

Health

Life Expectancy at Birth: 75 years (male); 81 years (female)

Infant Mortality: 6.43/1,000 live births

Physicians Available: 1/365 people

HIV/AIDS Rate in Adults: 0.06%

Education

Adult Literacy Rate: 97% (official)

Compulsory (Ages): 7–16; free

COMMUNICATION

Telephones: 268,000,000 main lines

Telephones: 219,000,000 cellular

Daily Newspaper Circulation: 238/1,000 people

Televisions: 776/1,000 people

Internet Users: 1,205,326,680 (2005)

TRANSPORTATION

Highways in Miles (Kilometers): 3,906,960 (6,261,154)

Railroads in Miles (Kilometers): 149,161 (240,000)

Usable Airfields: 14,695

Motor Vehicles in Use: 206,000,000

GOVERNMENT

Type: federal republic

Independence Date: July 4, 1776

Head of State/Government: President George W. Bush is both head of state and head of government

Political Parties: Democratic Party; Republican Party; others of relatively minor political significance

Suffrage: universal at 18

MILITARY

Military Expenditures (% of GDP): 4.6%

Current Disputes: various boundary and territorial disputes; "war on terrorism"

ECONOMY

Per Capita Income/GDP: $42,000/$12.31 trillion

GDP Growth Rate: 3.2%

Inflation Rate: 3%

Unemployment Rate: 5.1%

Population Below Poverty Line: 12%

Natural Resources: many minerals and metals; petroleum; natural gas; timber; arable land

Agriculture: food grains; feed crops; fruits and vegetables; oil-bearing crops; livestock; dairy products

Industry: diversified in both capital and consumer-goods industries

Exports: $723 billion (primary partners Canada, Mexico, Japan)

Imports: $1.148 trillion (primary partners Canada, Mexico, Japan)

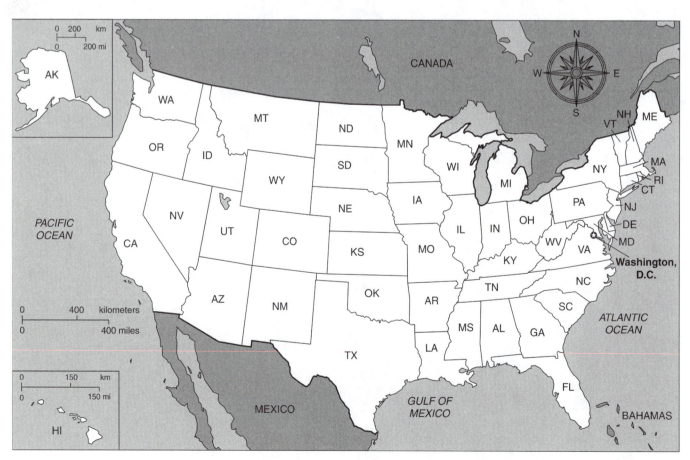

Canada

GEOGRAPHY

Area in Square Miles (Kilometers): 3,850,790 (9,976,140) (slightly larger than the United States)
Capital (Population): Ottawa (1,094,000)
Environmental Concerns: air and water pollution; acid rain; industrial damage to agriculture and forest productivity
Geographical Features: permafrost in the north; mountains in the west; central plains; lowlands in the southeast
Climate: varies from temperate to arctic

PEOPLE

Population
Total: 33,098,932
Annual Growth Rate: 0.88%
Rural/Urban Population Ratio: 23/77
Major Languages: both English and French are official
Ethnic Makeup: 28% British Isles origin; 23% French origin; 15% other European; 6% others; 2% indigenous; 26% mixed
Religions: 46% Roman Catholic; 36% Protestant; 18% others

Health
Life Expectancy at Birth: 77 years (male); 84 years (female)
Infant Mortality: 4.69/1,000 live births
Physicians Available: 1/534 people
HIV/AIDS Rate in Adults: 0.3%

Education
Adult Literacy Rate: 99%
Compulsory (Ages): primary school

COMMUNICATION

Telephones: 18,276,000 main lines
Telephones: 16,600,000 cellular
Daily Newspaper Circulation: 215/1,000 people
Televisions: 647/1,000 people
Internet Users: 16,840,000 (2002)

TRANSPORTATION

Highways in Miles (Kilometers): 559,240 (902,000)
Railroads in Miles (Kilometers): 22,320 (36,000)
Usable Airfields: 1,419
Motor Vehicles in Use: 16,800,000

GOVERNMENT

Type: confederation with parliamentary democracy
Independence Date: July 1, 1867
Head of State/Government: Queen Elizabeth II; Prime Minister Stephen Harper
Political Parties: Progressive Conservative Party; Liberal Party; New Democratic Party; Bloc Quèbècois; Canadian Alliance
Suffrage: universal at 18

MILITARY

Military Expenditures (% of GDP): 1.1%
Current Disputes: maritime boundary disputes with the United States

ECONOMY

Currency ($U.S. equivalent): 1.21 Canadian dollars = $1 (2005)
Per Capita Income/GDP: $27,700/$875 billion
GDP Growth Rate: 2.9%
Inflation Rate: 3%
Unemployment Rate: 7%
Labor Force by Occupation: 75% services; 14% manufacturing; 11% agriculture and others
Natural Resources: petroleum; natural gas; fish; minerals; cement; forestry products; wildlife; hydropower
Agriculture: grains; livestock; dairy products; potatoes; hogs; poultry and eggs; tobacco; fruits and vegetables
Industry: oil production and refining; natural-gas development; fish products; wood and paper products; chemicals; transportation equipment
Exports: $364.8 billion (primary partners United States, Japan, United Kingdom)
Imports: $317.7 billion (primary partners United States, European Union, Japan)

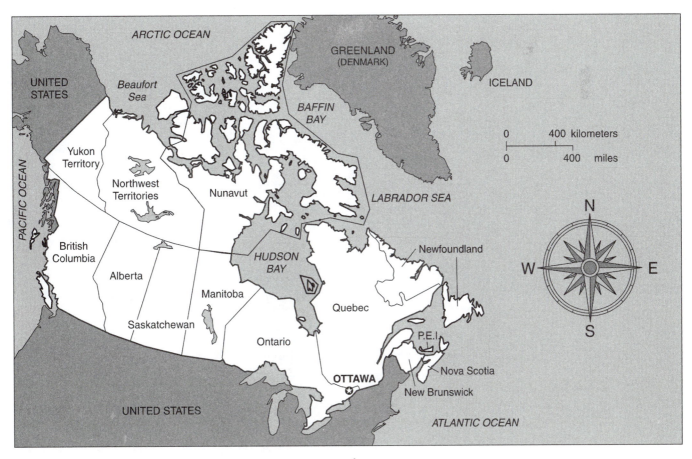

GLOBAL 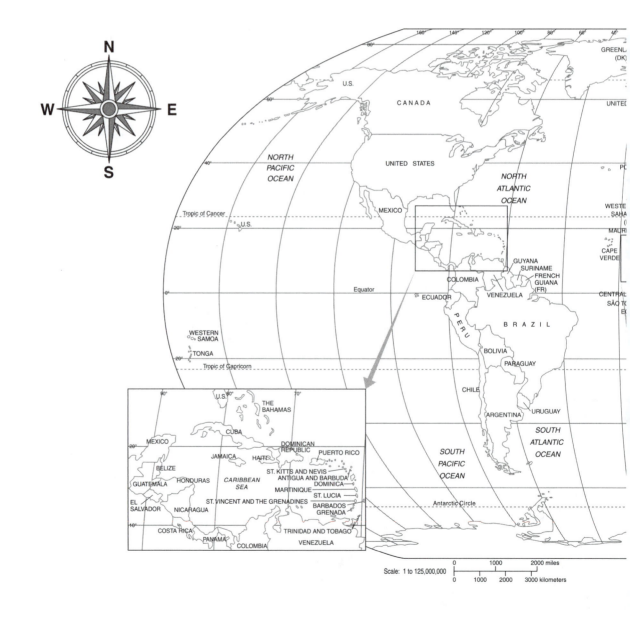 STUDIES

This map is provided to give you a graphic picture of where the countries of the world are located, the relationship they have with their region and neighbors, and their positions relative to major trade and power blocs. We have focused on certain areas to illustrate these crowded regions more clearly. China is shaded for emphasis.

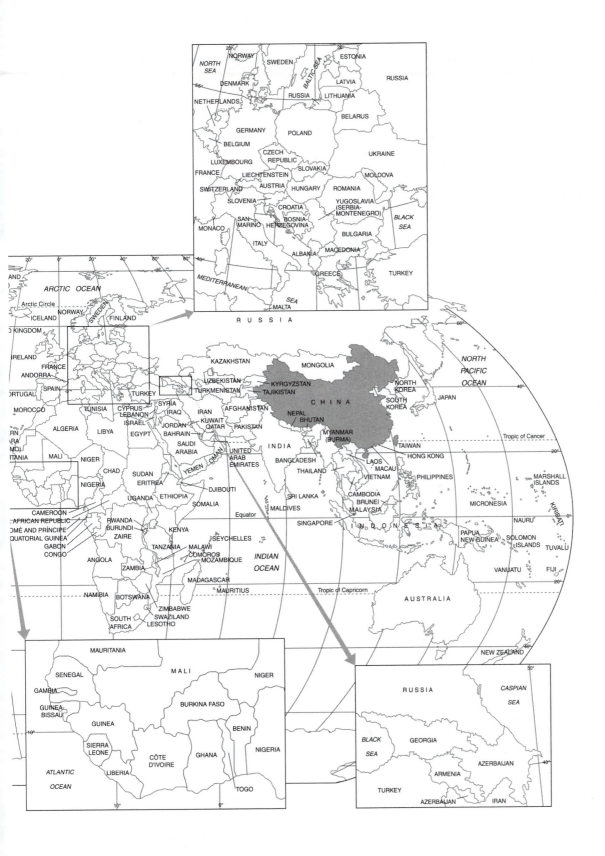

China Map

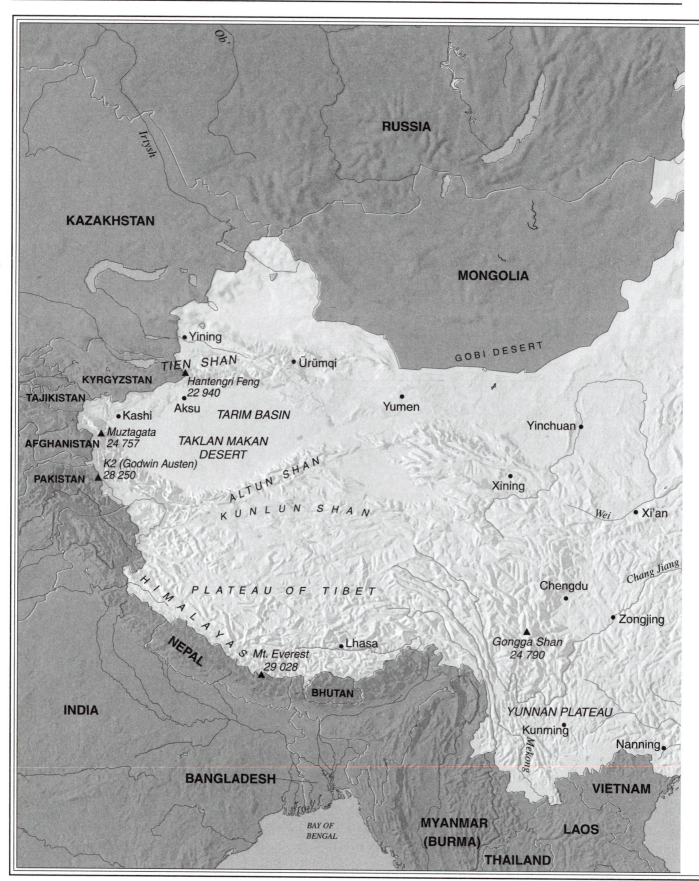

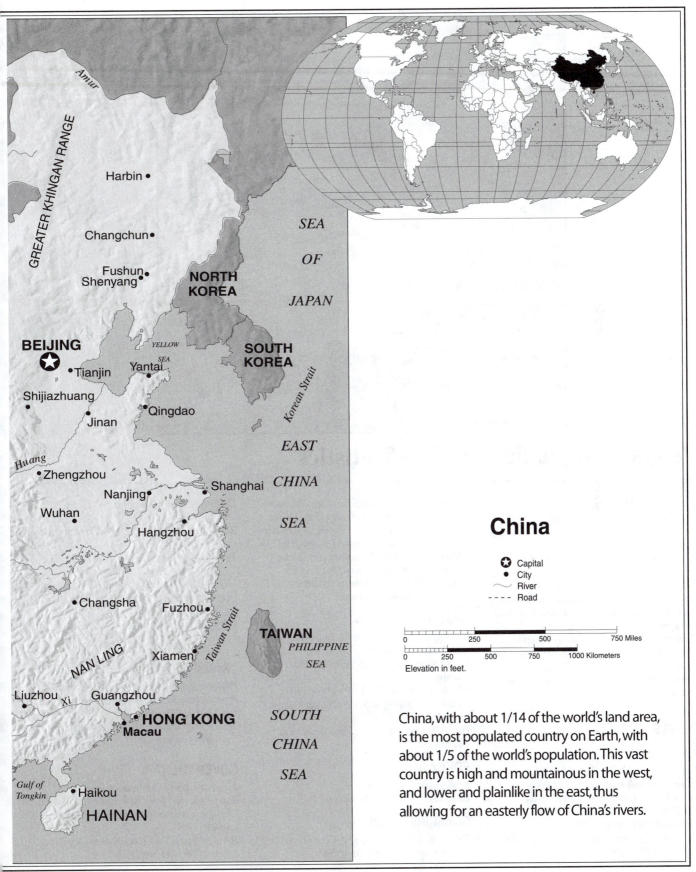

Greater Khingan Range

Amur

Harbin •

Changchun•

Fushun•
Shenyang•

NORTH KOREA

SEA

OF

JAPAN

BEIJING
⭐

• Tianjin

YELLOW
SEA

Yantai•

SOUTH KOREA

Korean Strait

Shijiazhuang•

•Qingdao

•Jinan

EAST

Huang

•Zhengzhou

CHINA

Nanjing•

•Shanghai

Wuhan•

SEA

•Hangzhou

•Changsha

Fuzhou•

Taiwan Strait

TAIWAN

PHILIPPINE

NAN LING

Xiamen•

SEA

Liuzhou•

Xi

Guangzhou•

HONG KONG

SOUTH

Macau

CHINA

*Gulf of
Tongkin*

•Haikou

SEA

HAINAN

China

⭐ Capital
• City
〜 River
- - - - Road

| 0 | | 250 | | 500 | | 750 Miles |

| 0 | 250 | 500 | 750 | 1000 Kilometers |

Elevation in feet.

China, with about 1/14 of the world's land area, is the most populated country on Earth, with about 1/5 of the world's population. This vast country is high and mountainous in the west, and lower and plainlike in the east, thus allowing for an easterly flow of China's rivers.

China (People's Republic of China)

People's Republic of China Statistics

GEOGRAPHY

Area in Square Miles (Kilometers):
3,705,386 (9,596,960) (about the same size as the United States)

Capital (Population): Beijing 6,619,000 (city proper) 9,376,200 (metro area)

Environmental Concerns: air and water pollution; water shortages; desertification; trade in endangered species; acid rain; loss of agricultural land; deforestation

Geographical Features: mostly mountains, high plateaus, and deserts in the west; plains, deltas, and hills in the east

Climate: extremely diverse, from tropical to subarctic

PEOPLE

Population

Total: 1,313,973,713 (July 2006 est.)
Annual Growth Rate: 0.59% (2006 est.)
Rural/Urban Population Ratio: 38.6/61.4
Sex Ratio of total population: 1.06 male(s)/1:0 female (2006 est.)
Major Languages: Standard Chinese (Putonghua) or Mandarin; Yue (Cantonese); Wu (Shanghainese); Minbei (Fuzhou); Minuan (Hokkien-Taiwanese); Xiang; Gan; Hahha

Ethnic Makeup: 92% Han Chinese; 8% minority groups (the largest being Chuang, Hui, Uighur, Yi, Miao, Mongolian, and Tibetan)

Religions: officially atheist; but Taoism, Buddhism, Islam, Christianity, ancestor worship, and animism exist

HEALTH

Life Expectancy at Birth: 71 years (male); 74.5 years (female)

Infant Mortality: 23.1 deaths/1,000 live births

Physicians Available: 1.39 million physicians; 1/628 people 5,535,682 health care personnel

HIV/AIDS Rate in Adults: less than 0.1% (2003 est.)

EDUCATION

Adult Literacy Rate: 90.9%
Compulsory Years of Schooling: 9

COMMUNICATION

Telephones: Landlines: 350,433 million; cell phones: 440,000 million (2006)

Daily Newspaper Circulation: 42.3 per 93.5 million

Radio stations: AM 369, FM 259, shortwave 45 (1998)

Television stations: 3,240 (of which 209 are operated by China Central Television, 31 are provincial TV stations, and nearly 3,000 are local city stations) (1997)

Televisions: 400 million
Internet Users: 123 million (2006)

TRANSPORTATION

Highways in Kilometers: 1,809,829 km
Railroads in Kilometers: 74,408 km
Usable Airfields: 486 (2006)
Motor Vehicles in Use: more than 30 million privately owned cars

GOVERNMENT

Type: one-party Communist state
Independence Date: unification in 221 B.C.; People's Republic established October 1, 1949
Head of State/Government: President Hu Jintao; Premier Wen Jiabao

Political Parties: Chinese Communist Party; eight registered small parties controlled by the CCP

Suffrage: universal at 18 in village and urban district elections

MILITARY

Military Expenditures (% of GDP): 4.3% (2005 est.)

Current Disputes: minor border disputes with a few countries, and potentially serious disputes over Spratly and Paracel Islands with several countries

ECONOMY

Currency ($ U.S. equivalent): = 7.71 yuan per one US dollar $1 (2007)

Per Capita Income/GDP (purchasing price parity): $6,800 PCI.

GDP (purchasing price parity): $8.883 trillion (2005 est.)

GDP (exchange rate based): $2.225 trillion (2005 est.)

GDP Growth Rate: 10.2% (2005 est.)

Inflation Rate: 1.8% (2005 est.)

Unemployment Rate: 9% official registered urban unemployment in 2004; substantial unemployment and underemployment in rural areas

Labor Force by Occupation: agriculture 49%; industry 22%; services 29% (2003 est.)

Natural Resources: coal; petroleum; iron ore; tin; tungsten; antimony; lead; zinc; vanadium; magnetite; uranium; hydropower

Agriculture: food grains; cotton; oilseed; pork; fish; tea; apples; peanuts

Industry: iron and steel; coal; machinery; light industry; textiles and apparel; food processing; consumer durables and electronics; telecommunications; armaments

Exports: $752.2 billion f.o.b. (2005 est.) (major purchaser of exports: United States, Hong Kong, South Korea, Japan, Germany)

Imports: $631.8 billion f.o.b. (2005 est.) (major sellers to China: Japan, Taiwan, South Korea, United States, Germany)

SUGGESTED WEB SITES

https://www.cia.gov/cia/publications/factbook/geos/ch.html

http://www.chinatoday.com/data/data.htm

People's Republic of China Country Report

Chinese civilization originated in the Neolithic Period, which began around 5000 B.C., but scholars know little about it until the Shang Dynasty, which dates from about 2000 B.C. By that time, the Chinese had already developed the technology and art of bronze casting to a high standard; and they had a sophisticated system of writing with ideographs, in which words are portrayed by picturelike characters. From the fifth to the third centuries B.C., the level of literature and the arts was comparable to that of Greece in the Classical Period, which flourished at the same time. Stunning breakthroughs occurred in science, a civil service evolved, and the philosopher Confucius developed a highly sophisticated system of ethics for government and moral codes for society. Confucian values were dominant until the collapse of the Chinese imperial system in 1911, but even today they influence Chinese thought and behavior in China, and in Chinese communities throughout the world.

From several hundred years B.C. until the 15th century, China was the world's leader in technology, had the largest economy, and enjoyed the highest GDP per capita income in the world. By 1500, however, the government had closed China's doors to broad international trade, and "Europe's" GDP per capita surpassed China's. Still, it remained the world's largest economy, accounting for some 30 percent of the world's GDP in 1820. Over the next 130 years, war, revolution, and invasions ate away at China's productive capabilities. By the time the Chinese Communist Party came to power in October 1949, China's share of the world's GDP had dropped to 5 percent.[1] The historical baggage that China carried into the period of the People's Republic of China in 1949 was, then, substantial. China had fallen from being

one of the world great empires—not just from an economic perspective, but also from cultural and scientific perspectives—before 1500, to one of the poorest countries in the world. When the Chinese Communists interpreted that history through the lens of Marxism and Leninism, they saw feudalism, capitalism, and imperialism as the cause of China's problem. They saw China as a victim both of exploitation within their own society, and from abroad.

The Chinese Empire

By 221 B.C., the many feudal states ruled by independent princes had been conquered by Qin Shi Huang Di, the first ruler of a unified Chinese Empire. He established a system of governmental institutions and a concept of empire that continued in China until A.D. 1911. Although China was unified from the Qin Dynasty onward, it was far less concrete than the term *empire* might indicate. China's borders really reached only as far as its cultural influence did. Thus China contracted and expanded according to whether or not other groups of people accepted the Chinese ruler and culture as their own.

Those peoples outside "China" who refused to acknowledge the Chinese ruler as the "Son of Heaven" or pay tribute to him were called "barbarians." In part, the Great Wall, which stretches more than 2,000 miles across north China and was built in stages between the third century B.C. and the seventeenth century A.D., was constructed in order to keep marauding "barbarians" out of China. Nevertheless, they frequently invaded China and occasionally even succeeded in subduing the Chinese—as in the Yuan (Mongol) Dynasty (1279–1368) and, later, the Qing (Manchu) Dynasty (1644–1911).

However, the customs and institutions of the invaders eventually yielded to the power-

ful cultural influence of the Chinese. Indeed, in the case of the Manchus, who seized control of the Chinese Empire in 1644 and ruled until 1911, their success in holding onto the throne for so long may be due in part to their willingness to assimilate Chinese ways and to rule through existing Chinese institutions, such as the Confucian-ordered bureaucracy. By the time of their overthrow, the Manchu were hardly distinguishable from the ethnic Han Chinese in their customs, habits, and beliefs. When considering today's policies toward the numerous minorities who inhabit such a large expanse of the People's Republic of China, it should be remembered that the central Chinese government's ability to absorb minorities was key to its success in maintaining a unified entity called China (*Zhongguo*—"the Central Kingdom") for more than 2,000 years.

The Imperial Bureaucracy

A distinguishing feature of the political system of imperial China was the civil service examinations through which government officials were chosen. These examinations tested knowledge of the moral principles embodied in the classical Confucian texts. Although the exams were, in theory, open to all males in the Chinese Empire, the lengthy and rigorous preparation required meant that, in practice, the sons of the wealthy and powerful with access to a good education had an enormous advantage. Only a small percentage of those who began the process actually passed the examinations and received an appointment in the imperial bureaucracy. Some of those who were successful resided in the capital to advise the emperor, while others were sent as the emperor's agents to govern throughout the far-flung realm.

The Decline of the Manchus

The vitality of Chinese institutions and their ability to respond creatively to new problems came to an end during the Manchu Dynasty (1644–1911). A stagnant agricultural system incapable of supporting the burgeoning population and the increasing exploitation of the peasantry who comprised the vast majority of Chinese people led to massive internal rebellions and the rise of warlords. As the imperial bureaucracy became increasingly corrupt and incompetent, the Manchu Dynasty gradually lost the ability to govern effectively.

China's decline in the nineteenth century was exacerbated by a social class structure that rewarded those who could pass the archaic, morality-based civil service examinations rather than those who had expertise in science and technology and could thereby contribute to China's development. An inward-looking culture contributed to the malaise by preventing the Chinese from understanding the dynamism of the Industrial Revolution then occurring in the West. Gradually, the barriers erected by the Manchu rulers to prevent Western culture and technology from polluting the ancient beauty of Chinese civilization crumbled, but too late to strengthen China to resist the West's military onslaughts.

The Opium War (1839–1842)

In the early nineteenth century, the British traded with China, but it was primarily a one-way trade. The British nearly drained their coffers buying Chinese silk, tea, and porcelain; China's self-satisfied rulers found little of interest to purchase from the rapidly industrializing British. The British were also frustrated by China's refusal to recognize the British Empire as an equal of the Chinese Empire, and to open up ports to trade with them along China's extensive coastline and rivers.

Opium, produced in the British Empire's colony India, proved to be the one product that the Chinese were willing to purchase, and it reversed the trade balance in favor of the British. Eventually they used the Chinese attack on British ships carrying opium as an excuse for declaring war on the decrepit Chinese Empire. The Opium War ended with defeat for the Chinese and the signing of the Treaty of Nanjing (sometimes called Nanking). This treaty ceded the island of Hong Kong to the British as a colony and allowed them to establish trading posts.

Subsequent wars with the British and other European powers brought further concessions—the most important of which was the Chinese granting of additional "treaty ports" to Europeans. The Chinese had hoped that they could contain and control Europeans within these ports. Although that was true to a degree, this penetration of China led to the spread of Western values that challenged the stagnant, and by then collapsing, Chinese Empire. As the West and, by the late nineteenth century, Japan,

nibbled away at China, the Manchu rulers made a last-ditch effort at reform to strengthen and enrich China. But it was too late, and the combination of internal decay, provincialism, revolution, and foreign imperialism finally toppled the Manchu Dynasty. Thus ended more than 2,000 years of imperial rule in China.

REPUBLICAN CHINA

The 1911 Revolution, which led to the overthrow of Manchu rule and derived its greatest inspiration from Chinese nationalist Sun Yat-sen, resulted in the establishment of the Republic of China (R.O.C.). It was, however, a "republic" only in name, for China was unable to successfully transfer Western forms of democratic governance to China. This was in no small part because of China's inability to remain united and to maintain law and order. China had been briefly united under the control of the dominant warlord of the time, Yuan Shikai; but with his death in 1916, China was again torn apart by the resurgence of contending warlords, internal political decay, and further Japanese territorial expansion in China. Efforts at reform failed in the context of China's weakness and internal division.

Chinese intellectuals searched for new ideas from abroad to strengthen their nation during the vibrant May Fourth period and New Culture Movement (spanning the period from roughly 1917 through the mid-1920s). In the process, the Chinese invited influential foreigners such as the English mathematician, philosopher, and socialist Bertrand Russell, and the American philosopher and educator John Dewey, to lecture in China. Thousands of Chinese traveled, worked, and studied abroad. It was during this period that ideas such as liberal democracy, syndicalism, guild socialism, and communism were put forth as possible solutions to China's many problems.

The Founding of the Chinese Communist Party

It was during that period, in 1921, that a small Marxist study group in Shanghai founded the Chinese Communist Party (CCP). The Moscow-based Comintern (Communist International) advised this highly intellectual but politically and militarily powerless group to join with the more militarily powerful Kuomintang (KMT or Nationalist Party, led first by Sun Yat-sen and, after his death in 1925, by Chiang Kai-shek) until it could gain strength and break away to establish themselves as an independent party. Thus it was with the support of the Communists in a "united front" with the Nationalists that Chiang Kai-shek conquered the warlords and reunified China under one central government. Chiang felt threatened by the Communists' ambitions to gain political power, however, so in 1927 he executed all but the few Communists who managed to escape.

(Public Domain)

CONFUCIUS: CHINA'S FIRST "TEACHER"

Confucius (551–479 B.C.), whose efforts to teach China's rulers how to govern well were spurned, spent most of his life teaching his own disciples. Yet 300 years later, Confucianism, as taught by descendants of his disciples, was adopted as the official state philosophy. The basic principles of Confucianism include hierarchical principles of obedience and loyalty to one's superiors, respect for one's elders, and filial piety; and principles and practices for maintaining social order and harmony; and the responsibility of rulers to exercise their power benevolently.

Members of the CCP continued to take their advice from Moscow; and they tried to organize an orthodox Marxist, urban-based movement of industrial workers twice more. Because the cities were completely controlled by the KMT, the CCP found it difficult to organize the workers, and ultimately the KMT's police and military forces decimated the ranks of the Communists. It is a testimony to the appeal of communism in that era that the CCP managed to recover its strength each time. Indeed, the growing power of the CCP was such that Chiang Kai-shek considered the CCP, rather than the invading Japanese, to be the main threat to his complete control of China.

Eventually the Chinese Communist leaders agreed that an urban strategy could not succeed. Lacking adequate military power to confront the Nationalists, however, they retreated. In what became known as the Long March (1934–1935), they traveled more than 6,000 miles from the southeast, through the rugged interior and onto the windswept, desolate plains of Yan'an in northern China.

OPIUM AS A PRETEXT FOR WAR

Although the opium poppy is native to China, large amounts of opium were shipped to China by the English-owned East India Company, from the British colony of India. Eventually India exported so much opium to China that 5 to 10 percent of its revenues derived from its sale.

By the late 1700s, the Chinese government had officially prohibited first the smoking and selling of opium, and later its importation or domestic production. But because the sale of opium was so profitable—and also because so many Chinese officials were addicted to it—the Chinese officials themselves illegally engaged in the opium trade. As the number of addicts grew and the Chinese government became more corrupted by its own unacknowledged participation in opium smuggling, so grew the interest of enterprising Englishmen in smuggling it into China for financial gain.

The British government was primarily interested in expanding trade with China. But it also wanted to establish a diplomatic relationship based on equality to supplant the existing one, in which the Chinese court demanded that the English kowtow to the Chinese emperor. In addition, it wanted to secure legal jurisdiction over its nationals residing in China to protect them against Chinese practices of torture of those suspected of having committed a crime.

China's efforts to curb the smuggling of opium and the Chinese refusal to recognize the British as equals reached a climax in 1839, when the Chinese destroyed thousands of chests of opium aboard a British ship. This served as an ideal pretext for the British to attack China with their sophisticated gunboats (pictured below destroying a junk in Canton's (Guangzhou's) harbor). Ultimately their superior firepower gave victory to the British.

Thus the so-called Opium War (1839–1842) ended with defeat for the Chinese Empire and the signing of the Treaty of Nanjing, which ceded the island of Hong Kong to the British and allowed them to establish trading posts on the Chinese mainland.

(Library of Congress Prints and Photographs Division/ LC-USZ62-86300)

It was during this retreat, in which as many as 100,000 followers perished, that Mao Zedong staged his contest for power within the CCP. With his victory, the CCP reoriented itself toward a rural strategy and attempted to capture the loyalty of China's peasants, then comprising some 85 percent of China's total population. Mao saw the downtrodden peasantry as the major source of support for the revolutionary overthrow of Chiang Kai-shek's government. Suffering from an oppressive and exploitative system of landlord control, disillusioned with the government's unwillingness to carry out land reform, and desirous of owning their own land, the peasantry looked to the CCP for leadership. Slowly the CCP started to gain control over China's vast countryside.

United Against the Japanese

In 1931, Japan invaded China and occupied Manchuria, the three northeastern provinces. In 1937, Japan attacked again, advancing southward to occupy China's heartland. Although the CCP and KMT were determined to destroy each other, Japan's threat to spread its control over the rest of China caused them to agree to a second "united front," this time for the purpose of halting the Japanese advance. Both the KMT and the CCP had ulterior motives, but according to most accounts, the Communists contributed more to the national wartime efforts. The Communists organized guerrilla efforts to peck away at the fringes of Japanese-controlled areas while Chiang Kai-shek, head of the KMT, retreated to the wartime capital of Zongjing (Chungking). His

elite corps of troops and officers kept the best of the newly arriving American supplies for themselves, leaving the rank-and-file Chinese to fight against the Japanese in cloth boots and with inferior equipment. It was not the Nationalist Army but, rather, largely the unstinting efforts and sacrifices of the Chinese people and the American victory over Japan that brought World War II to an end in 1945. With the demobilization of the Japanese, however, Chiang Kai-shek was free once again to focus on defeating the Communists.

The Communists Oust the KMT

It seemed as if the Communists' Red Army had actually been strengthened through its hard fighting during World War II, turning itself into a formidable force. Meanwhile, the relatively soft life of the KMT military elite during the war did not leave it well prepared for civil war against the Red Army. Chiang Kai-shek relied on his old strategy of capturing China's cities, but the Communists, who had gained control over the countryside by winning the support of the vast peasantry, surrounded the cities. Like besieged fortresses, the cities eventually fell to Communist control. By October 1949, the CCP could claim control over all of China, except for the island of Taiwan. It was there that the Nationalists' political, economic, and military elites, with American support, had fled.

Scholars still dispute why the Red Army ultimately defeated the Nationalist Army. They cite as probable reasons the CCP's promises to undertake land reform; the Communists' more respectful treatment of the

peasantry as they marched through the countryside (in comparison to that of the KMT soldiers); the CCP's more successful appeal to the Chinese sense of nationalism; and Chiang Kai-shek's unwillingness to undertake reforms that would benefit the peasantry, advance economic development, and control corruption. Still, even had the KMT made greater efforts to reform, any wartime government confronted with the demoralization of the population ravaged by war, inflation, economic destruction, and the humiliation of a foreign occupation would have found it difficult to maintain the loyal support of its people. Even the middle class eventually deserted the KMT. Many of those industrial and commercial capitalists who had supported the Nationalists now joined with the CCP to rebuild China. Others, however, stayed behind only because they were unable to flee to Hong Kong or Taiwan.

One thing is clear: The Chinese Communists did not gain victory because of support from the Soviet Union; for the Soviets, who were anxious to be on the winning side in China, chose to give aid to the KMT until it was evident that the Communists would win. Furthermore, the Communists' victory rested not on superior weapons but, rather, on a superior strategy, support from the Chinese people, and (as Mao Zedong believed) a superior political "consciousness." It was because of the Communist victory over a technologically superior army that Mao thereafter insisted on the superiority of "man over weapons" and the importance of the support of the people for an army's victory. The relationship of

MAO ZEDONG: CHINA'S REVOLUTIONARY LEADER

Mao Zedong (1893–1976) came from a moderately well-to-do peasant family and, as a result, received a very good education, as compared to the vast majority of the Chinese of his time. Mao was one of the founders of the Chinese Communist Party in 1921, but his views on the need to switch from an orthodox Marxist strategy, which called for the party to seek roots among the urban working class, to a rural strategy centered on the exploited peasantry were spurned by the leadership of the CCP and its sponsors in Moscow.

Later, it became evident that the CCP could not flourish in the Nationalist-controlled cities, as time and again the KMT quashed the idealistic but militarily weak CCP. Mao appeared to be right: "Political power grows out of the barrel of a gun."

The Communists' retreat to Yan'an in central China at the end of the Long March was not only for the purpose of survival but also for regrouping and forming a stronger Red Army. There the followers of the Chinese Communist Party were taught Mao's ideas about guerrilla warfare, the importance of winning the support of the people, principles of party leadership, and socialist values. Mao consolidated his control over the leadership of the CCP during the Yan'an period and led it to victory over the Nationalists in 1949.

From that time onward, Mao became a symbol of the new Chinese government, of national unity, and of the strength of China against foreign humiliation. In later years, although his real power was eclipsed, the party maintained the public illusion that Mao was the undisputed leader of China.

In his declining years, Mao waged a struggle, in the form of the "Cultural Revolution," against those who followed policies antagonistic to his own—a struggle that brought the country to the brink of civil war and turned the Chinese against one another. The symbol of Mao as China's "great leader" and "great teacher" was used by those who hoped to seize power after him: first the minister of defense, Lin Biao, and then the "Gang of Four," which included Mao's wife.

Mao's death in 1976 ended the control of policy by the Gang of Four. Within a few years, questions were being raised about the legacy that Mao had left China. By the 1980s, it was broadly accepted throughout China that Mao had been responsible for a full 20 years of misguided policies. Since the Tiananmen Square protests of 1989, however, there has been a resurgence of nostalgia for Mao. This nostalgia is captured in such aspects of popular culture as a tape of songs about Mao entitled "The Red Sun"—an all-time best-selling tape in China, at 5 million copies—that captures the

(Public Domain)

Mao cult and Mao mania of the Cultural Revolution; and in a small portrait of Mao that virtually all car owners and taxi drivers hang over their rear-view mirrors for "good luck." Many Chinese long for the "good old days" of Mao's rule, when crime and corruption were at far lower levels than today and when there was a sense of collective commitment to China's future. But they do not long for a return to the mass terror of the Cultural Revolution, for which Mao also bears responsibility.

the soldiers to the people is, Mao said, like the relationship of fish to water—without the water, the fish will die.

THE PEOPLE'S REPUBLIC OF CHINA

The Red Army's final victory came rapidly— far faster than anticipated. Suddenly China's large cities fell to the Communists, who now found themselves in charge of a nation of more than 600 million people. They had to make critical decisions about how to unify and rebuild the country. They were obligated, of course, to fulfill their promise to redistribute land to the poor and landless peasantry in return for the peasants' support of the Communists during the Civil War. The CCP leaders were, however, largely recruited from among the peasantry; and like revolutionary fighters everywhere, knew how to make a revolution but had little experience with governance. So,

rejected by the Western democratic/capitalist countries because of their embrace of communism, and desperate for aid and advice, the Communists turned to the Soviet Union for direction and support. They did this in spite of the Soviet leader Joseph Stalin's fickle support of the Chinese Communists throughout the 1930s and '40s.

The Soviet Model

In the early years of CCP rule, China's leaders "leaned to one side" and followed the Soviet model of development in education, the legal system, the economic system, and elsewhere. The Soviet economic model favored capital-intensive industrialization, but all the Soviet "aid" had to be repaid. Furthermore, following the Soviet model required a reliance on Soviet experts and well-educated Chinese, whom the Communists were not sure they

could trust. Without Soviet support in the beginning, however, it is questionable whether the CCP would have been as successful as it was in developing China in the 1950s.

The Maoist Model

China soon grew exasperated with the limitations of Soviet aid and the inapplicability of the Soviet model to Chinese circumstances. China's preeminent leader, Mao Zedong, proposed a Chinese model of development more appropriate to Chinese circumstances. What came to be known as the "Maoist model" took account of China's low level of development, poverty, and large population. Mao hoped to substitute China's enormous manpower for expensive capital equipment by organizing people into ever larger working units.

In 1958, in what became known as the "Great Leap Forward," Mao Zedong launched

RED GUARDS: ROOTING OUT THOSE "ON THE CAPITALIST ROAD"

During the Cultural Revolution, Mao Zedong called upon the country's young people to "make revolution." Called "Mao's Red Guards," their ages varied, but for the most part they were teenagers.

Within each class and school, various youths would band together in a Red Guard group that would take on a revolutionary-sounding name and would then carry out the objective of challenging people in authority. But the people in authority—especially school-teachers, school principals, bureaucrats, and local leaders of the Communist Party—initially ignored the demands of the Red Guards that they reform their "reactionary thoughts" or eliminate their "feudal" habits.

The Red Guards initially had no real weapons and could only threaten. Since they were considered just misdirected children by those under attack, their initial assaults had little effect. But soon the frustrated Red Guards took to physically beating and publicly humiliating those who stubbornly refused to obey them. Since Mao had not clearly defined precisely what should be their objectives or methods, the Red Guards were free to believe that the ends justified extreme and often violent means. Moreover, many Red Guards took the opportunity to take revenge against authorities, such as teachers who had given them bad grades. Others (at right) would harangue crowds on the benefits of Maoism and the evils of foreign influence.

The Red Guards went on rampages throughout the country, breaking into people's houses and stealing or destroying their property, harassing people in their homes in the middle of the night, stopping girls with long hair and cutting it off on the spot, destroying the files of ministries and industrial enterprises, and clogging up the transportation system by their travels throughout the country to "make revolution." Different Red Guard factions began to fight with one another, each claiming to be the most revolutionary.

Mao eventually called on the army to support the Red Guards in their effort to challenge "those in authority taking the capitalist road." This created even more confusion, as many of the Red Guard groups actually supported the people they were supposed to be attacking. But their revolutionary-sounding names and their pretenses at being "Red" (Communist) confused the army. Moreover, the army was divided within itself and did not particularly wish to overthrow the Chinese Communist Party authorities, the main supporters of the military in their respective areas of jurisdiction.

Since the schools had been closed, the youth of China were not receiving any formal education during this period. Finally, in 1969, Mao called a halt to the excesses of the Red Guards. They were disbanded and sent home. Some were sent to work in factories or out to the countryside to labor in the fields with the peasants. But

(Library of Congress Prints and Photographs Division/LC-USZ62-134168) Photograph shows leaders of "anti-revolutionary groups" wearing dunce caps being presented for public shame on the back of a truck on a Beijing street by members of the Red Guard.

the chaos set in motion during the Cultural Revolution did not come to a halt until the arrest of the Gang of Four, some 10 years after the Cultural Revolution had begun.

During the "10 bad years," when schools were either closed or operating with a minimal program, children received virtually no formal education beyond an elementary school level. Although this meant that China's development of an educated elite in most fields came to a halt, nevertheless it resulted in well over a 90 percent basic literacy rate among the Chinese raised in that generation.

his model of development. It was a bold scheme to rapidly accelerate the pace of industrialization so that China could catch up with the industrialized states of the West. In the countryside, land was merged into large communes, untested and controversial planting techniques were introduced, and peasant women were engaged fully in the fields in order to increase agricultural production. The communes became the basis for industrializing the countryside through a program of peasants building their own "backyard furnaces" to smelt steel. The Maoist model assumed that those people possessing a proper revolutionary, or "red" (communist), consciousness—that is, a commitment to

achieving communism—would be able to produce more than those who were "expert" but lacked revolutionary consciousness. In the cities, efforts to increase industrial production through longer work days, and overtaxing industrial equipment, likewise led to a marked decline in production and industrial wastage.

The Maoist model of extreme "egalitarianism"—captured in the Chinese expression "all eat out of the same pot"—and "continuous revolution," was a rejection of the Soviet model of development, which Mao came to see as an effort to hold the Chinese back from more rapid industrialization. In particular, the Soviets' refusal to give the Chinese the most advanced industrial-plant equipment and machinery, or

to share nuclear technology with them, made Mao suspicious of their intentions.

Sino–Soviet Relations Sour

For their part, the Soviets believed that the Maoist model was doomed to failure. The Soviet leader Nikita Khrushchev denounced the Great Leap Forward as "irrational"; but he was equally distressed at what seemed a risky scheme by Mao Zedong to bring the Soviets and Americans into direct conflict over the Nationalist-controlled Offshore Islands in the Taiwan Strait. The combination of what the Soviets viewed as Mao's irrational economic policy and his risk-taking confrontation with the United States prompted the Soviets to

(IISH Stefan R. Landsberger Collection (http://www.iisg.nl/~landsberger))
This poster, done in the style of the Cultural Revolution posters, was created sometime after the arrest of the Gang of Four in October 1976. These socialist-style workers are writing characters that read: "The Gang of Four (Wang, Zhang, Jiang, and Yao) are Krushchev-like bourgeois conspirators and demagogues." Below the poster, the inscription reads, "We must definitely carry forward the great struggle in thoroughly exposing and criticizing the Gang of Four."

THE GANG OF FOUR

The current leadership of the Chinese Communist Party views the Cultural Revolution of 1966–1976 as having been a period of total chaos that brought the People's Republic of China to the brink of political and economic ruin. While Mao Zedong is criticized for having begun the Cultural Revolution with his ideas about the danger of China turning "capitalist," the major blame for the turmoil of those years is placed on a group of extreme radicals labeled the "Gang of Four."

The Gang of Four consisted of Jiang Qing, Mao's wife, who began playing a key role in China's cultural affairs during the early 1960s; Zhang Chunqiao, a veteran party leader in Shanghai; Yao Wenyuan, a literary critic and ideologue; and Wang Hongwen, a factory worker catapulted into national prominence by his leadership of rebel workers during the Cultural Revolution. By the late 1960s,

these four individuals were among the most powerful leaders in China. Drawn together by common political interests and a shared belief that the Communist Party should be relentless in ridding China of suspected "capitalist roaders," they worked together to keep the Cultural Revolution on a radical course. One of their targets had been Deng Xiaoping, who emerged as China's paramount leader in 1978, after the members of the Gang of Four had been arrested.

Although they had close political and personal ties to Mao and derived many of their ideas from him, Mao became quite disenchanted with them in the last few years of his life. He was particularly displeased with the unscrupulous way in which they behaved as a faction within the top levels of the party. Indeed, it was Mao who coined the name Gang of Four, as part of a written warning to the radicals to cease

their conspiracies and obey established party procedures.

The Gang of Four hoped to take over supreme power in China following Mao's death, on September 9, 1976. However, their plans were upset less than a month later, when other party and army leaders had them arrested—an event that is now said to mark the formal end of the "10 bad years" or "Cultural Revolution." Removing the party's most influential radicals from power set the stage for the dramatic reforms that have become the hallmark of the post-Mao era in China. In November 1980, the Gang of Four were put on trial in Beijing. They were charged with having committed serious crimes against the Chinese people and accused of having had a hand in "persecuting to death" tens of thousands of officials and intellectuals whom they perceived as their political enemies. All four were convicted and sentenced to long terms in prison.

abruptly withdraw their experts from China in 1959. They packed up their bags, along with spare parts for Soviet-supplied machinery and blueprints for unfinished factories, and returned home.

The Soviets' withdrawal, combined with the disastrous decline in production resulting from the policies of the Great Leap Forward and several years of bad weather, set China's economic development back many years.

Population figures now available indicate that millions died in the years from 1959 to 1962, mostly from starvation and diseases caused by malnutrition. The catastrophic consequences of the Great Leap Forward resulted in the leadership paying no more than lip service to Mao Zedong's ideas. The Chinese people were not told that Mao Zedong bore blame for their problems, but the Maoist model was abandoned for the time being. More pragmatic

leaders took over the direction of the economy, but without further support from the Soviets. Not until 1962 did the Chinese start to recover their productivity gains of the 1950s.

By 1963, the Sino–Soviet split had become public, as the two Communist powers found themselves in profound disagreement over a wide range of issues: whether socialist countries could use capitalist methods, such as free markets, to advance economic development; appropriate policies toward the United States; whether China or the Soviet Union could claim to follow Marxism-Leninism more faithfully, entitling it to lead the Communist world. By the mid-1960s, the Sino-Soviet relationship had deteriorated to the point that the Chinese were worried that the Soviets might launch a military attack on them.

The Cultural Revolution

In 1966, Mao launched what he termed the "Great Proletarian Cultural Revolution." Whether Mao Zedong hoped to provoke an internal party struggle and regain control over policy, or (as he alleged) to re-educate China's exploitative, corrupt, and oppressive officials in order to restore a revolutionary spirit to the Chinese people and to prevent China from abandoning socialism, is unclear. He called on China's youth to "challenge authority," particularly "those revisionists in authority who are taking the capitalist road." If China continued along its "revisionist" course, he said, the achievements of the Chinese revolution would be undone. China's youth were therefore urged to "make revolution."

Such vague objectives invited abuse, including personal feuds and retribution for alleged past wrongs. Determining just who was "Red" and committed to the Communist revolution, and who was "reactionary" itself generated chaos, as people tried to protect themselves by attacking others—including friends and relatives. During that period, people's cruelty was immeasurable. People were psychologically, and sometimes physically, tortured until they "admitted" to their "rightist" or "reactionary" behavior. Murders, suicides, ruined careers, and broken families were the debris left behind by this effort to "reeducate" those who had strayed from the revolutionary path. It is estimated that approximately 10 percent of the population—that is, *80 million people*—became targets of the Cultural Revolution, and that tens of thousands lost their lives during these years of political violence.

The Cultural Revolution attacked Chinese traditions and cultural practices as being feudal and outmoded. It also destroyed the authority of the Chinese Communist Party, through prolonged public attacks on many of its most respected leaders. Policies changed frequently in those "10 bad years" from 1966 to 1976, as first one faction and then another gained the upper hand. Few leaders escaped unscathed. Ultimately, the Chinese Communist Party and Marxist-Leninist ideology were themselves the victims of the Cultural Revolution. By the time the smoke cleared, the legitimacy of the CCP had been destroyed, and the people could no longer accept the idea that the party leaders were infallible. Both traditional Chinese morality and Marxist-Leninist values had been thoroughly undermined.

Reforms and Liberalization

With the death of Mao Zedong and the subsequent arrest of the politically radical "Gang of Four" (which included Mao's wife) in 1976, the Cultural Revolution came to an end. Deng Xiaoping, a veteran leader of the CCP who had been purged twice during the "10 bad years," was "rehabilitated" in 1977.

By 1979, China once again set off down the road of construction and put an end to the radical Maoist policies of "continuous revolution" and the idea that it was more important to be "red" than "expert." Saying that he did not care whether the cat was black or white, as long as it caught mice, Deng Xiaoping pursued more pragmatic, flexible policies in order to modernize China. In other words, Deng did not care if he used capitalist methods, as long as they helped modernize China. He deserves credit for opening up China to the outside world and to reforms that led to the liberalization of both the economic and the political spheres. When he died in 1997, Deng left behind a country that, despite some setbacks and reversals, had already traveled a significant distance down the road to liberalization and modernization.

In spite of Deng Xiaoping's pragmatic policies, and Mao Zedong's clear responsibility for precipitating policies that were devastating to the Chinese people, Mao has never been defrocked in China; for to do so would raise serious questions about the legitimacy of the CCP. China's leaders have admitted that, beginning with the Anti-Rightest Campaign of 1957 and the Great Leap Forward of 1958, Mao made "serious mistakes"; but the CCP insists that these errors must be seen within the context of his many accomplishments and his commitment, even if sometimes misdirected, to Marxism-Leninism. In contrast to the Gang of Four and others who were condemned as "counter-revolutionaries," Mao has been called a "revolutionary" who made "mistakes." As recently as the Fourth Plenum of the 16th Party Congress of the CCP in 2004, Mao Thought (the Chinese adaptation of Marxism-Leninism to Chinese conditions) remained enshrined in the party's constitution as providing the foundation for continued CCP rule.

The Challenge of Reform

The erosion of traditional Chinese values, then of Marxist-Leninist values and faith in the Chinese Communist Party's leadership, and finally of Mao Thought, left China without any strong belief system. Such Western values as materialism, capitalism, individualism, and freedom swarmed into this vacuum to undermine both Communist ideology and the traditional Chinese values that had provided the glue of society. Deng Xiaoping's prognosis had proven correct: The "screen door" through which Western science and technology (and foreign investments) could

flow into China was unable to keep out the annoying "insects" of Western values. The screen door had holes that were too large to prevent this invasion.

China's leadership in the reform period has not been united. The less pragmatic, more ideologically oriented "conservative" or "hard-line" leadership (who in the new context of reforms could be viewed as ideologues of a Maoist vintage) challenged the introduction of liberalizing economic reforms precisely because they threatened to undo China's earlier socialist achievements and erode Chinese culture. To combat the negative side effects of introducing free-market values and institutions, China's leadership launched a number of "mass campaigns": the campaign in the 1980s against "spiritual pollution"—the undermining of Chinese values;[2] a repressive campaign following the brutal crackdown against those challenging the leadership in Tiananmen Square in 1989; on-going campaigns against corruption; and campaigns to "strike hard" against crime and to "get civilized."[3]

Since 1979, in spite of setbacks, China's leadership has been able to keep the country on the path of liberalization. As a result, the economy has had an average annual growth rate of 9.5% for the last 25 years. It is now ranked as the fourth largest economy in the world. China has dramatically reformed the legal and political system as well, even though much work remains to be done. When Deng Xiaoping died in 1997, he was succeeded in a peaceful transition by Jiang Zemin, another committed economic reformer. In turn, Jiang stepped down from his position as party leader in 2001, as president in 2002, and as the head of the Military Affairs Commission in 2004. China's leaders now operate within what is a younger and increasingly well-institutionalized and better-educated system of collective leadership. The problems that the leadership of President Hu Jintao and Premier Wen Jiabao faces as a consequence of China's rapid modernization and liberalization are formidable: massive and growing unemployment; increasing crime, corruption, and social dislocation; a lack of social cohesion; and challenges to the CCP's monopoly on power put into play by its policies of liberalization, pluralization, and modernization. The forces of rapid growth and social and economic modernization have taken on a momentum of their own. China's increasing involvement in the international community has also put into motion seemingly uncontrollable forces, some of which are destabilizing, and others that are contributing to demands for political reform. As will be noted below in the discussion of these issues, the real concern for China is not whether China will engage in further reform and democratization, but whether it can maintain stability in the context of this potentially destabilizing international and domestic environment.

The Student and Mass Movement of 1989

Symbolism is very important in Chinese culture; the death of a key leader is a particularly significant moment. In the case of Hu Yaobang, the former head of the CCP, his sudden death in April 1989 became symbolic of the death of liberalizing forces in China. The deceased leader's career and its meaning were touted as symbols of liberalization, even though his life was hardly a monument to liberal thought. More conservative leaders in the CCP had removed him from his position as the CCP's general-secretary in part because he had offended their cultural sensibilities. Apart from everything else, Hu's suggestion that the Chinese turn in their chopsticks for knives and forks, and not eat food out of a common dish because it spread disease, were culturally offensive to them.

Hu's death provided students with a catalyst to place his values and policies in juxtaposition with those of the then increasingly conservative leadership.[4] The students' reassessment of Hu Yaobang's career, in a way that rejected the party's evaluation, was in itself a challenge to the authority of the CCP's right to rule China. The students' hunger strike in Tiananmen Square—essentially in front of party headquarters—during the visit of the Soviet Union President, Mikhail Gorbachev, to China was, even in the eyes of ordinary Chinese people, an insult to the Chinese leadership. Many Chinese later stated that the students went too far, as by humiliating the leadership, they humiliated *all* Chinese.

Part of the difficulty in reaching an agreement between the students and China's leaders was that the students' demands changed over time. At first they merely wanted a reassessment of Hu Yaobang's career. But quickly the students added new demands: dialogue between the government and the students (with the students to be treated as equals with top CCP leaders), retraction of an offensive *People's Daily* editorial, an end to official corruption, exposure of the financial and business dealings of the central leadership, a free press, the removal of the top CCP leadership, and still other actions that challenged continued CCP rule.

The students' hunger strike, which lasted for one week in May, was the final straw that brought down the wrath of the central leadership. Martial law was imposed in Beijing. When the citizens of Beijing resisted its enforcement and blocked the armies' efforts to reach Tiananmen Square to clear out the hunger strikers, both students and CCP leaders dug in; but both were deeply divided bodies. Indeed, divisions within the student-led movement caused it to lose its direction; and

divisions within the central CCP leadership incapacitated it. For two weeks, the central leadership wrangled over who was right and the best course of action. On June 4, the "hard-liners" won out, and they chose to use military power rather than a negotiated solution with the students.

Did the students make significant or well-thought-out statements about "democracy" or realistic demands on China's leaders? The short and preliminary answer is no; but then, is this really the appropriate question to ask? One could argue that what the students *said* was less important than what they *did*: They mobilized the population of China's capital and other major cities to support a profound challenge to the legitimacy of the CCP's leadership. Even if workers believed that "You can't eat democracy," and even if they participated in the demonstrations for their *own* reasons (such as gripes about inflation and pensions), they did support the students' demand that the CCP carry out further political reforms. This was because the students successfully promoted the idea that if China had had a democratic system rather than authoritarian rule, the leadership would have been more responsive to the workers' bread-and-butter issues.

Repression Within China Following the Crackdown

By August 1989, the CCP leadership had established quotas of "bad elements" for work units and identified 20 categories of people to be targeted for punishment. But people were more reluctant than in the past to follow orders to expose their friends, colleagues, and family members, not only because such verdicts had often been reversed at a later time, but also because many people questioned the CCP's version of what happened in Beijing on June 4. Although the citizenry worried about informers, there seemed to be complicity from top to bottom, whether inside or outside the ranks of the CCP, in refusing to go along with efforts to ferret out demonstrators and sympathizers with the prodemocracy, antiparty movement. Party leaders below the central level appeared to believe that the central government's leadership was doomed; for this reason, they dared not carry out its orders. Inevitably, there would be a reversal of verdicts, and they did not want to be caught in it.

As party leaders in work units droned on in mandatory political study sessions about Deng Xiaoping's important writings, workers wondered how long it would be before the June 4 military crackdown would be condemned as a "counterrevolutionary crime against the people." Individuals in work units had to fill out lengthy questionnaires. A standard one had 24 questions aimed at "identifying the enemy." Among them were such questions as, "What did you think when

Hu Yaobang died?" "When Zhao Ziyang went to Tiananmen Square, what did you think? Where were you?" At one university, each faculty member's questionnaire had to be verified by two people (other than one's own family) or the individual involved would not be allowed to teach.[5]

As part of the repression that followed the military crackdown in June 1989, the government carried out arrests of hundreds of those who participated in the demonstrations. During the world's absorption with the Persian Gulf War in 1991, the government suddenly announced the trials and verdicts on some of China's best known leaders of the 1989 demonstrations. Of those who were summarily executed, available information indicates that almost all were workers trying to form labor unions. All the other known 1989 student and dissident leaders were eventually released, although some were deported to the West as a condition of their release. The government has also occasionally re-arrested 1989 protesters for other activities. In 1998, for example, some former protesters made bold attempts to establish a new party to challenge Chinese Communist Party rule. Although their efforts to register this new party were at first tolerated, several were later arrested, tried, and sentenced to prison. Finally, as discussed below, the government has attempted to ferret out and arrest activist leaders of the Falun Gong.

In spite of these important exceptions, many repressive controls were relaxed, and China's mass media have steadily expanded the parameters of allowable topics and opinions. Today, although there are occasional arrests of individuals who are blatantly challenging CCP rule, and although the establishment of a competing party is not tolerated, the leadership is more focused on harnessing the talents of China's best and brightest for the country's modernization than it is on controlling dissent. No longer a revolutionary party, the CCP is intent on effectively governing and developing China.

THE PEOPLE OF CHINA

Population Control

In 2007, China's population was estimated to be over 1.3 billion. In the 1950s, Mao had encouraged population growth, as he considered a large population to be a major source of strength: Cheap human labor could take the place of expensive technology and equipment. No sustained attempts to limit Chinese population occurred until the mid-1970s. Even then, because there were no penalties for those Chinese who ignored them, population control programs were only marginally successful.

In 1979, the government launched a serious birth-control campaign, rewarding couples giving birth to only one child with work bonuses and priority in housing. The only child was later to receive preferential treatment in university admissions and job assignments (a policy eventually abandoned). Couples who had more than one child, on the other hand, were to be penalized by a 10 percent decrease in their annual wages, and their children would not be eligible for free education and health care benefits.

The one-child policy in China's major cities was rigorously enforced, to the point where it was almost impossible for a woman to get away with a second pregnancy. Who was allowed to have a child, as well as when she could give birth, was rigidly controlled by the woman's work unit. Furthermore, with so many state-owned enterprises paying close to half of their entire annual wages as "bonuses," authorities came up with additional sanctions to ensure compliance. Workers were usually organized in groups of 10 to 30 individuals. If any woman in the group gave birth to more than one child, *the entire group* would lose its annual bonus. With such overwhelming penalties for the group as a whole, pressures for a couple not to give birth to a second child were enormous.

To ensure that any unauthorized pregnancy did not occur, women who had already given birth were required to stand in front of x-ray machines (fluoroscopes) to verify that their IUDs (intrauterine birthcontrol devices) were still in place. Abortions could and would be performed throughout the period of a woman's unsanctioned pregnancy. (The moral issues that surround abortions for some Christians are not concerns for the Chinese.)

The effectiveness of China's family planning policy in the cities has been due not merely to the surveillance by state-owned work units, neighborhood committees, and the "granny police" who watch over the families in their residential areas. Changed social attitudes also play a critical role, and urban Chinese now accept the absolute necessity of population control in their overcrowded cities.

The one-child policy in China's cities has led to a generation of remarkably spoiled children. Known as "little emperors," these only children are the center of attention of six anxious adults (the parents and two sets of grandparents), who carefully scrutinize their every movement. It has led to the overuse of medical services by these parents and grandparents, who rush their only child/grandchild to the doctor at the first signs of a sniffle or sore throat. It has also led to overfed, even obese, children. Being overweight used to be considered a hedge against bad times, and the Chinese were initially pleased that their children were becoming heavier. A common greeting showing admiration had long been, "You have become fat!" But as contemporary urban Chinese adopt many of the values associated in the developed world with

becoming wealthier, they are changing their perspectives on weight. Jane Fonda–style exercise programs are now a regular part of Chinese television, and weight-loss salons and fat farms are coming into vogue for China's well-fed middle class. Still, most people view the major purpose of exercise as staying healthy and keeping China a strong nation, not looking attractive.

The strictly enforced and administered family planning program has been undermined by a number of trends. First, in the cities, there are large migrant populations who are really under no one's control: the rural villages from which they fled have no responsibility for them; and the cities to which they migrate rarely issue them a "household registration" certificate, so they really belong to no official's jurisdiction. Yet, rural migrant families usually prefer to have only one child, as in their tenuous economic circumstances, taking care of more than one would make survival in a new city far more difficult. Second, well-to-do entrepreneurs who live in private housing can avoid population-control measures because they are not part of any public housing or work unit. They are willing to pay all the relevant fines and bribes necessary to have as many children as they want. Nevertheless, even they are unlikely to have more than two children. Indeed, some members of China's growing middle class are deciding not to have children, for the same reasons as in other more developed societies: they want to pursue careers and spend time and money in ways that leave little room for children. Third, in recent years, there has been a more relaxed enforcement of the one-child policy because of the demographic crisis on the horizon: too few young people to support the large number of elderly people in future years.

One step the government has taken to address this inverted population pyramid is to allow those married couples who both come from one-child families to have two children. The government has also tried to grapple with one of the unintended side-effects of the one-child policy: the aborting of female fetuses. Given the cultural preference for males, a certain percentage of female fetuses are aborted. (This has resulted in a lopsided male-female ratio of at least 105:100, although in some areas it is said to be as high as 125:100. These are, however, much debated figures. The problem of a lopsided sex ratio is true in many Asian countries, including India and South Korea.) The sex of fetuses is usually known because of the widespread use in China of ultrasound machines. To use these machines to reveal the sex of the child is illegal, but for a very small bribe, doctors will usually do so. In addition, although female infanticide is illegal, it sometimes happens, especially in rural areas. So the government

has promulgated several new laws and has investigated several thousand cases of alleged abuse of sex-identification of fetuses.

In the meantime, China's orphanages have absorbed some of the unwanted girl babies, now much sought after in the West. In 2007, however, China instituted new regulations that make it harder for foreigners to adopt Chinese babies (almost all of whom are girls—boys are usually only put up for adoption if there is a physical or mental defect). Arguably, one of the reasons for this change in policy is because of the other demographic crisis resulting from the one-child policy—tens of millions of men coming of marriage age without women to marry. Apart from societal unhappiness, the lack of brides has led to a sharp increase in the kidnapping of young women, as well as the practice of selling girls as brides in rural marketplaces when they reach marriageable age (usually to men who live in remote villages that have little to offer a new bride).

In the vast rural areas of China, where some three-quarters of the population still live, efforts to enforce the one-child policy have met with less success than in the cities, because the benefits and punishments are not as relevant for peasants. After the communes were disbanded in the early 1980s and families were given their own land to till, peasants wanted sons, to do the heavy farm labor. As a result, the government's policy in the countryside became more flexible. In some villages, if a woman gives birth to a girl and decides to have another child in hopes of having a boy, she may pay the government a substantial fee (usually an amount more than the entire annual income of the family) in order to be allowed to do so. Yet, in an ironic reflection of this still very male-dominant society, today's farming, which is far more physically demanding and less lucrative than factory jobs, is increasingly left to the women, while the men go off to towns and cities to make their fortunes.

Some analysts suggest that at least several million peasants have taken steps to ensure that their female offspring are not counted toward their one-child (and now, in some places, two-child) limit: One strategy is for a pregnant woman simply to move to another village to have her child. Since the local village leaders are not responsible for women's reproduction when they are not from their own village, women are not harassed into getting an abortion in other villages. If the child is a boy, the mother can simply return to her native village, pay a fine, and register him; if a girl, the mother can return and not register the child. Thus a whole generation of young girls is growing up in the countryside without ever having been registered with the government. Since, except for schooling, peasants have few claims to state-supplied benefits

FIRMLY IMPLEMENT
THE BASIC NATIONAL POLICY
OF FAMILY PLANNING!

(Alasdair Drysdale/DAL mhhe010359)

The Chinese government has made great efforts to curb the country's population growth by promoting the merits of the one-child family. Today, China has an average annual population growth rate of 0.59 percent.

anyway, they may consider this official non-existence of their daughters a small price to pay for having as many children as necessary until giving birth to a boy. And if this practice is as common as some believe, it may mean that China will not face quite such a large demographic crisis in the ratio between males and females as has been projected.

Males continue to be more valued in Chinese culture because only sons are permitted to carry on traditional Chinese family rituals and ancestor worship. This is unbearably painful for families without sons, who feel that their entire ancestral history, often recorded over several hundred years on village-temple tablets, is coming to an end. As a result, a few villages have changed the very foundations of ancestral worship: They now permit daughters to continue the family lineage down the female line. The government itself is encouraging this practice, and it is also changing certain other family-related policies. For example, it used to be the son who was responsible under the law for taking care of their parents. This meant that parents whose only child was a girl could not expect to be supported in their old age. Now, both sons and daughters are legally responsible. Furthermore, it is hoped that a new system of social security and pensions for retired people will gradually lead the state and employers to absorb the responsibility for caring for the elderly.

China's strict population-control policies have been effective: Since 1977, the popula-

tion has grown at an *average* annual rate of 1.1 percent, one of the lowest in the developing world. (As of 2006, the annual population growth rate was 0.59 percent—considerably below the fertility replacement rate of 2.1.) Yet, even this low rate works out to an average annual population *increase* for several years to come. (This is because previous generations had large numbers of offspring.) The dilemma is this: on the one hand, the growing population is a drain on China's limited resources and poses a threat to its environment and economic development. As China continues to provide a substantial percentage of its citizens with a higher standard of living, the continuing pollution of China's air, water, and land, and the depletion of nonrenewable resources and energy are leading to ecological crises that are increasingly difficult to redress. On the other hand, there are concerns that the population replacement rate is too low to provide enough workers to support the growing elderly population. Yet, arguably the productivity of new generations of workers will be far higher; for as farmers abandon the land and move into cities, their productivity (that is, their return on labor) increases; and so does the productivity of workers who move into less labor-intensive jobs, or move from manufacturing into the service sector. As a result, it could well turn out that it will take far fewer younger workers to support China's larger retired community than it did in the past. And, as is the case in developed

countries now facing problems of a burgeoning retired population, those beyond the retirement age who are still able may simply keep working.

Women

It is hardly surprising that overlaying (but never eradicating) China's traditional culture with a communist ideology in which men and women are supposed to be equal has generated a bundle of contradictions. Under Chinese Communist Party rule, women have long had more rights and opportunities than women in almost any other developing country, and in certain respects, more than women in some developed countries. For example, Chinese women were expected to work, not stay at home. And, in state-owned enterprises, they received from three to twelve months of paid maternity leave and child care in the workplace, decades before this became common practice in the Western countries. Although Chinese women rarely broke through the "glass ceiling" to the highest levels of the workplace or the ruling elite, and were often given "women's work," their pay scale was similar to that of men. Furthermore, an ideological morality that insisted on respect for women as equals (with both men and women being addressed as "comrades") combined with a de-emphasis on the importance of sexuality, resulted in at least a superficial respect for women that was rare before the Communist period.

The economic reforms that began in 1979, however, precipitated changes in the manner in which women are treated, and in how women act. While many women entrepreneurs and workers benefit as much as the men from economic reforms, there have also been certain throwbacks to earlier times that have undercut women's equality. Women are now treated much more as sex objects than they used to be; and while some women revel in their new freedom to beautify themselves, some companies will hire only women who are perceived as physically attractive, and many enterprises are now using women as "window dressing." For example, women dressed in *qipao*—the traditional, slim-fitting Chinese dress slit high on the thigh—stand outside restaurants and other establishments to entice customers. At business meetings, many women have become mere tea-pourers. In newspapers, employment ads for Chinese enterprises often state in so many words that only young, good-looking women need apply.

The emphasis on profits and efficiency since the reforms has also made state-run enterprises reluctant to hire women because of the costs in maternity benefits and because mothers are still more likely than fathers to be in charge of sick children and the household. Under the socialist system, where the purpose of an enterprise was not necessarily to make profits but to fulfill such socialist objectives as the equality of women and full employment, women fared better. Economic reforms, which emphasize profitability, have provided enterprise managers with the excuse they need not to hire women. Whatever the real reason, they can always claim that their refusal to hire more women or to promote them is justified: Women are more costly, or less competent, or less reliable.

National Minorities

Ninety-two percent of the population is Han Chinese. Although only 8 percent is classified as "national minorities," they occupy more than 60 percent of China's geographical expanse. These minorities inhabit almost all of the border areas, including Tibet, Inner Mongolia, and Xinjiang Province. The stability and allegiance of the border areas are important for China's national security. Furthermore, China's borders with the many neighboring countries are poorly defined, and members of the same minority usually live on both sides of the borders.

To address this issue, China's central government pursued policies designed to get the minorities on the Chinese side of the borders to identify with the Han Chinese majority. Rather than admitting to this objective of undermining distinctive national identities, the CCP leaders phrased the policies in terms of getting rid of the minorities' "feudal" customs, such as religious practices, which are contrary to the "scientific" values of socialism. Teaching children their native language was often prohibited. At times these policies have been brutal and have caused extreme bitterness among the minorities, particularly the Tibetans and the Uighurs (who practice Islam) in the northwest border province of Xinjiang. The extreme policies of the "10 bad years" that encouraged the elimination of the "four olds" led to the wanton destruction of minority cultural artifacts, temples, mosques, texts, and statuary.

In the 1980s, the Deng Xiaoping leadership conceded that Beijing's harsh assimilation policies had been ill-conceived, and it tried to gain the loyalty of the national minorities through more culturally sensitive policies. Minority children are now taught their own language in schools, alongside the "national" language (Mandarin). By the late 1980s, however, the loosening of controls had led to further challenges to Beijing's control, so the central government tightened up security in Xinjiang and reimposed martial law in Tibet in an effort to quell protests and riots against Beijing's discriminatory policies. Martial law was lifted in Tibet in 1990, but security has remained tight ever since. The terrorist attacks on the United States on September 11, 2001, led to even greater surveillance and controls on those minority groups that practice Islam and are believed to have ties with terrorist organizations in the Middle East.

Tibet

The Dalai Lama is the most important spiritual leader of the Tibetans, but he lives in exile in India, where he fled after a Chinese crackdown on Tibetans in 1959. He has stepped up his efforts to reach some form of accommodation with China. The Dalai Lama insists that he is not pressing for independence, only for greater autonomy; and that as long as he is in charge, Tibetans will use only non-violent methods to this end. The Dalai Lama believes that more Tibetan control over their own affairs is necessary to protect their culture from extinction. Nevertheless, the people who surround the Dalai Lama are far more militant and see autonomy as only the first step toward independence from China.

In the past, the Chinese government made a concerted effort to assimilate Tibetans by eradicating Tibetan cultural practices and institutions that differentiated them from the majority Han culture. These policies were largely abandoned during the 1980s. At this point, the major threat to Tibetan culture comes from globalization, and from Chinese entrepreneurs who, thanks to economic liberalization policies, have taken over many of the commercial and entrepreneurial activities of Tibet. Ironically, the Tibetan feelings about the Chinese mirror the feelings of the Chinese toward the West: The Tibetans want Chinese technology and commercial goods, but not the values that come with the people providing those goods and technology. And among Tibetans, as among the Chinese, the young are more likely to want to become part of the modern world, to be modern and hip, and to leave behind traditional culture and values. Young Tibetans in Lhasa have been swept up in efforts to make money, a pleasure somewhat reduced by the fact that the increasingly large number of Chinese entrepreneurs in Lhasa usually make higher profits than they do. If Tibetan culture is to survive, Tibetans need to take on a modern identity, one that allows them to be both Tibetan and modern at the same time. Otherwise, the sheer dynamism of Han Chinese culture and globalization may well overwhelm Tibetan culture.[6]

Not all Tibetans accept the Dalai Lama's preferred path of nonviolence. In 1996, Beijing revealed that there were isolated bombing incidents and violent clashes between anti-Chinese Tibetans (reportedly armed) and Chinese authorities. The government, in response, sealed off most monasteries in Lhasa, the capital of Tibet. Beginning in the late 1990s, however, China decided to restore many of Tibet's monasteries—in part to placate Tibetans, in part to attract tourists. China has also made it far easier for foreigners to travel to Tibet. By 2006 it had completed a new highway across the length of the vast Qinghai Province plateau to connect Tibet with the rest of China; and another engineering feat—a railroad through the Tibetan mountains to the capital, Lhasa.

As a result of a policy to alleviate poverty in Tibet, the autonomous region now receives more financial aid from the central Chinese government than any other province or autonomous region in China. Tibetans are better fed, clothed, and housed than in the past; but Tibet still remains China's poorest administrative region. Generous state subsidies have not generated development. This is largely because of disastrous, centrally conceived policies, a bloated administrative structure, a large Chinese military presence to house and feed, disdain for Tibetan culture, and incompetent Han cadres who have little understanding of local issues and rarely speak Tibetan.[7] Tibet's land-locked, remote location and its lack of arable land certainly exacerbate problems in development.

Nevertheless, in recent years, Tibetan farmers have discovered that they can produce a valuable caterpillar fungus, *Cordyceps sinensis* (also called "winter worm, summer grass"). The fungus consumes caterpillars, then produces a columnar growth that shoots through the soil. It can be harvested and dried. It is much sought after by the Chinese as an

This family lives in a commune in Inner Mongolia. China's policies have tended to undermine the distinctive national identities of those living close to its borders.

herbal remedy for enhanced health, longevity, and male potency. Overnight, some of Tibet's poorest farmers have gained considerable wealth from cultivation of the caterpillar. Tibet's tourist industry is also suddenly booming, thanks to an expanded airport, new hotels, fewer restrictions by the Chinese government, and the determination of both Chinese and Western travel agencies to provide opportunities for tourists to visit "Shangrila."

None of this is meant to suggest that Tibet is going to leave poverty behind any time soon, even though the Chinese government is fully engaged in an anti-poverty program in Tibet. Regardless of what actions the Chinese government takes to develop Tibet, moreover, it is viewed with suspicion: New roads or railroads? The better for the Chinese to exploit Tibetan resources and even to invade. Encouraging tourism in Tibet or sending Tibetans to higher-quality Chinese schools outside of Tibet? The better to destroy Tibetan culture. Allowing Chinese entrepreneurs to do business in Tibet or desperately poor youth from neighboring provinces to go to Tibet for work? The better to take away jobs from Tibetans. Projects to develop Tibet's infrastructure for development? The better to destroy its environment. In short, Tibetans tend to regard all of Beijing's policies, and Han cadres in Tibet, with suspicion.

Tibet's anger toward China's central government was exacerbated by Beijing's decision in 1995 not to accept the Tibetan

Buddhists' choice (chosen according to traditional Tibetan Buddhist ritual) of a young boy as the reincarnation of the second-most important spiritual leader of the Tibetans, the Panchen Lama, who died in 1989. Instead, Beijing substituted its own six-year old candidate. The Tibetans' choice, meanwhile, is living in seclusion somewhere in Beijing, under the watchful eye of the Chinese. China's concern is that any new spiritual leader could become a focus for a new push for Tibetan independence—an eventuality it wishes to avoid.

Inner Mongolia

Inner Mongolia (an autonomous region under Beijing's control) lies on the southern side of Mongolia, which is an independent state. Beijing's concern that the Mongolians in China would want to unite with Mongolia led to a policy that diluted the Mongol population with what has grown to be an overwhelming majority of Han Chinese. According to the 2000 national census, the national minority (largely Mongol) population was only 4.93 million—a mere 20.76% of the total population of 23.76 million. Inner Mongolia's capital, Huhhot, is essentially a Han city, and assimilation of Mongols into Han culture in the capital is almost complete. Mongolians are dispersed throughout the vast countryside as shepherds, herdsmen, and farmers and retain many of their ethnic traditions and practices.

Events in (Outer) Mongolia have led China's central leadership to keep a watchful eye on Inner Mongolia. In 1989, Mongolia's government—theoretically independent but in fact under Soviet tutelage until—decided to permit multiparty rule at the expense of the Communist Party's complete control; and in democratic elections held in 1996, the Mongolian Communist Party was ousted from power.

Beijing has grown increasingly concerned that these democratic inklings might spread to their neighboring cousins in Inner Mongolia, with a resulting challenge to one-party CCP rule. China's leadership worries that the Mongols in Inner Mongolia may try to secede from China and join with the independent state of Mongolia because of their shared culture. So far, however, those Inner Mongolians who have traveled to Mongolia have been surprised by the relative lack of development there and have shown little interest in drumming up a secessionist movement. Nevertheless, privatization of the economy, combined with an insensitivity to Mongolian culture have led to periodic demonstrations against the Han Chinese-dominated government.

Muslim Minorities

In the far northwest, the predominantly Muslim population—particularly the Uyghur minority—of Xinjiang Province continues to challenge the authority of China's central leadership. The loosening of policies aimed at assimilating the minority populations into the Han (Chinese) culture has given a rebirth to Islamic culture and practices, including prayer five times a day, architecture in the Islamic style, traditional Islamic medicine, and teaching Islam in the schools. With the dissolution of the Soviet Union in 1991 into 15 independent states, the ties between the Islamic states on China's borders (Kazakhstan, Kyrgyzstan, and Tajikistan, as well as Afghanistan and Pakistan) have accelerated rapidly.

Beijing is concerned that China's Islamic minorities may find that they have more in common with these neighboring Islamic nations than with the Chinese Han majority and may attempt to secede from China. Signs of a growing, worldwide Islamic movement have exacerbated Beijing's anxieties about controlling China's Islamic minorities. The 9/11/01 attacks by Islamic terrorists, followed by the U.S.–led "war on terrorism" throughout the world, have led China to intensify its efforts to root out Islamic radicals. Although some analysts argue that the war on terrorism has given Beijing an ideal pretext for cracking down on what is a legitimate desire for national independence by Uyghur Muslims in Xinjiang, others accept Beijing's view that those using violence (including bombs) are "terrorists," not "freedom fighters."

Uyghurs who have engaged in terrorism are not motivated by religious fanaticism, but rather, by a desire to achieve a concrete, pragmatic goal: Xinjiang's secession from China. Still, in the last decade, they have received funding from the Islamic world, including, it is believed, from terrorist groups located therein. The Uyghurs do not, however, accept the tenets of Islamic fundamentalists, nor that they view their struggle against Chinese rule as a struggle of good against evil. (Indeed, it has often been noted that Islam is much more moderate, tolerant, and progressive as it spreads eastward.) Evidence that the Uyghurs are engaged in an out-and-out political struggle for independence from Chinese rule would be that Uyghur violence in Xinjiang has not been in form of terrorist attacks on the local Han population but, rather, on the state structure of the governing Han. So it could be argued that, except for the 1997 attacks in Beijing on innocent bystanders, and several bus bombings in Xinjiang, Uyghur violence is not "terrorism" as it is now defined.

China's nearly 9 million Hui—Han Chinese who practice Islam—are also classified as a "national minority," but over many centuries, they have become so integrated into mainstream Chinese culture that at this point in history their only remaining distinct characteristic is their practice of Islam. They speak standard Chinese and live together with other Han. Although a large number of Hui live in one autonomous region, Ningxia, they are also spread out throughout China. In general, in spite of shared Islamic beliefs, they do not identify with Uyghur nationalism, which is seen as particular to Uyghur ethnicity, and not to a broader Islamic identity.

Religion

Confucianism

Confucianism is the "religion" most closely associated with China. It is not, however, a religion in Western terms, as there is no place for gods, faith, or many other beliefs associated with formal religions. But like most religions, it does have a system of ethics for human relationships; and it adds to this what most religions do not have, namely, principles for good governance that include the hierarchical ordering of relationships, with obedience and subordination of those in lower ranks to those in higher ranks.

The Chinese Communists rejected Confucianism until the 1980s, but not because they saw it as an "opiate of the masses." (That was Karl Marx's description of religion, which he viewed as a way of trapping people in a web of superstitions, robbing them of their money, and causing them to passively endure their miserable lives on Earth.) Instead, they denounced Confucianism for providing the ethical rationale for a system of patriarchy that allowed officials to insist on obedience from subordinates. During the years in which "leftists" such as the Gang of Four set the agenda, moreover, the CCP rejected Confucianism for its emphasis on education as a criterion for joining the ruling elite. Instead, the CCP favored ideological commitment—"redness"—as the primary criterion for ruling. The reforms since 1979, however, have emphasized the need for an educated elite, and Confucian values of hard work and the importance of the family are frequently referred to. The revival of Confucian values has, in fact, provided an important foundation for China's renewed emphasis on national identity and Chinese culture as a substitute for the now nearly defunct values of Marxism-Leninism-Mao Thought.

Buddhism

Buddhism has remained important among some of the largest of the national minorities, notably the Tibetans and Mongols. The CCP's efforts to eradicate formal Buddhism have been interpreted by the minorities as national oppression by the Han Chinese. As a result, the revival of Buddhism since the 1980s has been associated with efforts by Tibetans and Mongolians to assert their national identities and to gain greater autonomy in formulating their own policies. Under the influence of the more moderate policies of the Deng Xiaoping reformist leadership, the CCP reconsidered its efforts to eliminate religion. The 1982 State Constitution permits religious freedom, whereas previously only atheism was allowed. The state has actually encouraged the restoration of Buddhist temples, in part because of Beijing's awareness of the continuing tensions caused by its efforts to deny minorities their respective religious practices, and in part because of a desire to attract both tourists and money to the minority areas.

But Buddhism is far more widespread than in just Tibet and Inner Mongolia. Indeed, popular Buddhism, which is full of stories and Buddhist mythology, is pervasive throughout the rural population—and even among some urban populations. Popular Buddhist beliefs are even worked into many of the sects, cults, and folk religions in China. Today, Buddhist temples are frequented by increasingly large numbers of Chinese, who go there to propitiate their ancestors and to pray for good health and more wealth.

Folk Religions

For most Chinese, folk religions are far more important than any organized religion.[8] The CCP's best efforts to eradicate folk religions and to impart in their place an educated "scientific" viewpoint have failed. Animism—the belief that nonliving things have spirits that should be respected through worship—continues to be practiced by China's vast peasantry. Ancestor worship—based on the belief that the living can communicate with the dead and that the dead spirits to whom sacrifices are ritually made have the ability to bring a better (or worse) life to the living—once again absorbs much of the income of China's peasants. The costs of offerings, burning paper money, and using shamans and priests to perform rituals that will heal the sick, appease the ancestors, and exorcise ghosts (who are often poorly treated ancestors returned to haunt their descendants) at times of birth, marriage, and death, can be financially burdensome. But the willingness of peasants to spend money on traditional religious folk practices is contributing to the reconstruction of practices prohibited in earlier decades of Communist rule.

Taoism, Qigong, and Falun Gong

Taoism, which requires its disciples to renounce the secular world, has had few adherents in China since the early twentieth century. But during the repression that followed the crackdown on Tiananmen Square's prodemocracy movement in 1989, many Chinese who felt unable to speak freely turned to mysticism and Taoism. Qigong, the ancient Taoist art of deep breathing, had by 1990 become a national pastime. Some 30 Taoist priests in China took on the role of national soothsayers, portending the future of everything from the weather to China's political leadership. What these priests said—or were believed to have said—quickly spread through a vast rumor network in the cities. Meanwhile, on Chinese Communist Party–controlled television, qigong experts swallowed needles and thread, only to have the needles subsequently come out of their noses perfectly threaded. It is widely believed that, with a sufficient concentration of *qi* (vital energy or breath), a practitioner may literally knock a person to the ground.[9] The revival of Taoist mysticism and meditation, folk religion, and formal religions suggests a need to find meaning from religion to fill the moral and ideological vacuum created by the near-collapse of Communist values.

Falun Gong ("Wheel of Law"), which the government has declared a "sect"—and hence not entitled to claim a constitutional right to practice religion freely—has, however, been charged with involvement in a range of illegal activities. Falun Gong is a complex mixture of Buddhism, Taoism, and qigong practices—the last relying on many ideas from traditional Chinese medicine. According to its adherents, the focus is on healing and good health, but it also has a millennial component, predicting the end of the world and a bad ending for those who are not practitioners. According to the government, the sect's practices can endanger people's health and have in fact caused the deaths of hundreds. It also accuses the sect of being a front for antigovernment political activities.

In 1999, thousands of Falun Gong adherents, some from distant provinces, suddenly materialized in front of CCP headquarters, on the edge of Tiananmen Square in Beijing. Hundreds were arrested, but most were soon released and sent back to their home provinces. Others were sent to labor camps or jailed, and some died while incarcerated.[10] In many state-owned work units, officials continue to meet regularly to discuss the dangers of Falun Gong, to encourage followers to end their participation in Falun Gong, and to root out its leaders.

Religious practice often provides the foundation for illegal or "black" societies. Falun Gong and a number of other sects have been accused of using their organizations as fronts for drugs, smuggling, prostitution, and other illegal activities. Religious sects and black societies are widely believed to provide the basis of power for candidates for office. In the countryside, religion can become a tool of the family clans, who sometimes use it to pressure villagers to vote for their candidates.

Christianity

Christianity, which was introduced in the nineteenth and early twentieth centuries by European missionaries, has several million known adherents; and its churches, which were often used as warehouses or public offices after the Communist victory in 1949, have been reopened for religious practice. Bibles in several editions are available for purchase in many large-city bookstores. A steady stream of Christian proselytizers flow to China in search of new converts. Today's churches are attended as much by the curious as by the devout. As with eating Western food in places such as McDonald's and Kentucky Fried Chicken, attending Christian churches is a way that some Chinese feel they can participate in Western culture. Some Chinese want to become Christians because they see that in the West, Christians are rich and powerful. They believe that Christianity helps explain the wealth and power of Western capitalists, and hope that converting to Christianity will do the same for them.

The government generally permits mainstream Christian churches to practice in China, but it continues to exercise one major control over Roman Catholics: Their loyalty must be declared to the state, not to the pope. The Vatican is prohibited from involvement with China's priesthood, and Beijing does not recognize the validity of the Vatican's appointment of bishops and cardinals for China. Underground "house churches," primarily for smaller Christian sects, offshoots of mainstream Protestant religions, and papal Catholics, are forbidden. Nevertheless, they seem to flourish as officials busy themselves with addressing far more pressing social issues.

Since the mid-1990s, the government has tried to clamp down on non-mainstream Christian churches as well as religious sects, arresting and even jailing some of their leaders. They have justified their actions on the grounds that, as in the West, some of the churches are involved in practices that endanger their adherents; some are actually involved in seditious activities against the state; and some are set up as fronts for illegal activities, including gambling, prostitution, and drugs.

Marxism-Leninism-Mao Zedong Thought

In general, Marxists are atheists. They believe that religions hinder the development of "rational" behavior and values that are so important to modernization. Yet societies seem to need some sort of spiritual, moral, and ethical guidance. For Communist party–led states, Marxism was believed to be adequate to fulfill this role. In China, however, Marxism-Leninism was reshaped by Mao Zedong Thought to accommodate for Chinese culture and conditions. Paramount among these conditions was that China was a predominantly peasant society, not a society in which there was a capitalist class exploiting large numbers of urban workers. The re-packaged ideology

became known as Marxism-Leninism-Mao Zedong Thought. The Chinese leadership believed that it provided the ethical values necessary to guide China toward communism; and it was considered an integrated, rational thought system.

Nevertheless, this core of China's Communist political ideology exhibited many of the trappings of religions. It included scriptures (the works of Marx, Lenin, and Mao, as well as party doctrine); a spiritual head (Mao); and ritual observances (particularly during the Cultural Revolution, when Chinese were forced to participate in the political equivalent of Bible study each day). Largely thanks to the shaping of this ideology by Maoism, it included moral axioms that embodied traditional Chinese—and, some would say, Confucian—values that resemble teachings in other religions. Thus the moral of Mao's story of "The Foolish Old Man Who Wanted to Remove a Mountain" is essentially identical to the Christian principle "If you have faith you can walk on water," based on a story in the New Testament. Like this teaching, the essence of Mao Zedong Thought was concerned with the importance of a correct moral (political) consciousness.

In the 1980s, the more pragmatic leadership focused on liberalizing reforms and encouraged the people to "seek truth from facts" rather than from Marxism Leninism-Mao Zedong Thought. As a result, the role of ideology declined, in spite of efforts by more conservative elements in the political leadership to keep it as a guiding moral and political force. Participants in the required weekly "political study" sessions in most urban work units abandoned any pretense of interest in politics. Instead, they focused on such issues as "how to do our work better" (that is, how to become more efficient and make a profit) that were in line with the more pragmatic approach to the workplace. Nevertheless, campaigns like the "get civilized" and anticorruption ones retain a strong moralistic tone.

Ideology has not been entirely abandoned. In the context of modernizing the economy and raising the standard of living, the current leadership is still committed to building "socialism with Chinese characteristics." Marxist-Leninist ideology is still being reformulated in China; but it is increasingly evident that few true believers in communism remain. Rarely does a Chinese leader even mention Marxism-Leninism in a speech. Leaders instead focus on modernization and becoming more efficient; they are more likely to discuss interest rates and trade balances than ideology. Fully aware that they need something to replace their own nearly defunct guiding ideological principles, however, and fearing that pure materialism and consumerism are inadequate substitutes, China's leaders seem to be relying on patriotism, nationalism, and national iden-

DENG XIAOPING = TENG HSIAO-P'ING. WHAT IS PINYIN?

Chinese is the oldest of the world's active languages and is now spoken and written by more people than any other modern language. Chinese is written in the form of characters, which have evolved over several thousand years from picture symbols (like ancient Egyptian hieroglyphics) written on oracle bones to the more abstract forms now in use. Although spoken Chinese varies greatly from dialect to dialect (for example, Mandarin, Cantonese, Shanghai-ese), the characters used to represent the language remain the same throughout China. Dialects are really just different ways of pronouncing the same characters.

There are more than 50,000 different Chinese characters. A well-educated person may be able to recognize as many as 25,000 characters, but basic literacy requires familiarity with only a few thousand.

Since Chinese is written in the form of characters rather than by a phonetic alphabet, Chinese words must be transliterated so that foreigners can pronounce them. This means that the sound of the character must be put into an alphabetic approximation.

Since English uses the Roman alphabet, Chinese characters are Romanized. (We do the same thing with other languages that are based on non-Roman alphabets, such as Russian, Greek, Hebrew, and Arabic.) Over the years, a number of methods have been developed to Romanize the Chinese language. Each method presents what the linguists who developed it believe to be the best way of approximating the sound of Chinese characters. *Pinyin* (literally, "spell sounds"), the system developed in the People's Republic of China, has gradually become the most commonly accepted system of Romanizing Chinese.

Chinese characters are the symbols used to write Chinese. Modern Chinese characters fall into two categories: one with a phonetic component, the other without it. Most of those without a phonetic component developed from pictographs. From ancient writing on archaeological relics we can see their evolution, as in the examples shown (from left to right) above.

However, other systems are still used in areas such as Taiwan. This can cause some confusion, since the differences between Romanization systems can be quite significant. For example, in pinyin, the name of China's dominant leader is spelled Deng Xiaoping. But the Wade-Giles system, which was until recently the Romanization method most widely used by Westerners, transliterates his name as Teng Hsiao-p'ing. Same person, same characters, but a difference in how to spell his name in Roman letters.

---

tity as the key components of a new ideology. Its primary purpose is very simple: economic modernization and support of the leadership of the Chinese Communist Party.

Undergirding China's nationalism is a fierce pride in China's history, civilization, and people. Insult, snub, slight, or challenge China, and the result is certain to be a country united behind its leadership, against the offender. To oppose the CCP or its objective of modernization is viewed as "unpatriotic." China's nationalism, on the other hand, is fired by anti-foreign sentiments. These sentiments derive from the belief that foreign countries are—either militarily, economically, or through insidious cultural invasion—attempting to hurt China or to intervene in China's sovereign affairs by telling China's rulers how to govern properly. This is most notably the case whenever the Western countries condemn China for its human-rights record. U.S. support for Taiwan, and the U.S. bombing of the Chinese Embassy in Belgrade, Yugoslavia, during the Kosovo War in May 1999, fueled Chinese nationalism and injected even more tension into Sino–American relations. China's decision to join with the United States in its war on terrorism since 9/11 has, however, resulted in a toned-down nationalism and a less strident approach to international relationships. China's growing entanglement in a web of international economic and political relationships has also contributed to a softening of its nationalistic stance.

Language

By the time of the Shang Dynasty, which ruled in the second millennium B.C., the Chinese had a written language based on "characters." Over 4,000 years, these characters, or "ideographs," have evolved from being pictorial representations of objects or ideas into their present-day form. Each character usually contains a phonetic element and one (or more) of the 212 symbols called "radicals" that help categorize and organize them.[11] Before the New Culture Movement of the 1920s, only a tiny elite of highly educated men could read these ideographs, which were organized in the difficult grammar of the classical style of writing, a style that in no way reflected the spoken language. All this changed with language reform in the 1920s: The classical style was abandoned, and the written language became almost identical in its structure to the spoken language.

Increasing Literacy

When the Chinese Communists came to power in 1949, they decided to facilitate the process of becoming literate by allowing only a few thousand of the more than 50,000 Chinese characters in existence to be used in printing newspapers, official documents, and educational materials. However, since a word is usually composed of a combination of two characters, these few thousand characters form the basis of a fairly rich vocabulary:

Any single character may be used in numerous combinations in order to form many different words. The Chinese Communists have gone even further in facilitating literacy by simplifying thousands of characters, often reducing a character from more than 20 strokes to 10 or even fewer.

In 1979, China adopted a new system, *pinyin,* for spelling Chinese words and names. This system, which uses the Latin alphabet of 26 letters, was created largely for foreign consumption and was not widely used within China. The fact that so many characters have the same Romanization (and pronunciation), plus cultural resistance, have thus far resulted in ideographs remaining the basis for Chinese writing. There are, as an example, at least 70 different Chinese ideographs that are pronounced *zhu,* but each means something different. Usually the context is adequate to indicate which word is being used. But when it may not be clear which of many homonyms is being used, Chinese often use their fingers to draw the character in the air.

Something of a national crisis has emerged in recent years over the deleterious effect of computer use on the ability of Chinese to write Chinese characters from memory. Computers are set up to write Chinese characters by choosing from multiple Chinese words whose sound is rendered into a Latin alphabet. As a result, computer users no longer need to remember how to write the many strokes in Chinese characters—they simply scroll

COMMUNES: PEASANTS WORK OVERTIME DURING THE GREAT LEAP FORWARD

In the socialist scheme of things, communes are considered ideal forms of organization for agriculture. They are supposed to increase productivity and equality, reduce inefficiencies of small-scale individual farming, and bring modern benefits to the countryside more rapidly through rural industrialization.

These objectives are believed to be attained largely through the economies of scale of communes; that is, it is presumed that things done on a large scale are more efficient and cost-effective. Thus, using tractors, harvesters, trucks, and other agricultural machinery makes sense when large tracts of land can be planted with the same crops and plowed at one time. Similarly, a communal unit of 30,000 to 70,000 people can support small-scale industries, since, in such a large work unit, not everyone has to work in the fields.

Because of its size, a commune can support small-scale industries, as well as other types of organizations that smaller work units could not. A commune, for example, can support a hospital, a high school, an agricultural-research organization, and, if the commune is wealthy enough, even a "sports palace" and a cultural center for movies and entertainment.

During the Great Leap Forward, launched in 1958, peasants were—much against their will—forced into these larger agricultural and administrative units. They were particularly distressed that their small remaining private plots were, like the rest of their land, collectivized. Communal kitchens were to prepare food for everyone. Peasants were told that they had to eat in the communal mess halls rather than in the privacy of their own homes. And, they were ordered to build "backyard furnaces" to smelt steel and bring the benefits of industry to the countryside—part of Mao Ze-

dong's idea of "closing the gap" between agriculture and industry, and between countryside and city.

When the combination of bad policies and bad weather led to a severe famine, widespread peasant resistance forced the government to retreat from the Great Leap Forward policy and abandon the communes. But a modified commune system remained intact in much of China until the late 1970s, when the government ordered communes to be dissolved. A commune's collective property was then distributed to the peasants within it, and a system of "contract responsibility" was launched. Today, with the exception of a few communes that refused to be dissolved, agricultural production is no longer collectivized. Individual households are again, as before 1953, engaged in small-scale agricultural production on private plots of land.

---

down to the correct Chinese character under the sound of, say, "Zhen." Then they press the "enter" key. The problem is that, without regular practice writing out characters, it is easy to forget how to write them—even for Chinese people. It is a problem akin to the loss of mathematical skills due to the use of calculators and computers.

Spoken Chinese

The Chinese have shared the same written language over the last 2,000 years, regardless of which dialect of Chinese they spoke. (The same written characters were simply pronounced in different ways, depending on the dialect.) Building a sense of national unity was difficult, however, when people needed interpreters to speak with someone living even a few miles away. After the Communist victory in 1949, the government decided that all Chinese would speak the same dialect in order to facilitate national unity. A majority of the delegates to the National People's Congress voted to adopt the northern dialect, Mandarin, as the national language, and required all schools to teach in Mandarin (usually referred to as "standard Chinese").

In the countryside, however, it has been difficult to find teachers capable of speaking and teaching Mandarin; and at home, whether in the countryside or the cities, the people have continued to speak their local dialects. The liberalization policies that began in 1979 have had as their by-product a discernible trend back to speaking local dialects, even in the workplace and on the streets. Whereas a decade ago a traveler could count on the na-

tional language being spoken in China's major cities, this is no longer the case. As a unified language is an important factor in maintaining national cohesion, the re-emergence of local dialects at the expense of standard Chinese threatens China's fragile unity.

One force that is slowing this disintegration is television, for it is broadcast almost entirely in standard Chinese. As there is a growing variety of interesting programming available, it may be that most Chinese will make an effort to maintain or even acquire the ability to understand standard Chinese. Many television programs have Chinese characters (representing the words being spoken) running along the bottom of the screen. This makes it less necessary for viewers to understand spoken standard Chinese; but it makes it more necessary for those who do not speak standard Chinese to be literate in order to enjoy television programs.

Education

The People's Republic of China has been remarkably successful in educating its people. Before 1949, less than 20 percent of the population could read and write. Today, nine years of schooling are compulsory. In the larger cities, 12 years of schooling is becoming the norm, with children attending either a vocational middle school or a college-preparatory school. Computer use is increasingly common in urban schools.

It is difficult to enforce the requirement of nine years of school in the impoverished countryside. Still, close to 90 percent of those children living in rural areas attend at least primary school. Village schools, however,

often lack rudimentary equipment such as chairs and desks. Rural education also suffers from a lack of qualified teachers, as any person educated enough to teach can probably get a better-paying job in the industrial or commercial sector. But the situation is in flux, because as rural families are having fewer children than before, more can now afford the cost of educating their children. In 2006, the government abolished school fees, but there remain significant costs for poor villagers to educate their children. Still, as the goals of rural families have changed from preparing their children for farming to preparing them for factory work and office jobs in the towns and cities, education is seen as all the more important. So, at the same time that the collective basis for funding schools has deteriorated, in some villages many more farmers are able and willing to pay the necessary costs for schooling their children.

At the other end of the spectrum, many more students are now pursuing a college-oriented curriculum than will ever go on to college. From 1998 to 2004, China doubled the number of students it admitted to universities, from 2.1 to 4.2 million students.[12] Nevertheless, only about 5 percent of the senior middle school graduates will pass the university entrance examinations and be admitted. As a result, many who had prepared for a college curriculum are inappropriately educated for the workplace. The government is attempting to augment vocational training for high school students, but it is also increasing the number of slots available in colleges and universities. Private high schools and colleges are becoming increasingly popular

(D. Falcone/PhotoLink/DAL19099)

Communes were disbanded by the early 1980s. In some areas, however, farmers have continued to work their land as a single unit in order to benefit from the economies of scale of large tracts of land.

as parents try to optimize the chances for their only child to climb the academic ladder in order to gain social and economic success. Enrollments in on-line education courses, especially in business, have also soared in numbers as China's economy becomes increasingly specialized and demands greater skills and expertise for jobs.

Political Education

Until the reforms that began in 1979, the content of Chinese education was suffused with political values and objectives. A considerable amount of school time—as much as 100 percent during political campaigns—was devoted to political education. Often this amounted to nothing more than learning by rote the favorite axioms and policies of the leading faction in power. When that faction lost power, the students' political thought had to be reoriented in the direction of the new policies and values. History, philosophy, literature, and even foreign languages and science were laced with a political vocabulary.

The prevailing political line has affected the balance in the curriculum between political study and the learning of skills and scientific knowledge. Beginning in the 1960s, the political content of education increased dramatically until, during the Cultural Revolution, schools were shut down. When they reopened in the early 1970s, politics dominated the curriculum. When Deng Xiaoping and the "modernizers" consolidated their power in the late 1970s, this tendency was reversed. During the 1980s, in fact, schools jettisoned the study of political theory because both administrators and teachers wanted their students to do well on college-entrance examinations, which by then focused on academic subjects. As a result, students refused to clog their schedules with the study of political theory and the CCP's history. The study of Marxism and party history was revived in the wake of the events of Tiananmen Square in 1989, with the entering classes for many universities required to spend the first year in political study and indoctrination, sometimes under military supervision; but this practice was abandoned after two years. Today, political study has again been confined to a narrow part of the curriculum, in the interest of giving students an education that will help advance China's modernization.

Study Abroad

Since 1979, when China began to promote an "open door" policy, more than 100,000 PRC students have been sent for a university education to the United States, and tens of thousands more have gone to Europe and Japan. China has sent so many students abroad in part because the quality of education had seriously deteriorated during the "10 bad years" that included the Cultural Revolution, and in part because China's limited number of universities can accommodate only a tiny percentage of all high school graduates. Although an increasingly large number of Chinese universities are able to offer graduate training, talented Chinese students still travel abroad to receive advanced degrees.

Chinese students who have returned home have not always met a happy fate. Many of those educated abroad who were in China at the time of the Communists' victory in 1949, or who returned to China thereafter, were not permitted to hold leadership positions in their fields. Ultimately they were the targets of class-struggle campaigns and purges in the 1950s, '60s, and '70s, precisely because of their Western education. For the most part, those students who returned to China in the 1980s found that they could not be promoted because of the continuation of a system of seniority.

Since 1992, however, when Deng Xiaoping announced a major shift in economic and commercial policy to support just about anything that would help China become rich and powerful, the government has offered students significant incentives to return to China, including excellent jobs, promotions, good salaries, and even the chance to start new companies. Chinese students educated abroad are also recruited for their expertise and understanding of the outside world by the rapidly multiplying number of joint ventures in China, and by universities that are establishing their own graduate programs. Today, fully one third of students educated abroad return to live in China.

The Chinese government also now sees those Chinese who do stay abroad as forming critical links for China to the rest of the world. They have become the bridges over which contracts, loans, and trade flow to China, and are viewed as a positive asset. Finally, like immigrants elsewhere, Chinese who settle abroad tend to send remittances back to their families in China. These remittances amount to hundreds of millions of U.S. dollars in foreign currency each year and are valuable not just to the family recipients but also to the government's bank reserves.

Chinese studying abroad learn much about liberal democratic societies. Those who have returned to China bring with them the values at the heart of liberal-democratic societies. While this does not necessarily mean that they will demand the democratization of the Chinese political system, they do bring pluralistic liberal-democratic ideas to their own institutions. Some have been instrumental in setting up institutions such as "think tanks," have encouraged debate within their own fields, and have been insistent that China remain open to the outside world through the Internet, travel, conferences, and communications.

THE ECONOMIC SYSTEM

A Command Economy

Until 1979, the Chinese had a centrally controlled command economy. That is, the central leadership determined the economic policies to be followed and allocated all of the country's resources—labor, capital, land, and raw materials. It also determined how much each enterprise, and even each individual, would be allocated for production and consumption. Once the Chinese Communist Party leadership determined the country's political goals and the correct ideology, the State Planning Commission and the State Economic Commission would then decide how to implement these objectives through specific policies for agriculture and industry and the allocation of resources. This is in striking contrast to a capitalist laissez-faire economy, in which government control over both consumers and producers is minimal and market forces of supply and demand play the primary role in determining the production and distribution of goods.

The CCP leadership adopted the model of a centralized planned economy from the Soviet Union. Such a system was not only in accord with the Leninist model of centralized state governance; it also made sense for a government desperate to unify China after more than 100 years of internal division, instability, and economic collapse. Historically, China suffered from the ability of large

regions to evade the grasp of central control over such matters as currency and taxes. The inability of the Nationalist government to gain control over the country's economy in the 1930s and early 1940s undercut its power and contributed to its failure to win control over China. Thus, the Chinese Communist Party's decision to centralize economic decision making after 1949 helped the state to function as an integrated whole.

Over time, however, China's highly centralized economy became inefficient and too inflexible to address the complexity of the country's needs. Although China possesses a large and diverse economy, with a broad range of resources, topography, and climate, its economic planners made policy as if it were a uniform, homogeneous whole. Merely increasing production was itself considered a contribution to development, regardless of whether a market for the products existed or whether the products actually helped advance modernization.

State planning agencies, without the benefit of market research or signals from the marketplace, determined whether or not a product should be manufactured, and in what quantity. For example, the central government might set a goal for a factory to manufacture 5 million springs per year—without knowing if there was even a market for them. The factory management did not care, as the state was responsible for marketing the products and paid the factory's bills. If the state had no buyer for the springs, they would pile up in warehouses; but rarely would production be cut back, much less a factory be closed, as this would create the problem of employing the workers cut from the factory's payroll. Economic inefficiencies of this sort were often justified because socialist political objectives such as full employment were being met. Even today the state worries about shutting down a state-owned factory that is losing money, because it creates unemployment. In turn, unemployment leads to popular anger and provides a volatile, unstable environment, ripe for public political protest. Quality control was similarly not as important an issue as it should have been for state-run industries in a centrally planned economy. Until market reforms began in 1979, the state itself allocated all finished products to other industries that needed them. If a state-controlled factory made defective parts, the industry using them had no recourse against the supplier, because each factory had a contract with the state, not with other factories. It was the state that would pay for additional parts to be made, so the enterprises did not bear the costs.

As a result, China's economic development under the centralized political leadership of the CCP occurred by fits and starts. Much waste resulted from planning that did

not take into account market factors of supply and demand. Centrally set production quotas took the place of efficiency and profitability in the allocation of resources. Although China's command economy was able to meet the country's most important industrial needs, problems like these took their toll over time. Enterprises had little incentive to raise productivity, quality, or efficiency when doing so did not affect their budgets, wages, or funds for expansion.

Agricultural Programs

By the late 1950s, central planning was causing significant damage to the agricultural sector. Regardless of geography or climate, China's economic planners repeatedly ordered the peasants to restructure their economic production units according to one centralized plan. China's peasants, who had supported the CCP in its rise to power before 1949 in order to acquire their own land, had enthusiastically embraced the CCP's fulfillment of its pledge of "land to the tillers" after the Communists took over in 1949. But in 1953, the leadership, motivated by a belief that small-scale agricultural production could not meet the production goals of socialist development, ordered all but 15 percent of the arable land to be pooled into "lower-level agricultural producer cooperatives" of between 300 and 700 workers. The remaining 15 percent of land was to be set aside as private plots for the peasants, and they could market the produce from these plots in private markets throughout the countryside. Then, in 1956, the peasants throughout the country were ordered into "higher-level agricultural producer cooperatives" of 10 times that size, and the size of the private plots allotted to them was reduced to 5 percent of the cooperatives' total land.

Many peasants felt cheated by these wholesale collectivization policies. When in 1958 the central leadership ordered them to move into communes 10 times larger still than the cooperatives they had just joined, they were irate. Mao Zedong's Great Leap Forward policy of 1958 forced all peasants in China to become members of communes: enormous economic and administrative units consisting of between 30,000 and 70,000 people. Peasants were required to relinquish their private plots, and turn over their private utensils, as well as their household chickens, pigs, and ducks, to the commune. Resisting this mandate, many peasants killed and ate their livestock. Since private enterprise was no longer permitted, home industries ground to a halt.

CCP chairman Mao's vision for catching up with the West was to industrialize the vast countryside. Peasants were therefore ordered to build "backyard furnaces" to smelt steel. Lacking iron ore, much less any knowledge of how to make steel, and under the guidance of party cadres who themselves were ignorant of steelmaking, the peasants tore out metal radiators, pipes, and fences. Together with pots and pans, they were dumped into their furnaces. Almost none of the final smelted product was usable. Finally, the central economic leadership ordered all peasants to eat in large, communal mess halls. This was reportedly the last straw for a people who valued family above all else. Being deprived of time alone with their families for meals, the peasants refused to cooperate further in agricultural collectivization.

When the catastrophic results of the Great Leap Forward policy poured in, the CCP retreated—but it was too late. Three subsequent years of bad weather, combined with the devastation wreaked by these policies and the Soviet withdrawal of all assistance, brought economic catastrophe. Demographic data indicate that in the "three bad years" from 1959 to 1962, more than 20 million Chinese died from starvation and malnutrition-related diseases.

By 1962, central planners had condoned peasants returning to production units that were smaller than communes. Furthermore, peasants were again allowed to farm a small percentage of the total land as private plots, to raise domestic animals for their own use, and to engage in household industries. Free markets, at which the peasantry could trade goods from private production, were reopened. The commune structure was retained throughout the countryside, however; and until the CCP leadership introduced the contract responsibility system in 1979, it provided the infrastructure of rural secondary school education, hospitals, and agricultural research.

Other centrally determined policies, seemingly oblivious to reality, compounded the P.R.C.'s difficulties in agriculture. Maoist policies carried out during both the Great Leap Forward and renewed during the Cultural Revolution included attempts to plant three crops per year in areas that for climatic reasons can only support two (as the Chinese put it, "Three times three is not as good as two times five"); and "close planting," which often more than doubled the amount of seed planted, with the result that all of it grew to less than full size or simply wilted for lack of adequate sunshine and nutrients.

A final example of centrally determined agricultural policy bringing catastrophe was the decision during the Cultural Revolution that "the whole country should grow grain." The purpose was to establish China's self-sufficiency in grain. Considering China's immense size and diverse climates, soil types, and topography, a policy ordering everyone to grow the same thing was doomed to failure. Peasants were ordered to plow under fields of cotton and cut down rubber plantations and

(Courtesy of Ron Church/rchurcho1)
With economic-liberalization in the 1980s, shops such as this one were allowed to prosper.

fruit orchards, planting grain in their place. China's central planning was largely done by the CCP, not by economic or agricultural experts, and they ignored overwhelming evidence that grain would not grow well, if at all, in some areas. These policies ignored the fact that China would have to import everything that it had replaced with grain, at far greater costs than it would have paid for importing just grain. Peasant protests were futile in the face of local-level Communist Party leaders who hoped to advance their careers by implementing central policy. The policy of self-sufficiency in grain was abandoned only with the arrest of the Gang of Four in 1976.

Economic Reforms: Decentralization and Liberalization

In 1979, Deng Xiaoping undertook reform and liberalization of the economy, a critical component of China's modernization program. The government tried to maintain centralized state control of the direction of policy and the distribution and pricing of strategic and energy resources, while decentralizing decision making down to the level of the township and village. Decentralization was meant to facilitate more rational decision making, based on local conditions, needs, and efficiency. Although the state has retained the right to set overall economic priorities, township and village enterprises (TVEs), as well as larger state-owned enterprises, have been encouraged to respond to local market forces of supply and demand. Centrally determined quotas and pricing for most products have been phased out, and enterprises now contract with one another rather than with the

state. Thus the government's role as the go-between in commercial transactions—and as the central planner for everything in the economy—is gradually disappearing.

Since the introduction of market capitalism in the 1980s, the economy has become increasingly privatized. Some 70 percent of China's gross national product (GNP) is now produced by these nonstate enterprises. They compete with state-run enterprises to supply goods and services, and if they are not profitable, they go bankrupt.

On the other hand, some state-run enterprises that operate at a loss continue to be subsidized by the government rather than shut down. One reason is that the enterprises are in a sector over which the state wants to keep control, such as energy, raw materials, and steel production. Another reason is fear of the destabilizing impact of a high level of unemployment if the state closes down large state-run enterprises. Subsidies and state-owned bank loans (which will not be repaid) to unprofitable enterprises consume a significant portion of the state's budget. China's membership in the World Trade Organization (WTO) since 2001 has, however, forced China's large state-owned enterprises to become efficient, or else perish in the face of foreign competition. In the meantime, the government continues to close down the most unprofitable state-run enterprises, and it counts on the entrepreneurial sector and foreign investors to fuel economic growth and absorb the unemployed.

In addition, under a carefully managed scheme, the government has started to sell off some state-run industries to TVEs, the private sector, and foreign investors. Whoever buys them must in most cases guarantee some sort of livelihood, even if not full employment, to the former employees of the state-run enterprises. The new owners, however, have far more freedom to make a profit than did the enterprises when they were state-owned. The state is also slowly introducing state-run pension and unemployment funds to care for those workers who lose their jobs when state-owned enterprises are shut down.

Today, the agricultural sector is almost fully market-driven. The "10,000 yuan" household (about U.S. $1,200), once a measure of extraordinary wealth in China, has become a realizable goal for many peasants. Free markets are booming in China, and peasants may now produce whatever they can get the best price for in the market, once they have filled their grain quotas to the state. Wealthy rural towns are springing up throughout the agriculturally rich and densely populated east coast, as well as along China's major transportation routes.

Problems Created by Economic Reforms

Disputes Over Property

One downside of privatization and marketization is a distinct increase in disputes among villagers. There are disputes over who gets to use the formerly collectively owned goods, such as tractors, harvesters, processing equipment, and boats for transporting goods at harvest time. And with formerly collective fields turned into a patchwork of small private plots, villagers often protest when others cross their land with farm equipment. Theoretically, the land that is "leased" to the peasants is collectively owned by the village, but in practice the land is treated as the private property of the peasants. Those who choose to leave their land may contract it out to others, so some peasants have amassed large tracts of land suitable for large-scale farm machinery. To encourage development, the government has permitted land to be leased for as long as 30 years and for leased rights to be inherited. Furthermore, peasants have built houses on what they consider their own land, itself a problem because it is usually arable land. Nevertheless, the village councils also have some ability to reallocate land so that soldiers and others who return to settle in the villages can receive adequate land to farm.

With the growth of free enterprise in the rural towns since 1979, some 60 million to 100 million peasants have left the land to work for higher pay in small-scale rural industry or in cities. It is not just that the wages are higher, but also that the peasants are burdened by the arbitrary imposition of local taxes and fees. Combined with the low profits on agricultural products and the unpredictability of weather, farmers seek better wages in local enterprises or migrate to the

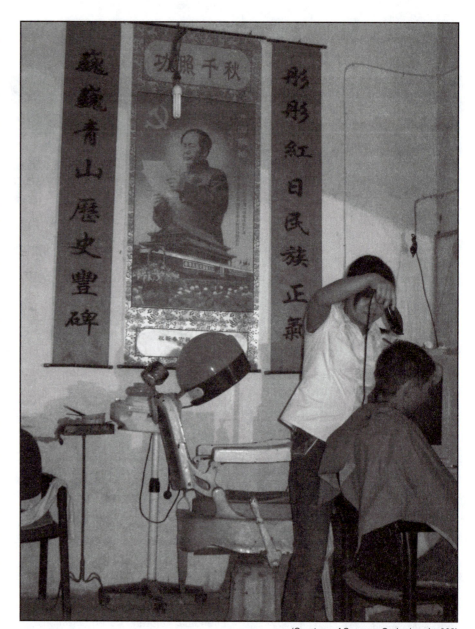

(Courtesy of Suzanne Ogden/sogden033)
Small private businesses in towns and cities are part of what is driving the growth of individual wealth in China. This hair-cutting salon is in a town in Anhui Province. A poster on the wall indicates the continuing reverence for Mao Zedong in many parts of China.

cities. Others leave because their land has been confiscated by the local government for development. Rarely compensated adequately, if at all, for their land, they are forced to leave the villages for towns and cities. Parents often migrate together, but are unable to bear the costs of taking their children with them, so they are left with their relatives or friends—or to fend for themselves, alone. To address the problems being created by the confiscation of agricultural land, as well as to stop the boom in building "development zones" for no specific need or purpose, the government cancelled some 4,800 of the 6,866 development zones that had sprung up throughout China. The Ministry of Land and Resources has discovered that, of the to-

tal zones, 70 percent had illegally acquired land, or had confiscated the land and then left it unused. The measure shut down about 65 percent of the total land area planned for development zones, and returned some of the land to agricultural use.[13]

Instability and Crime

For some, especially those able to find employment in the booming construction industry in many small towns and cities, migration has brought a far better standard of living. But tens of millions of unemployed migrants clog city streets, parks, and railroad stations. They have been joined by equally large numbers of workers from bankrupt state-owned enterprises. Together, they have contributed to a vast increase in criminality and social instability. According to Chinese government reports, there were more than 74,000 "mass incidents" (protests and riots) in 2004, a 30 percent increase over the 58,000 reported in 2003, and more than six times the number it reported 10 years earlier.[14]

Problems Arising From a Mixed Economy

Still other problems arose from the post–1979 reform policies that led to a mixed socialist and capitalist economy. For example, with decentralization, industrial enterprises tried to keep their profits but "socialize" their losses. That is, profitable enterprises (whether state-owned, collective TVEs, or private) try to hide their profits to avoid paying taxes to the state. State-owned enterprises that are losing money ask the state for subsidies to keep them in business. For this reason, the amount of profits turned over to the state was not commensurate with the dramatic increase in the value of industrial output since 1979. In the last decade, however, this situation has been ameliorated as China has become a primarily market-driven economy. Almost all prices are now market-determined, except for energy, water, and natural resources. Although it is common in almost all market economies for the state to regulate the prices of energy and utilities, the fact that certain other commodities and products in short supply are still regulated by the state continues to create problems in China.[15]

Products such as rolled steel, glass, cement, or timber are either hoarded as a safeguard against future shortages, or resold at unauthorized higher prices. By doing so, these enterprises make illegal profits for themselves and deprive other enterprises of the materials they need for production. In short, the remnants of a mixed economy, combined with the lack of a strong regulatory state to administer the economy, provide many opportunities for corruption and abuse of the system.

Further, while private and collective enterprises rely on market signals to determine whether they will expand production facilities, the state continues to centrally allocate resources based on a national plan. A clothing factory that expands its production, for instance, requires more energy (coal, oil) and water, and more cotton. The state, already faced with inadequate energy resources to keep most industries operating at full capacity, continues to allocate the same amount to the now-expanded factory. Profitable enterprises want a greater share of centrally allocated scarce resources, but find they cannot acquire them without the help of "middlemen" and a significant amount of under-the-table dealing. Corruption has, therefore, become rampant at the nexus where the capitalist and socialist economies meet.

Widespread corruption in the economic sector has led the Chinese government to wage a series of campaigns against economic crimes such as embezzlement and graft. An increasing number of economic criminals are going to prison, and serious offenders are sometimes executed. Until energy and transportation bottlenecks and the scarcity of key resources are dealt with, however, it will be extremely difficult to halt the bribery, smuggling, embezzlement, and extortion now pervasive in China. The combination of relaxed centralized control, the mandate for the Chinese people to "get rich," and a mixed economy have exacerbated what was already a problem under the

CHINA'S SPECIAL ECONOMIC ZONES

In 1979, China opened four "Special Economic Zones" (SEZs) within the territory of the People's Republic of China as part of its program to reform the socialist economy and to encourage foreign investment. The SEZs were allowed a great deal of leeway in experimenting with new economic policies. For example, Western management methods, including the right to fire unsatisfactory workers (something unknown under China's centrally planned economy), were introduced into SEZ factories. Laws and regulations on foreign investment were greatly eased in the SEZs in order to attract foreign capital. Export-oriented industries were established with the goal of earning large amounts of foreign exchange in order to help pay for importing technology for modernization. To many people, the SEZs looked like pockets of capitalism inside the socialist economy of the P.R.C.; indeed, they are often referred to as "mini-Hong Kongs." In 1984, 14 coastal cities were allowed to open up development zones to help attract foreign investment.

The largest of the Special Economic Zones is Shenzhen, which is located just across the border from the Hong Kong New Territories. Over several decades, Shenzhen was transformed from a sleepy little rural town to a large, modern urban center and one of China's major industrial cities. The city boasts broad avenues and skyscrapers, and a standard of living that is among the highest in the country.

But with growth and prosperity have come numerous problems. The pace of construction has outstripped the ability of the city to provide adequate services to the growing population. Speculation and corruption have been rampant, and crime is a more serious problem in Shenzhen than in most other parts of China. Strict controls on immigration help stem the flood of people who are attracted to Shenzhen in the hopes of making their fortune.

Nevertheless, the success of Shenzhen and other Special Economic Zones led the leadership to expand the concept of SEZs throughout the country. The special privileges, such as lower taxes, that foreign businesses and joint ventures could originally enjoy only in these zones were expanded first along the coast and then to the interior, so that it too could benefit from foreign investment. By 2004, there were 6,866 "development zones," formed largely by confiscating agricultural land from the peasantry. As a result of the anger this created among the peasants, which led to instability in the countryside, and because there were not enough investors to make the zones develop, the government shut down 4,800 of them in 2004.[16] Eventually, all of the special privileges given to SEZs and development zones will be eradicated.

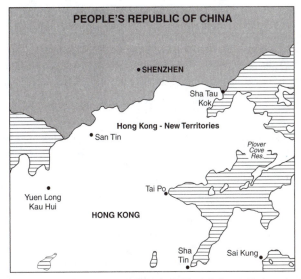

Shenzhen is the largest of China's SEZs. It is located close to the Hong Kong New Territories.

(Courtesy of Suzanne Ogden/sogden030)

Seventy percent of China's population still lives in the countryside. Mechanized farming is primarily for wealthier peasants with large tracts of land. Water buffalo are still widely used in cultivating rice.

socialist system. In a system suffering from serious scarcities but controlled by bureaucrats, it is political power, not the market, that determines who gets what. This includes not only goods, but also opportunities, licenses, permits, and approvals.

Although the Chinese may now purchase in the market many essential products previously distributed through bureaucratically controlled channels, there are still many goods available only through the "back door"—that is, through people they know and with whom they exchange favors or money. Scarcity, combined with bureaucratic control, has led to "collective corruption": Individuals engage in corrupt practices, even cheat the state, in order to benefit the enterprise for which they work. Since enterprises not owned by the state will not be bailed out if they suffer losses, the motivation for corrupt activities is stronger than under the previous system.

Liberalization of the economy is providing a massive number and variety of goods for the marketplace. The Chinese people may buy almost any basic consumer goods in stores or the open markets. But the nexus between continued state control and the free economy still fuels a rampant corruption that threatens the development of China's economy.

The mixed economy, then, provides the environment in which corruption has increased; but it is further exacerbated by the sheer amount of money in China today. Before 1979, corruption tended to involve exchanges of favors, many of which amounted to giving access, a privilege, or a necessary document to someone in exchange for another favor. Today, corruption is about getting large amounts of money through various deals. Further, unlike in most developing countries, corruption is not just at the top. It is widespread, all the way to the bottom of the economic ladder. Some argue that the fact that so many people at all rungs of the economic ladder can share in the cashing out of corrupt activities allows it to be tolerated.[17]

Still, there is a huge amount of wealth concentrated in the elite, if for no other reason than that they have the "connections" and access to gain wealth. Figures indicate that 90 percent of China's billionaires are, in fact, children of the senior party-state elite.[18] The ability of corrupt individuals to abscond to a foreign country has made capital flight an increasingly worrisome issue. China's Ministry of Commerce reported that thousands of corrupt officials (many of whom are said to be the children and relatives of political leaders) have illegally transferred China's wealth to companies registered in offshore tax shelters and financial havens.[19]

Unequal Benefits

Not all Chinese have benefited equally from the more than 25 years of economic reforms. Those who inhabit cities in the interior, and peasants living far from cities and transportation lines or tilling less arable land, have reaped far fewer rewards. And although the vast majority of Chinese have seen some improvement in their standard of living, short-term gains in income are threatened in the long term by the deterioration of the infrastructure for education and medical care in large parts of China's hinterland. This deterioration is due to the elimination of the commune as the underlying institution for funding these services. Wealthier peasants send their children into the larger towns and cities for schooling.

In healthcare, the Communist government has overseen dramatic improvements in the provision of social services for the masses. Largely because of its emphasis on preventive medicine and sanitation, life expectancy has increased from 45 years in 1949 to 72 years (overall) today. The government has successfully eradicated many childhood diseases and has made great strides against other diseases, such as malaria and tuberculosis. The privatization of medicine in recent years has, however, meant that many no longer have guaranteed access to medical treatment. The press has highlighted many cases in which, if they cannot pay, they will not be treated. Wealthier families, on the other hand, can travel to the more comprehensive health clinics and hospitals farther away, although in some areas, they have actually built local schools and private hospitals. In recent years, under the leadership of Hu Jintao and Wen Jiabao, the state has stepped back in to address these issues of unequal access, in part because they are giving rise to social instability. Among their many policies has been the elimination of school fees for children who attend rural schools.

Nevertheless, the visible polarization of wealth, which had been virtually eradicated in the first 30 years of Communist rule, continues to deepen in the context of capitalism and a poorly regulated free market. The creation of a crassly ostentatious wealthy class and a simply ostentatious middle class, in the context of high unemployment, poverty, and a mobile population, is breeding the very class conflict that the Chinese Communists fought a revolution to eliminate. When reforms began almost 30 years ago, street crime was almost unheard of in China's cities. Now it is a growing problem, one that the government fears may erode the legitimacy of CCP rule if left uncontrolled.

Mortgaging the Future

One of the most damaging aspects of the capitalist "get-rich" atmosphere prevailing in China is the willingness to sacrifice the future for short-term profits. The environment continues to be deeply degraded by uncontrolled pollution; the rampant growth of new towns, cities, and highways; the building of houses on arable land; the overuse of nonrenewable water resources; and the destruction of forests. Some state institutions, including schools, have turned the open spaces (such as playgrounds) within their walls into parking lots in China's crowded cities to provide spaces for the rapidly growing number of privately owned cars.

To sustain its rapid economic growth, China has had to add new power-generating capacity, 90 percent of which is from new coal-fired plants, at the *annual* rate (as of 2006) of "the entire capacity of the UK and Thailand combined, or about twice the generating assets of California."[20] China's primary source of energy is coal, followed by oil, both of which emit substantial greenhouse gases (such as carbon dioxide) to the environment. As of 2007, China was the world's second-largest producer of greenhouse gases, and was expected to surpass the U.S. by 2008. But regardless of how much it contributes to global warming, China is already suffering from its effects. The government is concerned about the impact of global warming on China's future economic growth and food security, as well as its role in generating severe weather patterns, desertification, and flooding. Environmental deterioration is, in turn, causing social instability. Indeed, each year there is an increasing number of major protests—often violent—from communities affected by environmental degradation. Since 1997, pollution disputes submitted to legal or administrative resolution have increased at an annual rate of about 25 percent. By 2002, the actual number of disputes reported as submitted for solution had reached 500,000.[21]

Health problems arising from polluted air and contaminated water are affecting both rural and urban populations. Cities that used to have clear blue skies before economic reforms began more than 25 years ago now infrequently see the sun. Coal-burning plants, which produce significant amounts of air particulates, supply two-thirds of China's energy needs. With close to 70 percent of China's rivers and lakes severely polluted, even boiled water is not fit to drink. In Beijing, 90 percent of the underground water supply on which it relies is contaminated. To add to its woes, a 60-billion-dollar pipeline is having to be built to transfer water from the south to the north, especially for Beijing.

So, even though China's government takes the same stance as most other developing countries—namely, that the *developed* countries should pay for their efforts to reduce greenhouse gases (and sulfur dioxide, which causes acid rain), China realizes it has to take its own actions before it is too late. Moreover, with Beijing hosting the 2008 Olympic Games, the government wants to be sure that air quality is improved quickly. The problem is that the State Environment Protection Agency (SEPA) is one of China's weakest ministries. It must compete against other powerful ministries that want to promote economic development, regardless of the environmental costs. The government also promotes car ownership and consumption of durable goods such as air conditioners and washing machines, all of which consume considerable energy and thereby exacerbate the pollution. In the meantime, officials receive promotion based on how much they have advanced economic growth in their localities. This puts them at cross purposes with SEPA's goals of regulating pollution, and causes them to blatantly ignore state environmental regulations.

Added to the demand for energy created by economic growth is the hugely inefficient use of energy, with some products requiring as much as 10 to 20 times more energy to produce than in more efficient economies, such as Japan, the U.S., and Germany. So, in 2006, environmental policy, instead of capping greenhouse gas emissions, chose to reduce the amount of energy used in the production of a product. The central government is now demanding that major state enterprises as well as provincial governors sign contracts in which they pledge "to reduce the amount of energy consumed relative to economic output by 20 percent over five years." If China succeeds in doing so, even though economic output will continue to grow, the amount of energy used will grow at a much slower rate.[22]

THE CHINESE LEGAL SYSTEM

Ethical Basis of Law

In imperial China, the Confucian system provided the basis for the traditional social and political order. Confucianism posited that good governance should be based on maintaining correct personal relationships among people, and between people and their rulers. Ethics were based on these relationships. A legal system did exist, but the Chinese resorted to it in civil cases only in desperation, for the inability to resolve one's problems oneself or through a mediator usually resulted in considerable "loss of face"—a loss of dignity or standing in the eyes of others. (In criminal cases, the state normally became involved in determining guilt and punishment.)

This perspective on law carried over into the period of Communist rule. Until legal reforms began in 1979, most Chinese preferred to call in CCP officials, local neighborhood or factory mediation committees, family members, or friends to settle disputes. Lawyers were rarely used, and only when mediation failed did the Chinese resort to the courts. By contrast, the West lacks both this strong support for the institution of mediation and the concept of "face." So Westerners have difficulty understanding why China has had so few lawyers, and why the Chinese have relied less on the law than on personal relationships when problems arise.

Like Confucianism, Marxism-Leninism is an ideology that embodies a set of ethical standards for behavior. After 1949, it easily built on China's cultural predisposition toward ruling by ethics instead of law. Although Marxism-Leninism did not completely replace the Confucian ethical system, it did establish new standards of behavior based on socialist morality. These ethical standards were embodied in the works of Marx, Lenin, and Mao, and in the Chinese Communist Party's policies; but in practice, they were frequently undercut by preferential treatment for officials.

Legal Reforms

Before legal reforms began in 1979, the Chinese cultural context and the socialist system were the primary factors shaping the Chinese legal system. Since 1979, reforms have brought about a remarkable transformation in Chinese attitudes toward the law, with the result that China's laws and legal procedures—if not practices and implementation—look increasingly like those in the West. This is particularly true for laws that relate to the economy, including contract, investment, property, and commercial laws. The legal system has evolved to accommodate its more market-oriented economy and privatization. Chinese citizens have discovered that the legal system can protect their rights, especially in economic transactions. In 2004, 4.4 million civil cases were filed, double the number 10 years earlier. This is a strong indication that the Chinese now are more aware of their legal rights, and believe they can use the law to protect their rights and to hold others (including officials) accountable for their actions.[23] Still, in many

(United Nations photo by John Isaac/UN161371)

Settling civil disputes in China today still usually involves neighborhood mediation committees, family members, or friends.

civil cases (such as disputes with neighbors and family members), the Chinese remain inclined to rely on mediation and traditional cultural values in the settling of disputes.

Law and Politics

From 1949 until the legal reforms that began in 1979, Chinese universities trained few lawyers. Legal training consisted of learning law and politics as an integrated whole; for according to Marxism, law is meant to reflect the values of the "ruling class" and to serve as an instrument of "class struggle." The Chinese Communist regime viewed law as a branch of the social sciences, not as a professional field of study. For this reason, China's citizens tended to view law as a mere propaganda tool, not as a means for protecting their rights. They had never really experienced a law-based society. Not only were China's laws and legal education highly politicized, but politics also pervaded the judicial system.

With few lawyers available, few legally trained judges or prosecutors in the courts, and even fewer laws to refer to for standards of behavior, inevitably China's legal system has been subject to abuse. China has been

ruled by people, not by law; by politics, not by legal standards; and by party policy, not by a constitution. Interference in the judicial process by party and local state officials has been all too common.

After 1979, the government moved quickly to write new laws. Fewer than 300 lawyers, most of them trained before 1949 in Western legal institutions, undertook the immense task of writing a civil code, a criminal code, contract law, economic law, law governing foreign investment in China, tax law, and environmental and forestry laws. One strong motivation for the Chinese Communist leadership to formalize the legal system was its growing realization, after years of a disappointingly low level of foreign investment, that the international business community was reluctant to invest further in China without substantial legal guarantees.

Even China's own potential entrepreneurs wanted legal protection against the *state* before they would assume the risks of developing new businesses. Enterprises, for example, wanted a legal guarantee that if the state should fail to supply resources contracted for, it could be sued for losses issuing from its nonfulfillment of contractual obligations.

Since the leadership wanted to encourage investment, it needed to supplement economic reforms with legal reforms. Codification of the legal system fostered a stronger basis for modernization and helped limit the party-state's abuse of the people's rights.

In addition, new qualifications have been established for all judicial personnel. Demobilized military officers who became judges and prosecutors during the Cultural Revolution have been removed from the judiciary. Judges, prosecutors, and lawyers must now have formal legal training and pass a national judicial examination. It is hoped that judicial personnel endowed with higher qualifications and larger salaries, as well as judicial systems that are financially autonomous from local governments will diminish judicial corruption and enhance the autonomy of judicial decisions.[24]

Criminal Law

Procedures followed in Chinese criminal courts have differed significantly from those in the United States. Although the concept of "innocent until proven guilty" was introduced in China in 1996, it is still presumed that people brought to trial in criminal cases are guilty. This presumption is confirmed by the judicial process itself. That is, after a suspect is arrested by the police, the procuratorate (*procuracy*, the investigative branch of the judiciary system) will spend considerable time and effort examining the evidence gathered by the police and establishing whether the suspect is indeed guilty. This is important to understanding why 99 percent of all the accused brought to trial in China are judged guilty. Indeed, had the facts not substantiated their guilt, the procuracy would have dismissed their cases before going to trial.

In short, then, those adjudged to be innocent would never be brought to trial in the first place. For this reason, court trials function mainly to present the evidence upon which the guilty verdict is based—not to weigh the evidence to see if it indicates guilt—and to remind the public that criminals are punished. A trial is a "morality play" of sorts: the villain is punished, justice is done, the people's interests are protected. In addition, the trial process continues to emphasize the importance of confessing one's crimes, for those who confess and appear repentant in court will usually be dealt more lenient sentences. Criminals are encouraged to turn themselves in, on the promise that their punishment will be less severe than if they are caught. Those accused of crimes are encouraged to confess rather than deny their guilt or appeal to the next level, all in hopes of gaining a more lenient sentence from the judge.

This type of system, which tends to focus on confession, not on fact finding, is weighted against the innocent. The result is that police are more inclined to use brutal tactics in order to exact a confession; but of course, police in Western liberal-democratic countries also have been known to use brutality, and even torture, to get a confession.

Another serious problem with the Chinese system was that the procuracy, which investigated the case, also prosecuted the case. Once the procuracy established "the facts," they were not open to question by the lawyer or the representative of the accused. (In China, a person may be represented by a family member, friend, or colleague, largely because there are not enough lawyers to fulfill the guarantee of a person's "right to a defense.") The lawyer for the accused was not allowed to introduce new evidence, make arguments to dismiss the case based on technicalities or improper procedures (such as wire tapping), call witnesses for the defendant, or make insanity pleas for the client. Instead, the lawyer's role in a criminal case was simply to represent the person in court and to bargain with the court for a reduced sentence for the repentant client.

The 1996 legal reforms were aimed at improving the rights of the accused: They may now call their own witnesses and introduce their own evidence, they cannot be held for more than 30 days without being formally charged with a crime, and they are supposed to have access to a lawyer within several days of being formally arrested. But many suspects are still not accorded these rights.

The accused have the right to a defense, but it has always been presumed that a lawyer will not defend someone who is guilty. Most of China's lawyers are still employed and paid by the state. As such, a lawyer's obligation is first and foremost to protect the state's interests, not the individual's interests at the expense of the state. Lawyers who acted otherwise risked being condemned as "counter-revolutionaries" or treasonous. Small wonder that after 1949, the study of law did not attract China's most talented students.

Today, however, the law profession is seen as potentially lucrative and increasingly divorced from politics. Lawyers can now enter private practice or work for foreigners in a joint venture. The All-China Lawyers Association, established in 1995 by the Ministry of Justice to regulate the legal profession, also functions as an interest group to protect the rights of lawyers against the state. Thus, when in recent years lawyers have found themselves in trouble with the law because they have defended the political rights of their clients against the state, the association tries to protect them.

Lawyers in Civil and Commercial Law

In the areas of civil and commercial law, the role of the lawyer has become increasingly important since the opening of China's closed door to the outside world. Because foreign trade and investment have become crucial to China's development, the government has made an all-out effort to train many more lawyers. In today's China, upholding the law is no longer simply a matter of correctly understanding the party "line" and then following it in legal disputes. China's limited experience in dealing with economic, liability, corporate, and contractual disputes in the courts, as well as the insistence by foreign investors that Chinese courts be prepared to address such issues, have forced the leadership to train lawyers in the intricacies of Western law and to draft countless new laws and regulations. To protect themselves against what is difficult to understand in the abstract, the Chinese used to refuse to publish their newly written laws. Claiming a shortage of paper or the need to protect "state secrets," they withheld publication of many laws until their actual impact on China's state interests could be determined. This practice frustrated potential investors, who dared not risk capital investment in China until they knew exactly what the relevant laws were. Today, however, the complexity of both foreign-investment issues and the entrepreneurial activities of China's own citizens have led the Chinese government to publish most of its laws as quickly as possible.

THE POLITICAL SYSTEM

The Party and the State

In China, the Chinese Communist Party is the fountainhead of power and policy. But not all Chinese people are party members. Although the CCP has some 60 million members, this number represents less than 5 percent of the population. Joining the CCP is a competitive, selective, rigorous process. Some have wanted to join out of a commitment to Communist ideals, others in hopes of climbing the ladder of success, still others to gain access to limited goods and opportunities. Ordinary Chinese are generally suspicious of the motives of those who do join the party. Many well-educated Chinese have grown cynical about the CCP and refused to join. Still, those who travel to China today are likely to find that many of the most talented people they meet are party members. Party hacks who are ideologically adept but incompetent at their work are gradually being squeezed out of a party desperate to maintain its leading position in a rapidly changing China.

Today's Party wants the best and brightest of the land as members, and it wants it to represent "the people" more broadly. In 2001, Jiang Zemin, then general-secretary of the CCP, laid the groundwork for this with his "theory of the three represents": The Party was from that point on to represent not just the workers and peasants, but *all* the people's interests, including both intellectuals and capitalists. This addition to party theory indicates that the Chinese Communist Party recognizes the important role that intellectuals and business people have played—and will play—in modernizing China; but it also acknowledges the reality that many individuals already within the Party have become capitalists. By enshrining this theory in the party constitution at the 16th Party Congress in 2002, the party was in effect attempting to shore up its legitimacy as China's ruling party. At the same time, it was in effect announcing that it had relinquished its role as a revolutionary party in favor of its new position as the *governing* party of China.

The CCP is still China's ultimate institutional authority. Although in theory the state is distinct from the party, in practice the two overlapped almost completely from the late 1950s to the early 1990s. Efforts to keep the party from meddling in the day-to-day work of the government and management of economic enterprises have had some effect; but in recent years, more conservative leaders within the CCP have exerted considerable pressure to keep the Party in charge.

The state apparatus consists of the State Council, headed by the premier. Under the State Council are the ministries and agencies and "people's congresses" responsible for the formulation of policy. The CCP has, however,

CENTRAL GOVERNMENT ORGANIZATION OF THE PEOPLE'S REPUBLIC OF CHINA

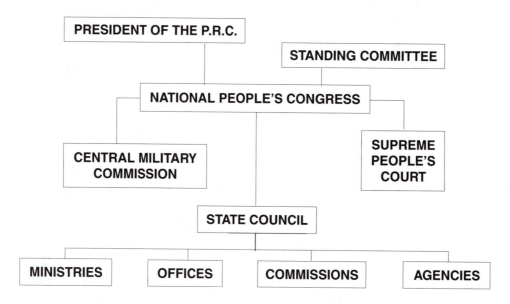

This central government organization chart represents the structure of the government of the People's Republic of China as it appears on paper. However since all of the actions and overall doctrine of the central government must be reviewed and approved by the Chinese Communist Party, political power ultimately lies with the party. To ensure this control, virtually all top state positions are held by party members.

THE CHINESE COMMUNIST PARTY (CCP)

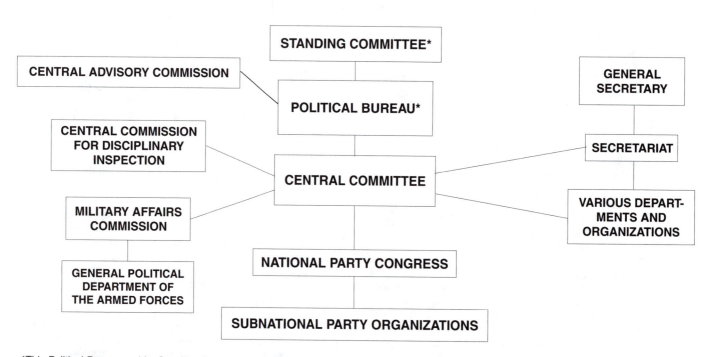

*This Political Bureau and its Standing Committee are the most powerful organizations within the Chinese Communist Party and are therefore the real centers of power in the P.R.C.

exercised firm control over these state bodies through interlocking organizations. CCP branches exist within all government organizations; and at every administrative level from the central government in Beijing down to the villages, almost everyone in a leadership position is also a party member.

Corruption in the Political System

China's political system is subject to enormous abuses of power. The lines of authority within both the CCP and the state system are poorly defined, as are the rules for selection to top leadership positions. In the past, this allowed individuals like Mao Zedong and the Gang of Four to usurp power and rule arbitrarily. By the late 1980s, China's bureaucracy appeared to have become more corrupt than at any time since the People's Republic of China came into being in1949. Anger at the massive scale of official corruption was, in fact, the major factor unifying ordinary citizens and workers with students during the antigovernment protests in the spring of 1989.

Although campaigns to control official corruption continue, the problem appears to be growing even worse. Campaigns do little more than scratch the surface. This is in part because with so many opportunities to make money in China, especially for party and state officials whose positions give them the inside track for making profitable deals, the potential payoff for corruption can be huge—and the risks of getting caught appear small. This is particularly true in the case of selling off of state-owned assets. In most cases, state-owned enterprises that have been closed down, or privatized, have been turned over to the relatives of China's leaders for managing. The same is true in real estate: land, which used to be completely state-owned, is now controlled by partly privatized land companies, run by the relatives of leaders, who take huge profits for themselves when they make deals with investors and real estate developers. One problem is that Chinese institutions lack the transparency, acquired through financial checks within the system and open access to accounting books, that could help rein in corruption. The situation is exacerbated by a society that by its complicity encourages official corruption.

Individuals may write letters to the editors of the country's daily newspapers or to television stations to expose corruption. Many Chinese, especially those living in the countryside, feel that the only way in which local corruption will be addressed is if the media send reporters to investigate and publicly expose criminality. The China Central Television station has aired a popular daily program in prime time that records the successes of China's public security system in cracking down on official corruption and crime. The press also devotes substantial space to sensational cases of official corruption, in part because it helps sell newspapers. The media only has the resources, however, to address comparatively few of the numerous cases begging for investigation. Furthermore, those reporters who have threatened to expose scandals, abuses of authority, and inappropriate local policies are often harassed, or even had violence used against them by those who might suffer from such a report. And in 2007, the government is reported to have shut down the investigative branches of the papers with more aggressive reporters. There is evidence, on the other hand, that some reporters have actually used the threat of reporting a scandal to extort money from local officials in order to cover it up.

So far, most efforts to control official corruption have had little effect. Officials continue to use their power to achieve personal gain, trading official favors for others' services (such as better housing, jobs for their children, admission to the right schools, and access to goods in short supply), or for wining and dining. Getting things done in a system that requires layers of bureaucratic approval still depends heavily upon a complex set of personal connections and relationships, all reinforced through under-the-table gift giving. This stems in part from the still heavily centralized aspect of Chinese governance, and in part from the overstaffing of a bureaucracy that is plagued by red tape. Countless offices must sign off on requests for anything from installing a telephone to processing a request for a license or additional electrical outlets. This gives enormous power to individual officials who handle those requests, allowing them to ask for favors in return, or to stonewall if the payoff is inadequate.

In today's more market-oriented China, officials have lost some of their leverage over the distribution of goods. Now, instead of waiting for a work unit official to decide whose turn it is to purchase a bicycle or who will have the right to live in a two-bedroom apartment, anyone with adequate funds may buy virtually anything they want. But as for electrical service, which is still controlled by the government, people must pay off an official to allow the electrical service to their apartment to be upgraded so they can actually use an air conditioner they have purchased. Similarly, brothels can be run in the open, virtually without interference from the police, who are bribed to look the other way. In short, officials may have lost control over the distribution of many consumer goods, but they have kept their ability to facilitate or obstruct access to many services, documents, licenses, and so on.

Controlling the abuse of official privilege is difficult in part because of the large discretionary budgets that officials have, and in part because the Chinese have made an art form out of going around regulations. For example, the government issued a regulation stipulating that governmental officials doing business could order only four dishes and one soup at a meal. But as most Chinese like to eat well, especially at the government's expense, the restaurants accommodated them by simply giving them much larger plates on which they put many different dishes, and then wrote it up as if it were just one dish.

The definition of corrupt behavior has also become more complex as the country moves from a socialist economy to a market economy. In the initial stages of introducing a market economy, selling imported goods in China for high profits was considered corrupt, as was paying middlemen to arrange business transactions. In the 1980s, some businesspeople were arrested, and even executed, for such activities. Now, it is assumed that those importing goods from abroad will make as large a profit as possible; and instead of looking at middlemen as the embodiment of corruption, government regulations allow them to be paid a transaction "fee." Yet, middlemen continue many activities considered corrupt, such as demanding a fee for introducing potential investors to appropriate officials—in part because the middlemen must in turn pay the officials for agreeing to meet with the potential investors—even though it is their job to do so.

Reform of party-state institutions and procedures has been an important avenue through which the government has attempted to curb corruption; but its broader goal in reforming the party state has been to improve the quality of China's leadership. Otherwise, China's leaders worry, the Chinese Communist Party may lose its legitimacy. Reforms have encouraged, even demanded, that the Chinese state bureaucracy reward merit more than mere seniority, and expertise more than political activism. And in 1996, the government's practice of allowing officials to stay in one ministry during their entire career was replaced by new regulations requiring officials from divisional chiefs up to ministers and provincial governors to be rotated every five years. Restrictions on tenure in office have brought a much younger generation of leaders into power; and they have placed a time limit on any one individual's access to power. The emphasis on a collective leadership since reforms began in 1979 has, moreover, made it virtually impossible for a leader to develop a personality cult, such as that which reached fanatical proportions around CCP chairman Mao Zedong during the Cultural Revolution. These reforms have dramatically reshaped the leadership structure and process. But other reforms, such as an antinepotism regulation that prohibits any high official from working in the same office as a spouse or direct blood relative, have seemingly had little effect on the overall pattern of officials using their power and access to put

The Chinese Communist Party is shown here at its 11th National Party Congress, which meets in the Great Hall of the People, located on one side of Tiananmen Square.

family members in positions where they can acquire significant wealth.

CONTEXT FOR DEMOCRACY

Cultural and Historical Authoritarianism

The Chinese political system reflects a history, political culture, and values entirely different from those in the West. For millennia, Chinese thought has run along different lines, with far less emphasis on such ideals as individual rights, privacy, and limits on state power. The Chinese political tradition is weighed down with a preference for authoritarian values, such as obedience and subordination of individuals to their superiors in a rigidly hierarchical system, and a belief in the importance of moral indoctrination. China's rulers have throughout history shown greater concerns for establishing their authority and maintaining unity in the vast territory and population they control than in protecting individual rights. Apart from some of China's intellectuals, the overwhelming majority of the Chinese people have appeared to be more afraid of chaos than an authoritarian ruler. Even today, the Chinese people seem more concerned that their leaders have *enough* power to control China than that the rights of citizens vis-à-vis their leaders be protected.

This is not to suggest that Confucianism and China's other traditions did not contain some mention of such rights. They did; but the *dominant* strand of Chinese political culture was authoritarian. It was critical in shaping the development of today's political system. As a result, when the Communists came to power in 1949, they were trying to operate within the context of an inherited patriarchal culture, in which the hierarchical values of superior–inferior and subordination, loyalty, and obedience prevailed over those of equality; and in which there was a historical predisposition toward official secrecy; a fear of officials and official power; and a traditional repugnance for courts, lawyers, and formal laws that protected individual rights. Thus, when Western democratic values and institutions were introduced, China's political culture and institutions were ill prepared to embrace them.

China's limited experience with democracy in the twentieth century was bitter. Virtually the entire period from the fall of China's imperial monarchy in 1911 to the Communist victory in 1949 was marred by warlordism, chaos, war, and a government masking brutality, greed, and incompetence under the label of "democracy." Although it is hardly fair to blame this period of societal collapse and externally imposed war on China's efforts to practice "democracy" under the "tutelage of the Kuomintang," the Chinese people's experience of democracy was nevertheless negative.

Moreover, the Chinese Communists condemned Western liberal democracy for being too weak a political system to prevent the Great Depression and two world wars in the twentieth century. In any event, foreign values were always suspect in China, as foreigners had repeatedly declared war on China in order to advance their own national interests. China was inclined to view the propagation of liberal democratic values as just one more effort by Western countries to enhance their own national power.

Experience with the Western powers and China's own efforts to implement democracy before 1949, together with China's traditional political culture, help explain the people's reluctance to embrace Western liberal democratic ideals. During the period of the Republic of China (1912–1949), China's "democratic" political and legal institutions proved inadequate to guarantee the nation's welfare, or to protect individual rights. Even under Communist rule, the one period described as "democratic mass rule" (the "10 bad years" or Cultural Revolution, from 1966 to 1976) was in fact a period of mass tyranny. For the Chinese, the experience of relinquishing power to "the masses" turned into the most horrific period of unleashed terrorism and cruelty they had experienced since the Communist takeover in 1949. Most analysts would argue that this was in no respect a "democracy," but rather the result of the

(Courtesy of Suzanne Ogden/sogden076)

This is a meeting room for the Chinese Communist Party branch in Huang village, Anhui Province. Below the banner for the "Mobilization committee for Huang village's progressive educational activities," is the oath for those who join the party.

Chinese people being manipulated by an ever-shifting nouveau elite, who were in a desperate competition with other pretenders to power. To those Chinese who experienced the Cultural Revolution first-hand, this was what could happen if China became democratic.

Socialist Democracy

When the CCP came to power in 1949, it inherited a country torn by civil war, internal rebellion, and foreign invasions for more than 100 years. The population was overwhelmingly illiterate and desperately poor, the economy in shambles. The most urgent need was for order and unity. China made great strides in securing its borders and ending internal fighting and chaos. Despite some serious setbacks and mistakes under the leadership of Mao Zedong, moreover, China also succeeded in establishing effective institutions of government and enhancing the material well-being of its people. But in the name of order and stability, China's leaders also severely limited the development of "democracy" in its Western liberal-democratic sense.

The Chinese people are accustomed to "eating bitterness," not to standing up to authority. The traditional Confucian emphases on the group rather than the individual

and on respect for authority continue to this day, although modernization, internationalization, and disenchantment with the CCP leadership have diminished their powerful cultural hold. Rapid modernization has likewise undermined Marxist Leninist-Maoist values, the glue that, along with traditional values, had helped hold China together. None of this, however, necessarily bodes well for the propagation of democratic values; for the destabilizing social effects of a loss of values, and the concomitant rise of aggressive nationalism and materialism, hardly provide a receptive environment for liberal democratic values.

Nevertheless, since 1949, and especially since the reform period began in 1979, there has been a gradual accretion of individual rights for Chinese people. These include greater freedom of speech; access to far more information and a diversity of perspectives; the right to vote in local elections; and development of the rights to privacy, to choose one's own work (as opposed to being assigned by the government), to move and work in different locations, to own private property, and many more. Moreover, the impersonal market forces of supply and demand, combined with an abundant variety of consumer goods, have undercut the power of officials to con-

trol the distribution of resources and opportunities in the society. The result is that the Chinese are no longer beholden to officials to supply them in exchange for favors, gift giving, banqueting, and outright bribery. This equality of access in the marketplace contributes to a greater sense of control by the people over their daily lives.

Unfortunately, even as such rights grow, other very important rights previously enjoyed by the Chinese people—such as a job, health care, housing, and education—are being eroded. Such "welfare rights" have provided the context in which other rights have gained meaning. At the same time that it has led to greater political and societal rights, then, economic liberalization has contributed to the polarization of wealth and destabilization of Chinese society.

Patterns of political participation are also changing. Participation in the political process at the local level has already led to greater responsiveness by local officials to the common people's needs. Village officials are more inclined than in the past to seek out advice for improving the economic conditions in their localities, and incompetent village officials are usually unable to gain reelection. In spite of local elections and other efforts to advance village democracy, however, villagers in

(Courtesy of Suzanne Ogden/sogden01)

Villagers wait patiently to cast their votes during the September 2001 election in a small village outside Shanghai.

many parts of China do not believe that elections have made much of a difference. Even in those areas where there has been extraordinary economic development, villagers do not necessarily see the connection of elections and democratization with prosperity.[25]

China has experienced only limited open popular demand for democracy. When the student-led demonstrations in Beijing began in 1989, the demands for democratic reforms were confined largely to the small realm of the intellectual elite—that is, students and well-educated individuals, as well as some members of the political and economic ruling elite. The workers and farmers of China remained more concerned about bread-and-butter issues—inflation, economic growth, unemployment, and their own personal enrichment—not democratic ideals.

By the mid-1990s, many Chinese had discovered that they could get what they wanted through channels other than mass demonstrations, because of the development of numerous alternative groups, institutions, and processes. Many of these groups are not political in origin, but the process by which they are pressing for policy changes in the government is highly political. When reforms began in 1979, there was only a handful of such groups. By the end of 2006, there were 346,000 interest groups and associations, commonly called NGOs (non-governmental organizations) in the West, but labeled as "civilian organizations" in China.[26]

While all such organizations are headed by a member of the CCP (usually a retired

person), they reflect and promote the interests of their membership. Indeed, it is in the self-interest of the appointed party head of the organization to advance its power and respond to the requests of the membership to represent their interests at higher levels. As an example, the party-state instituted an association to which small entrepreneurs in each city and town must belong. The association's purpose is to assert some level of control over a totally unsupervised arena of small business and commerce activity, but it also promotes the interests of its members; for entrepreneurs engaged in legitimate businesses do not want to have to compete against unregistered businesses that flog shoddy, illegal, and even dangerous products. Further, by helping crack down on those whose products violate copyright and trademark regulations, the association helps promote legitimate businesses.

In many areas, such as environmental protection, education, healthcare, and poverty reduction, interest groups, associations, foundations, and charities work together with the government to advance their causes. The fact that each group must be registered with the government and led by a party-state official need not, in most cases, be viewed as a negative factor. Indeed, the existence of a party-state official at the top ensures access to power that an organization would not otherwise have. Sometimes, the government has demanded that all "civilian associations," foundations, and charities re-register, in part because countless businesses have tried to avoid taxes by claiming to be "civilian organizations," charities, or

foundations. The government likewise prohibits democracy-promoting organizations from registering. Organizations that are funded by foreigners are always watched carefully, and when they appear to cross the line and become involved in sponsoring political movements, the government shuts them down.

It is perhaps ironic that the Chinese Communist Party's penchant for organizing people has resulted in teaching them organizational skills that they now use to pressure the government to change policy.[27] They work through these organizations to protect and advance their members' interests within the framework of existing law and regulations.

Even those Chinese not working through officially organized associations ban together to petition local officials using the organizational techniques they learned from the CCP. For example, urban neighborhoods join forces to stop local noise pollution emanating from stereos blasting on the street where thousands of Chinese engage in ballroom dancing, or from the cymbals, tambourines, gongs, and drums of old ladies doing "fan dancing" on the city streets.[28] In turn, the dancers petition the local officials to maintain their "right" to express themselves through dancing in the streets, some of the few public spaces available to them in a crowded urban environment.

The tendency to organize around issues and interests in China today is more than a reflection of the decline of the role of Communist ideology in shaping policy. It also reflects the government's focus on problem solving and pragmatic concerns in policy-making. Many constituencies take advantage of this approach to issues and policy. Although China has never been homogeneous and uncomplicated, it is certainly a far more complex economy, society, and polity today than it was before 1980. Today's China has far more diverse needs and interests than was the case previously, and specialized associations and interest groups serve the need of articulating these interests.

Compared to Western liberal democratic systems, Chinese citizens are politically passive. But is this a sign of satisfaction with the CCP regime? An indication that the Chinese are a "nation of sheep"? The outcome of their fear of the repercussions of being critical of the regime? Is Chinese submissiveness a sign of "collusion" with their oppressors? One could argue that, like Eastern Europeans, the Chinese have participated in their own political oppression simply by complying with the demands of the system. As the Czech Republic's then-president Vaclav Havel stated, "All of us have become accustomed to the totalitarian system, accepted it as an unalterable fact and therefore kept it running. . . . None of us is merely a victim of it, because all of us helped to create it together.[29]

Can we say that the Chinese, any more than the Czechs, collaborated with their authoritarian rulers if they did not flee into exile under Communist rule, or did not refuse to work? Is anyone who does not actively revolt against an oppressive system necessarily in collusion with it? In the case of China, one cannot assume that the major reason why people are not challenging the Communist system is out of fear of punitive consequences—although those who want to directly challenge CCP rule through the formation of new political parties or trade unions, or through the explicit public criticism of China's top political leaders do indeed risk punishment. The more logical explanation is that the Chinese have developed a completely different style from that of citizens in Western liberal democratic countries for getting what they want. This style is largely based on cultivating personal relationships rather than more formal and open institutionalized forms of political participation. More "democratic" behavioral skills can, of course, be acquired through practice; and as the Chinese political system gradually adopts more liberal democratic practices, the political culture is likely to evolve—indeed, it *is* evolving—in a more democratic direction.

Students, Intellectuals, and Business People as Potential Forces for Democratization

Democratization in China has been hampered by the people's inability to envision an alternative to CCP rule. What form would it take? How would it get organized? And if the CCP were overthrown, who would lead a new system? These questions are still far from being answered. So far, no dissident leadership capable of offering an alternative to CCP leadership, and laying claim to popular support, has formed. Even the mass demonstrations in 1989 were not led by either a worker, a peasant, or even an intellectual with whom the common people could identify:

[C]ompared with the intellectuals of Poland and Czechoslavakia, for example, Chinese intellectuals have little contact with workers and peasants and are not sensitive to their country's worsening social crisis; they were caught unawares by the democratic upsurge of 1989, and proved unable to provide the people with either the theoretical or practical guidance they needed.[30]

In fact, during the Tiananmen protests in 1989, students were actually annoyed by the workers' participation in the demonstrations. They wanted to press their own political demands—not the workers' more concrete, work-related issues. Some Chinese believe that the students' real interest in setting forth their own demands was because they wanted to enhance their own prestige and power vis-à-vis the regime: The students' major demands were for a "dialogue" with the government as "equals," and for free speech. These issues were of primary interest to them, but of little interest to the workers of China. Many Chinese believe that had the leaders of the 1989 demonstrations suddenly been catapulted to power, their behavior would have differed little from the ruling CCP elite. The student movement itself admitted to being authoritarian, of kowtowing to its own leaders, and of expecting others to obey rather than to discuss decisions. As one Beijing University student wrote during the 1989 Tiananmen Square protests:

The autonomous student unions have gradually cut themselves off from many students and become a machine kept constantly on the run in issuing orders. No set of organizational rules widely accepted by the students has emerged, and the democratic mechanism is even more vague.[31]

In any event, few of those who participated in the demonstrations in 1989 are interested in politics or political leadership today. Most have thrown themselves into business and making money.

Apart from students and intellectuals, some of the major proponents of democratic reform today hail from China's newly emerging business circles; but these groups have not united to achieve reform, as they neither like nor trust each other. Intellectuals view venture capitalists "as uncultured, and business people as driven only by crass material interests." The latter in turn regard intellectuals and students as "well-meaning but out of touch with reality and always all too willing and eager to serve the state" when it suits their needs.[32] Moreover, although the business community is interested in pushing such rights as the protection of private property and the strengthening of the legal system in the commercial and economic spheres, it tends to be more supportive of the regime's "law and order" values than of democratic values; for an unstable social and political environment would not be conducive to economic growth.

Those who wanted reforms (or even the overthrow of Communist Party rule) but left China and remain abroad have lost their political influence. Apart from everything else, it is difficult for those living abroad to make themselves heard in China, even if their articles are published or appear on the Web. Although they may keep in touch with the dissident movement in China, their influence is largely limited to their ability to supply it with funds. Doing so, however, often gets the recipients in China in trouble.

The Impact of Global Interdependency on Democratization

Since the late 1970s, the cultural context for democracy in China has shifted. The expansion of the international capitalist economy and increasing cultural and political globalization have led to a social and economic transformation of China. For the first time in Chinese history, a significant challenge to the "we–they" dichotomy—of China against the rest of the world—is occurring. This in turn has led many Chinese to question the heretofore assumed superiority of Chinese civilization.

Such an idea does not come easily for a people long-accustomed to hearing about China's greatness. Hence the fuss caused by *River Elegy*, a TV documentary series first shown on Chinese national television in 1988. In this series, the film producers argued that the Chinese people must embrace the idea of global interdependency—technological, economic, and cultural. To insist at that time in history on the superiority of Chinese civilization, with the isolation of China from the world of ideas that this implied, would only contribute to China's continued stagnation. The series suggested that the Chinese must see themselves as equal, not superior to, others; and as interdependent with, not as victims of, others. Such concepts of equality, and the opening up of China to ideas from the rest of the world, have led to a remarkable transformation of the Chinese political, cultural, and economic landscape.

In 2007, a 12-part TV documentary series, *Rise of the Great Powers,* aired by CCTV (China Central Television) examined how great powers have risen in history, and

Morning exercise time in the school yard of a school for children of migrants in Beijing. As with almost all public schools in China's cities, there is a set time and a specific set of exercises performed each day.

whether and why rising powers became involved in war. The fact that a television documentary, nearly ten years after the *River Elegy* series, was focused on a different set of issues and questions for China's role in the world in itself reflects how much China's self-perceptions and role in the world have changed.

The Press and Mass Media

At the time that the student-led demonstrations for democracy began in Beijing's Tiananmen Square in the spring of 1989, China's press had grown substantially and become increasingly liberalized. With some 1,500 newspapers, 5,000 magazines, and 500 publishing houses, the Chinese were able to express a wider variety of viewpoints and ideas than at any time since the CCP came to power in 1949. The production of millions of television sets, radios, short-wave radios, cassette recorders, and VCRs also facilitated the growth of the mass media in China. They were accompanied by a wide array of foreign audio and video materials. The programs of the British Broadcasting Corporation (BBC) and the Voice of America, the diversification of domestic television and radio programs (a choice made by the Chinese government and facilitated by satellite communication), and the importation and translation of foreign books and magazines—all contributed to a more pluralistic press in China. In fact, by 1989, the stream of publications had so overwhelmed the CCP Propaganda Department that it was simply no longer able to monitor their contents.

During the demonstrations in Tiananmen Square, the international press in Beijing, unlike the Chinese press, was freely filming the events and filing reports on the demonstrations. The Chinese press then took a leap into complete press freedom. With camera operators and microphones in hand, Chinese reporters covered the student hunger strike that began on May 13 in its entirety; but with the imposition of martial law in Beijing on May 20, press freedom came to a crashing halt.

In the immediate aftermath of the brutal crackdown on Tiananmen Square demonstrators in June 1989, the CCP imposed a ban on a variety of books, journals, and magazines. The government ordered the "cleansing" of media organizations, with "bad elements" to be removed and not permitted to leave Beijing for reporting. All press and magazine articles written during the prodemocracy movement, as well as all television and radio programs shown during this period, were analyzed to see if they conformed to the party line. If they did not, those individuals responsible for editing were dismissed. And, as had been the practice in the past, press and magazine articles once again had to be on topics specified by the editors, who were under the control of the Propaganda Department of the CCP. In short, press freedom in China suffered a significant setback because of the pro-democracy demonstrations in the spring of 1989.

In the new climate of experimentation launched by Deng Xiaoping in 1992, however, the diversity of television and radio programs soared. China's major cities now have multiple channels carrying a broad range of programs from Hong Kong, Taiwan, Japan, and the West. These programs, whether soap operas about the daily life of Chinese people living in Hong Kong and Taiwan, or art programs introducing the world of Western religious art through a visual art history tour of the Vatican, or in news about protests and problems faced by other nations in the world expose the Chinese to values, events, ideas, and standards of living previously unknown to them. They are even learning about the American legal process through China's broadcasting of American television dramas that focus on police and the judicial system. Chinese are fascinated that American police, as soon as they arrest suspects, inform them that they have "the right to remain silent" and "the right to a lawyer." Such programs may do more to promote reform of the Criminal Procedure Code than anything human rights groups do.

Today, television ownership is widespread. In addition to dozens of regular channels, China has numerous cable stations. And virtually all families have radios. Round-the-clock, all-news radio stations broadcast the latest political, economic, and cultural news and conduct live interviews; and radio talk shows take phone calls from anonymous listeners about everything from sex to political and economic corruption. There are even blatant critiques of police brutality,[33] and analyses of failed government policies on everything from trade policy to health care and unemployment. There is

STOCK MARKETS, GAMBLING, AND LOTTERIES

China has had two stock markets since the late 1980s. One was created in the Special Economic Zone (SEZ) of Shenzhen; the other in Shanghai. With only seven industries originally registered on them, strict rules about how much daily profit or loss (1.2 percent for the Shanghai exchange until July 1992) a stock could undergo, and deep public suspicion that these original issues of stocks were worthless, these markets got off to a slow start. But when these same stocks were worth five times their original value just a year later, the public took notice. Rumors—as important in China as actual news—took over and exaggerated the likelihood of success in picking a winning stock. The idea of investors actually losing money, much less a stock-market crash, did not seem to be an idea whose time had come.

Because China is still largely a cash economy, a stock-market transaction can be complicated. Instead of just telephoning a stockbroker and giving an order, with a simple bank transfer or check to follow shortly, many Chinese must still appear in person, stand in line, and pay cash on the spot. Taiwan has added its own angle to the stock-mania by selling to the Mainlanders small radios that are tuned in to only one frequency—stock market news. Local branches of the stock market and brokerages are popular places for retired people to spend the day watching their stocks on the boards. In Shanghai, they can also tune into "Stock Market Today," a popular local television program. Issuing, buying, and selling stocks has at times been a near-national obsession. Not only do ordinary companies selling commercial goods, such as computers and clothing, issue stocks. So do taxicab companies and even universities. Thus far, few such stocks are actually listed on the national stock exchanges; but employees of these work units are eager to purchase the stocks. In most cases, the original issues are sold at far higher prices than their face value, as employees (and even nonemployees) eagerly buy up fellow employees' rights to purchase stocks, at grossly inflated prices. Presumably, the right of employees to own stock in their own work unit will make them eager to have it do well, and thus increase efficiency and profits.

Even as China's economy continued to roar along with double-digit growth in the twenty-first century, the ardor for wheeling and dealing in the stock market cooled considerably. Companies were making money, but stock prices were in the doldrums, with a 2003 poll indicating that 90 percent of investors had lost money.[34] Then, in 2006, investors fueled a 130 percent surge. The bull market was largely due to a massive inflow of speculative funds from both foreign investment, and domestic investment from Chinese investors hoping to profit more from the stock market than from leaving their money in banks, where they rarely earn more than 2 percent per annum.

The underlying problems in China's stock markets, however, remain a concern. First, they are not regulated by outside auditors, which means that investors cannot trust the information in company reports. Scandals involving stocks all too often erupt in the Chinese media. Second, the state itself usually owns the majority of voting shares—often as much as two-thirds of the shares of China's leading companies. (These shares were until recently also "untradable" shares, meaning the companies were not really private at all, and should not have been listed on a public stock exchange.) This results in the state's preferred policies, which are often based on bureaucratic and political concerns, rather than private investors and the market determining company strategies and profitability for, say, the technology, telecommunications, or heavy industrial sector. Because a state enterprise or state agency is usually the majority stockholder, moreover, it can by its own purchases and sales determine the price of a stock. The small investor is simply a pawn, and really has little chance to make a profit.

Companies that are owned and run by state agencies and ministries, such as the Ministry of Defense, have used state funds to invest in both domestic and international stocks and real estate. They have sometimes lost millions of yuan in the process. As a result, the government now prohibits state-run units from investing state money in stocks and real estate. Nevertheless, some still do so indirectly, thereby evading the laws.

Learning from Western practices and catering to a national penchant for gambling (illegal, but indulged in nevertheless, in mahjong and cards), the Chinese have also begun a number of lotteries. Thus far, most of these have been for the purpose of raising money for specific charities or causes, such as for victims of floods and for the disabled. Recently, because the items offered, such as brand-new cars, have been so desirable, the lotteries have generated billions of yuan in revenue. The government has found these government-controlled lotteries to be an excellent way of addressing the Chinese penchant for gambling while simultaneously generating revenues to compensate for those it seems unable to collect through taxes.

Finally, companies follow such Western marketing gimmicks for increasing sales as putting Chinese characters on the inside of packages or bottle caps to indicate whether the purchasers have won a prize. With a little Chinese ingenuity, the world could witness never-before-imaged realms of betting and competitive business practices that appeal to people's desire to get something for nothing.

also far better coverage of social and economic news in all the media than previously, and serious investigative reporting on corruption and crime. A popular half-hour program during evening prime time looks at cases of corruption and crime that are being investigated, or have been solved. Figures indicate the exponential growth of the media. The number of books published annually in China rose from about 5,000 in 1970 to about 104,000 in 1995. The number of newspapers grew from 42 in 1970 to over 2,000 by the year 2005, with a circulation of over 100 million. (In China, almost all work units post a number of newspapers in glass cases outside, so the readership is far higher than the circulation numbers.) Most of the newspapers also have their own websites. Similarly, the number of magazines grew from a handful in 1970 to more than 9,000 by 2005—an official number that excludes the large number of nonregistered magazines and illegal publications. Xinhua (New China) News Agency has more than 100 branches throughout the world that report on news for the Chinese people. There are hundreds of radio stations, and the number of television stations grew to 3,000 by 2005. Close to 90 percent of the population has access to television. CCTV-9, the "CNN" of China, is a slick, English-language program that is watched in many parts of the world, and actually has broader viewership in Asia than does CNN. By 2005, there were 750 cable-television stations and an estimated 125 million households with cable television access, with millions of new subscribers being added each year. The government's National Cable Company is forming a countrywide network to expand services geographically and to include new Internet and telecommunications connections.[35]

This effort to expand Internet availability indicates the government's dilemma: It wants China to modernize rapidly, and to have the scientific, economic, commercial, and educational resources on the Internet available to as many as possible. It has demanded that all government offices be updated to use the Internet in order to improve communication, efficiency, and transparency. At the same time, it wants to control which websites can be accessed, and what type of material may be made available to China's citizens on those sites. In spite of the government's best efforts, the Internet is virtually uncontrollable. Angry and inflammatory commentary on events in China, and even criticism of China's leadership, appear with increasing regularity. Some sites are closed down because they violate the unstated boundaries of acceptable commentary; but it is difficult in a computer-saavy world to block access to all sites that the government might find irritating, if not downright seditious. China's Internet users know what is going on in the world; and they can spend their time chatting to dissidents abroad and at home on e-mail if they so choose. But most prefer to use the Internet for business, news, sports, games, music, socializing, and, of course, pornography. The Chinese, in fact, seem to spend most of their time on the Internet for entertainment and playing games, in contrast to Americans' preference for using it primarily for information. China's largest Internet company, Tencent, dominates 80 percent of China's market, far more than Google dominates in the U.S. market. This is due largely to the complete package of entertainment it offers (with a preference for playing games, forming communities, and adopting virtual personas—avatars), as well as its mobile instant-messaging service. In China, 70 percent of the Internet's users are under the age of 30; whereas in the U.S., some 70 percent are *over* the age of 30.[36] With print and electronic media so prolific and diverse, much of it escapes any monitoring whatsoever, especially newspapers, magazines, and books. Even the weekend editions of the remaining state-run newspapers print just about any story that will sell. Often about a seamier side of Chinese life, they undercut the puritanical aspect of communist rule and expanding the range of topics available for discussion in the public domain. Were the state able to control the media, it would, at the very least, crack down on pornographic literature on the streets.

The sheer quantity of output on television, radio, books, and the press allows the Chinese people to make choices among the types of news, programs, and perspectives they find most appealing. Their choices are not necessarily for the most informative or the highest quality, but for the most entertaining. Because the media (with few exceptions) are market-driven, consumers' preferences, not government regulations or ideological values, shape programming and publishing decisions.

This market orientation results from economic reforms. By the 1990s, the government had cut subsidies to the media, thereby requiring that even the state-controlled media had to make money or be shut down. This in turn meant that the news stories it presented had to be more newsworthy in order to sell advertising and subscriptions. Even in the countryside, the end of government subsidies to the media has spurred publication. Thinking there is money to be made, township and village enterprises, as well as private entre-

preneurs, have set up thousands of printing facilities during the last 10 to 15 years.[37] In short, "Even though China's media can hardly be called free, the emergence of divergent voices means the center's ability to control people's minds has vanished."[41]

The party tends, however, to concentrate its limited resources on the largest and most influential journals, magazines, newspapers, and publishing houses. It seems to have written off the rest as the inevitable downside of a commercialized media market—and the part that it no longer supports, nor controls, financially. Funded by advertising and consumer demand, the media must now "march to the market." Nevertheless, Beijing is trying to tighten its control over the media system by instituting a penalty point system. In 2007, the Chinese Communist Party's propaganda department announced the new system of points-based penalties, whereby each media outlet will be allocated 12 points. If it uses up its 12 points, it may be closed. Point deductions are based on the seriousness of the media outlet's action. This will supplement the existing system in which the CCP's propaganda department and the government's media regulator have jointly decided when to issue warnings, remove offending executives or reports, or otherwise punish a media organization. The new approach is portrayed as an effort to increase "social harmony," and seems to be increasing in intensity as the 17th National Party Congress and the Beijing 2008 Olympics draw closer in time.[38] As for China's film industry, because it produces relatively few films each year, it is more heavily censored than print media. Furthermore, all films are shot in a small number of studios, making control easier. Finally, a film is likely to have a much larger audience than most books, and so the censors are concerned that it be carefully reviewed before being screened.[39] Zhang Yimou, China's renowned film director and producer, and recipient of numerous international film awards, has had the screening in China of one after another of his films banned. A publication of the Party School of the Chinese Communist Party condemned his most recent blockbuster, *Curse of the Golden Flower*, as "ugly" and "bloodthirsty," transgressing the moral limits of Chinese art. And yet, the film has not been banned in China, and has wracked up tens of millions of dollars in profits.[40]

Human Rights and Democracy: The Chinese View

Surveys indicate that most urban Chinese citizens believe the government has adopted policies that have greatly improved their daily lives. Many have seen the government's law-and-order campaigns—which sometimes involve crackdowns on perceived dissidents (such as Falun Gong activists)—as necessary to Chi-

na's continued economic prosperity and political stability. They have tended to be far more interested in the prospect of a higher standard of living than in the rights of dissidents.

Even China's intellectuals no longer seem interested in protest politics. They do not "love the party," but they accept the status quo. Some just want a promotion and to make money. Others have become advisers to the government's think tanks and advisory committees. Many have gone into business. As one university professor put it, it is easy to be idealistic in one's heart; but to be idealistic in action is a sign of a true idealist, and there haven't been many of those in China since 1989. Today in China, it is difficult to find any student or member of the intellectual elite who demonstrated in Tiananmen Square in 1989 doing anything remotely political today.

Still, those who are discontent with party rule have far more outlets today for their grievances: the mass media, and journals, as well as think tanks, policy advisory committees, and professional associations that actually influence policy. Street protests are no longer considered the best way for the educated and professional classes to change policy, although ordinary workers and peasants resort to them with increasing frequency.

Many members of China's elites are committed to reform, but the number of idealists committed to democracy—or communism—is limited. Few Chinese, including government officials, want to discuss communist ideology, and even fewer agree on what democracy means. They prefer to talk about business and development, and do so in terms familiar to capitalists throughout the world, but also in terms of the overall objective of strengthening China as a nation. In this respect, they are appealing to the strong nationalism that has virtually replaced communism as the normative glue holding the country together.

Apart from their changed perspectives on what really matters, many Chinese feel that they do not know enough to challenge government policy on human rights issues. They assume that the government lies to them, and on such issues as the treatment of protesters and rights defenders, most Chinese know no more than what the government tells them. Why should they risk their careers to fight for the rights of jailed dissidents about whom they know almost nothing, they ask. They know of the abuse of human rights in Western liberal democracies, such as the killing of student protesters at Kent State by the National Guard during the Vietnam War, the many deaths attributed to the British forces in Northern Ireland, the torture of American-held prisoners in Iraq and in Guantanamo Bay. When the U.S. State Department issues its annual human rights report, which inevitably makes harsh criticism of China, Beijing replies with an equally damning condemnation of human

A crowded classroom in a school for children of migrants in Beijing. As of 2007, all migrant children are supposed to be put into the city's state-funded schools, but it is not clear this will happen immediately.

rights abuses by the United States. In 2007, it noted the "increased willingness by Washington to spy on its own citizens by monitoring telephone calls, computer connections, and travels."[42]

The Chinese people have heard of the unseemly behavior of several student leaders of the Tiananmen Square demonstrations, both during the movement in 1989 and after it. They wonder aloud if in the treatment of criminal suspects and those suspected of treason or efforts to harm the country—especially suspected terrorists—Western democratic states exhibit more virtuous behavior than does China. Some Chinese intellectuals argue that the recent difficulties in the United States and other Western democracies indicate that their citizens frequently elect the wrong leaders, people who not only make bad policies but who are also increasingly involved in corrupt money politics—the very issue of most concern to the Chinese. This, they suggest, indicates that democracy is no more able than socialism to produce good leaders. Furthermore, many support the view that the Chinese people are inadequately prepared for democracy because of a low level

of education. The blatant political maneuverings and other problems surrounding the 2000 U.S. presidential election hardly offered reassurance as to the virtues of American democracy; nor did the American 2003 invasion and subsequent occupation of Iraq. The minimal response by the U.S. government to those challenging the administration, and the unwillingness of Congress to debate the war for 4 years after the invasion give the Chinese the impression that "the people" were not necessarily listened to, and that a democracy does not necessarily have an effective system of "checks and balances."

Within China, it is frequently the people, rather than the government, who demand the harshest penalties for common criminals, if not political dissidents. And it is China's own privileged urbanites who often demand that the government ignore the civil rights of other citizens. For example, urban residents in Beijing have repeatedly demanded that the government remove migrant squatters and their shantytowns, asserting that they are breeding grounds for criminality in the city. And they resist the government allowing migrants to attend the city's public schools

or receive healthcare. Many ordinary people now seem to accept the government's overall assessment of the events of the spring of 1989, which is that the demonstrations in Tiananmen Square posed a threat to the stability and order of China and justified the military's crackdown. To many Chinese people, no less than to their government, stability and order are critical to the continued economic development of China. Advancement toward democracy and protection of human rights take a back seat.

INTERNATIONAL RELATIONS

From the 1830s onward, foreign imperialists nibbled away at China's territorial sovereignty, subjecting China to one national humiliation after another. As early as the 1920s, both the Nationalists and the Communists were committed to unifying and strengthening China in order to rid it of foreigners and resist further foreign incursions. When the Communists achieved victory over the Nationalists in 1949, they vowed that they would never again allow foreigners to tell China what to do. This historical background is essential to understanding

China's foreign policy in the period of Chinese Communist rule.

From Isolation to Openness

By the early 1950s, the Communists had forced all but a handful of foreigners to leave China. The target of the United States' Cold War policy of "isolation and containment," China under Chairman Mao Zedong charted an independent, and eventually an isolationist, foreign policy. Even China's relations with socialist bloc countries were suspended after the Cultural Revolution began in 1966. China took tentative steps toward re-establishing relations with the outside world with U.S. president Richard Nixon's visit to China in 1972, but it did not really pursue an "open door" policy until more pragmatic "reformers" gained control in 1978. By the 1980s, China was hosting several million tourists annually, inviting foreign investors and foreign experts to help with China's modernization, and allowing Chinese to study and travel abroad. Nevertheless, inside the country, contacts between Chinese and foreigners were still affected by the suspicion on the part of ordinary Chinese that ideological and cultural contamination comes from abroad and that association with foreigners might bring trouble.

These attitudes have moderated considerably, to the point where some Chinese are willing to socialize with foreigners, invite them to their homes, and even marry them. However, this greater openness to things foreign sits uncomfortably together with a new nationalism that has emerged since the West so heavily criticized, and punished, China for the military crackdown on Tiananmen Square demonstrators in June 1989. The broad masses of Chinese people remain suspicious, even disdainful of foreigners. A strong xenophobia (dislike and fear of foreigners) and an awareness of the history of China's victimization by Western and Japanese imperialism mean that the Chinese are likely to rail at any effort by other countries to tell them what to do. The Chinese continue to exhibit this sensitivity on a wide variety of issues, from human rights to China's policies toward Tibet and Taiwan; from intellectual property rights to prison labor and environmental degradation.

Ordinary Chinese people tended to concur with the government's anger over the U.S. threat of economic sanctions to challenge China's human rights policies (something that is no longer possible since China joined the World Trade Organization [WTO] in 2001). They were enraged by the American bombing of the Chinese Embassy in Belgrade during the war in Yugoslavia, which the U.S. government insisted was by error, not intent; the crash of a U.S. spy plane with a Chinese jet in 2001, which the Chinese believed to be in their own airspace; efforts to prevent China from entering the World Trade Organization or becoming a site for the Olympics; American accusations of Chinese spying and stealing of American nuclear-weapons secrets, charges that appeared to the Chinese to be motivated by hostility toward China, especially when they were ultimately dismissed for lack of evidence; American accusations of illegal campaign funding by the Chinese; the ongoing human-rights barrage; the strengthening of U.S. military ties with Japan and Taiwan; and continued American interference in China's efforts to regain control of Taiwan.

Only a narrow line separates a benign nationalism essential to China's unity, however, and a popular nationalism with militant overtones threatens to career out of control.[43] These aspects of nationalism worry China's government, whose primary concerns remain economic growth and stability. The government does not want to be forced into war by a militant nationalism. Nevertheless, China's xenophobia continues to show up in its efforts to keep foreigners isolated in certain living compounds; to limit social contacts between foreigners and Chinese; to control the import of foreign literature, films, and periodicals; and in general to limit the invasion of foreign political and cultural values in China. Since 1996, in an effort to protect China's culture, the government has ordered television stations to broadcast only Chinese-made programs during prime time. In 2007, the government limited television stations to showing "ethically inspiring TV series" during prime time. Programs broadcast during prime time must likewise "keep script and video records for future censorship against vulgarity."[44] The government has also attempted to enhance national pride through economic success; and by participation in international events, including the Olympic and Asian Games, music competitions, and film festivals.

Yet, in some respects, the resistance to the spread of foreign values in China is proving to be a losing battle, with growing numbers of foreigners in China; television swamped with foreign programs; Kentucky Fried Chicken, McDonald's, Starbucks, and Pizza Hut ubiquitous; "Avon calling" at several million homes;[45] and bodybuilding and disco (and even poll dancing!) becoming part of the culture. Further, with millions of Chinese tourists and officials tromping through the world, vast numbers of foreign investors in China, China's hosting of trade fairs, international meetings, and the 2008 Olympics, as well as a heavy reliance on foreign experts to help China reform its economic, legal, financial, and banking systems, and set up a commodities and futures market, China is awash with values that contend with traditional Chinese ones. China is now a full participant in the international economic and financial system: it is the third-largest global trading country, and gives foreign aid to developing countries, especially in Africa. It is an important participant in the war on terrorism, and a key player in Interpol and other efforts to control international crime syndicates, smuggling of weapons and drugs, and international trafficking in children and women. China today is seen by most countries as a partner rather than an adversary, a part of the solution, not the problem (such as in negotiations with the North Koreans over their nuclear weapons program). Its powerful economy and investments abroad have earned it respect (leavened with fear) worldwide. Today, China is a key international actor. It cannot be dismissed as a poor country without the wherewithal to enter the modern world.

China is a much more open country than at any time since 1949. This is in spite of the efforts by the party's more conservative wing to limit the impact of foreign ideas about democracy and individual rights on the political system, as well as the impact from "polluting" values embedded in foreign culture. Over time, however, conservatives have lost the battle to limit foreign influence, due more to the inexorable forces of globalization, communication, and the Internet than to any struggle behind closed doors with political adversaries. At the same time, although China's flourishing business community and growing middle class have little interest in disrupting the emphasis on stability by calling for greater political democracy, they nevertheless encourage, and benefit from, China's greater openness. Foreign investment in China (annual total foreign direct investment in the last few years has averaged around US$60 billion) far outstrips foreign investment in any other developing country. This is due not just to China's potential market size but also to the favorable investment climate created by the party-state. Fully one-third of China's manufacturing output is produced by foreign companies in China (both in the form of joint ventures with the Chinese, and wholly-owned foreign companies), indicating just how important foreign investment is to China's economy. (This is an important fact to remember when critics denounce China's trade surplus; that is, a considerable percentage of those exports are actually produced by companies wholly or partly owned by parent companies located in countries to which China exports its products.) China's openness, especially since joining the WTO in 2001, has forced its own enterprises to compete not just against imports, but also against foreign firms that have invested in China. China's service sector has been opened up to foreign competition. By 2007, foreign banks, insurance companies, securities firms, and telecommunications could compete on an increasingly equal basis.[46]

When it comes to the economy, then, the government has seemed less worried about the invasion of foreign values than anxious to attract foreign investment. China sees a strong economy as the key to both domestic stability and international respect. The government's view now seems to be: If it takes nightclubs, discos, exciting stories in the media, stock markets, rock concerts, the Internet, and consumerism to make the Chinese people content and the economy flourish under CCP rule, then so be it.

THE SINO–SOVIET RELATIONSHIP

While forcing most other foreigners to leave China in the 1950s, the Chinese Communist regime invited experts from the Soviet Union to China to give much-needed advice, technical assistance, and aid. This convinced the United States (already certain that Moscow controlled communism wherever it appeared) that the Chinese were puppets of the Soviets. Indeed, until the Great Leap Forward in 1958, the Chinese regime accepted Soviet tenets of domestic and foreign policy along with Soviet aid. But China's leaders soon grew concerned about the limits of Soviet aid and the relevance of Soviet policies to China's conditions—especially the costly industrialization favored by the Soviet Union. Ultimately, the Chinese questioned their Soviet "big brother" and turned to the Maoist model of development, which aimed to replace expensive Soviet technology with human labor. Soviet leader Nikita Khrushchev warned the Chinese of the dangers to China's economy in undertaking the Great Leap Forward; but Mao Zedong interpreted this as evidence that the Soviet "big brother" wanted to hold back China's development.

The Soviets' refusal to use their military power in support of China's foreign-policy objectives further strained the Sino–Soviet relationship. First in the case of China's confrontation with the United States and the forces of the "Republic of China" over the Offshore Islands in the Taiwan Strait in 1958, and then in the Sino-Indian border war of 1962, the Soviet Union backed down from its promise to support China. The Soviets also refused to share nuclear technology with the Chinese. The final blow to the by-then fragile relationship came with the Soviet Union's signing of the 1963 Nuclear Test Ban Treaty. The Chinese denounced this as a Soviet plot to exclude China from the "nuclear club" that included only Britain, France, the United States, and the Soviet Union. Subsequently, Beijing publicly broke party relations with Moscow.

The Sino–Soviet relationship, already in shambles, took on an added dimension of fear during the Vietnam War, when the Chinese grew concerned that the Soviets (and Americans) might use the war as an excuse to attack China. China's distrust of Soviet intentions was heightened in 1968, when the Soviets invaded Czechoslovakia in the name of the "greater interests of the socialist community"—which, they contended, "overrode the interests of any single country within that community." Soviet skirmishes with Chinese soldiers on China's northern borders soon followed. Ultimately, it was the Chinese leadership's concern about the Soviet threat to China's national security that, in 1971, caused it to reassess its relationship with the United States and led to the establishment of diplomatic relations with China in 1979. Indeed, the real interest of China and the United States in each other was as a "balancer" against the Soviet Union. Thus, in the midst of the Cold War, which began in 1947 and did not end until the late 1980s, China had moved out of the Soviet-led camp; yet China did not begin benefiting from friendship with Western countries in the power balance with the Soviet Union until it gained the seat in the United Nations in 1971.

The Sino–Soviet relationship moved toward reconciliation only near the end of the Cold War. In 1987, the Soviets began making peaceful overtures: They reduced troops on China's borders and withdrew support for Vietnam's puppet government in neighboring Cambodia. Beijing responded positively to the new *glasnost* ("open door") policy of the Soviet Communist Party's General Secretary, Mikhail Gorbachev. Border disputes were settled and ideological conflict between the two Communist giants abated; for with the Chinese themselves shelving Marxist dogma in their economic policies, they could hardly continue to denounce the Soviet Union's "revisionist" policies and make self-righteous claims to ideological orthodoxy. With both the Soviet Union and China abandoning their earlier battle over who should lead the Communist camp, they shifted away from conflict over ideological and security issues to cooperation on trade and economic issues. Today, China and Russia have significant trade, and their relationship is based on national interests, not ideology.

GUNS AND RICE

With the collapse of Communist party rule, first in the Central/Eastern European states in 1989, and subsequently in the Soviet Union, the dynamics of China's foreign policy changed dramatically. Apart from fear that their own reforms might lead to the collapse of CCP rule in China, the breakup of the Soviet Union into 15 independent states removed China's ability to play off the two superpowers against each other: The formidable Soviet Union simply no longer existed. Yet its fragmented remains had to be treated seriously, for the state of Russia still has nuclear weapons and shares a common border of several thousand miles with China, and the former Soviet republic of Kazakhstan shares a border of nearly 1,000 miles.

The question of what type of war the Chinese military might have to fight has affected its military modernization. For many years, China's military leaders were in conflict over whether China would have to fight a high-tech war or a "people's war," in which China's huge army would draw in the enemy on the ground and destroy it. In 1979, the military modernizers won out, jettisoning the idea that a large army, motivated by ideological fervor but armed with hopelessly outdated equipment, could win a war against a highly modernized military such as that of the Soviet Union. The People's Liberation Army (PLA) began by shedding a few million soldiers and putting its funds into better armaments. A significant catalyst to further modernizing the military came with the Persian Gulf War of 1991, during which the CNN news network broadcasts vividly conveyed the power of high-technology weaponry to China's leaders.

China's military believed that it was allocated an inadequate budget for modernization, so it struck out on its own along the capitalist road to raise money. By the late 1990s, the PLA had become one of the most powerful actors in the Chinese economy. It had purchased considerable property in the Special Economic Zones near Hong Kong; acquired ownership of major tourist hotels and industrial enterprises; and invested in everything from golf courses, brothels, and publishing houses to CD factories and the computer industry, as a means for funding military modernization. In 1998, however, President Jiang Zemin demanded that the military relinquish its economic enterprises and return to its primary task of building a modern military and protecting China. The promised payoff was that China's government would allocate more funding to the PLA, making it unnecessary for it to rely on its own economic activities.

In recent years, China's military has purchased weaponry and military technology from Russia as Moscow scales back its own military in what sometimes resembles a going-out-of-business sale; but in doing so, China's military may have simply bought into a higher level of obsolescence, since Russia's weaponry lags years behind the technology of the West. China possesses nuclear weapons and long-distance bombing capability, but its ability to fight a war beyond its own borders is quite limited. Asian countries, torn between wondering whether China or Japan will be a future threat to their territory, do not seem concerned by China's military modernization, except when China periodically makes threatening statements about Taiwan or the Spratly Islands in the South China Sea. Even here, however, Beijing usually relies on economic and diplomatic instruments. In the case of Taiwan, it is essentially tying Taiwan's economy to the mainland by welcoming economic investment and trade; the hope is ultimately to bring Taiwan under the control of Beijing without a war. In the case of the Spratlys, under whose territorial waters there is believed to be significant oil deposits, Beijing has reached tentative agreement with the five governments involved in competing claims to the Spratlys to avoid the possibility of armed clashes.

Nevertheless, in spite of China's remarkable economic and diplomatic gains since the reform period began in 1979, the leadership continues to modernize China's military capabilities. Beijing is ever alert to threats to its national security, but there are no indications that it is preparing for aggression against any country. China's military modernization is primarily aimed at defensive capabilities and maintaining its deterrent capability against an American nuclear attack. It has also increased the number of missiles it aims at Taiwan in response to repeated suggestions by Taiwan's President, Chen Shui-bian, that Taiwan would declare independence. With the arrival of the George W. Bush administration in Washington in early 2001, the American leadership began to seriously consider the possibility of deploying a limited "national missile defense" (NMD) in the United States, and even to deploy a "theater missile defense" (TMD) around Japan—and possibly Taiwan. Were a missile-defense system successfully deployed, it would limit the ability of China to prevent Japan or the United States from attacking it—or to prevent Taiwan from declaring independence. By providing a protective shield, TMD would allow Taiwan to declare independence with impunity. TMD is, then, perceived by Beijing as an aggressive move by the United States, and helps explain China's efforts to substantially increase the number of missiles it aims at Taiwan in order to overcome any defensive system (including "theater missile defense") that might be installed.

U.S. national missile defense and theater missile defense hardly provide the basis for confidence-building, peace, and security in Asia. Nevertheless, because the United States officially adopted a decision to deploy NMD within the context of international terrorism, and because the Chinese see themselves on the same side with the Americans in the war on terrorism, the Chinese have felt less threatened by NMD than they otherwise might.

China's leadership is, in any event, primarily concerned with economic development. China is working to become an integral part of the international economic, commercial, and monetary systems. It has rapidly expanded trade with the international community, even more so since joining the World Trade Organization in 2001. Today, China focuses its efforts primarily on infrastructure development and investment, not just in China but throughout the world. With the exponential growth in per capita income for more than 200 million Chinese, China is pressed to acquire natural resources to satisfy rocketing increases in consumer demand. It is investing heavily in resources for the future in Latin America, Southeast Asia, Africa, and the Middle East. It is ironic that China, considered "the sick man of Asia " in the early 20th century, should now in the 21st century be buying up companies not just in the developing world, but also in Europe and the United States; and that it has, along with Japan, become the "banker" for the United States, buying American debt and keeping the U.S. dollar from declining still further in value. For these reasons, China holds substantial bargaining power vis-à-vis the United States and many other countries in the world.

THE SINO–AMERICAN RELATIONSHIP

China's relationship with the United States has historically been an emotionally turbulent one.[47] It has never been characterized by indifference. During World War II, the United States gave significant help to the Chinese, who at that time were fighting under the leadership of the Nationalist Party, headed by General Chiang Kai-shek. When the Americans entered the war in Asia, the Chinese Communists were fighting together with the Nationalists in a "united front" against the Japanese, so American aid was not seen as directed against communism.

After the defeat of Japan at the end of World War II, the Japanese military, which had occupied much of the north and east of China, was demobilized and sent back to Japan. Subsequently, civil war broke out between the Communists and Nationalists. The United States attempted to reconcile the two sides, but to no avail. As the Communists moved toward victory in 1949, the KMT leadership fled to Taiwan. Thereafter, the two rival governments each claimed to be the true rulers of China. The United States, already in the throes of the Cold War because of the "iron curtain" falling over Eastern Europe, viewed communism in China as a major threat to its neighbors.

Korea, Taiwan, and Vietnam

The outbreak of the Korean War in 1950 helped the United States to rationalize its decision to support the Nationalists, who had already lost power on the mainland and fled to Taiwan. The Korean War began when the Communists in northern Korea attacked the non-Communist south. When United Nations troops (mostly Americans) led by American general Douglas MacArthur successfully pushed Communist troops back almost to the Chinese border and showed no signs of stopping their advance, the Chinese—who had frantically been sending the Americans messages about their concern for China's own security, to no avail—entered the war.

The Chinese forced the UN troops to retreat to what is today still the demarcation line between North and South Korea. Thereafter, China became a target of America's Cold War isolation and containment policies.

With the People's Republic of China condemned as an international "aggressor" for its action in Korea, the United States felt free to recognize the Nationalist government in Taiwan as the legitimate government to represent all of China. The United States supported the Nationalists' claim that the people on the Chinese mainland actually wanted the KMT to return to the mainland and defeat the Chinese Communists. As the years passed, however, it became clear that the Chinese Communists controlled the mainland and that the people were not about to rebel against Communist rule.

Sino–American relations steadily worsened as the United States continued to build up a formidable military bastion with an estimated 100,000 KMT soldiers in the tiny islands of Quemoy and Matsu in the Taiwan Strait, just off China's coast. Tensions were exacerbated by the steady escalation of U.S. military involvement in Vietnam from 1965 to the early 1970s. China, fearful that the United States was really using the war in Vietnam as the first step toward attacking China, concentrated on civil-defense measures: Chinese citizens used shovels and even spoons to dig air-raid shelters in major cities such as Shanghai and Beijing, with tunnels connecting them to the suburbs. Some industrial enterprises were moved out of China's major cities in order to make them less vulnerable in the event of a massive attack on concentrated urban areas. The Chinese received a steady barrage of what we would call propaganda about the United States "imperialist" as China's number-one enemy; but it is important to realize that the Chinese leadership actually *believed* what it told the people, especially in the context of the United States' steady escalation of the war in Vietnam toward the Chinese border, and the repeated "mistaken" overflights of southern China by American planes bombing North Vietnam. Apart from everything else, it is unlikely that China's leaders would have made such an immense expenditure of manpower and resources on civil-defense measures had they not truly believed that the United States was preparing to attack China.

Diplomatic Relations

By the late 1960s, China was completely isolated from the world community, including the Communist bloc. In the throes of the Cultural Revolution, it had withdrawn its diplomatic staff from all but one of its embassies. It saw itself as surrounded on all sides by enemies—the Soviets to the north and west, the United States to the south in Vietnam as well as in South Korea and Japan, and the Nationalists to the east in Taiwan. Internally, China was in such turmoil from the Cultural Revolution that it appeared to be on the verge of complete collapse.

In this context, Soviet military incursions on China's northern borders, combined with an assessment of which country could offer China the most profitable economic relationship, led China to consider the United States as the lesser of two evil giants and to respond positively to American overtures. In 1972, President Richard Nixon visited China, the first official American contact with China since breaking diplomatic relations in 1950. When the U.S. and China signed the Shanghai Communique at the end of his visit, the groundwork was laid for reversing more than two decades of hostile relations.

Thus began a new era of Sino–American friendship, but it fell short of full diplomatic relations, This long delay in bringing the two states into full diplomatic relations reflected not only each country's domestic political problems but also mutual disillusionment with the nature of the relationship. Although both sides had entered the relationship with the understanding of its strategic importance as a bulwark against the Soviet threat, the Americans had assumed that the 1972 opening of partial diplomatic relations would lead to a huge new economic market for American products; the Chinese assumed that the new ties would quickly lead the United States to end its diplomatic relations with Taiwan. Both were disappointed. Nevertheless, pressure from both sides eventually led to full diplomatic relations between the United States and the People's Republic of China on January 1, 1979.

The Taiwan Issue in U.S.–China Relations

Because the People's Republic of China and the Republic of China both claimed to be the legitimate government of the Chinese people, the establishment of diplomatic relations with the former necessarily entailed breaking them with the latter. Nevertheless, the United States continued to maintain extensive, informal economic and cultural ties with Taiwan. It also continued the sale of military equipment to Taiwan. Although these military sales are still a serious issue, American ties with Taiwan have diminished, while China's own ties with Taiwan have grown steadily closer since 1988. Taiwan's entrepreneurs have become one of the largest groups of investors in China's economy. More than one million people from Taiwan live on the mainland, with 500,000 living in Shanghai alone. Taiwan used to have one of the cheapest labor forces in the world; but because its workers now demand wages too high to remain competitive, Taiwan's entrepreneurs have dismantled many of its older industries

and reassembled them on the mainland. With China's cheap labor, these same industries are now profitable, and both China's economy and Taiwan's entrepreneurs benefit. Taiwan's businesspeople are also investing in new industries and new sectors, and they are competing with other outside investors for the best and brightest Chinese minds, so the relationship has already moved beyond simply exploiting the mainland for cheap labor and raw materials.

Ties with the mainland have also been enhanced since the late 1980s by the millions of tourists from Taiwan, most of them with relatives in China. They bring both presents and good will. Family members who had not seen one another since 1949 have reestablished contact, and "the enemy" now seems less threatening.

China hopes that its economic reforms and growth, which have substantially raised the standard of living, will make reunification more attractive to Taiwan. This very positive context has, however, been disturbed over the years by events such as the military crackdown on the demonstrators in Tiananmen Square in 1989, and efforts by Taiwan's leaders to declare independence. In 1996, China responded to such efforts by "testing" its missiles in the waters around Taiwan. High-level talks to discuss eventual reunification were broken off and now occur on a sporadic basis. The 2000 election of the Democratic Progressive Party candidate, Chen Shui-bian as president (and his re-election in 2004), led to still more diplomatic crises with Beijing. President Chen, who campaigned on the platform of an independent Taiwan, has refused to acknowledge Beijing's "one China" principle, and he has insisted that Taiwan negotiate with the P.R.C. as "an equal." This has further strained the relationship and led to raising the bellicosity decibel level in Beijing. Nevertheless, both sides recognize it is in their interests for the foreseeable future to maintain the status quo—a peaceful and profitable relationship in which Taiwan continues to act as an independent state, but does not declare its independence.

So far, the battle between Taipei and Beijing remains at the verbal level. At the same time, massive investments by Taiwan in the mainland and the 2000 opening of Taiwan's Offshore Islands of Quemoy and Matsu for trade with the P.R.C. are bringing the two sides still closer together. Their two economies are becoming steadily more intertwined, and both sides benefit from their commercial ties. This does not mean that they will soon be fully reunified in law. Furthermore, there remains the black cloud of Beijing possibly using military force against Taiwan if it declares itself an independent state. Beijing refuses to make any pledge never to use military force to reunify Taiwan with the mainland, on the grounds that what it does with

Taiwan is China's internal affair. In Beijing's view, no other country has a right to tell China what to do about Taiwan.

Human Rights in U.S.–China Relations

Since U.S. president Jimmy Carter established diplomatic relations with China in 1979, each successive American president has campaigned on a platform that decried the abuse of human rights in China and vowed, if elected, to take strong action, including economic measures, to punish China. The Chinese people have been confused and distraught at this prospect. They do not see the point in punishing hundreds of millions of Chinese for human rights abuses committed not by the people, but by their leadership. Nor do they necessarily believe that their own government has been more abusive of human rights than other states that seem to escape scrutiny. In any event, within a few months (if not sooner) of being sworn in, each successive president has abandoned his campaign platform and chosen to break the linkage between "most-favored-nation" trade status for China and its human rights record.

Why was this? Once inauguration day was over, it was quickly explained to the new president that the United States dare not risk jeopardizing its relations with an increasingly powerful state containing one-quarter of the world's population through punitive measures. Boycotts would probably give Japan and other countries a better trading position while undercutting the opportunity for Americans to do business with China. By 2000, President Bill Clinton had managed to get Congress to vote for "permanent normal trading relations" (PNTR). No longer would normal trade relations with China be subjected each spring to a congressional review of its human-rights record. This in turn cleared the way for China to join the World Trade Organization with an American endorsement in 2001. Under WTO rules, one country may not use trade as a weapon to punish another for political reasons.

Clinton's China policy was also shaped by a new strategy of "agreeing to disagree" on certain issues such as human rights, while efforts continued to be made to bring the two sides closer together. This strategy came out of a belief that China and the United States had so many common interests that neither side could afford to endanger the relationship on the basis of a single issue. The American policy of "engagement" with China, which began with the Clinton administration, was based on the belief that isolating China had proven counterproductive. The administration argued that human rights issues could be more fruitfully addressed in a relationship that was more positive in its broader aspects. "Engagement" allowed the two countries to work together toward shared objectives, including the security of Asia.

Timeline: PAST

1842

The Treaty of Nanking cedes Hong Kong to Great Britain

1860

China cedes the Kowloon Peninsula to Great Britain

1894–1895

The Sino–Japanese War

1895–1945

Taiwan is under Japanese colonial control

1898

China leases Northern Kowloon and the New Territories (Hong Kong) to Great Britain for 99 years

1900–1901

The Boxer Rebellion

1911

Revolution and the overthrow of the Qin Dynasty

1912–1949

The Republic of China

1921

The Chinese Communist Party (CCP) is established

1931

Japanese occupation of Manchuria (the northeast province of China)

1934–1935

The Long March

1937–1945

The Japanese invasion and occupation of much of China

1942–1945

The Japanese occupation of Hong Kong

1945–1949

Civil war between the KMT and CCP

The KMT establishes the Nationalist government on Taiwan. Keeps name of Republic of China

The People's Republic of China is established

1950

The United States recognizes the Nationalist government in Taiwan as the legitimate government of all China

1958

The "Great Leap Forward"; the Taiwan Strait crisis (Offshore Islands)

1963

The Sino–Soviet split becomes public

1966–1969

The "Cultural Revolution"

1966–1976

The "10 Bad Years"

The United Nations votes to seat the P.R.C. in place of the R.O.C.

1972

U.S. president Richard Nixon visits the P.R.C.; the Shanghai Communique

1976

Mao Zedong dies; removal of the Gang of Four

1977

Deng Xiaoping returns to power

1979

The United States recognizes the P.R.C. and withdraws recognition of the R.O.C.

1980s–1990s

Resumption of arms sales to Taiwan

The Shanghai Communique II: the United States agrees to phase out arms sales to Taiwan

China and Great Britain sign an agreement on Hong Kong's future Sino–Soviet relations begin to thaw

China sells Silkworm missiles to Iran and Saudi Arabia

Student demonstrations in Tiananmen Square; military crackdown; political repression follows

Deng encourages "experimentation" and the economy booms

The United States bombs the Chinese Embassy in Belgrade; says "an accident" Deng Xiaoping dies; Jiang Zemin assumes power

PRESENT

2000s

China bans the Falun Gong sect.

Terrorist attacks of 9/11 lead to stronger ties between China and the United States, but China opposes the war on Iraq

SARS (Severe Acute Respiratory Syndrome) outbreak

Hu Jintao and Wen Jiabao take over the reins of the party and government from outgoing Jiang Zemin in a peaceful transition of power

2006

China becomes the fourth largest economy, the third largest global trader.

2008

Olympics to be held in Beijing

---

ists, the United States was hardly in a position to be pressing for improved human rights in China. Just as important, the United States did not want to raise gratuitous questions concerning China's alleged derogation of human rights when it needed China on its side, not just in the war on terrorism, but on almost every issue of international significance.

In spite of the White House's tendency to be pro-China and avoid the issue of human rights, the U.S. Congress has been a different matter. It was Congress that pressed the human rights agenda, especially under President Clinton. Indeed, during his second term in office, Congress used Clinton's favorable treatment of China as one more reason for trying to force him out of office. All that changed with the Bush administration. With a Republican in the White House and a Republican-controlled Congress, there was no longer any need for Congress to use the China issue to attack the president.[48] Coupled with 9/11, the curtailing of American liberties, and numerous accusations of the American abuse of the rights of those under detention in Guantanamo and Iraq, the Chinese human rights issue virtually disappeared from the congressional agenda. U.S.–China relations today are more likely to suffer from trade and monetary issues than from human rights concerns.

THE FUTURE

Since 1979, China has moved from being a relatively closed and isolated country to one that is fully engaged in the world. China's agenda for the future is daunting. It must avoid war; maintain internal political stability in the context of international pressures to democratize; continue to carry out major economic, legal, and political reforms without destabilizing society and endangering CCP control; and sustain economic growth while limiting environmental destruction.

Since the death of Deng Xiaoping in 1997, China has carried out smooth leadership transitions. Although the central party-state leadership continues to be divided into opposing factions, due primarily to a difference of opinion over how to address growing economic polarization and social instability, and corruption, it has never deviated from the road of reform.

Strong economic growth has been crucial to the continuing legitimacy of the CCP leadership in the eyes of the Chinese people. The party may, however, some day change its name to one more reflective of its actual policies—not communism but capitalism, combined with socialist social policies. To some degree, it has adopted policies similar to those of European leftist parties, which tend to label themselves as "democratic socialist" or "socialist democratic" parties. Whatever name it adopts, the Chinese Communist Party

---

Although President George W. Bush initially appeared intent on ending engagement, and treating China as a "strategic adversary," the Bush administration soon abandoned this policy—an act made complete by the September 11, 2001 terrorist attacks on the United States. After those events, President Bush told the world, "You are either with us or against us." China, not wishing to needlessly bring trouble on itself, immediately sided with the United States in the war on terrorism. This had important implications for the role that human rights could play in the U.S.–China relationship; for with the focus on terrorism, human rights took a back seat, even in the United States itself. With critics across the political spectrum raising countless questions about the American government's treatment of suspected terror-is unlikely to allow the creation of a multiparty system that could challenge its leadership.

Governing the world's largest population is a formidable task, one made even more challenging by globalization. The integration of China into the international community has heightened the receptivity of China's leaders to pressures from the international system on a host of specific issues: human rights, environmental protection, intellectual property rights, prison labor, arms control, and legal codes. China's leadership insists on moving at its own pace and in a way that takes into account China's culture, history, and institutions; but China is now subject to globalizing forces, as well as internal social and economic forces, that have a momentum of their own.

In the meantime, China, like so many other developing countries, must worry about the polarization of wealth, high levels of unemployment, uncontrolled economic growth, environmental degradation, and the strident resistance by whole regions within China against following economic and monetary policies formulated at the center. It is also facing a major HIV/AIDS epidemic, a potential collapse of the banking and financial systems, the need to finance a social safety net and retirement pensions, a demographic crisis, and a looming threat to its state-owned enterprises as a result of China's entry into the WTO. To wit, the international community is pressing China to revalue the Chinese currency, the *yuan*, so that Chinese goods will be priced higher, thus making them less competitive internationally. Common criminality, corruption, and social instability provide additional fuel that could one day explode politically and bring down Chinese Communist Party rule.

At this time there is no alternative leadership waiting in the wings to take up the burden of leading China and ensuring its stability. An unstable China would not be in anyone's interest, neither that of the Chinese people, nor of any other country. An insecure and unstable China would be a more dangerous China, and it would be one in which the Chinese people would suffer immeasurably.

NOTES

1. Pam Woodall, "The Real Great Leap Forward, *The Economist*, October 2, 2004, p. 6.

2. A concern about "spiritual pollution" is not unique to China. It refers to the contamination or destruction of one's own spiritual and cultural values by other values. Europeans are as concerned about it as the Chinese and have, in an effort to combat spiritual pollution, limited the number of television programs made abroad (i.e., in the United States) that can be broadcast in European countries.

3. The essence of the "get civilized" campaign was an effort to revive a value that had seemingly been lost: respect for others and common human decency. Thus, drivers were told to drive in a "civilized" way—that is, courteously. Ordinary citizens were told to act in a "civilized" way by not spitting or throwing garbage on the ground. Students were told to be "civilized" by not stealing books or cheating, keeping their rooms and bathrooms clean, and not talking loudly.

4. The turmoil that ensued after his death had also ensued after the death of the former beloved premier, Zhou Enlai. Similar turmoil followed the death of another recently arrived hero of the students. Indeed, the central leadership was almost paralyzed when, in January 2005, Zhao Ziyang, the Premier of China at the time of the Tiananmen demonstrations in 1989, died. Zhao, who was dismissed from his position because in the end he supported the students' demands for political reform, had been accused of trying to "split" the party. He spent the next 15 years, until his death, under house arrest in Beijing.

5. "Campaign to Crush Dissent Intensifies," *South China Morning Post* (August 9, 1989).

6. Susan K. McCarthy, "The State, Minorities, and Dilemmas of Development in Contemporary China," *The Fletcher Forum of World Affairs*, Vol. 26:2 (Summer/Fall 2002).

7. June Teufel Dreyer, "Economic Development in Tibet under the People's Republic of China," *Journal of Contemporary China*, Vol. 12, no. 36 (August 2003), pp. 411–430.

8. For excellent detail on Chinese religious practices, see Robert Weller, *Taiping Rebels, Taiwanese Ghosts, and Tiananmen* (Seattle: University of Washington Press, 1994); and Alan Hunter and Kimkwong Chan, *Protestantism in Contemporary China* (Cambridge: Cambridge University Press, 1993). The latter notes that Chinese judge gods "on performance rather than theological criteria" (p. 144). That is, if the contributors to the temple in which certain gods were honored were doing well financially and their families were healthy, then those gods were judged favorably. Furthermore, Chinese pray as individuals rather than as congregations. Thus, before the Chinese government closed most temples, they were full of individuals praying randomly, children playing inside, and general noise and confusion. Western missionaries have found this style too casual for their own more structured religions (p. 145).

9. Professor Rudolf G. Wagner (Heidelberg University). Information based on his stay in China in 1990.

10. Richard Madesen, "Understanding Falun Gong," *Current History* (September 2000), Vol. 99, No. 638, pp. 243–247.

11. For a better understanding of how Chinese characters are put togther, see John DeFrancis, *Visible Speech: The Diverse Oneness of Writing Systems* (Honolulu: University of Hawaii Press, 1989); and Bob Hodge and Kam Louie, *The Politics of Chinese Language and Culture: The Art of Reading Dragons* (New York: Routledge, 1998.)

12. "Number of University Students Recruited Doubles in Six Years," *People's Daily Online* (December 7, 2004).

13. Cao Desheng, "China Cancels 4,800 Development Zones," *China Daily*, August 24, 2004.

14. Howard W. French "Alarm and Disarray on Rise in China," *The New York Times*, August 24, 2005.

15. Nicholas R. Lardy, "China's Economy: Problems and Prospects," *Foreign Policy Research Institute*, Vol. 12, no. 4 (Feb. 2007), online at www.fpri.org

16. Desheng Cao, "China cancels 4,800 Development Zones," *China Daily*, August 24, 2004.

17. Yan Sun, "Corruption, Growth, and Reform," *Current History*, September 2005, pp. 257–263.

18. According to research done by the Research Office of the State Council, the Chinese Academy of Social Sciences, and the Party School's Research Office, the main source of the billionaires' wealth was, among other things, "Legal or illegal commissions from introducing foreign investments . . . ; Importing facilities and equipment with . . . prices . . . usually 60 percent to 300 percent higher than market prices; . . . Developing and selling land with bank loans and zero costs; . . . Smuggling, tax evasion. . . . Obtaining and pocketing loans from banks without collateral." For this and other sources of wealth for Chinese billionaires, see Mo Ming, "90 Percent of China's Billionaires Are Children of Senior Officials," http://financenews.com/ausdaily/

19. Jonathan Watts, "Corrupt Officials Have Cost China 330 Million Pounds in 20 Years," *The Guardian* (August 20, 2004).

20. Richard McGregor, "China's Power Capacity Soars," *Financial Times*, February 6, 2007.

21. Yuanyuan Shen (Tsinghua University Law School), seminar, Harvard University Center for the Environment, China Project, October 20, 2005.

22. *Shai Oster,* "China Tilts Green: Climate Concerns Sway Beijing," *The Wall Street Journal,* February 13, 2007.

23. Philip P. Pan, "In China, Turning the Law into the People's Protector," *The Washington Post Foreign Service* (Dec. 28, 2004), p. A1.)

24. Suzanne Ogden, *Inklings of Democracy in China* (Cambridge: Harvard University Asia Center and Harvard University Press, 2002), pp. 234–236.

25. Based on the author's trip to interview village leaders in 2000 and the author's visit

with President Carter to monitor elections in a Chinese village in 2001. See Ogden, pp. 183–220.

26. "Chinese NGOs increase to 346,000 last year," posted February 4, 2007, at www.china elections.org

27. For an excellent analysis of how the "patterns of protest" in China have replicated the "patterns of daily life," see Jeffrey N. Wasserstrom and Liu Xinyong, "Student Associations and Mass Movements," in Deborah S. Davis, Richard Kraus, Barry Naughton, Elizabeth J. Perry, eds., *Urban Spaces in Contemporary China: The Potential for Autonomy and Community in Post-Mao China* (Cambridge: Cambridge University Press and Woodrow Wilson Center Press, 1995), pp. 362–366, 383–386. The authors make the point that students learned how to organize, lead, and follow in school. This prepared them for organizing so masterfully in Tiananmen Square. The same was true for the workers who participated in the 1989 protests "not as individuals or members of 'autonomous' unions but as members of *danwei* delegations, which were usually organized with either the direct support or the passive approval of work-group leaders, and which were generally led onto the streets by people carrying flags emblazoned with the name of the unit." p. 383.

28. In 1996–1997, the citizens of Beijing who were unable to sleep through the racket finally forced the government to pass a noise ordinance that lowered the decibel level allowed on streets by public performers, such as the fan and ballroom dancers.

29. Vaclav Havel, as quoted by Timothy Garton Ash, "Eastern Europe: The Year of Truth," *New York Review of Books* (February 15, 1990), p. 18, referenced in Giuseppe De Palma, "After Leninism: Why Democracy Can Work in Eastern Europe," *Journal of Democracy,* Vol. 2, No. 1 (Winter 1991), p. 25, note 3.

30. Liu Binyan, "China and the Lessons of Eastern Europe," *Journal of Democracy,* Vol. 2, No. 2 (Spring 1991), p. 8.

31. Beijing University student, "My Innermost Thoughts—To the Students of Beijing Universities" (May 1989), Document 68, in Suzanne Ogden, et al., eds., *China's Search for Democracy,* pp. 172–173.

32. Vivienne Shue, in a speech to a USIA conference of diplomats and scholars, as quoted and summarized in "Democracy Rating Low in Mainland," *The Free China Journal* (January 24, 1992), p. 7.

33. Joyce Barnathan, et al., "China: Is Prosperity Creating a Freer Society?" *Business Week* (June 6, 1994), p. 98.

34. Jim Yardley, "Chinese United by Common Goal: A Hot Stock Tip," *The New York Times* (January 30, 2007), pp A1, A10.

35. These figures are a composite, taken from the Chinese government website on "Mass Media," http://www.china.org.cn/english/features/Brief/193358.htm (Feb. 10, 2007); and "Lexis-Nexis Country Report, 1999: China," http://www.lexis-nexis.com.

36. David Barboza, "Internet Boom in China is Built on Virtual Fun," *The New York Times* (Feb. 5, 2007), pp. A1, A4.

37. Wang, in Davis, pp. 170–171.

38. Cary Huang, "Beijing Tightens Media Grip with Penalty Points System," *South China Morning Post,* Feb. 9, 2007.

39. Wang Meng (former minister of culture and a leading novelist in China), speech at Cambridge University (May 23, 1996). An example of a movie banned in China is the famous producer Chen Kaige's *Temptress Moon.* This movie, which won the Golden Palm award at the Cannes Film Festival in 1993, is, however, allowed to be distributed abroad. The government has adopted a similar policy of censorship at home but distribution abroad for a number of films, including *Farewell My Concubine,* by China's most famous film directors.

40. "Party Magazine Attacks Morality of Chinese Films," (article published on Feb. 9, 2007, posted Feb. 10, 2007), www.chinaelections.org). Zhang Yimou's film *House of Flying Tigers*, and Chen Kaige's

film *The Promise,* were also condemned by the party periodical, *The Study Times.*

41. Barnathan, et al., pp. 98–99.

42. For the Chinese response in 2007, see Edward Cody, "China: Bush Has No Right to Criticize on Human Rights," *Washington Post,* March 8, 2007.

43. For more on Chinese nationalism, see Suzanne Ogden, "Chinese Nationalism: The Precedence of Community and Identity Over Individual Rights," *Asian Perspective,* vol. 25, no. 4 (2001), pp. 157–185.

44. China to Show Only "Ethically Inspiring TV Series in Prime Time from Next Month" Published and posted Jan. 22, 2007 on www.chinaelections.org

45. In 1998, Avon was, at least temporarily, banned from China, as were other companies that used similar sales and marketing techniques. Too many Chinese found themselves bankrupted when they could not sell the products that they had purchased for resale.

46. Lardy, "China's Economy . . . ," (February 2007), ibid.

47. For excellent analyses of the Sino–American relationship from the nineteenth century, see Warren Cohen, *America's Response to China: A History of Sino–American Relations,* 3rd ed. (New York: Columbia University Press, 1990); Richard Madesen, *China and the American Dream: A Moral Inquiry* (Berkeley, CA: University of California Press, 1995); Michael Schaller, *The United States and China in the Twentieth Century,* 2nd ed. (New York: Oxford University Press, 1990); David Shambaugh, ed., *American Studies of Contemporary China* (Armonk, NY: M.E. Sharpe, 1993); and David Shambaugh, *Beautiful Imperialist: China Perceives America, 1972–1990* (Princeton, NJ: Princeton University Press, 1991).

48. Kenneth Lieberthal, the Charles Neuhauser Memorial Lecture, Harvard University (November 2002).

Hong Kong Map

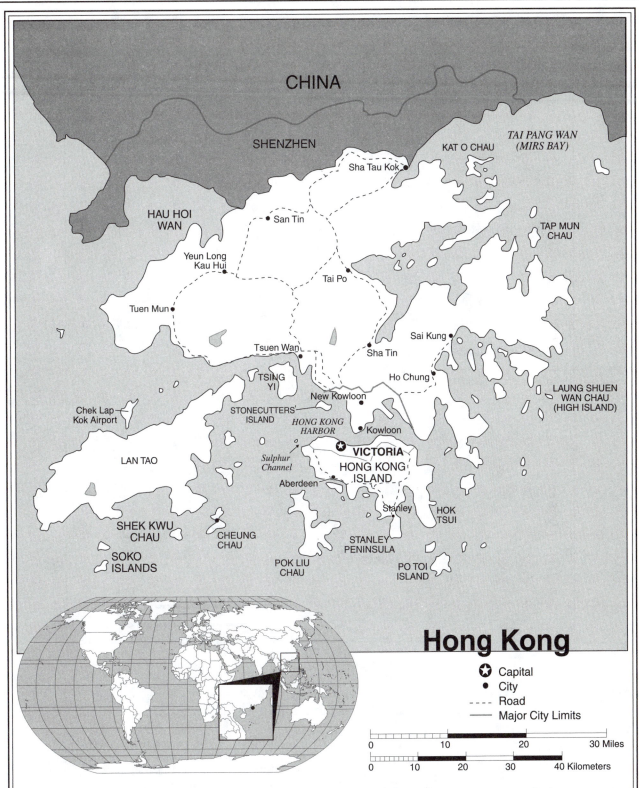

CHINA

SHENZHEN

TAI PANG WAN (MIRS BAY)

KAT O CHAU

Sha Tau Kok

HAU HOI WAN

San Tin

TAP MUN CHAU

Yeun Long Kau Hui

Tai Po

Tuen Mun

Sai Kung

Tsuen Wan

Sha Tin

Ho Chung

TSING YI

New Kowloon

LAUNG SHUEN WAN CHAU (HIGH ISLAND)

Chek Lap Kok Airport

STONECUTTERS' ISLAND

HONG KONG HARBOR

Kowloon

LAN TAO

Sulphur Channel

⭐ **VICTORIA**
HONG KONG ISLAND

Aberdeen

Stanley

HOK TSUI

SHEK KWU CHAU

CHEUNG CHAU

STANLEY PENINSULA

SOKO ISLANDS

POK LIU CHAU

PO TOI ISLAND

Hong Kong

⭐ Capital
● City
- - - Road
——— Major City Limits

0 10 20 30 Miles

0 10 20 30 40 Kilometers

Hong Kong is comprised of the island of Hong Kong (1842), the Kowloon Peninsula and Stonecutters' Island (1860), the New Territories (1898) that extend from Kowloon to the Chinese land border; and 230 adjacent islets. Land is constantly being reclaimed from the sea, so the total land area of Hong Kong is continually increasing by small amounts. All of Hong Kong reverted to Chinese sovereignty on July 1, 1997. It was renamed the Hong Kong Special Administrative Region.

Hong Kong (Hong Kong Special Administrative Region)

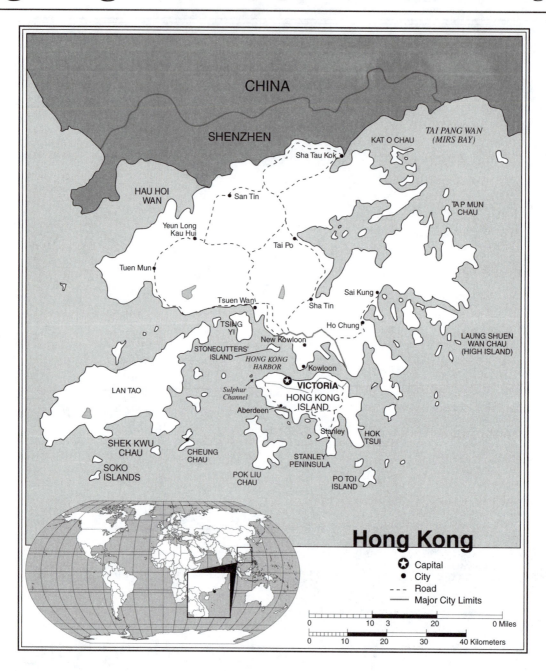

Hong Kong Statistics

GEOGRAPHY

Area in Square Miles (Kilometers):
671 (1,054) (about 6 times the size of Washington, D.C.)
Capital (Population): Victoria (na)
Environmental Concerns: air and water pollution
Geographical Features: hilly to mountainous, with steep slopes; lowlands in the north, more than 200 islands

Climate: tropical monsoon

PEOPLE

Population

Total: 6,940,400 (July 2006 est.)
Annual Growth Rate: .59%
Rural/Urban Population Ratio: 9/91
Major Languages: Chinese (Cantonese); English

Ethnic Makeup: 95% Chinese (mostly Cantonese); 5% others
Religions: 90% a combination of Buddhism and Taoism; 10% Christian

Health

Life Expectancy at Birth: 78.9 years (male); 84.5 years (female)
Infant Mortality: 2.95/1,000 live births
Physicians Available: 1.3/1,000 people
HIV/AIDS Rate in Adults: 0.1%

Education

Adult Literacy Rate: 93.5%

COMMUNICATION

Telephones: 3,794,600 (2005); mobile & cellular: 8.693 million (2005)
Internet Users: 3,212,800

TRANSPORTATION

Highways in Miles (Kilometers): 1,135 (1,831)
Railroads in Miles (Kilometers): 22 (34)
Usable Airfields: 4

GOVERNMENT

Type: Special Administrative Region (SAR) of China
Head of State: President of China HU Jintao (since March 2003)
Government: Chief Executive Donald Tsang (since June 2005)
Political Parties: Democratic Alliance for the Betterment of Hong Kong; Democratic Party; Association for Democracy and People's Livelihood; Hong Kong Progressive Alliance; Citizens Party; Civic Party; Frontier Party; Liberal Party
Suffrage: for direct elections, universal at 18 years of age for residents who have lived in Hong Kong for at least 7 years

MILITARY

Military Expenditures (% of GDP): defense is the responsibility of China
Current Disputes: none

ECONOMY

Currency ($ U.S. Equivalent): 7.81 Hong Kong dollars = $1 (March 2007)
Per Capita Income/GDP: 36,500/$253.1 billion (2006 est.) GDP, based on PPP (purchasing price parity)
GDP Growth Rate: 5.9% (2006 est.)
Inflation Rate: 2.2%
Unemployment Rate: 4.9%

Natural Resources: outstanding deepwater harbor; feldspar
Agriculture: vegetables; poultry; fish; pork
Industry: textiles; clothing; tourism; electronics; plastics; toys; clocks; watches
Exports: $611.6 billion (2006 est.) (primary partners: China, United States, Japan)
Imports: $329.8 billion (primary partners: China, Taiwan, United States, Japan, Singapore, South Korea)

SUGGESTED WEB SITES

http://www.civic-exhange.org/
https://www.cia.gov/cia/publications/factbook/geos/hk.html
http://www.cleartheair.org.hk/
http://www.epd.gov.hk/epd/english/
http://www.info.gov.hk/sitemap.htm
http://english.sz.gov.cn/
http://www.usc.cuhk.edu.hk/uscen.asp
http://www.state.gov
http://www.worldBANK.org

Hong Kong Report

Hong Kong, the "fragrant harbor" situated on the southeastern edge of China, was under British rule characterized as the "pearl of the Orient," a "borrowed place living on borrowed time," and a "den of iniquity." The British colonial administration supported a market economy in the context of a highly structured and tightly controlled political system. This allowed Hong Kong's dynamic and vibrant people to shape the colony into one of the world's great success stories. The history of Hong Kong's formation and development, its achievements, and its handling of the difficult issues emanating from a "one country, two systems" formula since it was returned to Chinese rule in 1997 provide one of the most fascinating stories of cultural, economic, and political transition in the world. Hong Kong's "borrowed time" has ended; but its efforts to shape itself into the "Manhattan of China" are in full swing.

HISTORY

In the 1830s, the British sale of opium to China was creating a nation of drug addicts. Alarmed by this development, the Chinese imperial government banned opium; but private British "country traders," sailing armed clipper ships, continued to sell opium to the Chinese by smuggling it (with the help of Chinese pirates) up China's coast and rivers.

In an effort to enforce the ban, the Chinese imperial commissioner, Lin Zexu, detained the British in Canton (Guangzhou) and forced them to surrender their opium. Commissioner Lin took the more than 21,000 chests of opium and destroyed them in public.[1] The British, desperate to establish outposts for trade with an unwilling China, used this siege of British warehouses as an excuse to declare war on the Chinese. Later called the Opium War (1839–1842), the conflict ended with China's defeat and the Treaty of Nanjing).

Great Britain did not wage war against the Chinese in order to sell an addictive drug that was banned by the Chinese government. Rather, the Chinese government's attack on the British opium traders, whose status as British citizens suddenly proved convenient to the British government, provided the necessary excuse for Great Britain getting what it really wanted: free trade with a government that had restricted trade with the British to one port, Canton. It also allowed London to assert Great Britain's diplomatic equality with China, which considered itself the "Central Kingdom" and superior to all other countries. The Chinese imperial government's demand that all "barbarians," including the British, kowtow to the Chinese emperor, incensed the British and gave them further cause to set the record straight.

The China trade had been draining the British treasury of its gold and silver species; for the British purchased large quantities of Chinese porcelain, silk, tea, and spices, while the Chinese refused to purchase the products of Great Britain's nineteenth-century Industrial Revolution. Smug in their belief that their cultural and moral superiority was sufficient to withstand any military challenge from a "barbarian" country, the Chinese saw no need to develop a modern military or to industrialize. An amusing example of the thought process involved in "Sinocentrism"—the belief that China was the center of the world and superior to all other countries—was Imperial Commissioner Lin's letter to Queen Victoria. Here he noted "Britain's dependence on Chinese rhubarb, without which the English would die of constipation."[2] China's narrow world view blinded it to the growing power of the West and resulted in China's losing the opportunity to benefit from the Industrial Revolution at an early stage. The Opium War turned out to be only the first step in a century of humiliation for China—the step that led to a British foothold on the edge of China.

For their part, the British public did not generally see the sale of opium as a moral issue, or that large-scale addiction was a possible outcome for China. Opium was available for self-medication in Britain, was taken orally (not smoked as it was in China), was administered as a tranquilliser for infants by the working class, and was not considered toxic by the British medical community at that time.[3] Great Britain's colonial government in Hong Kong remained dependent on revenues from the sale of opium until Hong Kong was occupied by Japan during World War II.[4]

The Treaty of Nanjing gave the British the right to trade with the Chinese from five Chinese ports; and Hong Kong, a tiny island off the southern coast of China, was ceded to them "in perpetuity." In short, according to the practices of the colonizing powers of the nineteenth century, Hong Kong became a British colony forever. The Western imperialists were still in the acquisition phase of their history. They were not contemplating that one day the whole process of colonization might be reversed. As a result, Great Britain did not foresee that it might one day have to relinquish the colony of Hong Kong, either to independence or to Chinese rule.

Hong Kong Island's total population of Chinese villagers and people living on boats then numbered under 6,000. From 1842 onward, however, Hong Kong became the primary magnet for Chinese immigrants fleeing the poverty, chaos, and cruelty of China in favor of the relatively peaceful environment of Hong Kong under British rule. Then, in 1860, again as a result of a British victory in battle, the Chinese ceded to the British "in perpetuity" Stonecutters' Island and a small (3 1/2 square miles) but significant piece of land facing the island of Hong Kong: Kowloon Peninsula. Just a few minutes by ferry (and, since the 1970s, by tunnel) from Hong Kong Island, it became an important part of the residential, commercial, and business sectors of Hong Kong. The New Territories, the third and largest part (89 percent of the total area) of what is now known as "Hong Kong," were not granted "in perpetuity" but were merely leased to the British for 99 years under the second Anglo–Chinese Convention of Peking in 1898. The New Territories, which extended from Kowloon to the Chinese land border, comprised the major agricultural area supporting Hong Kong.

The distinction between those areas that became a British colony (Hong Kong Island and Kowloon) and the area "leased" for 99 years (the New Territories) is crucial to understanding why, by the early 1980s, the British felt compelled to negotiate with the Chinese about the future of "Hong Kong"; for although colonies are theoretically colonies "in perpetuity," the New Territories were merely leased, and would automatically revert to Chinese sovereignty in 1997. Without this large agricultural area, the rest of Hong Kong could not survive; the leased territories had, moreover, become tightly integrated

into the life and business of Hong Kong Island and Kowloon.

Thus, with the exception of the period of Japanese occupation (1942–1945) during World War II, Hong Kong was administered as a British Crown colony from the nineteenth century onward. After the defeat of Japan in 1945, however, Britain almost did not regain control over Hong Kong because of the United States, which insisted that it did not fight World War II in order to return colonies to its allies. But Britain's leaders, both during and after World War II, were determined to hold on to Hong Kong because of its symbolic, economic, and strategic importance to the British Empire. India, Singapore, Malaya, Burma—all could be relinquished, but not Hong Kong.[5] Moreover, although during World War II, a U.S. presidential order had stated that at the end of the war, Japanese troops in Hong Kong were to surrender to Chiang Kai-shek, the leader of the Republic of China, it did not happen. Chiang, more worried about accepting surrender of Japanese troops in the rest of China before the Chinese Communist could, did not rush to Hong Kong. Meanwhile, a British fleet moved rapidly to Hong Kong to pre-empt Chiang occupying Hong Kong, even though Chiang averred he would not have stayed. The British doubted this, and argued that Hong Kong was still British sovereign territory and would itself accept the surrender of the Japanese.[6]

At the end of the civil war that raged in China from 1945 to 1949, the Communists' Red Army stopped its advance just short of Hong Kong. Beijing never offered an official explanation. Perhaps it did not want to get into a war with Britian in order to claim Hong Kong, or perhaps the Chinese Communists calculated that Hong Kong would be of more value to them if left in British hands. Indeed, at no time after their victory in 1949 did the Chinese Communists attempt to force Great Britain out of Hong Kong, even when Sino-British relations were greatly strained, as during China's "Cultural Revolution."[7]

This did not mean that Beijing accepted the legitimacy of British rule. It did not. After coming to power on the mainland in 1949, the Chinese Communist Party held that Hong Kong was a part of China stolen by British imperialists, and that it was merely "occupied" by Great Britain. Hence the notion of Hong Kong as "a borrowed place living on borrowed time." The People's Republic of China insisted that Hong Kong not be treated like other colonies; for the process of decolonization has in practice meant sovereignty and freedom for a former colony's people.[8] China was not about to allow Hong Kong to become independent. After the People's Republic of China gained the China seat in the United Nations in 1971, it protested the listing of Hong Kong and Macau (a Portuguese

THE SECOND ANGLO/CHINESE CONVENTION CEDES THE KOWLOON PENINSULA TO THE BRITISH

The second Anglo/Chinese Convention, signed in 1860, was the result of a string of incidents and hostilities among the Chinese, the British, and the French. Although the French were involved in the outbreak of war, they were not included in the treaty that resulted from conflict.

The catalyst for the war was that, during a truce, the Chinese seized the chief British negotiator and executed 20 of his men. In reprisal, the English destroyed nearly 200 buildings of the emperor's summer palace and forced the new treaty on the Chinese. This called for increased payments ("indemnities") by the Chinese to the English for war-inflicted damages as well as the cession of Kowloon Peninsula to the British.

colony) as colonies by the UN General Assembly's Special Committee on Colonialism. In a letter to the Committee, Beijing insisted they were merely

part of Chinese territory occupied by the British and Portuguese authorities. The settlement of the questions of Hong Kong and Macao is entirely within China's sovereign right and does not at all fall under the ordinary category of colonial territories. Consequently they should not be included in the list of colonial territories covered by the declaration on the granting of independence to colonial countries and peoples. . . . The United Nations has no right to discuss these questions.[9]

China made it clear that, unlike other colonies, Hong Kong's colonial subjects did not have the option of declaring independence, for overthrowing British colonial rule would have led directly to the re-imposition of China's control. And although there is for the Hong Kong Chinese a cultural identity as Chinese, after 1949 few wanted to fall under the rule of China's Communist Party government. Furthermore, Beijing and London as a rule did not interfere in Hong Kong's affairs, leaving these in the capable hands of the colonial government in Hong Kong. Although the colonial government formally reported to the British Parliament, in practice it was left to handle its own affairs. Still, the colonial government did not in turn cede any significant political power to its colonial subjects.[10]

No doubt the Chinese Communists were ideologically uncomfortable after winning control of China in 1949 in proclaiming China's sovereign rights and spouting Communist principles while at the same time tolerating the continued existence of a capitalist and British-controlled Hong Kong on its very borders. China could have acquired control within 24 hours simply by shutting off Hong Kong's water supply from the mainland. But China profited from the British presence there and, except for occasional flareups, did little to challenge it.

By 1980, the Hong Kong and foreign business communities had grown increasingly concerned about the expiration of the British lease on the New Territories in 1997. The problem was that all land in the New Territories (which by then had moved from pure agriculture to becoming a major area for manufacturing plants, housing, and commercial buildings) was *leased* to businesses or individuals, and the British colonial government could not grant any land lease that expired after the lease on the New Territories expired. Thus, all land leases—regardless of which year they were granted—would expire three days in advance of the expiration of the main lease on the New Territories on July 1, 1997. As 1997 grew steadily closer, then, the British colonial government had to grant shorter and shorter leases. Investors found buying leases increasingly unattractive. The British colonial government felt compelled to do something to calm investors.[11]

For this reason, it was the British, not the Chinese, who took the initiative to press for an agreement on the future status of the colony and the rights of its people. Everyone recognized the inability of the island of Hong Kong and Kowloon to survive on their own, because of their dependence upon the leased New Territories for food, and because of the integrated nature of the economies of the colonial and leased parts of Hong Kong. Everyone (everyone, that is, except for British prime minister Margaret Thatcher) also knew that Hong Kong was militarily indefensible by the British and that the Chinese were unlikely to permit the continuation of British administrative rule over Hong Kong after it was returned to Chinese sovereignty.[12] So, a series of formal Sino–British negotiations over the future of Hong Kong began in 1982. By 1984, the two sides had reached an agreement to restore all three parts of Hong Kong to China on July 1, 1997.

The Negotiations Over the Status of Hong Kong

Negotiations between the People's Republic of China and Great Britain over the future status of Hong Kong got off to a rocky start in 1982. Prime Minister Thatcher set a contentious tone for the talks when she claimed, after meeting with Chinese leaders in Beijing, that the three nineteenth century treaties that gave Great Britain control of Hong Kong were valid according to international law; and that China, like other nations, had an obligation to honor its treaty commitments. Thatcher's remarks infuriated China's leaders, who denounced the treaties that resulted from imperialist aggression as "unequal," and lacking legitimacy in the contemporary world.

Both sides realized that Chinese sovereignty over Hong Kong would be reestablished in 1997 when the New Territories lease expired, but they disagreed profoundly on what such sovereignty would mean in practice. The British claimed that they had a "moral commitment" to the people of Hong Kong to maintain the stability and prosperity of the colony. Both the British and the Hong Kong population hoped that Chinese sovereignty over Hong Kong might be more symbolic than substantive and that some arrangement could be worked out that would allow for continuing British participation in the administration of the area. The Chinese vehemently rejected what they termed "alien rule in Chinese territory" after 1997, as well as the argument that the economic value of a Hong Kong *not* under its administrative power might be greater.[13] Great Britain agreed to end its administration of Hong Kong in 1997, and together with China worked out a detailed and binding arrangement for how Hong Kong would be governed under Chinese sovereignty.

The people of Hong Kong itself did not formally participate in these negotiations over the colony's fate. Although the British and Chinese consulted various interested parties in the colony, they chose to ignore many of their viewpoints. China was particularly adamant that the people of Hong Kong were Chinese and that the government in Beijing represented *all Chinese* in talks with the British.

In September 1984, Great Britain and the People's Republic of China initialed the Joint Declaration on the Question of Hong Kong. It stated that, as of July 1, 1997, Hong Kong would become a "Special Administrative Region" (SAR) under the control of the central government of the People's Republic of China. The Chinese came up with the idea of "one country, two systems," whereby, apart from defense and foreign policy, the Hong Kong SAR would enjoy near autonomy. Hong Kong would maintain its current social, political, economic, and legal systems alongside China's systems; would remain an international financial center; and would retain its ability to establish independent economic (but not diplomatic) relations with other countries.

The Sino–British Joint Liaison Group was created to oversee the transition to Chinese rule. Any changes in Hong Kong's laws made during the transition period, if they were expected to continue after 1997, had to receive final approval from the Joint Liaison Group. If there were disagreement within the Liaison Group between the British and Chinese, they were obligated to talk until they reached agreement. This procedure gave China veto power over any proposed changes in Hong Kong's governance and laws proposed from 1984 to 1997.[14] When London's newly appointed governor, Christopher Patten, arrived in 1992 and attempted to change some of the laws that would govern Hong Kong after 1997, China had reason to use that veto power.

The Basic Law

The Basic Law is the crucial document that translates the *spirit* of the Sino–British Joint Declaration into a legal code. Often referred to as a "mini-constitution" for Hong Kong after it became an SAR on July 1, 1997, the Basic Law essentially defines where Hong Kong's autonomy ends and Beijing's governance over Hong Kong begins. The British had no role in formulating the Basic Law, as the Chinese considered it an internal, sovereign matter. In 1985, China established the Basic Law Drafting Committee, under the direction of the National People's Congress (NPC). The Committee had 59 members—36 from the mainland, 23 from Hong Kong. Of the latter, almost all were "prominent figures belonging to high and high-middle strata," with Hong Kong's economic elite at its core. In addition, China established a "Consultative Committee" in Hong Kong of 180 members. Its purpose was to function as a nonofficial representative organ of the people of Hong Kong from all walks of life, an organ that would channel their viewpoints to the Basic Law Drafting Committee. By so including Hong Kong's elite and a Hong Kong–wide civic representative organ in consultations about the Basic Law, China hoped to provide political legitimacy to the Basic Law.[15] Once the Basic Law was approved in April 1990 by China's NPC, the final draft was promulgated.

The Basic Law gave Hong Kong a high degree of autonomy after 1997, except in matters of foreign policy and defense, which fell under Beijing's direct control. The government was to be made up of local civil servants and a chief executive chosen by an "Election Committee" appointed by the Standing Committee of the National People's Congress.[16] The chief executive was given the right to appoint key officials of the Special Administrative Region (subject to Beijing's approval). Provisions were made to allow some British and other foreign nationals to serve in the administration of the SAR, if the Hong Kong government so desired. An elected Legislature was made responsible for formulating the laws.[17] The maintenance of law and order remained the responsibility of local authorities, but China took over from the British the right to station military forces in Hong Kong. The local judicial and legal system were to remain basically unchanged, but China's NPC reserved the right to approve all new laws written between 1990 and 1997.[18]

Thus, the Joint Declaration and Basic Law brought Hong Kong under China's rule, with the National People's Congress in Beijing accorded the right of the final interpretation of the meaning of the Basic Law in case of dispute; but the Basic Law allows Hong Kong considerable independence over its economy, finances, budgeting, and revenue until the year 2047. China is thus committed to preserving Hong Kong's "capitalist system and lifestyle" for 50 years and has promised not to impose the Communist political, legal, social, or economic system on Hong Kong. It also agreed to allow Hong Kong to remain a free port, with its own internationally convertible currency (the Hong Kong dollar), over which China would not exercise authority. The Basic Law states that all Hong Kong residents shall have freedom of speech, press, publication, association, assembly, procession, and demonstration, as well as the right to form and join trade unions, and to strike. Freedom of religion, marriage, choice of occupation, and the right to social welfare are also protected by law.[19]

Beijing agreed to continue to allow the free flow of capital into and out of Hong Kong. It also agreed to allow Hong Kong to enter into economic and cultural agreements with other nations and to participate in relevant international organizations as a separate member. Thus, Hong Kong was not held back from membership in the World Trade Organization (WTO) by China's earlier inability to meet WTO membership qualifications. Similarly, Hong Kong is a separate member of the World Bank, the Asian Development Bank, and the Asian-Pacific Economic Conference (APEC). Hong Kong is also allowed to continue issuing its own travel documents to Hong Kong's residents and to visitors.

When China promulgated the Basic Law in 1990, Hong Kong residents by the thousands took to the streets in protest, burning their copies of it. Some of Hong Kong's people saw Britain as having repeatedly capitulated to China's opposition to plans for political reform in Hong Kong before 1997, and as having traded off Hong Kong's interests in favor of Britain's own interests in further trade and investment in China. Hong Kong's business community, however, supported the Basic Law, believing that it would provide for a healthy political and economic environment for doing business. Other Hong Kong residents believed that it was Hong Kong's commercial value, not the Basic Law,

that would protect it from a heavy-handed approach by the Chinese government.

The Joint Declaration of China and Great Britain (1984), and the Basic Law (1990) are critical to understanding China's anger in 1992 when Governor Patten proceeded to push for democratic reforms in Hong Kong without Beijing's agreement—particularly since Patten's predecessor, Governor David Wilson, always did consult Beijing and never pushed too hard. After numerous threats to tear up the Basic Law, Beijing simply stated in 1994 that, after the handover of Hong Kong to Chinese sovereignty in 1997, it would nullify any last-minute efforts by the colonial government to promote a political liberalization that went beyond the provisions in the Basic Law. And that is precisely what China did on July 1, 1997. As is noted later in this report, the changes that Patten advocated were largely last-ditch efforts to confer on Hong Kong's subjects democratic rights that they had never had in more than 150 years of British colonial rule. These rights related largely to how the Legislature was elected, the expansion of the electorate, and the elimination of such British colonial regulations as one requiring those who wanted to demonstrate publicly to first acquire a police permit.

The Chinese people were visibly euphoric about the return of Hong Kong "to the embrace of the Motherland." The large clock in Beijing's Tiananmen Square counted the years, months, days, hours, minutes, and even seconds until the return of Hong Kong, helping to focus the Chinese people on the topic. Education in the schools, special exhibits, the movie *The Opium War* (produced by China), and even T-shirts displaying pride in the return of Hong Kong to China's control reinforced a sense that a historical injustice was at last being corrected. On July 1, 1997, celebrations were held all over China, and the pleasure was genuinely and deeply felt by the Chinese people. In Hong Kong, amidst a drenching rain, celebrations were also held. At midnight on June 30, 1997, 4,000 guests watched as the Union Jack was lowered, and China's flag, together with the new Hong Kong Special Administrative Region flag, were raised. President Jiang Zemin, and Charles, the Prince of Wales, and Tony Blair, Prime Minister of Great Britain, represented their respective countries, but the Hong Kong people were mere spectators, without an official representative at the handover.[20]

THE SOCIETY AND ITS PEOPLE

Immigrant Population

In 1842, Hong Kong had a mere 6,000 inhabitants. Today, it has almost 7 million people. What makes this population distinctive is its predominantly immigrant composition. Waves of immigrants have flooded Hong

Kong ever since 1842. Even today, barely half of Hong Kong's people were actually born there. This has been a critical factor in the political development of Hong Kong; for instead of a foreign government imposing its rule on submissive natives, the situation has been just the reverse. Chinese people voluntarily emigrated to Hong Kong, even risking their lives to do so, to subject themselves to alien British colonial rule.

In recent history, the largest influxes of immigrants came as a result of the 1945–1949 Civil War in China, when 750,000 fled to Hong Kong; as a result of the "three bad years" (1959–1962) following the economic disaster of China's Great Leap Forward policy; and from 1966 to 1976, when more than 500,000 Chinese went to Hong Kong to escape the societal turmoil generated by the Cultural Revolution. After the Vietnam War ended in 1975, Hong Kong also received thousands of refugees from Vietnam as that country undertook a policy of expelling many of its ethnic Chinese citizens. Many Chinese from Vietnam risked their lives on small boats at sea to attain refugee status in Hong Kong.

Although China's improving economic and political conditions after 1979 greatly stemmed the flow of immigrants from the mainland, the absorption of refugees into Hong Kong's economy and society remained one of the colony's biggest problems. Injection of another distinct refugee group (the Chinese from Vietnam) generated tension and conflict among the Hong Kong population.

Because of a severe housing shortage and strains on the provision of social services, the British colonial government first announced that it would confine all new refugees in camps and prohibit them from outside employment. It then adopted a policy of sending back almost all refugees who were caught before they reached Hong Kong Island and were unable to prove they had relatives in Hong Kong to care for them. Finally, the British reached an agreement with Vietnam's government to repatriate some of those Chinese immigrants from Vietnam who were believed to be economic rather than political refugees. The first few attempts at this reportedly "voluntary" repatriation raised such an international furor that the British were unable to systematize this policy. By the mid-1990s, however, better economic and political conditions in Vietnam made it easier for the British colonial government to once again repatriate Vietnamese refugees.

Before the July 1, 1997, handover, moreover, Beijing insisted that the British clear the camps of refugees. It was not a problem that China wanted to deal with. As it turned out, the British failed to clear the camps, leaving the job to the Chinese after the handover. The last one was closed in the summer of 2000.

(United Nations photo 74043)

The refugees who came to Hong Kong and settled in squatter communities such as the one shown above voluntarily subjected themselves to foreign (British) rule. Government-built housing has largely replaced areas like the one pictured above.

Today, China still maintains strict border controls, in an effort to protect Hong Kong from being flooded by Chinese from the mainland who are hoping to take advantage of the wealthy metropolis, or just wanting to look around and shop in Hong Kong.[21]

The fact that China's economy has grown rapidly for the last 25 years, especially in the area surrounding Hong Kong, has diminished the poverty that led so many Mainlanders to try illegally emigrating to Hong Kong. Nevertheless, overpopulation is still an important social issue because it stretches Hong Kong's limited resources and has contributed to the high levels of unemployment in recent years. Rulings that have greatly limited the right of Mainlanders with at least one Hong Kong parent (so-called "right-of-abode" seekers) to migrate to Hong Kong have eased concerns somewhat.

Today, the largest number of immigrants to Hong Kong are still Mainlanders; but they are more likely than in the past to come from distant provinces. Although Hong Kong is made up almost entirely of immigrants and their descendants, the older immigrants look down upon their non-Cantonese-speaking country cousins as "uncivilized." They are socially discriminated against and find it difficult to get the better-paying jobs in the economy. This is in striking contrast to past attitudes: From the 1960s to the 1980s, Hong Kong residents generally expressed deep

sympathy with Mainlanders, building roof-top schools for them, and throwing food onto the trucks when the British colonial government transported Mainlanders back to China against their will.[22]

Language and Education

Ninety-eight percent of Hong Kong's people are Chinese. The other 2 percent are primarily European and Vietnamese. Although a profusion of Chinese dialects are spoken, the two official languages, English and the Cantonese dialect of Chinese, predominate. Since the Chinese written language is in ideographs, and the same ideographs are usually used regardless of how they are pronounced in various dialects, all literate Hong Kong Chinese are able to read Chinese newspapers—and 95 percent of them do read at least one of the 16 daily newspapers available in Hong Kong.[23] Even before the handover, moreover, the people were intensively studying spoken Mandarin, the official language of China.

Since the handover in 1997, a source of bubbling discontent has been the decision of the Executive Council to require all children to be taught in Chinese. The government's rationale was that the students would learn more if they were taught in their own language. This decision caused an enormous

furor. Many Hong Kong Chinese, especially from the middle classes, felt that if Hong Kong were going to remain a major international financial and trading center, its citizens must speak English. Many suspected that the real reason for insisting on Chinese was to respond to Beijing's wishes to bind the Hong Kong people to a deeper Chinese identity. In response to strong public pressures, the Hong Kong government finally relented and allowed 100 schools to continue to use English for instruction. Many of the other schools are, Hong Kong parents complain, suffering from a decline in the quality of education generally, and language skills in particular. Those who can afford it now try to get their children into the growing number of private schools.

Chinese cultural values of diligence, willingness to sacrifice for the future, commitment to family, and respect for education have contributed to the success of Hong Kong's inhabitants. (The colonial government guaranteed nine years of compulsory and free education for children through age 15, helping to support these cultural values.) As a result, the children of immigrants have received one of the most important tools for material success. Combined with Hong Kong's rapid post–World War II economic growth and government-funded social-welfare programs, education improved the lives of almost all Hong Kong residents, and allowed remarkable economic and social mobility. A poor, unskilled peasant who fled across China's border to Hong Kong to an urban life of grinding poverty—but opportunity—could usually be rewarded by a government-subsidized apartment, and by grandchildren who graduated from high school and moved on to white-collar jobs.

Since the 1997 handover, the Hong Kong SAR has continued to support compulsory and free education. But in this rapidly changing society, juvenile delinquency is on the rise, because parents are working long hours and spend little time with their children, and an increasing number of those who finish the basic nine years of school now leave the educational system. Criminal gangs *(triads)* recruit them to promote criminal activities.[24]

For those who wish to continue their education beyond high school, access to higher education is limited, so ambitious students work hard to be admitted to one of the best upper-middle schools, and then to one of the even fewer places available in Hong Kong's universities. Hong Kong's own universities are becoming some of the best in the world, and admission is highly competitive. An alternative chosen by many of Hong Kong's brightest students is to go abroad for a college education. This has been important in linking Hong Kong to the West.

Living Conditions

Hong Kong has a large and growing middle class. By 1995, in fact, Hong Kong's per capita income had surpassed that of its colonial ruler, Great Britain.[25] Its people are generally well-dressed; and restaurants, buses, and even subways are full of people yelling into their cell-phones. Enormous malls full of fashionable stores can be found throughout Hong Kong. McDonald's is so much a part of the city-scape that most residents do not realize it has American origins. After school, the many McDonald's are full of teenagers meeting with their friends, doing homework, and sharing a "snack" of the traditional McDonald's meal—hamburgers, fries, and Coca-Cola (served hot or cold). The character Ronald McDonald, affectionately referred to by his Cantonese name, Mak Dong Lou Suk Suk (Uncle McDonald), is recognized throughout Hong Kong.[26]

Nevertheless, Hong Kong's people suffer from extremes of wealth and poverty. The contrast in housing that dots the landscape of the colony dramatically illustrates this. The rich live in luxurious air-conditioned apartments and houses on some of the world's most expensive real estate. They may enjoy a social life that mixes such Chinese pleasures as mahjong, banqueting, and participation in traditional Chinese and religious rituals and festivals with British practices of horseracing,

There are still some ethnic minorities in Hong Kong, such as this Hakka woman.

rugby, social clubs, yacht clubs, and athletic clubs for swimming and croquet.[27] (These practices have faded greatly with the exit of the British.) The Chinese have removed the name "Royal" from all of Hong Kong's old social clubs, including the Royal Jockey Club, which today is neither royal nor British. Times have changed: Hong Kong is no longer a colony, and exclusivity is a thing of the past. The mix of Hong Kong people and foreigners in business clubs reflects the fact that Hong Kong's

business elite is now both British and Chinese. Of course, memberships in some clubs are still all-British, like cricket clubs, because the Chinese are not interested.[28]

The wealthy are taken care of by cooks, maids, gardeners, and chauffeurs, most of whom are Filipino. The Hong Kong people—and the government—greatly prefer hiring Filipinos to hiring mainlander Chinese, as the former are better trained, speak English, and are less likely to try to apply for perma-

A fishing family lives on this houseboat in Aberdeen Harbor.

nent residency in Hong Kong. (The preference for hiring Filipinos adds to the sense the Chinese Mainlanders have of being discriminated against.) Virtually all members of the Filipino workforce (estimated to be about 200,000) have Sundays off, and they more or less take over the parks, and even the streets in Hong Kong Central, where they camp out for the day with their compatriots. The government dares not intervene to get them off the streets, lest it be accused of racism or violating their civil liberties. The Filippinos often complain about exploitation and abuse by Hong Kong employers.

There is a heavier concentration of Mercedes, Jaguars, Rolls Royces, and other luxury cars—not to mention cellular phones, car faxes, and fine French brandy—in Hong Kong than anywhere else in the world.[29] Some Hong Kong businessmen spend lavishly on travel, entertainment, and mistresses. Their mistresses, however, now tend to live in Shenzhen, the "Special Economic Zone" (SEZ) just 40 minutes by train from Hong Kong Central. Purchasing an apartment for them and paying for their upkeep are cheaper there, as are the karaoke bars, golf courses, bars, and massage parlors. Hong Kong is now for the wealthier and more sedate businessmen, while Shenzhen is more attractive to Hong Kong's young professionals.

The wealthiest business people have at least one bodyguard for each member of their families. Conspicuous consumption and what in the West might be considered a vulgar display of wealth are an ingrained part of the society. Some Hong Kong businesspeople, who have seemingly run out of other ways to spend their money, spend several hundred thousand dollars just to buy a lucky number for their car license plate. One Hong Kong businessman built a magnificent home in Beijing that replicates the style of the Qing Dynasty and features numerous brass dragons on the ceilings, decorated with three pounds of gold leaf.[30]

In stark contrast to the lifestyles of the wealthy business class, the vast majority of Hong Kong's people live in crowded highrise apartment buildings, with several poor families sometimes occupying one apartment of a few small rooms, and having inadequate sanitation facilities.[31] Beginning in the mid-1950s, the British colonial government built extensive low-rent public housing, which today accommodates about half of the population. These government-subsidized housing projects easily become run down and are often plagued by crime. But without them, a not-insignificant percentage of the new immigrant population would have continued to live in squalor in squatter villages with no running water, sanitation, or electricity.

When he took office in 1997, Hong Kong's chief executive, Tung Chee-hwa, made a significant commitment to provide more government-funded housing and social-welfare programs—some 85,000 new apartments were to be built each year. But in 2000, Tung suddenly announced that he had scrapped that policy two years earlier because of falling real-estate prices (owing to the Asian economic crisis)—without telling anyone. The result is a housing scarcity, and the rents for the apartments in the few new residential buildings are far beyond the means of the average Hong Kong resident.

The Economy

A large part of the allure of Hong Kong has, then, been its combination of a dynamic economy with enlightened social welfare policies. The latter were possible not just because of the British colonial government's commitment to them but also because the flourishing Hong Kong economy provided the resources for them. Hong Kong had a larger percentage of the gross domestic product (GDP) available for social welfare than most governments, for two reasons. First, it had a low defense budget to support its approximately 12,000 British troops (including some of the famous Gurkha Rifles) stationed in the colony for external defense (only 0.4 percent of the GDP, or 4.2 percent of the total budget available). Second, the government was able to take in substantial revenues (18.3 percent of GDP) through the sale of land leases.[32]

Now, of course, China is in charge of Hong Kong's defense. Land leases came to an end in 1997 with the return of Hong Kong's leased territories to China, but the sale of land is still the primary source of government revenue. Continuing the system established by the British colonial government, the Hong Kong government makes money by selling land one piece at a time to its handful of real-estate developers, who then build on the land.[33] This is how Hong Kong can continue to finance governmental expenditures without any income tax, sales taxes, or capital gains tax; and with a low profit tax (16.5 percent) for corporations, and a flat 15 percent tax on salaries that kicks in at such a high level that a large percentage of those working in Hong Kong pay nothing at all.

The result is that Hong Kong is a great place to do business, but the cost of private housing is beyond the means of most of Hong Kong's middle class; and, having made its money by selling land to the land developers, the government must then turn around and use a substantial portion of that money to subsidize public housing so that rent is affordable. Half of Hong Kong's populace receives housing free or at minimal (subsidized) rent, but the middle class cannot afford to buy housing. Many have moved to more affordable housing in the Shenzhen Special Economic Zone across the border in China. This may explain in part why the Hong Kong population has fallen by at least 300,000 people in the last few years.

Hong Kong's real estate system has affected the people's viewpoint on housing. Unlike in the West, people do not view the purchase of an apartment as a place where they might want to reside for an indefinite period. Rather, they see it more like buying a stock, and they might buy and sell it within one year in order to make a profit. Before the Asian financial crisis that hit Hong Kong in 1997, this was a fairly sure bet; but housing prices have been much lower, and many people have lost their savings by speculating in housing.

Beijing's greatest concern before the handover in 1997 was that the colonial administration had dramatically increased welfare spending—65 percent in a mere five years.[34] From Beijing's perspective, the British appeared determined to empty Hong Kong's coffers, leaving little for Beijing to use elsewhere in China. The Chinese believed that the British were setting a pattern to justify Hong Kong's continuing expenditures in the next 50 years of protected autonomy. As it turned out, however, the British did not try to deplete Hong Kong assets, and China's companies were deeply involved even in the vastly ex-

pensive new airport that the British insisted on building before their departure. (It opened in July 1998, one year after the handover.)

No sooner had China taken back Hong Kong than, suddenly, the Asian economic financial crisis broke out, first in Thailand, and then throughout Asia. It wreaked havoc on Hong Kong's economy and challenged its financial and economic system. Beijing, instead of interfering with the decisions made by Hong Kong to address the crisis, took a hands-off approach, except to offer to support the Hong Kong dollar against currency speculators by using China's own substantial foreign-currency reserves of U.S. $150 billion to sustain the Hong Kong dollar's peg to the U.S. dollar. Furthermore, China did not take the easy route of devaluing the Chinese yuan, which would have sent Asian markets, and Hong Kong's in particular, into a further downward spiral.

The Asian financial and economic crisis (1997–2002) brought a severe downturn in living conditions in Hong Kong. Growing increasingly anxious about the situation, the Hong Kong population pressured their government to intervene and do more to ease the pain. They demanded that the government take a more activist role in providing social welfare, controlling environmental degradation, and regulating the economy. In response to such pressure, the government required taxis to stop using diesel fuel and enacted some of the toughest emissions standards in the world.[35] The government also committed more to social welfare than it had under British rule. In addition, it intervened in the financial markets, purchasing large amounts of Hong Kong dollars to foil attempts by speculators to make a profit from selling Hong Kong dollars. It also intervened in the Hong Kong stock market, using up some 25 percent of its foreign-currency reserves to purchase large numbers of shares in Hong Kong companies in a risky but ultimately successful effort to prevent a further slide of the stock market.

Hong Kong's woes were aggravated, however, by the world economic turndown that began in 2000, made worse by the September 11, 2001 terrorist attacks on the United States, and by the outbreak of the SARS (severe acute respiratory syndrome) epidemic in early 2003 in the next-door Chinese province of Guangdong. It quickly spread to Hong Kong, showing the vulnerability of Hong Kong's geographical position on the edge of China. The life-threatening illness (with close to a 5 percent mortality rate) and the initial reluctance of China to furnish information about the spread of the epidemic in China led to disaster for Hong Kong's tourist industry and economy in 2003. Meanwhile, pollution from the coal-fired plants in the flourishing economy next door in southern China led to rapidly deteriorating air quality in Hong Kong. A survey taken each year from 1992

to 2007 indicates that by the end of 2003, the satisfaction of the Hong Kong people with the government reached its nadir, with only 51 percent of those surveyed "satisfied" with their life in Hong Kong.[36]

Before the 1997 return of Hong Kong to China, many analysts predicted that Beijing would undercut Hong Kong's prosperity through various political decisions limiting political freedom, tampering with the legal system, and imposing economic regulations that would endanger growth. Instead, Beijing left Hong Kong in the hands of its hand-picked Chief Executive, Tung Chee-hwa. Tung, however, proved unable to save Hong Kong's economy from the Asian financial crisis and rapidly lost popularity. To wit, although the economy recovered, its growth rate has remained only half that of the China mainland. The local press severely criticized Tung for having too literally interpreted Beijing's promise to the rest of the world in 1997 that Hong Kong would not change. Indeed, Hong Kong has changed so little in the years since the handover that it seems to be losing its dominant position in Asia as a major financial and commercial center to Shanghai and Singapore. Just as worrisome, Taiwan has emerged as the Asian leader in computer technology, while Hong Kong has fallen further behind in the technology sweepstakes.

The erosion of Hong Kong's leadership in Asia is blamed not on Beijing, but on the government's lack of vision and its catering to the real-estate "tycoons"—the mere half dozen individuals who hold the vast majority of Hong Kong's wealth in their hands.[37] More than anything else, Hong Kong's loss of its international character and relative decline as an Asian city are blamed on its "official obsession with mainland relations."[38] Yet, regardless of how others view Hong Kong, its citizens seem generally pleased with their government's relationship with the mainland, especially in the last few years.[39]

The collapse of Hong Kong's real estate prices in the wake of the Asian economic crisis did, however, result in their turning to technology as a new source of wealth for Hong Kong, and themselves. The Internet is empowering small entrepreneurs. But Hong Kong's economy is plagued with other problems emanating from monopolistic and duopolistic control of many sectors in the economy.[40] A more cynical view is that Hong Kong businesspeople are sycophants to both the Hong Kong and Beijing governments: their customary operating procedure is to make money not through creativity but through their connections—a practice common on the mainland as well.

Hong Kong's real estate and stock markets have bounced back from the Asian financial crisis, but remain volatile. For the time being, Hong Kong's greatest protection against substantial turmoil and a prolonged recession is the stability and growth of China's economy, which continues to bubble along at an average of 9 percent per year. Hong Kong businesspeople have heavily invested in China. Were its growth to falter, so would Hong Kong's.

Hong Kong as a World Trade and Financial Center

From the moment Hong Kong became a colony, the British designated it as a free port. The result is that Hong Kong has never applied tariffs or other major trade restrictions on imports. Such appealing trade conditions, combined with Hong Kong's free-market economy, deepwater harbor, and location at the hub of all commercial activities in Asia, have made it an attractive place for doing business. Indeed, from the 1840s until the crippling Japanese occupation during World War II, Hong Kong served as a major center of China's trade with both Asia and the Western world.

The outbreak of the Korean War in 1950 and the subsequent United Nations embargo on exports of strategic goods to China, as well as a U.S.–led general embargo on the import of Chinese goods, forced Hong Kong to reorient its economy. To combat its diminished role as the middleman in trade with the mainland of China, Hong Kong turned to manufacturing. At first, it manufactured mainly textiles. Later, it diversified into other areas of light consumer goods and developed into a financial and tourist center.

Today, Hong Kong continues to serve as a major trade and financial hub, with thousands of companies located there for the purpose of doing business with China. Even Mainland China companies try to have headquarters in Hong Kong, for reasons related to foreign exchange, taxes, and stock listing issues. Hong Kong also remains a middleman in trade with China, with more than one-third of China's total trade still flowing in and out of China through Hong Kong. A full 80 percent of Hong Kong's container port traffic, in fact, goes to and from Southern China. So Hong Kong's economy is still tied to China's economy doing well.

In addition, Hong Kong has actually shifted its own manufacturing base into China. Back in 1980, when almost half of Hong Kong's workforce labored in factories and small workshops, Hong Kong was on the verge of pricing itself out of world markets because of its increasingly well-paid labor and high-priced real estate. Just then, China, with its large and cheap labor supply, inexpensive land, and abundant resources, initiated major internal economic reforms that opened up the country for foreign investment. As a result, Hong Kong transferred its manufacturing base over the border to China, largely to the contiguous province of

(IMS Communication LTD/Capstone Design/Flat Earth Images/DAL022C19)
Land is so expensive in Hong Kong that most residences and businesses today are located in skyscrapers. While the buildings are thoroughly modern, construction crews typically erect bamboo scaffolding. The buildings in this photo are being built with this technique.

Guangdong. By the late 1990s, more than 75 percent of the Hong Kong workforce was in the service sector, with only 13 percent remaining in manufacturing. In short, the vast majority of Hong Kong workers in the manufacturing sector have been replaced by some 5 million Chinese laborers who now work in the tens of thousands of factories either owned or contracted out to Hong Kong businesses on the mainland.[41]

Hong Kong's many assets, including its hard-working, dynamic people, have made it into the world's tenth-largest trading economy. But it is facing much competition. In 2005, Singapore surpassed it to become the world's busiest container port, with Shanghai's and Shenzhen's ports (just across the Chinese border) hot on its heels. This does not mean that Hong Kong is not profiting from this shift, however, as it is Hong Kong investors who are helping the Mainland's ports grow. Similarly, as of 2007, Hong Kong had dropped from third to seventh as a place for foreign exchange trade. Still, it remains one of the world's largest (ranking 12th) banking centers, and has grown to become Asia's third-largest stock market, thanks to increased listings of companies from the China Mainland. Considering its tiny size and population, these are extraordinary achievements.

Hong Kong has, then, many competitors from other "dragons" in Asia; but given the rapid growth of the Asian economies over the last 25 years, there is no reason why other major financial and trade centers in Asia would necessarily harm Hong Kong's economy. Shanghai's or Shenzhen's growth need not come at Hong Kong's expense. In

fact, the booming SEZ of Shenzhen is really an extension of Hong Kong's growth and power, as is most of Southern China. Perhaps Singapore presents the greatest challenge to Hong Kong's position as a financial center. And changes in the trade environment, such as South Korea establishing full diplomatic relations with China in 1992, have allowed it to deal directly with China, thereby bypassing Hong Kong as an entrepôt for trade and business with China. But Hong Kong's entrepreneurs and businesses remain efficient, flexible, and able to incorporate such changes into their business strategies successfully.

The Special Economic Zones (SEZs)

As part of its economic reform program and "open door" policy that began in 1979, China created Special Economic Zones in areas bordering or close to Hong Kong in order to attract foreign investment. SEZs, until recent years under far more liberal regulations than the rest of China, blossomed in the 1980s and 1990s. Various branches of China's government themselves invested heavily in the SEZs in hopes of making a profit. In the 1990s, even China's military developed an industrial area catering to foreign investors and joint ventures in one of China's SEZs, Shenzhen, as part of its effort to compensate for insufficient government funding for the military. It called its policy "one army, two systems"—that is, an army involved with both military and economic development.[42] Brushing aside its earlier preference for a puritanical society, China's military was as likely to invest in nightclubs, Western-style hotels, brothels, and health spas in the SEZs as it was in the manufacturing sector. In 1998, however, Beijing ordered the military to divest itself of its economic enterprises, so it no longer runs nonmilitary enterprises in Shenzhen.

The bulk of foreign investment in the SEZs comes from Hong Kong Chinese, either with their own money or acting as middlemen for investors from Taiwan, the United States, and others. Most direct foreign investment in China, in fact, comes *through* Hong Kong, either by setting up companies in Hong Kong, or using Hong Kong companies as intermediaries. In turn, China is the single largest investor in Hong Kong, and its state-owned enterprises and joint ventures also set up companies in Hong Kong. Thus, this integrated area of south China, encompassing Hong Kong, the SEZs, and the provinces of Guangdong, Fujian, and Hainan Island, has become a powerful new regional economy on a par with other Asian "little dragons."

Indeed, even before China took over Hong Kong in 1997, south China had already become an integral part of Hong Kong's empire, with profound political as well as economic implications. Many Hong Kong people who regularly cross into Shenzhen SEZ (and even own property there) pressure the Shenzhen government to be responsive to their interests. Hong Kong's media coverage of Shenzhen affairs also puts pressure on the SEZ's administrators to be more responsive to public concerns, such as the exploitation of Mainlanders working under contract in Hong Kong–owned firms.[43]

At the same time, Hong Kong's growing ties with the SEZs and cross-border trade generally is causing serious problems, including the restructuring of the workforce as jobs in the manufacturing sector move across the Hong Kong border for cheaper labor. The result is a downward pressure on wages in Hong Kong, although many economists believe this will make Hong Kong more competitive. In any event, the Hong Kong business community is moving to integrate the economy even more fully with the mainland to take advantage of China's future growth.

Sensitivity of the Economy to External Political Events

Hong Kong's economic strength rests on its own people's confidence in their future—a confidence that has fluctuated wildly over the years. When Beijing undertook economic-retrenchment policies, partially closed the "open door" to international trade and investment, engaged in political repression, or rattled its sabers over Taiwan, Hong Kong's stock market would gyrate, its property values declined, and foreign investment would go elsewhere. Not knowing what the transition to Chinese sovereignty would bring, Hong Kong's professional classes emigrated at the rate of about 60,000 people per year between

1990 and 1997. This drain of both talent and money out of the colony was as serious a concern for China as it was for Hong Kong.

London's refusal to allow Hong Kong citizens to emigrate to the United Kingdom contributed to a sense of panic among the middle and upper classes in Hong Kong—those most worried about their economic and political future under Communist rule. Other countries were, however, more than willing to accept these well-educated, wealthy immigrants, who came ready to make large deposits in their new host country's banks. Once emigrants gained a second passport (a guarantee of residency abroad in case conditions warrant flight), however, they tended to return to Hong Kong, where opportunities abound for entrepreneurs and those in the professions, such as doctors, architects, and engineers.

Beijing's verbal intimidation of Hong Kong dissidents who criticized China in the period following the Tiananmen crackdown in 1989, and again when Governor Christopher Patten began whipping up Hong Kong fervor for greater democratic reforms from 1992 to 1997, also aroused anxiety in the colony. Hong Kong's anxiety that Great Britain would trade the colony's democratic future for good relations with China was later counterbalanced by concern that Patten's efforts to inject Hong Kong with a heavy dose of democratization before its return to China's control would lead to China dealing harshly with Hong Kong's political freedoms after 1997. In the end, Patten's blunt refusal to abide by the terms agreed to in the Basic Law, namely, that China would have to agree to any changes made before 1997, merely led to a reversal of Patten's changes after the handover, and no more.

China's sovereignty over Hong Kong has not had a negative effect on its economy. Occasionally China's statements concerning Hong Kong's economy, judicial system, or politics have sent shock waves throughout the colony, causing the Hang Sang stock market to take a nose dive out of fears that China would ignore the principles in the Basic Law guaranteeing Hong Kong's 50 years of autonomy. Similarly, the 2003 SARS epidemic had a catastrophic impact on Hong Kong's economy. Such volatility demonstrates just how sensitive Hong Kong is to Beijing's policies and actions. Nevertheless, in the years since the handover, millions of Hong Kong citizens have relinquished their British passports for Hong Kong Special Administrative Region passports. Apart from pressures from China for them to do so, it indicates a belief that their future lies with Hong Kong and China, not Great Britain.

China is sensitive to the possibility of its policies or statements destabilizing Hong Kong. Indeed, in the ten years since the handover, Beijing has exercised unusual restraint so as to avoid being seen to interfere in Hong Kong's affairs. For example, Beijing no longer permits Chinese ministry officials to visit or oversee their counterparts in Hong Kong without clearance, lest it be interpreted as interference. Furthermore, it is the Hong Kong government, not the Ministry of Foreign Affairs office in Hong Kong, that deals with all of the foreign consulates in Hong Kong. And, unlike the British Commonwealth Office, which always sent copies of government documents to the Hong Kong government, China's Ministry of Foreign Affairs does not, again to avoid being accused of interference.[44]

Because Beijing has tread lightly in Hong Kong, most businesses already located there have remained. In fact, many foreign corporations rushed to establish themselves in Hong Kong before the handover in order to avoid the unpredictable, lengthy, and expensive bureaucratic hassle of trying to gain a foothold in the China mainland lying beyond Hong Kong. Even Taiwan's enterprises in Hong Kong have stood firm; for without direct trade and transport links between China and Taiwan, Hong Kong is still the major entrepôt for trade between the two places. Many Chinese mainland corporations also establish footholds in Hong Kong to ease the problem of foreign hard-currency transfer and to avoid a host of other difficulties that plague mainland businesses.

Nevertheless, the overall profile of the foreign business community has changed substantially since 1997. Many British went home, leaving their companies in the hands of capable Hong Kong Chinese managers, a reflection of the end of the colonial era in the business community as well as in the political system; but the percentage of Americans and Europeans doing business in Hong Kong has increased significantly.

Crime

Although Hong Kong is still characterized by a high level of social stability, a high crime rate continues to plague society. For more than a decade, ordinary criminality has been steadily augmented by crime under the control of competing Chinese triads. This is in part because the housing and community and mutual-aid groups of the 1970s and 1980s, which used to help the police track down criminals, disappeared. Their disappearance also contributed to increasing juvenile delinquency.[45] Opium, largely controlled by the triads, continues to be used widely by the Chinese. As a commentator once put it:

> Opium trails still lead to Hong Kong . . . and all our narcotic squads and all the Queen's men only serve to make the drug more costly and the profits more worthwhile. It comes in aeroplanes and fishing junks, in hollow pipes and

bamboo poles and false decks and re-frigerators and pickle jars and tooth paste tubes, in shoes and ships and sealing wax. And even cabbages.[46]

Today, Hong Kong remains one of the largest entrepôts for drugs, and the number of drug addicts is skyrocketing. This is in no small part because social and economic lib-eralization on the mainland has allowed its people to move about freely. Hong Kong tri-ads work in collaboration with triads across the border. Young people cross the border to Shenzhen to buy drugs (originating in My-anmar (Burma), which they then smuggle back across Hong Kong's border. In turn, those recruited in Shenzhen provide a base in the mainland for Hong Kong triads to deal in drugs, prostitutes, and guns, and to set up underground banks and transport illegal im-migrants across the border.[47]

Cooperation between Hong Kong and Chi-nese mainland drug investigators is complicat-ed by Hong Kong's legal system, which still differs from the legal system of the rest of Chi-na. The critical difference is that Hong Kong does not have capital punishment. And China, committed to not changing Hong Kong's legal system for 50 years, has not pressured Hong Kong to change its law on the death penalty. Dozens of crimes such as drug dealing, pun-ishable by execution in the rest of China, will result at most in a life sentence in Hong Kong.

Before the handover, when Hong Kong investigators asked the Chinese to turn over drug dealers to the Hong Kong authorities, the Chinese expended significant resources to find the criminals and turn them over. But when the Chinese asked the Hong Kong drug authorities to do the same, they went so far as to arrest the suspects, but refused to turn them over to China's public security office because of the fairly strong chance that a person convicted on charges of selling drugs in China would be executed. At first China wanted to copy the Singapore model of executing drug dealers, but it soon real-ized that would mean the execution of thou-sands. Now only the biggest drug dealers are executed. (The problems emanating from cross-border crime are discussed further in this report, under the topic "The Legal Sys-tem and the Judiciary.")

Hong Kong's organized crime has long been powerful in the areas of real estate; extortion from massage parlors, bars, restau-rants, and clubs; illegal gambling; smuggling; the sale of handguns (illegal for ordinary people to purchase); prostitution; and drugs. And, as is common in other Asian countries, gangs are often hired by corporations to deal with debtors and others who cause them difficulties. Triads have also expanded into kidnapping for ransom, and taken on some unexpected roles. As an example, when the

British governor in Hong Kong, Christopher Patten, upset Beijing with his proposals for further democratization of Hong Kong before 1997, the Chinese Communist regime (by way of its estimated 60,000 supporters work-ing in Hong Kong) allegedly recruited triad members to begin harassing those within the Hong Kong government who were support-ing Patten's proposals. (And, when Patten's dog disappeared one day in 1992 during the crisis stage of Sino–British relations, one ru-mor had it that the Chinese Communists had kidnapped the dog and were going to ransom it in exchange for halting political reform in Hong Kong. The other rumor was that Pat-ten's pet had been flown into China to be served up for breakfast to Deng Xiaoping. Of course, neither rumor was true.)

POLITICS AND POLITICAL STRUCTURE

Politics and the political structure have changed greatly since the days of Hong Kong's colonial government, when the Brit-ish monarch, acting on the advice of the prime minister, would appoint a governor, who presided over the Hong Kong govern-ment's colonial administration. Colonial rule in Hong Kong may be characterized as be-nevolent, consultative, and paternalistic, but it was nonetheless still colonial. Although lo-cal people were heavily involved in running the colony and the colonial government inter-fered very little in the business activities and daily lives of Hong Kong Chinese, the Brit-ish still controlled the major levers of power and filled the top ranks in the government.

The colony's remarkable political sta-bility until the handover in 1997 was, then, hardly due to any efforts by the British to transplant a form of Western-style democ-racy to Hong Kong. But, the colonial Hong Kong government did seek feedback from the people through the hundreds of consulta-tive committees that it created within the civil service. Similarly, although the British ulti-mately controlled both the Legislative Coun-cil (LegCo) and Executive Council (ExCo), these governmental bodies allowed Hong Kong's socioeconomic elites to participate in the administration of the colony, even if they were unable to participate in the formula-tion of policy. Some 300 additional advisory groups as well as numerous partly elected bodies—such as the municipal councils (for Hong Kong Island and Kowloon), the rural committees (for the New Territories), and district boards—also had considerable au-tonomy in managing their own affairs. This institutionalized consultation among Chinese administrators and the colonial government resulted in the colony being governed by an elite informed by and sensitive to the needs of the Hong Kong people. As was common to

British colonial administration elsewhere, the lower levels of government were filled with the local people. Rarely was political dissent expressed outside the government.[48]

The relatively high approval rating of British colonial rule helps explain why only a small portion of the mere 6 percent of reg-istered voters actually voted. With the gov-ernment assuring both political stability and strong economic growth, the people of Hong Kong spent most of their time and energy on economic pursuits, not politics. In any event, given the limited scope of democracy in Hong Kong, local people had little incentive to be-come politically involved. For this reason, as the handover came nearer, Hong Kong resi-dents grew increasingly concerned that there were few competent and trustworthy leaders among the Hong Kong Chinese to take over.[49] They also worried that a government control-led by leaders and bureaucrats who held for-eign passports or rights of residence abroad would not be committed to their welfare. Al-though Beijing withdrew its demand before the handover that all governmental civil ser-vants swear an oath of allegiance to the gov-ernment of China and turn in their British passports, many did so anyway (including the first chief executive, Tung Chee-hwa).

The colonial government remained stable, then, because it was perceived to be trustwor-thy, competent, consultative, and capable of addressing the needs of Hong Kong's people. Most Hong Kong citizens also believed that a strong political authority was indispensable to prosperity and stability, and they worried that the formation of multiple political par-ties could disrupt that strong authority. Thus, what is seen in the West as a critical aspect of democracy was viewed by the people in Hong Kong as potentially destabilizing.

Nevertheless, by the late 1980s, many Hong Kong Chinese began to demand that democratic political reforms be institutional-ized before the Chinese Communists took over in 1997. The ability of the departing co-lonial government to deal with these increased pressures to democratize Hong Kong was, however, seriously constricted by the 1982 Joint Declaration and the Basic Law of 1990, which required Beijing's approval before the British could make any changes in the laws and policies governing Hong Kong. The peo-ple of Hong Kong awoke to the fact that their interests and those of the colonial government were no longer compatible. Britain's policy toward Hong Kong had become a mere ap-pendage of British policy toward China, and the status quo was frozen. The Hong Kong colonial government had, essentially, lost its independence to Beijing and London.[50]

What was "handed over" on July 1, 1997, was sovereign control of Hong Kong. Hong Kong became a Special Administrative Re-gion of China, with Beijing guaranteeing autonomy for 50 years in the political, legal, economic, and social realms. But Hong Kong would be governed by its new "constitution," the Basic Law, written by China's leaders. This document provided for certain changes to be made *after* the handover. Notably, Article 23 required the Hong Kong Legislative Council to outlaw treason, succession, subversion, and sedition, as well as other activities that could endanger China's national security. That is, Hong Kong was expected to outlaw, and punish, those individuals and organizations operating in Hong Kong who in the view of Beijing might pose a threat to China's security; but for five years, nothing was done to define how Article 23 could be implemented (see below).

Similarly, for five years after the 1997 handover, there was no real change in the government—except, of course, that Hong Kong's chief executive reported to Beijing, not London. The structure of the post-1997 government, outlined in great detail in the Basic Law, was to be, like Hong Kong's colonial government: structured on a separation of powers among the executive, legislative, and judicial branches of government, serving to check the arbitrary use of power by any single individual or institution of the government. This separation of powers, however, never did exist within the framework of a representative democracy. Thus, the government today remains similar in many respects to what it was under colonial rule, with power continuing to be centralized in the executive branch. LegCo cannot even initiate substantive legislation without the approval of the chief executive, or hold the chief executive accountable for his actions. In effect, Hong Kong under the Basic Law has retained the colonial model put in place by the British in the nineteenth century.

China has made some changes in Hong Kong's government to bring it into greater correspondence with its own government structure, even if in some cases this is merely a matter of changing names. In 2002, under a new "ministerial" system, Beijing changed the Basic Law to allow the chief executive to appoint all 14 policy secretaries in the cabinet of 20. (The others are leading politicians, including two heads of progovernment parties, and close personal advisers.) Previously, cabinet secretaries were senior civil servants who were, at least in theory, politically neutral. Now that they are appointed, they serve at the chief executive's discretion, which means that their political views weigh heavily in their selection. This has raised further questions concerning the accountability of the government to the Legislature.[51]

The Executive Council is run by Hong Kong's chief executive. Fortunately, continuity was maintained in the first years after the handover, when most of the cabinet heads

(Courtesy of Bruce Argetsinger)

Even under China's control, the strong work ethic of Hong Kong's small entrepreneurs continues.

under British colonial rule agreed to serve under the first chief executive. Sole decision-making authority remains vested in the chief executive, although ultimately Beijing must approve of any of ExCo's policies. So far, Beijing has chosen not to exercise this approval in a way that hampers the chief executive's policy-making authority.

Since 1982, the Hong Kong Transition Project has taken the pulse of Hong Kong each year through an extensive survey of public opinion on a variety of issues related to the impact of the transition of Chinese sovereignty. The level of satisfaction has been consistently much higher in the post-handover period than in the 15 years leading up to it.[52] Furthermore, the percentage of those satisfied with the performance of the PRC government in dealing with Hong Kong affairs

remained unusually high. In fact, Hong Kong public opinion in Nov. 2003 continued to give a far higher approval rating to Beijing's leadership than to Hong Kong's chief executive: Those "satisfied" or "very satisfied" with Beijing's dealing with Hong Kong affairs were 72 percent of those polled; whereas for Chief Executive Tung, the approval rating in the same 2003 poll was a humiliating 21 percent. Moreover, satisfaction with the overall performance of the Hong Kong government fell from 66 percent approval in June 1997 (still under British rule), to 20 percent by Nov. 2003.[53]

Problems with becoming the first chief executive of Hong Kong were understandable: As a colony, Hong Kong had bred strong civil servants, but no real political leaders who had had opportunities to make political decisions.

So Beijing had to pick someone whom they felt was safe, but who inevitably lacked real leadership experience. Tung Chee-hwa was a businessman, an elitist who opposed the welfare state and supported "Asian values" of a strong central leadership and obedient citizenry.[54] Tung Chee-hwa's popularity one year after he took office (49 percent were satisfied or very satisfied with his performance in July 1998) was quickly eroded by his inability to effectively address a number of problems, including fallout from the Asian financial and economic crisis that began within a few months of his entering office. Tung was blamed not only for plummeting land prices and the government's incompetence, but also for his reluctance to intervene in order to relieve the people's suffering that resulted from the crisis. The infrequency of his appearances in front of LegCo, and his refusal to consult with LegCo representatives, caused significant conflict and anger. Although it was the executive branch's role to deal with the financial crisis in Hong Kong, LegCo still believed that it should have been consulted.[55]

Although Beijing reappointed Tung for a second term in 2002, Beijing was not pleased with his performance. This was largely because of the growing number of demonstrations and protests directed at his government, and the dissatisfaction of the people of Hong Kong with his performance. By late 2003, some 58 percent of Hong Kong people polled said they would support China's President Hu Jintao and Premier Wen Jiabao if they were to dismiss Tung for his performance.[56]

Suddenly, in March 2005, Tung resigned, apparently under pressure from Beijing. Because two years remained in his term as Chief Executive, it led to a major constitutional crisis; for the Basic Law lacked procedures for dealing with a mid-term replacement. Beijing managed to engineer the choice of Donald Tsang, a member of the Executive Council, to fill out the term, which ends in 2007. Beijing has already ruled out any possibility that it will allow universal suffrage and full democracy for the elections of the next chief executive at that time (or of the Legislative Council in 2008—only 30 of its 60 legislators are directly elected at present), so the focus in Hong Kong is now on full democracy by the time of the 2012 elections. Although China has pledged significant autonomy for Hong Kong, Beijing argued that nothing in the Basic Law obligates it to allow Hong Kong to fully democratize on its own timetable. The real reason for China's reluctance to let Hong Kong move ahead is, no doubt, because it will put Hong Kong far in front of the pace of democratization in some of China's major cities, such as Beijing and Shanghai.[57]

Efforts to get the economy back on track were, as noted above, stymied greatly by events beyond the chief executive's control— the Asian financial crisis, the global reces-

sion that followed the terrorist attacks on the United States on September 11, 2001; and the SARS epidemic that erupted in 2003. Nevertheless, as the public and the press saw it, the fault for failure to revive the economy lay at the feet of the Hong Kong government, and especially the Chief Executive, not external forces (or Beijing). If, they argued, the Chief Executive had appointed advisers based on competence instead of politics, he would have received better advice.

Hong Kong residents generally believe, then, that Hong Kong's problems arise not from Beijing's control but, rather, from the incompetence of their own government. So the critical question for the Chief Executive is no longer how autonomous he is of Beijing's control. Instead, it is whether he can maintain his legitimacy as the head of Hong Kong's government. In this respect, Donald Tsang has thus far done quite well. In the most recent (March 2006) survey concerning his performance since taking office, fully 76 percent were "satisfied" with Tsang as Chief Executive.[58] But most Hong Kong people would prefer direct elections for all LegCo members and district council members, as well as for the chief executive. Presently, the latter is appointed by the Beijing-controlled Election Committee.

Article 23 of the Basic Law

As noted earlier, Article 23 outlaws treason, secession, subversion, and sedition. It also prohibits the theft of "state secrets," political activities of foreign political organizations in Hong Kong, and the establishment of ties with foreign political organizations by political organizations in Hong Kong. It had been left up to the Hong Kong government to give teeth to Article 23 so that it could be implemented, but it had not done so.

The purpose of Article 23 is to protect the national security of China as a whole by defining the types of activities in Hong Kong that would be punishable by law. It was one thing to define terms such as "subversion" as it applied to the rest of mainland China; it was another thing to define these terms for residents of Hong Kong. This had to be done without jeopardizing the fundamental rights given to Hong Kong people in the Basic Law, some of which have not been given to the rest of the Chinese.

The terrorist attacks of 9/11 spurred the Hong Kong government's Security Bureau to submit a bill to amend Article 23. In early 2003, after a year-long period of public consultation, Chief Executive Tung submitted a draft bill to LegCo. This predictably caused a public uproar, as it brought back fears that Beijing might have pressured the government to limit the guaranteed rights of people in Hong Kong. The public was particularly worried about a constriction of freedom of

the media to report news; and the rights to demonstrate and protest, to associate with foreign organizations or with organizations banned on the mainland, to access Internet sites, and to organize pressure groups and political groups. There was also concern that the new definitions of "treason," "subversion," and "sedition" might mean that journalists who managed to get hold of unpublished government documents, or refusal to reveal their anonymous sources, could be charged with "theft of state secrets."[59]

The concerns about the potential limits on individual freedom by Article 23 has spilled over into a concern for the rule of law in Hong Kong, which is the basis for protecting all other freedoms. The possibility that the Hong Kong government might resort to secret trials on cases relating to proscription of certain local organizations, and that "mere association between a local organization and a proscribed one on the Mainland" might be grounds for arrest, also caused anxiety. On July 1, 2003, 500,000 people demonstrated in Hong Kong against the draft bill. Finally, after further demonstrations, and Beijing's realization that the suggested amendments were destabilizing Hong Kong and causing hostility toward Beijing, the bill to amend Article 23 was withdrawn without any date for reconsideration. The impact of this is dramatically illustrated by polls that asked about the performance of China's government in dealing with Hong Kong affairs: In June 2003, before the July 1st demonstrations, there was a 57 percent satisfaction rate with Beijing; 6 months later, after the withdrawal of the legislation, the satisfaction rate shot up to 72 percent.[60] The fact that Beijing in this case catered to the will of the Hong Kong people seems to have won enormous good will for China.

Political Parties and Elections

On July 1, 1997, China immediately repealed Governor Patten's expansion of the franchise for the 1995 elections, which had lowered the voting age to 18 and extended the vote to all of Hong Kong's adult population (adding 2.5 million people to the voting rolls)—without consulting Beijing. As the Joint Declaration required that China had to agree to even a small increase in democracy in the Hong Kong colony, Beijing was within its rights when it repealed the changes and replaced the Legislature elected under those rules. A 400-member "Provisional Legislature," already selected by China's Preparatory Committee, replaced it on July 1, 1997.

Why did Beijing cancel the results of the 1995 elections? China's leaders viewed the last-ditch colonial government's efforts to install a representative government in Hong Kong as part of a conspiracy to use democracy to undercut China's rule in Hong Kong

(United Nations Photo 74037)

The Hong Kong government has constructed many apartment complexes in an effort to address the severe overcrowding in tenements and squatter communities.

after 1997. They believed that the last-minute political reforms could, in fact, jeopardize Hong Kong's prosperity and stability by permitting special interests and political protest to flourish; and that Hong Kong's social problems—narcotics, violence, gangs, prostitution, an underground economy—required that Hong Kong be controlled, not given democracy. China therefore adopted a status quo approach to Hong Kong. After all, Hong Kong's political system under British colonial control had been imposed from the outside. This system worked well and kept Hong Kong stable and prosperous. Beijing merely wanted to replace a colonial ruler with a Chinese Communist Party ruler.[61]

Nor did Beijing want a situation in which those citizens living in Hong Kong enjoyed substantially more rights than the rest of China's population. This could easily lead to pressure on Beijing to extend those rights to all Chinese. If Beijing is going to give greater political rights to its people, it would rather do so on its own timetable. Nevertheless, Beijing kept its promises not to interfere in Hong Kong's political system after the handover.

In the 1995 elections, Hong Kong's Democratic Party, whose political platform called for major changes to the Basic Law in order to give Hong Kong people more democratic rights, won two-thirds of the vote. Although Beijing

canceled the results of that election upon gaining control over Hong Kong in July 1997, Beijing immediately rescheduled the elections for May 1998; and when those elections led to the reelection of the same number of Democratic Party members as before, Beijing made no effort to remove them from the legislature.[62]

In the fall 2004 LegCo elections, the Democratic Party and their allies won 25 of the 60 seats, meaning that the pro-government/pro-Beijing parties still control the legislature after several rounds of elections. In that election, however, only 30 of the seats were chosen by direct election from the citizenry. The other 30 were chosen by what are called "functional constituencies," which tend to be more conservative, pro-business, and pro-Beijing. So, even though the democratic camp won the majority of the electoral vote, they still were not able to gain a majority of the seats.

It was, nevertheless, a disappointing showing for the democracy camp, which has been pressing to advance the timetable for direct elections, when the terms of the Chief Executive (2007) and members of LegCo (2008) expire. Many analysts attribute the electoral results to the preference of the electorate for better local governance over deadlines for democratization. The democracy camp lacks a meaningful platform of political, social, and economic policies that would improve condi-

tions in Hong Kong and be attractive to the electorate. Analysts also point to the disarray within the democracy camp, which seems unable to agree on anything other than that more democracy would be a good thing, and that they should stand in opposition to government policies.

Beijing has warned the pro-democracy group not to move forward with any plan to hold a referendum on direct elections before the original timetable called for them. Combined with this warning, however, have been significant efforts by China to enhance economic integration between Hong Kong and the mainland provinces bordering it. China has also made it easier for Chinese tourists to go to Hong Kong—a potential boon to the flagging tourist industry in Hong Kong.[63] This may help explain why the pro-Beijing forces maintained control of LegCo.

Under British colonial rule, ordinary citizens were rarely involved in politics. Today, there is much greater involvement, but a lingering suspicion of and lack of enthusiasm for politics and political parties in Hong Kong. The lack of a coherent platform and strong leadership in the democracy camp, as well as its failure to bring about change in government policies, contributes to a feeling of political inefficacy—a sense that there is little ordinary citizens can do to shape policy.

This view is also influenced by a belief that there is a not altogether healthy alliance between big business and government.

On the other hand, the government has the support of some remarkably strong pro-Beijing parties, especially the Democratic Alliance for the Betterment of Hong Kong (DAB). (It may not be appropriate to call the DAB pro-Beijing, but it does make more efforts to work with China for common goals and opposes it far less frequently than many in the democracy camp do.) The DAB has joined up with other "patriotic" (that is, pro-China/progovernment) parties in a loose coalition. The coalition works *with* the government to make policies focused on environmental, social, and economic issues. Many are suspicious of the DAB ties to the government, and concerned about the funding of the DAB by the Chinese government; but it and Hong Kong's "patriotic" organizations are highly effective at mobilizing people at the local level and responding to their concerns on issues important to their daily lives.

It is difficult for the Democratic Party to make inroads on the seats assigned to functional constituencies, which usually go to progovernment business people. This unfair, indeed undemocratic, system, whereby a mere 180,000 individuals could vote for the 30 functional constituency seats, while 3.5 million voted for the other 30 seats, is a residual system set up by the British colonial government.

The complicated electoral system virtually guarantees business groups dominance in the Legislature. This is one factor accounting for both Beijing and the Hong Kong government's tolerating the Democratic Party and its political protests, even when the protesters publicly denounce Beijing's leaders. That is, with rare exceptions (such as the protests led by the democracy camp against the bill to amend Article 23), their protests are without consequences. Besides, LegCo is a rather powerless political body. It is poorly funded, so legislators cannot afford the kind of research support that is essential to making effective policy proposals. And while in session, LegCo meets only once a week, at which time legislators give speeches written for them by their staffs.[64] This is hardly the stuff of impassioned legislative debate and policy making.

Beijing has tolerated the gadfly role of the Democratic Party, no doubt hoping that this hands-off policy will help bring Taiwan into negotiations for unification with the mainland sooner. The Hong Kong government has also kept channels open to Democratic Party leaders. The Democratic Party has, in turn, adopted a more moderate stance toward both Beijing and the government than it might otherwise have done—a position facilitated by the departure of several of the party's more radical leaders—and the public's concerns that it not stir up problems that could destabilize Hong Kong.[65]

The Democratic Party's minority position within the Legislature condemns it to the position of a critic and complainer.[66] In the post-transition period, the Hong Kong people believe that the party's demands for greater democracy have not been appropriate to the problems at hand. These problems include the "bird flu," which threatened public health and forced the government to kill the entire stock of chickens in Hong Kong; the red tide, which killed hundreds of thousands of fish; a disastrous opening of the new airport in 1998; the right-of-abode seekers in Hong Kong; the drop in real-estate values, increased unemployment, bankruptcies of retail stores, and a dramatic decline in tourism. These were not the sorts of problems for which the Democratic Party's call for changes in the Basic Law, a timetable for democratization, and opposition to Beijing have been relevant. Indeed, the vast majority of the public has wanted government intervention to address these problems. Thus, the many street demonstrations that occur tend not to be directed to broad demands for democracy but, rather, to pressing public policy issues. They reflect the frustration of the population in the legislature's ineffectiveness in shaping government policy.

The Legal System and the Judiciary

Under colonial rule, Hong Kong's judiciary was independent. After 10 years under the "one country, two systems" envisioned in the Basic Law, it has remained so. Judges are appointed and serve for life. English common law, partly adapted to accommodate Chinese custom, has been at the heart of the legal system. Much of the confidence in Hong Kong as a good place to live and do business has been based on the reputation of its independent judiciary for integrity and competence, the stability of the legal and constitutional system, and Hong Kong's adherence to the rule of law.

China has allowed Hong Kong's legal system to rely on such legal concepts as habeas corpus, legal precedent, and the tradition of common law, which do not exist in China. Beijing has not subjected Hong Kong's legal system to the Communist Party Politburo's guidelines for the rest of China. But on political matters such as legislation, human rights, civil liberties, and freedom of the press, the Basic Law offers inadequate protection. For example, the Basic Law provides for the Standing Committee of the National People's Congress (NPC) in Beijing, not the Hong Kong courts, to interpret the Basic Law and to determine whether future laws passed by the Hong Kong Legislature conflict with the Basic Law.

Furthermore, although Beijing had promised Hong Kong that the chief executive will be accountable to the Legislature, the Basic Law gives the chief executive—appointed by China's NPC until 2007—the power to dissolve the Hong Kong Legislature and veto bills. The relationship of Hong Kong's Basic Law to China's own Constitution remains in limbo. The fundamental incompatibility between the British tradition (in which the state's actions must not be in conflict with the laws) and China's practice of using law as a tool of the state, as well as China's conferring and withdrawing rights at will, is at the heart of the concern about Chinese rule over Hong Kong.[67]

The first case to be tried by the Hong Kong courts after July 1, 1997, was that of an American streaker who ran nude in crowded downtown Hong Kong and was easily apprehended. In this rather amusing case, the court fined and released the defendant. Serious questions soon arose, however, about the handling of cross-border crime. As noted earlier, the source of the problem is that Hong Kong does not have capital punishment, and China does. In the past, when Hong Kong has arrested a P.R.C. citizen wanted for a criminal activity that is punishable in China by execution, it has refused to turn the person over to China's judicial authorities.

The position of the Hong Kong courts is that a Hong Kong citizen cannot be tried in China for *any* crimes committed in Hong Kong, even if caught in China, because of its judicial independence under the "one country, two systems" structure. But, according to Article 7 of China's Criminal Code, China has the right to prosecute a Chinese national who commits a crime *anywhere* in the world, providing the crime was either planned in, or had consequences in, China.[68] The assertion of such a broad jurisdiction over Chinese nationals inevitably puts it in conflict with Hong Kong's judicial system. Because so many criminals straddle the border between the Hong Kong SAR and China, and because they have different criminal codes, there are many levels of conflict and ambiguity to resolve. In the ten years since the handover, the increasingly porous borders between Hong Kong and the rest of China, the greater mobility of the Chinese people, and the open market economy have seemed like an open invitation to Hong Kong's triads not only to expand their crime rings within China, but also to take refuge there. At the same time, citizens of China who commit capital crimes in China sometimes try to enter Hong Kong, where capital punishment is prohibited.

Polls over the years have indicated that residents (including those who really do not know anything about the Basic Law's provisions) are satisfied with the Basic Law and the rule of law in Hong Kong.[69] In addition, most residents think that Beijing has adhered to the Basic Law, but they have not been pleased that the Hong Kong government has several times dragged Beijing into Hong Kong affairs. One of the most notable examples was the Hong Kong government's request to China's National People's Congress in 1999 to rule on the "right of abode" for Mainlanders with at least one Hong Kong parent. (At the time of the NPC's ruling, 1.4 million Mainlanders were claiming eligibility.) The Hong Kong judiciary's decision was overturned, a result that came as a great relief to Hong Kong residents who were more afraid of overcrowding than they were of Beijing's interference. Nevertheless, as of 2007, the right to abode is still an uncomfortable issue; for although there is sympathy for these settlers' plight (many have lived and worked in Hong Kong for most of their lives), the settlers are usually the fruit of relationships between mainland Chinese women and married Hong Kong men who frequently go to the mainland for business, a point that does not sit well with many citizens, especially Hong Kong women.

Public Security

Under the "one country, two systems" model, Hong Kong continues to be responsible for its own public security. The British colonial military force of about 12,000 has been replaced by a smaller Chinese People's Liberation Army (PLA) force of about 9,000. The military installations used by the British forces were turned over to the PLA. In efforts to reassure the Hong Kong populace that the primary purpose of the military remains the protection of the border from smuggling and illegal entry, and for general purposes of national security, soldiers are mostly stationed across the Hong Kong border in Shenzhen. Some are also stationed, however, in heavily populated areas, to serve as a deterrent to social unrest and mass demonstrations against the Chinese government. No doubt the high cost of keeping soldiers in metropolitan Hong Kong was also a factor in the PLA decision to move most of its troops to the outskirts.

Apart from diminishing the interactions between the PLA soldiers and the Hong Kong people, China has done much to ensure that the troops do not become a source of tension. To the contrary, China wants them to serve as a force in developing a positive view of Chinese sovereignty over Hong Kong. As part of their "charm offensive," the soldiers must be tall (at least 5 feet 10 inches); have "regular features" (that is, be attractive); be well read (with all officers having college training, and all ordinary soldiers having a high school education); know the Basic Law; and be able to speak both the local dialect of Cantonese and simple English.[70] In short, the PLA, which has no such requirements for its regular soldiers and officers, has trained an elite corps of soldiers for Hong Kong. No doubt the hope is that a well-educated military will be less likely to provoke problems with Hong Kong residents. In fact, PLA troops are even permitted to date and marry local Hong Kong women!

Press, Civil Rights, and Religious Freedom

China's forceful crackdown on protesters in Beijing's Tiananmen Square in 1989 and subsequent repression traumatized the Hong Kong population. China warned the Hong Kong authorities that foreign agents might use such organizations as the Hong Kong Alliance in Support of the Patriotic Democratic Movement in China (a coalition of some 200 groups) to advance their intelligence activities on the mainland, and even accused that group of "playing a subversive role in supporting the pro-democracy movement."[71] China also announced that it would not permit politically motivated mass rallies or demonstrations against the central government of China after the handover. As it turns out, Beijing has done little to stop the rallies and protests by such diverse groups as doctors, students, property owners, social workers, and civil servants, Mainlanders demanding the right to abode in Hong Kong, or event protests against the bill to amend Article 23. Such protests occur regularly in Hong Kong. Indeed, even Jiang Zemin, during one of his final trips to Hong Kong as president of China, had to face the potential humiliation by the thousands of Falun Gong demonstrators protesting Beijing's crackdown on the religious group in China. (Rather than prohibiting the group members from protesting, Hong Kong authorities took Jiang along a route where they were not so visible.) Beijing has, however, used subtle and not-so-subtle intimidation to discourage Hong Kong from supporting prodemocracy activities, suggesting that such acts would be "treasonous." In addition, those individuals who assisted the Tiananmen demonstrators in Beijing in 1989, and those leaders of the annual demonstrations in Hong Kong to protest China's use of force to crack down on Tiananmen demonstrators, are blacklisted in China. Were they to try to go to the mainland, they could be arrested for sedition. Only when the chief executive himself has intervened on their behalf have they been allowed to cross the Hong Kong border.

One freedom that Hong Kong subjects under British rule had was freedom of the press. Hong Kong had a dynamic press that represented all sides of the political spectrum. Indeed, it even tolerated the Chinese Communist Party's sponsorship of both its own pro-Communist, pro-Beijing newspaper, and its own news bureau (the New China News Agency) in Hong Kong, which, until the handover, also functioned as China's unofficial foreign office in Hong Kong.

Concerns remain that China may one day crack down on Hong Kong's press, but they pale in comparison with other concerns. Indeed, when asked in a 2006 survey about 14 different issues, those evoking the lowest levels of concern were freedom of the press (8 percent), freedom of assembly (7 percent), and freedom of speech (7 percent). (By contrast, 48 percent were "very worried" about air and water pollution.)[72] This is not surprising, as China so far has done little to challenge Hong Kong's press freedom. The exceptions are primarily concerning matters that China considers "internal affairs." The Hong Kong press has received warnings not to speak favorably about Taiwan independence; but in general, members of the Hong Kong press have mastered the art of knowing where to draw the line so as not to offend Beijing. Self-censorship is nothing new for Hong Kong's (or China's) press; and even under the British, it was necessary. How Beijing will respond to a Hong Kong press that openly challenges the Chinese Communist Party remains to be seen; but in China itself, political analyses are no longer confined to parroting the Communist Party's line, and investigative reportage is encouraged. Further, the Hong Kong press does not hesitate to engage in searing criticisms of the chief executive, even though he is appointed by Beijing. In short, a major rollback of press freedom in Hong Kong seems unlikely.

As for religious freedom, Beijing has stated that as long as a religious practice does not contravene the Basic Law, it will be permitted. Given the fact that China's tolerance of religious freedom on the mainland has expanded dramatically since it began liberalizing reforms in 1979, this does not seem to be a likely area of tension. Even in the case of Falun Gong, a sect that is banned on the mainland but has strong support in Hong Kong, thus far Beijing does not seem inclined to pressure the Hong Kong government to restrict its activities.

THE FUTURE

The future is, of course, unpredictable; but so far, there is a "business as usual" look about Hong Kong. Hong Kong still appears much as it did before its return to China's sovereign control. And although some analysts believe that power is imperceptibly being transferred to Beijing, Deng Xiaoping's promise that "dancing and horseracing would continue unabated" has been kept. "U.S. aircraft carriers still drop anchor and disgorge their crews into the Wanchai district's red-light bars. Anti-China demonstrators continue their almost weekly parades through the Central district. . . . Meanwhile, the People's Liberation Army has made a virtue of being invisible."[73] It seems that fears of Hong Kong becoming just another Chinese city were misplaced.

China's leaders have promised that for 50 years after 1997, the relationship between China and the Hong Kong Special Administrative Region will be "one country, two systems." Moreover, China's leaders clearly want their cities to look more like Hong Kong, not the other way around. In fact, with China's commercial banks starting to act much the same as banks in any capitalist economy, the phasing out of China's state-run economy in favor of a market economy, a budding stock market, billions of dollars in foreign investment, and entry into the World Trade Organization, China's economy is looking more like Hong Kong's and less like a centrally planned socialist economy. China's leaders have repeatedly stated the importance of foreign investment, greater openness, and experimentation; and they are doing everything possible to integrate the country into the global economy. The imposition of a socialist economy on Hong Kong is, at this point, unthinkable.

China's political arena is also changing so profoundly that the two systems, which just 20 years ago seemed so far apart, are now much closer. China has undergone some political liberalization, (increasing electoral rights at the local level, permitting freedom in individual lifestyles, mobility, and job selection, and according greater freedom to the mass media). The rapid growth of private property and business interests is also bringing significant social change to China, including the proliferation of interest groups and associations to promote their members' interests.

Southern China's extraordinary economic boom has made Hong Kong optimistic about the future. Many of its residents see a new "dragon" emerging, one that combines Hong Kong's technology and skills with China's labor and resources. Others, however, do not see Hong Kong happily working as one unit with China. Instead, they see Hong Kong as a rival competing with Shanghai and with the many new ports that China is building; and even with Shenzhen, which borders Hong Kong and also now has a deepwater container port. Shenzhen is developing a high-quality pool of labor that costs just one-tenth that of Hong Kong, so many corporations are moving their operations—and their wealth—across the border to China. Moreover, the P.R.C. no longer needs Hong Kong as an entrepôt to export its products. Not only can it now do so through its own ports, but it is also building plants in other countries, such as India, where it will manufacture and export goods that otherwise would have gone through Hong Kong. In addition, China's membership in the WTO as of 2001, as well as its increasingly direct contacts and trade with Taiwan, could easily lead to a partial eclipse of Hong Kong.

Some Hong Kong analysts believe that the greatest threat to Hong Kong's success is not political repression and centralized control from Beijing; rather, it would take the more insidious form of China's bureaucracy and corruption simply smothering Hong Kong's economic vitality. One concern is that mainland companies operating in Hong Kong may be allowed to stand above the law or to use their Hong Kong ties to exert inappropriate influence on behalf of pro-China business interests and corrupt the Hong Kong economy.[74] So far, Hong Kong has escaped this fate, and is still considered one of the least corrupt business environments in the world. Another concern is that China may bring the features of the Singapore political model to Hong Kong, whereby it would be ruled by pro-China business tycoons who are insensitive to the political, social, and economic concerns of other groups, and where democratic parties would find it impossible to gain a majority in a legislative system stacked against them. Political rights and freedom would also be restricted by moving toward a Singapore political model.[75] Yet another worry is that the dangers lie *within* Hong Kong, notably the minimalist efforts of the Hong Kong government to reshape it in a way that allows it to remain competitive.

Beijing has an important stake in its takeover of Hong Kong not being perceived as disruptive to its political or economic system, and that Hong Kong's residents and the international business community believe in its future prosperity. Policies and events that threatened that confidence in the 1980s led to the loss of many of Hong Kong's most talented people, technological know-how, and investment. China does not want to risk losing still more.[76] Beijing also wants to maintain Hong Kong as a major free port and the regional center of trade, financing, shipping, and information—although it is also doing everything possible to turn Shanghai into a competitive center.[77]

William Overholt has labeled the major underlying sources of tension between Hong Kong and Beijing as the "Three Confusions:" Beijing's "confusion of Hong Kong, where there is virtually no separatist sentiment, with Taiwan;" confusion due to a failure to distinguish between the types of lawful demonstrations that have traditionally taken place in Hong Kong on a regular basis "with disruptive demonstrations in the mainland;" and confusion because of Beijing's failure to distinguish between some of the older leaders of the democracy movement "with the moderate loyal sentiments of the overwhelming majority of the democratic movement."[78] To the degree that China can eliminate such confusion, it will be able to avoid many problems with Hong Kong.

Finally, regardless of official denials by the government in Taiwan, Beijing's successful management of "one country, two systems" in Hong Kong will profoundly affect how Taiwan feels about its own peaceful integration with the mainland. If Beijing wants to regain control of Taiwan by peaceful means, it is critical that it handle Hong Kong well.

Timeline: PAST

A.D. 1839–1842
The first Opium War between China and Great Britain. Ends with Treaty of Nanjing, which cedes Hong Kong to Britain

1856
The Chinese cede Kowloon and Stonecutter Island to Britain. They became part of Hong Kong

1898
England gains a 99-year lease on the New Territories, which also became part of Hong Kong

1911
A revolution ends the Manchu Dynasty; the Republic of China is established

1941
The Japanese attack Pearl Harbor and take Hong Kong; Hong Kong falls under Japanese control

1949
The Communist victory in China produces massive immigration into Hong Kong

1980s
Great Britain and China agree to the return of Hong Kong to China

1990s
China resumes control of Hong Kong on July 1, 1997

PRESENT

1997–2002
Hong Kong's efforts to recover from the Asian economic and financial crisis are hindered by a worldwide economic downturn

2003
Outbreak of SARS. After massive demonstrations, government withdraws bill to amend the Basic Law, Article 23, on sedition from further consideration

2005
Chief Executive Tung Chee-hwa abruptly resigns. Donald Tsang becomes the new Chief Executive.

Notes

1. R. G. Tiedemann, "Chasing the Dragon," *China Now*, No. 132 (February 1990), p. 21.
2. Jan S. Prybyla, "The Hong Kong Agreement and Its Impact on the World Economy," in Jurgen Domes and Yu-ming Shaw, eds., *Hong Kong: A Chinese and International Concern* (Boulder, CO: Westview Special Studies on East Asia, 1988), p. 177.
3. Tiedemann, p. 22.
4. Steven Tsang, *A Modern History of Hong Kong* (New York: I.B.Tauris, 2004), p. 271.

5. Siu-kai Lau, "The Hong Kong Policy of the People's Republic of China, 1949–1997," *Journal of Contemporary China* (March 2000), Vol. 9, No. 23, p. 81.

6. Tsang, pp. 133–135.

7. Robin McLaren, former British ambassador to China, seminar at Cambridge University, Centre for International Relations (February 28, 1996).

8. Ambrose Y. C. King, "The Hong Kong Talks and Hong Kong Politics," in Domes and Shaw, p. 49.

9. Hungdah Chiu, Y. C. Jao, and Yual-li Wu, *The Future of Hong Kong: Toward 1997 and Beyond* (New York: Quorum Books, 1987), pp. 5–6.

10. Siu-kai Lau, "Hong Kong's 'Ungovernability' in the Twilight of Colonial Rule," in Zhiling, Lin and Thomas W. Robinson, *The Chinese and Their Future: Beijing, Taipei, and Hong Kong* (Washington, D.C.: The American Enterprise Institute Press, 1994), pp. 288–290.

11. McClaren.

12. McLaren noted that it was not easy to convince Prime Minister Thatcher in her "post-Falklands mood" (referring to Great Britain's successful defense of the Falkland Islands, 9,000 miles away, from being returned to Argentine rule), that Hong Kong could not stay under British administrative rule even after 1997.

13. T. L. Tsim, "Introduction," in T. L. Tsim and Bernard H. K. Luk, *The Other Hong Kong Report* (Hong Kong: The Chinese University Press, 1989), p. xxv.

14. Norman J. Miners, "Constitution and Administration," in Tsim and Luk, p. 2.

15. King, pp. 54–55.

16. Annex I, Nos. 1 and 4 of *The Basic Law of the Hong Kong Special Administrative Region of the People's Republic of China* (hereafter cited as *The Basic Law*). Printed in *Beijing Review*, Vol. 33, No. 18 (April 30–May 6, 1990), supplement. This document was adopted by the 7th National People's Congress on April 4, 1990.

17. For specifics, see Annex II of *The Basic Law* (1990).

18. Article 14, *The Basic Law* (1990).

19. Articles 27, 32, 33, and 36, *The Basic Law* (1990).

20. Tsang, p. 271.

21. Chinese cities on the mainland are overrun by transients. On a daily basis, Shanghai alone has well over a million visitors, largely a transient population of country people. Hong Kong does not feel that it can handle such an increase in its transient population.

22. James Tang and Shiu-hing (Sonny) Lo, University of Hong Kong, interview in Hong Kong (June 2000).

23. Michael E. DeGolyer, director, *1982–2007 Hong Kong Transition Project: Accountability & Article 23* (Hong Kong: Hong Kong Baptist University, December 2002), pp. 43–44. These newspapers include several that are pro-Beijing.

24. Tang and Lo.

25. In 1995, Hong Kong's per capita GDP was U.S.$23,500. Wang Gungwu and Wong Siu-lun, eds., *Hong Kong in the Asian-Pacific Region: Rising to the New Challenge* (Hong Kong: University of Hong Kong, 1997), p. 2.

26. James L. Watson, "McDonald's in Hong Kong: Consumerism, Dietary Change, and the Rise of a Children's Culture," in James L. Watson, ed., *Golden Arches East: McDonald's in East Asia* (Palo Alto, CA: Stanford University Press, 1997), pp. 77–109.

27. Tsim, in Tsim and Luk, p. xx.

28. Howard Gorges (South China Holdings Corporation), interview in Hong Kong (June 2000).

29. Wang and Wong, p. 3.

30. Keith B. Richburg, "Uptight Hong Kong Countdown," *The Washington Post* (July 2, 1996), pp. A1, A12.

31. An average apartment measures 20 feet by 23 feet, or 460 square feet.

32. Tsim, in Tsim and Luk, p. xxi.

33. The purchaser of the property pays tax, develops the property, and then pays a 2 percent tax on every real-estate transaction (renting or selling) that occurs thereafter.

34. Keith B. Richburg, "Chinese Muscle-Flexing Puts Hong Kong Under Pessimistic Pall," *The Washington Post* (December 26, 1996), p. A31.

35. For information on Hong Kong's problems with pollution, including from car emissions, see http://www.epd.gov.hk/epd/english/environmentinhk/air/air_maincontent.html

36. The Hong Kong Transition Project, *Parties, Policies, and Political Reform in Hong Kong* (Hong Kong: Hong Kong Baptist University, 2006), p. 15.

37. The six largest real-estate companies are among the top 20 companies in the Hang Seng Index of stocks. Others are banks and technology companies. The largest is Cheong Kong Holdings, under Li Kashing's control. Companies linked to him and his son accounted for 26 percent of the total market capitalization of the Hang Seng Index! *Asiaweek* (May 26, 2000), pp. 33–36.

38. Philip Bowring, "Meanwhile: China Changes, Not Hong Kong," *International Herald Tribune* (Feb. 12, 2007).

39. In surveys done since 1995, the percentage "satisfied" with the relationship with the mainland" has fluctuated widely. The lowest level of satisfaction (21 percent) was recorded in 1995, the highest (71 percent) in November 2005. The most recent survey, November 2006, recorded satisfaction at 62 percent. See The Hong Kong Transition Project, *Parties, Policies, and Political Reform in Hong Kong* (Hong Kong: Hong Kong Baptist University (2006), p. 51.

40. Al Reyes, journalist *(Asiaweek),* interview in Hong Kong (June 16, 2000).

41. "Is Hong Kong Ripe for a Bit of Central Planning?" *The Economist* (April 12, 1997).

42. Tammy Tam, "Shenzhen Industrial Estate Developed to Boost Military Funds," *The Hong-Kong Standard* (September 5, 1989), p. 1.

43. Shiu-hing Lo, "Hong Kong's Political Influence on South China," *Problems of Post-Communism,* Vol. 46, No. 4 (July/August 1999), pp. 33–41.

44. Tang and Lo; Christine Loh, LegCo legislator and founder of the Citizens' Party, interview in Hong Kong (June 2000). Loh did not run for reelection in September 2000. She is a businessperson-turned-politician. She has been a self-described "armchair critic" of the British and Hong Kong SAR governments, and is generally supportive of the business community.

45. Tang and Lo.

46. John Gordon Davies, "Introduction," *Hong Kong Through the Looking Glass* (Hong Kong: Kelly & Walsh, 1969).

47. Tang and Lo.

48. King, in Domes and Shaw, pp. 45–46.

49. Prybyla, in Domes and Shaw, pp. 196–197; and Lau, in Lin and Robinson, p. 302.

50. Lau, in Lin and Robinson, pp. 293–294, 304–305.

51. Willy Wo-Lap Lam, "New Faces to Star in Hong Kong's New Cabinet," CNN Web site (June 24, 2002).

52. In June 1997, just before the July 1 handover, only 45 percent were "satisfied," and 41 percent were "dissatisfied." DeGolyer, *Hong Kong Transition Project,* 1982–2007, Table 145, p. 103; http://www.hkbu.edu.hk/~hktp.

53. Hong Kong Transition Project, *Listening to the Wisdom of the Masses:Hong Kong People's Attitudes toward Constitutional Reforms* (Hong Kong: Civic Exchange and Hong Kong Transition Project, 2004), Tables 38, 135, 9, pp. 32, 68, 14.

54. Loh, interview.

55. "Silent Treatment: Hong Kong's Chief and Its Legislature Aren't Talking," *Far Eastern Economic Review* (September 17, 1998), p. 50. Hong Kong Transition Project, *Listening to the Wisdom,* Table 25, pp. 22–23.

56. Hong Kong Transition Project, *Listening to the Wisdom* (2004), Table 135, p. 68.

57. Frank Ching, "Beijing Loath to Cast the Fate of Elections in Hong Kong to the Wind," *The Japan Times,* August 2, 2006.

58. The Hong Kong Transition Project, *Parties, Policies, and Political Reform in Hong Kong,* (2006), p. 54.

59. Data based on surveys done in November 2002. The government submitted the proposed changes to Article 23 two months earlier. In almost all categories of rights, and across all occupations, ages, education, and so on, Hong Kong people showed an increase in concern about rights because of the potential amendments to Article 23. Hong Kong Transition Project, *Listening to the Wisdom,* (2004) pp. 36–39, 49–66.

60. Ibid., Table 38, p. 32.

61. King, in Domes and Shaw, pp. 51, 56, 57.

62. In the 1998 elections, 20 members of LegCo were for the first time elected directly; and of these, 13 seats went to the Democratic Party. Of the remaining 40 seats, which were indirectly elected, seven went to the Democratic Party.

63. Mark Magnier, "Hong Kong Warned to Drop Vote Idea," *LA Times,* Nov. 10, 2004.

64. Loh, interview (June 2000).

65. Alvin Y. So, "Hong Kong's Problematic Democratic Transition: Power Dependency or Business Hegemony? *The Journal of Asian Studies,* Vol. 59, No. 2 (May 2000), pp. 375–376.

66. According to the Hong Kong Transition Project 2000 polls, only 30 percent of the people believe that political parties wield significant influence on the government, whereas 74 percent think that Beijing officials do. Michael E. DeGolyer, director, *The Hong Kong Transition Project: 1982–2007* (Hong Kong: Hong Kong Baptist University, 2000), p. 25.

67. James L. Tyson, "Promises, Promises. . . ." *The Christian Science Monitor* (April 20, 1989), p. 2.

68. "Another Place, Another Crime: Mainland Trial of Alleged Gangster Puts 'One Country, Two Systems' to Test," *Far Eastern Economic Review* (November 5, 1998), pp. 26–27.

69. DeGolyer, The Hong Kong Transition (2000) 2000, pp. 3–8. Of students, 54 percent are satisfied, 28 percent neutral.

70. Kevin Murphy, "Troops for Hong Kong: China Puts Best Face on It," *The International Herald Tribune* (January 30, 1996), p. 4.

71. Miu-wah Ma, "China Warns Against Political Ties Abroad," *The Hong Kong Standard* (September 1, 1989), p. 4; and Viola Lee, "China 'Trying to Discourage HK People,' " *South China Morning Post* (August 21, 1989). The article, which originally appeared in an *RMRB* article in July, was elaborated upon in the August edition of *Outlook Weekly,* a mouthpiece of the CCP.

72. The Hong Kong Transition Project, *Parties, Policies, and Political Reform in Hong Kong* (2006), p. 19.

73. "Hong Kong: Now the Hard Part," *Far Eastern Economic Review* (June 11, 1998), p. 13.

74. Michael C. Davis, "Constitutionalism and Hong Kong's Future," *Journal of Contemporary China* (July 1999), Vol. 8, No. 21, pp. 271.

75. *Ibid.,* pp. 269, 273.

76. For extensive surveys on which types of people might want to leave Hong Kong, and for what reasons, see The Hong Kong Transition Project, *Parties, Policies, and Political Reform in Hong Kong* (Hong Kong: Hong Kong Baptist University, 2006.

77. Kai-Yin Lo, "A Big Awakening for Chinese Rivals: Hong Kong and Shanghai Look Afar," *International Herald Tribune,* January 20, 2005.

78. William Overholt, Testimony, "The Hong Kong Legislative Election of Sept 12, 2004: Assessment and Implications" (Testimony presented to the Congressional-Executive Commission on China on Sept. 23, 2004), (Santa Monica: RAND Corporation, 2004), p. 7.

Taiwan

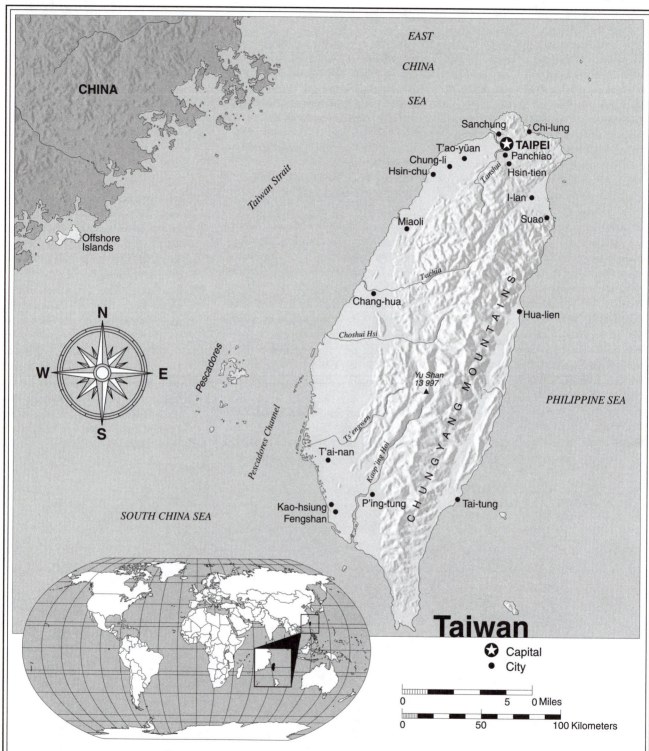

EAST CHINA SEA

CHINA

Taiwan Strait

Offshore Islands

Sanchung • Chi-lung
T'ao-yüan • ☆ **TAIPEI**
Chung-li • Panchiao
Hsin-chu • Hsin-tien
Tanshui
I-lan •
Miaoli • Suao •

Tachia

Chang-hua •

Choshui Hsi

Hua-lien •

Pescadores

N
W E
S

PHILIPPINE SEA

Yu Shan
13 997 ▲

Pescadores Channel

Ts'enzwen

T'ai-nan •

Kaoping Hsi

SOUTH CHINA SEA

Kao-hsiung •
Fengshan

P'ing-tung • Tai-tung •

CHUNGYANG MOUNTAINS

Taiwan

☆ Capital
• City

0 _____ 5 _____ 0 Miles

0 _____ 50 _____ 100 Kilometers

Taiwan was considered the center of the government of the Republic of China (Nationalist China) after 1949. Today according to international law, Taiwan is a province of China. Taiwan consists of the main island, 15 islands in the Offshore Islands group, and 64 islands in the Pescadores Archipelago. While the Pescadores are close to Taiwan, the Offshore Islands are only a few miles off the coast of mainland China.

Taiwan (Hong Kong Special Administrative Region)

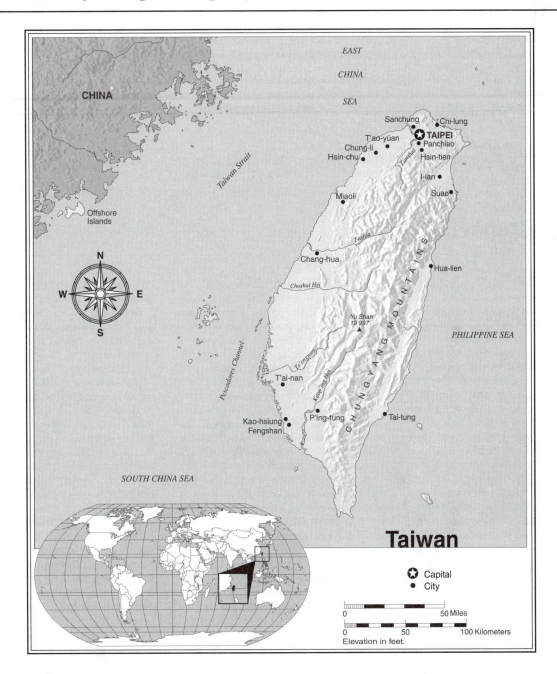

Taiwan

- ✪ Capital
- • City

0 — 50 Miles

0 — 50 — 100 Kilometers

Elevation in feet.

Taiwan Statistics

GEOGRAPHY

Area in Square Miles (Kilometers): 22,320 (36,002) (about the size of Maryland and Delaware combined)
Capital (Population): Taipei (2,596,000)
Environmental Concerns: water and air pollution; contamination of drinking water; radioactive waste; trade in endangered species

Geographical Features: mostly rugged mountains in east; flat to gently rolling plains in west
Climate: tropical; marine

PEOPLE

Population

Total: 23,036,087 (July 2006 est.)
Population Growth Rate: 0.61% (2006 est.)

Life Expectancy

Male: 74.67 years
Female: 80.47 years (2006 est.)

Education

Adult Literacy Rate: 96.1 percent
Suffrage: universal at 20 years of age

ECONOMY

Per Capita Income/GDP: GDP $353.9 billion (2006 est.) GDP per capita: $16,170 (2006 est.) GDP based on ppp (purchasing power parity): $29,000 (2006 est.)
GDP Growth Rate: 4.4% (2006 est.)
Unemployment Rate: 3.9% (2006 est.)

COMMUNICATION

Telephones: Main lines: 13.615 million (2005)
Telephones: Mobile Cellular: 22.17 million (2005)
Internet Users: 13.21 million (2005)
Radio Stations: 551
TV Broadcasting Stations: 29
Airports: 42 (2006)

GOVERNMENT

Type: Democratic Progressive Party, Taiwan Solidarity Union; Kuomintang, People First Party, New Party
Chief of State: President Chen Shui-bian (since 20 May 2000); Vice President Annette LU (LU Hsiu-lien) (since 20 May 2000)
Head of Government: Premier (President of the Executive Yuan) Su Tseng-chang (since 25 January 2006); Vice Premier (Vice President of the Executive Yuan) Tsai Ing-wen (since 25 January 2006)
Cabinet: Executive Yuan—(ministers appointed by president on recommendation of premier)

Elections: president and vice president elected on the same ticket by popular vote for four-year terms (eligible for a second term); election last held 20 March 2004 (next to be held in March 2008); premier appointed by the president; vice premiers appointed by the president on the recommendation of the premier.

SUGGESTED WEB SITES

http://www.taipeitimes.com/news/
http://www.mac.gov.tw/english/index1-e.htm.
http://www.taiwanheadlines.gov.tw/mp.asp
http://www.cia.gov/cia/publications/factbook/geos/tw.html
http://www.gio.gov.tw/
http://www.etaiwannews.com/Taiwan/

Taiwan Report

Taiwan, today a powerful economic center in Asia, was once an obscure island off the coast of China, just 90 miles away. (Taiwan has also been known as Formosa, Free China, the Republic of China, and Nationalist China. Recently, the government in Taiwan abandoned using the name the "Republic of China on Taiwan," in favor of simply "Taiwan.") It was originally inhabited by aborigines from Southeast Asia. By the seventh century A.D., Chinese settlers had begun to arrive. The island was subsequently "discovered" by the Portuguese in 1590, and Dutch as well as Spanish settlers followed. Today, the aborigines' descendants, who have been pushed into the remote mountain areas by the Chinese settlers, number under 400,000, a small fraction of the nearly 23 million people now living in Taiwan. Most of the population is descended from people who emigrated from the Chinese mainland's southern provinces before 1885, when Taiwan officially became a province of China. Although their ancestors originally came from China, they are known as *Taiwanese,* as distinct from the Chinese who fled the mainland from 1947 to 1949. The latter are called *Mainlanders* and represent less than 20 percent of the island's population. After 1949, the Mainlanders dominated Taiwan's political elite; but the "Taiwanization" of the political realm that began after Chiang Kai-shek's death in 1975 and the political liberalization since 1988 have allowed the native Taiwanese to take up their rightful place within the elite.

The Manchus, "barbarians" who came from the north, overthrew the Chinese rulers on the mainland in 1644 and established the Qing Dynasty. In 1683, they conquered Taiwan; but because Taiwan was an island 90 miles distant from the mainland and China's seafaring abilities were limited, the Manchus paid little attention to it and exercised minimal sovereignty over the Taiwanese people. With China's defeat in the Sino–Japanese War (1894–1895), the Qing was forced to cede Taiwan to the Japanese. The Taiwanese people refused to accept Japanese rule, however, and proclaimed Taiwan a republic. As a result, the Japanese had to use military force to gain actual control over Taiwan.

For the next 50 years, Taiwan remained under Japan's colonial administration. Taiwan's economy flourished under Japanese rule. Japan helped to develop Taiwan's agricultural sector, a modern transportation network, and an economic structure favorable to later industrial development. Furthermore, by creating an advanced educational system, the Japanese developed an educated workforce, which proved critical to Taiwan's economic growth.

With Japan's defeat at the end of World War II (in 1945), Taiwan reverted to China's sovereignty. In the meantime, the Chinese had overthrown the Manchu Dynasty (1911) and established a republican form of government on the mainland. Beginning in 1912, China was known as the Republic of China (R.O.C.). Thus, when Japan was defeated in 1945, it was Chiang Kai-shek who, as head of the R.O.C. government, accepted the return of the island province of Taiwan to R.O.C. rule. When some of Chiang Kai-shek's forces were dispatched to shore up control in Taiwan in 1947, tensions quickly arose between them and the native Taiwanese. The ragtag, undisciplined military forces of the KMT (the Kuomintang, or Nationalist Party) met with hatred and contempt from the local people. They had grown accustomed to the orderliness and professionalism of the Japanese occupation forces and were angered by the incompetence and corruption of KMT officials. Demonstrations against rule by Mainlanders occurred in February 1947. Relations were badly scarred when KMT troops killed thousands of Taiwanese opposed to mainland rule. Among those murdered were many members of the island's political and intellectual elite.

Meanwhile, the KMT's focus remained on the mainland, where, under the leadership of General Chiang Kai-shek, it continued to fight the Chinese Communists in a civil war that had ended their fragile truce during World War II. Civil war raged from 1945 to 1949 and diverted the KMT's attention away from Taiwan. As a result, Taiwan continued, as it had under the Qing Dynasty's rule, to function quite independently of Beijing. In 1949, when it became clear that the Chinese Communists would defeat the KMT, General Chiang and some 2 million members of his loyal military, political, and commercial elite fled to Taiwan to establish what they claimed to be the true government of the Republic of China. This declaration reflected Chiang's determination to regain control over the mainland, and his conviction that the more than 600 million people living on the mainland would welcome the return of the KMT to power.

During the McCarthy period of the "red scare" in the 1950s (during which Americans believed to be Communists or Communist sympathizers—"reds"—were persecuted by the U.S. government), the United States supported Chiang Kai-shek. In response to the Chinese Communists' entry into the Korean War in 1950, the United States applied its Cold War policies of support for any Asian government that was anti-Communist, regardless of how dictatorial and ruthless it might be, in order to "isolate and contain" the Chinese Communists. It was within this context that in 1950, the United States com-

MCCARTHYISM: ISOLATING AND CONTAINING COMMUNISM

The McCarthy period in the United States was an era of rabid anti-communism. McCarthyism was based in part on the belief that the United States was responsible for losing China to the Communists in 1949 and that the reason for this loss was the infiltration of the U.S. government by Communists. As a result, Senator Joseph McCarthy *(pictured here)* spearheaded a "witchhunt" to ferret out those who allegedly were selling out American interests to the Communists. McCarthyism took advantage of the national mood in the Cold War era that had begun in 1947. At that time, the world was seen as being divided into two opposing camps: Communists and capitalists.

The major strategy of the Cold War, as outlined by President Harry Truman in 1947, was the "containment" of communism. This strategy was based on the belief that if the United States attempted—as it had done with Adolf Hitler's aggression against Czechoslovakia (the first step toward World War II)—to appease communism, it would spread beyond its borders and threaten other free countries.

The purpose of the Cold War strategy was, then, to contain the Communists within their national boundaries and to isolate them by hindering their participation in the international economic system and in international organizations. Hence, in the case of China, there was an American-led boycott against all Chinese goods, and

(Wisconsin Historical Society (WHS8006))

the United States refused to recognize the People's Republic of China as the legitimate representative of the Chinese people within international organizations.

---

mitted itself to the military defense of Taiwan and the offshore islands in the Taiwan Strait, by ordering the U.S. Seventh Fleet to the Strait and by giving large amounts of military and economic aid to Taiwan. General Chiang Kai-shek continued to lead the government of the Republic of China on Taiwan until his death in 1975, at which time his son, Chiang Ching-kuo, succeeded him.

Two Governments, One China

Taiwan's position in the international community and its relationship to the government in Beijing have been determined by perceptions and values as much as by actions. In 1949, when the R.O.C. government fled to Taiwan, the Chinese Communists renamed China the "People's Republic of China" (P.R.C.), and they proclaimed the R.O.C. government illegitimate. Later, Mao Zedong, the P.R.C.'s preeminent leader until his death in 1976, was to say that adopting the new name instead of keeping the name "Republic of China" was the biggest mistake he ever made, for it laid the groundwork for future claims of "two Chinas." Beijing claimed that the P.R.C. was the legitimate government of all of China, including Taiwan. Beijing's attempt to regain de facto control over Taiwan was, however, forestalled first by the outbreak of the Korean War and thereafter by the presence of the U.S. Seventh Fleet in the Taiwan Strait.

Beijing has always insisted that Taiwan is an "internal" Chinese affair, that international law is therefore irrelevant, and that other countries have no right to interfere. For its

part, until 1995, the government of Taiwan agreed that there was only one China and that Taiwan was a province of China. But by 1995–1996, the political parties had begun debating the possibility of Taiwan declaring itself an independent state.

Although the Chinese Communists' control over the mainland was long evident to the world, the United States managed to keep the R.O.C. in the China seat at the United Nations by insisting that the issue of China's representation in the United Nations was an "important question." This meant that a two-thirds affirmative vote of the UN General Assembly, rather than a simple majority, was required. With support from its allies, the United States was able to block the P.R.C. from winning this two-thirds vote until 1971. Once Secretary of State Henry Kissinger announced his secret trip to Beijing in the summer of 1971 and that President Richard Nixon would be going to China in 1972, the writing was on the wall. Allies of the United States knew that U.S. recognition of Beijing as China's legitimate government would eventually occur, so there would no longer be pressure to block the P.R.C. from membership in the United Nations. They quickly jumped ship and voted for Beijing's representation.

At this critical moment, when the R.O.C.'s right to represent "China" in the United Nations was withdrawn, the R.O.C. could have put forward the claim that Taiwan had the right to be recognized as an independent state, or at least to be granted observer status. Instead, the R.O.C. steadfastly maintained

that there was but one China and that Taiwan was merely a province of China. As a result, today Taiwan has no representation in any international organization under the name of "Republic of China;" and it has representation only as "Chinese Taipei" in organizations in which the P.R.C. is a member—if the P.R.C. allows it any representation at all. With few exceptions, however, Beijing has been adamant about not permitting Taiwan's representation regardless of what it is called.[1]

It is important to understand that at the time Taiwan lost its seat in the United Nations, it was still ruled by the KMT mainlanders, under the name of the Republic of China. The "Taiwanization" of the ruling KMT party-state did not begin until the mid 1970s. As a result, the near 85 percent of the population that was native Taiwanese lacked the right to express their preference for rule by native Taiwanese rather than KMT mainlanders, much less their desire for a declaration of independent statehood. Under martial law, those who had dared to demand independence were imprisoned, forcing the Taiwan independence movement to locate outside of Taiwan. In short, most of the decisions that have shaped Taiwan's international legal standing through treaties and diplomatic relations were made when the KMT mainlanders held political power. Only after the abandonment of martial law in 1987, and the KMT's decision to allow competing political parties, did the Taiwanese start to assert a different view of Taiwan's future. By then, many would agree, it was too late.

CHIANG KAI-SHEK: DETERMINED TO RETAKE THE MAINLAND

Until his dying day, President Chiang Kai-shek, whose memorial hall is *pictured here*, maintained that the military, led by the KMT (Kuomintang, or Nationalist Party), would one day invade the mainland and, with the support of the Chinese people living there, defeat the Communist government. During the years of Chiang's presidency, banner headlines proclaimed daily that the Communist "bandits" would soon be turned out by internal rebellion and that the KMT would return to control on the mainland. In the last years of Chiang Kai-shek's life, when he was generally confined to his residence and incapable of directing the government, his son, Chiang Ching-kuo, always had two editions of the newspaper made that proclaimed such unlikely feats, so that his father would continue to believe these were the primary goals of the KMT government in Taiwan. In fact, a realistic appraisal of the situation had been made long before Chiang's death in 1975, and most of the members of the KMT only pretended to believe that an invasion of the mainland was imminent.

Chiang Ching-kuo, although continuing to strengthen Taiwan's defenses, turned his efforts to building Taiwan into an economic showcase in Asia. Taiwan's remarkable growth and a certain degree of political liberalization were the hallmarks of his leadership. A man of the people, he shunned many of the elitist practices of his father and the KMT ruling elite, and he helped to bring about the Taiwanization of both the KMT party and the government. The "Chiang dynasty" in Taiwan came to an end with Chiang Ching-kuo's death in 1988. It was, in fact, Chiang Ching-kuo who made

certain of this, by barring his own sons from succeeding him and by grooming his own successor, a native Taiwanese.

As the Taiwanese have gained an increasing amount of power in the last 20 years, they have reasserted their Taiwanese identity. This has led to a fading out of the two Chiangs from Taiwan's history books and public images.

INTERNATIONAL RECOGNITION OF THE P.R.C., AT TAIWAN'S EXPENSE

The seating of the P.R.C. in the United Nations in 1971 thus led to the collapse of Taiwan's independent political standing as the R.O.C. in international affairs. Not wanting to anger China, which has a huge and growing economy and significant military power, the state members of international organizations have given in to Beijing's unrelenting pressure to exclude Taiwan. Furthermore, Beijing insists that in bilateral state-to-state relations, any state wishing to maintain diplomatic relations with it must accept China's "principled stand" on Taiwan—notably, that Taiwan is a province of China and that the People's Republic of China is its sole representative.

Commercial ventures, foreign investment in Taiwan, and Taiwan's investments abroad have suffered little as a result of countries' severing their *diplomatic* relations with Taipei. After being forced to close all but a handful of its embassies as one state after another switched recognition from the R.O.C. to the P.R.C., Taipei simply substituted offices that function as if they are embassies. They handle all commercial, cultural, and official business, including the issuance of visas to those traveling to Taiwan. Similarly, the states that severed relations with Taipei have closed down their embassies there and reopened them as business and cultural offices.

The American Institute in Taiwan is a typical example of these efforts to retain ties without formal diplomatic recognition.

Still, Taiwan's government feels the sting of being almost completely shut out of the official world of international affairs. Its increasing frustration and sense of humiliation came to a head in early 1996. Under intense pressure to respond to demands from its people that Taiwan get the international recognition that it deserved for its remarkable accomplishments, Taiwan's president, Lee Teng-hui, engaged in a series of maneuvers to get the international community to confer de facto recognition of its statehood. Not the least of these bold forays was President Lee's offer of U.S. $1 billion to the United Nations in return for a seat for Taiwan—an offer rejected by the United Nations' secretary-general.

Lee's campaign for election in the spring of 1996 proved to be the final straw for Beijing. Lee had as one of his central themes the demand for greater international recognition of Taiwan as an independent state. Beijing responded with a military buildup of some 200,000 troops in Fujian Province across the Taiwan Strait, and the "testing" of missiles in the waters around Taiwan. Under pressure from the United States not to provoke a war with the mainland, and a refusal on the part of the United States to say exactly what it would do if a war occurred, President Lee

toned down his campaign rhetoric. A military conflict was averted. Since 1996, the pattern of Taiwan aggressively discussing independence, followed by China threatening the use of military force and the U.S. warning Taiwan to refrain from rhetoric about independence, has become well-established.

THE OFFSHORE ISLANDS

Crises of serious dimensions erupted between China and the United States in 1954–1955, 1958, 1960, and 1962 over the blockading of supplies to the Taiwan-controlled Offshore Islands in the Taiwan Strait. Thus, the perceived importance of these tiny islands grew out of all proportion to their intrinsic worth. The two major island groups, Quemoy (about two miles from the Chinese mainland) and Matsu (about eight miles from the mainland) are located about 90 miles from Taiwan. As a consequence, Taiwan's control of them made them strategically valuable for pursuing the government's professed goal of retaking the mainland—and valuable for psychologically linking Taiwan to the mainland.

In the first years after their victory on the mainland, the Chinese Communists shelled the Offshore Islands at regular intervals. When there was not a crisis, their shells were filled with pro-Communist propaganda materials, which littered the islands. When the Chinese Communists wanted to test the American commitment to the Nationalists in Taiwan and the Soviet commitment to their own objectives, they shelled the islands heavily and intercepted supplies to the islands. In the end, China always backed down; but in 1958 and 1962, it did so only after going to the brink of war with the United States. By 1979, most states had affirmed Beijing's claim that Taiwan was a province of China through diplomatic recognition of the P.R.C. Beijing's subsequent "peace initiatives" toward Taiwan moved the confrontation over the Offshore Islands to the level of an exchange of gifts by balloons and packages floated across the channel: As a 1986 commentary noted:

> The Nationalists load their balloons and seaborne packages with underwear, children's shoes, soap, toys, blankets, transistor radios and tape recorders, as well as cookies emblazoned with Chiang Ching-kuo's picture and audio tapes of Taiwan's top popular singer, Theresa Teng, a mainland favorite.
>
> The Communists send back beef jerky, tea, herbal medicines, mao-tai and cigarettes, as well as their own varieties of soap and toys.[2]

Because of the dramatic increase in contacts, tourism, trade, and smuggling since the early 1990s, however, such practices have ceased.

The lack of industry and manufacturing on the Offshore Islands led to a steady emigration of their natives to Southeast Asia for better jobs. The civilian population is about 50,000 (mostly farmers) in Quemoy and about 6,000 (mostly fishermen) in Matsu. Until the mid-1990s, the small civilian population in Quemoy was significantly augmented by an estimated 100,000 soldiers. Until recent years, the heavily fortified islands appeared to be somewhat deserted, since the soldiers lived mostly underground: hospitals, kitchens, sleeping quarters—everything was located in tunnels blasted out of granite, including two-lane highways that could accommodate trucks and tanks. Heavily camouflaged anti-artillery aircraft dotted the landscape, and all roads were reinforced to carry tanks.

Taiwan's military administration of Quemoy and Matsu ended in 1992.

Today, Taiwan's armed forces are streamlined, with only some 10,000 troops remaining on the Offshore Islands. Taiwan's Ministry of Defense believes, however, that these troops are better able than the former, larger forces to protect the Offshore Islands, because of improved weapons and technology. Many of the former military installations have become profit-making tourist attractions. Moreover, as of January 2001, the "three mini-links" policy was initiated, with both Quemoy and Matsu allowed to engage in direct trade, transportation, and postal exchange with the mainland. In truth, this change only legalized what had been going on for more than a decade—namely, a roaring trade in smuggled goods between the Offshore Islands and the mainland. Taiwan now seems far more interested in boosting the economy of these islands and increasing links with the mainland than it is concerned with the islands becoming hostages of the mainland. Indeed, Taiwan has moved forward with a plan to secure water for the islands from the mainland, to cope with an increased demand for water it assumes will be generated by growing tourism and business activities.[3] (The first PRC tourists went to Quemoy in Sept. 2004.)

Thus one fiction—that there was no direct trade between Taiwan's Offshore Islands and the mainland—has been abolished. Other fictions wait to be dismantled as Taiwan and the mainland move toward further integration. For example, there is still not supposed to be direct trade between the island of Taiwan and the mainland. All ships are supposed to transship their goods by way of another port, such as Hong Kong or the Ryuku Islands. But now, as soon as ships have left Taiwan, they simply process paperwork with port authorities in the Ryuku Islands by way of fax—that is, without actually ever going there—so they can go directly to the mainland. This eliminates the expensive formalities of transshipments via another port. In short, direct trade has actually been in existence for almost a decade.

CULTURE AND SOCIETY

Taiwan is a bundle of contradictions: "great tradition, small island; conservative state, drastic change; cultural imperialism, committed nationalism; localist sentiment, cosmopolitan sophistication."[4] Over time, Taiwan's culture has been shaped by various cultural elements—Japanese, Chinese, and American culture; localism, nationalism, cosmopolitanism, materialism; and even Chinese mainland culture (in the form of "mainland mania"). At any one time, several of these forces have coexisted and battled for dominance. As Taiwan has become increasingly affected by globalization, the power of the central government to control cultural development has diminished. This has unleashed not just global cultural forces but also local *Taiwanese* culture.[5]

The Taiwanese people were originally immigrants from the Chinese mainland; but their culture, which developed in isolation from that of the mainland, is not the same as the "Chinese" culture of the defeated "Mainlanders" who arrived from 1947 to 1949. Although the Nationalists saw Taiwan largely in terms of security and as a bastion from which to fight against and defeat the Chinese Communist regime on the mainland, "it also cultivated Taiwan as the last outpost of traditional Chinese high culture. Taiwanese folk arts, in particular opera and festivals, did thrive, but as low culture."[6]

The Taiwanese continue to speak their own dialect of Chinese (Holo, or Taiwanese), distinct from the standard Chinese spoken by the Mainlanders, and almost all Taiwanese engage in local folk-religion practices. However, until the mid-1990s, the Mainlander-controlled central government dictated a cultural policy that emphasized Chinese cultural values in education and the mass media. As a result, the distinctions institutionalized in a political system that discriminated against the Taiwanese were culturally reinforced.

The Taiwanese grew increasingly resistant to efforts by the KMT Mainlanders to "Sinify" them—to force them to speak standard Chinese and to adopt the values of the dominant Chinese Mainlander elite. By the 1990s, state-controlled television offered many programs in the Taiwanese dialect. Today, with the presidency in the hands of a Taiwanese, and the vast majority of seats held by native Taiwanese (regardless of party affiliation), they appear to have won the battle to maintain their cultural identity. Taiwanese legislators are refusing to use Chinese during the Legislature's proceedings, so now Mainlanders in the Legislative Yuan must learn Taiwanese. Indeed, the pendulum appears to have swung the other way, not just in language, but in terms of engineering an appropriate psycho-cultural milieu for an independent Taiwan. For example, Chen Shui-bian is going through with plans to "de-Sinicise" Taiwan by ridding it of any symbolic connections with the mainland. Thus, he has changed the names of government agencies and state-owned corporations that have "China" in them (including China Airlines, now called Taiwan Airlines; and China Steel Corporation, renamed Taiwan Steel Corporation). "De-Chiangification," echoing the unofficial but popular "de-Maoification" campaign on the Mainland in the early 1980s, has led to changing the name of the Chiang Kai-shek Airport to Taiwan Taoyuan International Airport, and the gradual disappearance of Chiang memorabilia and removal of icons and statues of Chiang K'ai-shek. Indeed the mayor of Kaoehsiung City personally oversaw the tearing down of a 24 foot high statue at the Chiang K'ai-shek Cultural Center, the second largest in Taiwan and then chopped it into two hundred pieces. Even Sun Yat-sen, the revolutionary who inspired the overthrow of the Manchu Dynasty in 1911, is fading from public memory. Sun Yat-sen established the Republic of China, and Chiang K'ai-shek was his heir to political power on the Mainland, and brought the rule of Chinese mainlanders to Taiwan under the name of Republic of China. In short, the DPP is trying to cut off Taiwanese from their Chinese heritage. Cynics say the real motivation is that the President would like to divert the Taiwanese from all the corruption charges he and other members of the DPP are facing. In any event, such changes are merely a change in window dressing, given the billions of dollars of investment flowing from Taiwan into the mainland. Investments are doing far more to link Taiwan with the mainland than any mere name change can counter. And, ironically, in the convoluted cultural politics of Taiwan-Mainland relations, the Chinese on the Mainland are busily sprucing up sites for tourists that feature where Chiang K'ai-shek was born, slept, or marched through, and are in the market for the statues of that defeated KMT Generalissimo!

Generally speaking, however, Taiwanese and Mainlander culture need not be viewed as two cultures in conflict, for they share many commonalities. Now that Taiwanese have moved into leadership positions in what used to be exclusively Mainlander institutions, and intermarriage between the two groups has become more common, an amalgamation of Taiwanese and traditional Chinese practices is becoming evident throughout the society. As is discussed later in this report, the real source of conflict is the Taiwanese insistence that their culture and political system not be controlled by Chinese from the mainland, whether they be Nationalists or Communists.

On the other hand, rampant materialism as well as the importation of foreign ideas and goods are eroding both Taiwanese *and* Chinese values. For example, there are more than 3,000 7-Eleven outlets in Taiwan, and customers in central Taipei rarely have to walk more than a few blocks to get to the next one. Starbucks coffee houses, often much larger than those in the United States, are usually so packed it is hard to find a seat. Most major American fast-food franchises, such as Kentucky Fried Chicken and McDonald's, are ubiquitous. They provide "snack" food for Taiwan's teenagers and children—before they settle down for "real" (Chinese) food. The Big Mac culture affects more than waistlines, contributing as it does to a more globalized culture in Taiwan. Although the government has at various times engaged in campaigns to reassert traditional values, the point seems lost in its larger message, which asks all to contribute to making Taiwan an Asian showplace. The government's emphasis on hard work and economic prosperity has seemingly undercut its focus on traditional Chinese values of politeness, the sanctity of the family, and the teaching of culturally based ethics (such as filial piety) throughout the school system. Materialism and an individualism that focuses on personal needs and pleasure seeking are slowly undermining collectively oriented values.[7] In many ways, this seems to parallel what is happening on the China Mainland. In the meantime, unlike their mainland cousins, who have had a 40-hour, five-day work week since 1996, the Taiwanese did not relinquish an exhausting six day, 48-hour work week until 2001. While playing a part in Taiwan's economic boom of the past decade, the emphasis on materialism has contributed to a variety of problems, not the least of which are the alienation of youth, juvenile crime, the loosening of family ties, and the general decline of community values. The pervasive spread of illicit sexual activities through such phony fronts as dance halls, bars, saunas, "barber shops," and movies on-video/DVD and music-video/DVD establishments, as well as hotels and brothels, grew so scandalous and detrimental to social morals and social order that at one point the government even suggested cutting off their electricity. They nevertheless continue to thrive. Another major activity that goes virtually uncontrolled is gambling. Part of the problem in clamping down on either illicit sexual activities or gambling (both of which are often combined with drinking in clubs) is that organized crime is involved; and that in exchange for bribes, the police look the other way.[8]

THE ENVIRONMENT

The pursuit of individual material benefit without a concomitant concern for the public good has led to uncontrolled growth and a rapid deterioration in the quality of life, even as the people in Taiwan become richer. As Taiwan struggles to catch up with its own success, the infrastructure has faltered. During the hot, humid summers in its largest city, Taipei, both electricity and water are frequently shut off; roads are clogged from 7:00 A.M. until 10:00 P.M.; and the city's air is so dense with pollution that eyes water, hair falls out, and many people suffer from respiratory illnesses. Inadequate recreational facilities leave urban residents with few options but to join the long parade of cars out of the city on weekends, often only to arrive at badly polluted beaches. Taiwan's citizens have begun forming interest groups to address such problems, and public protests about the government's neglect of quality-of-life issues have grown increasingly frequent. Environmental groups, addressing such issues as wildlife conservation, industrial pollution, and waste disposal, have burgeoned; but environmental campaigns and legislation have difficulty keeping pace with the rapid growth of Taiwan's material culture. According to Taiwan's Environmental Protection Agency, for example, from 1990 to 2000, the amount of garbage produced doubled, but without a doubling of capacity to dispose of it. Part of the problem is that in addition to being a very small island, Taiwan is mostly mountainous, so there is virtually nowhere to construct new landfills. Old landfills are filled to capacity and are leaching toxins into the soil. It is not uncommon for garbage simply to be dumped into a river, or left to rot in gullies or wherever it can be dumped unobserved.[9] Some is taken out to sea, and drifts back to the beaches. But new laws that require citizens to sort their garbage into three categories (regular waste, kitchen leftovers, and recyclable materials), and allow the government to fine citizens who do not sort properly, are intended to bring significant declines in the amount of garbage.[10]

Taiwan must continue to battle against the polluting effects of rapidly increasing wealth; for with almost all Taiwanese families owning a refrigerator, air conditioner, and a car or motorcycle (sometimes several), without a commensurate expansion of the island's roads, carbon emissions continue to grow, and air quality continues to deteriorate. Taipei's recent construction of a subway system has helped traffic flow and kept air pollution from worsening even more quickly. However, political roadblocks have confounded efforts to build a high-speed rail system, and efforts to build Taiwan's fourth nuclear-power plant, a critical project for providing clean electrical power, were plagued by political maneuvering. The Democratic Progressive Party (DPP) government, upon arrival in office, first cancelled the construction plan, and then, under pressure from the opposition and in consideration of the billions of dollars already invested in the plant, it overturned the cancellation. But in a sign of the strength of those environmentalists opposed to the building of the plant, the government made several concessions, including a pledge to a goal of a nuclear-free Taiwan in the future. In many respects, the government has shown good faith, and has supported the development of solar energy technology, in which Taiwan has become a leader.[11]

The public concerns about building nuclear-power plants are understandable. Taiwan sits astride an active earthquake zone, and the potential damage to the environment from a nuclear reactor hit by an earthquake is incalculable. Recent major earthquakes have measured as high as 6.7 on the Richter scale and caused significant damage to the island. The antinuclear movement is increasingly active, especially after an accident at one of Taiwan's nuclear-power plants and the discovery that there are more than 5,000 radioactive buildings in Taiwan, including more than 90 in the city of Taipei.[12] The antinuclear movement in Taiwan exemplifies the problem plaguing environmentalists elsewhere: those opposed to building nuclear plants out of fear of a nuclear accident are pitted against those who favor nuclear plants as a source of clean, carbon-free energy as the way to address the problem of carbon emissions and global warming gases.

The debate goes on while, in the meantime, Taiwan's environment continues to be severely damaged and long-term environmental sustainability is brought into question.

Taiwan is not alone in confronting the financial and political dilemmas caused by the need to create a sustainable environment in the context of a pro-growth economic policy, but its situation is perhaps more urgent because of its high population density and individual wealth. With a population of 1,600 persons per square mile, it is one of the most densely populated places in the world. When this is combined with Taiwan having "the highest density of factories and motor vehicles in the world," as well as being one of the highest per capita energy users in East Asia,[13] it is no surprise that the environment has become a serious mainstream issue. Decisions by tens of thousands of Taiwan's manufacturers to relocate abroad, especially to China, is one way Taiwan is able to "export" its pollution.

RELIGION

A remarkable mixture of religions thrives in Taiwan. The people feel comfortable with placing Buddhist, Taoist, and local deities—and even occasionally a Christian saint—together in their family altars and local temples. Restaurants, motorcycle-repair shops, businesses small and large—almost all maintain altars. The major concern in prayers is for the good health and fortune of the family. The focus is on life in this world, not on one's own afterlife. People pray for prosperity, for luck in the stock market, and even more specifically for the winning lottery number. If the major deity in one temple fails to answer prayers, people will seek out another temple where other deities have brought better luck. Alternatively, they will demote the head deity of a temple and promote others to his or her place. The gods are thought about and organized in much the same way as is the Chinese bureaucracy. In fact, they are often given official clerical titles to indicate their rank within the deified bureaucracy.

Numerous Taiwanese religious festivals honor the more than 100 local city gods and deities. Offerings of food and wine are made to commemorate each one of their birthdays and deaths, and to ensure that the gods answer one's prayers. It is equally important to appease one's deceased relatives. The annual Tomb-Sweeping Festival (*qing ming*) in April is when the whole family cleans up their ancestral grave sites, makes offerings of food, money, and flowers, and burns incense to honor their ancestors.[14]

If they are neglected or offered inadequate amounts of food, money, and respect, they will cause endless problems for their living descendants by coming back to haunt them as ghosts. Even those having trouble

(Courtesy of Suzanne Ogden/sogden02)

Religion is an integral part of everyday life in Taiwan. The inside of this busy Buddhist temple in Taipei shows the local people making offerings of food and burning incense.

with their cars or getting their computer programs to work will drop by the temple to pray to the gods and ancestors—just in case their problems have arisen from giving them inadequate respect. Whole businesses are dedicated to making facsimiles of useful or even luxury items out of paper, such as a car, a house, a computer, an airplane—and these days, paper Viagra as well—which are then brought to a temple and burned, thus sending them to their ancestors for their use.

The seventh month of the lunar calendar is designated "Ghost Month." For the entire month, most do whatever is necessary "to live in harmony with the omnipotent spirits that emerge to roam the world of the living." This includes "preparing doorway altars full of meat, rice, fruit, flowers and beverages as offerings to placate the anxious visitors. Temples [hang] out red lanterns to guide the way for the roving spirits. . . . Ghost money and miniature luxury items made of paper are burned ritualistically for ghosts to utilize along their desperate journey. . . ."[15]

In addition, the people heed a long list of taboos that can have an adverse effect on business during Ghost Month. The real estate industry is particularly hard hit, because people do not dare to move into new houses, out of fear that homeless ghosts might take up permanent residence. Many choose to wait until after Ghost Month to make major purchases, such as cars. Few choose to marry at this time as, according to folk belief, a man might discover that his new bride is actually a ghost! Pregnant women usually choose to undergo Caesarean sections rather than give birth during Ghost Month. And law suits de-

cline because it is believed that ghosts dislike those who bring law suits.[16] (On the mainland of China, the Chinese Communist Party's emphasis on science and the eradication of superstition means that it is far less common there than in Taiwan for people to worry in such a systematic way about propitiating ghosts.)

Finally, there continues to be a preference for seeking medical cures from local temple priests, over either traditional Chinese or modern Western medicine. The concern of local religion is, then, a concern with this life, not with salvation in the afterlife. The attention to deceased ancestors, spirits, and ghosts is quite different from attention to one's own fate in the afterlife.

What is unusual in the case of Taiwanese religious practices is that as the island has become increasingly modern and wealthy, it has not become less religious. Technological modernization has seemingly not brought secularization with it. In fact, aspiring capitalists often build temples in hopes of getting rich. People bring offerings of food; burn incense and bundles of paper money to honor the temple gods; and burn expensive paper reproductions of houses, cars, and whatever other material possessions they think their ancestors might like to have in their ethereal state. They also pay real money to the owner of their preferred temple to make sure that the gods are well taken care of. Since money goes directly to the temple owner, not to a religious organization, the owner of a temple whose constituents prosper will become wealthy. Given the rapid growth in per capita income in Taiwan since 1980, then, temples to local deities have proliferated, as a builder of a temple was almost guaranteed to get rich if its constituents' wealth grew steadily.

Christianity is part of the melange of religions. About 4 percent of the population is Christian; but it is subject to local adaptations, such as setting off firecrackers inside a church during a wedding ceremony to ward off ghosts, and the display of flashing neon lights around the Virgin Mary. The Presbyterian Church in Taiwan, established in Taiwan by missionaries in 1865, was frequently harassed by the KMT because of its activist stance on social and human rights issues and because it generally supported the Taiwan-independence viewpoint.[17] There are more than 1,200 Presbyterian congregations in Taiwan; but in recent years, there has been a 10 percent drop in members—apparently due to the aging church leaders' inflexibility in responding to modernization and ideas from the outside.[18] The Catholic Church in Taiwan is likewise witnessing a decline in membership; and it is also suffering from the aging of its priests, most of whom had emigrated in the 1940s from the China mainland and are now dying off. There is an ever smaller number of young priests in training to replace them.

As for Confucianism, it is more a philosophy than a religion. Confucianism is about self-cultivation, proper relationships among people, ritual, and proper governance. Although Confucianism accepts ancestor worship as legitimate, it has never been concerned directly with gods, ghosts, or the afterlife. In imperial China, if drought brought famine, or if a woman gave birth to a cow, the problem was the lack of morality on the part of the emperor—not the lack of prayer—and required revolt.

When the Nationalists governed Taiwan, they tried to restore Chinese traditional values and to reinstitute the formal study of Confucianism in the schools. Students were apathetic, however, and would usually borrow Confucian texts only long enough to study for college-entrance exams. Unlike the system of getting ahead in imperial China through knowledge of the Confucian classics, students in present-day Taiwan need to excel in science and math. Yet, although efforts to engage students in the formal study of Confucianism have fallen on deaf ears, Confucian values suffuse the culture. The names of streets, restaurants, corporations, and stores are inspired by major Confucian virtues; advertisements appeal to Confucian values of loyalty, friendship, and family to sell everything from toothpaste to computers; children's stories focus on Confucian sages in history; and the vocabulary that the government and party officials use to conceptualize issues is the vocabulary of Confucianism—moral government, proper relationships between officials and the people, loyalty, harmony, and obedience.

EDUCATION

The Japanese are credited with establishing a modern school system in Taiwan in the first part of the twentieth century. After 1949, Taiwan's educational system developed steadily. Today, Taiwan offers nine years of free, compulsory education. Almost all school-age children are enrolled in elementary schools, and most go on to junior high schools. More than 70 percent continue on to senior high school. Illiteracy has been reduced to about 6 percent and is still declining. Night schools that cater to those students anxious to test well and make the cut for the best senior high schools and colleges flourish. Such extra efforts attest to the great desire of Taiwan's students to get ahead through education.

Taiwan has one of the best-educated populations in the world, a major factor in its impressive economic development. Its educational system is, however, criticized for its insistence on uniformity through a unified national curriculum, a lecture format that does not allow for student participation, the grueling high school and university entrance examinations, tracking, rote memorization, heavy homework assignments, and humiliating treatment of students by teachers. Its critics say that the system inhibits creativity.[19] There is also a gender bias in education, which results in women majoring in the humanities and social sciences, while men choose science and math majors. Reforms in recent years have tried to modify some of these practices; and Taiwan's burgeoning information-technology and high-tech sectors have added to pressures to train more women in science and technology.

The number of colleges and universities has more than doubled since martial law was lifted. But the 120 colleges and universities now in existence cannot meet the demand for spaces for all qualified students. As a result, many students go abroad for study. From 1950 to 1978, only 12 percent of some 50,000 students who studied abroad returned, a reflection of both the lack of opportunity in Taiwan and the oppressive nature of government in that period. Beginning in the late 1980s, as Taiwan grew more prosperous and the political system more open, this outward flood of human talent, or "brain drain," was stemmed. Nevertheless, the system of higher education has been unable to keep up with the demand for high-tech workers. This has led to a loosening of restrictions on importing high-tech workers from mainland China.[20]

As the economies of mainland China and Taiwan become more intertwined, the options that Taiwanese have in the educational arena are increasing. A growing number of Taiwan's high school graduates choose to go to a university on the mainland. This is in no small part because the vast majority of Taiwan's businesspeople are investing their money in the mainland economy. However, in spite of the fact that many students from Taiwan attend China's leading universities, which produce outstanding graduates whose degrees are readily accepted in the West, Taiwanese students find that their degrees are not properly honored once they return to Taiwan. Indeed, in a poll conducted in Taiwan in 2000, 40.5 percent of respondents believed that academic credentials earned by Taiwan's students in the mainland should have a stricter standard applied than to students graduating in Taiwan; and 6.3 percent believed that they should not be recognized at all.[21] Students have to take a set of exams upon returning from the mainland to validate the legitimacy of their degrees. It would appear, however, that the real reason is political—namely, to challenge the quality of any institutions under the control of the Chinese Communist rulers.

HEALTH CARE AND SOCIAL SECURITY

Although Taiwan's citizens have received excellent health care for many years, the health-care system is now facing a crisis. Health care has been a major political issue for candidates running for office. But slower economic growth has produced lower governmental revenues for health care. The elderly, moreover, tend to visit their doctors on a weekly, if not a daily, schedule, not only because their visits are virtually free, but also because that's where all the other elderly people are! Lonely, with time on their hands and an obsession with longevity, the elderly often hang out at hospitals and health clinics. This contributes to the financial crisis of the "medicare" system, for doctors, who are paid by the number of patients they see, are more than happy to see dozens of patients each hour. Indeed, citizens complain that their visits usually last less than a minute!

Still, Taiwan's health care functions admirably. The one issue that continues to bedevil it is that the PRC continues to block its application for even a non-member "observer" status in the World Health Organization (WHO). It does so on the grounds that Taiwan is simply a province of China, not a sovereign state. The 2003 SARS (severe acute respiratory syndrome) epidemic in Hong Kong, China, and Southeast Asian countries also broke out in Taiwan. More recently, bird flu has shown up in Taiwan. But because of the lack of either membership or observer status in WHO, Taiwan's ability to receive or contribute important health data was minimal. This situation potentially jeopardizes not only health care in Taiwan, but health care in the entire world, especially during epidemics.

The Labor Standards Law requires that Taiwanese enterprises provide a pension plan for their employees; but under the old labor standards regulations, 90 percent of employees did not qualify for a pension because they had not worked in the same company for a minimum of 25 years. In 2005, the Labor Pension Retirement Act came into effect, with the result that everyone is now covered. As a result, Taiwan's citizens are not so reliant on their families for support in old age.

WOMEN

The societal position of women in Taiwan reflects an important ingredient of Confucianism. Traditionally, Chinese women "were expected to obey their fathers before marriage, their husbands after, and their sons when widowed. Furthermore, women were expected to cultivate the "Four Virtues": morality, skills in handicrafts, feminine appearance, and appropriate language."[22] In Taiwan, as elsewhere throughout the world, women have received lower wages than men and have rarely made it into the top ranks of government and business—this in spite of the fact that it was women who, from their homes, managed the tens of thousands of small businesses and industries that fueled Taiwan's economic boom.

In the workplace outside the home, women have been treated differently than men. For example, women are not allowed to serve in the armed forces; but until the 1990s, "all female civil servants, regardless of rank, [were] expected to spend half a day each month making pants for soldiers, or to pay a substitute to do this."[23] Women, who make up 40 percent of Taiwan's civil service, find themselves "walking on glue" when they try to move from the lower ranks to the middle and senior ranks of the civil service. By the beginning of 2000, only 12 percent of the total senior level civil service, and less than a third of intermediate ranks, were made up of women. Those figures had not changed at all by the end of 2004.[24] There have, however, been greater opportunities for women in the last decade. Women are more visible in the media and politics than before. In 2000, for the first time, a woman was elected as vice-president (and was re-elected in 2004); but since 1949, not one of the five branches of government has been headed by a woman. On the other hand, as of 2004, there were nine women in the Cabinet, seven with a ministerial post, and two without portfolio, as well as the first female vice premier. About 18 percent of the legislators in the Legislative Yuan were women; and an even higher percentage of women were city or county councilors. This training ground for leaders is, then, laying the basis for the advancement of women as leaders in the future.

Because women may now receive the same education as men, and because employment in the civil service is now based on an examination system, women's social, political, and economic mobility has increased.[25] Better education of women has been both the cause and the result of greater advocacy by Taiwan's feminists of equal rights for women. It has also eroded the typical marriage pattern, in which a man is expected to marry a woman with an education inferior to his own.

THE ECONOMY

The rapid growth of Taiwan's economy and foreign trade has enriched Taiwan's population. A newly industrialized economy (NIE), Taiwan long ago shed its "Third World," underdeveloped image. Today, the World Bank classifies it as a "high-income" economy. With a gross domestic product per capita income that rose from U.S.$100 in 1951 to U.S.$16,170 (equivalent in purchasing price parity dollars to $29,000) in 2006, and a highly developed industrial infrastructure and service industry, Taiwan sits within the ranks of some of the most developed economies in the world. As with the leading industrial nations, however, the increasing labor costs for manufacturing and industry have contributed to a steady decline in the size of those sectors as companies relocate to countries with cheaper raw materials and lower wages. Taiwan's economic growth rate from 1953 to 1997 had averaged a phenomenal 8-percent-plus annually; but it has slowed down since the Asian financial crisis that began in 1997. In recent years, a growing percentage of Taiwan's economic growth is due to production on the mainland, where most of Taiwan's manufacturing base has moved.

The government elite initiated most of the reforms critical to the growth of Taiwan's economy, including land redistribution, currency controls, central banking, and the establishment of government corporations. Taiwan's strong growth and high per capita income does not, however, bring with them a lifestyle comparable to that in the most developed Western states. The government has had limited success in addressing many of the problems arising from its breathtakingly fast modernization. In spite of—and in some cases because of—Taiwan's astounding economic growth, the quality of life has deteriorated greatly. Taiwan's cities are crowded and badly polluted, and housing is too expensive for most urbanites to afford more than a small apartment. The overall infrastructure is inadequate to handle traffic, parking, electricity, and other services expected in a more economically advanced society.

Only 3 percent of Taipei's sewage is treated, and diseases related to pollution have skyrocketed.[26] Massive air and water pollution; an inadequate urban infrastructure for housing, transportation, electricity, and water; and the rapid acquisition of carbon-emitting consumer goods, especially air conditioners, motorcycles, and automobiles, have made the environment unbearable and transportation a nightmare. Complaints of oily rain, ignitable tap water, stunted crops due to polluted air and land, and increased cancer rates abound. "Garbage wars" over the "not-in-my-back-yard" issue of sanitary landfill placement have led to huge quantities of uncollected garbage.[27] Numerous public-interest groups have emerged to pressure the government to take action. The government has tried to be responsive, but bitterly divisive politics and rampant corruption have complicated finding solutions to these woes, as everyone tries to get ahead in a now relatively open economy.

Taiwan's economic success thus far may also be attributed to a relatively open market economy in which businesspeople have developed international markets for their products and promoted an export-led economy. Taiwan's highly productive workers have tended to lack class consciousness, because they progress so rapidly from being members of the working-class "proletariat" to becoming capitalists and entrepreneurs. Even factory workers often become involved in small businesses.[28]

Now that Taiwan is privatizing those same government corporations that used to have complete control over many strategic materials as well as such sectors as transportation and telecommunications, workers are resisting the loss of their "iron rice bowl" of permanent employment in state enterprises and the civil service. Much like mainland China, the government is concerned that social instability may result if workers, instead of accepting the international trend toward privatization, resists it through street protests.[29] As an increasing number of industrial workers in Taiwan move into white-collar jobs and are replaced by relatively poorly organized immigrant laborers, who are often sent home when the jobs disappear, this problem seems to have been temporarily sidelined.

Sometimes called "Silicon Island," Taiwan has some 1.2 million small and medium-size enterprises, and only a handful of megagiants. Most of these smaller enterprises are not internationally recognized names, but they provide the heart and even the backbone of technological products worldwide. They make components, or entire products (such as computer hardware), according to specifications set by other, often well-known, large firms, whose names go on the final product. Furthermore, because Taiwan's firms tend to be small and flexible, they can respond quickly to changes in technology. This is particularly true in the computer industry. Thanks to the many students who have gone to the United States to study and then stayed to work in the computer industry's Silicon Valley, there are strong ties with Taiwan's entrepreneurs.[30] Taiwan's development of the information-technology sector has benefited from governmental incentives and from Taiwan's educated labor force. In this sector, low-wage labor is not yet an issue, and Taiwan has become the leading Asian center for information technology (IT) and software.

A stable political environment facilitated Taiwan's rapid growth. So did Taiwan's protected market, which brought protests over Taiwan's unfair trade policies from those suffering from an imbalance in their trade with Taiwan. Since joining the World Trade Organization (WTO) in 2002, Taiwan has shed most of the regulations that have protected its industries from international trade competition and has come into compliance with international intellectual property rights legislation.

After the 2000 elections, moreover, the "industrial policy" model, whereby the government, banks, and businesses essentially colluded for the purpose of economic growth, no longer worked because the new government under the Democratic Progressive Party (DPP) was unable to get the banks to give loans to declining industries to keep them alive. Furthermore, Taiwan's entry into the WTO required adjustments to the agricultural sector because Taiwan was no longer able to use import regulations to protect itself from a flood of agricultural goods from mainland China, where virtually every agricultural product is produced more cheaply. In particular, rice and poultry imports soared. But at the same time, agricultural exports increased, as Taiwan products, such as mango, tea and litchi, as well as other fruits, flowers and seeds, were promoted abroad.[31]

For the economy as a whole, there has been a dramatic turnaround since the 1997–2000 Asian financial crisis. By 2004, GDP growth has moved from negative numbers to a positive 3.2 percent. Taiwan came out of its economic downturn largely by increasing commercial links with China, where Taiwanese businesspeople can get better returns on their investment. There are more than 50,000 Taiwanese factories that have created more than 3 million jobs already in China. A 10 percent of China's IT products that are exported are made in Taiwanese factories on the mainland, and Taiwanese firms control a quarter of China's export licenses. Some 10,000 Taiwanese businesspeople travel to the mainland each day. In 2001, Taiwan's government lifted the limits on investment in China by companies and enterprises from U.S. $5 million to U.S. $50 million; but the likely KMT candidate for the presidency in 2008, Ma Ying-jeou, has said that if he wins, he will remove the remaining ceiling of a maximum of 40 percent of the net worth of a company.[32] In short, Taiwan's growth is coming from its investments in China.

Indeed, most of Taiwan's businesspeople are more concerned about the survival of their businesses than about national security vis-à-vis the mainland. As a result, they have been sending delegations to China (without authorization from the government) to reassure its leaders that they will not let Taiwan declare independence and will continue to develop economic ties with the mainland. They believe (as does Beijing) that once the two economies are fully integrated, a declaration of independence of Taiwan will be highly unlikely.[33]

By 2007, Taiwanese had invested well over U.S. $150 billion in China. Because of restrictions on trade with the mainland, however, money must first move to Hong Kong or elsewhere, and only then to China. These sorts of maneuvers complicate business investments and irritate Taiwan's business community. Critics contend that President Chen Shui-bian has been slow in fulfilling his promises to liberalize current restrictions on travel to and from mainland China, which still require that they travel first, like their money, to a country other than China. As part of his 2004 election campaign, President Chen promised to open direct air passenger and cargo links, to ease restrictions on travel to and from the mainland, and to liberalize regulations prohibiting Taiwanese from raising capital for their China businesses on the Taiwan Stock Exchange.[34] But, as of 2007, little progress had been made in these matters. Many in Taiwan's business community are, in fact, distressed that Chen is not doing more to protect and promote business ties with the mainland (which may explain why the business community generally supported the KMT in the 2004 elections).

Taiwanese enterprises run what amounts to a parallel economy on the mainland that is completely entangled with China's own. In fact, as of 2003, China had become Taiwan's number one trade partner. By 2006, over 22 percent of Taiwan's export trade was with China. Taiwan has a substantial trade surplus with the mainland. Much of China's trade surplus with the United States is, in fact, from Taiwan's enterprises doing business in China. It is estimated that up to one-third of exported consumer goods labeled 'Made in China' are actually made in firms owned by Taiwan's businesspeople in China. "Analysts attribute more than 70 percent of the growth in America's trade deficit with China to the exports of Taiwanese firms."[35] The result is that, as of the end of 2006, Taiwan held more than $280.6 billion in its central reserve bank—the third-largest holding of reserve currency and gold in the world. U.S. pressure on Taiwan to purchase $18 billion of military equipment originally offered for sale by the Bush Administration in 2001 in order to draw down some of these reserves has become an ongoing source of bitter contention between Taipei and Washington.[36] The stalemate has continued because the "pan-blue alliance," led by the KMT, continues to control the legislature, and views any such purchases as a waste of resources and of little real use to Taiwan's defense. Indeed, they argue that it will simply lead to an acceleration of the arms race with China, and could even lead to war.

Finally, although Taipei insists that the government will not establish direct trade links with China until Beijing meets certain conditions, it has passed legislation so that free-trade zones can be established near Taiwan's international airports and harbors. The purpose of these tax-free areas is to encourage foreign businesspeople, including Chinese from the Mainland, to establish companies in Taiwan for the purpose of trade, processing, and manufacturing.[37] Clearly Taipei is trying both to stem the outward flow of Taiwan's investment moneys and to lure more investors to Taiwan by making its business conditions competitive with those of the mainland, Hong Kong, and Asian countries with free trade zones.

Agriculture and Natural Resources

After arriving in Taiwan, the KMT government carried out a sweeping land-reform program: The government bought out the landlords and sold the land to their tenant farmers. The result was equalization of land distribution, an important step in promoting income equalization among the farmers of Taiwan. Today, farmers are so productive that Taiwan is almost self-sufficient in agriculture—an impressive performance for a small island where only 25 percent of the land is arable.

The land-reform program was premised upon one of Sun Yat-sen's famous Three Principles, the "people's livelihood." One of the corollaries of this principle was that any profits from the increase in land value attributable to factors not related to the real value of farmland—such as through urbanization, which makes nearby agricultural land more valuable—would be turned over to the government when the land was sold. As a result, although the price of land has skyrocketed around Taiwan's major cities, and although many farmers are being squeezed by low prices for their produce, they would get virtually none of the increased value for their land if they sold it to developers. Many farmers have thus felt trapped in agriculture. In the meantime, the membership of both China and Taiwan in the World Trade Organization means that cheaper mainland produce flows of the world. With Taiwan's important role in the international economy, it is virtually impossible for its trade, commercial, and financial partners to ignore it. This saves Taiwan from even greater international diplomatic isolation than it already faces in light of its current "non-state" status. In the meantime, its economy is becoming increasingly integrated with that of the Chinese mainland, to the mutual benefit of both economies.

Taiwan as a Model of Economic Development

Taiwan is often cited as a model for other developing countries seeking to lift themselves out of poverty. They could learn some useful lessons from certain aspects of Taiwan's experience, such as the encouragement of private investment and labor productivity, an emphasis on basic health care and welfare needs, and policies to limit gross extremes of inequality. But Taiwan's special advantages during its development have made it hard to emulate. These advantages include its small size, the benefits of improvements to the island's economic infrastructure and educational system made under the Japanese occupation, massive American financial and technical assistance, and a highly favorable international economic environment during Taiwan's early stages of growth.

What has made Taiwan extraordinary among the rapidly developing economies of the world is the government's ability—and commitment—to achieve and maintain a relatively high level of income equality. Although there are homeless people in Taiwan, their numbers are small. Government programs to help the disabled and an economy with moderate unemployment (3.9 percent in 2006) certainly help, as does a tight-knit family system that supports family members in difficult times. The government's commitment to Sun Yat-sen's principle of the "people's livelihood," or what in the West might be called a "welfare state," is still an important consideration in policy formation.

Like China's two stock markets, the regulatory regime of Taiwan's Stock Exchange Corporation (TSEC) is unreliable. Trading in Taiwan's stock market is highly speculative, and foreigners find it difficult to buy shares. The growth of Taiwan's stock market—a market often floating on the thin air of gossip and rumor—has created (and destroyed) substantial wealth almost overnight. Nevertheless, Taiwan's economic wealth remains fairly evenly distributed, contributing to a strongly cohesive social system.

At the same time, Taiwan's rapid economic growth rate, combined with a relatively low birth rate, has led businesses to import foreign laborers to do unskilled jobs that Taiwan's better-paid residents refuse to do. These foreign workers, largely from Thailand, the

(Courtesy of Suzanne Ogden/sogden03)

Motorcycles are parked on public sidewalks due to the lack of adequate parking facilities in Taipei. The 7-Eleven logo is ubiquitous in Taipei, one indication that Taiwan's economy is tied into the "global village."

quite freely into Taiwan. While this has undercut the profits of farmers in such areas as rice, their profits in fruits and other products have benefited by the lifting of trade barriers.

Natural resources, including land, are quite limited in Taiwan. Taiwan's rapid industrialization and urbanization have put a strain on what few resources exist. Taiwan's energy resources, such as coal, gas, and oil, are particularly limited. The result is that the government has had to invest in the building of four nuclear-power plants to provide sufficient energy to fuel Taiwan's rapidly modernizing society and economy. Taiwan has been able to postpone its energy and re-

source crisis by investing in the development of mainland China's vast natural resources. Taiwan's businesspeople have also moved their industries to other countries where resources, energy, land, and labor are cheaper. They now control a vast network of manufacturing and distribution facilities throughout the world.[38] Taiwan's economy has, in short, continued to grow while at the same time avoiding the problem of resource and energy scarcity through extensive participation in the global economy.

Internationalization of its economy is also part of Taiwan's strategy to thwart China's efforts to cut off its relationships with the rest

SUN YAT-SEN: THE FATHER OF THE CHINESE REVOLUTION

Sun Yat-sen (1866–1925) was a charismatic Chinese nationalist who, in the declining years of the Manchu Dynasty, played upon Chinese nationalist hostility both to foreign colonial powers and to the Manchu rulers themselves.

Sun (pictured at the right) drew his inspiration from a variety of sources, usually Western, and combined them to provide an appealing program for the Chinese. This program was called the Three People's Principles, which translates the phrase in the Gettysburg Address "of the people, by the people, and for the people" into "nationalism," "democracy," and the "people's livelihood."

This last principle, the "people's livelihood," is the source of dispute between the Chinese Communists and the Chinese Nationalists, both of whom claim Sun Yat-sen as their own. The Chinese Communists believe that the term means socialism, while the Nationalists in Taiwan prefer to interpret it to mean the people's welfare in a broader sense.

Sun Yat-sen is, in any event, considered by all Chinese to be the father of the Chinese Revolution of 1911, which overthrew the enfeebled Manchus. He thereupon declared China to be a republic and named himself president. However, he had to relinquish control immediately to the warlord Yuan Shih-K'ai, who was the only person in China powerful enough to maintain control over all other contending military warlords in China.

When Sun died in 1925, Chiang Kai-shek assumed the mantle of leadership of the Kuomintang, the Chinese Nationalist Party. After the defeat of the KMT in 1949, Sun's widow chose to remain in the People's Republic of China and held high honorary positions until her death in 1982.

(Library of Congress Prints and Photographs Division/LC-USZ62-5972)

Philippines, and Indonesia, work at wages too low, with hours too long and conditions too dangerous for Taiwan's own citizens. By the end of 2001, there were more than 304,000 legal foreign workers in Taiwan, and a growing number of illegal foreign workers.

Today, one in five marriages is to someone from outside Taiwan, primarily from China or Southeast Asian countries; and one in seven children is born in these marriages. Thus, the population of Taiwan, which used to be divided primarily along Mainlander-Taiwanese lines, has a fairly substantial immigrant compotent. Immigrants are still often looked down upon because they are seen as marrying Taiwanese to get ahead economically, and because they tend to come from relatively impoverished backgrounds. Some marry Taiwanese men who are from lower economic and social classes and may even be unemployed, or too sick or old to work). But these immigrant spouses, over 90 percent of whom are women, are essential to a society suffering from the same problems as Mainland China (from which so many of the brides come): a surplus of men of marriageable age, and a rapidly graying population because of a low birthrate.[39]

THE POLITICAL SYSTEM

From 1949 to 1988, the KMT justified the unusual nature of Taiwan's political system with three extraordinary propositions. First, the government of the Republic of China, formerly located on the mainland of China, was merely relocated temporarily on China's island province of Taiwan. Second, the KMT was the legitimate government not just for Taiwan but also for the hundreds of millions of people living on the Chinese mainland under the control of the Chinese Communist Party.[40] Third, the people living under the control of the Communist "bandits" would rush to support the KMT if it invaded the mainland to overthrow the Chinese Communist Party regime. Taiwan's political and legal institutions flowed from these three unrealistic propositions, which reflected hopes, not reality. Underlying all of them was the KMT's acceptance, in common with the Chinese Communist Party, that there was only one China and that Taiwan was a province of that one China. Indeed, until the early 1990s, it was a *crime* in Taiwan to advocate independence.

The Constitution

In 1946, while the KMT was still the ruling party on the mainland, it promulgated a "Constitution for the Republic of China." This Constitution took as its foundation the same political philosophy as the newly founded Republic of China adopted in 1911 when it overthrew China's Manchu rulers on the mainland: Sun Yat-sen's "Three People's Principles" ("nationalism," "democracy," and the "people's livelihood"). Democracy was, however, to be instituted only after an initial period of "party tutelage." During this period, the KMT would exercise virtually dictatorial control while in theory preparing China's population for democratic political participation.

The Constitution provided for the election of a National Assembly (a sort of "electoral college"); a Legislative Yuan ("branch") to pass new laws, decide on budgetary matters, declare war, and conclude treaties; a Judicial Yuan to interpret the Constitution and all other laws and to settle lawsuits; an Executive Yuan to run the economy and manage the country generally; a Control Yuan, the highest supervisory organ, to supervise officials through its powers of censure, impeachment, and auditing; and an Examination Yuan (a sort of personnel office) to conduct civil-service examinations. The Examination Yuan and Control Yuan were holdovers from Chinese imperial traditions dating back thousands of years.

Because this Constitution went into effect in 1947 while the KMT still held power on the mainland, it was meant to be applicable to all of China, including Taiwan. The KMT government called nationwide elections to select delegates for the National Assembly. Then, in 1948, it held elections for representatives to the Legislative Yuan and indirect elections for members of the Control Yuan. Later in 1948, as the Civil War between Communists and Nationalists on the mainland raged on, the KMT government amended the Constitution to allow for the declaration of martial law and a suspension of regular elections; for by that time, the Communists were taking control of vast geographical areas of China. Soon afterward, the Nationalist government under Chiang Kai-shek fled to Taiwan. With emergency powers in hand, it was able to suspend elections and all other democratic rights afforded by the Constitution.

By October 1949, the Communists had taken control of the Chinese mainland. As a result, the KMT, living in what it thought was only temporary exile in Taiwan, could not hold truly "national" elections for the National Assembly or for the Legislative and Control Yuans as mandated by the 1946 Constitution. But to foster its claim to be the legitimate government of all of China, the KMT retained the 1946 Constitution and governmental structure, as if the KMT alone could indeed represent all of China. With "national" elections suspended, those individuals elected in 1947 from all of China's mainland provinces (534 out of a total 760 elected had fled with General Chiang to Taiwan) continued to hold their seats in the National Assembly, the Legislative Yuan, and the Control Yuan—usually until death—without standing for re-election. Thus began some 40 years of a charade in which the "National" Assembly and Legislative Yuan in Taiwan pretended to represent all of China. In turn, the government of the island of Taiwan pretended to be a mere provincial government under the "national" government run by the KMT. At no time did the KMT government suggest that it would like Taiwan to declare independence as a state.

Although the commitment to retaking the China mainland was quietly abandoned by the KMT government even before Chiang Kai-shek's death, the 1946 Constitution and governmental structure remained in force. This was in spite of the fact that over those many years, numerous members of the three elected bodies died. Special elections were held just to fill their vacant seats. The continuation of this atavistic system raised serious questions about the government's legitimacy. The Taiwanese, who comprised more than 80 percent of the population but were not allowed to run for election to the Legislative Yuan or National Assembly, accused the KMT Mainlanders of keeping a stranglehold on the political system and pressured them for greater representation. Because the holdovers from the pre-1949 period were of advanced age and often too feeble to attend meetings of the Legislative Yuan (and some of them no longer even lived in Taiwan), it was virtually impossible to muster a quorum. Thus, in 1982, the KMT was forced to "reinterpret" parliamentary rules in order to allow the Legislative Yuan to get on with its work.

Chiang Ching-kuo, Chiang Kai-shek's son and successor, decided to concede reality and began bringing Taiwanese into the KMT. By the time a Taiwanese, Lee Teng-hui, succeeded Chiang Ching-kuo in 1988 as the new Nationalist Party leader and president of the "Republic of China," 70 percent of the party's membership was Taiwanese. Pressures therefore built for party and governmental reforms that would diminish the power of the old KMT Mainlanders. In July 1988, behind the scenes at the 13th Nationalist Party Congress, the leadership requested the "voluntary" resignation of the remaining pre-1949 holdovers. Allegedly as much as U.S. $1 million was offered to certain hangers-on if they would resign, but few accepted. Finally, the Supreme Court forced all those Chinese mainland legislators who had gained their seats in the 1948 elections to resign by the end of 1991.

Under the Constitution, the Legislative, Judicial, Control, and Examination branches hold certain specific powers. Theoretically, this should result in a separation of powers, preventing any one person or institution from the arbitrary abuse of power. In fact, however, none of these branches of government exercised much, if any, power independent of the KMT or the president who was chosen by the KMT until after the first completely democratic legislative elections of December 1992. In short, the KMT and the government were merged, in much the same way as the CCP was merged with the government on the mainland. Indeed, property and state enterprises owned by the government were claimed by the KMT as their own property when they lost control of the presidency in 2000 and the KMT was no longer the majority party.

Thanks to changes made by President Lee, however, Taiwan now has a far greater separation of powers as well as a two-headed government: The president is primarily responsible for Taiwan's security, and the prime minister (premier) is responsible for the economy, local government, and other broad policy matters. But problems remain because the president may appoint the prime minister without approval by the Legislature—yet the Legislature has the power to cast a no confidence vote and require new elections if it finds the government's actions unacceptable.

A final consequence of the three propositions upon which political institutions in Taiwan were created was that, after the KMT arrived in 1947, Taiwan maintained two levels of government. One was the so-called national government of the "Republic of China," which ruled Taiwan as just one province of all of China. The other was the actual provincial government of Taiwan, which essentially duplicated the functions of the "national" government, and reported to the "national" government, which for so many years pretended to represent all of China. In this provincial-level government, however, native Taiwanese always had considerable control over the actual functioning of the province of Taiwan in all matters not directly related to the Republic of China's relationship with Beijing. Taiwan's provincial government thus became the training ground for native Taiwanese to ascend the political ladder once the KMT reformed the political system. This expensive and unnecessary redundancy of governments has at long last been eradicated.

Martial Law

The imposition of martial law in Taiwan from 1948 to 1987 is critical to understanding the dynamics of Taiwan's politics. Concerned with the security of Taiwan against subversion, or an invasion by the Chinese Communists, the KMT government had imposed martial law on Taiwan. This allowed the government to suspend civil liberties and limit political activity, such as organizing political parties or mass demonstrations. Thus it was a convenient weapon for the KMT Mainlanders to control potential Taiwanese resistance and to quash any efforts to organize a "Taiwan independence" movement. Police powers were widely abused, press freedoms were sharply restricted, and dissidents were jailed. As a result, the Taiwan Independence Movement was forced to organize abroad, mostly in Japan and the United States. Taiwan was run as a one-party dictatorship supported by the secret police.

Non-KMT candidates were eventually permitted to run for office under the informal banner of *tangwai* (literally, "outside the party"); but they could not advocate independence for Taiwan; and they had to run as individuals, not as members of opposition political parties, which were forbidden until 1989. The combination of international pressures for democratization, the growing confidence of the KMT, a more stable situation on the China mainland, and diminished threats from Beijing led the KMT to lift martial law in July 1987. Thus ended the state of "Emergency" under which almost any governmental use of coercion against Taiwan's citizens had been justified.

Civil Rights

Until the late 1980s, the rights of citizens in Taiwan did not receive much more protection than they did on the Chinese mainland. The R.O.C. Constitution has a "bill of rights," but most of these civil rights never really existed until martial law was lifted in 1987. Civil rights were repeatedly suspended when their invocation by the citizenry challenged KMT power or policies; and opposition political parties were not allowed to organize. Because the "Emergency" regulations provided the rationale for the restriction of civil liberties, the KMT used military courts (which do not accord basic protection of defendants' civil rights) to try what were actually civil cases,[41] arrested political dissidents, and used police repression, such as in the brutal confrontation during the 1980 Kaohsiung Incident.[42]

Today, it is highly unlikely that individuals would be imprisoned for political crimes. Since Chen Shui-bian won the presidency in 2000 and the Democratic Progressive Party (DPP) became the largest party in 2001, there has been a far greater focus on civil and human rights. This reflects the sensitivity of the DPP to rights issues, since a number of its members were themselves deprived of civil and human rights because of their advocacy of Taiwan independence.

The 2002 survey by the Taipei-based Chinese Association for Human Rights, as well as the 2004 U.S. Department of State report on Taiwan's human rights indicated that the protection of judicial rights had improved somewhat. There was some improvement in the interrogation of suspects, but protection of suspects in police custody remained inadequate. Some cases of physical abuse of persons in police custody were reported, usually when lawyers were not present for the interrogation, or when the interrogation was not audio- and videotaped, as required by law. In 2003, a law was enacted to limit police powers. Search warrants and police raids of businesses suspected of illegal activities now require stricter proof of "probable cause." Furthermore, if police have failed to follow due process and therefore infringed on a suspect's rights, the suspect can immediately file an administrative appeal. In recent years, no reports of politically motivated disappearances or deaths have been made; and claims of unlawful dentention and arrest are rare.[43] Political rights (civil rights and freedom, equality, democratic consolidation, and media independence and objectivity) have progressed, if modestly. Improvement in the protection of women's rights has been attributed to better implementation of the Domestic Violence Prevention Law, and the promulgation of the Gender Equality Labor Law in 2002. The lat-

ter is aimed at eradicating sexual harassment and discrimination, requires employers to offer up to two years' paid maternity leave, and embodies principles of equal pay for equal work, and equal rights in places of employment. Taiwan also made progress in rights for children, elderly, and the handicapped.[44]

Political Reform in Taiwan

The Kuomintang maintained its political dominance until the turn of the century in part by opening up its membership to a broader segment of the population. It thereby allowed social diversity and political pluralism to be expressed *within* the KMT. The "Taiwanization" of both the KMT and governmental institutions after Chiang Kai-shek's death in 1975 actually permitted the KMT to ignore the demands of the Taiwanese for an independent opposition party until the late 1980s. The KMT also hijacked the most appealing issues in the platform of the Democratic Progressive Party—notably, the DPP's demand for more flexibility in relations with the P.R.C., environmental issues, and greater freedom of the press. By the time of the 1996 elections, the dominant wing of the KMT had even co-opted the DPP's platform for a more independent Taiwan. In short, as Taiwan became more socially and politically diverse, the KMT relinquished many of its authoritarian methods and adopted persuasion, conciliation, and open debate as the best means to maintain control.[45]

External pressures played a significant role in the democratization of Taiwan's institutions. American aid from the 1950s to the 1970s was accompanied by considerable American pressure for liberalizing Taiwan's economy, but the United States did little to force a change in Taiwan's political institutions during the Cold War, when its primary concern was to maintain a defense alliance with Taiwan against the Chinese Communists. Taiwan's efforts to bolster its integration into the international economy has allowed it to reap the benefits of internationalization. The government has also, after much prodding, responded positively to demands from its citizens for greater economic and cultural contact with China,[46] and for reform of the party and government. As a result, the KMT was able to claim responsibility for Taiwan's prosperity as well as for its eventual political liberalization; but as noted elsewhere, it must also take responsibility for the many problems it left on the platter for the incoming DPP administration in 2000.

The KMT's success in laying claim to key elements of the most popular opposition-party policies forced the opposition to struggle to provide a clear alternative to the KMT. Apart from the issue of Taiwan independence, when the DPP was acting as the opposition party it demanded more rapid politi-

cal reforms and harshly criticized the KMT's corrupt practices. The DPP's exposure of the KMT's corruption, and of the infiltration into the political system by criminal organizations, brought public outrage. Over the decades of its rule, the KMT used money and other resources to help tie local politicians and factions to itself. The KMT's power at the grassroots level was lubricated through patronage, vote buying, and providing services to constituents.[47] The public demanded that the interweaving of political corruption, gangsterism, and business (referred to as "black and gold politics" in Taiwan) be brought under control, and that the KMT divest itself of corporate holdings that involve conflicts of interest and permit it to engage in corrupt money politics. (When it also controlled the government, the KMT *as a political party* possessed an estimated U.S.$2.6 billion of business holdings, a sizable percentage of corporate wealth in Taiwan.) According to statistics published in the *Taipei Times*, "two-thirds of gangs in Taiwan have lawmakers running on their behalf in the legislature, while one-quarter of elected public representatives have criminal records . . . [T]hey are invulnerable because, as the KMT's legislative majorities have slowly declined, the ruling party needs the support of independent lawmakers—including those with organized crime backgrounds—to pass its legislative agenda."[48]

By the time of the first democratic elections for the president of Taiwan in 1996, much had changed in the platforms of both the KMT and the DPP. The KMT, which had by then developed a powerful faction within it demanding greater international recognition of Taiwan as an independent state, adopted what amounted to an "independent Taiwan" position. Although President Lee Teng-hui stated this was a "misinterpretation" by Beijing and the international community, and that Taiwan merely wanted more international "breathing space," his offer of U.S.$1 billion to the United Nations if it would give Taiwan a seat was hardly open to interpretation.

Angered by Lee's efforts to gain greater recognition for Taiwan as an independent state, China began missile "tests" in the waters close to Taiwan in the weeks leading up to the 1996 elections. Fortunately, none of the missiles accidentally hit Taiwan. As a result of Beijing's saber-rattling and pressures from the United States, the KMT had, by the time of the elections, retreated from its efforts to gain greater recognition as an independent state. Many members of the KMT regretted Lee's pushing for an independent Taiwan. By the 2000 election, moreover, many of those who did favor independence left the KMT to form a new party. In the 2004 legislative elections, the KMT ran on a platform rejecting independent statehood and supporting a positive and stable relationship with China to protect their business interests. It managed to keep the DPP and other parties sympathetic to declaring independence from winning a majority in the Legislative Yuan.

Taiwan's large middle class, with its diverse and complex social and economic interests arising from business interests and ownership of private property, has been a catalyst for political liberalization. Moreover, Taiwan has not suffered from vast economic disparities that breed economic and social discontent. The government's success in developing the economy meant at the least that economic issues did not provide fuel for political grievances. Thus, when martial law ended in 1987, the KMT could undertake political reform with some confidence. Its gradual introduction of democratic processes and values undercut much of its former authoritarian style of rule without its losing political power for more than a decade. Reform did generate tensions, but by the 1990s the KMT realized that street demonstrations would not bring down the government and that suppressing the opposition with harsh measures was unnecessary. This being the case, the KMT liberalized the political realm still further. Today, Taiwan's political system functions in most respects as a democracy; but as the KMT is the first to admit, it was so busy democratizing Taiwan that it neglected to democratize itself. Once it lost the presidency in the 2000 elections, and only narrowly remained in control of the Legislative Yuan, it rethought its political platform and tried to rid itself of the serious corruption and elitism that has alienated Taiwan's voters.[49] This may partially explain why in the 2004 legislative elections, the KMT, together with its political allies (the "Pan-Blue" alliance), was able to retain a narrow margin of control in the legislature.

Political Parties

Only in 1989 did the KMT pass laws legalizing opposition political parties. The Democratic Progressive Party, a largely Taiwanese-based opposition party, was for the first time recognized as a legal party. As with other political reforms, this decision was made in the context of a growing resistance to the KMT's continued restriction of democratic rights. Even after 1989, however, the KMT continued to regulate political parties strictly, in the name of maintaining political and social stability.

Angry factional disputes within both the DPP and the KMT have marred the ability of each party to project a unified electoral strategy. The KMT was particularly hurt by vitriolic disputes between pro-unification and pro-independence factions, and between progressive reformers who pushed for further liberalization of the economic and political systems, and conservative elements who resisted reform. These internal conflicts explain the KMT's inability to move forward on reform and its defeat in the presidential elections of 2000 and 2004.

In their first years in the Legislature, DPP legislators, no doubt frustrated by their role as a minority party that could not get through any of its own policies, sometimes engaged in physical brawls on the floor of the Legislature, ripped out microphones, and threw furniture. As the DPP steadily gained more power and influence over the legislative agenda, its behavior became more subdued, but its effectiveness was undermined by internal factionalism.[50]

Infighting became so serious in both parties that it led to the formation of three new breakaway parties, which competed for the first times in the 1998 elections. The Taiwan Independence Party, whose members had comprised the more radical faction within the DPP, refused to be intimidated by Beijing's possible military response to a public declaration of independence. Today, it has been renamed the Taiwan Solidarity Union. Within the KMT, members of the faction angered with the KMT leadership's slow-footedness in bringing about reunification with the mainland of China and its liberalizing reforms of the KMT, broke off to form the New Party, which first ran candidates in the 1994 elections. Its bitter disputes with former colleagues in the KMT made legislative consensus difficult. By the 2000 presidential elections, angry debates over who should lead the KMT led to the expulsion of James Soong, who then formed the People's First Party. Soong's effective campaign, which split the KMT vote, contributed to the victory of the DPP candidate, with Soong himself placing a close second and the KMT's candidate a distant third.[51] Today, the KMT, the New Party, and the People's First Party are in the "Pan-Blue" alliance in the Legislature, but are deeply divided on many issues.

Since the 1996 election, the most divisive issue has been whether or not to press for an independent Taiwan. Polls have indicated that although the Taiwanese people would like Taiwan to be independent, only a small minority has been willing to incur the risks of Beijing using force against Taiwan if the government were to endorse independence as a stated policy goal. The preference is for candidates who have promised a continuation of the status quo—namely, not openly challenging Beijing's stance that Taiwan is a province of China—but who favor Taiwan continuing to act as if it is an independent sovereign state.

The preconditions for reunification that the KMT set when it was in power are not likely to be met easily: democratization of the mainland to a (unspecified) level acceptable to Taiwan, and an (unspecified) level of economic development that would move the mainland closer to Taiwan's level of development. Ironically, although President Chen Shui-bian pushes aggressively to lay the groundwork for declaring independence, he has at the same time permitted, and even encouraged, investment in China (though not as much as Taiwan's business people would like). He accepts the argument that Taiwan's economy cannot continue to grow, or perhaps even survive, without commercial ties to the mainland. Symbolically, the most important step Chen made in advancing "the three links" (trade, postal, and transportation links) between China and Taiwan was allowing direct flights to accommodate citizens at both ends to visit the other over the Chinese New Year's period. Although direct flights were already permitted in 2003, there has been a huge leap in the details: now commercial airliners from *both* sides (not just Taiwan) may take passengers across the Taiwan Strait; passengers may board in multiple cities on both sides; and China's planes only have to fly *through the air space*, not land in, either Hong Kong or Macao on their way to Taiwan, saving considerable time. Extremists condemned Chen even for this modest concession as selling out Taiwan's interests and taking further steps toward unification; but members of the KMT have taken far bolder steps to improve relations and economic integration with the Mainland. Public opinion polls indicate that, as of December 2006, 70.3 percent of voters still believe direct transportation links should only be opened up conditionally.[52]

Money politics, vote-buying practices, and general dishonesty have plagued all of Taiwan's parties. In fact, they have burgeoned over the years, in part because of the growing importance of the legislature; for now that the Legislative Yuan is no longer a body of officials who fled the mainland in 1949 but a genuinely elected legislature with real power to affect Taiwan's policies, who wins really matters. As a result, candidates throw lavish feasts, make deals with business people, and spread money around in order to get the vote. Equally disturbing has been election-related violence, and the influence of the "underworld" on the elections.[53] The Chen administration has been plagued with corruption scandals in its second term, starting with what many commentators allege was a staged assassination attempt on the eve of the 2004 president election, to allegations throughout Chen's second term of family members engaging in insider trading and diverting public funds for private use. In 2006, there were two recall votes in the Legislative Yuan. Both failed to gain the two-thirds majority vote required to force Chen out of the presidency, but some opinion polls suggest

THE U.S. SEVENTH FLEET HALTS INVASION

In 1950, in response to China's involvement in the Korean War, the United States sent its Seventh Fleet to the Taiwan Strait to protect Taiwan and the Offshore Islands of Quemoy and Matsu from an invasion by China. Because of improved Sino–American relations in the 1970s, the enhanced Chinese Nationalist capabilities to defend Taiwan and the Offshore Islands, and problems in the Middle East, the Seventh Fleet was eventually moved out of the area. The U.S.S. Ingersol, a part of the Seventh Fleet, is shown at right. In 1996, however, part of the Seventh Fleet briefly returned to the Taiwan Strait when China threatened to use military force against Taiwan if its leaders sought independent statehood.

(Courtesy of US Navy)

that the majority of Taiwan's citizens think he should step down from the presidency before the end of his term in 2008.[54]

The positions of the KMT-led "pan-blue alliance," and the DPP-led "pan-green alliance" are far apart on the issue of Taiwan independence. The pan-blues do not support any policy that would risk a military confrontation with the PRC, and they are actively promoting "engagement" with China's officials. By contrast, the pan-greens have been highly confrontational, although there is considerable dissent about this strategy within its ranks. In part, this is because the people of Taiwan, regardless of how much they would like Taiwan to become an independent state, don't want to risk war. On social and economic issues, there is far less difference between the two major parties. Both are also committed to democracy, advocate capitalism, and support an equitable distribution of wealth. In these respects, the DPP has not significantly threatened policies that the KMT laid out during its many years in power.

Finally, although Chinese Mainlanders are almost all within the KMT or the New Party, the KMT has become so thoroughly "Taiwanized" that the earlier clear divide between the DPP and KMT based on Mainlander or Taiwanese identity has eroded considerably. Even those who strongly favor reunification with the mainland have for many years identified themselves not as Mainlanders but as "new Taiwanese." They are, in short, "born-again Taiwanese."[55]

Interest Groups

As Taiwan has become more socially, economically, and politically complex, alternative sources of power have developed that are independent of the government. Economic interest groups comprised largely of Taiwanese, whose power is based on wealth, are the most important; but there are also public in-terest groups that challenge the government's policies in areas such as civil rights, the environment, women's rights, consumer protection, agricultural policy, aborigine rights, and nuclear power. Even before the lifting of martial law in 1987, these and other groups were organizing hundreds of demonstrations each year to protest government policy.

On average, every adult in Taiwan today belongs to at least one of the thousands of interest groups. They have been spawned by political liberalization and economic growth, and in turn add to the social pluralism in Taiwan. They are also important instruments for democratic change. Taiwan's government, has then, successfully harnessed dissent since the 1990s, in part by allowing an outlet for dissent through the formation of interest groups—and opposition parties.

Mass Media

With the official end to martial law, the police powers of the state were radically curtailed. The media abandoned former taboos and grew more willing to openly address social and political problems, including corruption and the abuse of power. A free press, strongly critical of the government and *all* the political parties, now flourishes. Taiwan, with under 23 million people, boasts close to 4,000 magazines; about 100 newspapers, with a total daily circulation of 5 million; 150 news agencies, several with overseas branches; 29 television broadcasting stations, which are challenged by 75 cable stations that offer some 120 satellite channels; and more than 551 radio stations, which now include foreign broadcasts such as CNN, NHK (from Japan), and the BBC. More than 3,000 radio and 3,000 television production companies are registered in Taiwan. Although television and radio are still controlled by the government, they have become far more independent since 1988. About 75 percent of households buy a basic monthly package that gives them access to more than 70 satellite channels, many of which are operated by foreign companies. Programs from all over the world expose people to alternative ideas, values, and lifestyles, and contribute to social pluralism. Political magazines, which are privately financed and therefore not constrained by governmental financial controls, have played an important role in undercutting state censorship of the media and developing alternative perspectives on issues of public concern. New technology that defies national boundaries (including satellite broadcasts from Japan and mainland China), cable television, the Internet, and VCRs are diminishing the relevance of the state monopoly of television.[56]

THE TAIWAN–P.R.C.–U.S. TRIANGLE

From 1949 until the 1960s, Taiwan received significant economic, political, and military support from the United States. Even after it became abundantly clear that the Communists effectively controlled the China mainland and had legitimacy in the eyes of the people, the United States never wavered in its support of President Chiang Kai-shek's position that the R.O.C. was the legitimate government of all of China. U.S. secretary of state Henry Kissinger's secret trip to China in 1971, followed by President Richard M. Nixon's historic visit in 1972, led to an abrupt change in the American position and to the final collapse of the R.O.C.'s diplomatic status as the government representing "China."

Allies of the United States, most of whom had loyally supported its diplomatic stance on China, soon severed diplomatic ties with Taipei, a necessary step before they could, in turn, establish diplomatic relations with Beijing. Only one government could claim to represent the Chinese people; and with the KMT in complete agreement with the Chinese Communist regime that there was no such thing as "two Chinas" or "one Taiwan and one China," the diplomatic community had to make a choice between the two contending governments. Given the reality of the Chinese Communist Party's control over one billion people and the vast continent of China, and, more cynically, given the desire of the business community throughout the world to have ties to China, Taipei has found itself increasingly isolated in the world of diplomacy. It should be noted, however, that even when the R.O.C. had represented "China" in the United Nations, and at the height of the diplomatic isolation of the People's Republic of China from 1950 to 1971, Taipei was never officially recognized by any of its neighbors in Southeast Asia (unless they were in a defense alliance with the United States)—even though they distrusted China. That this was the case even at the height of China's unpopularity in the region was a bad omen for Taipei's dream of obtaining international legitimacy."[57]

Eventually the United States made the painful decision to desert its loyal Cold War ally, a bastion against communism in Asia, if not exactly an oasis of democracy. The United States had, moreover, heavily invested in Taiwan's economy. But on January 1, 1979, President Jimmy Carter announced the severing of diplomatic relations with Taipei and the establishment of full diplomatic relations with Beijing.

Taiwan's disappointment and anger at the time cannot be overstated, in spite of the fact that an officially "unofficial" relationship took its place. American interests in Taiwan are overseen by a huge, quasi-official "American Institute in Taiwan"; while Taiwan is represented in the United States by multiple branches of the "Taipei Economic and Cultural Office." In fact, the staffs in these offices continue to be treated in most respects as if they are diplomatic personnel. Except for the 25 countries that officially recognize the R.O.C. (primarily because they receive large amounts of aid from Taiwan), Taiwan's commercial, cultural, and political interests are represented abroad by these unofficial offices.

The United States's acceptance of the Chinese Communists' "principled stand" that Taiwan is a province of China and that the People's Republic of China is the sole legal government of all of China, made it impossible to continue to maintain a military alliance with one of China's provinces. Recognition of Beijing, therefore, required the United States to terminate its mutual defense treaty with the R.O.C. In the Taiwan Relations Act of 1979, the United States stated its concern for the island's future security, its hope for a peaceful resolution of the conflict between Taiwan's government and Beijing, and its de-

cision to put a moratorium on the sale of new weapons to Taiwan.

Renewal of Arms Sales

The Taiwan Relations Act was, however, largely ignored by the administration of President Ronald Reagan. Almost immediately upon taking office, it announced its intention to resume U.S. arms sales to Taiwan. The administration argued that Taiwan needed its weapons upgraded in order to defend itself. Irate, Beijing demanded that, in accordance with American agreements and implicit promises to China, the United States phase out the sale of military arms over a specified period. The U.S. has never actually agreed to this, but because of the gridlock in Taiwan's Legislative Yuan, in effect, U.S. arms sales have come to a halt (see below). Nevertheless, the fact that the U.S. *wants* to sell arms to Taiwan is a constant source of tensions with China. Similarly, the U.S. Congress's proposed Taiwan Security Enhancement Act in 2000—which, had it passed, would have amounted to a military alliance with Taiwan—and the possibility that Congress may authorize "theater missile defense" for the island, have been major irritants to the U.S.–China relationship.

When it took office in January 2001, the George W. Bush administration immediately stated its intention to go forward with deepening military ties with Taiwan. Tensions with Beijing generated by the U.S. sales of military equipment to Taiwan are aggravated by China's own sales of military equipment, such as medium-range missiles to Saudi Arabia, Silkworm missiles to Iran (used against American ships), nuclear technology to Pakistan,[58] and massive sales of semiautomatic assault weapons to the United States (one of which was used to attack the White House in 1994). These sales have undercut the P.R.C.'s standing on the moral high ground to protest American sales of military equipment to Taiwan. But views even within Taiwan concerning the purchase of U.S. military weapons and equipment are complicated. The DPP has argued that they are necessary to protect Taiwan against an attack by China. The KMT is, however, firmly opposed to further purchases, considering them a waste of money; for in the event of an attack, its defense would depend almost entirely on the United States—assuming that the Americans decided to come to its defense. Even worse, the KMT argues, additional arming of Taiwan would accelerate the arms race with China, and further destabilize the Taiwan Straits. The KMT has even accused President Chen of wanting greater military power as part of an effort to lay the groundwork for declaring Taiwan's independence.

This is a bizarre twist to the issue of Taiwan's defense; for in the past, the United

States and other countries have repeatedly backed out of proposed arms deals in the face of Beijing's threatened punitive measures. Now it is Taiwan that is backing out. U.S. policymakers are frustrated with Taiwan's falling military expenditures and the perception that Taiwan's defense readiness has declined as a result.[59] But most analysts agree that, with or without arms purchases from the U.S., Taiwan knows that its own defenses would be overwhelmed by a military onslaught from the mainland. As to the U.S. position on what it would do if Taiwan were attacked by China, it remains one of "strategic ambiguity"; for even though President Bush in 2001 stated the U.S. would come to Taiwan's aid if it were attacked, since that time, the administration has made it clear to Taiwan's president that the U.S. will not be pulled into a war with China to defend Taiwan if it declares independence. The U.S. also has to consider that, with more than 120,000 troops in Iraq, with others tied down in Afghanistan, and with no end in sight, the U.S. simply does not have the resources to participate in a conflict with China. This does not stop the U.S. military from portraying the Chinese buildup across the Taiwan Straits as a grave threat and, on this basis, requesting more of the budget for "defense."

The United States wants Beijing to agree to the "peaceful resolution of the Taiwan issue," but "on principle," China refuses to make any such a commitment. China insists that Taiwan is an "internal" affair, not an international matter over which other states might have some authority. From China's perspective, then, it has the right as a sovereign state to choose to use force to settle the Taiwan issue. There is general recognition, however, that the purpose of China's military buildup across from Taiwan is not as much to attack Taiwan as to prevent it from declaring independence as a sovereign state.[60] Indeed, apart from a mild statement from Japan protesting China's "testing" of missiles over Taiwan in 1996, no Asian country has questioned China's right to display force when Taiwan pressed for independent statehood. Still, Beijing knows that American involvement may be critical to getting Taiwan to agree to unification with the mainland. One thing is certain: the day Beijing no longer threatens to use force against Taiwan if it declares independence, Taipei *will* declare independence. So we can expect Beijing to continue its bluster about using military force until Taiwan is reunified with the mainland.

Minimally, Taiwan wants the United States to insist that any solution to the China unification issue be *acceptable to the people of Taiwan*. One possible solution would be a confederation of Taiwan with the mainland: Taiwan would keep its "sovereignty" (that is to say, govern itself and formulate its own foreign policy), but China could say there was only one China. An interim solution bandied about by the KMT in 2006–2007 is that Taiwan would promise not to declare independence for 50 years, and Beijing would promise not to use force to gain control of Taiwan for 50 years. Then, in that context, both sides would go about their business of furthering the integration of the two economies and deepening cultural ties. Neither this proffered solution, or one that promotes the idea of a Chinese commonwealth for the relationship of Taiwan to China, will likely be adopted until President Chen Shui-bian leaves office in 2008.[61]

CHINA'S "PEACE OFFENSIVE"

Since the early 1980s, Beijing has combined its threats and warnings about Taiwan's seeking independence with a "peace offensive." This strategy aims to draw Taiwan's leaders into negotiations about the future reunification of Taiwan with the mainland. Beijing has invited the people of Taiwan to visit their friends and relatives on the mainland and to witness the progress made under Communist rule. The vast majority of Taiwan's adult population has traveled to the mainland. In turn, a mere trickle of Chinese from the mainland has been permitted by Taipei to visit Taiwan. The government did allow mainland Chinese students studying abroad to come for "study tours" of Taiwan. They have treated them as if they were visiting dignitaries, and the students usually returned to their universities full of praise for Taiwan. They also eventually loosened visa restrictions for those Mainland Chinese who had become residents of Hong Kong, Macao, or another country. By 2005, the number of Chinese visitors had increased to 5,000 per month. Taipei has said it is willing to increase that number to 30,000 per month, a decision motivated, it appears, by Taiwan's economy, which could use an infusion of tourist dollars to get it moving.[62] Economic issues have, at long last, trumped Taipei's worries about tourists overstaying their visas to find work, as well as political and security concerns.

China's "peace offensive" is based on a nine-point proposal originally made in 1981. Its major points include Beijing's willingness to negotiate a mutually agreeable re-integration of Taiwan under the mainland's government; encouragement of trade, cultural exchanges, travel, and communications between Taiwan and the mainland; the offer to give Taiwan "a high degree of autonomy as a special administrative region" within China after reunification (the status it offered to Hong Kong when it came under Beijing's rule in 1997); and promises that Taiwan could keep its own armed forces, continue its

socioeconomic systems, maintain political control over local affairs, and allow its leaders to participate in the national leadership of a unified China. This far exceeds what China offered Hong Kong.

The KMT's original official response to the Beijing "peace offensive" was negative. The KMT's bitter history of war with the Chinese Communists, and what the KMT saw as a pattern of Communist duplicity, explained much of the government's hesitation. So did Beijing's refusal to treat Taiwan as an equal in negotiations. Nevertheless, since 1992, Taiwan has engaged in unofficial "track 2" and "track 3" discussions on topics of mutual interest, such as the protection of Taiwan's investments in the mainland, tourism, cross-Strait communication and transportation links, and the dumping of Taiwan's nuclear waste on the mainland.

Taipei remains sensitive, however, to the Taiwanese people's concern about the unification of Taiwan with the mainland. The Taiwanese have asserted that they will never accede to rule by yet another mainland Chinese government, especially a Communist one. With the DPP in power, Taiwanese have fewer fears that the leadership will strike a deal with Beijing at their expense; for, as the long-time advocate of the interests of the Taiwanese people and an independent Taiwan, the DPP is trusted not to sell out their interests. To speak of the "Taiwanese" as a united whole is, however, misleading; for it must be remembered that the overwhelming majority of members in the KMT, which favors stronger integration with the mainland, are Taiwanese, and that Taiwanese who do business with the mainland are eager to see integration—if not necessarily political unification at this point in history—progress much more rapidly. In addition, the political influence of those age cohorts most opposed to improving cross-Strait ties is waning. For younger Taiwanese, "loving Taiwan does not mean hating China. If the PRC refrains from acting in ways that provoke negative reactions from young Taiwanese, current trends suggest that Taiwan's public will demand better relations between the two sides in the future."[63] An increasing Taiwanese identity does not, then, necessarily mean greater support for a pro-independence policy. Indeed, public opinion polls indicate that support for declaring independence, in spite of the fact that 80 percent of the population today was born on Taiwan, has rarely exceeded 10 percent of voters.[64]

With only a handful of countries recognizing the R.O.C., and with Beijing blocking membership for the R.O.C. in most international organizations, Taipei is under pressure to achieve some positive results in its evolving relationship with Beijing. While

officially the "three mini-links" (trade, postal exchange, and transportation) are unacceptable to Taiwan, they are in fact developing rapidly. The introduction of direct commercial flights from Taiwan to Shanghai over the 2003 Chinese New Year was one of the first steps toward direct air links,[65] but there has been little progress in this regard since that time. On the other hand, "indirect" trade between China and Taiwan by way of Hong Kong has continued to soar, although the opening of Taiwan's Offshore Islands (Quemoy and Matsu) to direct trade with the mainland in 2001 has somewhat undercut the need for the Hong Kong connection.

Although China has become Taiwan's largest export market and the single largest recipient of investment from Taiwan, Taipei still hesitates to move forward on many issues that would further bind Taiwan with the mainland. Its policy on mainland spouses is particularly stringent and clearly indicates a perception that China's citizens are potential enemies, not compatriots. In the 1990s, relatively few Taiwanese residents who married individuals from the mainland were permitted to live with them in Taiwan. By contrast, Beijing's policy was to welcome Taiwan spouses to come live on the mainland. Taiwan's government argued that the mainland spouses could be spies and that internal security forces were inadequate to follow them around. Over time, however, this policy has relaxed, and as of 2007, there were 240,000 Chinese spouses of Taiwan citizens. This number, expected to grow by the time of the 2012 election to 300,000 to 400,000 eligible to vote (though they may only vote after 8 years of residency in Taiwan), is causing concern to the ever-paranoid Taiwanese that they might vote as a block for political unity with the mainland.[66] As Mainlanders are smuggled into Taiwan in ever-larger numbers (primarily to satisfy the needs of entrepreneurs in Taiwan for cheap labor), and the number of fake marriages (marriages of convenience) with Taiwan's citizens grows (more than 16,000 had been discovered as of 2005),[67] the issue of surveillance has become a growing concern. At the same time, Taiwan spying on the mainland has grown steadily as its contacts with the mainland have increased. The Military Intelligence Bureau recruits from its approximately one million citizens who work, live, and tour on the mainland. They in turn form Taiwan spy networks that recruit local Chinese with sex, money, and "democratic justice" (an appeal to their sense of injustice at the hands of the Chinese government).[68]

In the meantime, China continues to deepen and widen harbors to receive ships from Taiwan; wine and dine influential Taiwanese; give preferential treatment to Taiwan's entrepreneurs in trade and investment on the mainland; open direct telephone links between Taiwan and the mainland; rebuild some of the most important temples to local deities in Fujian Province where Taiwanese like to visit; establish special tourist organizations to care solely for people from Taiwan; and refurbish the birthplace of Chiang K'ai-shek, the greatest enemy of the Chinese Communists in their history.

Taiwan's businesspeople and scholars are eager for Taiwan's relationship with the mainland to move forward. They seek direct trade and personal contacts, and try to separate political concerns from economic interests and international scientific exchanges. The manufacturing and software sectors are particularly concerned with penetrating and, if possible, controlling the China market. Otherwise, they argue, businesspeople from other countries will do so.

The business community, faced with Taiwan's ever-higher labor cost and Taiwan's lack of cheap raw materials, has flocked to China. Whether they move outdated labor-intensive factories and machinery to the mainland, or invest in cutting-edge technology, Taiwan's businesspeople benefit from China's cheap, hard-working labor force.

Others are concerned, however, that, with more than 15 percent of its total foreign investment in the mainland, Taiwan could become "hostage" to Beijing. That is, if China were to refuse to release Taiwan's assets or to reimburse investors for their assets on the mainland in case of a political or military conflict between Taipei and Beijing, Taiwan's enterprises would form a pressure point that would give the advantage to Beijing. Any military defensive capabilities either Taiwan or the U.S. could offer are useless to counter possible Mainland economic warfare, such as an economic blockade, when most of Taiwan's trade is with the mainland itself and 60 percent of its investments are in the mainland.[64] Furthermore, without diplomatic recognition in China, Taiwan's businesses on the mainland are vulnerable in case of a conflict with local businesses or the government. High-level members of the government have even denounced those who invest in the mainland as "traitors." And members of the pro-independence press have attempted to whip up fear among its citizens that with Beijing's new anti-secession law, Taiwanese visiting or living in China will be vulnerable to "shakedown artists."[69] So far, affairs have turned out quite the opposite: China has actually *favored* Taiwan's businesses over all others; and Taiwan's investors have tended to turn a quick profit, and to construct many safeguards, so that any seizure of assets would result in negligible losses. To wit, Beijing learned that its heavy-handed approach to Taiwan in passing an anti-secession law was counter-productive, and now relies more on "soft power" in its relations with Taipei.

PROSPECTS FOR THE REUNIFICATION OF TAIWAN WITH THE MAINLAND

The December 2004 legislative elections kept an anti-independence majority in the legislature, but most Taiwanese remain opposed to reunification. Most agree that, given China's threats to use force if Taiwan were to declare independence, it would be foolish to do so; and that the government's policy toward China should be progressive, assertive, and forward-looking. Lacking a long-term plan and simply reacting to Beijing's initiatives puts the real power to determine the future relationship in China's hands.

For the last 20 years, reform-minded individuals in Taiwan's political parties have insisted that the government needs to actively structure how the cross-Straits relationship evolves. One of the most widely discussed policies favored by those who opposed a declaration of independence has been a "one country, two regions" model that would approximate the "one country, two systems" model China has with Hong Kong. The problem is determining who would govern in that "one China" after reunification with the mainland. To call that country the People's Republic of China would probably never find acceptance in Taiwan—a point understood by Beijing. As a result, it now frequently drops the "people's republic" part of the name in its pronouncements. Symbolically, this eliminates the issue of two different governments claiming to represent China, and whether that China would be called a "people's republic" or a "republic." It would be called neither. But, would Beijing be in charge of the new unified government? Would the government of the "Republic of China," even were free and democratic elections for all of the mainland and Taiwan to be held, be the winner? There is certainly no evidence to suggest that most people on the mainland would welcome being governed by Taiwan's leaders.

In spite of the negative rhetoric, changes in Taipei's policies toward the P.R.C. have been critical to improving cross-Strait ties. For example, Taiwan's government ended its 40-year-old policy of stamping "communist bandit" on all printed materials from China and prohibiting ordinary people from reading them; Taiwan's citizens, even if they are government officials, are now permitted to visit China; scholars from Taiwan may now attend international conferences in the P.R.C., and Taipei now permits a few P.R.C. scholars to attend conferences in Taiwan; and KMT retired veterans, who fought against the Communists and retreated to Taiwan in 1949, are actually encouraged to return to the mainland to live out their lives because their limited KMT government pensions would buy them a better life there! Certainly some members of Taiwan's upper class are acting as if the relationship will eventually be a harmonious one when they buy apartments for their mistresses and purchase large mansions in the former international sector of Shanghai and elsewhere. (It is estimated that there are more than one million individuals from Taiwan living in China.) One survey indicated, in fact, that after the United States and Canada, mainland China was the preferred place to emigrate for Taiwan's citizens![70] And, from the perspective of the Democratic Progressive Party, things are getting worse: hundreds of thousands more Taiwanese are relocating to the mainland, and they are taking with them venture capital estimated at well over U.S.$100 billion—money that might otherwise be pumped into Taiwan's economy.

Some Taiwanese share with Beijing a common interest in establishing a Chinese trading zone in East Asia. A "Chinese common market" would incorporate China, Taiwan, Hong Kong, Macau, and perhaps other places with large ethnic-Chinese communities such as Singapore and Malaysia. Economically integrating these Chinese areas through common policies on taxes, trade, and currencies would strengthen them vis-à-vis the Japanese economic powerhouse, which remains larger than all the other Far Eastern economies put together.

Yet, with an ever-smaller number of first-generation Mainlanders in top positions in the KMT and Taiwan's government, few are keen to push for reunification. Indeed, the majority of people in Taiwan still oppose reunification under current conditions. They are particularly concerned about two issues. The first is the gap in living standards. Taiwan is fully aware of the high price that West Germany paid to reunify with East Germany. Obviously the price tag to close the wealth gap with mammoth China would be prohibitive for tiny Taiwan; and any plan that would allow Beijing to heavily tax Taiwan's citizens would be unacceptable. Yet China is developing so quickly, at least along the densely populated eastern coast that faces Taiwan, that this issue should disappear. Indeed, at this point it might be predicted that Shanghai will easily match Taipei's living standard within this generation's lifetime.

The second issue is democracy. Fears that they might lose certain political freedoms and control over their own institutions have made the Taiwanese wary of reunification. Finally, whether or not "one country, two systems" succeeds in protecting Hong

Kong from Beijing's intervention, Taiwanese reject a parallel being drawn between Hong Kong and Taiwan. Hong Kong was, they argue, a British colony, whereas Taiwan, even if only in the last ten years, is a fledgling democracy. When the KMT was in power, it stated that once China had attained a certain (unspecified) level of development and democracy, China and Taiwan would be reunified; but the DPP has made no such statement. In any event, with so much left open to its own arbitrary interpretation as to what is sufficient development and democracy, even the KMT seems to have made no real commitment to reunification. For its part, the DPP-led government has been pressured into accepting greater interdependency with China, yet has tried desperately to move toward the formal declaration of an independent state, to no avail.

China's significant progress in developing the economy and increasing the rights of the Chinese people in the last 25 years should make reunification more palatable to Taiwan. Greater contacts and exchanges between the two sides should in themselves help lay the basis for mutual trust and understanding.

Many members of Taiwan's political and intellectual elite, including the DPP and KMT party leaders, think tanks, and the Ministry of Foreign Affairs, seem to spend the better part of each day pondering the meaning of "one China." In general, they would like China to return to the agreement that they reached with Beijing in 1992: namely, that each side would keep its own interpretation of the "one China" concept: Beijing would continue to see "one China" as the government of the P.R.C. and would continue to deny that the R.O.C. government existed. Taipei would continue to hold that Taiwan and the mainland are separate but politically equivalent parts of one China. Unfortunately for Taipei, Beijing no longer embraces this view. Instead, it states that no further negotiations can occur until Taipei accepts that it is not a state, and hence not the equal of Beijing at the negotiating table.

Today, it is estimated that China has more than 900 (non-nuclear) missiles pointed at Taiwan; but unless Taiwan again pushes seriously for recognition as an independent state, an attack is unlikely; for the mainland continues to benefit from Taiwan's trade and investments, remittances and tourism; and it is committed to rapid economic development, which could be seriously jeopardized by even a brief war—a war that it might not win if the United States were to intervene on behalf of Taiwan. In spite of the fact that the U.S. has repeatedly made it clear to President Chen Shui-bian that it is angered by his efforts to advance the cause of inde-

pendence, Beijing could well worry that the U.S. might suddenly be persuaded to come to Taiwan's support.

It is in Taiwan's best interests for the relationship with China to develop in a careful and controlled manner, and to avoid public statements on the issue of reunification versus an independent Taiwan, even as that issue haunts every hour of the day in Taiwan. It is also in Taiwan's interest to wait and see how well China integrates Hong Kong under its formula of "one country, two systems." In the meantime, Taiwan's international strategy—agreeing that it is a mere province of China, while acting like an independent state and conducting business and diplomacy with other states as usual—has proved remarkably successful. It has allowed Taiwan to get on with its own economic development without the diversion of a crippling amount of revenue to military security. A continuation of the status quo is clearly the preferred alternative for Taiwan, the United States, and mainland China; for it avoids any possibility of a military conflict, which none would welcome; and it does not interrupt the preferred strategy of both the DPP and the KMT—"closer economic ties, lower tensions, and more communication with the mainland."[71]

At the same time, this strategy allows time for the mainland to become increasingly democratic and developed, in a way that one day might make reunification palatable to Taiwan. Meanwhile, Beijing's leadership knows that Taiwan acts as a de facto independent state, but it is willing to turn a blind eye as long as Taipei does not push too openly for recognition. Thus far, the reality has mattered less to Beijing than recognition of the symbolism of Taiwan being a province of China. Beijing's leadership is far more interested in putting resources into China's economic development than fighting a war with no known outcome. In part for this reason, and in part because of continuing efforts of the U.S. to sell armaments to Taiwan, Beijing has made it clear to Washington that China's own buildup of missiles targeted at Taiwan would be linked to American sales and efforts to install a theatre missile defense system around Taiwan.

Because China's sovereignty over Taiwan has been an emotional, patriotic, even nationalistic, issue for the Chinese people, however, Beijing does not make a "rational" cost-benefit analysis of the use of force against a rebellious Taiwan. Taiwan does not like Beijing's militant rhetoric, but some mainland Chinese analysts believe that China's leadership is forced to sound more militant than it feels, thanks to the militant nationalism of ordinary Chinese people and the Chinese military. Indeed, some go so far as to say that, were Chi-

na an electoral democracy, the people would have voted out the CCP leadership because it has done little to regain sovereignty over Taiwan.

As Taiwan's relationship with China deepens and broadens, it is possible that

Timeline: PAST

A.D. 1544
Portuguese sailors are the first Europeans to visit Taiwan

1700s
Taiwan becomes part of the Chinese Empire

1895
The Sino-Japanese War ends; China cedes Taiwan to Japan

1945
Japan is forced to return the colony of Taiwan to China when Japanese forces are defeated in World War II

1947–49
Nationalists, under Chiang Kai-shek, retreat to Taiwan

1950s
A de facto separation of Taiwan from China; The Chinese Communist Party is unable to bring its civil war with the KMT to an end because the U.S. interposes its 7th Fleet between the mainland and Taiwan in the Taiwan Straits

1971
The People's Republic of China replaces the Republic of China (Taiwan) in the United Nations as the legitimate government of "China"

1975
Chiang Kai-shek dies and is succeeded by his son, Chiang Ching-kuo

1980s
40 years of martial law end and opposition parties are permitted to campaign for office

1990s
Relations with China improve; the United States sells F-16 jets to Taiwan; China conducts military exercises to intimidate Taiwanese voters. Democratization develops. The Asian financial crisis deals a setback to Taiwan's economic growth.

PRESENT

2000s
Trade and communication with China continue to expand and economy recovers. The opposition Democratic Progressive Party wins the presidency but the Legislature remains controlled by the KMT. Taiwan refuses to buy significant amounts of military equipment from the United States. President Chen Shui-bian's efforts to assert Taiwan's independence cause splits within the governing party. Corruption scandals plague the DPP and calls for President Chen to step down before his term expires in 2008 grow.

more arrangements could be made for the representation of both Taiwan and China in international organizations, without Beijing putting up countless roadblocks. Indeed, Beijing welcomed Taiwan's membership in the WTO, if for no other reason that that it allows it to pry open Taiwan's market. Further, Taiwan's WTO membership has led to even more investments in the mainland and further economic integration.

Taiwan eagerly embraced membership in the WTO, not because it would necessarily benefit from WTO trade rules, but so that it could become a player in a major international organization. But, the very trade practices that led to Taiwan's multibillion-dollar trade surplus will have to be abolished to gain compliance with WTO regulations. Still, had Taiwan not joined the WTO, it would have eventually lost its competitiveness in agriculture and the automobile industry anyway.

To conclude, the benefits of Taiwan declaring independence would be virtually nil. Already Beijing refuses to have diplomatic relations with any country that officially recognizes the Republic of China. Those countries that do recognize the R.O.C., or Taiwan, as a sovereign state also cannot trade with the P.R.C. Given the size of the China market, this is an unacceptable price for most countries to pay. Beijing would no doubt use this trump card to punish those that would dare to recognize Taiwan as an independent and sovereign state, just as it does now.

Taiwan is looking for a place for itself in the international system, and it can't seem to find it. But its government realizes that the island is a small place, and that if Taiwan ever were to stop demanding international status and attention, it might well discover that it had suddenly become, de facto, a province of China while the international community looked the other way. If only for this reason, it is in Taiwan's interest to continue to press its case for greater international recognition, and to continue to engage in pragmatic unofficial diplomacy and trade with states throughout the world. It may not buy Taiwan statehood, but it may well buy the government's continued independence of Beijing.

NOTES

1. Before it won its bid to host the 2008 Olympics, Beijing had said that it would not allow Taipei to co-host them unless it first accepted the "one China" principle. Taipei did not accept it, so Beijing is the sole host of the 2008 Olympics.

2. John F. Burns, "Quemoy (Remember?) Bristles with Readiness," *The New York Times* (April 5, 1986), p. 2.

3. Mainland Affairs Council, "Report on the Preliminary Impact Study of the 'Three Mini-links' Between the Two Sides of the Taiwan Strait" (October 2, 2000); and discussions at The National Security Council and Ministry of National Defense in Taiwan (January 2001)

4. Edwin A. Winckler, "Cultural Policy on Postwar Taiwan," in Steven Harrell and Chun-chieh Huang, eds., *Cultural Change in Postwar Taiwan* (Boulder, CO: Westview Press, 1994), p. 22.

5. *Ibid.*, p. 29.

6. Thomas B. Gold, "Civil Society and Taiwan's Quest for Identity," in Harrell and Huang, p. 60.

7. Thomas A. Shaw, "Are the Taiwanese Becoming More Individualistic as They Become More Modern?" Taiwan Studies Workshop, *Fairbank Center Working Papers*, No. 7 (August 1994), pp. 1–25.

8. "Premier Hau Bristling about Crime in Taiwan," *The Free China Journal* (September 13, 1990), p. 1; and Winckler, p. 41.

9. Paul Li, "Trash Transfigurations," *Taipei Review* (October 2000), pp. 46–53.

10. Central News Agency, Taipei, "Nearly 90% support new garbage classification policy, survey finds," *Taiwan News Online* (December 27, 2004). http://www.etaiwannews.com/Taiwan/Politics/2004/12/27/1104112881.htm

11. U.S. Energy Information Administration. Report on Taiwan, available at http://www.eia.doe.gov/emeu/cabs/taiwanenv.html

12. A dormitory for employees of Tai Power is one of these buildings. Ninety percent of Taiwan's nuclear waste is stored on Orchid Island, where one of Taiwan's 9 aboriginal tribes lives. Christian Aspalter, *Understanding Modern Taiwan: Essays in Economics, Politics, and Social Policy* (Burlington, Vt.: Ashgate Publishers, 2001), pp. 103–107.

13. U.S. Energy Information Administration. Report on Taiwan, op.cit.

14. http://www.settlement.org/cp/english/taiwan/holidays.html

15. Lee Fan-fang, "Ghosts' Arrival Bad for Business," *The Free China Journal* (August 7, 1992), p. 4.

16. Ibid.

17. Marc J. Cohen, *Taiwan at the Crossroads* (Washington, D.C.: Asian Resource Center, 1988), pp. 186–190. For further detail, see his chapter on "Religion and Religious Freedom," pp. 185–215. Also, see Gold, in Harrell and Huang, p. 53.

18. "Presbyterian Church in Taiwan Calls for Reform," (February 18, 2004). Posted on http://www.christiantoday.com/news/asip/42.htm

19. See *Free China Review*, Vol. 44, No. 9 (September 1994), which ran a series of articles on educational reform, pp. 1–37.

20. Brian Cheng, "Foreign Workers Seen as a Mixed Blessing," *Taipei Journal* (October 20, 2000), p. 7.

21. Election Study Center, National Chengchi University, *Taipei: Face-to-Face Surveys* (February 2000). Funded by the Mainland Affairs Council.

22. Cohen, p. 107.

23. *Ibid.*, p. 108. For more on women, see the chapter on "Women and Indigenous People," pp. 106–126.

24. Jim Hwang, "The Civil Service: Walking on Glue," *Taipei Review* (October 2000), pp. 22–29; and "Taiwan's Civil Service Makes Headway on Gender Equality," *Taiwan Update*, Vol. 5, No. 3 (March 30, 2004), p. 7).

25. Cher-jean Lee, "Political Participation by Women of Taiwan," *Taiwan Journal* (August 20, 2004), p. 7.

26. Lynn T. Whyte III, "Taiwan and Globalization," in Samuel S. Kim, ed., *East Asia and Globalization* (New York: Rowman & Littlefield, 2000), p. 163.

27. Robert P. Weller, "Environmental Protest in Taiwan: A Preliminary Sketch," Taiwan Studies Workshop, *Fairbank Center Working Papers*, No. 2 (1993), pp. 1, 4.

28. Taiwan's workers could not get higher wages through strikes, which were forbidden under martial law. The alternative was to try starting up one's own business. Gold, in Harrell and Huang, pp. 50, 53.

29. Kelly Her, "Not-So-Iron Rice Bowl," *Free China Review* (October 1998), pp. 28–35.

30. "Taiwan: In Praise of Paranoia," *The Economist* (November 7, 1998) pp. 8–15.

31. William C. Pao, "COA (Council of Agriculture) to help agriculture sector upgrade its competitiveness," *The China Post* (Taipei), 2003. On line http://www.gio.gov.tw/taiwan-website/5-gp/apec/ap3_12.htm

32. Tim Culpan Bloomberg, Ma pledges to ease China investment ceiling, *The China Post* (Taipei), (March 21, 2007). Available at http://www.chinapost.com.tw/news/archives/business/2007321/105185.htm

33. Since 2005, a steady stream of high level KMT political and economic leaders have gone to China to assure China that they do not support Taiwan independence and want

to expand their economic relations with China.

34. Peter Morris, "Taiwan business in China supports opposition," *Asia Times Online* (Feb. 4, 2004). http://www.atimes.com/atimes/China/FB04Ad04.html

35. "Taiwan: In Praise of Paranoia," p. 17. For 2004, Taiwan had an overall trade surplus (with all countries) of well over US$7 billion.

36. Kerry Dumbaugh: *China-U.S. Relations: Current Issues and Implications for U.S. Policy* (Washington: Congressional Research Service Report for Congress (February 2007), pp. 2, 9. Available at http://fpc.state.gov/documents/organization/81340.pdf.

37. Francis Li, "Taiwan to Set Up Free-Trade Zones," *Taipei Journal* (October 11, 2002), p. 3.

38. "Taiwan: In Praise of Paranoia," p. 16.

39. Editor, "Standard-bearers for the Future," *Taiwan Review* (February 2007), p. 1; and Zoe Cheng, "The Biggest Leap," *Taiwan Review* (February 2007), pp. 4–11.

40. Until the DPP came into power in 2000 and began to promote the concept of Taiwan as an independent state, Taiwan was always shown on the map as a part of China, as were Tibet, Inner Mongolia, and even Outer Mongolia, which is an independent state.

41. From 1950 to 1986, military courts tried more than 10,000 cases involving civilians. These were in violation of the Constitution's provision (Article 9) that prohibited civilians from being tried in a military court. Hung-mao Tien, *The Great Transition: Political and Social Change in the Republic of China* (Palo Alto, CA: Hoover Institution, Stanford University, 1989), p. 111.

42. The Kaohsiung rally, which was followed by street confrontations between the demonstrators and the police, is an instance of KMT repression of *dangwai* activities. These activities were seen as a challenge to the KMT's absolute power. The KMT interpreted the Kaohsiung Incident as "an illegal challenge to public security." For this reason, those arrested were given only semi-open hearings in a military, not civil, tribunal; and torture may have been used to extract confessions from the defendants. Tien, p. 97.

43. Bureau of Democracy, Human Rights, and Labor, U.S. Department of State, *China (Taiwan only): Country Report on Human Rights Practices (2003)*, (Washington D.C. 2004). Available at: http://www.state.gov/g/drl/rls/hrrpt/2003/27767.htm; and Lin Fang-yan, "Rights Group Reports on ROC Progress," *Taipei Journal* (January 3, 2003), p. 1.

44. Lin Fangyan, Ibid.

45. Tien, p. 72.

46. A February 2000 poll conducted in Taiwan indicated that only 6.1 percent of the respondents opposed conditional or unconditional opening up of direct transportation links with the mainland. Election Study Center, National Chengchi University, Taipei. Face-to-face surveys. Funded by the Mainland Affairs Council, Executive Yuan (February 2000).

47. Shelley Rigger, "Taiwan: Finding Opportunity in Crisis," *Current History* (September 1999), p. 290.

48. Shelley Rigger, "Taiwan Rides the Democratic Dragon," *The Washington Quarterly* (Spring 2000), pp. 112–113. Reference is to the editor, *Taipei Times* (January 4, 2000).

49. Discussions with Shaw Yu-ming, deputy secretary-general of the KMT, at KMT headquarters, Taipei, 2001.

50. Myra Lu and Frank Chang, "Election Trends Indicate Future of Taiwan Politics," *Free China Journal* (November 27, 1998), p. 7.

51. According to Shaw Yu-ming, the KMT was defeated not because of its policies but because it was the KMT leadership who chose the candidates to run in the election. The implication was that if instead, the KMT membership had chosen candidates, they would have picked candidates who had a better chance of winning.

52. Charts of poll results available at http://www.mac.gov.tw/english/index1-e.htm.

53. Cal Clark, "Taiwan in the 1990s: Moving Ahead or Back to the Future?" in William Joseph, *China Briefing: The Contradictions of Change* (Armonk, NY: M. E. Sharpe, 1997), p. 206; and Myra Lu, "Crackdown on Vote-Buying Continues," *Free China Journal* (November 27, 1998), p. 2.

54. One poll, conducted by *The China Times* (June 18, 2006) indicated that 53 percent of respondents thought Chen should resign. Referenced in Kerry Dumbaugh: *China-U.S. Relations: Current Issues and Implications for U.S. Policy* (Washington: Congressional Research Service Report for Congress (February 2007), p. 9. Available at http://fpc.state.gov/documents/organization/81340.pdf.

55. Lee Chang-kuei, "High-Speed Social Dynamics," *Free China Review* (October 1998), p. 6.

56. *Taiwan Yearbook, 2007*, (Government Information Office, Taipei, 2007). Available at http://english.www.gov.tw/Yearbook/index.jsp?categid=28&recordid=52736; and Chin-chuan Lee, "Sparking a Fire: The Press and the Ferment of Democratic Change in Taiwan," in Chin-chuan Lee, ed., *China's Media, Media China* (Boulder, CO: Westview Press, 1994), pp. 188–192.

57. Chen Jie, *Foreign Policy of the New Taiwan: Pragmatic Diplomacy in Southeast Asia* (Northampton, MA: Edward Elgar Publishing, 2002), pp. 63–64.

58. In 2000, however, China agreed to stop selling nuclear and missile technology to Pakistan.

59. Kerry Dumbaugh: *China-U.S. Relations: Current Issues and Implications for U.S. Policy* pp. 2, 9.

60. Thomas J. Christensen, "The Contemporary Security Dilemma: Deterring a Taiwan Conflict," *The Washington Quarterly* (Autumn 2002), pp. 7–21.

61. Patrick L. Smith, "For Many in Taiwan, Status Quo with China Sounds Fine," *International Herald Tribune*, December 11, 2006.

62. Jimmy Chuang, "A 'foreigner's point of view' can boost tourist numbers: [Premier] Su," *Taipei Times* (January 4, 2007), p.4; Kathrin Hille, "Taiwan May Allow More Mainland Chinese Visitors," *Financial Times*, October 21, 2005.

63. Shelley Rigger, *Taiwan's Rising Rationalism: Generations, Politics, and "Taiwanese Nationalism,"* Policy Studies 26 (Washington D.C.: East-West Center Washington, 2006), p. 84.

64. Robert S. Ross, "Explaining Taiwan's Revisionist Diplomacy," *Journal of Contemporary China*, Vol. 15, no. 48 (August 2006), pp. 446–447, 450. Ross (2006), pp. 452–454. See the charts based on public opinion polls by the Mainland Affairs Council, done 3 to 4 times per year from May 2000 through December 2006, in which the highest percentage of those polled who wanted to declare independence immediately only reached more than 10 percent once (10.3 percent in November 2005). Charts available at http://www.mac.gov.tw/english/index1-e.htm.

65. Taiwan's own airlines are now permitted to continue on to Shanghai.

66. China News Agency (Taipei), "Chinese Spouses of Taiwan Citizens Wont Sway Elections: Official," *Taiwan Headlines* (January 5, 2007). Available at http://www.taiwanheadlines.gov.tw/ctasp?xItem=57629&CtNode=5

67. Yulin County Government, "Over 16,000 PRC Citizens Found in Fake Marriages with Taiwanese" (2005). Available at http:// en.yunlin.gov.tw/index3/en/03Bulletin/03Bulletin_01_01.asp?id=686. However, "fake marriages" are more likely to be related to human trafficking and prostitution than spying. See Zoe Cheng (Feb. 2007), p. 9.

68. Wendell Minnick, "The Men in Black: How Taiwan Spies on China," *Asia Times Online Co.*, (http://www.atimes.com), 2004.

69. Editorial, "The Chinese Gulag Beckons," *Taipei Times*, (January 10, 2005). http://www.taipeitimes.com/News/edit/archives/2005/01/10/2003218825

70. Chien-min Chao, "Introduction: The DPP in Power," *Journal of Contemporary China*, vol. 11, no. 33 (November 2002), p. 606.

71. "Taiwan Stands Up," *The Economist* (March 25, 2000), p. 24.

The Mao® Industry

"One can indeed say that political reform has been visited upon China. It came, however, not in the form of an institutional transformation of the state-based political system . . . but in a far subtler yet profoundly life-transforming manner. No longer are people enthralled by the political, or even intimidated by it."

MICHAEL DUTTON

In 1984, I was a student at Beijing University when China's official de-Maoification program was at its height. Throughout the city, statues of Chairman Mao were being torn down. It seemed as if the reassessment of the chairman's thought (70 percent correct, 30 percent incorrect) advanced by the Communist Party's new, reform-era central committee had been transformed into a plan for urban renewal. The cult of Mao that the new central committee wanted to dismantle had left China awash with images of the chairman. A Mao statue could be found in the heart of every town square, another at every work unit entrance and, once inside these compounds, one in every office, as well as in every home. Invariably the statues stood in places formally occupied by ancestral shrines. It was not just Mao's thought that needed moderating, but also his omnipresence.

It was around this time that a Slovenian student friend discovered something that she knew would be of interest to me. At the back of the university campus, outside an old 1950s-style administration building, she found a huge pile of smashed white plaster statues. On closer inspection, the pile turned out to be the university's own contribution to the de-Maoification program. On the ground beneath our feet lay the splintered remains of hundreds of little Mao statues that had been taken down from their exalted positions in administrative offices and unceremoniously dumped into piles awaiting collection. In effect, what my friend had discovered was, if not the burial ground of Chairman Mao, then at the very least, the beginnings of a graveyard of his auric presence. As foreigners, we felt no qualms scavenging about in the pile looking for body parts to souvenir. Soon, we were joined by a couple of inquisitive primary school children. They asked us what we were up to and when we told them, they joined in. Before long, we were happily trading body parts: "I'll give you an arm and a leg of the chairman for his nose," said one child. "No, I want his ear," came my reply. Such irreverence didn't last long.

A Communist Party cadre came screaming out of the administrative building: "You are not allowed to touch the chairman's parts, it's disrespectful." The kids scampered but we held our ground. "We're not being disrespectful," we responded. "That honor goes to the cadre who had the chairman's statues removed from the offices, smashed to pieces, then shoveled into this pile." Our response did little to appease the cadre on what was clearly a sensitive issue. He ordered us off the little Mao mountain with the warning that security guards were on their way. Gathering up what booty we could, we loaded it onto our bikes and tried to make a run for it, but a detachment of security officers pursued and caught us. So we were ourselves "de-Mao-ified," sent back to our respective departments and criticized by our teachers and fellow students.

Mystical Mao, Sentimental Mao

That was China in 1984. Less than 10 years later it was a different story. In 1993 one did not have to dig to find the chairman's image on the campuses of Beijing. He was, once again, just about everywhere. He re-emerged when a growing wave of popular nostalgia was bolstered by official party promotions to mark the one-hundredth anniversary of his birth. With the party sanctioning a variety of activities that were centered around Mao, the popular response was to join in with alacrity. A decade later, in 2003, he would return once more, but this time accompanied by marketing strategists and advertising executives. Where 1993 had the air of spontaneity and the hint of trouble, 2003 had only the hallmarks of a well-oiled advertising campaign.

There is something odd in this constant reappearance of Mao during the long march toward consumerism. Perversely, the chairman's return is more a sign of his fall from grace than of any lingering sense of revolutionary devotion.

No one really knows how the current Mao craze started. Most commentators agree that it probably began after a multicar pileup on a Guangdong highway in 1989. The crash was fatal for many, and the only person to walk away unscathed was the driver of a car with a Mao talisman. With this story, the mystical Mao was born. Transformed from revolutionary leader into a god of good fortune, Mao became a soothsayer for troubled times. From then on other "miracles" confirmed his beatification. His shadowy apparition appeared on the surface of a pebble drawn from the waters of the Yangtze River; it reappeared as a ghostly image on the surface of a peasant's household wall where his portrait once hung; it even resurfaced as nature's own handiwork, etched onto the rock face of a mountainside in Hainan Island that has become known as Mao Mountain (Maogongshan).

This spirit figure, however, was not the only guise in which the chairman re-emerged. Indeed, a wide range of different Maos made their debut in this early phase of the Mao craze. Popular movies and books started to appear. These tell of a very different Mao from the mystic and suggest, as well, a different origin.

Like the mystic Mao, this other, more sentimental Mao came to prominence in 1989. In that year a new "post-scar" literary trend described by Geremie Barmé in *Shades of Mao* as a "search for Mao" began to emerge.[1] This literary movement broke the mold of Mao writing, for rather than adding to the chairman's mystique as both scar literature and party hagiography had done in their different ways, it offered a radical dénouement.

Greatness (hagiography) and great excess (scar literature) were now replaced by a focus on the everydayness of Mao. A *Woman's Day* voyeurism combined with nostalgia for simpler times to produce this new and highly popular genre. Perversely, this nostalgia also had a political face, which reached its apogee in 1989 in the protests at Tiananmen Square.

While students fought party corruption with calls for democracy and liberty, the pragmatic worker participants fell back on nostalgia, resurrecting the image of the chairman to remind the party of their now forgotten obligations to the working class. For years, Mao's image had been the flag under which labor disputes in the reform era had been used to dramatize the loss of worker security and welfare provisions. With the Tiananmen Square protests, this well-worn weapon of worker protest reappeared in the heart of the capital. From such political nostalgia, a more general and genteel form of longing for past security and lost youth fed into a growing romanticism already seduced by movies, magazines, and novels.

By the early 1990s, these aberrant and contradictory trends started to congeal. What tied them together had less to do with the fact that they were all about Mao, and more to do with what they produced: sales. In this respect, origins are unimportant because what is central to this craze is the entrepreneurial discovery that Mao sells. Slowly, the hallowed images of Mao and the revolution were being transformed. They were now well on their way to becoming pure commodities.

Money in the Bank

This process of commodification began innocently enough. In the spring of 1990, a number of publishing houses discovered that the republication of Mao's official portrait had a greater market appeal than they had initially imagined. As many as 3.5 million copies of Mao's official poster portrait were sold in that first year of republication and, in the three years that followed, more than 11 million copies were sold. Seizing the opportunity, other entrepreneurs began to produce their own tokens of Mao.

Indeed, almost anything revolutionary now seemed to have a market. Even the songs of that era began to be sung again. Naturally, they were songs with a very different beat from those of the past. A 1992 remake of revolutionary tunes put to a disco beat was an overnight karaoke sensation, selling 70,000 to 80,000 copies in its first week of release, and over 1 million copies in its first month. In addition, long-neglected revolutionary sites started to become tourist attractions. By 1990, Shaoshan, the place of Mao's birth, boasted around 2,500 visitors per day, reaching a peak of nearly 3,000 per day the following year.

As this "love of Mao" grew, so, too, did the fears and suspicions of party cadres, who were still hostage to the belief that any revival of his image must mean a revival of his politics. Initially, the Communist Party read the various heterodox trends that fed into the Mao craze not as fashion or as fad, but as potentially troublesome and political. Party leaders grew concerned that they could well be looking into the image of a backlash against their liberal economic reform policies. Mao's image, they feared, might become the clarion call that would rally the masses to revolution once more.

They were not the first ruling class to be worried about mass entertainment providing a venue for popular unrest and revolution: from the very first moment business began promoting mass entertainment and the mass tourist industry, political rulers had worried about its effects. The first world trade exhibition at London's Crystal Palace in 1852 provoked anxiety within the political elite. Fearful of gathering together so many proletarians for leisure rather than work, the English ruling class at first tried to limit worker entry.

Soon, however, it discovered that far from fomenting revolution, mass entertainment actually quelled it. Once the mesmeric effects of the culture industry were fully appreciated by political leaders, they did a complete about-face. Instead of limiting participation, the English ruling classes started giving away tickets! Such generosity did not last long. Realizing that workers would pay for their enchantment, Thomas Cook began organizing train-travel tours to the exhibition site and, in so doing, initiated the modern tourist industry.

In China, the Communist Party simply skipped a few stages. It never gave away free tickets and instead moved directly into hiring marketing consultants to manage the growth of this new industry. From this, the so-called Red industry was born. It was brought to consumers, not by the bottlers of Coca-Cola, but by those who would bottle the revolution: the Communist Party.

With an official endorsement of Shaoshan as a national tourist site in 1993, the party fully embraced the Mao craze. By that stage, however, almost anything that made money seemed to be permissible. Even the most heterodox and mystical of Mao sites seemed able to gain official endorsement at this time. In November 1992, the State Environmental Protection Bureau even put a protection notice on Hainan's Mao Mountain and upgraded it from a county- and provincial-level site to one of national significance. By this stage, Mao was becoming irrelevant. Anything that promoted local tourism seemed to be acceptable, and Mao Mountain was certainly doing that. Indeed, Hainan's Mao Mountain became something of a pacesetter with at least three other rival Mao Mountain bids emerging in other parts of China.

While the party showed an initial reluctance to officiate over the spread of the burgeoning Mao business, Chinese entrepreneurs exhibited no such constraint. For them, the growth of Mao iconography and paraphernalia was money in the bank. One of the earliest entrepreneurs to cash in on the late chairman's earning potential was "Old Lady Tang" of Shaoshan, who renamed her capitalist enterprise "Maoist." Beginning as a humble greenbean noodle-soup stall owner, she started to repackage her business in 1978 as a Mao restaurant selling his favorite dishes. It proved a huge commercial success. Having conquered Mao's hometown of Shaoshan, she then moved on to bigger and better things. Currently she operates a franchise of more than 40 Mao-themed restaurants throughout China.

The Great Logo

During the Mao era, the chairman sang a siren song, enchanting the masses with his politics and poetry. Later, he would orchestrate the marshal music that was the Cultural Revolution. Millions would join his choir, march in step, and fight and die in his name. The re-emergence of his face on billboards and posters thus carries special significance—not because it threatens a new wave of radicalism, but because it does the opposite. Through the years of reform, Mao's siren song of revolution has been transformed into simply another soothing love song. He has become, in effect, a mere commodity-shell through which the very idea of being for sale is offered for sale. This is the chairman's afterlife in the era of reform, the foundation for the Mao Industry.

No longer is every event the basis of a political question. Now every event is a question of market opportunity.

As economic reform developed into a consumer revolution, Mao's image was transformed from Great Helmsman to great logo. He became the fashionable embodiment of that mass-produced art form of the common and the everyday: kitsch. The production of kitsch plays on his shadow-image afterlife, and its import lies in the fact that it is not just born on the gravesite of revolutionary siren politics, but actually constitutes one of its most determined gravediggers.

Like the chairman himself, this siren form of politics—a form in which millions expressed an undying faith in their political cause and a willingness to die for it—has been reduced to an artless art form that merely entertains. What we are witnessing, the German sociologist Ulrich Beck would argue, is a very

political form of depoliticization. In this sense, one can indeed say that political reform has been visited upon China. It came, however, not in the form of an institutional transformation of the state-based political system that swept away the Communist Party, but in a far subtler yet profoundly life-transforming manner. No longer are people enthralled by the political, or even intimidated by it.

Turning Revolution into Money

There is no better example of this political depoliticization of the masses than what has happened to the once taboo subject of the Cultural Revolution. In 1986, the Chinese author and critic Ba Jin controversially called for a Cultural Revolution museum to be built along the lines of the Holocaust Museum under construction in Washington, D.C. History, he argued, must never be repeated; a site where "real objects" and "striking scenes" would bring forth feelings of discomfort offered the best guarantee that the Chinese would never forget their own past atrocities. "Masks would fall, each will search his or her conscience, the true face of each one will be revealed, large and small debts from the past will be paid," Ba Jin wrote, and "the flowers that bloom in blood" that appear "bright and beautiful" but that are, ultimately, poisonous will never be planted again. For years, Ba fought official opposition to his idea. The Communist Party did not want to be reminded of its own past failings. Silence reigned while the party struggled with the fear that any revival of that memory spelled trouble. By 2004, all such fears were gone—swept from the party's thoughts by the profit motive.

In April 2004, entrepreneurs in Dayi county, Sichuan Province, turned the earth on a site that became China's first Cultural Revolution museum complex. Consisting of a restaurant, a hotel, and a teahouse, this "museum" was suitably outfitted so that it could take its place as part of a broader theme-park experiment to create the experience of revolutionary extremism without the excess. Promoting nostalgia rather than revolution, the museum was designed to appeal to tourists in need of a break from the capitalist rat race. With suitably attired staff and the accoutrements of revolution adorning its walls, the museum complex's restaurant was a perfect simulacrum of the "worker-peasant-soldier large canteen" (*gong nong bing dashitang*) and the complex's hotel, a Red Guard "reception center" (*Hongweibing jiedaizhan*); the teahouse was renamed Chunlai (Spring Cometh) after one made famous in a Jiang Qing (Madam Mao) model opera, Shajiabang. "This venture definitely isn't just about social service, but about remembering the past, and, most importantly, about the management of a museum business," said one of the investors bankrolling the project. As a cynical reporter from the Qianlong web news service noted when he covered the opening of the "museum," "It was more than social service all right, it was about profit!"

Perversely, it is the very profit orientation and theme-park quality of the museum that makes it so politically powerful—but always in an antipolitical way. What might at first appear as little other than a parody of Ba's solemn vow to remember the victims offers quite literally the best antidote available to the infectious allure of the revolutionary sirens' song.

Ba Jin's solemnity was little different from the anger displayed by the responsible cadre who pulled me off the Mao rubbish pile at Beijing University. Both remain caught in the aura of politics in a way that the tourists of the museum, the karaoke crooners of Mao songs, or the diners at Old Lady Tang's Mao restaurant chain are not. While the former still pick at the scars of the sirens' return, the latter relax at the crossroads of distraction and nostalgia. Fear is replaced by fetishization. Such forms do not merely attract paying customers—they help produce a consumer mentality. In the process of producing this commodity mentality, they bring forth a far more effective and life-changing antidote to the Cultural Revolution than solemnity or outrage could ever evince. In speaking to an everyday anti-politics of fashion and fad, seriousness is caught off-guard. Yet the cost of this anti-political subversion is the reification of the commodity form.

The Politics of Distraction

It is in this ability to transform even the greatest expressions of political commitment and political terror into items of consumption and enjoyment that one can see the power of the culture industry. This power to diminish our capacity to be thrown by the sirens' song of politics lies precisely in the ability it has to make even the most horrendous political event seem, in the eyes of the moderns, unthinkable. The commodified simulacrum of the Cultural Revolution makes the past unthinkable as a horrendous event by remembering it nostalgically, and by offering it to modern consumers as a light-hearted form of distraction.

Politically, this proves far more effective in halting the reemergence as horror than any truth or revelation. Truths can always be contradicted and countered in ways that commodities cannot. After all, how does one challenge a theme park? How does one reverse the trend that makes remnants of siren politics fashionable or "cool?"

In transforming events like the Cultural Revolution and figures such as Mao Zedong into forms of consumer distraction and nostalgia, the commodity process actually robs them of their original transformative ability. In making everything into a commodity, that which is commodified is itself transformed. No longer is every event the basis of a political question. Now every event is a question of market opportunity. Our ears become plugged to the music of the political precisely because we are deafened by the hip-hop or disco versions of the revolutionary song. Increasingly, even when we desire change, we become tied to the very logic that stops it from taking effect. It is this political reform that the Mao Industry has helped solidify, and it is this that constitutes the long-term political legacy of economic reform.

In 1992, Deng Xiaoping undertook his now famous southern tour of China, effectively launching the consumer revolution in China. With this in mind, the dates of the Mao craze suddenly take on added significance. That craze constitutes the first postliberation consumer frenzy witnessed in China. The leader who once made the siren call to politics and then directed politics against capitalism now becomes the image form that leads the counterrevolution. In this new consumer counter-revolution, forms of enchantment remain. Nevertheless, like rootless migrant workers, the forms have left the tightly knit village of commitment politics and moved to the polymorphous consumer capitals of the eastern coastal cities. These are the places of seduction—seductive because they offer forms of enchantment that do not confront the political. Instead, they morph politics into a safer form of dreaming.

They do this by bleaching away the unnatural power of the political and replacing it with the artificial power of the simulacra. The aura remains but the passion is drained away. In each and every domain, and irrespective of their particular localized distinctions, the practices once undertaken out of passionate commitment to a political program are forgotten. Instead of political distinction, we now have economic distractions; instead of being uplifted, we are now stupefied. Caught between the Scylla of passion and excess and the Charybdis of alienation and order, China heads for the latter.

This dilemma is a feature of all liberal democracies. It is now beginning to emerge within the Chinese state. It is the Mao Industry that puts it into focus, for it is the Mao Industry that has led the charge. In this new, passionless world of the commodity, the life-affirming exhilaration of revolution gives way to the faux excitement of manufactured desire. The excesses of the past have gone, but so too have the life-affirming victories of revolutionary zeal. Perhaps this is the cost of any ethic of limit. Life-threatening intensity can only be limited by limiting life itself.

Note

1. Revolutionary realism dominated art and literature during the Cultural Revolution. When it came to an end in 1976, a new form of realism emerged. Called "scar," it described the psychological traumas suffered by intellectuals, rusticated youth, and the common people during the Cultural Revolution. The name for this genre came from a short story by Lu Xinhua called "Scar" that was published in the *Wenhui Daily* on August 11, 1978.

MICHAEL DUTTON is an associate professor in political science at the University of Melbourne. He is the author most recently of Streetlife China (Cambridge University Press, 1998) and *Policing Chinese Politics: A History* (Duke University Press, forthcoming, 2005). He is also the coeditor of the journal *Post-colonial Studies*.

"Let Us Speak!"

Social Debate is Opening up China . . . but the Communist Party Still Dictates

Chris Richards tracks the boundaries of the new political space.

You could not help but notice it. A huge red banner—always popular in Beijing—strung high over the entrance of Renmin University, welcoming NGOs to a meeting about the environment. Inside more than 200 people from 150 organizations from all over China (with a sprinkling of international representatives) talk for two days about strategies to raise public awareness of environmental issues and lobby government officials.

Within minutes of arriving, a group of activists are telling me about the Nujiang river: "As big, as amazing as the Yangtze and the Mekong, but little known outside China." And—at the time we are speaking—soon to be dammed. Wen Bo (who was the first Greenpeace worker in China and now represents Pacific Environment) suggests I write an article about it. "The Government takes its international image very seriously," he calls over his shoulder as he runs to answer his mobile phone. "We need international coverage to bring pressure to bear."

And so it happened. After that conversation in November last year, the NI was one of a number of international outlets that publicized the proposal to dam this recently listed World Heritage Site. By April this year, Premier Wen Jiabao had called a halt to the project for further assessment.

Here was a side of China not reported in the Western press. A forum that nurtures civil society and welcomes debate. A government sensitive enough to critics to reverse a major plan.

As the country hurtles towards a capitalist economy, the ability of the Chinese people to debate social and economic issues is beginning to blossom. Many will tell you that in the 55-year rule of the Chinese Communist Party (CCP) they have never felt so free to exchange views amongst themselves.

Go Directly to Jail!

But this new-found freedom to speak is fragile. China is, after all, still a one-party dictatorship. Any activists worth their salt can explain the clearly defined no-go zones. Challenging the supremacy of the CCP (the Chinese Communist Party) is off-limits. So are statements that undermine the unity of the Republic. Those who step outside these boundaries can expect a reaction that's swift and brutal.

The CCP has maintained stable government since 1949 by wiping out perceived opponents before their views gain any support amongst the people. Those who propose another Party or suggest alternatives to the authority of the CCP are destined for jail.

Since 1998, there have been at least 71 people detained for their use of the Internet. Almost all have been found guilty of subversion and sentenced to between 2 and 12 years jail. Most of them can be linked to one of three categories: banned groups like the China Democracy Party (whose members are amongst those receiving the harshest sentences); criticism of a high-ranking Party official; or the 4 June 1989 Tian'anmen Square protest (when the State stepped in to shut down democracy demonstrators and in the process killed and injured hundreds).[1] Indeed, just the act of demonstrating in the Square now is enough to get you arrested.

Also heading for prison are those who speak about territorial independence from China in Tibet, Xinjiang and Inner Mongolia. Government reactions range from high-powered international diplomacy to direct internal repression. The blood that has flowed from the Tibetan independence movement is known worldwide. The lesser-known struggle by the Uighur in the northwestern province of Xinjiang—just above Tibet has also left many dead. Of those Uighur whose fates are known (and many are not) 134 have been charged with separatist-related activities over the past five years. Twenty-nine received the death penalty while the rest are serving sentences from one year to life.[2]

In deciding what other groups constitute a threat, more unlikely contenders can be caught in the net. Falun Dafa (also known as

Falun Gong) is a practice of purification through exercise and meditation. As a movement, it is about individual spirituality and health as opposed to social reform. Up until 25 April 1999—when more than 10,000 practitioners held a peaceful gathering in Beijing outside the Chinese leadership compound—Falun Gong was freely practised. Within two months of the gathering, the practice was declared illegal. The ability of the movement to mobilize such large numbers of people—rather than the beliefs of its members—is thought to be what the CCP has found so threatening.[3] The movement is now brutally suppressed.

This subjectivity and uncertainty means there are no guarantees. While you may think that you're on the acceptable side of the public debate line, the Government may not end up agreeing with you. A 'freedom' like this—allowing views to be expressed that can be arbitrarily and instantaneously removed later—is no freedom at all. How could anyone argue otherwise?

Then I meet 'Dan'.

Redefining Democracy

Dan says it's not as black and white as I paint it. He challenges me to step outside my usual frameworks to assess the rights that the Chinese can and do enjoy. Dan's an information technology executive who got a Masters degree in the US in the 1960s and later returned to work in China. He's not a Party man himself. But he puts a view that he says is controversial to Westerners like me; a view I hear time and time again. He says that—in judging whether the people have a voice in how they are governed—there is a form of democracy in China. No, it is not a representative democracy with directly elected politicians gathering in a Parliament or Congress. Nationally, he points out how difficult that would be. In a population of 1.3 billion, if you had, say, 1,000 elected representatives, each would need to represent the views of 1.3 million people. "But amongst ourselves we do debate our views freely. We can have an impact at a local level and on government officials. We can be heard." He then relates his recent meeting with CCP officials in which there was a healthy difference of opinion about policy issues, argued without adherence to a Party line.

Let a hundred flowers bloom and a hundred schools of thought content . . . Questions of right and wrong in the arts and sciences should be settled through free discussion.*
Mao Zedong, February 1957

Other NGOs in Beijing also report how the bureaucracy and Party welcome a debate about issues and new ideas. And, as a window to Party policy, *China Daily*—the country's officially sanctioned English language newspaper—presently promotes discussion over a range (albeit limited) of social issues. Nowhere

is this more prevalent than with the environment. For it is here that the Government needs all the help it can get. Of the world's 20 most polluted cities, 16 are in China. Western analysts now estimate that 300,000 people will die prematurely here from air pollution and that more than 20 million people will have to leave their homes because of lack of access to water or degraded land over the next 15 to 20 years.

"In fact, one of the nice things about having a one-party system is that you always have a range of different views in government so that you always have someone who is sympathetic to your views," Greenpeace campaigner Sze Pang Cheung says. Sze thinks that political lobbying in China is easier than in the US where politicians have an eye on donations rather than issues. "A lot of officials here are prepared to take our views very seriously. They give you an opportunity to be heard." In addition to Greenpeace, international NGOs like WWF, Oxfam, ActionAid and Médecins Sans Frontières now openly work in China as a civil society starts to grow.

Civil Society Emerges

Indigenous NGOs have mushroomed: between 1965 and 1996 national social associations grew from 100 to 1,800 while local groups ballooned from 6,000 to 200,000.

The attraction of these organizations to the CCP is more about their potential to offer resources that can absorb the burden of a downsized government than it is about a desire to promote community participation or listen to the people. Since the 1989 protests in Tian'anmen Square, clamps on advocacy are tight. Organizations must register. To do this, they must have a sponsor: a government body or an organization authorized by government to oversee its day-to-day activities. The search for a sponsoring agency—called 'finding a mother-in-law'—is difficult, particularly for organizations that want a national profile and therefore must find a national sponsor. And even if a sponsoring organization can be found, security is tenuous: sponsors are authorized to unilaterally terminate the relationship if the sponsored group acts or speaks out of line.

For the CCP, it is a system that encourages social assistance to individuals while keeping down groups with 'undesirable' messages. The regulations can react to prevailing conditions. After a tightening of the system in 1998, by 2000 the number of social organizations plummeted to just under 137,000.[4]

Despite these constraints, the mere process of running such a huge number of civil society groups is starting to train people about a range of issues—the rights of women, people with disabilities, rural workers, the unemployed and children. Such skills and knowledge will increase the likelihood of their becoming effective advocates when the time is ripe.

'He who is not afraid of death by a thousand cuts dares to unhourse the emperor'—this is the indomitable spirit needed in our struggle to build socialism and communism.
Mao Zedong, 1949

---

*Many of Mao's thoughts and predictions about China—some written over 80 years ago—are surprisingly relevant today, a selection of them appears throughout this issue.

The Communications Revolution

Transnationals like to brag that China's integration into the global economy will help propel the Government to observe human rights. The argument is that free markets and free speech are travelling companions: if one develops, the other will naturally follow. This position has many flaws. Nevertheless, there are a number of indirect consequences flowing from the opening-up of China's markets that should push China closer to a free speech climate.

First, the diaspora. According to official figures, more than 20 million Chinese went overseas last year. This record number included students, tourists, businesspeople and tens of thousands of workers. They are building highways and bridges in the United Arab Emirates, Jordan and Yemen, drilling for oil in Sudan and Venezuela, mining ore in Peru and Australia and picking fruit in England and Israel.[5] Those that return will have a different view of the world and changed expectations.

Second, as China embraces capitalism, an important reason for the people to accept a curtailment of freedom to speak is disappearing.

A postgraduate student at the Peking University who talked frankly and openly to me about a range of issues nevertheless felt uncomfortable discussing human rights in public. She described it as the dominance of 'the Big I over the Little I'. She believed that the Government is justified in setting aside individual rights if it means that the collective good is promoted.

This feeling, still prominent, is nevertheless in retreat. As the market economy pushes the gap between rich and poor further and further apart, the belief that the CCP continues to champion the collective good is diminishing. Workers are no longer able to rely on an 'iron rice bowl'. Previously expected employment rights to job security, healthcare, housing, pay and pensions are receding as the number of people employed by state-owned enterprises falls. Rising in its stead is a new industrial workforce that gets rock-bottom pay, sweatshop conditions, and little (if any) education or pension rights.

The Little I Battles the Big I

The health system is already based on user fees. Recent research says that, as a consequence, as much as 30 percent of poverty in China is directly attributable to medical bills.[6] And as the State provides less and less for the collective good, the justifications for sacrificing individual rights are also retreating. As a result, public resistance is becoming more visible. Nicola Bullard points out that: "In 2001 the Chinese Ministry of Social Security reported an average of 80 'daily incidents' but by December 2002 this had swelled to 700 per day." And, over time, it looks likely there will be less community tolerance for harsh action being directed at those who publicly criticize the authority of the CCP. This will leave the CCP in a much more difficult climate in which to silence its critics.

The exponential growth in the market for Chinese people to communicate with each other must also help free up expression. Officially, the mainland has more than 300 million mobile phone subscribers. They sent a staggering 10 billion SMS (text) messages during this year's seven-day Spring festival, which is 7.7 messages for every one of China's citizens.[7]

It is a communications revolution that even the Chinese authorities will not be able to contain, giving new potential to individuals who are not yet organized into a group with common goals. He Xiaopei, a lesbian organizer in Beijing since 1994, describes the mobile phone as offering an immediately accessible, but largely invisible, way for tongzhi (homosexuals) to obtain information and support in a previously hostile environment. Volunteers who provided counselling and advice for a mobile hotline were confronted by personal problems that they hadn't expected, which provoked group discussions over a range of issues. Out of this: "We have moved from being alone to helping others, from struggling for survival to seeking liberation, from rescuing ourselves to liberating others."[8]

For women's groups, labour and human rights activists; for those who wish to start building a democracy with Chinese characteristics in all areas where debate is not yet welcomed, the potential is enormous.

Then there is the power of the words themselves. Not just the words being heard through mobile phones. Also those in teahouses and kitchens, factories and bedrooms, spoken by farmers and workers. The thoughts previously hidden that are now being spoken. Having taken form, these words are slowly seeping out from the private into the public domain. A growing bulk of articulated opposition pressing against the boundaries that the State has erected.

Poetic justice waiting to be done.

Notes

1. Bobson Wong, 'The Tug-of-war for Control of China's Internet' in *China Rights Forum*, No 1, 2004.
2. The full list can be read in 'In Custody: Recent Arrests in Xinjiang' in *China Rights Forum*, No 1, 2004.
3. Hu Ping 'The Falungong Phenomenon', *China Rights Forum*, No 4, 2003.
4. J Howell, 'Women's Organizations and Civil Society in China' in *International Feminist Journal of Politics*, 5:2, July 2003; S Liang 'Walking the tightrope: civil society organizations in China' in *China Rights Forum*, No 3, 2003.
5. *South China Post*, 24 June 2004.
6. N Young, 'The physician will not heal himself', *China Development Brief*, July 2003.
7. South China Post, 23 June 2004; *China Daily*, 28 January 2004 and 5 February 2004.
8. He Xiaopei, 'Chinese Queer Women Organizing in the 1990s' in *Chinese Women Organizing: cadres, feminists, muslims, queers*, Berg, Oxford, 2001.

Home Alone

Twenty-five years ago, faced with a dizzying population crisis, China banned its citizens from having more than one baby. The policy was a huge success—but what of the children who grew up without siblings? And what are the implications for society of millions of young people who never learned to share? Beginning the second day of our week-long special report, Catherine Bennett talks to Shanghai's 'little emperors.'

Catherine Bennett

Soon after China implemented its one-child policy in 1979, reports reached the west of a new breed of plump, pampered creatures who had never learned to share. They were called Little Emperors, and nobody ever said "No" to them. It was as if our own country had decided to spawn millions of Prince Andrews. As these children have grown older, they have not, according to many bulletins, grown nicer. They are said to be in love with consumer durables and so obese, due to routine parental overfeeding, that they require regular sessions in fat farms. After the terracotta warriors, its army of spoilt tinies is now one of the most famous things about China. But like real emperors, these miniatures seem to avoid the vulgar gaze.

Because among the crowds loitering on the Bund, which once, according to Shanghai historians, swarmed with ragged, insistently begging juveniles, the number of promenading babies, each with a retinue of doting adults, can be counted on one hand. They are held up to be photographed against Pudong's brazen spikes and pinnacles. Elsewhere, in Shanghai's malls, parks and cafes, little children are rarer than British sparrows. In one big toy and baby shop there is not so much as a laden buggy, not even a glimpse of a pregnant stomach containing an embryonic emperor. The city looks as if the Pied Piper of Hamelin has just been through it. Or like a city with a very, very low birthrate. Professor Peng Zizhe, a demographer and director of the Institute of Population Research at Shanghai's Fudan University, thinks it may be as low as 0.7.

Although the contribution of a majority of larger, rural families keeps China's overall birthrate at an estimated 1.8, in urban Shanghai, the one-child policy is well on the way to becoming a half-a-child policy. The ruthless suppression of breeding may have succeeded almost too well. "Twenty or 30 years of propaganda and government implementation of the policy has really changed people's minds about reproduction," explains Peng. "The problem for demographers and policymakers in Shanghai is not, 'Will these children have two or three kids?'—but whether they will have any kids."

Nowadays, he says, it is not uncommon for people in their late 20s still to be living like children with their parents: "They still get enough love from their mothers, so they don't need to create the solid marriage unit." The fact that any couple wanting two children must file an application to the people's government, supported by the relevant documentation, probably doesn't help create the additional citizens Shanghai needs to avert a future pensions and labour crisis. Citizens who pledge to reproduce just once are still rewarded with a Certificate of Honour for Single-Child Parents, and a lump sum at retirement.

So it is likely that most classes, in most city schools, will continue to be composed of only children: individuals who were once pathologised by the psychologist and birth-order obsessive Alfred Adler as typically selfish loners, prone to exaggerated feelings of superiority and liable to have trouble building close relationships. Outwardly, of course, you would never know. No one in the group of 14-year-olds I meet at No 2 Fudan Affiliated middle school is even fat. Do they live like little emperors? Maybe, given that many Chinese emperors succeeded the throne as children and suffered thereafter an oppressed, semi-adult existence, they do.

"We don't sound like children, do we?" asks one boy, Zhang Zhe Yuan, who, like several of these children, has lived abroad. (Even those who haven't speak to me in astonishingly fluent, expressive English.) In their uniform of blue and white tracksuits, with red scarves at the neck, they have a keen, active look, but they say they do nothing but study. "For us it's a very hard life now," says another child. "The competition is intense." One girl, Xie Lu, lived in Leeds for a while. "It's so much pressure; the child has too much to live up to," she says.

Yes, the children say, their parents love them. "They put so much love on us that love becomes a reason to do everything," Xie Lu explains. In particular, love is the reason they must work hard at school. "One of the things that happens when you're an only child, the thing that happens in China," says Zheng Xiu Yi, a boy who has lived in the States, "is that everything is focused on your grades, every aspect of expectation is focused on your grades. If you don't have good grades, you aren't a good child."

The good parent's job, accordingly, is to create a perfect studying environment. "Our parents sometimes do lots of things that we should be doing for ourselves because they want us to concentrate on our grades," says Zheng Xiu Yi. "For instance, my mom pushes my bike out of the door, presses the elevator button and waits for me to finish my breakfast and go out. It's just study, study, study, study and nothing else."

If they are, in every other respect, incompetent, it's not their fault. "The one-child policy is a good way to reduce the population," says Zheng, judiciously, "but everything has its good side and bad side, and what may become of this generation of people is that when we grow up, we may not know how to do laundry, or wash our socks, or tidy up our rooms."

They will, on the other hand, be academically able to a degree that is almost chilling when you imagine them competing against British teens, with their collections of indulgently marked GCSEs. The scores of Chinese students now studying in Britain present a misleading picture. Everyone in China knows that the cleverest, most ambitious students choose top universities at home first; the US—where there are scholarships—second; and English universities only third or fourth. Chinese students know our speciality is selling prestige for money.

At No 2 Fudan Affiliated, where entrance exams for high schools are coming up, the 14-year-olds say it is normal to work 14 hours a day. I must look disbelieving. "We do!" insists Zhang Zhe Yuan. "We wake up at 6.30 am, we don't have enough hours to eat, I skip my dinners for homework. We're not supposed to have this much pressure at school, because we're kids, we're children!" Another boy, taciturn until now, speaks up: "I think I'm just like a robot."

If they finish their school homework, their parents produce home-made extras. "They want more and more," says Zheng Xiu Yi. "You give 'em As, they want A-plus, you give them A-pluses, they want A-plus plus plus. Maybe I'll get 98%, and my dad goes, 'What went wrong?'" It is common, apparently, to score 100% in a school test, then be urged to try harder next time.

Sunny, a solemn girl who says her pocket money is stopped when she fails to excel, is one of thousands of Chinese children who find themselves the family raison d'être. "Chinese people always have new year dinner," she says. "When we eat dinner, my grandmother, grandfather, uncle, aunt, parents and other people always ask me, 'How is your study?' It is the only topic. There is not any other topic. They like to have this topic for a long time, and I can't eat. When I get a bad mark in my examinations, they always say, 'If you don't get good marks, your future is dark'."

It is tempting to attribute some of this grumbling to general 14-year-old disgruntlement. Doesn't Britain also have its quota of pushy parents? But at another Shanghai middle school, Ying Chang Qi Weiqi, where large portraits of Mao, Lenin, Trotsky and Engels preside over the consuming struggle to come top, the fiftyish headmaster, Mr Jin Weiliang, says the parental pressure is "unprecedented in China."

These days, the headmaster says, the government's directive is to alleviate, rather than increase academic pressure on students. It is the parents, many of whom belong to the "lost generation", born into famine, their own prospects sacrificed to the cultural revolution or the economic upheavals which followed it, who focus relentlessly on the exam marks required for a successful life. And, in the absence of guaranteed state pensions, many of them are being realistic.

Once, they would probably have had six children, not just one. "If one child didn't do very well," says Jin Weiliang, "you could put your expectations on another child. Now, if you have only one child, it's succeed or fail. Parents value the success of their children more than their own success. To some extent, the success of a child's education decides whether the family is happy or not. So a very poor family, if their child is doing well, may be very happy—and even a rich family may be unhappy."

Ying, a 22-year-old student, must have made his parents happy by winning a place reading English literature at Fudan, one of the top three universities in China. He is already considering the best way to repay their investment. He remembers when he was 12 and won a free place at a good middle school, that his parents thanked him: "You save us money."

"It's a huge burden for us," he says, "to take care of our mother and father. At our age, you have to start thinking about that. When I get married, my wife and I will have to take care of four old people, so I am deliberately screening out certain jobs already. That's the kind of thing we have to think about, before we think about our own interests. There is a saying: if you are a good student, you earn money for your parents. This has become part of our consciousness."

How much this joyless, long-term planning is a response to China's exiguous welfare system, and how much it illustrates the only child's over-intense parental bond, it's too early to say. Longitudinal studies on some of China's only children are incomplete. Early findings are equivocal. What did we expect them all to be like—Churchill or Stalin? Most of the traits we associate with the only child are anecdotal, or were just made up by people like Adler or the early American psychologist, G Stanley Hall, who said: "Being an only child is a disease in itself."

For every person who believes that only children are loners, there's someone else to argue that they form stronger friendships to compensate for not having siblings. Susan Branje of Utrecht University, who has a paper in this month's *Journal of Child Psychology and Psychiatry* on "Perceived Support in Sibling Relationships", tells me that, "The differences are very small between children with and without siblings. If a child has a good relationship with parents, and companionship from friends, there don't have to be any negative effects from not having siblings."

Some have questioned whether the Chinese should even be concerned. "In countries all over the world you will find more and more single children," Professor Peng points out, rattling off a few low-fertility competitors—Japan, 1.2; Italy, 1.3; Spain, 1.3. "So sometimes the Chinese say, 'In other countries they do not worry about the mentality of the single child, why should the Chinese worry so much?'"

But the savage pruning of aunts, uncles and cousins from the family tree, creating families in which the interest and expectation of six adults all bear down on a single child, is utterly new. And it is in China, where the decline in fertility has been so ruthlessly enforced, that families once worshipped their ancestors. Back in the 70s, says Peng, while mathematicians extolled the one-child plan, some people did wonder what it might do to the Chinese tradition of the family. "But no one paid serious attention to that, because at that time China was in the aftermath of the cultural revolution, the Chinese had just experienced great destruction of Chinese traditional culture, so no one realised there would be further destruction of the traditional norms of Chinese society." He wonders about a lack of kinship and sense of belonging in these children with no relatives except parents and grandparents.

In the professor's experience, the students he teaches are less sociable than generations before them—but then, they grew up in changing times. "We really don't know whether this is caused by the single child [policy], or by the openness to the outside world." A Fudan student has a different explanation for his generation's reserve. "I think the cultural revolution largely destroyed the trust between people, that's why I personally don't feel so secure." Another 14-year-old says it's just that their parents see their friends as academic rivals: "Your parents think they are telling lies, and perhaps your friends are working hard, but they don't want you to know."

Whatever it is, exactly, that has made this generation so self-sufficient, the result is something which Mao would surely have recognised as a threat to the collective life of the party. "Liberalism," he wrote in his 1937 tract, *Combat Liberalism*, "stems from petit bourgeois selfishness, it places personal interests first and the interests of the revolution second . . ." And had his successors wanted to design a generation of people who behaved in this lamentable way, they could not have done better, surely, than enforce a policy which filled the cities and universities with striving only children. The population planners may even have created a generation which will one day render their own style of authoritarian birth control, enforced with fines, utterly unworkable. For rich people, those fines are irrelevant. Equally, it is hard to imagine some of the 14-year-olds I met in Shanghai meekly filling in an application form for a second child.

"I would say [this generation] are more innovative, more creative, they have a very strong self-identity," says the headmaster of Ying Chang Qi Weiqi. "They are more individual." And even with the compulsory Mao studies, which still go beyond school into university, it could be a challenge to keep them on the right path. "We have a lot of pressure and competition," says one of these 14-year-olds, pondering on the character of 100 million only children. "That makes us stronger."

Probably One

A Generation Comes of Age Under China's One-Child Policy

CLAUDIA MEULENBERG

The Chinese population-control policy of one child per family is 25 years old this year. A generation has come of age under the plan, which is the official expression of the Chinese quest to achieve zero population growth. China's adoption of the one-child policy has avoided some 300 million births during its tenure; without it, the Chinese population would currently be roughly 1.6 billion—the number at which the country hopes to stabilize its population around 2050. Many experts agree that it is also the maximum number that China's resources and carrying capacity can support. Standing now at a pivotal anniversary of the strategy, China is asking itself, Where to from here?

China's struggle with population has long been linked to the politics of national survival. China scholar Thomas Scharping has written that contradictory threads of historical consciousness have struggled to mold Chinese attitudes towards population issues. China possesses a "deeply ingrained notion of dynastic cycles" that casts large populations as "a symbol of prosperity, power, and the ability to cope with outside threat." At the same time, though, "historical memory has also interpreted a large population as an omen of approaching crisis and downfall." It was not until economic and development issues re-emerged as priorities in post-Mao Zedong's China that the impetus toward the one-child policy began to build rapidly. During Mao's rule population control was often seen as inhibiting the potential of a large population, but in the years following his death it became apparent that China's population presented itself as more of a liability than an asset. Policymakers eager to reverse the country's backwardness saw population control as necessary to ensure improved economic performance. (In 1982, China's per-capita GDP stood at US$218, according to the World Bank. The U.S. per-capita GDP, by way of comparison, was about $14,000.)

> **Had China not imposed its controversial but effective one-child policy a quarter-century ago, its population today would be larger than it presently is by 300 million—roughly the whole population of the United States today, or of the entire world around the time of Genghis Khan.**

The campaign bore fruit when Mao's successor, Hua Guofeng, along with the State Council, including senior leaders such as Deng Xiaoping, decided on demographic targets that would curb the nation's high fertility rates. In 1979 the government announced that population growth must be lowered to a rate of natural increase of 0.5 percent per year by 1985. In fact, it took almost 20 years to reach a rate of 1 percent per year. (The overestimating was in part due to the lack of appropriate census data in 1979; it had been 15 years since the last population count and even then the numbers provided only a crude overview of the country's demography.) Nevertheless the Chinese government knew that promoting birth-planning policies was the only way to manifest their dedication and responsibility for future generations. In 1982 a new census was taken, allowing for more detailed planning. The government then affirmed the target of 1.2 billion Chinese for the year 2000. Demographers, however, were skeptical, predicting a resurgence in fertility levels at the turn of the century.

The promotion of such ambitious population plans went hand in hand with the need for modernization. Though vast and rich in resources, China's quantitative advantages shrink when viewed from the per-capita perspective, and the heavy burden placed on its resources by China's sheer numbers dictates that population planning remain high on the national agenda. The government has also stressed the correlation between population control and the improved health and education of its citizens, as well as the ability to feed and employ them. In September 2003, the Chinese magazine *Qiushi* noted that "since population has always been at the core of sustainable development, it is precisely the growth of population and its demands that have led to the depletion of resources and the degradation of the environment. The reduction in birth rate, the changes in the population age structure, especially the improvement in the quality of the population, can effectively control and relieve the pressure on our nation's environment and resources and strengthen our nation's capability to sustain development."

The Reach of the One-Child Policy

Despite the sense of urgency, the implementation of such a large-scale family planning program proved difficult to control, especially as directives and regulations were passed on to lower levels. In 1981, the State Council's Leading Group for Birth Planning was transformed into the State Population and Family Planning Commission. This allowed for the establishment of organizational arrangements to help turn the one-child campaign into a professional state family planning mechanism. Birth-planning bureaus were set up in all counties to manage the directives handed down from the central government.

Documentation on how the policy was implemented and received by the population varies from area to area. There are accounts of heavy sanctions for non-compliance, including the doubling of health insurance and long-term income deductions as well as forced abortions and sterilizations. Peasant families offered the most significant opposition; rural families with only one daughter often insisted that they be given the right to have a second child, in hopes of producing a son. On the other hand, in some regions married couples submitted written commitments to the birth-planning bureaus stating they would respect the one-child policy. Despite this variation, it is commonly accepted that preferential treatment in public services (education, health, and housing) was normally given to one-child families. Parents abiding by the one-child policy often obtained monthly bonuses, usually paid until the child reached the age of 14.

Especially in urban areas it has become commonplace for couples to willingly limit themselves to one child. Cities like Shanghai have recently eased the restrictions so that divorcees who remarry may have a second child, but there, as well as in Beijing and elsewhere, a second child is considered a luxury for many middle-class couples. In addition to the cost of food and clothing, educational expenses weigh heavily: As in many other countries, parents' desire to boost their children's odds of entering the top universities dictates the best available education from the beginning—and that is not cheap. The end of free schooling in China—another recent landmark—may prove to

be an even more effective tool for restricting population growth than any family planning policy. Interestingly, the *Frankfurter Allgemeine Zeitung* has reported that Chinese students who manage to obtain a university education abroad often marry foreigners and end up having more than one child; when they return to China with a foreign spouse and passport they are exempt from the one-child policy.

There are other exceptions as well—it is rumored that couples in which both members are only children will be permitted to have two children of their own, for instance—and it is clear that during the policy's existence it has not been applied even-handedly to all. Chinese national minorities have consistently been subject to less restrictive birth planning. There also appears to have been a greater concentration of family planning efforts in urban centers than in rural areas. By early 1980, policy demanded that 95 percent of urban women and 90 percent of rural women be allowed only one child. In the December 1982 revision of the Chinese constitution, the commitment to population control was strengthened by including birth planning among citizens' responsibilities as well as among the tasks of lower level civil administrators. It is a common belief among many Chinese scholars who support the one-child policy that if population is not effectively controlled the pressures it imposes on the environment will not be relieved even if the economy grows.

More Services, Fewer Sanctions

Over time, Chinese population policy appears to have evolved toward a more service-based approach consistent with the consensus developed at the 1994 International Conference on Population and Development in Cairo. According to Ru Xiaomei of the State Population and Family Planning Commission, "We are no longer preaching population control. Instead, we are emphasizing quality of care and better meeting the needs of clients." Family planning clinics across the country are giving women and men wider access to contraceptive methods, including condoms and birth-control pills, thereby going beyond the more traditional use of intrauterine devices and/or sterilization after the birth of the first child. The Commission is also banking on the improved use of counseling to help keep fertility rates down.

Within China, one of the most prevalent criticisms of the one-child policy has been its implications for social security, particularly old-age support. One leading scholar envisions a scenario in which one grandchild must support two parents and four grandparents (the 4-2-1 constellation). This development is a grave concern for Chinese policymakers (as in other countries where aging populations stand to place a heavy burden on social security infrastructures as well as the generations now working to support them).

A related concern, especially in rural China where there is a lack of appropriate pension systems and among families whose only child is a daughter, is that it is sons who have traditionally supported parents in old age. The one-child policy and the preference for sons has also widened the ratio of males to females, raising alarms as the first children born into the one-child generation approach marriage age. The disparity is aggravated by modern ultrasound technology, which enables couples to abort female fetuses in hopes that the next pregnancy produces a son; although this practice is illegal, it remains in use. The 2000 census put the sex ratio at 117 boys to 100 girls, and according to *The Guardian* newspaper, China may have as many as 40 million single men by 2020. (There are several countries where the disparity is even greater. The UN Population Fund reports that countries such as Bahrain, Oman, Qatar, Saudi Arabia, and United Arab Emirates have male-to-female ratios ranging between 116:100 and 186:100.)

A Younger Generation: Adapting Tradition

However, the traditional Chinese preference for sons may be on the decline. Dr. Zhang Rong Zhou of the Shanghai Population Information Center has argued that the preference for boys is weakening among the younger generation, in Shanghai at least, in part because girls cost less and are easier to raise. The sex ratio in Shanghai accordingly stands at 105 boys to every 100 girls, which is the international average. Shanghai has distinguished itself over the past 25 years as one of the first urban centers to adopt the one-child policy, and it promises to be a pioneer in gradually relaxing the restrictions in the years to come. Shanghai was the first region in China to have negative fertility growth; 2000 census data indicated that the rate of natural increase was −0.9 per 1,000.

A major concern remains that as the birth rate drops a smaller pool of young workers will be left to support a large population of retirees. Shanghai's decision to allow divorced Chinese who remarry to have a second child is taking advantage of the central government's policy, which lets local governments decide how to apply the one-child rule. Although Shanghai has devoted much effort to implementing the one-child policy over the past 25 years, the city is now allowing qualifying couples to explore the luxury of having a second child. This is a response to rising incomes (GDP has grown about 7 percent per year over the past 20 years) and divorce rates. As noted above, however, many couples, although often better off than their parents, remain hesitant to have more than one child because of the expense.

The first generation of only children in China is approaching parenthood accustomed to a level of economic wealth and spending power—and thus often to lifestyles—that previous generations could not even have imagined. However, China also faces a rapidly aging population. In the larger scheme of things, this may be the true test of the government's ability to provide for its citizens. The fate of China's family planning strategy—in a context in which social security is no longer provided by family members alone but by a network of government and/or private services—may be decided by the tension between the cost of children and the cost of the elderly. There seems little doubt, however, that family planning will be a key element of Chinese policymaking for many years to come.

CLAUDIA MEULENBERG, a former Worldwatch intern, received her master's degree from the George Washington University's Elliott School of International Affairs in May and now works at the Institute for International Mediation and Conflict Resolution at The Hague in her home country of the Netherlands.

Where the Broom Does Not Reach, the Dust Will Not Vanish

To whose voices is the Chinese Communist Party listening—the capitalists' or the workers'?

CHRIS RICHARDS

She is only 36 years old. Yet when you look at her, you know that every part of her is wearing out. Her whole body sags.

Sometimes she works all day and through the night into the early hours of the morning. After all, there are many costs that come with living in the city. And she has many people in her family to support.

Li Siuling is a migrant worker: just one of 130 million who have left their rural communities to find work in the prosperous eastern cities. The money that she and others like her send back now makes up more than half of the income of the peasants and rural workers in the Chinese hinterland.

Suiling was only 15 when she left Anhui province, not far from Shanghai. It was soon after her father had died. On offer in the city were the menial, dangerous or difficult jobs that are always poorly paid. At first she worked in a restaurant, making 100 yuan ($12.10) a month while the city citizens working with her earned five times that amount. Then she sold clothes, earning 350 yuan ($42.35) while her urban colleagues took home 900. It was just one of the prejudices that she has had to face.

There are four others. After 20 years—like most Chinese citizens who move away from the household where they are officially registered—she still pays an annual fee for a temporary residence permit. Effectively, it registers her as a second-class citizen within her own country. It deprives her of a vote in local elections. It deprives her children of the right to free education. It exposes her to harassment from a police force strapped for cash. Indeed, the police came to her house around midnight once, demanding to see her permit. When she produced it, they tore it up in front of her. Then they fined her for not being able to produce her documents, and jailed her when she wouldn't pay.

The fifth prejudice cursing migrant workers has largely escaped her. Many who have lived in the city for as long as she has done are often unmarried and socially dislocated. But she has a husband—a migrant worker like her, from her province.

Li Siuling lives in Beijing. In Guangzhou, the capital of the southeastern province of Guangdong, I sit at a table with seven representatives of the All China Federation of Trade Unions (ACFTU) to find out whether her story is a common one here, too. Yes, they say, except that after seven years of working in Guangzhou, migrant workers can apply for permanent residence and the social entitlements that go with it.

They tell me that in March last year, Sun Zhigang—a young man from a northern province who worked in a Guangzhou garment company—was taken to a police station because he didn't have a temporary residence permit. He later died from the beating he received there. The public outcry that followed has led to reform of, but not an end to, the system of citizen registration.

The New Face of Labour

Migrant workers now form the country's main industrial workforce. There are an estimated 20 million of them presently in Guangdong alone. And they are in high demand. China is the factory of the world's manufacturers, and this province is one of its main production lines.

The transnational brands pouring from Guangdong's factories read like a corporate who's who. Economic growth here is staggering. It took Britain most of the 19th century to increase its per capita income by two and a half times, and Japan from 1950 to 1975 to improve its by six. Guangdong's per capita income since 1978 has increased 60-fold. A promotional book about the province says that by 2002, the amount of the province's import and export transactions with countries around the world totalled as much as that of Russia and twice that of India.[1]

The road from the coastal city of Shenzhen (another economic power-zone within the province) to Guangzhou is just over 200 kilometres: a virtually uninterrupted line of factories. A grey haze folds over the horizon. At the halfway mark, the factories seem to take up all the space that the eye can see—blocks after blocks after yet more blocks of grey cement and grey corrugated iron line up into the distance. Inside the larger factories 20,000, 30,000, even 70,000 people work. To an entrepreneur, this must be nirvana. To me it looks like hell.

Capitalism Speaks

Taking this journey, the conclusion that corporations have freedom to speak and be heard in this country is inescapable. Local authorities here have been given special powers to govern their own economies. They have long ago learnt the language that attracts investment: special economic zones, tax havens and neglected labour regulations.

So too the Chinese Communist Party, whose government has nurtured this new culture. In November 2002, Jiang Zemin—the country's President at the time—announced that entrepreneurs would henceforth have both membership and a voice in making decisions within the Party. This only formalized what had already been happening. In the *Forbes* magazine list of China's 100 richest in 2002, a quarter said they were CCP members,[2] and nine were delegates to China's law-making body, the National People's Congress.[3]

The most outstanding thing about China's 600 million people is that they are 'poor and bland'. . . . On a blank sheet of paper free from any mark, the freshest and most beautiful characters can be written, the freshest and most beautiful pictures can be painted.

Just as big business is now being officially heard in Government, workers' representative committees and trade unions have a legal right to be heard in management. The catch is that there's only one recognized workers' voice: the ACFTU. Other labour unions must be affiliated to it in order to be recognized.

The ACFTU and the CCP are closely intertwined. At the union table in Guangzhou, I'm sitting opposite Chen Weiguang, who chairs the Guangzhou Trade Union Council and is also the convenor of this region's CCP (ACFTU branch). He smiles at any suggestion of conflict, and says the two should work as one. As for the CCP's ties with capital and management: "On the surface there is conflict, but these must be resolved."

Inside the Larger Factories 20,000, 30,000, Even 70,000 People Work

Ma Xiao Xin, a manager with Panasonic, is also sitting at the union's table. He outlines his company's "particular attention to labour relations." Whenever there are issues affecting workers, the company approaches the union. He describes a proactive union response—for instance, negotiating a drop in the temperature in a too-hot factory by 4 degrees. So who is the union representative in the factory he manages? He is. When I express surprise, he explains: "When we wear the union hat, we have to fight for workers' rights." International investors would be hard pressed to come up with a more attractive way of doing business with unions.

What should one make of such systems? China's paramount leader during the late 1970s and 1980s, Deng Xiaoping, dubbed the country's new capital-driven economy as "socialism with Chinese characteristics." He explained: "It does not matter whether the cat is white or black; if it catches mice it is a good cat." In other words, the primary concern should be the betterment of the people. And if the system that delivers the goal is driven by a free market economy, then that's considered appropriate in a socialist government agenda.

According to the World Bank, China's economic transformation has helped the Communist Party Government to deliver people from starvation. The Bank estimates that over the past 20 years between 300 and 400 million people have been lifted out of poverty.[4] In Guangdong province alone the GDP per head in 1978 was less than a dollar a week and well under the international poverty line. By 2000, its 87 million people enjoyed an average annual GDP income of 12,973 yuan (a little more than $30 a week): three times that amount for those who were living in the provincial capital, Guangzhou.

This city—with its row upon row of high-rise buildings reaching to the clouds—looks like any modern capital in the rich world. Its streets throng with an emerging middle class. But like any city, Guangzhou's buildings and streets hide the underclass that capitalism creates to survive: the groups of migrants who will do the menial and dirty work shunned by the locals. They sweat it out in nearby factories and dormitories.

On the Factory Floor

Overwhelmingly, rural migrants work the factory production lines. In some, 80 percent are migrants. In others, 90 percent. Most are young women under 25 years of age: as workers they are cheap and compliant. They come here willingly, most knowing that they will work 10 or 11 hours a day, six days a week. In busy times, some will regularly work all night. Tired and bleary, they are accidents waiting to happen.

I visit a chemical factory, passing by a sign that warns workers that if they use the lift 'inappropriately' they will be fined (a common way for employers to regulate their employees in these provincial factories). The sign is on the way to the factory floor where male workers with scant protection in stifling heat pack chemicals into bags. I see a toy factory where rows of migrant workers sit at tables, applying glue and paint with fine brushes to tiny resin soldiers. Again, the heat is stifling: the smell from the solvents inescapable. The workers have no protection. When I talk to one of the employers, he explains that there is ventilation "and they have a break every 5 hours." I wonder what the continual whiffs of glue must do to their brains.

These are the better places to work.

On average these workers earn less than 600 yuan ($73) a week; up to 800 ($97) with overtime.[5] The system maximizes employer control. During busy times temporary employees—who can be sacked when production falls—make up a large proportion of the workforce (40 percent is not uncommon). Accommodation is tied to employment, giving employers extended control over the lives of workers outside their factories and minimizing the opportunity for employees to find out about other—more appealing—workplaces.[6] The workers live together in dormitories—some attached to the factory, some in nearby towns. In the less restricted ones, there are only six people to a room. All are sex-segregated. Even if the workers were given the choice (and few are), the workers could not afford to live in a house with a partner as a family. Exhausted after long workdays, many have never been to nearby towns. The factories and the dormitories define their lives.

Industrial action appears a remote prospect. Less than 30 percent of foreign factories in Guangdong have an ACFTU representative. Indeed, it was not until last year that membership of the ACFTU was even open to migrant workers.

In any event, a priority for both the CCP and the ACFTU is courting capital. Their policies for the modernization of China depend on it. To attack the chronic underemployment in the countryside (where 30 million still have inadequate food and clothes) surplus rural labour needs to be sucked into the cities. But to support the rural influx, jobs must be attracted—and lots of them. China's labour laws must be the trade-off. Both the Chinese Government and the ACFTU know that if factory wages and standards are raised, capital investment will go elsewhere—to other parts of China, or worse still, to other countries.

Left to their own devices, with no ability to form their own associations, there'll be no real change for migrant workers—in the short term, at least. But as the Chinese saying goes: Water supports a boat; it can also capsize it. China's rural workforce was 488 million in 2003, with over 300 million of them underemployed. As a consequence, the number of rural workers leaving the countryside to seek work in the cities is increasing exponentially: estimated to grow to 200 million in the next decade. Just as the peasants and farmers provided the vital support needed for the Communists to take power, the migrant workers they have become can take it away.

Resentment and frustration are spilling over. There have been sporadic strikes and walkouts. Reports of vandalism, sabotage and violence by workers are seeping past the factory doors and on to the desks of NGOs. If the legitimate grievances of migrant workers remain unresolvable, they are likely to pose a long-term problem for the stability of the Government.

Occasionally there is an encouraging sign from the CCP. Xiong Deming, a woman in a remote village in Chongqing province, complained to Premier Wen Jiabao last October that her husband, who was working on a nearby construction site, had not been paid for several months. This is a common tale: in the construction industry alone, payments in arrears owing to workers have accumulated to 30 billion yuan ($3.6 billion). After Premier Wen's direct intervention, the money owed to Xiong's family was paid that night. It sparked a Government-led campaign to help migrant workers retrieve the arrears owed to them.[7]

The ACFTU too is working to improve living standards: running model dormitories and setting up health schemes for the workers.

But these responses dance around the central issue. To pull a few up to riches, the money that is being made through the sweat of the migrant workers pushes many down to appalling pay and conditions.

To an Entrepreneur, This Must Be Nirvana. It Looks Like Hell

It is still not too late. The CCP's public embrace of the market economy does not mean that it needs to trash socialist principles completely. It could resist the present economic orthodoxy overseen by the World Trade Organization, the World Bank and the International Monetary Fund that the state should refrain from any intervention in the market. It could then reach into the factories and dormitories with laws and inspectors to guarantee better, safer working conditions and a more equitable share of income. However, if it accepts the prevailing capitalist view and takes a 'hands-off' approach, the voices of the migrant workers are likely to remain unheard in the crowded factories and dormitories where they are presently trapped.

Notes

1. Jin Huikang, *Aspects of Guangdong*, Cartographic Publishing House of Guangdong Province, Guangdong, 2002.
2. J Chan 'Chinese Communist Party to declare itself open to the capitalist élite.' *World Socialist Web Site*, wsws.org, November 2002.
3. China's 100 Richest 2002, *Forbes*, forbes.com, 24 October 2002. This was a fall from 2000, when 12 of the 50 richest were delegates to the Congress—see R Hoogewert 'China's 50 Richest Entrepreneurs' *Forbes*, forbes.com, 27 November 2000.
4. World Bank President, James Wolfensohn, speech to a Poverty Reduction Conference in Shanghai on 26 May 2004.
5. Research conducted by Kai Ming Liu, Executive Director of the Institute of Contemporary Observation, Shenzhen.
6. Pun Ngai 'The Precarious Employment and Hidden Costs of Women Workers in Shenzhen'. The Chinese Working Women Network, September 2003.
7. *China Daily*, 19 January 2004.

Discontent in China Boils into Public Protest

David J. Lynch

Wanli, China—When the local government announced it was going to confiscate their homes and businesses to make room for a new development, residents of this village in southeastern China fought back.

They complained to five levels of local government. They sued officials in charge of the relocation effort. They journeyed to Beijing to petition central authorities. And when all that failed, they staged a sit-in on the grounds of a local factory that they had built with their pooled savings.

All but one of the demonstrators were women, many middle-aged or older. But that didn't stop more than 100 police officers, backed by thugs led by a notorious local criminal, from busting through a locked gate and beating them into submission.

"They bent my arm and threw me on the ground. I started to cry when I fell on the ground," says 54-year-old Huang Yaying, who suffered a broken arm.

After a half-hour melee in which 15 people were injured, authorities seized control of the four-story liquor factory. And in the weeks since the Aug. 1 incident, relocation crews have returned again and again to knock down nearby homes and businesses. Today, blue metal construction fences line Wanli's narrow streets, shielding piles of cement and brick rubble.

The continuing siege in this village of 600 people illustrates that beneath a veneer of authoritarian rule, economic strength and Olympic success, popular discontent is bubbling in China. Last year, there were 58,000 "mass incidents" across China, according to government statistics cited in the Chinese magazine *Outlook*. That's more than six times the number of protests and demonstrations the authorities admitted to in 1993.

The increasing willingness of individuals to confront state authority is powerful evidence of the emergence of what political scientists have labeled "rightful resistance." As China's economy grows freer and more tumultuous, these government-tolerated grievances are starting to hint at what a more open political environment might entail. They illustrate both the partial loosening of restraints on popular action and the very real limits that remain.

The disturbances—by farmers upset over high taxes, laid-off workers demanding overdue pensions and residents outraged over improper land grabs—have been carefully limited to economic issues. Even the most ill-educated peasant understands that the Communist government would swiftly crush any organized demand for political liberalization.

That doesn't mean China's rulers regard the complaints with indifference. Last month, Zhou Yongkang, minister of public security, listed such protests as one of several factors potentially threatening the country's stability.

Once a rarity, examples of public disobedience are now plentiful. Earlier this year, 2,000 workers and retirees at a textile plant in Suizhou in central Hubei province took to the streets to demand unpaid benefits. In November 2003, thousands of people in Zoucheng, Shandong province, stormed a government building, smashing windows and office equipment, after a sidewalk vendor was accidentally run over when city officials tried to enforce a new policy against such sales. And in March of 2002, tens of thousands of workers in Liaoyang massed against corruption and unpaid wages in the longest-lasting protests in China since the 1989 "Democracy Wall" campaign.

"They are very concerned about it," says Murray Scot Tanner, a China specialist at the Rand Corp, a think tank. "Unrest has gone up every year by at least 9% or 10% since they started keeping these numbers in 1993."

The central government in recent years, however, has relaxed its view of people who balk at official actions. Beijing established "letters and visits" offices to receive citizen complaints and seems to understand that the dislocation caused by China's unprecedented capitalist evolution, not foreign agents, explains much of the discontent.

At the same time, Chinese protesters also have become adept at choosing their targets. To increase their chances of success, they usually argue that unjust local officials are failing to implement the central government's policies. "When you protest and wave the central government's policies as your shield, it provides some sort of political protection," says Minxin Pei of the Carnegie Endowment for International Peace.

Since taking office two years ago, Communist Party General Secretary Hu Jintao and Premier Wen Jiabao often have spoken publicly of the need to address legitimate citizen complaints. Ensuring that the ruling party is more responsive to those being left behind in China's pell-mell capitalist surge is likely to be emphasized at a high-level party meeting in Beijing.

Still, local officials don't always handle citizen disputes with the sophistication Beijing would prefer. And, as Wanli demonstrates, they don't hesitate to employ brute force to get their way.

"Take him out and beat him."

Wanli once was a farming village outside of Fuzhou, the bustling capital of Fujian province. In the 1980s, the Cangshan district government confiscated almost 500 acres of village farmland to use for a new university, hospital and other institutions. As their vegetable farms kept shrinking, villagers decided in 1985 to pool their savings and invest in a series of shops, factories and six-story apartment buildings. Four years later, the enterprise, similar to village-level commercial ventures sprouting throughout China, was formalized by the local government as the Wanli Group.

By the mid-1990s, rent from these properties was the villagers' main source of income. By then, continued development in the area had turned the former farming village into an urban neighborhood on the outskirts of Fuzhou.

In 2000, villagers began hearing that the local government planned to evict them to make way for unspecified redevelopment. It's a familiar story in contemporary China. Roughly 20 million of China's 900 million farmers already have lost their land to commercial projects, according to the state-run Xinhua news agency. Often these disputes pit developers and their government allies against some of the least powerful people in China.

Almost everyone in Wanli was opposed to the project, fearing it would eliminate the businesses that are their only source of income and leave them without enough money to buy new homes elsewhere. With their farms gobbled up by China's insatiable urban development, many residents survive on the 330 yuan ($39.85) they receive each month as their share of income from the village enterprise.

Villagers say they receive 100 yuan ($12) per month in compensation for some of the businesses that already have been torn down. And they have been offered 1,300 yuan per square meter ($14.59 per square foot) for their homes. That's less than half the amount they say they need to buy comparable new housing.

But as is routine amid China's construction binge, local officials rejected the residents' complaints about improper treatment and insisted they evacuate. Villagers, displaying a surprisingly strong faith in the central government, blame corrupt local officials for their predicament. Earlier this year, the villagers sued the Cangshan district government office that is directing the relocation. But the case has languished. "We think it's useless. The government and the court, they're the same thing," Li Hua says.

On March 18, the first wrecking crews arrived in the neighborhood and began tearing down several buildings. In their wake, one despondent resident, Jiang Biquan, 45, died after drinking a bottle of agricultural chemicals. His suicide did nothing to slow the redevelopment. Several weeks later, about 300 police officers and men in civilian clothes surrounded the village and beat residents trying to halt additional demolition efforts.

On July 17, a group of villagers flew to Beijing and spent 11 days fruitlessly making the rounds of relevant ministries. One official at the Ministry of Construction even telephoned the Fujian Construction Bureau to inquire about the situation. But demolition work continued. "The Cangshan district government doesn't care what the law says. Their attitude is, 'We want this land and you have to give it to us,' " villager Li Wu says.

On Aug. 1, the dispute finally boiled over. Villagers had learned that the relocation office staff was preparing to seize the liquor factory to serve as its headquarters during the final stages of clearing Wanli. Relocation officials told villagers their existing office suffered from poor feng shui, meaning the building's design lacked harmony.

Local residents, who had invested as much as 10,000 yuan each in the village enterprise, feared the loss of their financial stake. So a few minutes past 8 a.m., about 20 people assembled inside the compound, which is ringed by a cement wall.

About 8:30 a.m., Shen Li, an official with the Cangshan district government, arrived and demanded to be let in. The villagers refused to unlock the gate, so Shen clambered over the wall and ordered an underling to break the lock with a hammer. "We tried to stop them from breaking open the lock. Some of us surrounded the lock," says a woman who gave only her surname, Jing, saying she feared retaliation from officials.

At that point, officials began roughly pulling the women away. As the skirmish intensified, says Jiang Bibo, the only male villager inside the compound, "You can't beat people like that!"

Villagers say Shen responded by ordering another man to punish Jiang, who was sitting nearby, saying, "Take him out and beat him."

Jiang, 50, was punched in the face and hurled to the ground. As he lay there, wrapping his arms protectively around his head, several men kicked and struck him repeatedly, witnesses say. Jiang was later hospitalized with a concussion and internal bleeding. "If it wasn't for another woman who went over and covered Jiang Bibo with her body, somebody could have died that day," Jing says.

Operating alongside the police that day were 14 recently released prisoners headed by Zhao Zhenguang, a local mobster. With ambulances parked nearby, the authorities seemed prepared for violence, witnesses say. One of the vehicles was needed to ferry Pan Lanfang, 56, to the hospital. The local resident had gone to the factory to look for a friend, not to protest. She ended up badly beaten.

Efforts to reach Shen at his office and on his cellphone for his account of the August 1 events were unsuccessful. Authorities in Beijing say they were unable to provide any immediate comment on an individual relocation dispute.

Retaliation by officials alleged.

Despite central government directives to take a more subtle approach to quelling protest, such violent repression remains all too common, analysts say. "The use of hoodlums, really violent criminals, against peaceful civilians is quite prevalent," says Pei, the Carnegie analyst.

Chinese authorities have ordered local police to defuse protests without violence, according to Tanner. But the message doesn't appear to be getting through. "In the last couple of months, I've heard several cases of very deliberate use of harsh forces by the police and very undisciplined use of force," he says. "That's absolutely the sort of thing that, officially, they've been discouraging."

Following the attack, 60 villagers went to the Fujian province's Public Security Bureau to file a complaint. They also penned an open letter to authorities in Beijing seeking an investigation. Human Rights in China, a New York-based group, released an account of the dispute on Aug. 25. There has been no formal response to the villagers' letter.

But on Aug. 2, the day after the assault, relocation office officials staged a banquet at the factory compound for the police and other government officials who evicted the demonstrators. And in the intervening weeks, several villagers say, provincial officials have threatened them with prosecution for talking about the case with foreign reporters or other outsiders. "Everybody here is in great danger now. They could just put us in jail for seven or eight years. You never know," Zheng Rong says.

Already, one villager, whose home was demolished earlier this month, has been detained along with his wife and sister. Officials reportedly are pressing him to admit he helped organize recent protests, which would leave him open to prosecution. As part of their strategy to quell protest, Chinese officials customarily punish organizers more harshly than mere participants.

Officials are keeping the pressure on in other ways. In early September, as the temperature hovered around 97 degrees, they interrupted the public water supply for several days. Villagers also say their sleep has been interrupted by people knocking on their doors before dawn.

Amid continued clearance work, desperation is growing. On Sept. 8, Jiang Zongzhong, a retiree in his 70s, had had enough. As workers moved to demolish his home, the elderly man tried to kill himself by igniting a propane tank used for cooking fuel. Witnesses say a fireman knocked him to the ground, slapped him in the face and removed him from the home. The structure and the possessions of a lifetime were flattened.

Still, the villagers continue to profess faith in the central government in Beijing.

"We hope the real Communist Party can send us a Bao Qingtian," Li says, referring to a 12th-century Chinese imperial official renowned for his honesty and integrity. "We hope they send somebody like that to give us justice."

Beijing's Ambivalent Reformers

"The party has implemented various modest reforms in recent years. Some are designed to allow the party to implement its policy agenda more efficiently. Others aim to make it more responsive to a changing society, or at least to appear so. All are designed to perpetuate the Communist Party's rule, not necessarily to make China more democratic."

BRUCE J. DICKSON

China's leaders have been exceedingly cautious about embarking on extensive political reforms, and not without good reason. There is no guarantee that reform efforts will succeed, or that China will be better or more easily governed as a consequence of reform. There is certainly no guarantee that the Chinese Communist Party will survive as the ruling party if it initiates fundamental reform of the political system.

The leadership is acutely aware that even good intentions can have disastrous consequences: when Soviet Communist Party leader Mikhail Gorbachev launched his reforms in the Soviet Union, he did not envision the collapse and dissolution of his country, and yet that was the result. Even though the immediate causes of the Soviet collapse are not as salient in China (economic stagnation, separatism, populist leaders, Gorbachev himself), the country's leaders are concerned that political reform could lead to the same fate. With few examples of authoritarian parties sponsoring democratization and surviving as the ruling parties of their countries, the Chinese Communist Party is still searching for a suitable role model to emulate.

What kinds of reforms are necessary to keep the party in power, and what reforms would jeopardize its tenure? These are questions that bedevil the current "fourth generation" of leaders just as they did their predecessors. Both Deng Xiaoping and Jiang Zemin, leaders of the second and third generations, respectively (Chairman Mao, of course, was the first generation leader) believed that economic modernization had to precede political change, and took the Soviet collapse as a cautionary tale. The current leadership, symbolized by party General Secretary Hu Jintao and Prime Minister Wen Jiabao, has not made its full intentions clear, but it has not yet shown any inclination to experiment with bold political reforms.

Even though China has not experienced the kinds of democratization that most observers have in mind when they look for signs of political reform, the party has implemented various modest reforms in recent years. Some are designed to allow the party to implement its policy agenda more efficiently. Others aim to make it more responsive to a changing society, or at least appear so. All are designed to perpetuate the Communist Party's rule, not necessarily to make China more democratic.

Adapting the Party to the New Agenda

At the beginning of the post-Mao period, Deng Xiaoping and other reformers recognized that their goal of modernizing China's economy with "reform and opening" (*gaige kaifang*) policies could be undermined both by remnant Maoists, who did not support their policies, and by veteran cadres, who were not qualified to carry out reform even if they supported it. For their economic reforms to be successful, therefore, they changed the party's policies regarding recruiting of new members and appointments of officials. After removing the Maoists from their posts and easing the veteran cadres into retirement, they transformed the composition of the cadre corps and rank-and-file membership.

At all levels, party members and officials have become on average younger and better educated. To make the Communist Party younger, leaders assured that roughly two-thirds of new recruits each year were no older than 35. To prevent local officials from remaining in office indefinitely, the party instituted a two-term limit on all posts and required officials to retire once they reached a certain age and were not promoted (65 for provincial-level officials, younger for lower levels of the bureaucracy).

The emphasis on education is even more apparent. Whereas less than 13 percent of party members had a high school or better education in the late 1970s, by the time of the sixteenth party congress in November 2002, the figure had risen to 53 percent. Within the central committee—which comprises the party's top 150 to 200 leaders—the proportion of those with a college degree rose from 55 percent in 1982 to 99 percent in 2002. Improvements in the education qualifications of local officials from the provincial to the county level were even more dramatic: in 1981, only 16 percent had a college education; 20 years later in 2001, 88 percent did.

The current generation of leaders is often referred to as "technocrats," meaning they hold bureaucratic posts and have technical backgrounds in the sciences and engineering. As Li Cheng has noted in the *China Leadership Monitor*, all nine members of the Politburo's standing committee, the very top elite of the party, are technocrats, as are eight of the ten members of the State Council, China's cabinet. Below this top level, however, the growing dominance of technocrats has abated. According to Li, the proportion of technocrats on the central committee dropped from 52 percent at the fifteenth party congress in 1997 to 46 percent at the sixteenth party congress in 2002. Similarly, among provincial party secretaries and governors, the proportion of technocrats has declined from about 75 percent in 1997 to only 42 percent in 2003. Moreover, *none* of the provincial leaders appointed after March 2003 (the likely candidates for the fifth generation of leaders) are engineers. For this younger generation of leaders, educational backgrounds in economics, the social sciences, humanities, and the law are increasingly common.

Many Chinese now believe that economic success is based on personal connections with party and government officials, not individual initiative or quality work.

While it is dangerous to infer political preferences from academic backgrounds, this change in the composition of local leaders is a trend worth following. Many observers have predicted that the technocratic background of fourth generation leaders makes them more disposed to practical problem solving than bold experimentation. But the next generation of leaders comes from very different formative experiences. They have different educational backgrounds, have had greater exposure to international influences, and have enjoyed deeper experience in local administration. They may be more inclined to not just make the political system work more efficiently but to change it to make it more responsive to societal demands.

For these leaders, the key political event was not the Cultural Revolution (they are too young to have had their careers affected by those tumultuous years between 1966 and 1976 as previous generations of leaders did) but the popular demonstrations of 1989. The challenge facing the party is not to undo the mistakes of the Maoist period or to achieve rapid economic growth, but to prepare the political system for the consequences of modernization. How the party addresses this challenge will largely determine whether China will become more democratic, and more important, how systemic change may come about.

The best example of the party's change in recruitment strategy is the proportion of worker and farmers in the party. In 1994,

they comprise 63 percent of all party members; by the end of 2003 their proportion had dropped to 44 percent in a party that had grown to over 68 million members. In less than 10 years, these representatives of the proletarian vanguard had become a minority in the Chinese Communist Party. The party now focuses on educational credentials and professional accomplishments in its recruitment strategy. Increasingly, that has meant turning to the urban entrepreneurial and technological elites.

These changes in the composition of the rank-and-file party members, local officials, and top leaders were designed specifically to promote economic reform. In this regard, the party reform was certainly successful. Over the past 25 years, China's economy has grown by 8 percent annually, lifting per capita income from $190 in 1978 to $960 (according to the World Bank, using current dollars) and shifting the bulk of economic activity from agriculture to industry, commerce, and services, and from the state sector to the nonpublic sector. Rapid economic change has also led to the emergence of new social groups, and the party has switched from excluding them from the political arena to actively incorporating them. It has co-opted these new elites by recruiting them into the party, appointing them to official posts, and creating corporatist-style organizations to integrate state and society.

The Rise of the Red Capitalists

In August 1989, soon after the end of popular demonstrations in Tiananmen Square and elsewhere, the Communist Party imposed a ban on recruiting private entrepreneurs into the organization. Party leaders were concerned that the economic interests of businessmen conflicted with the political interests of the party. This was not just Marxist paranoia: several prominent businessmen publicly supported the Tiananmen demonstrators and later fled the country to avoid arrest. Although the ban remained in place for more than 10 years, it was not very successful in keeping entrepreneurs out of the party. As I noted in my recent book, *Red Capitalists in China: The Party, Private Entrepreneurs, and Prospects for Political Change*, local officials had an incentive to reach out to entrepreneurs even if central leaders disapproved. Creating economic growth is now a key criterion for career advancement, and throughout the 1990s most economic growth and job creation came from the private sector.

Because of this, local officials in some communities—but by no means all—began to recruit successful entrepreneurs into the party despite the formal ban. The percentage of private entrepreneurs who belonged to the party—a group known as "red capitalists"—grew from around 13 percent in 1993 to more than 20 percent in 2000. Not all were new party members, however; most red capitalists had been members before going into business, but about one-third were co-opted after becoming successful businessmen. Orthodox Marxists harshly criticized the emergence of red capitalists and warned that it would spell the demise of the Chinese Communist Party.

As the economic clout of the private sector has grown, the political roles filled by private entrepreneurs have also increased. In addition to being members of the party, many entrepreneurs also belong to local party committees, the major decision-making bodies in China, further integrating them into the political system. At the sixteenth party congress in November 2002, entrepreneurs were among the delegates for the first time, although none were named to the central committee. When China's legislature, the National People's Congress, met in spring 2003, 55 entrepreneurs were selected as deputies. Entrepreneurs have been asked to serve in local legislatures in even larger numbers: over 17 percent of entrepreneurs belong to local people's congresses, and 35 percent belong to local people's political consultative conferences, a body designed to allow discussion between the party and other local elites. Many have been candidates in village elections, and most of the successful candidates are also party members, showing the party's desire to keep all political participation under its control.

In addition to bringing new social strata into the political arena, the party has also developed institutional ties with a variety of new social organizations. These groups are designed to be the party's bridge to society, allowing it to monitor what is occurring without directly controlling all aspects of daily life. China has tens of thousands of civic and professional organizations and hundreds of thousands of nonprofit organizations, such as private schools, medical clinics, job-training centers, and community groups, that provide a variety of social welfare services.

This vast number of organizations may create the foundations of a fully developed civil society, but at present they do not enjoy the kind of autonomy normally expected to be found in the groups that compose a civil society. All organizations must be formally registered and approved, and have a sponsoring governmental organization. They are also not supposed to compete with each other for members or for governmental approval. Where more than one similar group exists in a community, they may be pressured to merge or disband. These restrictions on social organizations suggest a corporatist logic to state-society relations, with controls over which organizations can exist and what kinds of activities they can engage in.

At the same time, many of these new groups are unlike the Communist Party's traditional "mass organizations," such as the All-China Federation of Trade Unions, which are seen by their nominal members as tools of the state rather than representing members' interests. Many professional organizations are not simply transmission belts for the party line, but instead are able to provide tangible benefits for their members. As Scott Kennedy shows in his forthcoming *The Business of Lobbying in China*, a variety of business associations have sprung up, often industry-specific, organized from the bottom up, and active at lobbying the state and in some cases unilaterally setting industry standards and regulations. These associations are more autonomous, more assertive, and less interested in simply representing the state's interests. This may complicate the party's strategy of creating new institutional links to monitor and control the private sector, but at present these business associations limit their activities to issues within their sphere and are not involved in larger public policy issues.

That behavior remains the key to success for both individuals and organizations: do not stray into political matters, and do not challenge the Communist Party's monopoly on political power. While much has changed in China in recent years, this basic political rule has not. Yet most of these new organizations are more inclined to succeed within the existing boundaries than try to change them. This also is a function of civil society: not just to challenge the state, but to find ways of working with the state to pursue common interests. Most writing on contemporary China focuses largely on the conflictual nature of civil society, but the potential for cooperation is just as important and certainly more prevalent today.

Courting New Elites

As economic development created a more complex society, with new social strata that did not fit neatly into old class categories, third generation leader Jiang Zemin and his colleagues recognized that they relied on these new elites to maintain rapid economic growth and could not continue excluding them from the party. Beginning in early 2000 and culminating in his speech on the eightieth anniversary of the Chinese Communist Party's founding on July 1, 2001, Jiang laid out a new definition of the party's relationship with society, which became known as "the important thinking of the 'Three Represents.'" According to this formulation, the party no longer represented only farmers and workers, its traditional base of support, but now also incorporated, first, the advanced productive forces (referring to entrepreneurs, professionals, high-tech specialists, and other urban elites); second, the most advanced modern culture; and third, the interests of the vast majority of the Chinese people.

This was a very inclusive definition of the party's role, and while often ridiculed as an empty slogan, it indicates a serious effort to update the party's relationship with a changing society. It acknowledged that what brought the party to power in 1949 was substantially different from what the party faces in the twenty-first century. If the party's guiding ideology no longer fit China's economic and social conditions, then the ideology needed to be updated—but not abandoned altogether. The party still goes to great lengths to show how its ideology remains consistent with its Marxist origins, even if China's few remaining ideologues believe the party has already abandoned its traditions and betrayed its revolutionary goals.

After Jiang's Party Day speech in 2001, in which he recommended lifting the ban on recruiting entrepreneurs and other new social strata into the party, and after the sixteenth party congress in 2002, when the "Three Represents" was added to the party constitution, large numbers of these "advanced productive forces" were expected to join the party. That did not happen, but it is not clear why. It may have been that local officials were not enthusiastic about this new policy and resisted implementing it. While some local leaders had ignored the ban on recruiting private entrepreneurs into the party, other leaders adamantly believed that capitalists did not belong in the Communist Party.

After the "Three Represents" became official party doctrine, a small number of cities was chosen to experiment with recruiting members from among these new urban elites. The public media did not report on the results of these experiments, indicating little progress was made. The party's organization department issued new directives on recruiting private entrepreneurs in 2003, but the message was ambiguous. Local party committees were advised not to be so eager to recruit new members that they lowered the standards for party membership, nor so strict that they did not let in any. Without clearer guidelines, the adoption of the "Three Represents" slogan was not fully integrated into the party's recruitment strategy.

However, the lack of progress may have been due to declining interest among private entrepreneurs themselves in joining the party. The number of red capitalists has continued to grow in 2003—up to 30 percent of entrepreneurs were party members—but most of the growth has come not from new recruitment, but from the privatization of state-owned enterprises. As these enterprises were converted into private firms, their former managers, almost all of whom were party members, became owners of private firms, automatically becoming red capitalists. Other entrepreneurs, however, seem to have lost interest in joining the party. Some claimed that they did not want to belong to a party that seems increasingly corrupt. Others did not want to be subject to party scrutiny of their business practices.

In a more general sense, party membership has become less valuable for many entrepreneurs. When the party was more ambivalent about the private sector, membership was useful for promoting business interests, such as securing loans, finding new investors, limiting outside competition, and above all protecting them from predatory actions of local officials. Reports of the confiscation of private property and financial assets remain common, showing that many local officials are more concerned with profiting from the private sector than promoting it. As the party's commitment to the private sector grew, and the interests of businessmen became better protected in party policy as well as laws and regulations, party membership became a less valuable commodity for private entrepreneurs. Still, the slowdown in co-opting entrepreneurs into the party—which seemed to be the main motivation behind the "Three Represents" in the first place—remains something of a mystery.

> **While many no longer believe Marxism remains a relevant doctrine in contemporary China, there is no doubt that Leninism remains the guiding influence in the political system.**

Even so, in the years after 1978, the party has steadily become younger, better educated, more professionally experienced, and more diverse as the farmers and workers, the traditional mainstays of the party, have been replaced by entrepreneurs, high-tech specialists, managers, and other new social strata. These changes have reinforced the commitment of party members and officials to the "reform and opening" policies. As a result, party adaptation has been generally successful by one measure: the changes have allowed the party to pursue its new goals more efficiently. However, a more challenging test of the party's adaptability is whether it is responsive to the changing wants and needs of society, and here the results have been more ambiguous.

Restoring Balance

Under the leadership of Jiang Zemin, the Communist Party had a distinctly elitist orientation, emphasizing the first of the "Three Represents": the advanced productive forces, which are primarily the urban entrepreneurial and technological elites. In recent years, private entrepreneurs in particular have become more assertive in seeking political and legal protection of their economic interests, and the party has been very responsive to their interests. To further symbolize the party's commitment to the private economy, in November 2003 it decided to revise the state constitution to protect private property and to promote the interests of the private sector.

This increasingly close relationship between the party and the private sector has created the widespread perception that the benefits of economic growth are being monopolized by a small segment of the population while the rest of the Chinese people are being left behind. Many Chinese now believe that economic success is based on personal connections with party and government officials, not individual initiative or quality work. As people come to believe that the benefits of the economic reform policies are unfairly distributed, the legitimacy of the party's policy of letting some get rich first is jeopardized.

In response to this perception, the new leadership of General Secretary Hu and Prime Minister Wen has shifted the focus away from the elitist orientation of the Jiang era to the third of the "Three Represents": the interests of the vast majority of the Chinese people. Hu and Wen, along with many others, concluded that the pendulum had swung too far in recent years, favoring the elites over the general population. They now want to create a new image for themselves and the party. This can be seen in Hu's speech on Party Day in 2003. Like Jiang just two years earlier, Hu concentrated exclusively on the "Three Represents." But whereas Jiang had emphasized the advanced productive forces, Hu mentioned the new social strata only once in passing. Instead, he focused on the "fundamental interests of the vast majority of the people," a phrase he repeated 13 times. In doing so, he was not rejecting an important symbol of the Jiang era, but he was reinterpreting it to signal a shift in priorities.

Hu and Wen have done more than simply speak on behalf of the majority. They have also shown their support—or at least their sympathy—for the disadvantaged in their public appearances and activities. During the 2003 Chinese New Year, Wen visited and shared a meal with miners. During the 2003 SARS crisis, Hu and Wen visited SARS patients in hospitals. They fired the minister of public health and the mayor of Beijing for covering up the extent of the epidemic. On World AIDS Day in December 2003, Wen visited and shook hands with HIV/AIDS patients, the first top leader to recognize China's AIDS crisis. In January 2004, the Communist Party issued a new policy directive on improving rural conditions that included policies aimed at alleviating income inequality. The Hu-Wen team has also tried to alleviate regional inequalities by promoting development in the northeast rustbelt and the less developed western provinces. This effort was begun under Jiang but expanded under Hu and Wen. Experiments with local elections, also started under Jiang, have continued with the fourth generation. In recent years, there have been elections for party secretaries, township leaders, urban neighborhood committees, and other positions.

Mixed Signals

Along with hints of change came signs of the enduring features of the political system. The doctor who exposed the SARS cover-up and became a national hero, Jiang Yanyong, was taken into custody by military officials in June 2004 and held for six weeks for advocating a reassessment of the official verdict on the 1989 Tiananmen demonstrations. Although the extent of the AIDS crisis has been gradually but not yet fully acknowledged, HIV/AIDS victims still rarely get the treatment they need and official culpability in the spread of the virus has yet to be admitted, much less punished. AIDS activists, most notably Wan Yanhai, have been harassed and imprisoned, and reporters who have tried to expose the policies of local governments that allowed the virus to spread have been fired and their stories suppressed. Residents of "AIDS villages" in rural Henan, where the AIDS virus has spread widely through blood donations that use unsanitary practices, have been beaten, arrested, and had their homes destroyed for seeking medicine and financial assistance from higher levels of government, for meeting with journalists to publicize their plight, or for attempting to gain the attention of investigating groups visiting China from the World Health Organization.

Efforts by top leaders to compensate the disadvantaged continue to be hampered by the failure of local leaders to act on new initiatives. For example, Wen may order local leaders to pay IOU's and unpaid wages to specific individuals in specific cases when they come to his attention, but similar cases that do not get singled out are rarely addressed. Local governments are themselves often starved of cash and cannot be as generous and proactive in identifying and addressing the many injustices that exist in their jurisdictions. And candidates in local elections are still either Communist Party members or independents; no new political parties have been allowed to form, and there has not even been official discussion of such a possibility. Efforts to create the China Democracy Party went for naught, as petitions to register the party were denied and the activists who were behind the effort were arrested and sentenced to jail terms of more than 10 years.

At the same time, Hu and Wen seem determined to shift away from the elitist orientation within the party. There is now frequent media coverage of Politburo meetings. Hu reported on the work of the Politburo to the most recent central committee meeting in fall 2003, and lower-level party committees are also expected to give regular reports to the bodies that formally elected them. Hu also canceled the annual meetings in the resort city of Beidaihe, which have traditionally been held each August to decide major policy and personnel issues. Because they are more informal than Politburo meetings and central committee plenums, they have been frequently used by senior party leaders to influence decision making, even after these officials have formally retired from office. The decision to cancel the meetings gives greater emphasis to the formal meetings in Beijing, and may curtail the informal influence of retired elders.

These changes are designed to promote the transparency and accountability of top-level decision making and to give greater weight to formal processes over informal politics. While the party has described these changes as improving inner party democracy, a dubious claim to be sure, they should at least be recognized as creating greater institutionalization in the Chinese system, which by itself would be a generally positive trend.

But these changes occur within clear limits. Reports on Politburo meetings reveal little beyond the topic under discussion and the theme of Hu's remarks to the group. Work reports by themselves do not provide for much accountability, and in any event the central committee only "elected" the Politburo after top leaders agreed among themselves who would belong to it. And media coverage of the November 2003 central committee plenum highlighted again the party's secretive nature. Although the media reported that the central committee had approved major constitutional revisions, they did not report on the content of those revisions. Speeches were given by top leaders, but the texts of the reports—including Hu's report on the work of the Politburo—were not published.

These mixed signals are the result of several factors. First is the leadership's ambivalence about pursuing any one course exclusively, with the danger that concessions to some individuals or groups may be used as a precedent for others to make claims against the state, or might raise expectations that more expansive political reforms are being considered. Second is the fragmented nature of political authority in China. Not all actions are the result of coherent decisions by unified leaders; they are also the result of different parts of the state taking actions that other parts of the state, and other leaders, may be unaware of or even oppose. Third is the consequence of political decentralization. Policies announced in Beijing are not immediately or even inevitably implemented by local governments. Finally, the transition from the third to the fourth generation of leaders is still incomplete. Jiang retains his post as chairman of the Central Military Commission, the Communist Party's top body for military matters, and continues to intervene in domestic and foreign policies—he was reportedly behind the detention of Dr. Jiang (no relation). Hu and Wen, perhaps recognizing that time is on their side, have not directly challenged Jiang's interventions even when they run contrary to the new leaders' preferred direction. Which of these causes is behind each zig and zag is often difficult to determine by outside observers and even by the victims and beneficiaries of these steps and missteps within China.

Benevolent Leninists?

While many no longer believe Marxism remains a relevant doctrine in contemporary China, there is no doubt that Leninism remains the guiding influence in the political system. There is still no organized opposition of any kind, and no public lobbying for policy change is visible outside the economic realm. But for those who do not choose to challenge the Communist state—and this involves the vast majority—the party is increasingly less pervasive and less intrusive. This is not to suggest that the party is seen as legitimate, much less popular. But it points to a fact that is often overlooked in most criticisms of China: although freedoms of all kinds are sharply delimited, and not well protected by law, it is nevertheless true that the degree of mobility, expression of ideas, and access to information is increasing, not contracting. When compared to the freedoms enjoyed, even taken for granted, by citizens of democratic countries, this progress seems halting and minuscule. But when compared against China's own past, the changes are dramatic.

Whether they will be sufficient to forestall popular demands for more significant change, and to prolong the Communist Party's tenure as China's ruling party, remains a key question in Chinese politics. In short, it is still not clear if we are seeing a more benevolent form of authoritarianism or signs of more significant political reform yet to come.

BRUCE J. DICKSON is an associate professor of political science and international affairs at George Washington University. His most recent book is *Red Capitalists in China: The Party, Private Entrepreneurs, and Prospects for Political Change* (Cambridge University Press, 2003).

From *Current History*, September 2004, pp. 249–255. Copyright © 2004 by Current History, Inc. Reprinted by permission.

Letter From Beijing
China's New Left

JEHANGIR S. POCHA

With its soaring glass towers and giant neon signs, Beijing looks like the new mecca of global capitalism. But behind the glitz there's growing disenchantment with relentless market reforms that have shrunk social services and thrown at least 20 million people out of work. Within intellectual circles, the echo of this disillusionment has become the rallying cry of a group known as China's New Left. This loose coalition comprises leading academics, many of whom have studied in the West and are disenchanted by it. They're challenging China's current market reforms with a simple message: China's failed twentieth-century experiment with Communism cannot be undone in the twenty-first century by embracing nineteenth-century-style laissez-faire capitalism. China is "caught between the two extremes of misguided socialism and crony capitalism, and suffering from the worst of both systems," says Wang Hui, a professor of literature at Beijing's Tsinghua University. His passionate denunciations of China's market reforms in *Du Shu*, a magazine he edits, are partly credited with energizing China's New Left intellectuals. "We have to find an alternate way. This is the great mission of our generation."

Such grand visions notwithstanding, the New Left's adherents don't have a unified ideology beyond the broad brush strokes, or a coherent set of alternate policies. Some are hardliners who find common cause with China's "old" leftists, who remain faithful to Mao's radical "Communism with Chinese characteristics." Though they say they rue the violence of the Maoist years, they remain enchanted with the sociopolitical initiatives of that period, such as collectivization. But the majority of New Left intellectuals are moderates who recognize that old Communist dogma lies discredited, and who simply want to rein in the excesses of China's market reforms. Their main complaint is that China's export-led growth strategy skews society and allows the fruits of reform to be harvested by urban residents and by government and Communist Party officials.

That criticism resonates increasingly with both discontented workers and peasants. "This is now an unjust society," says Lu She Zhong, 55, a village leader in central Henan province, who's been battling local authorities for six years over unpaid compensation after his entire village was resettled to make way for the giant Xiao Langdi dam on the Yellow River. "I know such projects are important, but why were we cheated in the bargain?" Public anger over illegal demolitions, withheld pensions and corruption led to more than 50,000 protests in 2003, seven times the number from a decade before, according to official reports, including those from the Ministry of Public Security.

But significantly, public security officials and police who used to crack down hard on such protests and blame external forces for trying to destabilize China now apply New Left thinking to explain the causes of the unrest and urge a kinder, gentler response. "Surprising numbers of analysts in the public security system display an undisguised sympathy for the very worker and peasant protestors the police are supposed to suppress," wrote Murray Scot Tanner, senior political scientist at the RAND Corporation in Washington, DC, in an article in the Summer 2004 issue of *Washington Quarterly*. "In their writings, they characterize laid-off demonstrators as 'exploited,' 'marginalized,' 'socially disadvantaged,' 'victims' and 'losers' in economic competition, driven to protest by social distrust and the 'heartlessness' of the free market. They frankly concede that many protesters are victims of crooked managers who drove their factories into bankruptcy through illicit dealings or who absconded with company assets."

Indeed, the degree to which the New Left's rhetoric meshes with that of the government's indicates that President Hu Jintao and his team are tacitly supporting the New Left. Part of Hu's motivation is to discredit previous President Jiang Zemin, who committed the country to his awkwardly named "Three Represents" theory. Generally dismissed in the West as a euphemism for Reaganesque trickle-down economics, Jiang's theory is enshrined in China's Constitution, even though it is widely blamed for the deep inequalities gripping the country.

The argument that economic changes were forced 'by the discipline of the market' has angered many Chinese.

Though China is one of the world's fastest-growing economies, it is also one of the world's most unequal societies. In a country where people used to save for months to buy a Flying Pigeon bicycle, the roads are jammed with gleaming Audis and Buicks. But among them, the unlucky ones who have missed the opportunities that have come with economic reforms still pedal their now-rusty Flying Pigeons. Free access to education and healthcare has been drastically cut, especially in rural areas, and property that was once seized from the rich and redistributed to the poor is being taken from farmers and given to developers.

The argument that these changes were forced by "the discipline of the market" has angered many Chinese, causing party leaders to worry about the nation's stability. Chen Xin, a professor of sociology at the Chinese Academy of Social Sciences in Beijing and a self-described New Lefter, says Hu realizes he must correct the imbalances created during Jiang's term because while a democracy can balance between extremes by throwing a party or a president who's gone too far out of power, "in a one-party system, the party must have its own self-correcting mechanisms—or else it will lose touch with the people."

Emboldened by such tumult, New Left intellectuals, who have been questioning China's market reforms from the sidelines since the early 1990s, have stepped up their criticism. Wang says it's time for people to understand that China's problems are not merely fallout from market mechanics but the result of "bad policies and bad governance." He and other New Lefters have begun educating the public about the faults they see in China's reforms through a series of well-publicized articles. "The government is more focused on helping export manufacturers than agriculture and rural welfare," which affect far more people, says Cui Zhi Yuan of Tsinghua University, a leading New Left thinker. "[One of] the largest expenditure items in the budget is not education or healthcare but tax rebates to exporters. So essentially the government is returning money to [domestic and multinational] exporters while cutting welfare programs."

With businesspeople now allowed to join the Communist Party, New Left intellectuals are also challenging what Cui calls the growing "nexus between corrupt politicians, bankers and businessmen who in the name of reform are looting China." Though both Wang and Cui say there is no doubt that China's state-owned enterprises (SOEs), which generally lose vast amounts of money every year, need change, they are calling for a process of "institutional renovation" that would allow SOEs to restructure without surrendering ownership or abdicating responsibilities to workers.

Critics of the New Left, such as Professor Shi Yinhong, director of the Center for American Studies at the People's University in Beijing, dismiss their talk as fluff and say New Lefters "criticize but have no real alternative" to the current global economic system, based on the Washington Consensus.

While Wang accepts that the major focus of the New Left is constructive criticism, he says a new economic framework is being created. "Just because those without imagination cannot see it doesn't mean it isn't being formed," he says.

At the core of the New Left's policy recommendations is a focus on what they call the *San Nong* (or Three Nongs): issues concerning the plight of the *Nong Min* (peasants), *Nong Ye* (agriculture) and *Nong Cun* (rural communities). Currently the average annual rural income in China is the equivalent of about $355, and China's 786 million farmers, who are 70 percent of the population, account for only 39 percent of domestic consumption and hold just 19 percent of all deposits in the country's individual bank accounts, according to government reports. More than 50 million people still live in poverty, according to government figures, and the real number is likely much higher. Cui says that focusing on the *San Nong* will allow China to make the transition from an economy based on foreign direct investment to one based on organic growth and driven by domestic investment, which will raise local salaries and standards of living.

New Left thinkers say their strident criticism, coupled with increasing protests in villages, is succeeding in leading the government to soften some of its earlier policies. For example, China's National People's Congress recently passed a new bankruptcy law that will give primacy to workers' rights when a company goes bust. Financial support to farmers has also increased, and now fewer migrate to cities looking for work as daily wage earners. That's shrinking China's pool of cheap labor and upsetting factory owners. But championing such causes and arguing in favor of development that is "less GDP-focused and more people-focused" is what the New Left sees as its immediate role, says Cui.

Still, dissent is a delicate business in China, and sociology professor Chen Xin is quick to point out that the New Left's concern "is not politics but social welfare. We're only amplifying what we see happening around us. Hopefully, that will aid and guide the government." With the Chinese government congenitally opposed to any sort of unsanctioned organization, Wang also emphasizes that "we're not a group . . . just a loose affiliation of people with similar beliefs." He adds, "Even the term 'New Left' is not ours. It was first used to discredit us and to portray us as the old socialists. But I don't really mind. When something new is happening, it's normal for people to try to define it in old terms."

If Wang's benevolence toward his labelers seems magnanimous, it is partly because the "left" label has begun to work in favor of the intellectuals. "I've been reading some New Left articles, and they make me feel very warm because they remind me of the values my parents used to talk to me about," says Maria Zhang, 24, a student at the Beijing Forestry University. "I feel like China has lost its bearing by bending too much toward Western ways. We're out of touch with our past and core values."

With such sentiments increasing, President Hu, who took over from Jiang two years ago, has brought a different tone to decision-making in Beijing. His government has said it will look beyond GDP growth to address such issues as environmental decay, regional inequality and unemployment. Lu, the village leader in Henan, dismisses this as "only words" to mollify restive groups. But Chen says rhetoric is always the first step toward change in China. "That sets the national mood," he says. "Then there are some broad changes in policy and then, over many years, detailed changes in governance and implementation of laws. Right now, I think we are already at the second stage." Indeed, Hu is currently overseeing a massive reshuffle of officials and replacing older and discredited officials with a younger generation of technocrats.

But even Hu's public indications that he intends to steer China more toward a German-style socially responsive state doesn't entirely satisfy Cui. "The truth is that even the Western left's policies [like progressive taxes] are only reactive and aimed at correcting imbalances caused by a capitalistic system," he says. "Our ultimate goal should be to develop a new theory of poverty and an independent society where such massive imbalances do not occur in the first place."

Despite his seemingly anti-Western stance, Cui, whose school works closely with Harvard University's John F. Kennedy School of Government, admits that most of the essential principles the New Left is advocating have come from the West: full-cost pricing (which passes on the costs of environmental and health damages caused by products to their manufacturers); full financial disclosure (which reins in potentially destabilizing financial tools such as hedge funds); dismantling of tax loopholes and havens (in countries like Switzerland); new definitions of patents, copyrights and royalties (which emphasize their productive use rather than restricting ownership); and new salary schemes (which emphasize wages plus a share in profits). That these principles are still not widely accepted even in the West doesn't daunt him. "China is finding itself," he says. "We have a new will to build a certain kind of society—a better society."

JEHANGIR S. POCHA is the Beijing-based China correspondent for the *Boston Globe*.

Chinese Nationalism: Challenging the State?

"It would be a mistake to attribute to the Communist Party complete control over Chinese nationalism today. With the emergence of the Internet, cell phones, and text messaging, popular nationalists in China are increasingly able to act independently of the state."

PETER HAYS GRIES

In July 2003, 66 years after the Marco Polo Bridge incident that led to Japan's invasion of central China, a group of Chinese nationalists organized an Internet petition. Their goal: to prevent Japan from winning a $12 billion Chinese government contract for the construction of a high-speed Beijing-Shanghai rail link. Featuring an image of a clenched fist evocative of socialist propaganda, their campaign logo read: "Heaven and Earth will not tolerate traitors. We *don't want* the Japanese *bullet train*. We refuse the use of Japanese products for the Beijing-Shanghai line." In just one week, the organizers gathered 90,000 e-signatures, which they publicly submitted to the Ministry of Railways in Beijing on July 29.

Visiting the Chinese capital the next week, Chikage Ogi, Japan's minister of transportation, discovered that her appointments had been cancelled: she was unable to meet with Prime Minister Wen Jiabao or even any Railway Ministry officials. The press in both China and Japan described the cancellations as a snub. The rail contract decision, furthermore, was suddenly deferred. Petition organizer and "nationalist hero" Feng Jinhua declared that the Internet petition had a "clear impact."

That very week of Ogi's visit, construction workers in Qiqihar in China's northeast uncovered and ruptured five drums of mustard gas left from the wartime Japanese occupation. Dozens were injured and one man died. The popular Chinese reaction to the news was fast and furious. Internet chatrooms were filled with anti-Japanese invective. A million e-signatures were gathered on a second petition demanding that the Japanese government thoroughly resolve the chemical weapons issue. It was delivered to the Japanese embassy in Beijing on September 4, 2003, as Chinese and Japanese diplomats were negotiating compensation for the victims of the Qiqihar accident. Petition

organizer Lu Yunfei later said that he and his followers sought to "put pressure on the Japanese government."

Domestic Chinese analysts were quick to note the significance of the online petitions, declaring 2003 to be the beginning of a "new chapter" or "second wave" of Chinese nationalism. In this view, books like *China Can Say No*, which appeared in 1996, and *Behind the Demonization of China*, published a year later, marked the "first wave" of recent popular nationalism. The first wave was largely anti-American and centered on events such as US involvement in the 1996 Taiwan Strait crisis, the 1999 bombing of the Chinese embassy in Belgrade, and the 2001 collision of an American surveillance plane with a Chinese fighter jet. This nationalist outpouring was concentrated in books and magazines and thus largely confined to intellectuals. The current second wave, by contrast, focuses on Japan and is more Internet-based. This new "Internet nationalism," the analysts argued, is "more influential" than the earlier wave, better able to convert popular opinion into political action.

They turned out to be right. April 2005 witnessed three successive weekends of anti-Japanese protests involving tens of thousands of Chinese in cities as diverse as Beijing, Shanghai, Canton, Shenzhen, and Chengdu. The protests were organized almost exclusively by e-mail, text messaging, and online chatrooms, and were notable for their lack of a clear leadership. While the street demonstrations did die down in May, Internet activity did not. Indeed, on July 1, 2005, activists presented an e-signature petition with 46 million names to an aide to UN Secretary General Kofi Annan. The petition stated that "Japan thus far shows no remorse [for] its past misdeeds, refuses to repent, and appears to be untrustworthy. The international community cannot and must not designate such [a] state to [a permanent] seat on the Security Council." The vast majority of the 46 million signatures came from China. (According to the China Internet Network Information Center's latest report this January, China has 96 million "Internet users," loosely defined as those who use the Internet at least an hour per week. It is thus highly likely that many Chinese "netizens" signed the petition more than once; the 46 million figure is nonetheless astounding.)

The Internet clearly is altering the nature of politics in the People's Republic. Chinese Internet petitions are not just getting larger; their targets are also changing, first presented to the Chinese government, then to the Japanese embassy, then to the United Nations. And the Internet has transformed the ways that Chinese protest in the streets, facilitating larger and more decentralized demonstrations.

Popular nationalists—not the Communist Party—initiated and organized the April 2005 anti-Japanese protests.

What should we make of the emergence of Internet nationalism in twenty-first century China? First, Western analysts must move beyond reductionist, top-down understandings of Chinese politics to embrace the complexity of state-society legitimacy dynamics in China. Nationalist opinion is an increasingly important constraint on China's elite decision-makers. Western analysts and policy makers ignore this new development at their own peril.

Cyber-Libertarian Dreams

When the Internet first emerged as a significant technology in the 1990s, many Westerners optimistically predicted that it would be a potent force for political change. Authoritarian regimes, in this view, could not survive the free flow of information that the Internet allows. Indeed, US Secretary of State George Shultz had suggested as early as 1985 that "totalitarian societies face a dilemma: either they try to stifle the [information and communication] technologies and thereby fall further behind in the new industrial revolution or else they permit these technologies and see their totalitarian control inevitably eroded." In the extreme cyber-libertarian view, the Internet would topple tyrannies around the globe.

But authoritarian regimes endured. Indeed, some appeared to be using new Internet technologies to their advantage. In a 2002 *Weekly Standard* cover article, Ethan Gutmann argued that the Internet in China was "a tool of the Beijing government, not a force for democracy." Tamara Shie, a researcher at National Defense University, has even declared that in the Chinese context, "arguments for the emancipatory power of the Internet are merely utopian political rhetoric." The Internet, in this pessimistic view, cannot overcome China's authoritarian political culture.

The idea that the Chinese people are largely impotent before the vast coercive apparatus of the Oriental state has a long history in the Western study of Chinese politics, and it continues to impede Western studies of state legitimation in China today. In the eighteenth, nineteenth, and early twentieth centuries, an "Oriental despotism" view of Chinese politics prevailed, depicting Asian absolutism as the opposite of Western liberalism. American freedom, in particular, has long been constructed against the foil of Chinese tyranny.

During the cold war, "totalitarianism" replaced "Oriental despotism" as the predominant paradigm for studying China, but the state dominance thesis persisted. Since the cold war's end, new approaches have focused on civil society and the public sphere in state-society relations, but the thesis of state dominance endures. The Western media and academics alike still largely depict the Chinese people as defenseless against the coercive power of an omnipotent Chinese state.

Western analysis of Chinese nationalism exhibits this same tendency. The dominant view today depicts Chinese nationalism as "party propaganda": the Communist elite constructing nationalism to use it in its domestic and foreign policies. Thomas Christensen expressed this view succinctly in an influential 1996 *Foreign Affairs* article: "Since the Chinese Communist Party is no longer communist, it must be even more Chinese." Chinese nationalism is largely reduced to "state" or "official" nationalism, a top-down party affair that leaves little room for popular participation.

This "state nationalism" view is not wrong. The Chinese Communist Party came to power based in large part on its nationalist credentials, leading the Chinese peasantry during the victorious "War of Resistance Against Japan." And nationalism has been central to Chinese Communist claims to legitimacy since. School textbooks indoctrinate a nationalist vision of the Chinese nation. Following the 1989 Tiananmen massacre, the party initiated a "Patriotic Education Campaign" to shore up its shattered legitimacy.

But the top-down state nationalism view is incomplete. Nationalist politics is never a one-way street. As e-petition organizers like Feng Jinhua and Lu Yunfei show, popular nationalists play a central role in Chinese nationalist politics today. If the state nationalism thesis were the end of the story, then the state should have both the ability and the willingness to manipulate Chinese nationalism at will, turning it on and off as it sees fit. Recent petitions and protests clearly demonstrate that this is not the case. The state is not the only actor in Chinese nationalism and does not have complete control over it. A more dynamic analysis of Chinese nationalist politics, therefore, is needed.

Power, Party, and Public

How can we move beyond state dominance approaches to bring the Chinese people back into the study of Chinese politics? We can begin by reexamining the neglected core of the discipline of political science: power.

"Power grows out of the barrel of a gun." Mao Zedong said and wrote many, many things. And yet this quote is among the best known of his remarks in the West. Why? Because it fits with prevalent Western views of Chinese politics, and therefore resonates with Western audiences. As Richard Madsen argued in

China and the American Dream, Americans continue to construct and treasure American liberty in opposition to the "Red menace" of communism: Americans can freely participate in politics, but Chinese are mere slaves to China's authoritarian rulers.

In this common view, power in Chinese politics can be reduced to coercion: the Communist Party endures solely because of the coercive power of the state. Little wonder that the image of a People's Liberation Army tank facing down a single Chinese man, Wang Weilin, remains the most enduring image of the 1989 Tiananmen massacre in the West. In the Western imagination, communism = tyranny = tanks = coercive power.

But Mao also said, "When you make revolution, you must first manage popular opinion." Western analysts have tended to treat "Chinese popular opinion" as an oxymoron. Mao knew better. All regimes require the consent of the governed—legitimate power—to endure for long. It is extremely costly to have to constantly coerce compliance; it is much cheaper and more practical to persuade. Resorts to coercion, furthermore, undermine regime legitimacy.

Mao understood the importance of persuasive forms of power. His "manage popular opinion" remark came from the period just before the Cultural Revolution when he was busy cultivating his charismatic and traditional authority. The *Little Red Book* of Mao quotations and the Mao cult helped to persuade an entire generation of China's youth, many of whom were soon to become Red Guards, to voluntarily do Mao's bidding. Indeed, the Cultural Revolution would never have been possible without Mao's careful cultivation of popular opinion.

Power, at its simplest, is the ability to get others to do what they would not otherwise do. It is thus relational. Power does not exist in isolation, but only if others accept it. And it occurs along a continuum, from more coercive to more persuasive or legitimate forms.

"The People Are Very Angry"

These two aspects of power—its relational nature and the tension between its coercive and legitimate forms—are central to an understanding of the dynamics of nationalist politics in China today.

The April 16, 2005, anti-Japanese demonstrations in downtown Shanghai illustrate the argument. "The Chinese people are very angry; there will be serious consequences!" read a long banner held aloft by a dozen marching demonstrators. Another banner revealed the object of their anger: "Oppose Japanese imperialism!" Other banners displayed a variety of specific grievances: "Oppose Japan entering the Security Council!" "Boycott Japanese goods, revitalize China!" "Oppose Japan's history textbooks!" "Protect our Diaoyu Islands!"

Other protesters held high a variety of handmade placards and posters. The most persistent messages focused on a proposed May 2005 boycott: "Boycott Japanese goods for a month, and Japan will suffer for a whole year." "Boycotting Japanese goods will castrate Japan!" Images of butcher knives, swords, and arrows were painted piercing the rising sun of Japan's national flag.

But it was the image of Japan's Prime Minister Junichiro Koizumi that incurred the greatest wrath from the young demonstrators. One protester gave him a mustache to make him look like Adolf Hitler. Others went further, dehumanizing the prime minister. One placard painted a pig's snout and ears onto his face and declared in large characters, "Death to Koizumi the pig!" The most ominous images evoked a deceased Koizumi, with tombstones bearing his name, and a photo of a funeral with Koizumi's picture at the center.

In addition to peacefully waving Chinese flags, singing the Internationale, and chanting anti-Japanese slogans, the demonstrators engaged in a number of less benign activities. On their way to the Japanese consulate, they smashed the windows of Japanese stores and restaurants, overturned Japanese cars, and burned Japanese flags and photos, as well as placards of Koizumi. When they arrived at the consulate, they hurled eggs and pelted it with paint bombs.

Why do so many Chinese today hate the Japanese? After a quarter-century of unprecedented economic growth, most Chinese no longer fear Japan, and a long suppressed anger at Japan has resurfaced. The Maoist "victor narrative" about heroic Chinese triumphs over Western and Japanese imperialism, dominant from the 1950s through the 1980s, has been challenged since the mid–1990s by a new "victim narrative" about Chinese suffering during the "century of humiliation." To most Chinese, the Japanese are "devils"—not just because of the brutality of the Japanese invasion of China and the sheer numbers of Chinese killed by Japanese troops, but also because of an ethical anger with earlier origins. The perceived injustice of "little brother" Japan's impertinent behavior toward "big brother" China, starting in the late nineteenth century and running through World War II atrocities like the "Rape of Nanking," helps to sustain deep anti-Japanese sentiments, setting them apart from other, more fleeting anti-foreign feelings.

China's cyber-nationalists, armed with PCs and cell phones, are increasingly contesting party claims to nationalist legitimacy.

But what about the state's role in the protests? If the government did not initiate the demonstrations, why did it not stop them? "Why Didn't," as Japan's *Asahi Shimbun* put it in the title of an editorial, "the Chinese Authorities Do Something?"

A common view is that the Chinese government encouraged the anti-Japanese protests for both domestic and international purposes. Domestically, the Communist Party is seen as using Japan as a scapegoat to preempt popular criticisms of the Chinese government itself. Tokyo Mayor Ishihara Shintaro quickly declared that the Chinese "government is initiating a dangerous kind of nationalism in order to divert public frustration." Internationally, the party is seen as using popular anti-Japanese protests to achieve specific foreign policy goals, such as denying Japan a permanent seat on the UN Security Council.

State nationalism arguments do of course tell an important part of the story. There is no question that the party has deployed its educational and propaganda systems to inculcate anti-Japanese views. But it would be a mistake to attribute to the Communist Party complete control over Chinese nationalism today. With the emergence of the Internet, cell phones, and text messaging, popular nationalists in China are increasingly able to act independently of the state. Popular nationalists—not the Communist Party—initiated and organized the April 2005 anti-Japanese protests.

And the critical question is not so much who initiated the demonstrations as why did the party not stop them sooner? The answer is that the party's hands were tied. It did not want to see Sino-Japanese relations deteriorate, but was forced to allow the anti-Japanese protests for fear of losing the consent of the Chinese people. "The basic policy of our government has been to be conciliatory to the Japanese and the rest of the world, but that policy has become less viable today, when people are demanding a tougher line," Beijing University's Pan Wei told *The New York Times* during the April protests.

Many in the Chinese elite may have found the anti-Japanese protests gratifying, for they largely share the popular nationalists' hatred of Japan. But these sentiments are outweighed by the elite's number one goal: regime survival. And members of China's elite know that their continued rule depends in large part on continued economic development—which requires stable relations with Japan. Sino-Japanese trade benefits both countries enormously, and conflict with Japan is certain to disrupt China's economic growth. That the government sent text messages urging restraint by the April demonstrators reveals both the elite's desire to keep the protests within acceptable bounds and its weak position: forced to plead with the protesters for calm.

The Chinese state had the capability to clamp down on popular nationalists. The People's Armed Police could have stepped in to prevent protesters from hurling eggs and rocks at the Japanese consulate in Shanghai. But any blatant use of force to suppress the demonstrators could have backfired. Because anti-Japanese sentiment is widespread in China today, had the Chinese state deployed force, its legitimacy in the eyes of the Chinese people would have been seriously undermined. And few regimes last for long by force alone; stable governments require some degree of consent of the governed.

The Communists Constrained

Because the Communist Party's legitimacy is based in large part on nationalist claims—to make China rich and strong and, more fundamentally, to restore China's respect in the international community—it is increasingly stuck between the rock of domestic nationalists and the hard place of international politics. The tough foreign policies that domestic opinion often demands can arouse fears among its neighbors about China's rise, undermining the leadership's stated foreign policy goal of creating a peaceful environment for China's development. Nationalist opinion is increasingly constraining the ability of China's elite to coolly pursue China's national interest.

This argument runs counter to a long-standing Western view that democracies are constrained by elections and public opinion and thus at a disadvantage in foreign policy making.

Authoritarian regimes, conversely, are seen as free of domestic constraints and thus at a diplomatic advantage. "In the conduct of their foreign relations," US Secretary of State Dean Acheson asserted during the cold war, "democracies appear to me decidedly inferior to other governments."

Popular opinion, in this view, can compel both aggression and nonaggression against the will of foreign policy makers in democratic states. The *Maine* and "Munich" incidents serve as useful shorthand for these twin arguments. The sinking of the USS *Maine* in Havana harbor (mistakenly attributed to Spanish subterfuge) and popular outrage over Spanish atrocities against the Cubans forced President William McKinley to launch the Spanish-American War of 1898, "a war which he did not want," according to historian Ernest May, "for a cause in which he did not believe." "Munich" is short for the 1938 acquiescence of Great Britain and France to the German annexation of Czechoslovakia. Pacifist British and French publics are frequently blamed for Prime Ministers Chamberlain and Daladier's decisions to appease Hitler.

The "democratic disadvantage"/"authoritarian advantage" logic continues to drive American visions of Chinese foreign policy today. Viewing China as a dictatorship, many Americans hold that the Chinese Communist Party, unlike the US government, can calmly construct China's foreign policies unfettered by domestic constraints. One example was the US-China Security Review Commission's report submitted to Congress in 2002. It expressed concern that, in contrast with America's China policy, which lacks consistency and is beset by rivalries between Congress and the Bush administration and among various interest groups, China's America policy is driven by a coherent set of expansionist goals. Free of domestic constraints, Chinese foreign policy makers are seen as better able to pursue their objectives.

The emerging role that popular nationalism is playing in Chinese foreign policy making challenges the "authoritarian advantage" view. It is clear that the April 2005 anti-Japanese protests influenced China's Japan policy. China's evolving policy toward Japan's bid to become a permanent member of the UN Security Council can serve as a case study. On April 13, during a state visit to India, Chinese Prime Minister Wen Jiabao publicly announced that China would oppose Japan's bid to become a permanent member of the Security Council: "Only a country that respects history, takes responsibility for the past, and wins over the trust of the people of Asia and the world at large can take greater responsibilities in the international community."

China and Japan are rivals for dominance in the newly emerging East Asian security order. Wen's opposition to Japan's Security Council bid should thus come as little surprise. The timing and context of Wen's announcement, however, do call for explanation: Why had China not come out against Japan's bid earlier? And why would China's leadership choose to make its announcement so publicly, during an official state visit abroad?

Circumstantial evidence suggests that popular nationalism played a significant role in elite decision making on this Japan policy issue. While members of China's elite did not wish to see Japan become a permanent member of the Security Council, they also did not want to jeopardize China's lucrative trade and investment relations with Japan. Until April 13, therefore, they had chosen to take a backseat on the issue, allowing other governments, like South Korea's, to take the lead in publicly opposing Japan's UN bid. China's policy toward Japan's quest for a Security Council seat had thus followed a common Chinese foreign policy tactic: allowing others to take the heat for positions that China shared. (China had, for instance, deployed this strategy during the 2003 Iraq War debate. Although China opposed U.S. unilateralism on Iraq, it remained largely silent, allowing France and Germany to take the lead—and the heat—in opposing US policy.)

So why did China's leadership not maintain this "lay low while others take the lead" policy when it came to Japan and the UN? While it is impossible to know for sure—we simply do not have sufficient access to the inner workings of Zhongnanhai, China's leadership compound in Beijing—the circumstantial evidence is compelling: China's elite was responding to the pressures of domestic nationalist opinion. By early April, the Internet petition opposing Japan's Security Council bid had gathered a staggering 30 million signatures from irate Chinese netizens. And Prime Minister Wen's announcement came after two successive weekends of popular anti-Japanese demonstrations in China that had focused on opposing Japan's seat on the Security Council. "China must vote no and not just abstain," said popular nationalist Tong Zeng. "The government may not want to take the lead, but the Chinese people have taken the lead." This popular pressure forced the leadership—against its own will—to come out very publicly against Japan's bid.

Lacking the procedural legitimacy accorded to democratically elected governments and facing the collapse of communist ideology, the Chinese Communist Party is increasingly depen-dent on its nationalist credentials to rule. But bottom-up popular pressures are increasingly threatening the party's nationalist legitimacy. And those pressures tend to be of the aggressive *Maine* variety—not the pacifist Munich type. Chinese nationalism, therefore, can no longer be described as a purely "state" or "official" top-down affair. Aware that popular nationalists now command a large following, China's Ministry of Foreign Affairs is actively seeking to appease them. China's foreign policy makers, it appears, do not enjoy a "nondemocratic advantage" over their counterparts in democracies; as they make policy, they too must be responsive to domestic opinion.

The Dance of Politics

At its core, politics in China today is like politics everywhere: it involves contestation over power. Seeking power on the cheap, the Communist Party makes a variety of claims, including nationalist claims, to legitimate rule and the voluntary consent of the Chinese people.

The party's nationalist claims, however, are increasingly falling on deaf ears. Few now accept the decades-old Chinese communist mantra that only the party can save China. Moreover, many popular nationalists are beginning to articulate their own nationalist counterclaims—often employing the regime's own nationalist grammar—to argue that they have the nationalist right to participate in Chinese politics. The party is thus losing its hegemony over Chinese nationalist discourse, weakening the hyphen that holds the Chinese Party-nation together.

China's cyber-nationalists, armed with PCs and cell phones, are increasingly contesting party claims to nationalist legitimacy. So far, the party has done a masterful job of containing popular nationalism. But it is forced to walk a fine line. Let the next nationalist protests spin out of control, and the party could become a target of popular criticism, whether for failure to uphold China's national dignity, or corruption, or social injustice. But should the party resort to force to suppress nationalist protesters, its legitimacy in the eyes of the Chinese people could receive a mortal blow. Either scenario could lead to regime change. The party and nationalist protesters are engaged in a very subtle dance, both seeking to use each other to achieve their goals, but also fearful of the threat each represents to their own survival.

PETER HAYS GRIES is an assistant professor of political science at the University of Colorado, Boulder, and director of the Sino-American Security Dialogue. He is the author of *China's New Nationalism: Pride, Politics, and Diplomacy* (University of California Press, 2004).

Reprinted from *Current History*, September 2005, pp. 251–256. Copyright © 2005 by Current History, Inc. Reprinted with permission.

China's Conservative Middle Class

JONATHAN UNGER

In the literature on democratization, the rise of a large middle class is often seen as a precursor for the development of civil society and a well-functioning democracy. In East Asia, the cases of Taiwan and South Korea have been pointed to as examples. Is a similar future scenario on the cards for China?

Certainly, the urban middle class has grown very rapidly in the years since the massive Tiananmen protests more than a decade and a half ago, when angry university students were joined by throngs of middle-class protesters. In the major cities of China today, the expansion of the middle class is obvious. The major thoroughfares of cities like Chengdu in Sichuan province, where I have lived on and off in recent years, are lined by vast new gated housing projects built to accommodate a burgeoning population of middle-class professionals. Beijing contains 40 new mega-malls, and similar temples to consumerism are springing up in dozens of other cities.

These newly affluent middle-class households possess family incomes of at least 80,000 yuan ($10,000) per year, according to recent studies by Chinese sociologists. This marks the lowest income at which a household can afford to purchase both an apartment and a small car, the *sine qua non* of middle-class prosperity.

The prosperous shoppers and residents of the gated high-rises are not principally businesspeople or members of the Party elite. They include these groups, to be sure, but most of them are salaried employees, and among these the greatest number are public servants. They are academics and high-school teachers, doctors, engineers, and the white-collar staffs of state-owned enterprises, as well as government administrators of all stripes. Their numbers are large enough that they set the tone and tastes of respectable urban society.

They distinguish themselves from the businesspeople who crowd the same shops and restaurants. They view the latter as parvenus and hold in disdain the uneducated business class's supposed lack of taste. The well-educated salaried middle class perceives its status as superior.

In 2000, the anthropologist William Jankowiak asked hundreds of young adults in one large city to lay out dozens of cards, each bearing the title of an occupation, in descending order from most to least admired. The four most admired occupations turned out to be those of professor, lawyer, doctor and middle-school teacher, listed above the province's party secretary, the mayor, an international businessman, or the director of a joint-venture company. Much lower was the esteem held for a low-level official (who ranks below a barber).

Strategic Generosity

At the time of the Tiananmen protests in 1989, China's urban educated populace had good reason to be angry. Their salaries were low, and sour jokes circulated about private barbers earning more with their razors than hospital surgeons with their scalpels. They were bitter that the sons and daughters of senior Party officials were doing well in private business, which they thought smacked of corruption, and rumors circulated about how these "princelings" were living high off the hog. The urban educated were furious that "political connections" took precedence over their own expertise and loyal service when it came to determining living standards.

But in the years since, as China's economy has continued to expand at a breakneck pace, there has been a deliberate government policy to favor them through their pay slips and perks. Year after year those on government payrolls have been offered higher salaries. During one year in the late 1990s, the pay of all of the academics at China's most prestigious public universities was literally doubled in one go.

Even earlier, in the first half of the 1990s, a huge government-endorsed construction program was initiated to build vast numbers of pleasant new apartment blocks, which were immediately sold off to favored state-sector employees at knockdown prices, sometimes as low as 20% of construction costs. Some of the most recent high-rises are truly fancy, with Japanese-style garden ponds and waterfalls, ornate statuary and health clubs. Thanks to the hefty subsidies to purchase flats, the most fortunate members of the salaried middle class can afford to live in comparative luxury alongside wealthy businesspeople who earn many times more.

They also have enough cash left at their disposal to buy autos, and in the early 2000s the sale of cars began leaping by close to 40% a year. State employees who in the 1980s could not afford a fridge or color TV or even leather shoes and who lived in dreary walk-ups now have gained a material life that they had never imagined possible. They do not want to upset the apple cart. If the government's plan was to co-opt the salaried middle class, it has worked.

If unrest like 1989 occurs again, much of the middle class would be on the government's side.

China's intellectuals are part of this educated middle class. Their writings today in academic journals and high-brow magazines are imbued with a sense of satisfaction. There are, of course, exceptions, but most intellectuals tend to accept and approve of the status quo and see the straitened circumstances of China's peasants and workers as the necessary price to be paid for China's modernization.

Throughout the 20th century, Chinese intellectuals and university students have been at the forefront of organized unrest. This involvement reaches back to the liberal May Fourth Movement protests of 1919 and the 1920s, to the Communist-aligned student agitations of the 1930s and 1940s, to the Hundred Flowers Movement outcries of 1957 against the Party's deadening style of rule, and more recently the Tiananmen protests of 1989. In view of this history, China's rulers have learned to worry about the potential of the educated as catalysts and organizers. The feeling within China today, valid or not, is that without their participation any surge of major social unrest would be incapable of toppling a government—that it would be leaderless, disorganized and local. But as of now there is very little chance of mass participation by the urban educated. In fact, if there is another outbreak like Tiananmen, many would prefer to be on the government side of the barricades.

This is true not just of the middle-aged among them, but also of the university students. They are, after all, the incoming generation of the educated middle class, and most of them look forward to their own material futures. In one survey of university students, about half said that money is as important as, or more important than, having ideals or friends. In another survey, 83% of the students at a teachers' training university chose the following value statement above any other: "A modern person must be able to make money."

Middle Class vs. Democracy

The educated middle class is elitist. Many of its members do not want democracy—that is, multiparty elections for the nation's top leaders. Nor did they want this at Tiananmen a decade and a half ago. They did not and do not want China's peasant majority to play a decisive hand in deciding who rules. Most of them hold the rural populace in disdain, and their fear is that the peasants would be swayed by demagogues and vote-buying. They believe that the rural populace is not yet ready to participate in elections. This is ironic, since villagers have been the

only ones in China who have been allowed to cast secret ballots to elect their locality's leader.

Many members of the educated middle class are vaguely pro-democratic just so long as democracy can be put off to a future time. This is not only the case today, but also was true at the time of Tiananmen. The then Party Secretary Zhao Ziyang favored a policy called "neo-authoritarianism," under which the Party would act as a benevolent autocracy until such time as the middle class had developed sufficiently to predominate in a democratized polity. Until then, China would remain in a state of tutelage, much as Sun Yat-sen had proposed in the 1920s. This was the program of the Party elite's reform camp, and it drew support from among the urban, educated elite.

At Tiananmen, what many of the university students and their middle-class supporters wanted, instead of multiparty democratic elections, was political relaxation in ways that concerned themselves. They wanted to be able to play a role in organizing their own clubs and associations. They wanted "personal space"—to have the government not interfere in their personal lives. They wanted access to more interesting magazines and films, and the freedom to have public intellectual discussions (just as today, they want their own Web sites and access to Web chatrooms). As patriotic citizens, they wanted their expertise to be listened to in the making of government policy. They also wanted what they considered a more fair distribution of incomes, in which they would be beneficiaries. In all these respects, they are largely getting today what they wanted then.

If anything, many protesters at Tiananmen were more in favor of political liberalization than they are now. At the time, they admired Mikhail Gorbachev and the political reforms he was carrying out. But the collapse and dismemberment of the Soviet Union in the early 1990s and the corruption and plunging living standards that soon followed under Boris Yeltsin's rule soured China's educated on the idea of Party-led political liberalization along Gorbachev's lines. By the mid-1990s, young Russian women were flowing into China in large numbers to work as prostitutes. Chinese considered this shocking evidence of Russia's penury and humiliation. Many of the urban educated who had demonstrated in 1989 began to feel relieved that China had followed Deng Xiaoping's policy of economic rather than political reform.

Nevertheless, many today still think of themselves as pro-reform, albeit in modest ways. They are apt to shake their heads in dismay at China's environmental problems and express hopes that the government will give greater priority to the issue. Those with expertise are often eager to offer up suggestions on how to enact this or that small, incremental reform. What pass in China for academic papers are often really policy prescriptions on how to improve one or another aspect of China's physical or administrative infrastructure, or relieve traffic congestion, or provide for a more effective education curriculum.

A small number of writers go further. They worry in print about corruption, and about the awful working conditions faced by many millions of migrant workers, and about the plight of farmers. Gutsy journalists, bona fide members of the educated middle class, have written exposés about the seamier side of the Chinese economic miracle; and exposé TV programs similar to

60 Minutes are popular. But these often are loyal expressions of concern that exploitation, corruption and grinding poverty might lead to instability. China's top leaders have publicly expressed similar concerns about corruption and the difficult situation of struggling farmers. Barely any of the exposé journalism hints at displeasure with the national leadership, and this does not just seem to be a question of censorship. Even the exposé journalists appear to live comfortably within the boundaries of China's status quo.

Middle Class and Leadership

The government has consistently pushed patriotism as a means to prop up public support. In encouraging nationalism, though, Beijing has run the risk of seeming too mild in its actual reactions in the international arena, and a portion of the middle class has felt uncomfortable whenever this occurs.

But the grumblings have been fleeting. Few among the middle class actually put great stock in nationalism as an ongoing political concern. They look approvingly on most things foreign and modern, and are eager to sample foreign foods, fashions and fads. The best of the university students eagerly prep for the TOEFL exams so that they can study abroad, and many are quite happy ultimately to settle abroad, with their parents' encouragement.

Most members of the educated middle class find little to be irritated about on a daily basis in regard to the central government. This is quite unlike earlier times. Under Mao in the 1970s, when the government directly controlled almost all economic activity and was responsible for all services, it naturally took the blame whenever there were shortages or inadequate services. This was a problem all Communist political systems have faced.

But as the central government in China has pulled back from dominating everything directly and has devolved responsibilities to lower levels or to the private sector, it can no longer be blamed by the populace for the various frustrations of daily life. It is now the private employer, or the school head, or a local official who is perceived as blameworthy; the central government is no longer the lightning rod for people's frustrations and anger. This is especially true among the urban middle class, which has little to feel resentful about in any case.

Instead, when the educated middle class sees the national leaders on the evening television news, they are perceived in a generally favorable light. The current leaders fit the image of the type of people the middle class wants to see in charge. The President and Party Secretary Hu Jintao and Prime Minister Wen Jiabao are university-educated technocrats who rose to the very top through what has increasingly become a Party meritocracy. They look like members of the educated middle class, and share many of its values. This is their leadership.

The Chinese educated middle class has become a bulwark of the current regime. Summarizing a large survey of political attitudes in Beijing, a recent book by the political scientist Chen Jie concludes that, among all urban groups, "those who perceive themselves to belong to the middle class and who are government bureaucrats are more likely to support the incumbent authorities." Don't expect regime change or democratization any time soon. The rise of China's middle class blocks the way.

MR. UNGER is professor and head of the Contemporary China Centre at the Australian National University.

Finding China's Missing Farmers

WILLIAM MACNAMARA

"This is the countryside, you know. You can throw your trash wherever you want," says the old woman helpfully. So I drop the grapefruit rinds on the floor. Grapefruits are the freshest thing in her noodle shop, which is otherwise thick with dust, stale cigarette smoke and motorcycle exhaust. Along with oranges, grapefruits are a mainstay of the rural economy in Wuyang Village, Jiangxi Province, and they are given out to strangers in abundance.

These fruits have benefited some local farmers, like the man who built the town's one guesthouse and installed his elderly mother in a noodle shop on the bottom floor. He sits beside her and lazily gazes at his grimy property. By all accounts this should be a banner year for him. Citrus, as always, is fetching higher prices than the staple crops his neighbors grow.

Most dramatically, the government has abolished agricultural taxes throughout most of China in the past year and is even paying a small subsidy to farmers. "Before, I had to pay taxes on my fields of 100 yuan per year, and now I pay nothing and the government gives me 20 yuan per year," he says between drags on his cigarette. But he doesn't sound very enthusiastic. "It's helped a little," he allows.

Outside in the twilight, farmers are returning from their rice paddies, which by the beginning of November are harvested and only require a bit of manure and scything of dry stalks. The hilly countryside and its tillers show no sign that a historic change has occured here. Yet the recent tax reforms overturn 3,000 years of practice. Since the beginning of recorded history, all Chinese dynasties from the primeval Shang to the Communists have relied on often crushing taxes levied on the peasantry.

That state of affairs will officially cease in 2006. Already, 27 out of China's 31 provinces and municipalities, including Jiangxi, have abolished agricultural taxes, with the rest soon to follow. "The agricultural tax will be exempted throughout the country next year," announced Premier Wen Jiabao at the National People's Congress in March 2005. Finally, the state media proclaimed, farmers can boost their incomes and build a decent life.

However, many farmers here remain unimpressed, as a relative decline in the prices for their crops in comparison to the cost of their daily needs makes life still more difficult. Indeed, the tax abolition appears to be a belated recognition of a new reality—farmers are moving off the land so quickly and Chinese agriculture is so moribund that such taxes don't serve any useful purpose anymore.

One of the deeper motives behind tax abolition is the Chinese Communist Party's alarm over the widening gap in income between the cities and countryside. This imbalance is immediately obvious wandering through a place like Wuyang—despite the new highway that runs near it, this is still a place where black-toothed men lug water from wells to Qing-era houses whose collapsed sections are covered by tin roofing, and where villagers, if they can afford a television, watch images of affluent Beijing youths falling in love via cell phone text messaging.

The potential of these imbalances to breed strife was shown in a bombshell of a book released in early 2004, as tax abolition was starting implementation. The book, *An Investigation of the Chinese Peasantry*, is based on rural research conducted during 1998–2001, by which time unrest was intensifying across the countryside. It details the plight of peasants who were paying higher taxes than their entire incomes, who died due to their inability to pay medical expenses, and who rallied against arbitrary taxes levied on them by corrupt officials only to be beaten to death for their temerity.

Agricultural tax abolition is just one of many proactive measures that the Communist Party has adopted recently to redress the kinds of vicious problems portrayed in this book and defuse the potential for rural rebellion. The government hopes to demonstrate that marginal enrichment will breed contentment.

The area around Wuyang Village is the cradle of the Communist Revolution. It was here, in the hills of southeastern Jiangxi province, that Mao Zedong first put into practice his idea for an agrarian revolution by founding the Jiangxi Soviet in 1931. This prototypical Chinese Communist state, with its "red capital" in the town of Ruijin, lasted for four years before Chiang Kai-shek drove the revolutionaries out and forced them to embark on the journey now known as the Long March.

The area was desperately poor back then, and it remains so today. True, farmers are no longer in danger of starving to death, and tax collectors can no longer be seen confiscating pigs in lieu of cash, as one farmer says used to happen there several years ago. But new phenomena show the depth of dissatisfaction. The biggest puzzle: Where are all the farmers?

Plenty of old men, and women of all ages, are out working the fields around Wuyang at this time of year. But the young men are gone. One of the few around is Guo Jian'an, a 32-year-old native of Wuyang, and even he is at home against his will, and not farming. Instead, he drives a motorcycle taxi.

Making 300 yuan ($37) per month hauling goods and people around the neighboring villages, Mr. Guo is distressed that his job earns him barely more than working the fields. "Do you have any friends in the cities?" he asks. He is trying to get back to Guangzhou.

Mr. Guo's parents could not afford to feed him when he was born, so he was sent as a baby to his mother's family in Wuyang. He worked in the rice paddies there until he was a teenager, but from age 18 until this year he spent most of the year working around the metropolis of Guangzhou at a tire factory and a light-bulb factory. He was able to earn a minimum of 500 yuan ($62) a month.

"Every youngster in Wuyang, 99% of them, leaves town at around 16 to 18 years old and goes to work in the factories in Shantou, Shanghai, Zhejiang," he says, describing humming industrial regions on the coast hundreds of kilometers away. Mr. Guo is explaining the Chinese migrant phenomenon to me in the house of a friend who has also "gone off" and opened a restaurant in Shishi, a city on the coast of adjoining Fujian province. Mr. Guo clearly envies his friend's prosperity.

The house, in a hillside hamlet barely accessible even by motorcycle, is unfinished, its walls bare brick and its floors roughly hewn rock, but it is a potent sign of a farmer who has made good in the big city and returned to his native acreage. Below us, dotting the old villages across the valley, are the shells of other new houses whose construction resumes, brick by brick, as soon as distant children mail more money home to their parents and wives. In this way, migrant workers gradually realize hopes for a permanent homecoming.

"My big hope is that I'll be able to make enough money by the time my son reaches 18 so that we can stay here at home together, and do business together, and not have to go far away to work. But to find that good life, and to build the highest house possible, we all have this dream: to go 'abroad' and make the most money."

The problem for peasants who want to match this formula for success, Mr. Guo says, is that "work is now extremely difficult to find in the cities. The economy has slowed down. I'm stuck here. The only place to go now is Shenzhen," the mother of all Chinese boomtowns, "but I don't know anyone there." Mr. Guo is one of many young peasants eating a new kind of bitterness—having grown used to a tough industrial life that carries possibilities, he can hardly return in peace to an even tougher agricultural life that spells a dead end.

When China's leaders announced the agricultural tax abolition, they were also acknowledging that the fundamentals of the Chinese economy have changed. According to the government's own statistics, the agricultural tax was contributing only

1% of state revenues by 2003. The economy has outgrown its traditional agricultural roots, and state leaders can afford to feel generous when relieving a marginalized and stagnant sector.

The abolition of agricultural taxes represents an acknowledgment of changes in the economy.

Meanwhile, the dynamic sectors of the economy, especially construction and export manufacturing, keep sucking in farmers. Over the past 25 years, this has created one of the greatest internal migration flows in Chinese history. Today, an estimated 100 million "floating" people identify themselves as farmers but spend most of the year working at more lucrative city jobs.

In this changed rural world, farmers in Wuyang and nearby villages tend to see tax abolition and agricultural subsidies as a few drops of water in a glass still more than half empty.

"What do you mean, 'life here'?" demands the rice farmer in Dabodi Village. I am struggling to articulate a long question, but he stops me at the first phrase. "There's no kind of life to be had here, just look around you." It is almost dark, and I can barely see the edge of the fields. We have drunk too much moonshine sorghum wine during our afternoon talk, and seemingly sensing that he is about to rail too loudly, he quiets down and chuckles instead. "Life is a little more carefree now, for sure. . . . Things are better than before when we were paying the government 100 yuan per year and making 300 yuan per year, and when corrupt officials would come here and say 'tax on your grain yield, tax on your acreage, tax on your livestock, tax this, tax that. But the land is no way to make a living. Life here is bitter. There's simply no money to be had in the country."

The farmer, surnamed Liu, has the distinction of living next door to the one site that puts his 300-person village on the map: a hut where Mao passed a couple of days in 1929, when the Jiangxi Soviet was being formed. The house is now a storage shed with a slowly rotting roof. Mr. Liu, 37, usually spends only three months of the year at home, during harvest time. He worked throughout the roaring 1990s, and until recently, "all over the country": in Xiamen, cooking at a hotel and doing demolition for the government; in the Pearl River Delta cities of Shenzhen and Dongguan, carting rice and lumber; and in Harbin, the capital of northeastern Heilongjiang province, selling oranges over the Siberian winters.

"I have friends all over the country, and we help each other out with work leads," he says over a hearty meal prepared by his wife, who helps him read (Mr. Liu is mostly illiterate) and reins in his smoking and drinking. "But I've been very unlucky recently. . . ." He idly shoos away the flies that are nibbling on the braised pig ears in front of us. "There's no work to be found right now. That's why I'm at home." He is frustrated, and says he would jump on a train that evening if he heard of a good lead.

"Most farmers in this village are taking in around 300 yuan per month," he says, echoing a figure heard in villages throughout the region. Since their gross income goes almost entirely for basic costs of farming and living, they only clear a net income of around 300 to 400 yuan per year, which made their old tax rates of about 100 yuan per year particularly onerous.

However, the elimination of these taxes "still doesn't help," Mr. Liu says, "because prices on everything are rising. A *jin* [equivalent to one pound] of fish used to cost three yuan—now it's five yuan. Even fruit is more expensive." He can sell 100 jin of rice for 80 yuan nowadays, whereas 10 years ago it would only fetch 40 yuan, but this increase still does not cover his costs, he says. When I bring up the new farm subsidy initiative, he scoffs. The subsidies only amount to 20 to 30 yuan per year, which is hardly effective, he says.

The most fundamental problem facing farmers, explains Mr. Liu, is also a very old one: Few have enough land to farm on. The average acreage per family in Dabodi Village is about one *mu* of land. A mu is roughly equivalent to one-tenth of an acre, or a little smaller than an Olympic-size swimming pool. This might be enough to feed and clothe one person depending on the crop, Mr. Liu says, but "it's hardly enough for a family of five or six to live on."

Despite the bleak picture Mr. Liu paints, it is still possible for Chinese farmers to eke out an existence off the land, as their forebears did for millennia under much worse conditions than those prevailing today. However, their concept of *ganhuo*—"to make a living"—has fundamentally changed. Even if young farmers enjoy better lives than their parents, they have had two decades of exposure and access to a wider world of livelihoods that have inevitably raised the standard of what is considered a life at all.

On the night train to Shishi, Jiangxi peasants are returning to the "better life," which is dismal in its own way. Shishi, a nondescript city on the Fujian coast, is one of China's newest boom towns, having risen from the marshes in the past 10 years on the basis of one industry alone—clothing. It is one of the world's lesser-known major manufacturing centers. Within the city, clothes spill from every other storefront, and many store signs are in English and Arabic to cater to wholesale buyers from abroad.

Thousands of migrant garment workers are now unemployed in Shishi, and the local opinion is that this is due to the U.S. and EU reimposing import quotas on Chinese textiles. The jobless congregate in a dark, dirty lane off 92 Road, the city's major avenue named after the seminal year when Deng Xiaoping jumpstarted economic reforms.

Most of the men are migrant farmers from Jiangxi province, and would have their listeners believe that China's agricultural economy is doomed. One of them, a 39-year-old farmer from Yugan County in northern Jiangxi, was employed in a wool-clothing factory until three weeks ago. He has worked in Shishi for 12 years, only returning home each year for the Spring Festival. "I'm building a house at home," he says, "and there's still one floor to go." If he can find another job, he will be able to finish the house by this time next year and return home for good, and he is considering boarding a train for Shanghai or

Beijing to find whatever factory job he can—an uncertain prospect that others on laid-off lane were discussing as they jerkily smoked cigarettes and waited for job-hawking recruiters to show up with the right offer.

"The land is no way to make a living. Life here is bitter. There's simply no money to be had in the country."

In his factory, the farmer from Yugan County worked 13-hour days sewing clothes seven days a week. This earned him 1,200 to 1,400 yuan ($148 to $173) per month, of which he mailed 1,000 yuan home to his parents, wife, and young son, who farm one mu of land.

"To leave the land isn't our ideal," he says. "I'd much rather be in the country. Here, you work until you drop asleep, and everyone in the city looks down on you, and just going out at night you have to spend 20 yuan. At home, there's nothing to do at night but chat, read, cook. The country has everything—it has mountains, water, your family around you. But the thing it doesn't have is money. . . . I sincerely wish for the best for Jiangxi, and hope that it's able to make good for itself to the point that you don't have to send money home. But in Jiangxi, it's a lifetime of awful poverty. . . ."

He surprises me by saying that he has not heard of the government's tax abolition scheme and its potential to alleviate the rural miseries he described. At the mention of taxes, however, he launches into a diatribe against corrupt officials. He is one of many Chinese his age who bitterly deride the government's supposedly reformist policies. A teenager who had stopped to listen to the migrant farmer's speech starts teasing the man, saying that he was exaggerating how corrupt local officials are nowadays—"and anyway," the youth says, "[President] Hu Jintao cancelled taxes in the countryside last year, and it's a lot better than before."

The farmer from Yugan County has a particular grievance against the government, however. Last year, local officials confiscated a total of 18 mu of land that had been farmed by his extended family. "The district government said no one was there to farm it, so they just took it away! It's like I said—corruption has no end out in the countryside." The relatives who held the user rights to the 18 mu had, like him, been living "abroad" working in the factories for over a decade, and their children were doing the same. Except for his parents, no one, in fact, *was* there to work the land.

One fresh face in Shishi who offers a sense of rural opportunities is Huang Linsheng, a soft-spoken, 23-year-old migrant from Yudu, a town in southern Jiangxi. Until being laid off the previous week, he earned 2,000 to 2,600 yuan per month, and has been sending 600 yuan home per month. Now he is considering returning home permanently, far before his prime working years are over. He is homesick and tired of his 16-hour days in the factory, and anyway he has a clever scheme to make a living off the land. He and his parents are investigating how to cultivate *ziyacai*, a medicinal plant that is fetching high prices from pharmaceutical companies.

He is encouraged to return home to what he affirms is an "enriched countryside." The agricultural tax abolition, he says, is as important a factor in enriching the modern countryside as the money sent home by migrant workers. His work in the Shishi garment factories has allowed him and his family to save enough money to experiment with their ziyacai scheme, and on top of that, "my parents are saving 1,000 yuan per year since the tax relief began."

While tax relief partly motivates him to return to his roots, Mr. Huang is one of several migrant workers who offer insights into how the government continues to tax the peasantry in its "floating" form. One way it does so in Shishi, Mr. Huang says, is by requiring migrant farmers to pay 600 to 700 yuan a year for a "work and living permit." Another way is by fining farmers for having more than one child.

The farmer from Yugan County is anticipating his wife giving birth again soon: "There's nothing to be done about it—of course I'll pay the fine," he says. "What would I do, not raise a good family because of the government?" In some cases the fines reach 6,000 yuan, a huge sum but one that an increasing number of farmers are willing to pay in order to make life's ultimate investment.

The most ingenious method the government has devised of tapping into the new peasantry's pockets, however, is through the tax levied on house construction. As more migrant farmers direct their incomes toward building the modest dream homes they will settle in one day, officials are seizing on these most tangible symbols of the urban-to-rural cash stream—and taxing their construction to the tune of 30,000 yuan ($3,700).

When I finally am able to visit one of Shishi's factories, I am startled to see that it is not unlike a home itself. A migrant worker I meet on "laid-off lane" takes me on a motorcycle tour all over the city on night, and our last stop, at midnight, is the garment factory where his sister works. It is not a gargantuan warehouse somewhere outside town, but rather an unassuming building close to downtown with the look of a typical apartment block. On the ground floor, a family is glumly eating dinner in a bare room lit by one bulb. On the second floor is a dormitory where two workers sleep to a bed. On the third floor, stacks of army camouflage cloth are piled to the ceiling. And on the fourth floor, we open an unmarked door to a bright room filled with seven rows of workers, none of them past 30, hunched over identical sewing machines producing identical camouflage jackets.

My new friend introduces me to his sister, who at midnight is in the middle of her 18-hour work day. The workers joke around in Jiangxi accents. As they spin the machines hour by each monotonous hour, they are winning more and more money to buy food, fertilizer, televisions, and houses for their families far away. It is these people, not the government, who are ushering in the revolution in the countryside.

Mr. MacNamara is a recent graduate of Princeton University and a Princeton in Asia fellow at the *Review*.

Corruption, Growth, and Reform
The Chinese Enigma

"The cumulative unfolding of corruption's many paradoxes in China has, above all, built up momentum and public support to improve state capacities, rather than further weaken them. Beijing does not suffer a legitimacy deficit despite corruption's staying power as a top public concern."

YAN SUN

Corruption, an epidemic afflicting almost all postsocialist societies, is often blamed as the major factor undermining transitions to market economies. China after Mao is no exception. Long before the recent "colorful" revolutions to overthrow corrupt leaders in three post-Soviet states, the Chinese people in 1989 staged their famous Tiananmen protests. Though typically portrayed in the Western media as a prodemocracy movement, the protests in reality were fueled by public outrage at the unprecedented corruption that had arisen out of economic liberalization in the 1980s.

Yet this corruption, which has continued to grow, seems hardly to have hampered China's economic strides over the past two decades. Annual growth rates have averaged 8 to 9 percent during this period, the highest in the world. A country of such enormous size and complexity, and without fundamental political change, has been able to successfully make the transition to a market environment and achieve record economic growth despite massive, widespread corruption.

This may be one of the most enigmatic developments of our times. Indeed, corruption in reformera China presents a number of paradoxes that defy conventional wisdom and require nuanced assessment. The key to the Chinese enigma is that corruption has varied, in breadth and intensity, across reform periods, economic sectors, and regions. And the nature of this variation has made the difference, economically and politically.

The Economic-Reform Paradox

The first paradox is that more economic liberalization has led to more corruption in China over the past two decades. This fact has cast doubt on the neoliberal logic that economic liberalization will automatically reduce bureaucratic intervention, open up competition, and bring about free markets. Since economic reform began there has been a steady rise in the number of Chinese cadre disciplined for abuses, especially at senior levels. The increase has occurred even though the bar for disciplinary action and legal proof in the courts has been raised over the years. In the 1980s, illicit proceeds amounting to the equivalent of a few thousand US dollars were considered major cases and entailed criminal punishments. Since the mid-1990s they would likely result in dismissals. Among the highest officials disciplined for official corruption—those at the deputy governor or minister level and higher—the average take in the 1980s was about $5,000. Since the 1990s, the average has approached $250,000, or 50 times as much. This surge of corruption has stemmed from a continuing expansion of incentives and opportunities created by economic liberalization. Correspondingly, the forms and scale of abuse have worsened over time.

In the early period of economic reform from 1984 to 1992, corruption largely resulted from the exploitation of loopholes in China's "dual-track" reform policy. Created to encourage flexibility and initiative outside the planned economy, the dual-track system allowed central planners to continue to set commodity prices and production quantities and decide who benefited from them. State-owned enterprises (SOEs) that fulfilled their quotas could, however, sell in the marketplace. The price differential between planned and market sales spurred an explosion of profiteering activities. Shrewd individuals sought production quotas and goods at state prices, often by offering bribes to officials and managers in charge of those items, then sold them in the market at prices several times higher.

A parallel dual-track policy spurred a robust demand side for corruption. Non-state small businesses now were allowed to coexist with SOEs and operate outside central plans. To offset their lack of access to state prices and allocations, these new players readily offered inducements to snatch raw materials, financing, and distribution channels. For a while in the late 1980s, China seemed to be on a profiteering frenzy. Middlemen and speculative businesses proliferated. The children of party leaders became involved, giving rise to the "princely party" label. And officials in various state functions caught on. Whether it was in licensing new businesses or regulating new commercial activities, they found fresh opportunities for rent seeking—that is, exchanging official power for material gain. The public backlash came vehemently in the form of the 1989 Tiananmen protests.

Family members and cronies of top leaders are no longer seen as running or profiteering from connection-based businesses.

While many blamed the incomplete market under the dual-track system for inviting corruption, the scrapping of central planning after 1992 did not halt or reduce it. On the contrary, this second phase of economic liberalization set off a new wave of corruption unprecedented in scale and kind. The end of central planning devolved economic and fiscal power to localities and markets. Today, in place of central planners and administrators, local officials make decisions and assume rights over factors of production (land, assets, and personnel); capital markets allocate loans and investment; SOE managers implement shareholding reforms; local offices interpret tax liabilities; and regulatory officials arbitrate rule compliance. The central government retains its developmental role over infrastructure, dams and waterworks, poverty reduction, and rural relocation, but local agencies administer the projects. In each of these areas, local officials have found new and more lucrative opportunities for self-enrichment. In place of profiteering, the post-1992 period has witnessed the rise of grand-level corruption, involving major government projects, land, loans, and privatization processes. No longer is rent seeking the prerogative of executives in state economic agencies or manufacturing SOEs, nor does it involve only the planned-from-above portion of the economy.

Instead, corruption has exploited the void vacated by the planned economy and has shifted to broader layers of officials, mostly at subnational levels: chief executive offices and officers, executives in capital-intensive sectors and SOEs, and regulatory and law enforcement personnel. If, in the 1980s, officials collected small bribes for doling out manufactured goods, now they collect huge bribes for signing off on a variety of capital-intensive goods: land, property rights, investment funds, loans, SOE shares and assets, construction and infrastructure projects, commercial judgments, tax breaks, and developmental aid. Cheng Kejie, the former governor of Guangxi autonomous region and the highest-ranking official executed for corruption, accepted $5 million for interceding on behalf of businesspeople to secure land, loans, contracts, and official appointments. His deputy governor took in $100,000 in 53 separate bribes to provide loan guarantees and intervene in smuggling investigations for private entrepreneurs.

On the demand side, favor seekers are no longer predominantly small-scale businesses and individuals. They may be ambitious developers, dubious construction contractors, land speculators, public office buyers, struggling SOEs, organized smugglers, or any business trying to grab a project or loan. Besides such two-way exchanges, opportunities have also arisen for officials to pillage public resources directly. It is not uncommon for executives at smaller SOEs to strip their firms of substantial assets, or to engage in stock flipping by reselling initial public offerings of their firms in the market for personal profits. Local state agencies can hike fees on public services so they can set up slush funds for various amenities.

The economic consequences of corruption are significant. Authoritative Chinese estimates put corruption-related losses of state revenue at around 4 percent of GDP annually, and corruption-related capital flight at around 2 percent of GDP. The economist Fan Gang estimated that capital flight in 2000 surpassed China's capital inflow for the year, $48 billion versus $41 billion. This capital flight often takes the form of private tuition in Western countries for the offspring of corrupt officials. Another top destination is gambling houses in Las Vegas and China's neighboring countries. Chinese gamblers account for an estimated 5 percent of annual earnings by the world's gambling businesses.

High Corruption, High Growth

Another paradox presents itself. If the combined corruption-related capital losses at home and overseas could be, at worst, large enough to cancel out the advantages of China's famed capital inflow, why has China sustained phenomenal economic growth? The most important reasons are that China has avoided the most destructive kinds of corruption at the national level and the worst types in the most productive sectors.

So-called kleptocracy and bilateral monopoly are the most destructive forms of corruption at the national level. In the first model, which is found in many African states, the ruler monopolizes his ability to use personal power for material gain. In the second model, the ruler and a few private interests share in the spoils. The latter approximates the arrangements between Boris Yeltsin's political cronies and the new economic oligarchs during Yeltsin's presidency in Russia in the 1990s. Even Yeltsin came to depend on economic powerbrokers—the oligarchs—for his electoral fortunes, rendering his government vulnerable to the group's demands for economic and political concessions. This pattern was repeated in Russia's regional governments.

In post-Mao China, the top leadership at the national level has been clean and devoted to national development, as has most of the top leadership at the provincial level. The children of Deng Xiaoping, the man who instituted China's reform program, and party leader Zhao Ziyang were tarnished during the period of "official profiteering," a main complaint of the

Tiananmen protesters. But the leaders themselves remained credibly clean and firmly willing to ban family members from doing business, unlike Yeltsin or Indonesia's Suharto. The difference may be attributed to Chinese Confucianism, nationalism, and communism. Confucianism has instilled an ethos of rule by moral mandate. The country's top communist leadership has been at its core a group of nationalists devoted to national modernization and revival. And the communist ethic has reinforced discipline.

Below the top leadership, several deputy ministers of central ministries, along with dozens of deputy provincial governors, have been brought down by corruption. But just one central minister—of the Ministry of Land and Resources, established in 1998—has been stained. (Cheng Kejie was a deputy chair of the National People's Congress when he was exposed and eventually executed for corruption in 2000, but his misdeeds occurred prior to his promotion to the center.) Four governors and one provincial party secretary have fallen because of corruption. All but one ruled in regions remote from Beijing's control: Hainan, Yunnan, Guangxi, Guizhou, and Liaoning (later Hunan). Hainan was a free economic zone, while Yunnan and Guangxi were ethnic regions with greater autonomy. In short, the Chinese state is not itself organized for rent seeking, nor does it depend on the exchange of official favors for political survival.

A competitive model, instead, characterizes the dominant patterns of Chinese corruption, with rent seeking shared among multiple officials and private interests. The "competitive" nature of Chinese corruption is evident in the range of offenders and in the absence of concentrated rent capture among political or economic elites. The type of competitive corruption, moreover, has also made a difference. During the era of dual-track reform policies before 1992, competition was for a fixed supply of government benefits: state-priced and -regulated commodities. In this situation, illegal payoffs for goods should ideally act like market prices in an efficient market. In reality, insider dealings rendered official profiteering less competitive, but it still served a sort of "market clearing" function and helped to erode central planning eventually.

Since the end of central planning, competitive corruption has sought a variable supply of government benefits. With no more commands from on high, local officials now enjoy discretion over the quantity and quality of services they provide. Their greater autonomy has entailed a greater ability to manipulate rents. They can arbitrarily decide whom to award land, projects, or contracts and at what prices; whom to grant loans, shares, and services and on what terms; or how much in fees and levies to demand or absolve. Because the stakes are so much larger now, involving capital goods rather than manufactured goods, the payoffs for officials and the costs for businesses escalate as well. This entails greater waste and burden on the economy. Which raises the question: Why then has China's post-1992 economy managed to grow so fast?

Winners and Losers

One important reason is China's avoidance of the worst types of corruption in its most productive sector: non-state enterprises.

This is a significant point because the non-state sector has been the larger and more efficient contributor to reform-era growth, especially since the 1990s. That so many SOEs are ailing is often linked to managerial corruption, and usually the most destructive kind: misuse of company funds, partial privatization or theft of SOE assets, hoarding of revenue, and appointment of cronies. This predatory abuse aggravates the problems of inefficiency and bankruptcy that already plague many SOEs, a third of which may be loss-making and another third latent loss-making. Credits and subsidies to prop up feeble SOEs have been responsible for much of the government's deficits. These loans often become nonperforming as SOEs fail to pay them back, which has caused China's infamous banking crisis. This in turn has seriously hindered the development of a sound financial system.

While non-state enterprises are not free of corruption, they only have incentives for the competitive kind: offering inducements to secure contracts, loans, or markets; evading taxes; or influencing regulatory decisions. These practices do not contribute to an orderly market. And bad contractors have accounted for many "tofu" (easily collapsible) construction projects. But, overall, corruption is far less detrimental to the non-state sector's productivity and growth.

If the combined corruption-related capital losses at home and overseas could be, at worst, large enough to cancel out the advantages of China's famed capital inflow, why has China sustained phenomenal economic growth?

There is also a cultural explanation for China's overall less-destructive corruption. The Chinese emphasis on *guanxi* (connections) is well known. Implicit in this idea is not only respect for social relations but also for reciprocity. The latter has meant that, despite a decline in affective incentives (that is, motives based on social or emotional ties) in corrupt exchanges, services are still performed after payoffs are offered or made. Defrauding would amount to unpredictability, extortion, or absolute losses for businesses. Indeed, in thousands of actual cases I have surveyed from corruption casebooks published in China, defrauding or outright extortion (both of which are common in post-Soviet Russia) is rare. The predictable delivery of services, along with rather predictable levels of payoffs, has ensured a stable, if less than optimal, business environment.

More harmful corruption still abounds. And where it does, growth suffers. In addition to the SOEs, the economies of remote, underdeveloped, and often rural regions are seriously afflicted. These regions, like the SOEs, tend to have public funding and "soft" budgets, cushioned by funds for development, infrastructure, poverty relief, and resettlement, usually from the central and provincial governments. Lacking the alternative routes to enrichment available in booming regions and often far from the higher administrative and disciplinary agencies of the state, many local officials have resorted to raiding developmental funds. A National Audit Office investigation in 2003 found that $7.7 billion worth of government funds had been misused and some $580 million for poverty-alleviation projects had vanished. Some 40 million farmers may have lost their land to illegal confiscations by officials who resold the land to developers, a transaction that often involves kickbacks. In these sectors, a cycle of corruption further retards real reform and development.

Ultimately, the paradox of corruption and growth in the Chinese case must be weighed in terms of the distributional consequences obscured by overall growth rates. Although per capita income has increased by tens of times since economic reforms began, not everyone's income has grown on such a scale, especially for SOE workers and rural residents. Many Chinese analysts and citizens view corruption as an important cause of unwarranted quick wealth and of social polarization. Although corruption no longer is seen as the main avenue to wealth, as it was a decade ago, these perceptions persist among many ailing SOEs and poor regions. Not surprisingly, displaced SOE workers and disgruntled farmers have largely fueled the periodic protests and unrest at local levels in recent years. They are most agitated when they see their plight as linked to local cadre corruption. Because SOEs still employ half of the national workforce, and poor regions still hold at least half of the nation's rural population, the impoverishment of even a third of these two sectors constitutes a significant distributional problem.

The Central-Authority Paradox

Why has the Chinese regime not been more effective at deterring corruption, given that the leadership cares as much about social stability as economic growth? Herein lies a third paradox from the Chinese case. Neoliberal orthodoxy dictates a reduction in the scope of the state, especially central authority, in the transition to the market. But the steady erosion of state authority has not reduced bureaucratic arbitrariness. Rather, it has weakened deterrence against it. Assertions of central authority, meanwhile, have helped to enhance deterrence.

Institutional continuity at the center is the reason deterrence against abuse has not deteriorated in China to the point that systemic collapse occurs, as in Russia and other post-Soviet republics. The Chinese state has preserved two fundamental capacities critical to anticorruption efforts: law making and institution building. In contrast to the parliamentary paralyses and intra-elite polarization evident in other postsocialist states, the Chinese leadership has shown a strong consensus against corruption and an effectual capacity to create oversight laws and agencies. The central state has adopted a range of new laws to reduce irregularities in public tendering, project approval, and fiscal extraction. It has set up new institutions to increase the audit, inspection, and monitoring of administrative matters and personnel. It has elevated the importance and power of disciplinary agencies in local administrations and SOEs.

Without these efforts, corruption might easily have escalated to uncontrollable levels. China has avoided the state capture (buying off of politicians by economic oligarchs to shape the legal, policy, and regulatory environments in their own interests), the mafia rampancy, and the routine need for private security protection that have plagued, for example, Russia's transition to the market.

In the enforcement of anticorruption laws and bans, however, central authority remains seriously challenged. A major problem is the supervision of the chief executive at each local administrative level to which state authority has devolved. Local oversight mechanisms are ineffective because they are subordinate to, rather than independent of, the local chief executive office. In response, the Communist Party has formed a central inspection team, with power independent of localities, which conducts periodic and targeted scrutiny of local officialdom. This serves to channel upward grass-roots complaints and abuse cases.

An alternative anticorruption mechanism—popular control from below—can also suffer from insufficient state strength. Direct elections, first implemented at the village level, are now also held at township levels. Indirect elections are the norm at other levels of the party, state, and people's congresses. However, where central authority and legal enforcement are weak, vote buying has become a problem in township, county, and even city-level elections. Shrewd operators have also managed to get elected through cultivated public images and private maneuverings, even at senior ranks. A former Hunan governor built a reputation as a tough corruption fighter and won overwhelming reelection in the provincial people's congress in 2001. Yet privately he garnered more than $100,000 in bribes as governor of Liaoning and Hunan provinces. A former deputy mayor of Shenyang, who had ties to organized crime and was to gamble away millions in public funds in Macao, was elected by the provincial people's congress over another candidate who later died fighting floods as leader of a lesser city.

Although China does not yet have its share of oligarchs like those who have secured elections as governors and senators in Russia, vote buying by private businessmen has increased in local elections. On the promising side, direct elections have improved administrative and fiscal transparency in many villages. On balance the various problems do not discredit elections, but they do suggest that elections will not provide a panacea, and they will continue to require rigorous central oversight.

Assertions of state authority also seem necessary to bolster another liberal guarantor of accountability: the media. For the first time in its history, the party in April 2005 issued a decree to encourage and legitimize the monitoring and exposure of cadre abuse by the media. The decree urges all levels of the party and state to support the media's work in this area. The background to this new policy is the rise of corruption exposure in China's news media in recent years. Yet, without legal guarantees of their rights, the media have often encountered intimidation by local officials, or lost defamation lawsuits filed by exposed officials.

Corruption and Political Reform

The realities of other postsocialist states have taught China's leaders and many of its intellectuals to be cautious about rapid democratization. Many of the new democracies not only have grown more slowly economically, but also have seen more corruption and have been ruled by corrupt "elected autocrats." Experience suggests that drastic political change may worsen rather than alleviate corruption. So far, incremental change has proved a workable strategy for China. It appears to be what most Chinese want, and they likely will continue to rely on the state as the engine of change.

The cumulative unfolding of corruption's many paradoxes in China has, above all, built up momentum and public support to improve state capacities, rather than further weaken them. Beijing does not suffer a legitimacy deficit despite corruption's staying power as a top public concern. The government is still looked on as a solution to social ills. Family members and cronies of top leaders are no longer seen as running or profiteering from connection-based businesses. Indeed, they hardly run any of China's major corporations, in contrast with a good deal of the postsocialist world. Many ordinary Chinese have become successful and affluent entrepreneurs, making the "princely party" indistinct or even extinct. As corrupt exchange has become mostly materially based, it is also more accessible, thus less exclusive or inflammatory than in the early years of economic reform. Unlike the dual-track policies of the 1980s, moreover, contemporary corruption no longer is caused by central policies, but by errant officials at local levels. In fact, when local protesters and rioters complain about localized injustices, they are likely to demand that central policies be upheld.

For the first time in its history, the party in April 2005 issued a decree to encourage and legitimize the monitoring and exposure of cadre abuse by the media.

An important segment of Chinese liberal intellectuals also supports strengthening central capacities. Unlike their counterparts in the former socialist regimes of Eastern Europe and Russia, Chinese intellectuals are not united around a liberal political agenda. They diverge into two broad camps: the liberal left (the so-called new left or social democrats) and the liberal right (the new right or neoliberals). For the roots of corruption, the new left faults the government's blind faith in the market, especially after 1992, pointing to the erosion of state authority and loss of control over local officialdom. In the new left's view, the Tiananmen crackdown made it safe for unbridled capitalism and a right-wing Communist Party.

The new right, by contrast, faults government power itself, rather than the way it is used. The reduction of corruption, in this view, requires the reduction of state power itself. If the new left blames the government for being too neoliberal, the new right blames it for not being neoliberal enough. As remedies, the new right proposes "property rights," or allowing SOEs to be "spontaneously privatized" by cadre abuse. Corruption's destructiveness here is seen as positive: helping to replace SOEs, giving rise to private ownership, and acting as a driving force for change. Yet who would benefit and lose from a bargain

transfer of public enterprises? Would it, the new left asks, not simply benefit a class of bureaucratic capitalists and entrench crony capitalism? Rather than destroying state power, the new left sees an important role for government in correcting market failures and redressing social inequalities.

The emergence of new left intellectuals in China challenges the lingering American view of a monolithic and ruthless Communist Party pitted against pro-democracy and Western-oriented intellectuals. Rather than being socialist diehards, the new left thinkers have usually been educated in the West. Some were participants in the Tiananmen protests. One participant and new left thinker, Wang Hui, has published an impassioned critique of the government's neoliberalism: *China's New Order: Society, Politics, and Economy in Transition.* Wang blames ideological and partisan interests at home and abroad for a failure to appreciate the neoliberal bias of the Tiananmen crackdown, which allowed the state to impose more sweeping economic liberalization policies. He calls these policies neoliberal because they radically devolved economic and political power, promoted markets, and sought the economic withdrawal of the state in the midst of globalization—all of which have helped increase corruption after 1992. Still more revealing is Wang's view on the source of growing Chinese disillusion with the liberal democratic paradigm the many crises of Chinese and Russian reform on the one hand, and American foreign policies and military hegemonism on the other. The attractiveness of the liberal model, for the time being, is not taken for granted.

The presence of a new left and a new right places the ruling party in the ideological middle. The two groups help legitimize the party in different ways. The new right helps the party explain away the rampant corruption and shirk its social responsibility. The new left helps the party justify strengthening its capabilities. One might add that both groups need the party as well: the new right needs it to continue devolving political power and pushing economic liberalization; the new left needs the party to curtail the excesses of this process. Given that not only efficiency but its own legitimacy is at stake, the ruling party has shown a consistent determination to fight corruption and introduce anticorruption reforms. These reforms have been along the lines that new left thinking has emphasized: state building. In other words, while the party proceeds economically in the direction desired by the new right, it proceeds politically in the direction urged by the new left on anticorruption, though in neither case as much as each group would like to see.

Changing the Landscape

Anticorruption reform is one area in which a US role could be constructive and welcomed in China. In contrast to their usual annoyance with US lecturing about democracy and human rights, the Chinese are impressed with America's efforts to bring its own companies to justice for illegally pursuing commercial advantages in China. Under the US Foreign Corrupt Practices Act of 1977, which prohibits US companies and their subsidiaries (including officers, directors, employees, and agents) from bribing foreign officials, the Chinese subsidiary of Lucent Technologies was forced to fire four top executives for commercial bribery in

2004. In 2005, Diagnostic Products Corporation was fined $4.8 million by the us Justice Department for kickbacks to Chinese medical personnel. By punishing its own companies, the United States sets a credible example and demonstrates compellingly the paramount importance of rule of law. The Bush administration's tightened control of illegal monetary inflows can also be useful for deterring capital flight.

Beyond these steps, however, little concrete assistance for anticorruption efforts comes from the West, despite profuse public posturing and chastening about China. In fact, thanks to mistrust of Chinese laws in the West, Chinese perpetrators have found Western countries a safe haven where they enjoy some measure of protection. Even those apprehended face little prospect of being extradited.

To fundamentally change its corruption landscape, China needs to learn from successful examples, including America. Singapore and Hong Kong offer realistic and effective models from China's own vicinity. The two city-states rank among the least corrupt states in the world according to Transparency International, and the best among non-Western governments. Both share China's cultural heritage yet have managed to change tenacious cultural attitudes—that is, weak respect for the rule of law and an emphasis on informal practices and social relations. Both instituted effective anticorruption mechanisms at developmental stages similar to China's. Both have relied on strong state capacities for strict enforcement and prevention, under authoritarian rule, yet have maintained highly independent anticorruption agencies and relatively independent legal systems. Even the democratic Philippines has recently tapped a top anticorruption official from Hong Kong to help with its anticorruption work.

China should embrace this approach the way it welcomes foreign investment. Along with the increasing role of the media, popular elections, and expanding privatization, greater initiative against corruption would serve well the building of what the Chinese themselves consider to be good government: accountable, just, and devoted to the welfare of the people. Memories of Tiananmen and periodic peasant rebellions in Chinese history will keep the regime on its toes in any event, because anticorruption is one battle it cannot afford to lose.

YAN SUN is a professor of political science at City University of New York, Queens College, and the Graduate Center. She is the author of *Corruption and Market in Contemporary China* (Cornell University Press, 2004) and *The Chinese Reassessment of Socialism* (Princeton University Press, 1995).

Managing China's Rise

Contending effectively with China's ambitions requires a better understanding of our own.

BENJAMIN SCHWARZ

When President Bush took office, in 2001, the dominant national-security issue for his administration—and for most foreign-policy analysts, whether Republican or Democrat—was not terrorism or even Iraq but China. The issue, specifically, is that China will eventually emerge as what Pentagon planners call a "peer competitor" to the United States in East Asia—that is, a great power with the economic and military muscle to challenge America's preponderant position in a region that is sure to be the economic pivot of the new century.

When "eventually" may roll around is a matter of intense debate between moderates and hardliners. The moderates have a better case. Hardliners, some of whom hold powerful positions in the current administration, see a hegemon on the horizon. But China is a defense-minded state, vulnerable to domestic turmoil and burdened with colossal environmental problems and natural-resource demands. True, over the past several years China has selectively and impressively modernized its armed forces, but they're still debilitated by pervasive corruption and are organizationally and technologically far behind not only America's but also Japan's and South Korea's. Hardliners point, correctly, to Beijing's ambitions to play a more active role in the eastern Pacific. But they exaggerate when they claim that soon China will be able to disrupt sea-lanes and intimidate Malaysia, Singapore, the Philippines, and even Australia and Japan—because the problems posed by projecting air and naval power far from home waters are a good deal more complicated than those in a game of Risk. To bid for mastery of East Asia, China will have to fundamentally transform the doctrine, training, and structure of its military (which has traditionally focused on defending home territory), not to mention acquire aircraft carriers—no easy task in itself. Hardliners warn that China has recently bought first-rate fighter planes from Russia, but America's fighter pilots are vastly superior, owing to their incomparably better experience, tactics, and training (the Chinese air force has been training to fly over open waters for only seven years, and its pilots can devote barely half the hours to flight training that U.S. pilots can). Forget about fighting the United States or Japan; today China's navy would lose a battle in the home waters of Singapore or Malaysia. To be sure, China's newly acquired midrange missiles, and even its diesel submarines, complicate aspects of U.S. naval planning in the eastern Pacific. The United States, however, has such a jump on Beijing in its command, control, communications, computer, and intelligence capabilities—by far the most vital elements of a modern military's effectiveness, and by far the most difficult to develop—that American strategic supremacy in East Asia will grow, not diminish, in the coming years.

Far from discouraging the rise of China and other powers, Washington should recognize the significant benefits that can result.

But these points merely deflate alarmist arguments. Given its economic dynamism, China probably will—in twenty-five years or longer—become a powerful and militarily sophisticated geopolitical actor in East Asia and the eastern Pacific. And so America's overwhelming military and political influence in the region will decline. But the United States has plenty of time to consider the implications of China's rise before it is complete. We must examine our own stance toward the world, and the way we define threats to our national security. In other words, to understand the consequences of China's (slowly) growing ambitions, we have to understand our own.

We should first acknowledge that the pace of China's military modernization and the nature of its geopolitical alignments are very much tied to the post–Cold War imbalance of power in Washington's favor. Never before in history has one state held so pre-eminent a position as that which America has enjoyed since the collapse of the Soviet Union. Of course, both Democratic and Republican administrations hold that other countries regard us as a "benevolent hegemon." But in fact states must always be more concerned with a predominant power's capabilities than with its professed intentions. China and Russia saw the U.S. intervention in Kosovo as a dangerous precedent establishing Washington's asserted right to interfere in other countries' internal affairs; and although long estranged, they formed a nascent alliance aimed expressly at re-establishing a "multipolar world." With the invasion of Iraq, of course, the world's suspicion of American hegemony intensified enormously, and now China and Russia have expanded their military cooperation and are conducting joint military exercises. Similarly, the wars in both Kosovo and Iraq spurred Chinese military planners to focus on countering America's high-tech dominance on the battlefield. The United States should conduct whatever foreign policies it deems appropriate—but it must recognize that actions it perceives as selfless, others will most likely see in an entirely different light. An interventionist global role may serve a number of American interests, but history has repeatedly shown that intervention by a dominant power accelerates the rise of other great powers and ensures their wariness, if not their hostility, toward it.

We should also rigorously examine how Washington defines a "China threat." Hardliners and moderates, Republicans and Democrats, agree that America is strategically dominant in East Asia and the eastern Pacific—China's back yard. They further agree that America should retain its dominance there. Thus U.S. military planners define as a threat Beijing's efforts to remedy its own weak position in the face of the overwhelming superiority that they acknowledge the United States holds right up to the edge of the Asian mainland. This probably reveals more about our ambitions than it does about China's. Imagine if the situation were reversed, and China's air and naval power were a dominant and potentially menacing presence on the coastal shelf of North America. Wouldn't we want to offset that preponderance? America's direct sphere of influence extends from the Canadian Arctic to Tierra del Fuego, and from Greenland to Guam. Surely we can tolerate other great powers' enjoying spheres of influence in other parts of the world. China's sphere certainly includes Taiwan, which is just a hundred miles off its shore.

More generally, we have to examine the strategic implications raised when regional and great powers emerge. Americans are understandably happy with U.S. global hegemony. It's a misreading of history, however, to suggest that the rise of new great powers will perforce engender conflict. Admittedly, German interests in the late nineteenth and early twentieth centuries could not be accommodated without hazarding the interests of others, because several great powers were crowded onto a small continent. But it's also true that in the same period the United States peacefully rose to be a great power in a region far from other great powers. Britain, the dominant naval power in the Western Hemisphere, wisely acquiesced to U.S. ascendancy there and, more important, recognized that America could collaborate with rather than challenge the effort to maintain international stability. London thereby transformed a potential conflict into a strategic partnership that has served it well for a century.

China's emergence as a great power may be inevitable, but it's going to be a long process, which we should seek to manage with Beijing. Far from discouraging the rise of Ghina and other independent powers, such as the European Union and Japan, Washington should recognize the significant benefits that can result. There will be more jockeying for advantage in global politics; but accommodating other powers, giving them a stake in the stability of the international system, and making them share the responsibility for maintaining it can substantially reduce America's globe-girdling defense commitments and the concomitant international suspicion toward the United States. The alternative in the long run is to create enemies where none need exist.

BENJAMIN SCHWARZ is the literary editor and national editior of *The Atlantic*.

China's "Peaceful Rise" to Great-Power Status

ZHENG BIJIAN

Getting the Facts Right

China's rapid development has attracted worldwide attention in recent years. The implications of various aspects of China's rise, from its expanding influence and military muscle to its growing demand for energy supplies, are being heatedly debated in the international community as well as within China. Correctly understanding China's achievements and its path toward greater development is thus crucial.

Since starting to open up and reform its economy in 1978, China has averaged 9.4 percent annual GDP growth, one of the highest growth rates in the world. In 1978, it accounted for less than one percent of the world economy, and its total foreign trade was worth $20.6 billion. Today, it accounts for four percent of the world economy and has foreign trade worth $851 billion—the third-largest national total in the world. China has also attracted hundreds of billions of dollars of foreign investment and more than a trillion dollars of domestic nonpublic investment. A dozen years ago, China barely had mobile telecommunications services. Now it claims more than 300 million mobile-phone subscribers, more than any other nation. As of June 2004, nearly 100 million people there had access to the Internet.

Indeed, China has achieved the goal it set for itself in 1978: it has significantly improved the well-being of its people, although its development has often been narrow and uneven. The last 27 years of reform and growth have also shown the world the magnitude of China's labor force, creativity, and purchasing power; its commitment to development; and its degree of national cohesion. Once all of its potential is mobilized, its contribution to the world as an engine of growth will be unprecedented.

One should not, however, lose sight of the other side of the coin. Economic growth alone does not provide a full picture of a country's development. China has a population of 1.3 billion. Any small difficulty in its economic or social development, spread over this vast group, could become a huge problem. And China's population has not yet peaked; it is not projected to decline until it reaches 1.5 billion in 2030. Moreover, China's economy is still just one-seventh the size of the United States' and one-third the size of Japan's. In per capita terms, China remains a low-income developing country, ranked roughly 100th in the world. Its impact on the world economy is still limited.

The formidable development challenges still facing China stem from the constraints it faces in pulling its population out of poverty. The scarcity of natural resources available to support such a huge population—especially energy, raw materials, and water—is increasingly an obstacle, especially when the efficiency of use and the rate of recycling of those materials are low. China's per capita water resources are one-fourth of the amount of the world average, and its per capita area of cultivatable farmland is 40 percent of the world average. China's oil, natural gas, copper, and aluminum resources in per capita terms amount to 8.3 percent, 4.1 percent, 25.5 percent, and 9.7 percent of the respective world averages.

Setting the Priorities

For the next few decades, the Chinese nation will be preoccupied with securing a more comfortable and decent life for its people. Since the Third Plenary Session of the Eleventh Central Committee of the Chinese Communist Party, held in 1978, the Chinese leadership has concentrated on economic development. Through its achievements so far, China has blazed a new strategic path that suits its national conditions while conforming to the tides of history. This path toward modernization can be called "the development path to a peaceful rise." Some emerging powers in modern history have plundered other countries' resources through invasion, colonization, expansion, or even large-scale wars of aggression. China's emergence thus far has been driven by capital, technology, and resources acquired through peaceful means.

The most significant strategic choice the Chinese have made was to embrace economic globalization rather than detach themselves from it. In the late 1970s, when the new technological revolution and a new wave of economic globalization were unfolding with great momentum, Beijing grasped the trend and reversed the erroneous practices of the Cultural Revolution. On the basis of the judgment that China's development would depend on its place in an open world, Deng Xiaoping and other Chinese leaders decided to seize the historic opportunity and shift the focus of their work to economic development. They carried out reforms meant to open up and foster domestic markets and tap into international ones. They implemented the household contracting system in rural areas and opened up 14 coastal cities, thus ushering in a period of economic takeoff.

In the 1990s, China once again confronted a strategic choice, due to the Asian financial crisis and the subsequent struggle between the forces for and against globalization. China's decision to participate in economic globalization was facing a serious challenge. But by carefully weighing the advantages and disadvantages of economic openness and drawing lessons from recent history, Beijing decided to open up China even more, by joining the World Trade Organization and deepening economic reform at home.

China has based its modernization process mainly on its domestic resources. It has relied on ideological and institutional innovations and on industrial restructuring. By exploring the growing domestic market and transferring the huge personal savings of its citizens into investment, China has infused its economy with new momentum. Its citizens' capacities are being upgraded and its technological progress expedited. Even while attempting to learn from and absorb useful products from other societies, including those of the advanced capitalist countries, China has maintained its independence and self-reliance.

In pursuing the goal of rising in peace, the Chinese leadership has strived for improving China's relations with all the nations of the world. Despite the ups and downs in U.S.-Chinese relations over the years, as well as other dramatic changes in international politics, such as the collapse of the Soviet Union, Beijing has stuck to the belief that there are more opportunities than challenges for China in today's international environment.

The Road Ahead

According to China's strategic plans, it will take another 45 years—until 2050—before it can be called a modernized, medium-level developed country. China will face three big challenges before it gets there. As described above, China's shortage of resources poses the first problem. The second is environmental: pollution, waste, and a low rate of recycling together present a major obstacle to sustainable development. The third is a lack of coordination between economic and social development.

This last challenge is reflected in a series of tensions Beijing must confront: between high GDP growth and social progress, between upgrading technology and increasing job opportunities, between keeping development momentum in the coastal areas and speeding up development in the interior, between fostering urbanization and nurturing agricultural areas, between narrowing the gap between the rich and the poor and maintaining economic vitality and efficiency, between attracting more foreign invest-

ment and enhancing the competitiveness of indigenous enterprises, between deepening reform and preserving social stability, between opening domestic markets and solidifying independence, between promoting market-oriented competition and taking care of disadvantaged people. To cope with these dilemmas successfully, a number of well-coordinated policies are needed to foster development that is both faster and more balanced.

The policies the Chinese government has been carrying out, and will continue to carry out, in the face of these three great challenges can be summarized as three grand strategies—or "three transcendences."

The first strategy is to transcend the old model of industrialization and to advance a new one. The old industrialization was characterized by rivalry for resources in bloody wars and by high investment, high consumption of energy, and high pollution. Were China to follow this path, it would harm both others and itself. China is instead determined to forge a new path of industrialization based on technology, economic efficiency, low consumption of natural resources relative to the size of its population, low environmental pollution, and the optimal allocation of human resources. The Chinese government is trying to find new ways to reduce the percentage of the country's imported energy sources and to rely more on China's own. The objective is to build a "society of thrift."

The second strategy is to transcend the traditional ways for great powers to emerge, as well as the Cold War mentality that defined international relations along ideological lines. China will not follow the path of Germany leading up to World War I or those of Germany and Japan leading up to World War II, when these countries violently plundered resources and pursued hegemony. Neither will China follow the path of the great powers vying for global domination during the Cold War. Instead, China will transcend ideological differences to strive for peace, development, and cooperation with all countries of the world.

The third strategy is to transcend outdated modes of social control and to construct a harmonious socialist society. The functions transformed, with self-governance supplementing state administration. China is strengthening its democratic institutions and the rule of law and trying to build a stable society based on a spiritual civilization. A great number of ideological and moral-education programs have been launched.

Several dynamic forces are noticeable in the carrying out of the three strategies. For example, there are numerous clusters of vigorously developing cities in the coastal areas of eastern and southern China, and similar clusters are emerging in the central and western regions. They constitute the main engines of growth, are the major manufacturing and trading centers, and absorb surplus rural labor. They also have high productivity, advanced culture, and accumulated international experience that the rest of China can emulate and learn from. The expansion of China's middle-income strata and the growing need for international markets come mainly from these regions.

China's surplus of rural workers, who have strong aspirations to escape poverty, is another force that is pushing Chinese society into industrial civilization. About ten million rural Chinese migrate to urban areas each year in an orderly and protected way.

They both provide Chinese cities with new productivity and new markets and help end the backwardness of rural areas. Innovations in science and technology and culture are also driving China toward modernization and prosperity in the twenty-first century.

The Chinese government has set up targets for development for the next 50 years. This period is divided into three stages. In the first stage—2000 to 2010—total GDP is to be doubled. In the second stage, ending in 2020, total GDP is to be doubled again, at which point China's per capita GDP is expected to reach $3,000. In the third, from 2020 to 2050, China will continue to advance until it becomes a prosperous, democratic, and civilized socialist country. By that time, China will have shaken off underdevelopment and will be on a par with the middle rung of advanced nations. It can then claim to have succeeded in achieving a "peaceful rise."

Impact on the World

China's peaceful rise will further open its economy so that its population can serve as a growing market for the rest of the world, thus providing increased opportunities for—rather than posing a threat to—the international community. A few figures illustrate China's current contribution to global trade: in 2004, China's imports from members of the Association of Southeast Asian Nations increased by 33.1 percent, from Japan by 27.3 percent, from India by 80 percent, from the European Union by 28 percent, and from the United States by 31.9 percent.

China is not the only power that seeks a peaceful rise. China's economic integration into East Asia has contributed to the shaping of an East Asian community that may rise in peace as a whole. And it would not be in China's interest to exclude the United States from the process. In fact, Beijing wants Washington to play a positive role in the region's security as well as economic affairs. The beginning of the twenty-first century is seeing a number of countries rising through different means, while following different models, and at different paces. At the same time, the developed countries are further developing themselves. This is a trend to be welcomed.

China does not seek hegemony or predominance in world affairs. It advocates a new international political and economic order, one that can be achieved through incremental reforms and the democratization of international relations. China's development depends on world peace—a peace that its development will in turn reinforce.

ZHENG BIJIAN is Chair of the China Reform Forum, a nongovernmental and nonprofit academic organization that provides research on and analysis of domestic, international, and development issues related to China. He has drafted key reports for five Chinese national party congresses and held senior posts in academic and party organizations in China.

Cultural Revolution
How China Is Changing Global Diplomacy

Joshua Kurlantzick

At a major Asian security conference this month, Secretary of Defense Donald Rumsfeld was typically blunt. Discussing China's military modernization, Rumsfeld said that China's upgrade of its military technology was a threat to countries across Asia. "Since no nation threatens China, one wonders: Why this growing investment?" Rumsfeld asked.

Unfortunately, he is focused on the wrong problem. China is indeed on the verge of posing a major threat to U.S. power and could potentially dominate parts of the developing world. But the real concern is not that China's armed forces will challenge the mighty U.S. military, which soon may spend more on defense than the rest of the world combined.

No, China's rising power is reflected in a different way. In late 2003, Australia hosted back-to-back state visits by two world leaders. The first to head down under was George W. Bush, a staunch ally of Australia, which, along with the United Kingdom, was a major provider of non-U.S. troops for the invasions of Iraq and Afghanistan. On arrival, however, Bush was treated like a boorish distant cousin; his official reception was polite, but barely so. He stayed just 21 hours, and, speaking before the Australian parliament, faced protests outside and inside the chamber, where Green Party senators repeatedly interrupted him with catcalls.

The treatment was far different when Chinese President Hu Jintao arrived for a more extended stay. Though, less than a decade ago, fear of being swamped by Asians was a potent electoral issue in Australia, now Canberra threw open its arms to the Chinese leader. For days, Australia's business and political elite fêted Hu at lavish receptions. And, at China's request, Australian lawmakers barred potential irritants—like Tibetan activists—from parliament, as Hu became the first Asian leader to address the Australian legislature, receiving a 20-minute standing ovation. Perhaps this differing treatment shouldn't have been surprising. Australia's leaders were simply following their people's lead. Recent polls suggest that, despite decades of close American-Australian relations, Australians generally have a more favorable view of China than of the United States.

China has also scored diplomatic successes in Latin America, long thought to be within Washington's sphere of influence. During a highly successful twelve-day Latin America trip, which, like his visit to Australia, coincided with a brief Bush trip to the region that received a cool reception, Hu signed some $30 billion in new investment deals and subtly staked a claim that the United States was failing as the major power in the region. Hu stopped in regional giant Brazil, where President Luiz Inácio Lula da Silva upgraded bilateral trade ties with Beijing and decided to send Brazilian advisers to Beijing to study Chinese economics. During an earlier trip to China, Lula had cooed to Hu: "We want a partnership that integrates our economies and serves as a paradigm for South-South cooperation."

Most important for Beijing, in oil-rich Venezuela, a nation increasingly shunned by the United States—which tacitly condoned a 2002 coup attempt against Venezuelan leader Hugo Chávez—Chinese officials are solidifying an alliance with Caracas while providing Chávez an opportunity to point out Washington's failures in the region. While Chávez talks of slashing oil deliveries to the United States, he promises Beijing a long-term supply of petroleum. "China is a world power. She doesn't come here with imperialist airs," announced the Venezuelan leader, leaving the distinction with another world power unsaid. Chávez also plans to send advisers to Iran to help Tehran funnel *its* oil to Beijing. (Iran has inked deals to supply China with natural gas and to provide the Chinese state oil company, Sinopec, with a stake in one of Iran's biggest oil fields.)

Beijing's inroads with Australia and Latin America, two vastly different regions of the world, signify aspects of the same sea change. For the first time in centuries, China is becoming an international power, a nation with global foreign policy ambitions. In fact, China may become the first nation since the fall of the Soviet Union that could seriously challenge the United States for control of the international system.

As it develops, China has several key interests in the world. Because of China's booming economy and lack of domestic resources, securing stable supplies of oil, natural gas, and other natural resources—as well as safe passage for these resources—is of primary interest to Beijing. Second, as China's leading companies continue to grow and improve the quality of their products, Beijing clearly needs access to foreign markets. Less obviously, but no less significantly, China seeks to demonstrate that it is an international power, worthy of the same respect as the United States and capable of projecting enough power to limit U.S. intentions in Asia and other parts of the developing world. And, perhaps most important, Beijing wants to bring its own socioeconomic and political models to other developing countries, just as the United States historically has been committed to—at least rhetorically—the spread of democracy.

Beijing is pursuing these interests through a two-pronged strategy. On the one hand, China appears to be building a string of alliances across the globe with nations shunned by the United States—nations like Venezuela, Iran, Sudan, Burma, and Zimbabwe. At the same time, China appears to be wooing non-rogue developing nations—both democracies like Brazil and stable pseudo-authoritarian states like Malaysia. Beijing does so by championing a vision of international relations centered on national sovereignty—one that contrasts sharply with recent U.S. doctrine, by leveraging China's economic successes to win over foreign leaders and by using Chinese soft power to win hearts and minds even in places like Australia, once considered firm American allies.

China's rise may have significant positive effects. As China takes on a larger role in the world, it may come to assume a large role in peacekeeping, global aid disbursements, and other responsibilities currently handled by the United States and other wealthy nations. China even contributed funding to elections in Iraq. Because it straddles both the rich and the poor world, China could also help mediate between developed and developing countries at institutions like the World Trade Organization (WTO).

Yet China's more prominent international footprint is likely to threaten U.S. interests seriously. Beijing's quest for natural resources will thrust it into competition with the United States, particularly in crucial regions like West Africa and the Middle East. China's emergence as a growing power could threaten America's role as the primary guarantor of stability in Asia. Its increasing access to international markets could damage U.S. corporations, especially if Chinese businesses were subsidized by Beijing through soft loans that would allow them to operate unprofitably, at least for a time, and squeeze competitors' margins. And China's power could damage one of the most important U.S. interests of all: the spread of democracy, which will ultimately enable us to win the war on terrorism. Despite stumbles in Uzbekistan, Saudi Arabia, and other places where the White House continues to choose stability or cooperation on counterterrorism over liberalization, the United States remains the major force for democratization in the world.

Though hawks have been warning of a "China threat" for over a decade, they usually focus on China's military capabilities, not its diplomatic skills. The view elaborated in Rumsfeld's speech will likely be reflected in an upcoming Defense Department report on China's military intentions, programs, and strategies. Hawks have pushed to make the report as dire as possible, portraying China as a military threat that has sized up the weaknesses of the U.S. Armed Forces. Similarly, a recent *Atlantic Monthly* piece by Robert Kaplan forecasts a military showdown with Beijing. Yet, while China probably has the world's third-largest military budget, in most respects, Beijing badly lags the U.S. military. The Chinese military still relies too heavily on conscripts and wastes time and resources forcing troops to study political doctrine. Beijing probably spends less than $80 billion per year on its military, according to a RAND study, in contrast to over $400 billion that the White House requested for the Pentagon's fiscal year 2006 budget. (China's defense spending as a percentage of GDP is also smaller than that of the United States.) In fact, a 2003 report on the Chinese military by the Council on Foreign Relations concluded that Beijing was at least two decades from closing the gap on the United States.

In reality, an insecure Beijing, weakened by 150 years of foreign incursions into China, historically pursued a relatively nonaggressive foreign policy, focusing on defending core interests but rarely seeking influence over issues outside its borders and usually abstaining from important debates at the United Nations. In launching China's reforms in the late '70s, Deng Xiaoping pushed the country to develop its domestic economic and social resources, and not to focus on foreign affairs. In fact, Deng often explicitly warned China not to be a world leader—at least not for now—and, during Deng's time, China remained a poor, inward-looking nation.

That has begun to change. In May alone, China ran a trade surplus of almost $9 billion, and it sits atop the second-largest pile of currency reserves on earth. High growth—combined with intensive inculcation of nationalism via the Chinese press and education system—has created a self-confident populace more insistent that China play a major role in the international system, as University of Colorado Sinologist Peter Hays Gries notes in his book, *China's New Nationalism*. And, though this nationalism sometimes lies dormant beneath the surface of Chinese society, it can explode with little warning, as with the anti-Japan protests this spring—when I witnessed Beijingers, who normally brag about their Sony DVD players, scrambling over each other to try to smash up the Japanese embassy.

Meanwhile, two decades of development have also sharply raised the education level of Chinese leaders and diplomats. As former *Time* foreign editor Joshua Cooper Ramo notes in a fascinating new essay called "The Beijing Consensus," "In 1982 only 20 percent of China's provincial leaders had attended college. In 2002, this number was 98 percent." The Chinese government has made a concerted effort to upgrade its diplomatic corps, boosting their language fluency and other important skills. As a result, today Chinese leaders and diplomats are savvier and more knowledgeable about the outside than the men of Deng's generation. As one former American diplomat in China told me, Chinese officials can now describe in detail the splits within the U.S. neoconservative movement, a grasp of nuance sorely lacking in Beijing just ten years ago.

Richer, more worldly, more confident, China's mandarins have begun to reassess their place in the world. As Ramo writes, China is pursuing a deliberate policy to bolster its role in the international system and project its development model abroad. It is enunciating a new foreign policy doctrine, just as a young United States once did. The China doctrine has several components. One is the idea of "peaceful rise"—that China is growing into a preeminent power but would never use its strength unilaterally to threaten other countries, supposedly a sharp distinction from U.S. policy. Second is the notion that China has created a model of socioeconomic development that can be applied elsewhere—what Ramo calls the "Beijing consensus" of development for poor nations. This model argues that developing nations must pursue innovation-led growth by obtaining the latest technology; must control development from the top, so as to avoid the kind of chaos that comes from rapid economic opening; and must rely on links with other developing nations to counter the economic advantages of Western states. In controlling development from the top, of course, the Beijing model implicitly rejects both the free market and the idea that ordinary citizens, not a small elite of rulers, should control countries' destinies.

China then wields its policy doctrine, along with other weapons like trade and aid, to draw developing nations to its side. Beijing focuses in part on countries like Iran and Sudan, which are shunned by the United States, but it also aims closer to Washington's heart, seeking, if not to win over U.S. allies, then at least to complicate their loyalties by emphasizing that gains for developing nations come at the expense of arrogant Western powers. Playing off Western powers works: As prominent Indian economist Jayanta Roy said after visiting China, "I was happy to see that there is a hope for a developing country to outstrip the giants in a reasonably short period of time."

The Chinese challenge is most obvious in three areas of the world: Asia, Latin America, and Africa. Asia is China's natural sphere of influence and the one with the largest number of ethnic Chinese living outside China's borders. Asia is also the area in which China has made up the most ground on the United States. At first, China concentrated on Asian nations alienated from Washington. Since 1997, the United States has enforced severe sanctions against Burma's dictatorship. China has unsurprisingly paid the sanctions no mind. Instead, Beijing has sold Burma's military junta over $1 billion in military equipment. In return, Chinese businesses have gained access to Burma's valuable natural resources, while Chinese diplomats have become almost the only foreigners with insight into the workings of the secretive Burmese government. Today, wealthy Chinese businesspeople cruise the streets of Rangoon, Burma's impoverished capital, in late-model Mitsubishi jeeps, gabbing on ultra-pricey cell phones.

In Laos, until recently blocked by Congress from enjoying normal trade relations with the United States, China has become one of its largest trade partners. In Cambodia, where Prime Minister Hun Sen's poor human rights record—including alleged involvement in a grenade attack that maimed an American citizen—has led to frosty relations with Washington, China has given Phnom Penh at least $200 million in loans. Likewise, after the recent Uzbekistan crackdown on demonstrators, China quickly welcomed Uzbek autocrat Islam Karimov to Beijing. Across the Pacific Ocean, meanwhile, China has become a major aid donor to countries like Fiji—countries that could be crucial to U.S. military basing and missile defenses but that Washington has essentially ignored.

But, in the past five years, Beijing has also honed in on countries with close relationships with the United States, nations like South Korea, Thailand, and Mongolia. Again, understanding that leveraging Beijing's policy doctrine is crucial, Chinese diplomats repeatedly contrast China's "peaceful rise"—and its supposedly nonthreatening posture—with an aggressive, unilateralist United States. "We Asian countries" must work more closely together, at this time of "new manifestations of power politics," Chinese Premier Wen Jiabao told Southeast Asian leaders at a 2003 summit, using typical Chinese coded language to refer to the United States. What's more, Chinese diplomats emphasize that China does not prod foreign nations to pursue political reform or market-driven economic liberalization. This reassurance is popular among Asian nations—such as Cambodia or Thailand—that have poor human rights records, that resent U.S. criticism of their domestic affairs, and that have a history of centralized economic planning, which makes China's Beijing consensus economic model appealing.

The response to Beijing has been overwhelming. As Southeast Asia scholar Carlyle Thayer has reported, China has inked long-term bilateral cooperation agreements with Indonesia, the Philippines, and Singapore. The Philippines, a former U.S. colony, has, for the first time, accepted military aid from China. At the same time, while progress on several prospective trade pacts between the United States and Thailand have stalled, trade between China and Southeast Asia is growing by nearly 20 percent per year, and ten Southeast Asian nations have agreed to join a free-trade zone with China. China's trade with the rest of Asia is also expanding. Even India, which has a long-standing border dispute with China, has established new trade ties with Beijing.

Asian leaders increasingly look to China for economic and political cues as well. Though, less than a decade ago, Beijing maintained icy relations with Jakarta—strained by periodic attacks on Indonesia's ethnic Chinese—today, Indonesia's president publicly praises China's emergence as a leader in Asia. Singapore's senior minister, Goh Chok Tong, has expressed similar sentiments, saying, "China's extraordinary development sets the example for other Asian countries to follow." Ramo has reported that Vietnam, which fought a border war with China only 25 years ago, is now studying China's economic models for clues to faster development. In South Korea, President Roh Mun-Hyun has led Seoul toward Beijing's orbit, looking to China for help handling North Korea. In Thailand, which, during the cold war, was probably America's staunchest ally in Southeast Asia, Prime Minister Thaksin Shinawatra has said that China and India are now the "most important countries for Thailand's diplomacy." Meanwhile, Central Asian nations have formed a regional security group with China, the Shanghai Cooperation Organization—an organization in which China takes the lead, pushing the group to focus on issues of concern to Beijing, such as the restive ethnic minority Uighur population in western China.

As they look to China, Asian leaders are increasingly willing to do Beijing's bidding. Nations from Nepal to Singapore have restricted the activities of Tibetan and Falun Gong activists. Presumably at China's insistence, Malaysia's deputy prime minister publicly warned Malaysian politicians to avoid official visits to Taiwan, while Thailand tried to deny a visa to a top Taiwanese labor official.

Average Asians, too, look to China, which is building up its soft power in the region. In one poll, three-quarters of Thais said they considered China Thailand's closest friend, while less than 10 percent picked the United States. Asian businesspeople covet invites to the Boao Forum for Asia, a conference about Asia's future held on a Chinese resort island to which Beijing invites thousands of business and political leaders. Asian students increasingly seek out education in China, rather than the United States, and Chinese-language schools are gaining popularity in South Korea, Malaysia, and other countries. Meanwhile, ethnic Chinese living outside the Chinese mainland, once afraid to showcase their heritage for fear of being singled out as a wealthy minority, have become increasingly outspoken about their roots. In part, they are more comfortable with their heritage, because China has begun actively promoting Chinese culture through new cultural centers and TV stations. (By contrast, the United States has cut back on its cultural centers in Asia, many of which used to be affiliated with the United States Information Service.) "It looks like being Chinese is cool," publisher Kitti Jinsiriwanich told *The Wall Street Journal*, explaining his decision to produce a glossy magazine about ethnic Chinese life in Bangkok and why advertisers were lapping up his copy.

In Africa and Latin America, where post-independence economic models imposed by Western international financial organizations have failed to raise living standards, China's ideas, its companies, and its emphasis on a multipolar international system are also increasingly welcome. Beijing has signed trade deals with 40 African states. In many resource-rich African countries—including pariah nations like Sudan, where Beijing covets Sudanese oil—China has dramatically bolstered its diplomatic and economic presence, as Stéphanie Giry has reported in these pages ("Out of Beijing," November 15, 2004). In Zimbabwe, Beijing has become a major provider of military hardware, including fighter jets. "Suffering under the effects of international isolation, Zimbabwe has looked to new partners, including China, who won't attach conditions [to aid]," one Western diplomat told *The Christian Science Monitor*.

Hu's 2004 trip to Latin America highlighted China's growing power there as well, even as the Bush administration neglects the region. As Ramo notes, China's enormous consumption of natural resources, such as steel, oil, and copper, makes it an essential ally and trading partner of nearly any nation in Latin America and Africa. Indeed, not only did Hu sign $30 billion in new investment deals during his Latin trip, but China has become Brazil's second-biggest trading partner. By comparison, during his 2004 Latin America swing, Bush spent little time

anywhere other than Colombia and Chile (and almost got in a fistfight in the latter). Furthermore, the American president has failed to persuade Latin nations to back his proposed Free Trade Area of the Americas pact, one of the White House's main goals for the Western Hemisphere.

As in Asia, China's education system and culture—components of its soft power—have become attractive to African and Latin American elites. Beijing has developed a proposal to bring over 10,000 African professionals to China for human resources development. And, as in Asia, key African and Latin leaders, awed by China's economic success, praise Beijing's foreign policy doctrine and development model. "China is doing a wonderful job," Muyingo Steuem, a Ugandan government adviser dazzled by China's big cities, told *The Financial Times* during last year's World Bank conference on poverty alleviation, held in bustling Shanghai. "In developing countries, China is regarded with a mixture of envy, admiration, and awe," U.N. Development Program chief Mark Malloch Brown told the *FT* during the same conference.

In some respects, China's new foreign policy assertiveness is only natural, and it could benefit the developing world. Until 150 years ago, China was one of the world's most powerful nations, and Beijing is, in many respects, regaining the position in foreign affairs and global trade it enjoyed for centuries. As China engages more with the developing world, it is beginning to project its power for the good of others. It has been expanding its participation in U.N. peacekeeping operations. Beijing has also started playing a larger, more positive role in global trade talks and could help to bridge the gap between richer nations and the developing world on tough issues like agricultural subsidies; China has also lived up to its WTO commitments, in some cases more so than the United States. After the Asian tsunami, China offered significant aid disbursements to affected nations (though Beijing's pledge of roughly $85 million in initial government aid was dwarfed by the U.S. offer). China also has become more of a player on the U.N. Security Council, a role it traditionally abdicated—Beijing has backed antiterrorism resolutions and avoided blocking the U.S.-led war in Iraq. As China becomes more powerful, it may take on a more beneficent role at Turtle Bay.

But, despite significant political opening over the past two decades, China remains a highly authoritarian state, one in which individuals who try to form national political organizations are suppressed. In recent months, the government has launched a new strike against dissent, detaining prominent intellectuals, upping its crackdown against the Uighurs and other ethnic minorities, increasing press censorship, and bolstering its Internet firewalling. China also canceled an international human rights conference due to be held in Beijing and arrested a Hong Kong-based journalist for the Singapore *Straits Times* and a Chinese researcher for *The New York Times*. Today, China has the largest number of journalists in jail of any country.

This is hardly an ideal political model for developing nations—following the Chinese model might forestall democratization. Indeed, African, Asian, and Latin American democrats certainly can take no comfort in their leaders moving closer to Beijing, since China places no priority on human rights in its decisions about its allies. Beijing's aid and trade prop up the brutal Burmese and Sudanese regimes, allowing them to ignore Western sanctions, and Beijing reportedly has helped prevent the U.N. Security Council from taking tougher action against genocide in the Sudanese region of Darfur.

What's more, China's talk of noninterference may be just that—talk. As the University of Colorado's Hays Gries writes, China historically has practiced a politics defined by the term *biao li bu yi*—"surface and reality differ." After all, Chinese academics at government-linked think tanks say that, ultimately, China will surpass the United States in Asia and control the region. Some foreign leaders recognize that China's kinder face abroad may mask a desire to increase Chinese power across the developing world. A classified report by the Philippine armed forces captures the difference between Beijing's statements and actions. It notes: "China's actions are widely viewed as a doubled-edge[d] diplomatic strategy aimed at furthering its strategic goals in the region."

Unfortunately, though some nations may resent China's growing power, too often they resent the United States more. The United States has all but abdicated its presence in parts of the developing world, and Washington seems unprepared for China's emergence as a more aggressive foreign policy actor. Washington lacks enough diplomats who truly understand China's foreign policy intentions and how it executes its ambitions on the ground. *Foreign Affairs* editor James Hoge has noted that the workforce at the U.S. Embassy in Beijing is half the size of the one assigned to the new embassy in Baghdad.

At the same time that China's influence has grown, the U.S. means of leverage—aid allocations, trade deals, academic ties, popular culture—are weakening, undermined by everything from new restrictions on student visas to the prisoner abuse scandals at Guantánamo Bay and Abu Ghraib. Worse, when dealing with longtime allies like Thailand, Washington too often talks about little other than terrorism. Asians find the American "obsession" with terrorism tedious, Karim Raslan, a prominent Malaysian writer, told *The New York Times*. "We've all got to live. We've all got to make money," he said. "The Chinese want to make money, and so do we."

Savvy American officials are beginning to understand how China is switching from a defensive to an offensive foreign policy. During an important visit to Southeast Asia earlier this year, new Deputy Secretary of State Robert Zoellick, a former trade negotiator, tried to recapture lost ground. He emphasized not only counterterrorism cooperation but also economic ties, aid disbursements, and other issues of importance to Asian nations. The mild-mannered Zoellick was a hit. "The Zoellick road show was an important signal from Washington that Southeast Asia was not being ignored by the world's No. 1 superpower," enthused the Singapore *Straits Times*.

Meanwhile, administration hawks—who concentrated on China early in Bush's first term—are beginning to refocus their attention on Beijing. Even as Rumsfeld talks about China's military power, other hawks are trying to more effectively leverage key foreign allies against China. They are doing so by drawing important nations more tightly under the U.S. security umbrella. Washington appears to have convinced Tokyo to move closer to the U.S. position on Taiwan—as reflected in a joint statement issued in February—and the Bush administration is reaching out to India, with Rumsfeld calling for closer ties with New Delhi.

But these are only initial steps. Is Washington up to the task of reorienting foreign policy to handle a competitor like the cold war–era Soviet Union, one with a defined foreign policy doctrine and allies across the globe?

Too often, official Washington, whether focused on China's military or awed by China's booming economy, simply disregards the gravity of China's changing foreign policy. During a private luncheon last year for the American ambassador to Thailand, one person asked about recent unrest in southern Thailand, where the United States closed its consulate a decade ago—and where the region has become a potential hotbed of Islamic extremism. The ambassador mentioned that the United States was still trying to exert influence in the south and had reopened a program in southern Thailand, a small "American corner" where Thais could read English-language books to learn about the United States. What happened to the U.S. consulate, asked someone else in the audience. The ambassador paused. "I think it's the Chinese consulate now," he said. Everyone in the room laughed.

The Ambiguous Arsenal

Recent reports warn that China is aggressively building up its nuclear forces. Don't believe the hype.

JEFFREY LEWIS

If you read the *Washington Times*, in addition to believing that Iraqi weapons of mass destruction are hidden somewhere in Syria, you might believe that "China's aggressive strategic nuclear-modernization program" was proceeding apace.[1] If munching on freedom fries at a Heritage Foundation luncheon is your thing, you might worry that "even marginal improvements to [China's intercontinental ballistic missiles (ICBMs)] derived from U.S. technical know-how" threaten the United States.[2]

So, it may come as a shock to learn that China's nuclear arsenal is about the same size it was a decade ago, and that the missile that prompted the *Washington Times* article has been under development since the mid-1980s. Perhaps your anxiety about "marginal improvements" to China's missile force would recede as you learned that China's 18 ICBMs, sitting unfueled in their silos, their nuclear warheads in storage, are essentially the same as they were the day China began deploying them in 1981. In fact, contrary to reports you might have recently read that Chinese nukes number in the hundreds—if not the thousands— the true size of the country's operationally deployed arsenal is probably about 80 nuclear weapons.

Estimating the size, configuration, and capability of China's nuclear weapons inventory is not just an exercise in abstract accounting. The specter of a robust Chinese arsenal has been cited by the Bush administration as a rationale for not making deeper cuts in U.S. nuclear deployments. Likewise, opponents of the Comprehensive Test Ban Treaty (CTBT) point to China in making the case for maintaining U.S. deterrent capabilities. Others portray China's modernization program as evidence of the country's increasingly hostile posture toward Taiwan—adding a sense of urgency to developing missile defenses. And, more recently, these concerns have raised the temperature in transatlantic relations as the European Union contemplates lifting the arms embargo imposed on China in the wake of the Tiananmen Square massacre.

The true scope of China's nuclear capabilities are hidden in plain sight, among the myriad declassified assessments produced by the U.S. intelligence community. Yet, such analyses have run afoul of conservative legislators, who express dismay when threat assessments don't conform to their perceptions of reality. Congressional Republicans, for instance, in 2000 created the China Futures Panel, chaired by former Gen. John Tilelli, to examine charges of bias in the CIA assessments of China. In 2002, Bob Schaffer, a Republican congressman from Colorado, complained about the latest National Intelligence Estimate (NIE) of foreign ballistic missile development in a letter to CIA director George Tenet: "The lack of attention to the pronounced and growing danger caused by China's ballistic missile buildup, and its aggressive strategy for using its ballistic missiles cannot go unchallenged. The report is misleading, and, because it understates the magnitude of threat, is profoundly dangerous."

With a very small nuclear arsenal relative to the United States and Russia, China seems intent on letting ambiguity enhance the deterrent effect of its nuclear forces.

Consequently, many defense analysts simply ignore what the intelligence community has to say. For example, two scholars in a peer-reviewed international security journal cited *Jane's Strategic Weapon Systems* to suggest that China's future submarine-launched ballistic missile (SLBM)—the Giant Wave, or Julang-2 (JL-2)—may carry "three to eight multiple independent reentry vehicles." They failed to mention the consensus judgment of the U.S. intelligence community that Chinese warheads are so large that it is impossible to place more than one on the JL-2.

In another instance, a student from the National University of Singapore posted an essay on a web site claiming that China had more than 2,000 warheads. His figure was based on amateurish fissile material production estimates that incorrectly identified several Chinese fissile material facilities.[3] (Classified estimates by the Energy Department, leaked to the press, estimate the Chinese plutonium stockpile at 1.7–2.8 tons.[4] Assuming 3–4 kilograms of plutonium per warhead, China could deploy, at most, a nuclear force of 400–900 weapons.) Despite such obvious mistakes, experts from the Heritage Foundation, the Institute for Defense Analyses, the Institute for Foreign Policy Analysis, and the Centre for Defence and International Security Studies all cited the Singapore essay to suggest that China might have substantially more nuclear warheads than widely believed.[5] David Tanks, then with the Institute for Foreign Policy Analysis, called the essay "convincingly argued."

Iraq debacle or not, the estimates of the U.S. intelligence community are still a better place to start than, say, some college kid's essay posted on the Internet. These analysts have unparalleled access to the full array of information-gathering technology available to the federal government. For example, the intelligence community monitors ballistic missile tests with satellite images to detect test preparations, signals intelligence sensors to intercept telemetry data, and radars to track missile launches and collect signature data on warheads and decoys. No comparable unclassified source of such data exists, unless it is released by the government conducting the test.

Moreover, the intelligence community employs well-known methods that can be evaluated for gaps or bias. Although intelligence estimates are sometimes politicized or agenda driven, systematic bias is often evident and can be observed by comparing estimates over time. For example, the intelligence community has tended to exaggerate future Chinese ballistic missile deployments, in part because Chinese industrial capacity has tended to exceed production. This information is useful when considering estimates about future Chinese deployments. Establishing a baseline consensus estimate about the size and composition of Chinese nuclear forces would allow analysts to lodge specific objections to intelligence community judgments. More broadly, a deeper understanding of the true scope of China's arsenal and its modernization efforts provides a clearer picture of Beijing's strategic intentions.

Minimum Means of Reprisal

Beijing doesn't publish detailed information about the size and composition of its nuclear forces. With a very small nuclear arsenal relative to the United States and Russia, China seems intent on letting ambiguity enhance the deterrent effect of its nuclear forces. Chinese force deployments suggest that Beijing's leadership believes that even a very small, unsophisticated force will deter nuclear attacks by larger, more sophisticated nuclear forces. While some Western analysts spent the Cold War fretting about the "delicate balance of terror," the Chinese leadership appears to have concluded that technical details such as the size, configuration, and readiness of nuclear forces are largely irrelevant. China's declaration that it would "not be the first to use nuclear weapons at any time or under any circumstances" reflects the idea that nuclear weapons are not much good, except to deter other nuclear weapons. In deciding what sort of nuclear arsenal to build, China settled on what Marshal Nie Rongzhen, the first head of China's nuclear weapons program, called "the minimum means of reprisal."[6]

China's reluctance to provide numerical information about its nuclear forces relaxed a bit this past spring, when its foreign ministry released an April 2004 statement that, "Among the nuclear weapon states, China . . . possesses the smallest nuclear arsenal." That statement suggests China possesses fewer than 200 nuclear weapons, the generally accepted size of the British nuclear arsenal.

The intelligence community does not publish a single, detailed assessment of China's nuclear arsenal. Instead, these estimates are scattered across multiple documents, including the 2001 edition of the Defense Department's *Proliferation: Threat and Response* and the National Air and Space Intelligence Center's (NASIC) 2003 *Ballistic and Cruise Missile Threat*. Some information, such as the National Intelligence Council's *Tracking the Dragon* series, has been released through the natural process of declassification. But much more information was released—or leaked—during the 1990s amid debates over allegations of Chinese nuclear espionage, ballistic missile defenses, and the CTBT.

Based upon these various assessments, a realistic estimate of China's nuclear arsenal is a total force of 30 nuclear warheads operationally deployed on ICBMs and another 50–100 on medium-range ballistic missiles (MRBMs), for a total force of 80–130 nuclear weapons.

Estimates provided by many nongovernmental organizations—such as the Council on Foreign Relations, the Natural Resources Defense Council, and the International Institute for Strategic Studies (IISS)—are much higher (albeit, not as high as their more zealous conservative counterparts). They typically describe the People's Republic of China as the world's third largest nuclear power, ahead of Britain and France, with 400 or so warheads.[7] Such estimates often assume deployment of three other categories of nuclear weapons—aircraft-delivered weapons, SLBMs, and tactical nuclear weapons.

Yet, in the 1980s, the Defense Intelligence Agency (DIA) found no evidence that China had deployed nuclear bombs to airfields and, based on the antiquity of the aircraft, concluded that China did not assign nuclear missions to any of its planes—a conclusion reiterated in a declassified 1993 National Security Council report. The most recent edition of the Pentagon's *Chinese Military Power* suggests that China has yet to deploy the Julang-1 (JL-1) ballistic missile on its solitary ballistic missile submarine. And, in 1984, the DIA acknowledged that it had "no evidence confirming production or deployment" of tactical nuclear weapons. To the contrary, *Chinese Military Power* notes that the country's short-range ballistic missiles are conventionally armed, thereby freeing Beijing from "the political and practical constraints associated with the use of nuclear-armed missiles."

Room for Expansion?

Over the next 15 years, the intelligence community expects China's ICBM force to expand from 18 to 75–100 strategic nuclear warheads targeted primarily against the United States and from 12 shorter-range ballistic missiles capable of reaching parts of the United States to "two dozen."[8]

Beijing's modernization plan centers on a mobile, solid-fueled ballistic missile under development since the mid-1980s called the Dong Feng (DF)-31. The intelligence community believes the DF-31 could be deployed during the next few years. Since 2002, IISS has cited "reports" that the DF-31 is deployed, but that assessment appears based on a pair of 2001 news stories in the *Taipei Times* and *Washington Times*, neither of which actually claims the missile is deployed.[9]

The intelligence community believes China is also developing follow-on versions of the DF-31: the extended-range DF-31A to replace the DF-5 (currently its longest-range ICBM) and a submarine-launched version (JL-2). The DF-31A may have a range of 12,000 kilometers and could be deployed before 2010. China is also designing a new nuclear ballistic missile submarine to carry the JL-2, which is expected to have a range of more than 8,000 kilometers. China will likely develop and test the JL-2 and the new sub (Type 094) later this decade.[10]

One senior intelligence official described the 75–100 warhead estimate to the *New York Times*: "[China would] add new warheads to their old 18 [DF-5s], transforming them from single-warhead missiles into four-warhead missiles," or "double the size of their projected land-based mobile missiles."[11] The estimate of 75 warheads assumes that China will supplement its existing ballistic missile force with the DF-31 ICBMs; the estimate of 100 warheads is based on the assumption that China would build half as many DF-31 ballistic missiles, but place multiple warheads on existing DF-5 ICBMs.

China has not placed multiple warheads on its silo-based ICBMs and has not begun to deploy the DF-31. Therefore, these predictions are little more than informed speculation, based on how the intelligence community imagines China *might* respond to missile defense and other changes in U.S. nuclear posture. Past intelligence community estimates, however, have overstated future Chinese ICBM deployments. The number of Chinese strategic ballistic missiles has actually declined, from 145 in 1984 to 80 today.

China tested its smallest nuclear warhead from 1992–1996.[12] Developed for China's DF-31 ICBM, NASIC estimated that the reentry vehicle has a mass of 470 kilograms—too heavy to place more than one on any of China's solid-fueled ballistic missiles.[13] Placing multiple warheads on China's solid-fueled ballistic missiles would probably require Beijing to design and test a new warhead, which is currently prohibited by China's signature on the CTBT.[14]

Dangerous Incentives

So, let's review: China deploys just 30 ICBMs, kept unfueled and without warheads, and another 50–100 MRBMs, sitting unarmed in their garrisons. Conventional wisdom suggests this posture is vulnerable and invites preemptive attack during a crisis. This minimal arsenal is clearly a matter of choice: China stopped fissile material production in 1990 and has long had the capacity to produce a much larger number of ballistic missiles.[15] The simplest explanation for this choice is that the Chinese

leadership worries less about its vulnerability to a disarming first strike than the costs of an arms race or what some Second Artillery officer might do with a fully armed nuclear weapon. In a strange way, Beijing placed more faith in Washington and Moscow than in its own military officers.

Washington has never reciprocated that trust. Instead, the United States has embarked on a major transformation of its strategic forces that is, in part, driven by concern about the modernization of China's strategic forces. President Bill Clinton reportedly directed U.S. Strategic Command in 1998 to include plans for strikes against China in the U.S. nuclear weapons targeting plan. The 2001 Nuclear Posture Review (NPR) identified China as one of seven countries "that could be involved in an immediate or potential contingency" with nuclear weapons.[16]

Chinese strategic forces are increasingly supplanting Russia as the primary benchmark for determining the size and capabilities of U.S. strategic forces—at least in administration rhetoric. China's nuclear arsenal is reflected in the 2001 NPR in two ways. First, the review recommends reducing the 6,000 deployed U.S. nuclear weapons to no less than 1,700–2,200. In response to criticism that these cuts didn't go low enough, Defense Secretary Donald Rumsfeld warned that further reductions might encourage China to attempt what he termed a "sprint to parity"—a rapid increase in nuclear forces to reach numerical parity with the United States.[17]

Second, the 2001 NPR recommends the addition of ballistic missile defenses and non-nuclear strike capabilities to help improve the ability of the United States to extend nuclear deterrence to its allies.[18] Here too, concern over China's arsenal lurked in the background. Shortly before he was nominated as Deputy Assistant Secretary of Defense for Forces Policy (with responsibility for overseeing the NPR), Keith Payne argued that the United States, in a crisis with China over Taiwan, must possess the capability to disarm China with a first strike if U.S. deterrence is to be credible. Despite overwhelming U.S. nuclear superiority, he has argued, "China's leadership may not be susceptible to U.S. deterrence threats, regardless of their severity, largely because denying Taiwan independence would be a near-absolute goal for Chinese leaders." Thus, the United States "would have to make blatantly clear its will and capability to defeat Chinese conventional and [weapons of mass destruction] attacks against Taiwan and against its own power projection forces."[19]

Yet, if the United States were truly interested in discouraging a Chinese sprint to parity or the development of a Chinese ballistic missile force that could undertake coercive operations, the president would disavow the vision for nuclear forces outlined in the NPR. The Chinese leadership chose their arsenal in part on the belief that the United States would not be foolish enough to use nuclear weapons against China in a conflict. By asserting that Washington *may be* that foolish, and by attempting to exploit the weaknesses inherent in China's decision to rely on a small vulnerable force, the NPR creates incentives for Beijing to increase the size, readiness, and usability of its nuclear forces.

Larger, more ready Chinese nuclear forces would not be in the best interests of the United States. In the midst of a crisis, any attempt by Beijing to ready its ballistic missiles for a first strike against the United States, let alone to actually fire one, would be suicide. The only risk that China's current nuclear arsenal poses to the United States is an unauthorized nuclear launch—something the intelligence community has concluded "is highly unlikely" under China's current operational practices. That might change, however, if China were to adopt the "hair trigger" nuclear postures that the United States and Russia maintain even today to demonstrate the "credibility" of their nuclear deterrents. China might also increase its strategic forces or deploy theater nuclear forces that could be used early in a conflict—developments that might alarm India, with predictable secondary effects on Pakistan.

So far, none of this has happened. Chinese nuclear forces today look remarkably like they have for decades. The picture of the Chinese nuclear arsenal that emerges from U.S. intelligence assessments suggests a country that—at least in the nuclear field—is deploying a smaller, less ready arsenal than is within its capabilities. That reflects a choice to rely on a minimum deterrent that sacrifices offensive capability in exchange for maximizing political control and minimizing economic cost—a decision that seems eminently sensible. The great mystery is not that Beijing chose such an arsenal, but that the Bush administration would be eager to change it.

Notes

1. Bill Gertz and Rowan Scarborough, "Inside the Ring: Failed DF-31 Test," *Washington Times*, January 4, 2002, p. 9.
2. Richard D. Fisher Jr., "Commercial Space Cooperation Should Not Harm National Security," Heritage Foundation Backgrounder, no. 1198, June 26, 1998.
3. Yang Zheng, *China's Nuclear Arsenal*, March 16, 1996 (www.kimsoft.com/korea/ch-war.htm).
4. David Wright and Lisbeth Gronlund, "A History of China's Plutonium Production," pp. 61–80; see also David Albright, Frans Berkhout, and William Walker, *Plutonium and Highly Enriched Uranium 1996: World Inventories, Capabilities and Policies* (New York: Oxford University Press, 1997), pp. 126–130.
5. See: Fisher, "Commercial Space Cooperation Should Not Harm National Security"; Richard D. Fisher Jr. and Baker Spring, "China's Nuclear and Missile Espionage Heightens the Need for Missile Defense," Heritage Foundation Backgrounder, no. 1303, July 2, 1999; David R. Markov and Andrew W. Hull, "The Changing Nature of Chinese Nuclear Strategy," Institute for Defense Analyses, January 1997; David R. Tanks, "Exploring U.S. Missile Defense Requirements in 2010: What Are the Policy and Technology Challenges?" Institute for Foreign Policy Analysis, April 1997; and "Size of China's Ballistic Missile Force," Centre for Defence and International Security Studies, no author, no date.
6. Nie Rongzhen, *Inside the Red Star: The Memoirs of Marshal Nie Rongzhen*, Zhong Rongyi, translator (Beijing: New World Press, 1988). See also: Nie Rongzhen, "How China Develops Its Nuclear Weapons," *Beijing Review*, April 29, 1985, pp. 15–18.
7. Such estimates are often based on two comments in the open literature: In 1979, a senior Defense Department official described the nuclear forces deployed by China, France, and Britain as "more or less comparable with China perhaps being the leader of the three. So it is possible that China might be the third nuclear power in the world." See: Defense Department, *Department of Defense Authorization for Appropriations for FY80; Part 1: Defense Posture; Budget Priorities and Management Issues; Strategic Nuclear Posture* (Washington,
D.C.: Government Printing Office (GPO), 1979), p. 357. See also John W. Lewis and Xue Litai, *China Builds the Bomb* (Stanford: Stanford University Press, 1988), p. 253. A "senior Chinese military officer" purportedly told Lewis and Xue that China maintained "a nuclear weapons inventory greater than that of the French and British strategic forces combined."
8. Unless otherwise noted, this estimate is derived from: Senate Committee on Homeland Security and Governmental Affairs, *CIA National Intelligence Estimate of Foreign Missile Developments and the Ballistic Missile Threat through 2015*, Senate Hearing 107-467, 107th Cong., 2nd sess., 2002.
9. Bill Gertz, "China Ready to Deploy its First Mobile ICBMs," *Washington Times*, September 6, 2001.
10. Senate Committee on Intelligence, *Current and Projected National Security Threats to the United States*, Senate Hearing 107-597, 107th Cong., 2nd sess., 2001, p. 79.
11. Michael R. Gordon and Steven Lee Myers, "Risk of Arms Race Seen in U.S. Design of Missile Defense," *New York Times*, May 28, 2000, p. A1. An earlier National Air Intelligence Center (NAIC) estimate, however, suggested that the DF-5A (CSS-4) might carry up to three 470-kilogram DF-31 (CSS-X-10)-type reentry vehicles—although one assumption of this analysis was that a "minimum number of changes" were made to modify a Smart Dispenser upper stage for use as a post-boost vehicle. See Bill Gertz, *Betrayal: How the Clinton Administration Undermined American Security* (Washington, D.C.: Regnery, 1999), p. 252.
12. Defense Department, *Future Military Capabilities of the People's Republic of China, Report to Congress Pursuant to Section 1226 of the FY98 National Defense Authorization Act* (Washington, D.C.: GPO, 1998), p. 5.
13. The NAIC estimate is found in NAIC-1442-0629-97 (no title), December 10, 1996, cited in Gertz, *Betrayal*, pp. 251–252.
14. John M. Shalikashvili, *Findings and Recommendations Concerning the Comprehensive Nuclear Test Ban Treaty* (Washington, D.C.: GPO, 2001).
15. Defense Department, *Chinese Military Power* 1997, p. 4.
16. Presidential Decision Directive (PDD)-60 (1998) returned China to the Single Integrated Operational Plan after a reported 16-year absence. Although classified, the *Washington Post* reported that PDD-60 directed "the military to plan attacks against a wider spectrum of targets in China, including the country's growing military-industrial complex and its improved conventional forces." See: R. Jeffrey Smith, "Clinton Directive Changes Strategy on Nuclear Arms Centering on Deterrence, Officials Drop Terms for Long Atomic War," *Washington Post*, December 7, 1997, p. A1; and Hans M. Kristensen, *The Matrix of Deterrence: U.S. Strategic Command Force Structure Studies* (Berkeley: Nautilus Institute, 2001), pp. 14–15. The revelation produced a confidential State Department memorandum, now partially declassified, concerning targeting policy. See: State Department, *Targeting Policy*, March 17, 1998 (SEA-23820.9).
17. Senate Committee on Foreign Relations, *Treaty on Strategic Offensive Reduction: The Moscow Treaty*, Senate Hearing 107-622, 107th Cong., 2nd sess., 2002, pp. 81, 111.
18. These quotations are drawn from the unclassified cover letter that accompanied the 2001 Nuclear Posture Review. See: Donald H. Rumsfeld, Foreword, Nuclear Posture Review Report, January 2002 (www.defenselink.mil/news/Jan2002/d20020109npr.pdf).
19. Keith B. Payne, "Post–Cold War Deterrence and a Taiwan Crisis," *China Brief*, vol. 1, no. 5, September 12, 2001.

Jeffrey Lewis is a research fellow at the Center for International and Security Studies at the University of Maryland School of Public Policy in College Park, Maryland.

From *Bulletin of the Atomic Scientists*, vol. 61, no. 3, May/June 2005, pp. 52–59. Copyright © 2005 by Bulletin of the Atomic Scientists, Chicago, IL 60637.
Reprinted by permission of the *Bulletin of the Atomic Scientists: The Magazine of Global Security, Science and Survival*.

Fueling the Dragon: China's Strategic Energy Dilemma

"Unless the world's existing powers are prepared to descend into the sort of resource driven geopolitical competition that resulted in World War I . . . they must make room at the table for an energy hungry China."

MICHAEL T. KLARE

The draft proposal for China's 11th five-year plan for economic and social development, covering the period from 2006 to 2010, sets only two specific, quantitative objectives: that per capita gross domestic product in 2010 should be double that of 2000; and that energy input per unit of GDP should be 20 percent lower than it was in 2005.

In a sense, these two ambitious goals highlight the central dilemma facing Chinese policy makers in the years ahead. Although the Communist Party leadership seeks to steadily improve the livelihood and lifestyle of ordinary Chinese citizens, thereby ensuring their support for (or acquiescence to) the regime, it must somehow find a way to deliver the vast increases in energy that will be needed to satisfy the first goal. With the recent increases in energy prices and growing concern about the future adequacy of global oil stocks, China's leaders will have to walk a precarious tightrope to balance these competing and very demanding objectives.

Securing the additional supplies of energy needed to sustain growth and satisfy consumer demand will pose both an economic and a political challenge for the Chinese leadership. The economic challenge arises from the mammoth financial investments that will be required: hundreds, perhaps thousands of new electricity-generating plants will have to be built, along with numerous oil refineries, natural gas facilities, coal mines, and hydroelectric dams, all costing in the billions of dollars.

The political challenge derives from the fact that China will not be able to rely exclusively on domestic sources to satisfy its future energy requirements but will have to obtain ever-increasing supplies of oil and natural gas from abroad—in many cases, from the same sources that are also the target of avid acquisition efforts by American, European, and Japanese firms.

The older industrial nations have long consumed the lion's share of world energy supplies; as recently as 1990, they ac-

counted for three-fourths of total global energy usage. But now they face increasingly fierce competition from the newly industrialized countries of Asia. India, South Korea, Taiwan, and the Southeast Asian nations have joined the world-wide quest for additional energy—and the largest energy consumer by far among the emerging powers is China.

The resulting competition is driving up global energy prices and generating intense geopolitical friction among the major energy-importing states. In some instances, this friction has taken on a worrisome military aspect, as rival suitors offer various forms of military aid to potential suppliers of energy and so fuel regional tensions and arms rivalries. Although China is a relative newcomer to this sort of geopolitical contest, its pursuit of energy-cum-military ties with such countries as Iran, Sudan, Uzbekistan, and Venezuela has become a significant irritant in US-China relations.

Further complicating the picture is the environmental impact of China's surging energy use. Because Beijing seeks to rely on domestic supplies for as large a share of its total energy mix as possible, and because the only source of energy that China possesses in great abundance is coal, the government's future plans call for a substantial increase in coal consumption—from 1.4 billion tons in 2002 to an estimated 3.2 billion tons in 2025. If this projection proves accurate, and if Chinese utilities continue to rely on existing coal-burning technology, China will overtake the United States as the world's leading emitter of climate-changing carbon dioxide by 2025. Only if Beijing can be persuaded to curb its consumption of coal or to adopt clean-coal technology on a very large scale will it be possible to avert a substantial buildup of greenhouse gases in the atmosphere.

How the Chinese leadership manages these competing goals and interests will prove to be one of the greatest tests facing Beijing in the years to come. At the same time, Chinese energy behavior will raise significant political and environmental concerns for the United States, Europe, Japan, and the rest of the world.

The Big Picture

As might be expected, China's energy dilemma begins with the country's large population and rapid economic growth. Although Chinese citizens, on average, use considerably less energy than citizens of the United States and other highly developed countries—per capita energy consumption in China is about one ton of oil equivalent per year, compared to eight tons in the United States—the combined consumption of 1.3 billion people is bound to be substantial. More important than population, however, is the country's fastpaced economic growth, now averaging between 9 and 10 percent per year. Every increment in economic activity generates a comparable increase in energy demand, pushing the nation's total requirements ever higher.

Disputes arising from the competitive pursuit of foreign oil will play an increasingly critical role in the US-China relationship.

The striking increase in China's energy demand is evident in data provided by the US Department of Energy (DoE). In the 12 years between 1990 and 2002, net energy consumption in China rose by 60 percent, from 27 to 43 quadrillion British thermal units (BTUs). It is projected to grow by another 153 percent by 2025, reaching 109 quadrillion BTUs. To better appreciate the scale and rapidity of this increase, consider that in 1990, China consumed less than half as much energy as the Western European nations; by 2025 it is projected to consume 44 percent *more* energy than all of those nations combined.

To satisfy this vast increase in demand, Chinese suppliers will have to increase their delivery of all forms of energy, including oil, coal, natural gas, hydropower, nuclear, and renewables such as solar and wind. As noted, the largest additional increment to China's net energy supply is likely to be provided by coal. But even if Beijing were to overlook the environmental consequences of depending so heavily on coal, it cannot rely on coal alone to provide all of the extra energy that it will need. For some purposes, including transportation, it will also have to obtain expanded supplies of oil and natural gas, and this is where the geopolitical aspect enters the picture.

Oil is likely to be in particularly strong demand. Petroleum products are the main source of fuel for China's road, air, rail, and sea transportation systems, which are among the fastest-growing components of its vast and expanding infrastructure. To put this in perspective, China had only 14.5 million registered motor vehicles on the road in 2001; by 2030, this number is expected to jump to 130 million. The country is also building about 30,000 miles of highway every year to make room for all these additional vehicles. And it is building new or expanded airports to accommodate a sudden surge in domestic airline traffic (the number of air travelers in China more than tripled from 1990 to 2002, from 27 million to 84 million).

More cars and more air travel can only mean one thing: an ever-increasing thirst for petroleum products. At 4.5 percent per year, the growth rate of China's oil consumption is now the highest of any country in the world. Assuming this rate continues unabated, the country's net consumption will jump from 5.2 million barrels per day in 2002 to a projected 14.2 million barrels in 2025—at which point its total oil usage will exceed that of all other countries, save the United States.

China was once self-sufficient in petroleum: as recently as 1993, it produced and consumed approximately 3 million barrels per day. But Chinese oil output has increased only slightly, reaching just 3.5 million barrels per day in 2004, while consumption has soared. As a result, the gap between production and consumption has grown larger every year—and the only way Beijing has been able to fill this yawning gap has been through increased imports of foreign oil. In 2004, China's net oil imports amounted to 3.2 million barrels per day, or 48 percent of its total consumption; by 2025, its daily import requirement is expected to reach 10.7 million barrels, or 75 percent of consumption.

It is to procure all of these additional quantities of foreign oil that Chinese leaders and energy firms have been scouring the world for new supply sources—in some cases signing long-term contracts for the delivery of crude, in other cases acquiring equity shares in foreign oil fields.

In Search of Oil

American observers are uncertain as to how much the Chinese government directly oversees the pursuit of foreign energy assets by Chinese firms. The three major Chinese oil companies—the China National Petroleum Corporation (CNPC), the China National Petrochemical Corporation (Sinopec), and the China National Offshore Oil Corporation (CNOOC)—are said to operate like independent, profit-making enterprises, conducting their own international operations. However, the government owns a very large stake in these firms, ranging from 80 to 90 percent, and chooses their top leaders. Government-owned banks provide low-cost loans to the firms, and Chinese diplomats often facilitate their efforts to negotiate exploration and drilling rights in foreign countries.

Although Chinese officials have never spelled out their objectives in wielding influence over the overseas operations of the major oil companies, their intentions are clear: to increase the number of countries supplying oil and gas to China and, wherever possible, to gain direct ownership over key foreign reserves. As recently as 1996, China imported 70 percent of its oil from just three countries: Indonesia, Oman, and Yemen. By 2003, it had established ties with a much broader range of suppliers, including Saudi Arabia (providing 17 percent of China's imports), Iran (14 percent), Angola (11 percent), and Sudan (5 percent). Chinese officials have traveled the world in pursuit of other sources of oil and gas, establishing supply arrangements and acquiring drilling rights in Brazil, Canada, Ecuador, Kazakhstan, Nigeria, Russia, and Venezuela.

That China is vigorously seeking to enhance its access to foreign sources of energy is not, in itself, a source of friction in international relations. After all, the United States, Britain, France, Japan, and other Western oil-importing countries have long competed among themselves for drilling rights in overseas producing areas, and have managed to divvy up the available supplies in a (relatively) amicable fashion. China may be a newcomer to this contest, but is not behaving noticeably differently from the other oil-seekers. Indeed, the "National Energy Policy" announced by President George W. Bush on May 17, 2001, calls for US officials to conduct the same sort of diplomatic quest in pursuit of foreign energy as that now being undertaken by Chinese officials.

In a world of ever-expanding petroleum supplies, China would simply use its abundant stockpiles of cash to buy up whatever energy it requires. There are, however, two major problems with this picture. First, there are growing indications that global oil supplies are not expanding fast enough to keep up with rising international demand. And second, many of the world's most prolific sources of supply are already controlled by Western energy firms or by producer-owned national oil companies, forcing China to seek development opportunities in marginal areas or "pariah" states shunned by the other major importers.

The Competition Heats Up

For decades, the world supply of petroleum has grown in tandem with the steady rise in international demand. This has made possible the vast expansion of the global economy over the past 60 years and the emergence of the new Asian economic powerhouses, including China, India, Taiwan, and South Korea. Recently, however, significant doubts have arisen as to the oil industry's ability to continue boosting the available world supply at a rate commensurate with global demand. While some energy analysts insist that this is not a problem and that world supplies will continue to expand as needed, others believe that the growth rate of global oil supplies will soon begin to slacken and eventually reach zero—a condition known as "peak" oil output—after which the supply will begin to contract.

Until recently, most oil company executives and government energy experts have sided with those who believe that the moment of peak oil is still safely in the distant future. But lately there have been some conspicuous defections from this consensus. For example, the CEO of Chevron, David O'Reilly, has signed his name to full-page advertisements in leading newspapers expressing concern about oil's future availability. "One thing is clear," the advertisements state, "the era of easy oil is over."

It is impossible now to predict exactly how much oil will be available in the decades ahead to meet anticipated demand. The US DoE contends that there will be sufficient supply in the market in 2025 to satisfy projected demand of 119 million barrels per day—an increase of 35 million to 36 million barrels over current levels of output. If this projection proves accurate, there will be enough oil to meet China's projected demand of 14.2 million barrels per day, as well as the 27.3 million barrels sought by the United States, the 14.9 million sought by Western Europe, and the 6.8 million sought by Japan. Under this comfortable scenario, prices will remain relatively stable and severe energy shortages will be averted.

Unfortunately, given the concerns raised by Chevron's O'Reilly and other skeptics, one can have no confidence that this scenario will prevail. Indeed, it would be far more prudent to assume that global supplies will *not* expand sufficiently to satisfy anticipated demand, that prices will rise significantly, and that the competition for whatever supplies are available will grow more intense and fractious. It is in this context that China's efforts to secure increased supplies of oil (along with the efforts of India, South Korea, and the other rising Asian economic powers) must be viewed.

How, exactly, this will play out cannot be foreseen. But we already have some early indications. One is price: with China and India becoming ever more significant players in an already crowded energy market, oil prices have risen much faster than expected even one year ago. In January 2005, the DoE projected prices in the $30 to $35 per barrel range for the period between 2005 and 2025; this January, it raised its projection for this period to between $50 and $55 per barrel.

Even more worrisome was the hysterical reaction in Congress to CNOOC's June 2005 effort to purchase the Unocal Corporation, a mid-sized American oil and gas producer. Although CNOOC's bid for Unocal was $2 billion higher than that proffered by Chevron, the other major suitor, US lawmakers were so incensed by the possibility that a Chinese company might gain control of American energy assets that they voted in August to place insurmountable obstacles in the way of CNOOC's purchase, forcing the company to withdrew its offer. The fact that Unocal's oil and gas reserves were mostly located in Asia to begin with, and played a negligible role in satisfying US energy demand, made little difference to those who voted against CNOOC.

The risk of crisis and conflict over access to vital resources will become increasingly severe.

The Unocal affair did not, in the end, produce a significant breach in US-China relations, and CNOOC has gone on to buy energy assets in other countries, including Nigeria. Nevertheless, the episode demonstrates just how intense the international competition over energy assets has become and highlights the very real possibility that this competition will inflame political ties among the major oil-importing countries. One analyst, Kurt Barrow of Purvin and Gertz (a Singapore-based consultancy), characterized the Unocal affair as the opening salvo in a new "war" over global oil supplies. "CNOOC lost the battle over Unocal," he told *The New York Times*, "but will continue to wage the war toward acquiring overseas energy assets to support China's growing energy needs."

This may seem overly rhetorical—but it is not seen that way by those in Congress who view China's avid pursuit of foreign oil assets as a "national security" matter, since it poses a threat to America's own essential energy supplies.

Where Others Fear to Go

The potential for friction arising from an increasingly competitive search for diminishing supplies of oil is made more severe by the second key aspect of this equation: the fact that many of the world's most prolific fields are controlled by the major Western oil firms or the producing countries' state-owned firms (such as Saudi Aramco and the Kuwait Petroleum Corporation). State-owned firms dominate production in most of the Middle East, while the Western firms have established a commanding position in such other producing areas as sub-Saharan Africa and the Caspian Sea basin.

Chinese energy officials would no doubt like to obtain a foothold in these areas, but have often been frustrated by the well-entrenched presence of these competing firms. For example, when CNOOC and Sinopec jointly sought to purchase a one-sixth stake in the consortium developing the large Kashagan reservoir in Kazakhstan's sector of the Caspian Sea, the original members of the consortium, including Exxon-Mobil, Royal Dutch/Shell, and Conoco-Philips, exercised their "right of first refusal" to exclude the Chinese firms and acquire the stake for themselves.

Having been excluded in this manner from many of the more attractive producing areas, the Chinese have opted for the only path that appears open to them: the pursuit of reserves in marginal producing areas and in "pariah" states like Iran, Sudan, and Uzbekistan. These countries have been largely shunned by firms from the United States and its allies, whether for human rights reasons or, in Iran's case, the pursuit of nuclear weapons.

China's position in Sudan is particularly noteworthy. CNPC currently holds a 40 percent stake in the Greater Nile Petroleum Operation Company, the leading producer in Sudan, and a substantial stake in other Sudanese fields; it has also constructed a 930-mile pipeline from southern Sudan to Port Sudan on the Red Sea and a refinery in Khartoum. In Iran, Sinopec has helped build a pipeline from the Caspian Sea to Tehran and is involved in the development of natural gas reserves.

The fact that China has established such close ties to countries considered unfriendly to the United States is seen in Washington as provocation enough. But, in its efforts to cement relations with these suppliers, Beijing has also provided them with military and diplomatic aid, further provoking ire in Washington. "In countries like Uzbekistan, Sudan, and Burma, China has openly supported regimes whose human rights violations, support for terrorism, or proliferation activities have engendered worldwide opposition," the DoE observed in a 2006 congressionally mandated review of Chinese energy policy. "As a long-term trend, China's behavior in this respect runs counter to key strategic goals of the United States."

The seriousness with which top US officials view these activities was evident in a 2005 Pentagon analysis of Chinese strategy and capabilities, *The Military Power of the People's Republic of China,* which for the first time highlighted energy competition as a significant factor in US-Chinese security affairs. In a section on "Resource Demand as a Driver of Strategy," the report observed, "Beijing's belief that it requires such special relationships in order to secure its energy access could shape its defense strategy and force planning"—thus, presumably, posing a potential threat to US national security.

This concern is being expressed at a time when China is importing only about 3 million barrels of oil per day, less than one-third of the current US import tally. Imagine the degree of alarm one might expect in 2025, when China's oil imports are expected to have risen to 11 million barrels per day, or two-thirds of America's projected imports. Although it is impossible to predict the future course of international relations, it would appear safe to assume that disputes arising from the competitive pursuit of foreign oil will play an increasingly critical role in the US-China relationship, possibly eclipsing such other concerns as Taiwan and the bilateral trade imbalance.

The Struggle for Gas

As time goes on, China will not only show an increasing thirst for petroleum. It also will need expanded supplies of natural gas. This, too, could produce significant friction in international affairs.

At present, China consumes a relatively small quantity of natural gas, about 1.2 trillion cubic feet per year, which is a mere 5 percent of the amount consumed in the United States. But China is expected to consume far more natural gas in the future, mostly to fuel electrical power plants but also as a source for fertilizer, hydrogen, and assorted petrochemicals. As Beijing becomes more aware of the environmental effects of over-reliance on coal, moreover, it is likely to depend increasingly on natural gas to generate electricity, further ramping up demand. As a result, China's gas consumption is expected to grow by 7.8 percent per year—the highest rate of any large economy. Just as in the case of oil, supplying all of this additional natural gas will prove a major challenge for the Chinese government.

Chinese officials would prefer to rely on domestic sources for as large a share of the needed gas as possible, and so have invested considerable funds in efforts to develop promising fields in the Tarim Basin of Western China and to transport this gas to energy-starved areas on the coast. But these sources are not sufficient to satisfy China's growing needs, and so Beijing has had to look elsewhere for additional supplies—once again, generating various forms of international antagonism.

The world's largest reservoirs of natural gas are found in Iran and Russia, and China has sought supplies from both—causing problems with the United States in the case of the former, and with Japan in the case of the latter. In October 2004, Sinopec signed a 25-year, $100 billion contract with Tehran for the production and export of up to 10 million tons per year of liquefied natural gas to China and for participation in the construction of a refinery for natural gas condensates. Although details of this plan are still being worked out, it could result in a major infusion of new capital into Iran, thus frustrating US efforts to isolate that country and thereby impede its efforts to acquire nuclear weapons.

The problem with Japan is of a different character, entailing competition over the ultimate destination of the vast gas supplies recently discovered off the coast of Sakhalin Island, in Russia's Far East. Japanese firms have provided much of the capital and technology for development of these fields, and Tokyo has always assumed that the resulting output would be carried southward by pipeline to Japan. Recently, however, Chinese officials have been negotiating with the Sakhalin consortium for a substantial share of the field's gas supplies and for the construction of a pipeline heading west, to China. Although the Russian government and its corporate partners in the Sakhalin project have yet to decide on the ultimate destination of this gas, the very fact that China has swooped in and attempted to capture a large share of it has produced considerable anger and resentment in Japan.

An even more serious dispute with Japan has arisen over the development of offshore gas fields in contested waters of the East China Sea. Chinese and Japanese geologists believe that considerable gas lies in the Xihu Trough, a deep undersea strip located roughly midway between China's east coast and Japan's southernmost islands. Citing provisions of the United Nations Convention on the Law of the Sea, Japan claims that its offshore boundary lies at the median line between the Chinese and Japanese coasts, putting it over or adjacent to the Xihu Trough. China, citing an older rule, insists that its outer boundary extends to the very edge of the continental shelf, much farther to the east.

Recently, CNOOC and Sinopec have been drilling right at the edge of the median line claimed by Japan, drawing gas from what Tokyo believes is Japanese territory but China claims is its own. Both sides have periodically deployed warships in the area, provoking a number of threatening naval encounters—none of which has yet entailed actual gunfire, but creating a very real risk of someday doing so. The gas dispute has also helped stoke rising anti-Chinese hostility in Japan and anti-Japanese hostility in China, complicating efforts to resolve the dispute peacefully.

The World's Dilemma

With China's need for imported energy certain to grow, and the future availability of abundant oil increasingly in doubt, the risk of crisis and conflict over access to vital resources will become increasingly severe. Viewed in this light, the potential for conflict is not a "China problem" but a global dilemma. Unless the world's existing powers are prepared to descend into the sort of resource-driven geopolitical competition that resulted in World War I and many lesser conflicts, they must make room at the table for an energy-hungry China. Efforts to exclude China from promising energy deals, such as the Kashagan field in the Caspian Sea and the Unocal sale in the United States, will only inflame tensions and drive Beijing to pursue more risky arrangements, with unpleasant international repercussions.

At the same time, the eventual peaking of world oil production and the environmental consequences of global reliance on fossil fuels can only be addressed on the international level, involving close cooperation among all key parties, including China.

It is essential, therefore, that the international community view China's strategic energy dilemma in a sympathetic manner. The international community needs to work with Beijing to help diversify its sources of energy and, along with everyone else, accelerate the development of environmentally friendly energy alternatives such as clean-coal technologies, biofuels, wind, solar, and hydrogen.

MICHAEL T. KLARE, a *Current History* contributing editor, is a professor at Hampshire College and the author of *Blood and Oil: The Dangers and Consequences of America's Growing Dependency on Imported Petroleum* (Owl Books, 2005).

China's Changing Landscape

NAOMI LUBICK

China is changing. The past several decades have seen immense booms in the country's demand for energy, steel, water and other natural resources that were already in scarce supply, in a country that is almost the size of the United States but has more than four times the population. Worries over the giant nation's need for oil peaked with the U.S. and Chinese governments' strange dance over Unocal last summer (see *Geotimes*, August 2005), and with China's consumption of steel, which sent the American government into a defensive stance several years ago.

"China has become, in the last five to 10 years, an enormous powerhouse and driver of resource exploitation and use around the Pacific Rim," says David Gordon, executive director of Pacific Environment, a nonprofit group in San Francisco, from "forests in Russia and southeast Asia, fisheries of the western Pacific, [and] oil resources around the world."

As China continues its economic metamorphosis into the gorilla in the global sandbox, it has rapidly changed its physical environment. Home to some of the world's largest cities, the country contains several of the most polluted cities in the world, partly because of its reliance on coal for energy. Wood and water needs have led to increased erosion and desertification, and the country sends dust from its quickly growing western desert across the Pacific, carrying sulfate and other polluting particulate matter.

Yet as the most populated country in the world moves ahead with its ambitious economic-growth agenda, it is also taking steps to address environmental impacts of that growth, sometimes in unexpected ways.

Thinking Big

Emblematic of the scale of its environmental issues and the will that can be applied to fix them, the government is transforming Beijing, one of China's most polluted cities, for the 2008 Olympics. The effort "illustrates some of the opportunities and the challenges" of China's environmental situation, says Ruth Greenspan Bell, an international development expert with Resources for the Future in Washington, D.C.

China's environment minister has promised that the capital city's notorious smog would be cleared before the world gathers for the games. The government continues to raze centuries-old neighborhoods, fueled by coal stoves, to replace them with massive high rises that have more emissions-efficient heating systems. Some of Beijing's industrial sites have been forced to relocate outside the city, shifting their pollution elsewhere. The government also initiated a massive tree-planting campaign several hundred kilometers from the urban center, to the west of the city, in an effort to slow the desertification of the region that has led to intense dust storms that pass through Beijing.

Since the Great Wall was built around 1000 B.C., massive human impacts on China's landscape have been the norm. Migrating populations that settled in southern China a millennium ago, for example, deforested the region that was once home to the soon-to-be-extinct South Chinese Tiger.

"The forests in the south, where it's tropical and semitropical, were extensive until about 1,000 years ago," says Walter Parham, a geologist affiliated with the Federation of American Scientists in Washington, D.C., who has used paintings from the 1700s and 1800s to show that treeless hills and erosion were widespread even then. Now only about 10 square kilometers (4 square miles) are left of South China's native forest. Local governments have been planting nonnative fast-growing trees such as eucalyptus, as well as grasses and other plants to halt erosion.

The loss of agricultural land—tens of millions of hectares over the past decade, according to the Chinese government—is drawing rural dwellers into the cities, lured by the industrial economy that is now running full steam ahead. Megacities that house millions of people might produce only several items—such as Datang, one of China's sock-producing cities, or Wenzhou, which makes most of the metal cigarette lighters in the world, both south of Shanghai.

To fuel that industry, China needs power, on a huge scale. "China is very poorly endowed with natural resources, with the exception of coal," says Nicholas Lardy, a senior fellow at the Institute for International Economics. About 60 to 70 percent of China's energy comes from coal. The country's coal consumption outstrips the rest of the world, and is projected to increase by 50 percent while the rest of the world drops by 15 percent, according to estimates by the U.S. Energy Information Administration (EIA).

In addition to coal, hydropower and damming have provided electricity necessary for industrial sites. According to the International Rivers Network, more than 20,000 large dams more than 15 meters (49 feet) tall sit on many of China's rivers. The Chinese government, which is in a "mega-projects" phase according to many analysts, is still in the process of building the Three Gorges Dam, which will be the largest dam in the world once completed in 2009, providing more than 18 gigawatts of electricity to six provinces, according to the U.S. Embassy (see *Geotimes*, August 2003). In the end, more than 1.3 million people could be displaced, in addition hundreds of villages and towns flooded for a reservoir that will be about 550 kilometers long, an area several times the size of Washington, D.C.

Despite such dramatic water infrastructure, China still does not have enough water to meet its needs in the north, which has severely depleted groundwater stores. To help with the water supply problem, the government has decided to reverse the flow of some of its rivers, spending more than $59 billion on three canals, each more than 1,000 kilometers long. Accompanying engineering efforts will link the country's four major rivers (including the Yangtze), which generally flow from north to south—reversing the flow of water from the south to the north. The Chinese Embassy in the United States projects that every year, 44.8 billion cubic meters of water will be channeled from the Yangtze to northern China. According to the Xinhua News Agency, the Yangtze River Water Resources Committee projects that more than 200,000 people, most of them farmers, will have to move to make way for the middle canal alone.

Some of these large-scale changes have yet to occur. More immediately visible may be the issue of air quality, one of the biggest worries for China before the Olympics.

Up in the Air

Over the past 50 years, Beijing has suffered the onslaught of anywhere from five to 15 dust storms a year (see *Geotimes*, June 2004). These storms deliver thousands of tons of dust, lifted from the desiccating northwestern plains, where demand for water, wood and agricultural land have decimated the forests and grasslands that used to keep the soils in place.

Sulfates and so-called black carbon—elemental carbon that contributes to global greenhouse warming because it absorbs and traps heat from sunlight in the atmosphere—as well as other kinds of particulate matter are carried by the dust storms. Scientists have tracked the dust all the way to California.

Along with dust, China has been creating acid rain that affects its own land and the countries surrounding it. The impacts may be most evident in soil acidification of forests, particularly in Chongqing, as well as in the South China Sea. The Chinese government has a 10-year plan in place to reduce acid rain by controlling sulfur emissions through tracking the quality of coal burned.

But that could prove difficult, partly because despite the Chinese government's ability to create massive changes, it also has a difficult time tracking what occurs at the local level. Researchers from China and the United States, led by David Streets of Argonne National Laboratory in Illinois, have shown that carbon dioxide and methane emissions took a dip at the end of the 1990s, as China took efforts to cut back on its coal

---

China's Facts and Figures

Population: Most populous country in the world with more than 1.3 billion people

Population Density: Ranked 77th in the world with 140 people per square kilometer

City Population with Highest Density: Shanghai; with about 2,700 people per square kilometer, followed by Beijing with about 860 people per square kilometer

Gross Domestic Product Per Capita: Ranked 121st worldwide at $5,600

Energy Consumption: 10.8 percent of world total

Coal Consumption: Accounts for 28 percent of the world's total coal use, and for 65 percent of the China's total energy consumption

Acid Rain: Occurs in 54 percent of 265 monitored cities in 2003, a 4.1 percent increase over the previous year

Cities Attaining Acceptable Air Standards: 41.7 percent of the 340 cities monitored

Days in Beijing with Air Quality Above National Standards: 229 for the year 2004

Forested Area: Ranked 5th in the world

Soil Erosion Area: Affects 3.56 million square kilometers, or 37.1 percent of China

Dust Storms: 100 dust storms are expected between 2000 and 2009, up from 23 over the previous decade; a March 2002 storm dropped 30,000 tons of dust on Beijing

Sources: CIA World Fact Book, Statistical Communiqué of the People's Republic of China, the American Embassy in China, the Earth Policy Institute and China's State Environmental Protection Administration.

---

burning—even as other countries steadily increased their carbon dioxide output. Those efforts included shutting down small mining operations in the late 1990s, and tracking what kind of coal larger mines shipped and in what quantities.

But small unregistered rural mines remained active, says Jonathan Sinton, a scientist with the China Energy Group at the Lawrence Berkeley National Laboratory in California. The government data show "a big gap between production and consumption," Sinton says. Also, tracking the quality of the coal is difficult, with implications for emissions estimates, which are made directly from energy statistics reported to various Chinese bureaus.

EIA says that China's carbon dioxide emissions started to increase again in 2002 and 2003. The Chinese government has endorsed emissions trading schemes adapted from U.S. systems to control sulfur emissions, Bell says. However, she and other observers question whether such plans are appropriate, "in view of China's weak record of tracking emissions and enforcing pollution controls," she says.

The need for alternative power sources is reflected in interest in liquefied natural gas pipelines, as well as the drive for hydropower and nuclear power, Sinton says. Local leaders are "actively pushing to have nuclear plants sited in their provinces."

National alternative energy plans, just approved to take effect at the beginning of next year, include commitments to build 20 to 25 nuclear plants in the next few decades, as well as hydropower and wind power projects and other measures, says Christopher Flavin, president of the Worldwatch Institute in Washington, D.C., and although such ventures are promising, they are only a small part of China's energy needs. Still, "the commitment to renewable energy is certainly a real one on the part of officials in China," he says. "They don't have much choice."

In the meantime, massive environmental impacts are sparking environmental awareness among China's residents.

Raising the Stakes

In the fall of 1999, 2,700 ducks from farmer Zhang Jinhu's flock, living in the Huai River in Hairou County, Beijing, died from the changing pH of the river. Zhang successfully sued the Gaoliang River Aquatic Farm, raising awareness of the problem of alkaline wastewater discharges.

Zhang's path-breaking case was represented by a volunteer law group in Beijing, the Center for Legal Assistance to Pollution Victims, which works to bring such issues to court in cases structured like tort actions in the United States, seeking damages from the effects of pollution. But current environmental laws require that a victim must bring the lawsuit, unlike in the United States, where cases may be brought for the public good, often by environmental activist groups, such as the Natural Resources Defense Council and Sierra Club.

Observers say that China may never allow such lawsuits, and meanwhile, its governing bodies are in transition. The central government is attempting to distribute some of the environmental responsibilities once consolidated in Beijing, but it has difficulty tracking what local governments might do. Although the local environmental protection bureaus ultimately are responsible for enforcing what the Chinese State Environmental Protection Agency decrees, they must report to provincial or local governments that control their finances.

Those local governments may be run or influenced by owners of industrial sites, says Jennifer Turner, coordinator of the China Environment Forum at the Woodrow Wilson Center in Washington, D.C. And the local bodies may do what they think is best for the economy of a region, but not necessarily for its environment, says Wen Bo, a Beijing-based environmental activist who is affiliated with the Global Greengrants Fund in Boulder, Colo., and who works with Pacific Environment to develop environmental nongovernmental organizations (NGOs) in China. "The [central] government knows what's going on, but is not necessarily able to control it," Turner says.

However, publicity surrounding cases like that of the duck farmer, paired with local awareness of water quality issues and other concerns that directly impact citizens, has kindled a nas-

cent grassroots environmental movement, where individuals and nonprofit groups find ways to get local industries to comply. "The critical issue that the [environmental] movement and society there is facing is how to deal with and manage their development in such a way as to not create public health problems and environmental problems," says Gordon of Pacific Environment. The issues "are getting too large for the government to ignore," he says. "People are hungry for more information, what they can do to ensure that something is done."

Wen says that the environmental groups that are NGOs number in the hundreds, and each might have several hundred members. "They cannot be too big, otherwise they would attract negative attention from the central government," says Wen, whose activities occasionally have been considered "sensitive" and "pro-democracy." (The Chinese government has tracked pro-democracy activists since the Tiananmen Square protests in 1989.) More than 400 student groups, for example, with 50 to 100 members apiece, may join under one banner, the China Green Student Forum, but they remain separate organizations, sometimes with their own pet causes.

Despite continued difficulties in gaining legal status (China requires NGOs to register, but they must be government-sponsored to do so), Wen says that environmental NGOs "have more power" and are "becoming watchdogs that pressure government on certain topics." One such case was an effort to redirect a highway project slated to go through protected mangroves in southern China. Documents collected by local NGOs uncovered the local government's illegal actions, garnering attention from the media and citizens—and from officials at the national and provincial government level who intervened.

Such incidents, along with some violent protests by villagers and communities downstream of chemical plants and other polluters, reported recently in the international press, are something that the Chinese government would like to avoid.

Continued Growth

"The maxim 'First development, then environment,' was a common refrain throughout the 1980s and much of the 1990s," wrote Elizabeth Economy in her book *The River Runs Black*. But China's "leadership has also begun to witness the broader social and economic costs of its environmental failure," she wrote. More than 300,000 premature deaths a year can be attributed to air pollution, not including other health costs incurred, noted Economy, who is director of Asia studies for the Council on Foreign Relations in New York. The World Health Organization and the United Nations Development Programme estimate that such annual losses amount to up to $19.3 billion, accounting for up to 2 percent of China's gross domestic product.

"China has certainly almost every kind of environmental problem that's been invented," says Flavin of the Worldwatch Institute. But even though the country is using a lot of resources on the whole, usage is "extremely low" on a per capita basis, he says. "The United States is using 10 times as much oil per person." If China approaches those rates, with 22 percent of the world's population (versus the United States at 4.5 percent), then there will be reason to worry.

Although oil remains "much less important" to China's economy than it is in the United States, says Lardy of the Institute for International Economics, the country is "building highways at a prodigious rate." These thoroughfares already are "thick with trucks" for interstate commerce, particularly in coastal areas. Car purchases in the country have been steadily increasing, although only around 7.6 million cars are in the country, according to the World Resources Institute. EIA expects China's demand for oil to increase annually by almost 10 percent until 2010, when it will settle back to an almost 3-percent increase annually for the next decade or so.

Efforts by China's central government to control its emissions and energy use, as well as its environmental impacts, are commendable and sweeping, but whether they will be successful and sustainable is uncertain, observers say, in much the same way as the government's attempts to rework Beijing's environment in time for the Olympics. Political will is critical, Bell says, but "as a practical matter, the environment more often gets short shrift against the government's desire to grow the economy and keep people employed."

LUBICK is a staff writer for *Geotimes*.

Article 19

Will China Go to War Over Oil?

Wu Lei, Shen Qinyu

As the global energy markets undergo radical changes and oil prices remain near record highs, the "China energy threat" has emerged as a new fear in Washington's corridors of power. China's quest for energy security, conducted through aggressive "bilateral energy diplomacy," has attracted worldwide attention. Many analysts argue that the trajectories of the U.S. and China, the world's two most voracious energy consumers, will inevitably lead to a clash over resources in the future.

Energy security is already playing an increasingly important role in Sino-U.S. relations, intensifying friction on regional issues. For instance, Sudan is one area of dispute in which oil is a key to China's interest. At present, Sudan is China's largest overseas production base, and more than half of the country's oil exports go to China, accounting for 5% of China's total oil imports. The genocide and humanitarian disaster in oil-rich Darfur in southern Sudan has given rise to concern in the U.S., which proposed sanctions on Sudan by the United Nations. In September 2004, the Security Council voted to threaten sanctions on Sudan's oil industry if Khartoum failed to rein in Janjawid militiamen in Darfur. Shortly after the vote, China announced that any attempts to actually impose sanctions would be met with a Chinese veto.

Iran is a more troublesome and dangerous test of Sino-U.S. relations, however. Iran is now China's biggest foreign-oil supplier, and its relations with China in the political, economic and military arenas have intensified. On Oct. 28, 2004, China signed an agreement with Iran worth between $70 billion and $100 billion to develop the giant Yadavaran natural-gas field and Beijing agreed to buy 250 million tons of liquefied natural gas from Iran over 25 years. Beijing wants to construct a 386-kilometer pipeline from Iran to the northern Caspian Sea to connect with the Kazakhstan-Xinjiang pipeline, bringing more Middle East oil to China. This would have lasting strategic benefits for China, since a pipeline reduces reliance on shipped oil.

China's increasing energy investment and trade breakthrough with Iran obviously clashes with America's Iran-Libya Sanctions Act. The U.S. and the European Union are pressuring Iran to give up its nuclear power program, and Washington wants to refer the case to the U.N. Security Council to impose sanctions on Tehran.

Since Sudan and Iran together supply China with 20% of its oil imports, U.S. attempts to contain these regimes bring it into direct confrontation with China's energy-security policies. Washington has warned Beijing that the two countries would be on a collision course if China continues to pursue energy deals in places like Iran and Sudan. U.S. Deputy Secretary of State Robert Zoellick has said that Beijing's ties with "troublesome" states would have repercussions elsewhere, and the Chinese would have to pay the "price."

The potential friction does not end there. China has also made moves into Latin American oil-producing countries, an area which is traditionally within the U.S. "sphere of influence" and is a major oil supplier to the U.S. In the search for fuel and minerals for its booming economy, China is disregarding U.S. objections by courting these countries.

It is too soon to draw conclusions from the above stories that the rise of China as a new mover of global energy markets is bound to lead to war over energy. At the very least, a few more complications will have to be added to the mix. In truth, the United States and China are not really in direct competition on many energy issues, even though China's practices of energy diplomacy do undermine U.S. goals of isolating or punishing "rogue states."

The biggest challenge still arises from the Taiwan issue, which Beijing regards as an issue of life and death. The Bush administration has threatened China by urging Japan to rearm and by promising Taiwan that, should China use force to prevent a Taiwanese declaration of independence, the U.S. will go to war on its behalf. It seems that the U.S. and Japan might actually precipitate a war with China over Taiwan. If the "cold war" between the U.S. and China on the Taiwan issue turns hot to some degree, the U.S. and Japan would likely move to cut off China's overseas "oil lifeline." That would be a huge blow to Beijing, making a wider war over energy inevitable.

After all, with a widening gap between domestic supply and demand, energy is being recognized as a core national interest among China's national security apparatus. As such, energy security is not only economically vital, but also has political, diplomatic and military implications. The legitimacy of the Chinese Communist Party is largely based on rapid and sustained economic growth. That is why China's top leaders have been paying full attention to this issue and becoming actively involved in energy diplomacy toward Russian and states in the Middle East, Central Asia, West Africa and even Latin America. This is also the motivation behind a major 2004 reshuffle of China's energy-related agencies in a bid to allow better management of future energy security. The new ministerial-level State Energy Office under the leadership of Premier Wen Jiabao will focus on broad energy decision-making.

Therefore, the U.S. needs to understand China's quest for energy security and the Chinese top leaders' insecurity vis-à-vis the U.S. The fear is that the U.S. might try to cut off China's overseas oil lifeline in order to destabilize the country. The fact that China's future energy supply is overly dependent on the sea lanes and the fear that the U.S. might cut them off as a result of the deterioration of Sino-U.S. relations over the Taiwan issue drives much of Beijing's modernization of its navy and air forces.

It must be made clear that China is not a small regional power like Iraq or North Korea. If confronted with serious threats to its energy security, it will mobilize all its economic, political and military resources to ensure a secure energy supply, or to interfere in the energy supply chains of the U.S. and its allies like Japan in key chokepoints such as the South China Sea, the Strait of Malacca or even the Taiwan Strait. These counterbalancing measures would, of course, be a last resort.

Being major energy importers, China and the U.S. are finding more common interests with regard to energy affairs. Both countries face similar problems: Domestic oil resources are declining, domestic energy supplies fall short of demand, and there is an increasing need for imports. Both hope for a stable supply and fair price in international markets.

China should actively expand its coordinative relations with the U.S. In fact, as long as the U.S. does not embarrass China on the Taiwan issue, it is possible for the two powers to carry out comprehensive dialogue and even cooperation. After all, common interest in stabilizing energy supply and price makes it necessary for two powers to exercise strategic cooperation.

For China, international cooperation in energy security should become part of its energy-security strategy. China's decision makers should keep in mind that energy security is a global issue and no single energy-importing country can remain immune from an oil crisis. In an era of globalization, a single nation's policy no longer works well to address oil security.

The U.S. and its allies, accordingly, should gradually lead Beijing onto the right track by, for instance, taking China into the "oil club," the International Energy Agency, in order to turn China's unilateral energy policy into a multilateral one. This move would not only alleviate U.S. concerns about China's unilateral energy diplomacy, it would also help to prevent future energy crises and minimize the security risks. China's membership in the "oil club" would enable Beijing to obtain or share energy market information. And cooperation with the West would bring energy-tapping technology, investment knowledge and environment-protection know-how, all of which are priorities of China's new energy strategy. Most importantly, through cooperation, China and the U.S. can minimize disputes and possible conflicts over energy.

MR. WU is director of the Centre for Energy Security and Strategy at the School of International Studies, Yunnan University, Kunming, China, and is author of *China's Oil Security*. Mr. Shen is a lecturer at Capital University of Economics and Business in Beijing.

Article 20

The Gramercy Round

China Goes Global

Implications for the United States

Chaired by Ian Bremmer and Fareed Zakaria, the Gramercy Round convenes over dinner in New York's historic Gramercy Tavern to consider issues which have received insufficient attention from the established foreign policy community but which have a direct impact on the peace and prosperity of the United States. The Round meets to discuss questions with an eye to promoting realistic assessments and innovative approaches for American policy.

Harry Harding

China is increasingly "going global." As part of a state policy to secure markets, technology and resources abroad, Chinese firms—primarily its largest state-owned enterprises—are making direct investments overseas and signing long-term contracts to acquire key natural resources from foreign producers. The numbers are still relatively small (a total of stock of less than $40 billion by the end of 2004) but they are expected to grow rapidly.

China's outbound foreign investment represents the beginning of a second stage in China's strategy of relying on integration with the global economy to promote its economic development. The earlier stage was one of "bringing in"—what the Chinese called *kaifang*, or "opening." Foreign investors were invited to establish operations in China while Beijing sought to create the international environment that would facilitate its access to foreign markets, capital and technology. This meant China adopted an omnidirectional foreign policy, in which it sought to reduce tensions with virtually every potential trade and investment partner; it also meant Beijing was willing to join existing international institutions (such as the World Bank and the World Trade Organization) and to accept "rules of the game" written primarily by the United States.

Now, Chinese firms are "going out" (a literal translation of the Chinese phrase *zou chuqu*). Increasingly, the Chinese want to capture a greater portion of the "value chain" in the production of goods, no longer concentrating on providing low-cost labor (what the Chinese call *jiagong* or "adding labor") to assemble products.

China seems largely intent on what some describe as a mercantilist, as opposed to a purely market-oriented, strategy. That is, China is not willing to rely simply on the international marketplace to gain indirect access to the resources it wishes to import, but prefers to gain direct access by acquiring those materials at the source.

Moreover, since the Chinese government is the majority owner of many firms, questions are raised not only about unfair trading practices (for example, if the state provides below-market financing) but the interrelationship between Chinese business interests and foreign policy objectives. There are reports, for example, that the Australian government has become far more guarded about supporting the U.S. commitment to the security of Taiwan as a result of growing Chinese investment in that country. Conversely, there is also the possibility that the Chinese government will be more supportive of the host governments of the countries in which it has key investments or contracts, regardless of those government's international orientations or domestic human rights records; China's energy relationships with countries like Iran, Burma and Sudan pose these kinds of concerns.

As China goes global, it may increasingly seek to create new international institutions and norms, rather than simply accepting those already in existence. China is actively engaged in creating new organizations—from a new Asian free trade area (ASEAN+China) to a regional security entity, the Shang-

HARRY HARDING is director, Research and Analysis, at the Eurasia Group, and University Professor of International Affairs at The George Washington University.

hai Cooperation Organization. Significantly, many of these new groupings explicitly exclude the United States. At some point, China may also attempt to define international norms differently than the United States, whether these are technical standards for key manufactured goods or the principles by which the international community is governed.

Finally, China is now in a position to make major investments in the United States itself. Two kinds of investment may be of particular concern: strategic and iconic. Strategic investments are those by which China seeks to acquire, and thereby to control, critically important resources. Oil is one obvious example, but I suspect that Chinese attempts to acquire American high-technology firms will be the more common way in which this issue gets raised. Iconic investments would involve the acquisition of companies or other assets of particular symbolic importance to the United States: imagine a Chinese attempt to buy a well-known American automobile or equipment manufacturer, a major shopping center or resort, or an American film studio.

The efforts of Japanese firms a decade or so ago to make similar strategic and iconic investments in the United States were controversial enough—and Japan was a fellow democracy and a strategic ally of the United States. Nor is China unique; increasingly, India is also "going global" while the emergence of a form of "state capitalism" in Russia raises similar concerns about the intersection of a country's business interests and foreign policies. All of this presents a new set of challenges and opportunities to the United States, which have not yet been adequately identified or addressed.

Ian Bremmer

For the first time in history, China has gone global. Its strategy to secure the commodities, market access and new technologies needed to fuel sustainable economic growth has exposed China to unprecedented levels of political risk in every corner of the world. Its leadership has little experience in managing these risks, or the conflicts with the United States the new policy has generated. For its part, Washington has yet to formulate a coherent strategy to meet the challenges China's foreign investment strategy poses for U.S. interests, or to profit from the opportunities it offers.

At the core of current U.S. policy towards China's global strategy is an admonition that Beijing must act as a "responsible stakeholder" in international politics. In practice, this means China should accept responsibility for key elements of global stability (as defined in Washington). It also means there are red lines China should not cross as it seeks to lock down long-term access to key commodities and a larger share of the global value chain. But Washington has yet to clearly define where these red lines are.

If the United States could magically overcome all diplomatic misunderstanding, communicate clearly what it wants from China, and win unconditional Chinese support for this formulation, what precisely would Washington ask of Beijing? Are Iran, Venezuela, Sudan, Burma and Zimbabwe off limits for Chinese investment? May Chinese firms compete with American companies in West Africa and Latin America? Should China restrict

its commercial dealings to developed economies? If so, would the United States welcome/accept Chinese investment in Canadian energy? May Chinese firms offer competitive bids for American firms? Recent history suggests Washington takes a dim view of all these options.

But steady, sustainable Chinese growth is in America's interest. It is crucial for the health of the global economy and for the future of a growing list of U.S. companies. China's economic expansion requires that its international investment strategy succeed.

Will U.S. policymakers see past protectionist politics if Hugo Chavez decides to sell a Chinese state-owned company a major stake in Citgo? If a Chinese automaker bids for a stake in a struggling General Motors? Or a U.S. airline? Beijing (and many in the United States) is waiting for Washington to define which assets the U.S. government considers "critical infrastructure."

The United States needs a balanced approach. Washington is wise to insist that China develop a political system supportive of long-term stability. But China must know where its investment policy will bring it into conflict with the United States—and where it will not.

Sloganeering will not persuade China to become a responsible stakeholder. But long-term Sino-American cooperation on the development of sustainable trade practices could. When U.S. firms invest in a foreign country, they take a holistic political approach to development there. They try to help improve local school systems, secure labor rights for women, encourage transparency and anti-corruption efforts, and address environmental problems, not because they set a premium on democracy and high-mindedness, but because politically active, better-educated citizens living in communities free of corruption and pollution offer a better environment for sustainable commercial relations.

China's state-owned companies lack experience in establishing such relationships. They are generally intent only on locking up deals, developing strong relations with local elites and supplying these elites with what they want—often at the expense of local stability. Because Chinese companies neglect the need to establish footholds in local communities, anti-Chinese sentiment in many of these states is growing.

The same is true for the Chinese government. When the tsunami devastated Indonesia and other Southeast Asian states in 2004, the United States and Asian/Pacific democracies (Australia, Japan and India) were quick to respond with badly needed help for local populations. China was nowhere to be found. But the Chinese were not invited to participate. They should have been.

If the United States wants China to adopt this sort of responsible role in the countries in which it is now investing, American companies and the U.S. government should offer their Chinese counterparts the chance to learn from America's experience investing abroad—its successes and its mistakes. This process won't be easy. China envisions itself as America's partner, not its student. But Beijing is well aware that Chinese firms are operating in uncharted foreign waters. If China's lead-

Ian Bremmer is president of the Eurasia Group and a contributing editor to *The National Interest*.

ers had more confidence that Washington understood the need to coordinate their interests abroad, the relationship might grow much more smoothly.

Coordination, not competition, can help both states realize their shared goal of better relations. And a clearer definition from Washington of where, and under what circumstances, U.S. and Chinese goals conflict can help Beijing grow its economy in ways that serve the long-term interests of both.

Thomas Stewart

Americans spend a good deal of time worrying about China, yet we are not doing enough to develop our own strategies for competing in the globalized world of the 21st century. We have no one speaking up intelligently on the question of domestic competitiveness. Many American businesses now get half their sales or more from overseas; in a sense they have become stateless. The same is true of business schools. They won't advocate for one nation's competitiveness as they used to. Who's left to speak for America? Lou Dobbs and a Congress and an administration that have never demonstrated expertise in foreign economic policy. We cannot blame the Chinese for having a strategy.

The United States continues to take in more capital than it exports, and increasingly it seems that these resources are being used to support current consumption and government deficits rather than being directed into investment. But as the Chinese and Indian economies continue to expand, they will become increasingly attractive destinations for capital—and big enough to absorb a lot of it. What impact will this have on the dollar? Over time, investor economies in the Middle East and Asia may seek to develop an alternative that would enable them to bypass the United States and reduce the use of the dollar as a de facto international currency.

We have a theology that says the expansion of the free market system leads to democracy, and in turn that democracies do not fight each other. I think these premises should be questioned—because I think all premises should always be questioned—but if you accept them, the logical course of action *vis-à-vis* China is maximum engagement and to encourage China's deeper integration into the global system.

David Lipton

When discussing the economics of foreign investment, we need to be clear in the terminology that we use. The Chinese are not engaged in much foreign direct investment in the sense of building new factories or bringing in fresh investment; they are engaged in acquisition of existing assets, so the impact on jobs and output is less than greenfield FDI.

The CFIUS process has served well in identifying the acquisition of U.S. companies that threaten our national security interests, while avoiding undesirable obstacles to useful investments. [CFIUS (Committee on Foreign Investment in the United States) is an interagency mechanism that evaluates the national security risk of

U.S. assets being acquired by foreign firms.] In thinking through the challenge of dealing with prospective Chinese investments, it might be useful to distinguish three categories of targets: firms that have control over critical parts of the infrastructure, assets that secure access to energy and other raw materials, and firms that enhance Chinese manufacturing capabilities. In the first, there may be legitimate objects of concern for CFIUS. In the second, China is unlikely to acquire enough to materially affect energy market pricing and supply, and for now there is less rationale for concern over national security. In the third, acquisitions are likely to be mainly commercial. There is a more general need to update the CFIUS process. We have never defined what constitutes national security—and to some extent, that lack of definition has served us well, giving us a certain degree of flexibility. But we run the risk of too broad of a definition of "national security" or "critical infrastructure"; we need an evolution in both the case law and procedures, given that the nature of national security concerns is changing as globalization progresses and various new threats emerge.

The whole debate about China reflects a larger unease with globalization. The economies of Europe and Japan have not been growing satisfactorily and the U.S. economy has not been generating satisfactory job growth. The economic rise of China and India has led to downward pressure on domestic wages and over time may increase the cost of capital because of the rapid investment needed to support growth.

We have to find ways to bring more Americans into the "capital game." Politicians will face pressures to react to these forces, and those pressures will be for protection against low-wage imports and against capital acquisitions. It will be important to accept and make the best of globalization despite its adverse by-products, because consumers will gain so much. It is preferable to find ways to live with globalization rather than try to impede it. It may be ironic for a Democrat to be advocating this, but we do need some version of the "Ownership Society" to expand the number of Americans with a stake in capital assets.

We need to help U.S. politicians to better explain to their constituents the new and different world we live in, and to lay out what the risks and gains are from the globalized system that has emerged. We also have to be able to make the case for the Sino-American relationship. Adjusting to the rise of China may be strange and difficult, but ultimately China going global is good for us.

Robert D. Hormats

We are not engaged in a zero-sum game with China. It is highly unlikely that there is a central grand plan where the Chinese state is coordinating the activities of all state-owned companies. The State Council did not sit down and dictate that Lenovo should purchase IBM's personal computer and laptop unit. Chinese state-owned firms make decisions based on what is good for the company, and managers have a good deal of discretionary authority; the government has far less control than many Americans assume.

THOMAS STEWART is editor and managing director of the *Harvard Business Review*.

DAVID LIPTON is managing director and head of Global Country Risk Management at Citigroup. He served as undersecretary of the treasury for global affairs in the Clinton Administration.

This is not like the challenge posed by Japan during the 1970s: with an economy expanding outward yet relatively closed at home to foreign investment and imposing limitations to foreign penetration of its domestic markets. China may be "going global" but it is open for business at home. American businesses can invest in China and can benefit from access to the Chinese domestic market.

One potentially divisive issue is energy. Here the Chinese government has been making decisions that are frequently based on strategic rather than market calculations, a preference for acquiring equity stakes in oil rather than trusting market mechanisms. This is because the Chinese believe that in a crisis international oil companies might not be able to provide deliveries of energy to China.

We also need to put things into perspective. Americans tend to panic because China seeks to buy a company that produces the equivalent of 1 percent of the U.S. oil supply and portray this as a threat to national security. The vastly bigger national security issue is that the United States continues to rely on imports for 60 percent of its oil needs. That is where our strategic focus should be.

There are overlapping interests between Washington and Beijing. Both countries want a stable supply of oil in global markets. The task is getting China to think of itself as a global consumer, who shares interests with other consumers, and to trust the markets, rather than try to lock up resources using equity arrangements. And we can help China with clean coal technology.

Energy could be a contentious issue in the Sino-American relationship, but it is also a good prospect for cooperation. Here, a more creative institutional framework, perhaps a high-level cabinet committee, could be created to deal with questions such as the sale of clean coal technology to China as well as ways to ensure supply stability in both oil and natural gas markets. Otherwise, we will have dispute after dispute on energy issues.

The crux of the matter is this: We need to create a dialogue about how Beijing plans to use its growing economic and political power and to encourage it to do so in a way that creates a more stable and prosperous global economy.

In the end, I do not think we need to worry very much about China's increased global economic presence. But we do need to see it as a challenge to us to boost our competitive capabilities and improve our education system. Beijing is still inclined to participate in the international system. Washington, and specifically the Congress, however, must be more patient; we will need a more sophisticated diplomacy. It will take time for China to follow the path to becoming a stakeholder. Our watchword should be engagement, not containment.

Robert Friedman

In assessing the challenge of a China going global, we are very far from any sort of threat situation. China is still in an immature stage in terms of its outward investments, and its track record, so far, is poor. TCL acquired RCA but still has no profits to show; Lenovo has seen profits go down by 85 percent after it purchased IBM's PC division. Indeed, we should be thankful that Chinese firms are willing to take bankrupt or troubled U.S. assets off of our hands; if these are companies in which China can use its labor advantage to make them more productive, then "bring 'em on." The selling companies benefit by disposing of assets that are no longer profitable.

It is not necessarily the smartest strategy for Beijing to try to lock up natural resources in various parts of the world. China is opening itself up to all sorts of political risks its policymakers and business figures have not foreseen in places like Nigeria and Pakistan, where the Chinese are beginning to encounter a backlash to their presence. Rebels in the Niger Delta seeking more autonomy and greater control over their resources have targeted Chinese oil workers as well as those from Shell, which suggests that China's desire for energy security may link it more closely with the interests of the U.S. and other consuming countries than with those of revolutionary movements it once supported.

Joel Rosenthal

In his 2000 campaign for president, Governor Bush never missed an opportunity to define China as a "strategic competitor." This position seemed to be part of an overall foreign policy orientation that claimed the mantle of " realism" and took the practical form of "anything but Clinton."

As we approach 2008, any realist assessment would have to feature two observations. First, the United States and China are in fact competing for global power and influence. The competition at this point in time is most fierce over soft power issues that will determine the rules of the game for the global economy as it evolves for next generation. Second, the United States and China are the biggest beneficiaries of the process of economic integration that is called globalization. With this common interest established, one can see that the competition over rules and norms of global economic integration may turn out to be the main game rather than a sideshow.

All of this means that U.S.-China relations will play out under a complicated constellation of rivalry and strong mutual interest. The challenge and opportunity for policy makers on both sides is to see this moment clearly and to identify and lock in common goals and common interests. As the two biggest winners in the globalization sweepstakes, there is much to gain by engaging in a "concert" approach, based on win-win scenarios.

The United States and China have much to gain by forging a 21st century globalization that will continue to benefit its peoples and help to raise the fortunes of the least well off around the world. Further, Chinese investment in the global economy can be an opportunity to encourage China's emergence as a responsible stakeholder in the global system. This outcome would

ROBERT D. HORMATS is vice chairman of Goldman Sachs (International).

ROBERT FRIEDMAN is the international editor of *Fortune*.

JOEL ROSENTHAL is president of the Carnegie Council for Ethics in International Affairs.

depend not only on China itself, but also on U.S. leadership that will show the way and insist on human rights and related ethical standards as the basis for a stable and just world system. In the end, the power of principle will prevail. A global system that does not reflect basic human values, justice and fairness will not be sustainable over the long term.

Nader Mousavizadeh

Containment of China is not a realistic option, given Chinese access to global markets and resources, especially in Europe and Latin America—not to mention East Asia. Nor, is it, in all likelihood, an effective one, given the web of relationships China is forming around the world—leveraging diplomacy in trade negotiations and vice versa—a world which is growing increasingly susceptible to multiple sources of power.

Integrating and nurturing China's emerging managerial class should form a central part of our strategy toward China. To the extent that the Chinese are engaged in acquisitions of Western firms, they are doing so in part to gain Western experience, knowledge and expertise, and improve their ability to manage the power and risk of market forces. Given the integrated nature of the global economy, the world as a whole stands to benefit from the development of these skills in China.

From the perspective of the (in many cases U.S.-educated and free-market-oriented) managers of China's emerging global companies, the United States and its most successful companies are models to emulate. They want to compete and win on the global playing field, which is why there is a great risk involved in protectionist measures that could signal a double standard for global M & A.

In potentially overreacting to a perceived threat from China, the United States may undertake policies that will send precisely the wrong message to China's modernizing managerial class and encourage highly damaging (to the United States, as well as the rest of the world) tendencies in China, including nationalism, mercantilism and distrust of the international markets. To the extent that some U.S. politicians define foreign— and in this case, Chinese—acquisitions of U.S. assets as threats for domestic political purposes, they are jeopardizing a relationship—and a larger open global market—from which the United States has gained the most, and from whose weakening it has the most to lose.

Ruchir Sharma

Everyone seems to be convinced that a new superpower is on the verge of overtaking the United States. History, of course, never plays out in purely linear fashion. We've seen this before. In the 1990s it was the small economies of East Asia, the "Asian tigers", which were the wave of the future. Recall that in the 1950s, based on linear projections, Burma and

the Philippines were supposed to become the most developed countries of the region. And in the early 1980s the CIA was projecting that the Soviet economy was nearly as large as that of the United States.

Linear projections are not the entire story; they do not encompass the quality of growth or social benefits. It takes a lot more than uninterrupted growth rates to match or even surpass the United States. We don't focus on the very real challenges China faces in making it to the next level of development. I wonder how, in five years time, we are going to evaluate some of these overblown expectations about China.

It is popular to underestimate how well the U.S. economy is doing, and to be worried about the Chinese juggernaut. China is still very dependent on exports to the United States to sustain its economic growth. Domestic demand in China is flat. For a long time to come, China is going to need a healthy, strong and prosperous United States to ensure its own prosperity and development.

Fareed Zakaria

Washington has an unsatisfactory way of conceiving the "China challenge" and for coping with it. The discussion tends to focus on the military growth or on the trade deficit. Those aren't the real issues. The real issue is that of size and scope. China poses a multidimensional challenge to the United States: it possesses an almost limitless amount of inexpensive labor for manufacturing as well as a growing high-technology sector (small as a percentage of the Chinese population but large by any other measure). This means China can combine research and development with labor arbitrage. When combined with China's growing surpluses, this means China is in a position to acquire U.S. assets, particularly in the high-technology sector, and move them offshore. Take one example: a firm like JDS Uniphase. This is a company that does high-tech optical physics. It's about as high up on the value chain as you can get. But cost pressures have made it outsource almost all its research and production to China, which happens to be strong in optical-physics research. The shell of the company remains American, but it is essentially a Chinese technology company. The Chinese are in a position to use their labor advantage to produce products more cheaply, and their research and engineering base to imitate American-developed technology. This is a challenge on a different scale than Japan or Germany ever posed. And it can have national security implications when we are considering dual-use technologies. I know the Ricardian answer to all this. But I do wonder if China's size makes things different.

Another aspect of the problem of scale is that China will not be a rich country per capita when it becomes a rich country in tort. China may not be an advanced industrial power, but when its per capita GDP (real) reaches approximately $4,000 or $5,000, it becomes the world's second largest economy. Is it going to think like a rich country, concerned about global rules and norms, or is it going to see itself as a developing country

NADER MOUSAVIZADEH, an investment banker at Goldman Sachs & Co., served from 1997–2003 as a special assistant to UN Secretary-General Kofi Annan.

RUCHIR SHARMA is a managing director at Morgan Stanley.

with its narrow interests dominating? I think the latter. This is a unique situation, where India and China will both cast huge shadows on the global economy but still be poor or middle-income countries.

The United States talks about upholding a broad, liberal, international order; Beijing is concerned with how it can get oil from Sudan back to the mainland. Even domestically, China's interests are not necessarily defined in the same way as American ones. The state is very concerned to use economic growth and prosperity to sustain the existing regime. A U.S. company will try to make profits and not be worried about contributing to "full employment" but this is still very much a concern for China. China's state-owned and state-funded firms operate to full employment rather than return on investment.

There is a great deal of concern about China signing natural resource contracts with "rogue" states around the world. I think we need to put this in perspective. I see China less as an evil mastermind signing deals with rogue states to thwart Washington's geopolitical ambitions and more as a scavenger. The United States and Europe have locked up the choicest oil suppliers in the world. China is looking for equity stakes wherever it can find them. If we are concerned about Chinese involvement with less than desirable regimes, then we need to find a way to collaborate with them as consumers. I've always thought that a consumers' cartel of petroleum is a better solution than to have individual countries try to freelance.

In New York, especially in financial and business circles, there is a "thin, wonky consensus" about China reflected in our discussions: promoting engagement with China and facilitating its continued integration, as opposed to a confrontational approach defined in terms of containment and protectionism. This consensus does not necessarily hold when one travels to Washington, particularly when one reaches the Congress. But politicians have to deal with realities. China and India are not going to stop growing, they are not going to "disappear." Our political leaders cannot escape the very clear intersection between domestic and foreign policy in dealing with the China challenge. This includes moving beyond talking about competitiveness to having the political courage to prescribe the remedies (some of which may be unpleasant in the short run) needed to heal an ailing American economy.

China certainly benefits from having low wage workers and Chinese firms can sometimes turn to the state for assistance, but Beijing is not responsible for a low savings rate in the United States, or the costs of our hyper-litigiousness, or our lack of investment in education and research.

Nikolas K. Gvosdev

If war is too important to be left to the generals, China policy may be too important to be left to the politicians. It is unrealistic to expect that the solution to the challenges posed by "China going global" is to convince China to "stay at home", or that tightening energy markets can be corrected by beseeching the Chinese (or Indians for that matter) to forego an American-style, middle-class lifestyle. Yet the temptation for both political parties to succumb to demagoguery about a "China threat" to the United States is very real.

It is important not to overestimate China's progress or to elevate them to the position of America's new superpower rival. But we are approaching the point where we can no longer compartmentalize the Sino-American relationship into neat "economic" and "political" boxes, and we cannot expect that as China begins to accumulate leverage (as Beijing acquires more U.S. debt, for example) that it will refrain from seeking to influence U.S. policy. Either we have to accept the political consequences of the growing economic interdependence between the United States and China, or we have to change our domestic patterns of consumption that create our dependency on foreign sources of energy and on inexpensive consumer goods from Chinese sources.

Barry Lynn made a cogent observation about the U.S.-China relationship in the Winter 2005/06 issue of *The National Interest:* "The two nations share absolutely no political framework in which to manage a deeply interdependent economic relationship." One of the recurring themes of our discussion was that a course of action that makes perfect sense from a macroeconomic standpoint may at the same time be highly undesirable from a foreign policy perspective. Currently we have an unbalanced relationship, which cannot be sustained indefinitely.

We have a mindset that conflates competition with hostility. In "going global", Beijing is signaling that it intends to compete, for markets, for resources, for influence, not simply in East Asia, but around the world, including in our own backyard of Latin America and in the United States itself. Will we be able to duplicate the success of the post-1895, Anglo-American rapprochement with China in this century? Or will China become the equivalent of Wilhelmine Germany, seeking its place in the sun? Much depends on whether America's politicians are prepared to lead, to make the case for a Sino-American *modus vivendi.*

FAREED ZAKARIA is editor of *Newsweek International* and host of the public-television show *Foreign Exchange.*

NIKOLAS K. GVOSDEV is editor of *The National Interest.*

China as No. 1

Bush wants freedom everywhere. But the world's biggest dictatorship is now one of America's biggest creditors. Guess who has the leverage on whom?

CLYDE PRESTOWITZ

In the 15th century, Venice was one of the world's richest cities and ranked among the great powers because its navy controlled the Mediterranean and its merchants controlled the trade in goods, especially spices. Then Portuguese Captain Vasco da Gama arrived in India in 1498. By 1515, the Portuguese controlled the Straits of Hormuz, the Indian Ocean, the Moluccas (or Spice Islands), and the trade with China. The spices, gems, and silks that for centuries had passed from Asia through the Middle East to Venice and then to the rest of Europe were now carried around Africa on Portuguese caravels. The Egyptian sultans had been able to keep the price of pepper for Europe very high by limiting shipments to 210 tons annually. With the Portuguese in the game, the price of pepper in Lisbon dropped swiftly to one-fifth the price in Venice. The Egyptian-Venetian trade was destroyed overnight, and Portugal knocked Venice out of the ranks of the great powers without firing a shot.

That history came to mind during President Bush's recent inaugural address. His assumptions of indefinite American hegemony were quite at odds with what I have been seeing on recent trips to Asia, and especially to China.

In Singapore, high officials describe the recent rise of China as akin to the arrival of a new sun in the solar system. All over Asia, one hears talk of a shift, not in the balance of power but in the "balance of influence." In a poll asking Thais which nation they considered their country's closest ally, the response was 75 percent for China against 9 percent for the United States. In the Philippines, pop stars from China have risen to the top of the ratings. Filipino businessman John Gokongwei says, "China isn't interested in military expansion. It will seek tribute through trade, like it did before the Western powers came to Asia."

During a recent trip to Australia to meet with business, government, academic, and media leaders, I was told repeatedly that America must not ask Australians to choose between the United States and China. Two years before, President Bush traveled Down Under only to be followed within a week by Chinese President Hu Jintao. Whereas Bush stayed only a couple of days, held no press conferences, and got a distinctly cool reception, Hu kissed babies, toured the country, and was treated like a conquering hero.

Go to Newman in Australia's big-sky country. There you can watch as the front-end loaders take big bites out of the 60-foot walls of iron ore in the open strip mines and load the trains that will take the ore on the first leg of its trip to China. Or just drive north of the U.S. border to Alberta, Canada, where provincial officials are deep in negotiations to strike large deals giving China access to Canadian oil reserves previously destined exclusively for the U.S. market. Brazil, South Korea, and even Japan all now export more to China than to the United States. After more than 20 years of rapid growth, the Chinese economy has become the world's second-largest behind the United States in terms of purchasing power parity.

No one wants to alienate a good customer. And China is quite simply becoming everyone's best customer. Well, almost everyone's.

In contrast to many other countries, the United States has seen its exports to China increase only modestly in recent years while its imports have gone off the chart. Last year China passed Mexico and Japan to become the second-largest exporter to the U.S. market after Canada. Because Canada also buys a lot from U.S. suppliers, however, China now has by far the largest trade surplus ($1150 billion) with the United States that any country has ever had. Behind this statistic lie several powerful new forces.

First, China has become the location of choice for global manufacturing. This is usually attributed to its low wages. Chinese factory workers today earn 50 cents to $2 an hour and often work long shifts, getting minimal time off for weekends and holidays. But low wages are not the only factor; after all, wages in places like Vietnam, Myanmar, and Africa are even lower. China's workers are not just inexpensive but literate, hard working, already reasonably skilled, and eager—nay, desperate—to be trained. There is also a sizable and growing cadre of university-educated technologists and professionals. For example, China is now graduating 330,000 engineers and scientists annually, as compared with 398,622 for the United States. China has also invested extensively in infrastructure and now has a very workable system of airports, harbors, communications, and roads. Indeed, your mobile phone will work a lot better in China than in the United States, and you'll get from the airport to downtown in Shanghai a lot faster than in any major U.S. city.

Today, China is already the largest market in the world for steel, mobile phones, cement, aluminum, and electronic components. Within 20 years, it will likely be the largest market in the world for just about everything. If you are a manufacturer, you will pretty much have to succeed in the China market to have a chance of surviving anywhere else. In theory, you can serve the China market by exporting, but there are some good reasons why you might not. Because Chinese labor is inexpensive, production processes that are capital-intensive in the advanced countries can be "dumbed down" and made much less capital-intensive in China. As a manufacturer, you cut both your wage and your investment costs. On top of that, the Chinese government at local, provincial, and national levels will offer substantial investment incentives—such as long tax holidays, capital grants, free land, low utility rates, worker training, and other benefits—to companies willing to put plants and research-and-development facilities in China.

These investment incentives confound free-trade theory. They are, in fact, distortions of the market, and therefore of questionable legitimacy under the rules of the World Trade Organization. This has never been challenged because other countries have investment subsidies, too. (American states offer tax deals to induce companies to invest.) China, however, subsidizes investment strategically to capture new industries at higher levels than anyone else.

China is a symptom and a cause of America's vulnerability. Our retailers depend on China, our high-tech companies cede important know-how, and our debt depends on Chinese financing.

But why is the United States the outlier when it comes to China trade? Why isn't every nation running a large trade deficit with the Chinese? Commodity suppliers like Australia, Brazil, and Chile, of course, have trade surpluses with China because China needs their materials. But what of Japan, Korea, Taiwan, and the European nations? Their industries are also locating plants in China. But there are mitigating circumstances. A big one is that these countries have maintained a broader, more robust manufacturing base than the United States. One of America's biggest exports to China and the rest of Asia is waste paper. Germany exports high-speed trains, specialty steels, and machine tools. In addition to these, Japan exports loads of electronic components and ships. America long ago gave up making any of this stuff.

A second factor is differing business and government attitudes. Japanese executives, for example, make a point of saying that they "keep the brain work in Japan." Indeed, Canon has publicly stated that it is bringing formerly outsourced work back to Japan in order to keep key technologies proprietary in Japan. Some European companies take a similar attitude. But given the shareholder-as-king basis of U.S. business, this is a very difficult position for U.S. executives to take. Nor are there government policies to maintain U.S. advantage; it is assumed that American genius and free markets will automatically result in U.S. leadership. If the Chinese are foolish enough to exchange low-priced consumer goods for cheap U.S. paper, let the party continue.

That brings us to the 800-pound gorilla of the story—the dollar. It is, of course, the world's money. As such, it allows Americans to buy things in international markets simply by printing green pictures of presidents and exchanging them for real goods and services. Unlike others who have to make and sell something to earn dollars with which to buy oil or soybeans or whatever, the Americans only have to run the printing presses.

In the short run, the U.S. budget and trade deficits can be financed at unprecedented levels by the foreigners who lend us money. The U.S. trade deficit is exacerbated by the fact that China keeps its currency artificially low to promote exports. But because the United States needs a net inflow from abroad of about $2 billion every day to keep itself afloat, it doesn't seriously complain. Worse, the U.S. government actually likes a strong dollar, to keep the price of imported goods and the cost of borrowing low. Of course, such a dollar absolutely kills the export and manufacturing industries, but it makes consumers and the government feel very good, so the government doesn't want to do anything that might interrupt the flow of that foreign capital. Besides, to do so could throw the U.S. economy into a nasty recession, if not a depression. Obviously, this cannot continue indefinitely.

The second-biggest lender to the United States after Japan is China. Those who think this dependence has no diplomatic consequences are naive. For more than 50 years, American policy was to keep China out of the Korean Peninsula. Today, the U.S. government has outsourced the handling of North Korea to Beijing. When Chinese Prime Minister Wen Jiabao came recently to Washington, American supporters of Taiwan were shocked and disappointed by his warning to the Taiwanese against any deviation from the long-standing "one China" formulation. American trade officials who ask Beijing to offer more protection for U.S. intellectual property, or to revalue its currency, are politely rebuffed.

The United States has lost substantial leverage with China, along with our loss of manufacturing industry and dependence on Chinese loans. China is both symptom and cause of America's dwindling economic leadership. This loss has geopolitical consequences far beyond our relations with Beijing, and it mocks Bush's hegemonic grand design. At this rate, we risk becoming the Venice of the 21st century.

CLYDE PRESTOWITZ is president of the Economic Strategy Institute and author of the forthcoming *3 Billion New Capitalists*.

New Ripples and Responses to China's Water Woes

Jennifer L. Turner

China's environmental problems are increasingly in the international limelight, as reports of the country's mounting pollutants and stories of the choking air in major Chinese cities have made their way into newspapers throughout the world. The most serious of these challenges have been linked to the country's dwindling water supply, which not only suffers from considerable pollutants, but also is insufficient for the country's rapidly growing economy and its massive population. While the Chinese government has finally recognized the seriousness of these environmental issues and has even begun to address them through various top-down efforts, its responses remain hampered by the local government's protectionism of its polluting industries as well as the crippling weakness of the State Environmental Protection Administration (SEPA). Furthermore, even as grassroots environmental efforts have grown during the last decade and have had notable successes in combating environmental woes, they are still viewed with suspicion by the government and are even sporadically harassed. If China is to combat its environmental challenges successfully, it must provide for stronger environmental regulations and enforcements as well as empower grassroots environmental efforts.

Black Rivers and a Growing Health Crisis

China's pollution trends are sobering, threatening economic growth, human health and watershed ecosystems. Urban and rural areas are both facing equally serious water pollution problems. Urban inhabitants in China draw 70% of their drinking water from groundwater sources. Between 50% and 90% of urban groundwater, however, is contaminated by agricultural runoff, industrial and municipal wastewater and in some municipalities, even toxic mine tailings. In rural areas, 700 million citizens lack access to safe water. Besides agricultural runoff and pollutants from small and medium industries, a large (and perhaps now the largest) source of water pollution is from ani-

mal factory farms, better known as confined animal feeding operations (CAFOs). Today, China's CAFOs produce a total of 2.7 billion tons of livestock manure annually; 3.4 times the industrial solid waste generated nationwide (*China Watch*, December 12).

Another relatively unknown type of water pollution is occurring in karst landscape areas of southwest China. Karst landscapes—where much of the water flows underground through caves rather than at the surface—have shallow and porous bedrock, which means surface pollutants are easily able to contaminate the underground rivers, upon which millions of poor farmers depend. Water quality of rivers flowing above ground is likewise severely degraded by pollution, with nearly 50% running black at grade 5 (not suitable for agriculture or industry). Since 2002, approximately 63 billion tons of wastewater flow into China's rivers each year, of which 62% are pollutants from industrial sources, and 38% are poorly treated or raw sewage from municipalities [1].

Rivers in China are also increasingly degraded by the growing frequency of chemical spills. In November 2005, an explosion occurred at a PetroChina chemical plant in Jilin Province that released over a hundred tons of benzene into the Songhua River. The enormous benzene slick then flowed through the Heilongjiang Provinces' capital Harbin and into Russia. A mere three months after the Songhua benzene accident, a plant in Sichuan Province spilled toxins into the upper reaches of the Yuexi River, disrupting the water supply of 20,000 people in the city of Yibin. In early 2006, SEPA released a survey, revealing that over half of China's 21,000 chemical plants are located along the Yellow and Yangtze rivers (*China Watch*, February 23). Few of these plants have conducted the required environmental impact assessments and almost all are weakly regulated.

Such widespread pollution to China's water supplies has resulted in troubling social and economic repercussions. Anecdotal evidence reported by Chinese and international news media, Chinese water non-governmental organizations (NGOs) and—albeit rarely—the Ministry of Health points to a disturbing trend of higher than normal rates of tumors, cancer, spontaneous abortions and diminished IQs among populations living near polluted rivers and lakes. Water pollution is also causing agricultural losses, sparking protests against industries by farmers who have lost the use of land and water and cannot sell their "toxic" crops. The Chinese government admitted that 50,000 environmental-related protests occurred in 2005, many of which were most likely related to water degradation.

Water Scarcity—Eco-refugees and Thirsty Cities

Water scarcity is also a growing crisis, exacerbating the severe water pollution problems throughout China. China's annual per capita water supply is a quarter of the global average and is even lower in China's arid north. While agriculture still consumes nearly 70% of water resources in China, water consumption in industrial and domestic sectors has been quickly rising, and none of these sectors uses water efficiently [2]. In 2002, the amount of water used for every $10,000 worth of GDP in China was 537 m³, four times the world's average and nearly 20 times that of Japan and Europe (*Economic Daily*, August 8, 2005).

China's booming demand for water and lack of conservation are accelerating the depletion of its water resources, particularly in the dry north where grain production accounts for more than 45% of China's GDP [3]. In northern and western China, the overdrafting of water and land degradation has caused desertification to advance at an annual rate of 1,300 square miles, affecting 400 million people (*China Daily*, July 1, 2002). The economic impact of this desertification in China's breadbasket is growing, as is the human suffering from the loss of homes and livelihoods. For example, 24,000 villages in northern and western China have been abandoned or partially depopulated due to growing desertification [4]. Continued desertification will exacerbate rural migration into cities as well as increase the severity of the spring sandstorms [5]. While most severe in the north, water scarcity has become a major obstacle to sustainable development throughout the country. Besides human suffering from water shortages, river ecosystems have also been damaged from excessive withdrawals. Most alarming has been the damage to the Yellow River, which, since the mid-1990s, often does not flow to the ocean for up to 200 days a year [6].

Yet, rather than emphasizing water conservation, increasing the country's water supply through major dam and water diversion projects continues to be a cornerstone of Beijing's response to the water shortage. Shortly after China was awarded the 2008 Olympics, the government finalized a decision to begin construction on the South-North Water Transfer project—three canals that will bring water from the Yangtze River to quench the thirst of the arid north and ensure Beijing sufficient water for the Games. Part of the rationale for damming the stunning Tiger Leaping Gorge, one of the more than 200 dams planned in southwest China, is to divert its reservoir water to Lake Dianchi in Kunming, the capital of Yunnan, to dilute its pollution problems. These enormous water transfer and dam projects are costly—in terms of money, loss of agricultural land, ecological damage and hardships on relocated people—and increasingly spark protests by unwilling relocatees.

Top-down Responses to the Water Crises

The Chinese central government has recognized and is beginning to address the serious threats that water degradation and river mismanagement are posing to the economy, human health and—of perpetual concern—social stability. The government has been adopting new laws, such as the Environmental Impact Assessment (EIA) Law, and updating old ones to strengthen water pollution enforcement (*China Brief*, November 22). The strengthening of such top-down water protection measures is critical for reforming the water management laws and institutions and improving the water pollution prevention infrastructure. To stem the growing threats of industrial pollution emissions and spills, in July, SEPA announced it would tighten the supervision of polluting industries and wastewater emissions affecting major drinking water sources. In addition, the central government is revising its national standards on drinking water quality, catalyzing collaboration among SEPA, the Standardization Administration and the ministries of construction and health. The new standards will increase the number of pollutants tested from the current amount of 35 to 107 (*China Watch*, August 3). Water shortages, primarily in northern China, have also served as the catalyst for attempts to reform the existing river basin commissions responsible for the management of the country's seven main rivers. Water protection has been increasingly prioritized with ambitious goals for river clean ups in the 10th and 11th Five-Year Plans.

Many such water protection investments and targets, however, fell short in the 10th Five-Year Plan, and expensive supply-side management projects still dominate as the primary solution to water shortages. Years of major central government investments and campaigns to protect shallow lakes suffering from serious eutrophication (e.g., Dianchi, Chaohu and Taihu) or toxic rivers (e.g., Huai River) have done little to mitigate the pollution and nutrient runoff that have turned them into nearly dead watersheds. The Huai River is the poster child of China's failing environmental governance system. Despite a decade-long central government campaign that began in 1993 to clean up the river, it is still one of the most polluted in China and citizens in the basin suffer from significantly higher rates of cancer as well as other health problems. The failures of this campaign and many of the other ambitious pollution prevention laws stem largely from the difficulties in pressuring local governments to regulate the very industries that prop up the local economy. Attempts at compelling local governments to enforce environmental laws by linking "green GDP"—economic growth and improvements in environmental quality—to individual promotions have failed. Moreover, local governments have pushed for limits on the ability of lawyers to bring class action lawsuits, which have become relatively successful in recent years in punishing polluting industries.

Grassroots Efforts—China's Water Warriors

Acknowledging their inability to enforce environmental laws at the local level, central government officials have permitted the growth of "green" NGOs beginning with the passage of a registration system in 1994. Already the largest sector of China's civil society, green NGOs spent their first decade of development focused on relatively "safe" issues, such as environmental education and animal protection issues. Yet, the growing seriousness of water degradation and the threats to river ecosystems have catalyzed a number of Chinese NGOs and even individual citizens to become "water warriors," pursuing more aggressive activities and empowering citizens through existing environmental laws. For instance, Yu Xiaogang, the director of Green Watershed in Yunnan and the winner of the prestigious Goldman Environmental Prize in 2006, brought villagers from the Nu basin to visit villages at the Manwan and Xiaowan dams, enabling them to see first-hand the detrimental effects of dam building (*China Brief*, November 22). In addition, Yu also assisted the villagers in understanding their rights in demanding input into environmental impact assessments and greater transparency in dam building projects. Likewise, Zhang Changjian, a local doctor in Xiping Village in Fujian Province, with assistance from the Beijing NGO Center for Legal Assistance to Pollution Victims, successfully sued the Rongping chemical plant, China's largest chlorate manufacturer, forcing it to compensate villagers for health and environmental damages.

China's green NGOs have also successfully pushed to make more environmental information accessible to the public, a remarkable achievement for a society whose access to information is often restricted. For example, the Institute of Public and Environmental Affairs, a Beijing-based environmental organization directed by a long-term water researcher and activist Ma Jun, launched China's first online public database of water pollution. This digital water pollution map enables Internet users to survey water quality and monitor pollution discharges. While this database represents a significant step toward information transparency, it requires more extensive data inputs and cooperation from other environmental NGOs (*China Watch*, September 26). The creation of such information-sharing platforms has begun to yield tangible results in the forms of media coverage and government action. Based on the health surveys of over 100 villages in the Huai River basin conducted by the Huai River Protectors, Chinese news media, including the state-owned CCTV, have reported on the abnormally high cancer rates in the villages, most likely caused by the extensive pollution of the Huai River. Such news reports have forced local governments to invest in the drilling of deep wells to supply safe and clean water for its villagers.

While the central leadership has tolerated the creation of green groups to help implement and monitor environmental laws, there are instances when environmental NGOs, lawyers and citizens tackling pollution issues have been subjected to major backlash or harassment from local governments or industries. Over the past two years, even the central leadership has become concerned with what it perceives as excessive social activism. This wariness stems from the growing number of protests throughout China on a wide range of issues, such as land grabs, corruption and pollution. In addition to the external constraints, green NGOs in China are also hampered by certain internal shortcomings that threaten their sustainability in the long run, including an overdependence on foreign assistance, the lack of internal transparency and a high turnover in staff due to low paying positions.

Closing Thoughts

China's severe water pollution, shortages and watershed destruction contribute to population movements, health risks, food security problems and rising income disparities. These problems raise humanitarian concerns and have the potential to affect China's economic, political and social stability. In order to strengthen the environmental governance system for water protection, the Chinese government must find ways to drastically improve law enforcement at the local level, which demands not only better regulations but also the true empowerment of NGOs and citizens to become even more effective watchdogs. Recent moves to limit the ability of the media to report on pollution accidents, discourage class action cases and intimidate NGOs are regrettable steps backwards. China's watersheds and citizens cannot wait too long for the needed political reforms.

Notes

1. U.S. Department of Commerce, International Trade Administration, 2005 *Water Supply and Wastewater Treatment Market in China*, Washington, DC.

2. For example, only 43% of the water consumed in agriculture is used efficiently for irrigation, compared to 70% to 80% in developed countries. See U.S. Embassy in Beijing, *China's Water Supply Problems*, 2003, available at http://www.usembassy-china.org.cn/sandt/ptr/water-supply-prt.htm. Chinese urbanites have increased their per capita daily water consumption about 150% between 1980 and 2000—from less than 100 liters in 1980 to 244 liters in 2000. At least 20% of the water supplies to cities are lost through leaky pipes, so this official per capita consumption figure underestimates total urban water use. See Dabo Guan and Klaus Hubacek. (2004). "Lifestyle Changes and its Influences on Energy and Water Consumption in China," Proceedings of the 6th Conference for postgraduate students, young scientists and researchers on Environmental Economics, Policy and International Environmental Relations, Prague (October 7–8), p. 389. Guan Xiaofeng. (2005). "Water Crisis Needs Urgent Solutions," *China Daily*, November 1, available online at http://www.chinadaily.com.cn/english/doc/2005-11/01/content_489327.htm.

3. Lohmar, Bryan, Jinxia Wang, Scott Rozelle, Jikun Huang, and David Dawe, *China's Agricultural Water Policy Reforms: Increasing Investment, Resolving Conflicts, and Revising Incentives*, 2003. Economic Research Service Agriculture Information Bulletin Number 782. (Washington, DC: United States Department of Agriculture), p. 3.

4. Lester Brown, *Outgrowing the Earth: The Food Security Challenge in an Age of Falling Water Tables and Rising Temperatures* (New York: W.W. Norton & Company, 2005).

5. 100 sandstorms are expected between 2000 and 2009, a marked increase over the 23 in the previous decade (*Geotimes*, October 18–21, 2005). The impact of these sandstorms extends well beyond China's borders to Korea, and Japan, and the U.S. west coast.

6. Wang Yahua, "River Governance Structure in China: A Study of Water Quantity/Quality Management Regimes," 2005. In *Promoting Sustainable River Basin Governance: Crafting Japan-U.S. Water Partnerships in China*, IDE Spot Survey No. 28, Jennifer L. Turner and Kenji Otsuka (Ed.), (Chiba, Japan: Institute of Developing Economies/IDE-Jetro, 2005), p. 23–36.

DR. JENNIFER L. TURNER has directed the China Environment Forum at the Woodrow Wilson International Center for Scholars since 1999. In addition to editing the yearly publication, the *China Environment Series* (www.wilsoncenter.org/cef), she has recently begun a new China Environmental Health project with Western Kentucky University, focusing on health challenges in karst water regions and coal emissions in Atthui Province.

Article 23

Perpetual Challenges to China's Education Reform

WILLY LAM

A recent talk by Premier Wen Jiabao illustrates Beijing's failure to undertake comprehensive reforms in perhaps the most critical area of Chinese life: education. While meeting with several university presidents, Wen recalled a discussion that he had with Qian Xuesen, the revered "Father of the Chinese A-Bomb," during which Qian complained that "China still has not fully developed." The scientist cited the fact that "Chinese universities have failed to produce distinguished talent," adding, "None of China's universities have adopted a model [that is geared toward] propagating creative and innovative minds" (Xinhua, November 27). China's Minister of Education Zhou Ji has also been forthcoming about the nation's inability to propagate first-class research. Zhou, who holds a Ph.D. from a U.S. institution, pointed out that the results of scientific research as well as other pursuits in institutions of higher education "can neither touch the sky nor [are they] down to earth." China's research, he explained, falls woefully short of international standards; it is incapable of producing market-oriented products that can be of benefit to people's everyday needs (China Youth Daily, December 3). Zhou also deplored the fact that the morality and integrity of a sizeable number of professors and researchers have been called into question. Last month, the Ministry of Science and Technology, a major source of funding for high-level research, published a tough regulation that targeted plagiarism and other infractions of academic ethical standards (Xinhua, November 9).

In theory, China's spending on advanced research and development (R&D) as well as general education has risen in tandem with the fast-paced growth of the economy. According to the State Council's long-term plans, government outlay on research R&D is due to make up 2.5% of GDP by the year 2020, by which time some 900 billion yuan (US$115 billion) will be spent every year on advanced research. Currently, more than 23 million students are enrolled in China's institutes of higher learning; and 21% of those who take part in college entrance examinations are allotted slots in its universities. The government even claims that China has "the world's biggest pool of technological personnel," around 32 million people. Of these, 1.05 million are engineers and scientists whom the authorities have classified as "R&D specialists" (People's Daily, January 31; Xinhua, November 27).

Moreover, it would be misleading to say that, despite Professor Qian and Minister Zhou's unusual frankness about the shortcomings in academia, there has been little progress on the higher education and research fronts. Chinese scientists and engineers boast what some cadres have termed "innate superiorities," that is, qualities that are part of the socialist system. Thanks to the abilities of the government, academic and industrial units to quickly pool human as well as financial resources, astonishing results have been produced in gargantuan projects that require large-scale mobilization. Examples of these remarkable successes include the country's state-of-the-art space program, genetic engineering projects and the domestic development of sophisticated weaponry. Last week, a group of researchers who represented 20-odd top medical and herbal-medicine institutes announced that they had produced new and more effective AIDS-treatment drugs.

It is nonetheless true that across the board, the standard of China's higher education in fields ranging from molecular physics to political science remains dissatisfactory. The biggest shortfalls are found in areas that require plenty of individual initiative, creativity and the ability to challenge established authority. 27 years after Deng Xiaoping began his reforms and open-door policy, academic institutions still encourage conformity and frown on potentially heretical—and politically incorrect—experimentation. All colleges and research institutes are governed by CCP committees, whose chief functions include the weeding out of "dangerous ideas" as well as "anti-party elements" from within academia. This stultifying atmosphere has spread to fields supposedly less prone to political controversy, such as the physical sciences and technology.

The crisis of confidence in China's education system came to a head last year after several Chinese newspapers and websites printed the harsh criticisms that Harvard mathematician

Yau Shing-tung leveled at Chinese universities and research institutes. Professor Yau noted that despite the increased levels of funding and much-improved facilities, the standards of research in China have continued to deteriorate. "Many professors of famous universities spend the bulk of their time making money—or trying to boost their reputation overseas," he told the Chinese media. Yau added that bureaucrats and apparatchiks still maintain a significant amount of authority in allocating research funds and deciding which academics would receive promotion. In the meantime, corrupt phenomena, such as plagiarism, have mushroomed, and Yau predicted a further decline in standards unless dramatic remedial steps were adopted (http://www.edu.cn website, August 19, 2005).

The time-honored tendency of Chinese scholars of all specialties to toe the party line has paradoxically been reinforced by the current leadership's penchant for seeking the views of a large number of academics and specialists. President Hu Jintao, Premier Wen and quite a few Politburo members maintain large think tanks, many of whose members come from academia. Once they have been consulted by top party and government leaders, however, China's scholars often believe they have an obligation to at least refrain from criticizing these cadres or their policies. According to well-known writer Yu Jie, Chinese intellectuals have yet to shed the age-old tradition of relying upon the established authority for recognition and sustenance. "Most scholars will think twice about engaging in research deemed politically suspect," Yu added [1].

Reflecting the massive disparities between rich and poor—as well as between the wealthy coastal regions and the impoverished hinterland—"First World-standard" educational and research opportunities are only available in several universities and cities, such as Beijing, Shanghai, Nanjing and Guangzhou, in addition to the military-run institutes. Moreover, education has become so expensive that students from ordinary families are self-selected against enrollment. College tuition has soared 25 times in 20 years, and if living expenses are included, an average university student is required to pay 40,000 yuan ($5,000) a year just to cover basic bills. The annual per capita income for rural Chinese, however, is less than 3,000 yuan ($380) (Xinhua, March 7). Even more shocking is the fact that in the vast central and western provinces, most schools lack well-qualified teachers and up-to-date course material.

Despite the Hu-Wen administration's rhetoric about "putting people first" and "giving priority to rural areas," high-quality basic-level education is not available in the 11 western provinces. Premier Wen has not hidden the fact that in quite a number of poor counties, a free nine-year education, which is guaranteed by the constitution, is far from being instituted. Many impoverished villages rely on donations from foreign countries in addition to the wealthier provinces, such as Guangdong, to keep their poorly equipped schools running.

Educators were recently shocked by a scandal in Minqin County, Gansu Province, where authorities mobilized 40,000 secondary- and primary-schoolchildren to collect the season's cotton crop. One student died when a tractor driven by his classmate accidentally rolled over him. Yet, despite the number of brutal accidents, it is not uncommon for administrators in poor, remote areas to ask students to "contribute to the common good" by spending several hours a week working in factories, including those that lack proper industrial-safety standards. Moreover, given the near-universal gender discrimination, it is routine for rural families to keep their girls at home, rather than send them to school. Minister Zhou admits that in particularly impoverished villages, the dropout rate in junior high schools can be as high as 10% (Lanzhou Morning Post, December 1; Xinhua, April 27).

In a special measure designed to assist rural regions, the State Council decided earlier this year to launch a campaign to "encourage" up to 10,000 college graduates a year to teach in remote, countryside schools. As an incentive, the Education and Finance Ministries have guaranteed them an annual salary of at least 15,000 yuan ($1,900), which is on par with what university graduates earn in the larger cities (Xinhua, May 19). Given that the future of China hinges on the competitiveness of its scientists, engineers and workers, few doubt the eagerness of the party and state officials to boost the standards of its schools and universities. Yet, instead of relying on stop-gap measures such as "special funding" for various emergency projects, it is imperative that top cadres such as Premier Wen tackle the crux of the matter: de-linking education from the country's orthodox socialist system.

Note

1. Personal communications with the author.

The Development of Environmental NGOs in China
A Road to Civil Society?

NAMJU LEE

There has been an upsurge of environmental movements in China over the past several years. During the spring of 2005, environmentalists staged a series of protests that eventually halted a construction project in Yuanmingyuan. Just one year earlier, Green Peace China prevented the Asian Pulp & Paper Company from illegally deforesting the Yunnan Province. Yet perhaps the most notable of these demonstrations were those undertaken to protect the Nu River from the construction of mega dams, which activists claimed would threaten the Three Parallel Rivers World Heritage Site in Yunnan Province. The State Development and Reform Commission had approved of the dam construction plans prepared by the Huadian Corporation and the local government in August 2003, in spite of the fact that just one month before, the area had been designated a World Natural Heritage Site. Under pressure from Chinese environmental non-governmental organizations (NGOs) and the international community, however, Premier Wen Jiabao suspended the original project in February 2004 with the instructions to "Study Carefully, Decide Scientifically."

These movements distinguish themselves from other patterns of resistance in contemporary China in two ways. Unlike the "unauthorized" protests that have often been brutally suppressed by the government, many of these efforts have been relatively successful in influencing government policies. More importantly, the NGOs, which emerged after the mid-1990s, have played a pivotal role in leading and organizing these environmental movements. As a result, 2004 has been dubbed by the media as "Year One of the NGO Era" (*NGO Yuannian*). According to the Development Situation Report on China's Civil Environmental Organizations (*zhongguo huanbao minjia zuzhi fazhan zhuangkuang*) released by the Government Organized Non-Governmental Organization (GONGO) All China Environmental Federation (*zhonghua huanbao lianhehui*) in April 2006, the total number of "Civil Environmental Organizations" amounted to 2,768. Of these organizations, government-initiated groups and student clubs accounted for 49.9% and 40.3%, respectively, while civil-initiated organizations and international NGOs, which are eligible to be categorized as NGOs, accounted for 7.2% and 2.6% [1]. Although civil-initiated organizations and international NGOs remain in the minority, they are nevertheless significant given that there were only a handful of NGOs just a decade before.

The Development of NGOs

The tremendous growth in the number of NGOs can be accounted for primarily by the need to facilitate the interactions between the state and society. Up until recently, the state-centered approach (e.g., state corporatism), which placed a priority on the state's ability to maintain control over society, possessed the upper hand in the ongoing debates regarding the relationship between state and society in China. Yet, beginning in the late 1990s, the society-centered approach gained currency, as it became clear that a number of the social problems and conflicts were often beyond the grasp of the state. Last year, for instance, Public Security Minister Zhou Yongkang noted that the number of "mass incidents"—including protests, riots and mass petitions—had risen by 28% in 2004 to 74,000; only 10,000 such cases had been reported a decade before (*South China Morning Post*, February 8).

In light of the growing domestic turbulence, the state has begun to acknowledge its need to collaborate with "healthy" social forces to maintain stability. For example, "The Guideline for the Development of Charities (2006–2010)" emphasizes the potential for charitable civil organizations to plug gaps in the development of a state social welfare system (China Development Brief, December 2005/January 2006). Nevertheless, the state remains caught between contradictory views. On the one hand, there is the view that fostering a charitable sector within society could reduce the government's burden. Yet, there is also a fear that the growth of independent environmental groups promoting an agenda separate from that of the government could eventually erode the political monopoly of the Chinese Communist Party (CCP) and therefore should be suppressed.

While the development of NGOs in China has certainly been facilitated by the shift in the state's attitude toward social organizations, much of the progress has largely been the result of the activists' strategic decision to use NGOs as an instrument in promoting social and political progress while avoiding direct challenges to the state. Some NGO activists see the activities of NGOs as a platform for political and social progress. One NGO activist whom this author interviewed in 2003 pointed out the impact that the 1995 Fourth UN Conference on Women in Beijing had on the development of NGOs in China. Beijing had applied for this conference primarily to increase its influence in the international arena. Yet, during the conference, the criticism that the international NGOs lodged against the Chinese government's policies, such as its coercive birth control program, drew far more attention than any of the conference's other events. Many of the Chinese participants discovered the potential of using NGOs to develop and strengthen civil society, while avoiding an outright challenge to the government. It is, therefore, no accident that a number of the important NGOs emerged and developed after the 1995 UN Conference, such as Friends of Nature (1995), Green Village in Beijing (1996) and Center for Legal Assistance to Pollution Victims (1998).

A number of changes in China's environmental policy have particularly accelerated the development of environmental NGOs. Since 2003, new policies highlighting the necessity to harmonize economic development with the protection of the environment have been adopted by Wen and President Hu Jintao, such as "scientific development" and a "harmonious society," which in turn have strengthened the legitimacy of the environmental movement. The State Environment Protection Administration (SEPA) has also been a supporter of the environmental movement, and its vice director, Fanyue, was quoted more than once declaring that the SEPA and NGOs are natural friends. Moreover, a number of significant environmental laws have been enacted in recent years. For instance, the September 1, 2003 Environmental Impact Assessment (EIA) Law requires that comprehensive environmental reviews be undertaken during the planning stages of major public and private development projects. The Provisional Rule for Public Participation in Environmental Impact Assessment, enacted on March 17, requires the government to provide the public with open information and to hold public hearings over issues that may affect the people. Against this backdrop, the amount of collaboration between the government and NGOs has increased, particularly on the subject of environmental issues. The government-NGO cooperation peaked when 56 environmental NGOs published a letter supporting SEPA's decision to suspend 30 construction projects on the charges of violating the EIA law in January 2005.

Promoting Civil Rights through the Environmental Movement

It is interesting to note that rather than dealing solely with ecological issues, the environmental movement in China has increasingly incorporated the issue of civil rights into its arguments. The aforementioned case of the Nu River movement demonstrates this point clearly. In the beginning, the opposition to the dam project was largely based on the necessity to conserve the natural environment around the Nu River and the fact that it was a part of the Three Parallel Rivers World Heritage Site. As debates proceeded, however, environmentalists realized that the rationale of natural conservation alone could not prevail against the argument of economic development, which implied improved conditions for the poor peasants residing near the Nu River. Those supporting the construction of the dam accused the environmentalists of ignoring the people's needs for economic development and of focusing exclusively on nature.

The stalemate was broken when the environmentalists introduced the concerns of the local people. Citing examples of previous dam projects, the environmentalists argued that the construction of the dam would actually exacerbate the condition of the local residents. Professor Zhou Tianyong at the Central Party School, for instance, discovered that residents in China's western Qinghai province had an average net income of 1,772 yuan (US$220) per head in 2004—about half the national average—despite the 50 billion yuan ($6.2 billion) project to build 13 hydropower dams along the Yellow River. In addition, he found that the loss of land and roads from the dams left many even poorer after the construction was completed (*Jingjicankaobao*, February 15).

In April 2004, Yu Xiaogang, a founder of the NGO Green Watershed in Yunnan Province, took peasants to the site of Manwan Dam where most of the rural residents were barely managing to make ends meet since the construction of the dam in 1993. The peasants were shocked by how the government had made promises, yet had not followed through (*The New York Times*, December 27, 2005). In October 2004, Yu led a small group of peasants to a Beijing hydropower conference jointly sponsored by the UN and China's National Development and Reform Commission. They held a press conference to claim their rights to information, participation and decision-making. Along with a riot in Hanyuan, Sichuan Province in October 2004 caused by the Baopu dam project, the environmentalists' activities led the government to increase the amount of compensation provided in cases of expropriation. Environmental activists have also staunchly supported the right of the public to participate in governmental affairs. In the 2005 Yuanmingyuan case demand for "public participation in decision-making" became very salient and even forced a public hearing to be held in April 2005. On August 25, 2005, an open letter signed by 66 NGOs and 99 individuals was sent to the government, demanding that the environmental assessment report on Nu River dams be made public according to related laws.

The Future of NGOs in China

The prospects of the environmental movement and civil and political progress are not always promising in China, as many NGOs must selectively choose their battles in order to prevent themselves from being shut down. For instance, China's environmental NGOs were not willing to involve themselves in the Songhua river debacle in November 2005. According to an editorial published in the China Development Brief, the primary reason for their refrain was their fear of a governmental backlash, similar to Beijing's heightened scrutiny of NGOs in 2005 following the "color revolutions" in Central Asia and Eastern Europe (China Development Brief, March 2006). The Songhua incident reveals the true limits of autonomy for the "Green NGOs."

In spite of these challenges, there are a number of promising signs for the development of NGOs and civil society. NGOs have demonstrated a willingness to oppose the local and even provincial governments, exploiting differences between state apparatuses. Moreover, NGOs have developed autonomous networks throughout China and continue to organize coordinated activities such as joint signature gatherings. Although these may not be purely collective actions, they would have been unthinkable only a few years before. These autonomous NGO networks have also increased the profile of other civil rights issues. NGOs, though nascent, are already having an impact on the Chinese society and are only likely to increase the dialogue and action on political, civil and environmental problems.

Note

1. The Development Situation Report on China's Civil Environmental Organization is available online at: http://www.acef.com.cn/ngo. asp?productSort=490.

Dr. Namju Lee is a visting scholar at Harvard University's Fairbank Center for East Asian Research and an associate professor in the department of Chinese Studies at Sungkonghoe University in South Korea.

The "Latin-Americanization" of China's Domestic Politics

WILLY LAM

The good news is that the Chinese Communist Party (CCP) has finally recognized the need to rein in the exploitative practices of the "new classes" in Chinese society. The theme of the recently concluded plenary session of the CCP Central Committee, "Constructing a Harmonious Socialist Society," indicated that the party and government leadership will no longer stand idly by when "disadvantaged sectors"—peasants and migrant workers—are being bullied by the "new classes"—business interests that are often collaborating with corrupt officials. The bad news, however, is that President Hu Jintao and Premier Wen Jiabao have once again chosen insufficient measures to deal with the challenges instead of more effective and comprehensive steps such as political liberalization.

The concept of "Socialist Harmony with Chinese Characteristics" is central to the statecraft of the Hu-Wen team. It is intimately tied to many of the populist slogans that the Fourth Generation leaders have coined since coming to power in November 2002, including "put people first," "pursue a scientific theory of development," "construct new socialist villages" and "raise the party's governance ability." These rallying cries stem from Hu's realization that the CCP's mandate of heaven is being jeopardized by growing schisms, if not full-fledged class warfare, in Chinese society. The "unholy alliance" between the fast-rising business sector, on the one hand, and the opportunistic cadres on the other, has spawned a new class that has carved out for itself a disproportionately big share of the pie.

The "Latin-Americanization" of China—a label that has been popular with Western Sinologists since the late 1990s—is by no means a far-fetched phenomenon. In fact, it is now being used more and more frequently by Chinese commentators. Take, for example, the views of experts at the Central Party School (CPS), which doubles as a public-policy think tank for the Hu team. Professor Wu Zhongmin pointed out earlier this month that while China is going through a "golden era of development," it is also facing "a period of exacerbated contradictions" among disparate power blocs and social groupings. Wu, who heaped lavish praise on Hu's "harmonious society"

concept, warned that China could become like "some countries in Latin America if [the leadership] fails to come up with appropriate measures" (People's Daily, October 4). Another CPS academic, Xin Ming, noted that the goal of harmony presupposed benevolent and symbiotic interactions among China's disparate interest blocs. "Different groups can realize the goal of win-win or become multiple winners," he said, adding that these blocs can, through cooperation, "make the cake bigger so that each can have a bigger share" (People's Daily, September 27).

To address this challenge, the Central Committee plenum adopted a landmark "Resolution on Certain Major Questions Concerning the Construction of a Socialist Harmonious Society." It spelled out specific measures for narrowing the rich-poor gap, as well as that between the rich coastal region and the disadvantaged, primarily rural hinterland. These have included mechanisms to lower the exorbitantly high education, housing and health-care costs that peasants as well as urban workers have to contend with. Moreover, the Central Committee discussed the ways and means to curb the growth of "groups with special interests and privileges," a euphemism for the business sectors that enrich themselves through preying upon the public. As renowned Chinese Academy of Social Sciences sociologist Lu Xueyi noted, "Special interest groups easily emerge at a time when the structure of the market economy is far from perfected." As examples, Lu cited largely state-held conglomerates that enjoy monopolistic powers in areas such as energy, transport and telecommunications (Wen Wei Po, October 5).

Moreover, the CCP leadership pledged that economic development would be pursued in tandem with safeguarding social justice. Central Committee members, particularly those from the central and western provinces, urged that legal and other means be used to ensure that all social sectors and groups are able to count on "equality in [socio-economic] rights, equality in opportunities, equality in [the degree to which they are being protected or constrained by] regulations and equality in distribution [of national resources]." Thus, in addition to setting up a social security net, the Hu leadership is thrashing out a mechanism to enhance social justice (Xinhua, October 7). To this end, the Central Committee vowed for the first time to create a level-playing field by "constructing scientific and efficient mechanisms for mediating among different interest [groupings] and for handling contradictions [among them]" (Xinhua, October 19).

Yet even as the CCP attempts to play the role of a fair mediator or arbiter, many of its party factions and senior cadres have become patrons as well as joint-venture partners of semi-monopolistic business groups and other interest blocs. To dissociate the party from powerful commercial conglomerates, the Hu-led Politburo decided in mid-year to launch a nationwide anti-corruption campaign, which climaxed in the dismissal of Shanghai party secretary and Politburo member Chen Liangyu last month. Shanghai, whose streets seem to be paved with gold, offers the best opportunities for businessmen—especially those in the real estate and securities fields—to make obscenely high profits thanks to their sterling connections with corrupt local officials. After Chen's disgrace, dozens of other provincial officials have also been arrested for colluding with real-estate businessmen in property-related racketeering. Isolated actions to penalize high-ranking corrupt officials, however, cannot whitewash the CCP's large-scale involvement in businesses that at times take advantage of society's disadvantaged sectors.

The big question, therefore, remains: Can a harmonious society be constructed in the absence of democracy, or at least a pluralized socio-political structure? On the issue of political reform, the plenum resolution merely repeated the well-known cliché: "We will expand [ways in which] citizens take part in politics in an orderly manner." During the past year, both Hu and Premier Wen have reiterated that "Western" democratic ideas and practices are unsuitable for China, and that most Chinese lack the economic and educational standards to experiment with institutions such as universal-suffrage elections. To forestall criticism from Western governments and scholars, however, members of Hu's think tanks have claimed that the CCP is open-minded enough to learn from the socialist-democratic parties in Europe.

CPS sociologist Qing Lianbin alleged that there were similarities between Hu's views on social justice on the one hand, and principles advocated by socialist democratic parties in Europe on the other. Qing noted that in Western Europe, quite a few political parties championed the precepts of ensuring that citizens would have "equality in the starting points [of their careers], equality during the process [of competition], and equality [regarding opportunities for achieving] results" (China News Service, October 7).

Qing and other Hu publicists, however, have failed to mention that in Western Europe, it is only through democratic systems and institutions, including multi-party politics and the liberal media, that social justice is guaranteed and exploitative "special interest groups" can be reined in. The bitter Chinese reality was illustrated graphically on October 8, when the plenary session opened at the well-guarded Xijiao Hotel, a People's Liberation Army facility in western Beijing. Dozens of members from disadvantaged sectors—mostly peasants with grievances against either corrupt officials or unscrupulous businessmen—had gathered there to try to deliver petitions to Central Committee members; they were all taken away by police and paramilitary People's Armed Police officers (Ming Pao, October 9).

For decades, CCP leaders ranging from Mao and Deng to ex-president Jiang Zemin and Hu have taken "stability" and "harmony" to mean the entire country subserviently toeing the line from the CCP's dominant faction. After sacking Shanghai's party secretary Chen, President Hu is certainly much better positioned to fill top central and regional posts with more of his protégés. Another key theme of the just-finished party plenum was the discussion of personnel movements in the run-up to the 17th CCP Congress next year, which will elect a new Central Committee, Politburo and Politburo Standing Committee (PBSC). To some extent, the Hu-Wen leadership will observe the CCP's long-standing tradition of picking younger leaders from the proverbial "five lakes and four seas." This means that for the sake of stability—and harmony—even cliques competing with Hu's dominant Communist Youth League Faction will be awarded at least a token number of slots in the Central Committee and Politburo.

For the same reason of maintaining a façade of unity to the outside world, Hu has for the foreseeable future decided not to incriminate another cadre with as high a rank as Shanghai's Chen. This is despite the rising expectations among cadres and ordinary Chinese alike that the CCP leadership should adopt a comprehensive anti-graft campaign. Since the 1990s, widespread rumors and allegations have linked two PBSC members—Executive Vice-Premier Huang Ju and Chinese People's Political Consultative Conference Chairman Jia Qinglin—to real estate and other rackets in the cities of Shanghai and Beijing. Both Huang, a former Shanghai party boss, and Jia were close to the Shanghai Faction led by ex-president Jiang. Political analysts in Beijing said, however, that Hu was able to remove Chen only with the acquiescence of Shanghai Faction-affiliated Politburo Standing Committee members. Moreover, as long as Huang and Jia agree to step down at the 17th CCP Congress—and not interfere with his plans to elevate his protégés to the top—Hu will observe the rules of "intra-party harmony" and allow them to quietly retire next year.

US-China: Quest for Peace
Taiwan a Deal-Breaker for U.S. Security

Henry C K Liu

The United States argues that the terms and validity of the 1982 communique—one of three documents setting forth the terms of the US-China-Taiwan relationship—depend upon assurances from the People's Republic of China (PRC) to resolve "the Taiwan question" by peaceful means only.

On July 14, 1982, the US gave Taiwan the Six Assurances that it:

- Had not agreed to a date for ending arms sales to Taiwan.

- Had not agreed to hold prior consultations with the PRC regarding arms sales to the Republic of China (ROC).

- Would not play any mediation role between the PRC and the ROC.

- Would not revise the Taiwan Relations Act.

- Had not altered its position regarding sovereignty over Taiwan.

- Would not exert pressure on the ROC to enter into negotiations with the PRC.

It has further been revealed in recent years that US president Ronald Reagan also secretly assured Taipei that if Beijing ceased its commitment to peaceful resolution of the Taiwan question, the August 17, 1982, US-PRC communique would become null and void.

As is well known, the PRC has never rejected the use of force as an option in resolving the Taiwan question, calling into dispute US good faith in signing the 1982 communique while secretly assuring Taiwan of a precondition. Moreover, the current US administration of President George W Bush has declared that there should be no unilateral change in the status quo by either party.

This policy entails three elements:

- Taiwan should not declare independence.

- Neither side should use force.

- Taiwan's future should be resolved in a manner mutually agreeable to the people on both sides of the Taiwan Strait.

In addition, the US has said it does not "support" Taiwanese independence. This means that Washington does not support Taiwanese independence unless all the people on both sides of the Strait agree to it, which in reality could mean never.

Bush Flouts Accord on Taiwan Non-recognition

The Bush administration, in defiance of the basic precondition of non-recognition of Taiwan for normalization of US-China relations, also believes that Washington should maintain robust, albeit unofficial, diplomatic relations with Taipei, on the grounds that peace across the Taiwan Strait is an important US interest and Taiwanese actions, especially provocative ones, fundamentally affect US interests. Regular dialogue and contact with Taiwanese officials are rationalized as necessary to improve communications and limit political surprises. This is a flimsy excuse, since there are already adequate unofficial channels of communication between Washington and Taipei without ostentatious visits between government officials designed merely to boost Taiwan's official status.

The Bush administration has been clear that it expects the parties on both sides of the Strait to act responsibly in support of regional stability, as if they were equal parties. Furthermore, Washington continues to encourage dialogue between Beijing and Taipei on political as well as security issues. This is in contradiction even to Reagan's Six Assurances to Taipei, which maintained that the US would not play any mediation role between the PRC and the ROC and would not exert pressure on the ROC to enter into negotiations with the PRC.

The Bush administration also believes that the United States should assist in finding opportunities for greater international representation for Taiwan in such organizations as the World Health Organization. Its argument for this belief is that it is the right thing to do for the 22 million people of Taiwan, who deserve representation in the international community, especially on issues affecting their health, their economic welfare and the security of their planes and ships. Another reason is that the less Taiwan feels diplomatically isolated and the more it feels part of the international community, the less likely it will be dissatisfied with the status quo and the less likely to undertake provocative actions that could undermine peace and stability across the Strait.

But China only opposes Taiwan's participation in international organizations as an independent entity. Taiwan can participate in international organizations the same way Hong Kong does, as a highly autonomous part of China. But Taipei not only refuses to participate as Taiwan, China, it is even beginning to decline the appellation of Taiwan, Republic of China, and wants to be known only as Taiwan, thus turning the issue to one of independence.

More US Moral Imperialism Directed at China

Finally, US policy encourages political liberalization on the mainland as the best hope for a peaceful resolution of the cross-Strait relationship. This of course is mere moral imperialism in the form of peaceful evolution. Political developments in China will respond only to internal Chinese needs, and are not undertaken to enhance US geopolitical interests. This policy of moral imperialism unwittingly has the counter-effect of deterring political liberalization in China by casting it as a movement against Chinese national interests.

Last June 1, Bush discussed Taiwan with Chinese President Hu Jintao on the sidelines of the Group of Eight summit of industrialized nations in France. In a press briefing later that day, a senior Bush administration official described Bush's comments, triggering speculation on whether US policy toward Taiwan had changed. Within a few days both Taiwan's cabinet spokesman Lin Chia-lung and American Institute in Taiwan chair Therese Shaheen said there had been no harmful change in US policy toward Taiwan.

On the other hand, the *People's Daily* noted on June 13 that after deviating from the policy of the previous six US administrations, Bush's Taiwan policy had now moved back to the mainstream. It described Bush's "non-support" as "opposition" to Taiwan independence and aligned the United States' "one-China policy" more closely with Beijing's "one China principle". Without directly correcting the Chinese interpretation, the same US senior official said: "On Taiwan, the president repeated our policy of a 'one China' policy based on the three communiques, the Taiwan Relations Act [TRA], no support for Taiwan independence . . . The president also said . . . if necessary, we will help Taiwan to the extent possible to defend itself."

Bush's remarks were widely interpreted as a softening in US support for Taiwan. This was the first time "no support for Taiwan's independence" had been elevated to the level of the TRA and the three communiques, and Bush did not mention

peaceful resolution with the assent of the people on Taiwan. The April 2001 Bush promise of "whatever it took" to help defend Taiwan, committing the United States to maximum effort in Taiwan's defense, was replaced with the new wording, "If necessary, we will help Taiwan to the extent possible to defend itself" with two qualifications. The phrase "if necessary" is superfluous if it simply means "if China were to attack Taiwan" because US intervention presupposes Chinese military aggression. There is little question that if the People's Liberation Army (PLA) were to launch a blitzkrieg against Taiwan, the island could not alone repel the invading forces.

Taiwan would clearly need US assistance. China has always insisted on its right to the force option on the independence issue. Beijing in fact has put a still-unspecified time limit on peaceful resolution by warnings of military action if Taiwan refuses to acknowledge Chinese sovereignty indefinitely. The qualifying phrase "if necessary" can be interpreted as a US hedging against Taipei's opting unilaterally to make accommodations with Beijing. Similarly, the phrase "to the extent possible" could be a hedge against the eventuality of Taiwan's leadership caving in to PLA actions so quickly that US intervention would make no difference.

Would Taiwan Really Fight for Independence?

Although not publicly acknowledged, Washington is reported to be steadily losing confidence in Taiwan's resolve to fight for its survival as a de facto independent nation. With economic integration with the mainland, Taiwan's economy is increasingly dependent on the motherland. Because of massive outflow of capital, technology and people from Taiwan to the mainland, the Taiwanese economy is being hollowed out of manufacturing. And yet all the island's political parties are intent on early implementation of direct links, further weakening Taiwan's desire for political independence and US-backed security.

After a US B-2 (mistakenly, the United States said) bombed the Chinese Embassy in Belgrade in May 1999 during the North Atlantic Treaty Organization military action in Kosovo, the administration of President Bill Clinton worked to rebuild its relationship with the PRC. Taiwan "president" Lee Teng-hui's July 9 statement that Taiwan and China should deal with each other on a "special state-to-state" basis upset the US State Department. While Washington and Beijing have restored some momentum to their bilateral ties with a landmark agreement on China's entry into the World Trade Organization, the relationship between Washington and Taipei continues to drift.

Lee's "state-to-state" announcement created serious strains between Taiwan and the United States. His provocative statement, so soon after the embassy bombing, could not have come at a more sensitive time for Washington, which viewed Lee's behavior as reckless. The Clinton administration delayed a trip to Taiwan by a Pentagon delegation and leaked to the media the possible scaling back of deliveries of F-16 spare parts, sending a clear signal that Taiwan could not go too far down the "state-to-state" road without risking its security ties to the US. Even some of Taiwan's longtime supporters in Congress criticized Lee's remarks as being unhelpful.

In June 1998, Clinton publicly stated the "Three Nos":

- No support for Taiwan independence.
- No support for "two Chinas".
- No support for Taiwan's participation in state-based international organizations.

Taiwan also sensed US pressure for an interim arrangement whereby Taipei would agree not to declare independence in exchange for Beijing's pledge not to use force. Faced with these developments, Lee chose to assert that Taiwan was already an independent, sovereign state and Beijing and Washington needed to deal with this reality. Nevertheless, it is a de facto sovereignty that depends directly on the US skirting official non-recognition of Taiwan.

Cross-Strait Status Quo Unacceptable to Beijing

The interim agreement proposals from US academics and officials actually fanned misunderstanding. Assistant secretary of state Stanley Roth and other US diplomats suggested that an interim agreement might be useful for improving cross-Strait relations, in the spirit of buying time and stabilizing the status quo. But the status quo was a continuing state fundamentally unacceptable to Beijing.

Lee's "state-to-state" announcement was coached by Republican China hand James Lilley, a former Central Intelligence Agency director with close ties to Taiwan and former ambassador to China in the administration of President George H W Bush, in order to give the Clinton administration a diplomatic headache—and it went further than a declaration of "independence." In alluding to the German model of reunification, Lee identified Taiwan with West Germany, reuniting with a poorer and less developed mainland, as East Germany.

Taiwan realizes that it will need to enter into political discussion with the Beijing government sooner or later and the "state-to-state" formula is a strategy to reject Beijing's idea that it is merely a province. Meanwhile, as Beijing insists on Taiwan being a Chinese province, Taipei insists on being an independent state.

Taiwan's adoption of a "state-to-state" formula was triggered by a perceived softening of US support as the Clinton administration in its second term became more receptive to China's "one country, two systems" formula, as applied to Hong Kong, as a possible solution to the Taiwan issue. Taiwan's state-to-state formulation, in turn, increased US annoyance at Taipei acting as an unwelcome obstacle to US global geopolitical strategy that requires Chinese cooperation. Washington's desire to restrain Taipei's provocative behavior fueled Taiwan's anxieties, and caused Taipei to exert increasing independence even from Washington with the support of the right wing in US domestic politics. "Selling out Taiwan" became a campaign issue in the 2000 presidential election.

The Bush administration's robust support of Taiwan has been diluted primarily because of Taipei's failure to commit unequivocally to non-provocative acceptance of the status quo and secondarily because of America's need to elicit China's help in fighting global terror after September 11, 2001, in resolving the North Korean nuclear standoff, and in supporting (or not opposing) the United States on Iraq in the United Nations Security Council. This shift in the US stance is tactical, however, rather than strategic. The US still perceives geopolitical interests in maintaining the status quo on Taiwan. The recent appointment of Princeton professor and prominent sinologist Aaron Friedberg to the post of deputy national security adviser and director of policy planning on Vice President Dick Cheney's staff tends to support this interpretation (see The Struggle for Harmony Part 1: Myths and realities about China, June 13, 2003, and Part 2: Imagined danger, June 14).

Some See Inevitable US-China Confrontation

Friedberg sees potential long-term dangers that a modernized PLA may pose to US security and has written about the inevitability of a US-China confrontation. After the September 11, 2001, attacks, world geopolitics has become highly volatile. The US-Taiwan relationship is not exempt from the dynamics of changing international relations. After a private meeting in the White House with Chinese Premier Wen Jiabao last December 11, during Wen's state visit, Bush told the press: "We oppose any unilateral decision by either China or Taiwan to change the status quo. The comments and actions made by the leader of Taiwan indicate that he may be willing to make decisions unilaterally to change the status quo, which we oppose." Thus "oppose" has officially replaced "non-support" for Taiwan independence.

The area of converging US-Taiwan interests is shrinking because of changing geopolitics. The single most important consideration remaining is US concern that allowing Taiwan to fall back into the arms of the PRC by force or coercion could prove detrimental to US leadership in East Asia, particularly in terms of security arrangements with US allies, especially Japan and South Korea. Yet the test of maintaining security is in US diplomatic skill in avoiding war, not its war-winning capability. US allies in East Asia know that while a victory in war may protect US prestige, it would nevertheless leave their respective countries in ruins.

Such war-deterring diplomatic skill requires yielding to China on issues of its fundamental and vital national interest, such as the issue of Taiwan. Taiwan is a deal-breaking issue, as the American saying goes. Pushing the Taiwan issue to a military solution would represent a massive failure of US diplomacy in Asia. Even if the US 7th Fleet with its two carrier groups and the overwhelming force-projection capabilities from US bases in Japan should manage to thwart a PLA invasion of Taiwan, the Taiwan that was left after the bomb smoke clears would not resemble anything worth defending. On the other hand, even if China should succeed in regaining Taiwan through military conquest, the gain of a war-torn economy would be a Pyrrhic victory.

The Taiwan issue is a political issue, and all parties agree that it needs to be solved with political accommodation. Yet political options exist only within limits. Failure to exercise political options will lead to war. Clausewitzian concepts of war notwithstanding, war is not diplomacy by other means (Karl von Clausewitz, a Prussian military officer, wrote on military strategy). War is the product of failed diplomacy. The legacy of war is international hatred that fuels future wars while the legacy of diplomacy is international harmony that fuels stability. A war over the Taiwan Strait has no winners. All will lose more than they hope to gain.

HENRY C K LIU is chairman of the New York-based Liu Investment Group.

They Can't Handle the Truth

Taiwan's media go all out for a story, even if the facts aren't there. Reformers don't have much clout in a culture that's so freewheeling.

MARK MAGNIER
Times Staff Writer

Taipei, Taiwan—When Sir Elton John arrived here shortly before midnight in a bright blue track suit and dark glasses, he was greeted at the airport by local reporters who jostled him, slammed cameras in his face and barked questions.

The pop star tried to hide but was soon flushed out and started yelling obscenities.

Not known for taking an insult lying down, the Taiwanese journalists yelled back. Some suggested that he consider going elsewhere.

"We'd love to get out of Taiwan if it's full of people like you. Pig! Pig!" the knighted entertainer screamed last fall.

"The television and the photographers at the airport were the rudest I have ever met, and I've been to 60 countries," John said at his piano bench at a concert a few hours later. "I'm sorry if I offended anyone in Taiwan, I didn't mean to. But to those guys, I meant every word."

Celebrity histrionics aside, Taiwan's media have the reputation of being among the most aggressive in Asia. In a region where print and broadcast reporters are often de facto cheerleaders for governments and billionaires, Taiwan's no-holds-barred journalism is alternately seen as a gutsy check on authority and the embodiment of chaos.

Concerned about the media's excesses and ability to ruin reputations and lives, reformers in and outside the industry are trying to stem the sensationalism, partisanship and corruption that characterize the business. Some argue that the media are merely a reflection of Taiwanese society, which is one of the most freewheeling in Asia.

Foreign luminaries aren't the only ones trying to hide from the island's aspiring Woodwards and Bernsteins, who've been called man-eaters, bloodsuckers and worse. Several years ago, when Taiwan's then-vice president and prime minister, Lien Chan, gave his traveling herd of reporters the slip on a trip to the Dominican Republic and secretly traveled to Ukraine, newspapers summoned all their troops to search for him.

A few months later, then-Foreign Minister John Chang pulled a similar Houdini act during a visit to South Africa. Hounded by angry reporters when he returned to Taipei after a stealth visit to Belgium, Chang defended himself with what is now known here as the "rice cooker" theory of diplomacy. Making policy while one is barraged by reporters, he said, is like trying to boil rice with someone constantly lifting the lid.

Wary of angering those who buy ink by the barrel, however, he quickly apologized and begged the scribes' forgiveness.

The media's willfulness had a deadly outcome, or so some charged, when the daughter of television star Pai Ping-ping was kidnapped a few years ago. The singer criticized the media for following the family in cars, vans and helicopters, even hounding it during the ransom drop.

"Were you helping me or hurting me?" Pai asked at a news conference.

When her daughter was found dead, the accusations grew more pointed. "Reporters are guilty!" screamed placards hoisted by neighbors around Pai's house.

Journalists showed little remorse, citing pressure from their editors.

"If you fail to get this story, jumping from the 14th floor is too good for you," an editor at the *United Daily News* was quoted—in a well-cited essay on media reform—as saying during a meeting on the newspaper's 14th floor. "You should climb up to at least the 20th floor and jump from there."

In a market of 23 million people, Taiwan has six 24-hour television news channels, 4,185 magazines, 172 radio stations, 135 cable TV channels, 2,524 newspapers and 977 domestic news agencies, the government says. The desperate struggle for ratings results in stories on sex, murder, corruption and kidnappings and not much else, critics charge.

Kuan Chung-hsiang, a journalism professor at Shih Hsin University in Taipei, recounted that one of his top students landed a job at a local TV station but quit a few months later. She'd been told to wear a short skirt and to walk over a hidden camera positioned in a drain for an "investigative" piece about how hidden cameras all over Taiwan were secretly recording lewd scenes. The station couldn't find videos of lewd scenes, so it was staging one.

When the former student strongly objected, Kuan said, her boss asked her, "Do you want conscience or do you want ratings?"

Part of the Taiwanese media's character reflects its evolution, what some refer to as the transition from lapdog to mad dog. Until 1988, major newspapers and TV stations served as government mouthpieces controlled by the ruling Nationalist Party, which had maintained an iron grip for decades.

Less government control has led to privatization, but several important stations are still owned by political parties. In a polarized society where politics is a blood sport—fistfights in the legislature were not uncommon up until a few years ago—media objectivity is spotty at best.

President Chen Shui-bian's ruling Democratic Progressive Party has its own tools to manipulate the media, and, some say, the truth. "The Taiwan media is truly scandalous in its behavior," said Bonnie Glaser of the Center for Strategic and International Studies in Washington. "But the government often joins in. None of them have any scruples."

Journalism watchdogs cite a $250-million budget for "persuading" stations to invite generals and other people the government wants on talk shows, to write dramatic scripts favorable to its policies and to otherwise promote its agenda.

"The Taiwanese government has been doing dollar diplomacy so long overseas, it thinks it's natural to do it at home," said Hu Yu-wei, a journalism professor at National Taiwan Normal University, referring to the government's practice of paying other governments to give it diplomatic recognition.

Small payoffs to journalists for favorable treatment—hardly unusual in many Asian cultures with strong gift-giving traditions—remain a problem, although media experts say the practice is on the wane.

When Lu Shih-hsiang, a professor and head of Taiwan's Foundation for the Advancement of Media Excellence, offered a course on media ethics two years ago, none of his journalism students signed up. Asked why, several said they didn't want to become "schizophrenic," constrained by boring niceties that had no place in the real world.

Double-checking information is a rarity at many news organizations, as are corrections. Reporters acknowledge big rewards in gaining an edge over competitors and little cost for getting it wrong. There's no tradition of libel suits.

"Many reporters don't check their facts," said Chen Chao-jen, a senior reporter with the TVBS network who recounted a story about a bombing in Taipei. Competitors ran a report on their 9 o'clock news saying authorities had arrested a suspect.

"I told my boss it was wrong, but he said write it anyway," Chen said. "Then at 10 o'clock, everyone runs a story saying he's not a suspect."

During last year's presidential election, stations raced to get the results first. Some reported that the Nationalists had garnered 8 million votes. After it was reported that only 6 million people had actually voted, the stations, embarrassed by their error, withheld results and announced that the data had simply stopped coming in.

In a part of the world where national politicians are rarely challenged, however, Taiwanese reporters are as confrontational toward their leaders as they are toward pop stars. Information flows freely, some of it true. Soon after taking office in 2002, Douglas Paal, director of the American Institute in Taiwan, the de facto U.S. embassy, fretted about how quickly sensitive information leaked out.

Taiwanese media enjoy some of the world's strongest press freedoms, according to 2004 surveys by watchdog groups Reporters Without Borders, the International Press Institute and Freedom House.

Some continue to hope, however, that the media will adopt meaningful changes.

"From political shows to news and entertainment, local television programming as a whole is terrible in the extreme, indeed," Lin Chia-lung, an official in the government information office, wrote in an essay urging reform. "The restructuring of the media environment and institutions has become essential."

Calls for change have been growing amid concern that partisanship and excessive commercialism are undermining the media's ability to inform people. A new law requires all political parties to divest their media holdings by the end of this year. The media excellence foundation has encouraged citizens to boycott irresponsible outlets and start filing libel suits. People whose reputations have been besmirched are starting to win verdicts.

Other proposals to improve programming and accountability are also under discussion, including a public network modeled after Britain's BBC or Japan's NHK that would be funded by the government or subscriber fees.

In 2003, the government decided to scrap a program that rated Taiwan's six largest Chinese-language newspapers for accuracy and objectivity after critics charged that it was pursuing its own agenda under the guise of neutrality. In response, policymakers called for better self-policing.

How quickly reforms take hold remains to be seen, but some observers believe that the media are a reflection of broader social forces.

"We have a poor democracy and a poor media," said Chen Hao, senior vice president of CTI Television. "Taiwan is unstable and partisan, and we need to find a middle ground. There's no easy solution."

Until then, celebrities and politicians will have to contend with the media's bulldog tactics. Said Chen, the television reporter: "We give them popularity. That's the price they have to pay."

Special correspondent Tsai Ting-I in Taipei contributed to this report.

Preventing a War Over Taiwan

Kenneth Lieberthal

Strait Talk

One of the greatest dangers to international security today is the possibility of a military confrontation between China and Taiwan that leads to a war between China and the United States. Such a war would be not only tragic but also unnecessary, since it would result from a failure of imagination and diplomacy—fought because a place that has long declared itself independent was attacked for doing so again.

Neither Beijing nor Taipei wants a war, but both sides have adopted policies that run an unacceptably high risk of bloodshed over the next several years. The Bush administration should therefore take steps now to reduce the prospect of conflict across the Taiwan Strait. Understanding what those steps should be, however, requires getting past the rhetorical constructs that have dominated discussion to date.

China says that it wants stability across the Taiwan Strait, that it can postpone final resolution of the cross-strait issue for a long time, that it is developing its regional military capabilities solely to deter Taiwanese independence, and that it will use force if necessary to prevent or reverse a declaration of independence. But these positions have not served China's interests well, because it has failed to make clear exactly what "declaring independence" involves.

By not doing so, Beijing has risked miscalculation by a Taiwanese leadership that does not want to provoke a military response but continues to push the envelope just short of one. The fact that for more than a decade Taiwan's leaders have declared Taiwan to be "an independent, sovereign country" without dramatic consequences adds to the confusion. Beijing's stance now runs the risk that Taiwanese President Chen Shui-bian will consider Chinas threats a bluff. (Chen's pro-independence predecessor Lee Teng-hui, for example, has said that Beijing is nothing more than a "paper tiger.") Ironically, Beijing's position also enhances the stature and leverage of the pro-independence elements in Taiwan. Since China says war and peace will be determined by what these individuals say and do, they attract enormous domestic and international attention.

China may be able to continue on its current course, expanding trade and investment ties with Taiwan while insisting that the island's leaders accept the "one-China principle" as a precondition for any political talks and threatening the use of force in response to a declaration of independence. But if it does, it will be tying both its credibility and the chances of a confrontation to forces beyond its control.

Triangulation

Over the past two decades, Taiwan has moved from dictatorship to democracy. It has achieved this transition with remarkably little political disruption, a fact that is rightfully a source of pride for the island's people and leaders. But Taiwan's democracy is still very young, and it is experiencing growing pains. Political parties remain weak and faction-ridden, the notion of cross-party compromise to produce legislation is not well established, and leaders have been moving toward the use of referendums as a way to get around obstreperous opposition in the legislature.

Cross-strait relations, meanwhile, have become deeply intertwined in intensive partisan maneuvering for electoral advantage. Chen has proven very effective at appealing to the supporters of full independence while not alienating those fearful of rocking the boat with China. In the process, he has created a record that seems to support almost any position on the spectrum.

If his tactics have benefited Chen, however, their results have been less happy for Taiwan. Beijing has lost all trust in him, making it hard for Chen to initiate a meaningful dialogue even if he were to try. Beijing supports various multilateral initiatives in Asia and free-trade agreements in the region, but all of these exclude Taiwan, to the latter's growing economic and political disadvantage. And many corporations are moving activities from Taiwan to the mainland because the costs and bother of doing business across the strait are too high.

Meanwhile, whereas Chinas military has been gaining in strength and operational capability, Taiwan's defense budget has been declining (it is currently at its lowest level, in real purchasing power, since 1992), and Taiwan still lacks defenses well suited to fend off a mainland attack. Chen also has lost a great deal of support from the Bush administration, which has no desire to see regional tensions rise. Although he is now in his second term of office and prohibited from running for a third in

2008, Chen still has more than two years left to ensure a lasting legacy on the cross-strait issue before he steps down.

Washington has traditionally adhered to a cross-strait relations policy of dual deterrence and dual reassurance. It has signaled that Beijing cannot count on the United States' standing by if China attacks Taiwan and has signaled to Taiwan that it cannot count on U.S. forces to defend it regardless of the circumstances that precipitate the fighting. Washington has also assured Beijing that it will not change its one-China policy unilaterally and assured Taiwan that it will not sell out the island's interests. And it consistently suggests that both sides resolve their differences through negotiations. The United States, in short, has a one-China policy, insists on peaceful resolution of the cross-strait issue, and encourages dialogue as a path to that resolution.

The U.S. stance has probably helped keep the peace in the region until now, but it has not solved the underlying standoff. As a result, the United States now finds itself with a conditional commitment to protect a government in Taiwan that pushes the envelope on independence well beyond what Washington wants, while fending off constant requests from Beijing to do more to rein in Taiwan's actions. However loath Washington is to see the risk of instability grow across the Taiwan Strait, its traditional posture can no longer guarantee that the situation will not deteriorate.

Further complicating matters is a series of misguided assumptions in each capital that could easily lead to war. Many in Beijing believe that the White House seeks to encourage Taiwanese independence and uses its ongoing weapons sales to do so; that Taiwan can be defeated before U.S. military power can be brought into play; and that even if the United States did engage militarily, Beijing could force it to withdraw through a dramatic act such as the sinking of an aircraft carrier.

In Taipei, meanwhile, many think that Beijing is so focused on economic growth, domestic political stability, and the 2008 Olympics that it will do anything to avoid a war. Even if Beijing does make good on its threats, the reasoning goes, Washington will step in to defend Taiwan. And, in this view, Taiwan's independent defense capabilities are largely irrelevant, since any conflict will end in either a quick Chinese win or a Sino-American war. Weapons purchases are thus more important for their political symbolism than for their military utility.

In Washington, finally, many officials believe that U.S policy has "worked" for decades and remains robust. Thus there is no compelling need to engage the Chinese military to increase mutual understanding, and the mixed messages that unavoidably emerge from various parts of Washington are unimportant. Ultimately, if any cross-strait conflict did erupt, the United States could settle the matter for the long term by achieving a decisive military victory.

The tragedy is that all of these assumptions are questionable and most are simply wrong. Yet taken together they could lead to the only outcome that nobody wants: a major war between the United States and China over Taiwan.

A Fork in the Road

Two developments in December set the stage for possible improvements in the cross-strait relationship. Unfortunately, they could just as easily move things in the opposite direction. On December 11, Taiwan held legislative elections that, to the surprise of nearly all observers, preserved the anti-independence Pan-Blue parties' slim majority in the legislature. Later that month, China's government submitted to its parliament a new anti-secession law that, when adopted, will legally commit China to use force should any part of its territory, explicitly including Taiwan, secede.

The Pan-Blue victory virtually eliminates the chance that Chen can push through pro-independence changes to the constitution during his second term. As a result, he might dampen cross-strait tensions in order to get enough Pan-Blue cooperation to pass at least some of his domestic agenda. Alternatively, Chen might decide to adopt a strongly pro-independence posture in the hope of fully capturing this issue for his party's supporters in the next legislative and presidential elections.

China and Taiwan have long pursued policies that raise the risk of miscalculation and bloodshed.

Although Beijing recognizes that the election results have greatly reduced the chances of a crisis-inducing constitutional change in Taiwan, different observers draw contrasting operational lessons about whether to pursue a tough line with Taiwan. Some believe that Pan-Blue's triumph reflects the success of Beijing's refusal to deal with Chen, whereas others see it as vindication of China's having adopted a relatively low profile on cross-strait issues in the months before the election.

Likewise, Chinas impending adoption of the anti-secession law has ambiguous implications. By legally mandating the use of force to prevent secession, the law is designed to clear up any uncertainty over whether China is willing to sacrifice peace to preserve territorial integrity. (In a loose sense, it is China's counterpart to the U.S. Taiwan Relations Act, which credibly constrains Washington's options.) The law could reduce Beijing's fears that Chen would misinterpret conciliatory gestures as indications of China's lack of resolve. It could also enhance Chinese President Hu Jintao's ability to take the initiative on cross-strait issues, now that he has demonstrated his willingness to commit himself to the use of force if things go badly.

On the other hand, the anti-secession law may also increase the influence of China's military on the Taiwan issue, since it creates an explicit national mandate to use force if necessary. Some Chinese leaders might view the law as an additional instrument for pressuring Chen should they decide to do so. And although many in Taiwan are likely to view the law as increasing the credibility of Beijing's threats, it will not draw a clear enough red line to eliminate the possibility of future Taiwanese misjudgment.

Thus the December 2004 developments have increased the chances of serious movement in relations between Beijing and Taipei without predetermining the direction the movement will take. They have created the potential for grudging cross-party cooperation in Taiwan to seek cross-strait stability, and even for China to move forward. But they have also created the possibility that Taiwan's pro-independence Democratic Progressive Party will turn even more strident and that China's policy will become more muscular and hard-line.

Here is where U.S. initiatives can help tilt the outcome in a more benign direction. Right now, there appears to be an unusual two-year window of opportunity to change the underlying cross-strait dynamic because the top leaders in Beijing, Taipei, and Washington now have terms of office that stretch until at least late 2007, with no elections coming beforehand that could present major obstacles. Within this context, two broad approaches could eliminate the possibility of war across the Taiwan Strait. Both are feasible, for they do not require any of the players to repudiate existing core principles. Nevertheless, each requires considerable political initiative and courage.

The first approach, which could be adopted by Beijing largely on its own, consists of embracing an "international" definition of Taiwanese independence instead of an "ideational" or "juridical" one. The second approach would rely on getting Beijing and Taipei to negotiate a long-term agreed framework for stability across the strait, perhaps with the help of U.S. diplomacy.

Thinking about Independence

On close examination, Beijing can think about Taiwan's independence in three separate ways, each with very different repercussions for China's interests. The first, which is common in international relations, considers a country independent only if other countries recognize it as such and grant it diplomatic recognition. By this definition, Beijing has already won and Taiwan has already lost. Every single major country in the world not only recognizes Beijing as China's legitimate government but also shares the view, articulated by former Secretary of State Colin Powell in his last official trip to Beijing, that "Taiwan is not independent."

If it accepted this standard, China could declare that it had already succeeded in preventing Taiwan's independence and that nothing Taiwan does could change that reality. China could thus assure Taiwan that it would not need to use force because the goal of preserving territorial integrity had already been achieved (whether or not the residents of Taiwan agreed). Only a move by other governments to recognize an independent Taiwan would change the status quo.

Unfortunately, Beijing is highly unlikely to adopt this simple, elegant, and powerful solution to the independence issue. Having ignored it for years, China's leaders would be hard-pressed to embrace it now. China's powerful military, moreover, would probably vehemently oppose any shift. And such a move might have undesirable effects, from Beijing's perspective, on the political dynamics in such areas as Tibet, Xinjiang, and Inner Mongolia.

The second, or ideational, definition considers a country independent if its own people accept and promote the view that they are a distinctive community constituting an independent political entity. By this definition, however, Beijing has already lost the game, since a sense of independent identity is widespread and growing within Taiwan. At times, Beijing seems to expect the United States to stop Taiwan's nationalistic tendencies, but that hope is unrealistic. Yet if this definition prevails, Beijing will inevitably feel that it must resort to force to impose its will—which, of course, would only increase, not decrease, Taiwan's sense of its separate identity.

According to the third, or juridical, definition, a country is considered independent if it takes some formal legal action to declare itself so. With respect to Taiwan, such action would likely come in the form of changes to Taiwan's constitution that clearly create a political entity distinct from the government that has been ruling Taiwan since 1949, after fleeing the Chinese mainland (where it was established in the early twentieth century as "the Republic of China"). Beijing has hinted that any such constitutional change would cross a red line and spark a crisis.

The juridical definition seems extremely artificial, even arbitrary, and thus may feed a sense of unreality on Taiwan. It virtually invites salami tactics, such as constitutionally changing Taiwan's name to "Republic of China (Taiwan)" instead of to "Republic of Taiwan." The latter would apparently induce a Chinese use of force and so should be avoided. But would the former? If not, what lesson should Taiwan draw?

Nevertheless, Beijing regularly asks the United States to make sure that Taiwan does not cross the juridical independence line. Washington has made clear to Taipei that it does not want games played on this issue, but Taipei has repeatedly pushed the envelope, evidently feeling confident of Washington's support should the mainland respond aggressively to another seemingly minor Taiwanese initiative.

In sum, by embracing the international definition of independence, Beijing could ignore independence activities on Taiwan. On the other hand, asserting the ideational definition would inevitably result in Chinese defeat on Taiwan's independence, and accepting the juridical definition would perpetuate the current lack of clarity and the risk of salami tactics. Thus only the first definition would clearly avoid war, but, unfortunately, China will not adopt that approach.

Agreeing to Disagree

A second and politically more feasible approach would be to lock in the status quo by having Beijing and Taipei negotiate a 20-to-30-year "agreed framework" for stability across the Taiwan Strait. Such an agreement would eliminate the things that each side fears the most: for Taiwan, the threat that Beijing will attack; and for Beijing, the threat that Taiwan will cross the independence red line.

Such an agreement would be built on the recognition that deep-rooted political factors in both Beijing and Taipei preclude negotiating a peaceful resolution to the cross-strait issue for at least another generation—something that officials on both sides acknowledge privately. It would also be rooted in a sense that the current obsession with final-status issues ("reunification" for Beijing and "independence" for Taiwan) has made the situation pregnant with catastrophe. There is every reason to believe, in contrast, that, two or three decades down the road, things will have changed significantly. At that point, the two sides might be able to hold more fruitful final-status negotiations.

Only Beijing and Taipei could determine the details and scope of any such long-term agreement, but presumably it would encompass a variety of issues, including confidence-building measures in the security arena, provision for increased economic and political contact across the strait, and consideration of more international space for Taiwan politically. Its core, however, would consist of credible commitments to take the issues of independence and the use of force off the table.

Each side has already seriously considered a long-term stability framework agreement in private, but it remains unclear how compatible their respective positions on it are. Neither, moreover, has yet figured out how to start dialogue on the subject given their extraordinary levels of mutual distrust and the lack of a reliable and secret channel of communication between them.

To lock in today's fragile status quo, Taipei should forgo full independence and Beijing should stop threatening to use force.

This is where the United States comes in. Washington can play two potentially important roles in reducing the chances of military conflict. It could strongly encourage each side to focus on achieving a cross-strait stability framework agreement as its major objective, stating that, if either side does not, it will pay a price in its bilateral relations with the United States. Washington could also offer its good offices to facilitate the necessary, delicate, and secret communications that would have to take place before either side is prepared to commit publicly to such a plan.

If both sides agreed, moreover, Washington could help create the mutual confidence necessary to make the core commitments in the agreement credible. Taipei might ask, for example, that all major governments promise to take Beijing's use of force against Taiwan as a matter of grave concern and to react accordingly (the current U.S. commitment). Beijing, in turn, might demand a commitment from all major governments to cut off ties with Taiwan and remove it from all international organizations if it asks for recognition as an independent country while the agreement is in force.

These comments are suggestive, not prescriptive, but they indicate the ways in which outside actors might play a helpful role. Washington could indicate from the outset its willingness, in principle, to help line up international support.

Out of the Box

A framework agreement would be difficult to negotiate and, given the countries' respective electoral calendars, would have to be completed before the middle of 2007. Furthermore, the substance of the agreement would have to prove broadly acceptable to each country's public, lest opposition politicians in Taiwan, for example, manage to win the 2008 elections on a platform rejecting it.

Is such an agreement even conceivable? It should be. The main obstacle in China would likely be Beijing's position that Taiwan must accept the one-China principle before any negotiations begin. But Beijing has always asserted this condition in the context of efforts designed to address final-status issues. If the sole purpose of the proposed agreement is to assure stability for a defined period of time and the agreement includes Taiwan's commitment not to declare independence for the entire term, the one-China principle will not be violated by the outcome of the negotiations.

The main obstacles in Taiwan would likely be the government's position that Taiwan is already an independent country and the public's increasing sense of a separate Taiwanese identity. But because Beijing does not consider Taiwan to have already declared independence, the practical task will be for the two sides to negotiate a definition of "declaring independence" clear enough to determine what future acts would cross the red line. Issues such as Taiwan's domestic identity and China's development of its overall (as opposed to cross-strait) military capabilities could be deemed beyond the scope of the agreement and thus not up for discussion.

This approach has the virtue of turning all the participants' attention to the most urgent task at hand—reducing the risks of a cross-strait conflict without compromising either side's core objectives—and dealing with it for at least a generation. It also provides an opportunity for Chen to establish a legacy and for leaders in Beijing to ensure that the Taiwan issue will not hinder their nation's overall aspirations. Indeed, it could lay the groundwork for the 2008 Olympics in Beijing to mark the beginning of a new geopolitical era in cross-strait relations.

Wars sometimes occur because of miscalculations influenced by the weight of historical legacies. In the case of the Taiwan Strait, the dangers of such a conflict are so clear and the potential consequences so dire, that all three major players should summon the courage to think creatively about how to prevent it. Because neither Beijing nor Taipei is likely to make the first move even if they recognize such a plan's potential benefits, Washington will have to jump-start the process. Given the relatively brief window of opportunity during which a stable framework agreement can be reached, as well as the still-ambiguous implications of recent developments, the Bush administration should move quickly.

KENNETH LIEBERTHAL teaches political science and business at the University of Michigan and is currently a Visiting Fellow at the Brookings Institution. In 1998–2000, he served as Special Assistant to the President for National Security Affairs and Senior Director for Asia on the staff of the National Security Council.

Reprinted by permission of *Foreign Affairs*, vol. 84, no. 2, March/April 2005, pp. 53–63. Copyright © 2005 by the Council on Foreign Relations, Inc.

Taiwan: The Tail That Wags Dogs

Michael McDevitt

Executive Summary

This essay explores how Taiwan has been able to seize the political initiative from China, Japan, and the United States.

Main Argument

Taiwan has attained this leverage due to the interrelationship of four factors:

- Strategic considerations stemming from Taiwan's geographic position lead Tokyo and Washington to prefer the status quo, while leading China to strive for reunification. China's increasing military power, however, may suggest a Chinese intention to change the status quo.

- Shared democratic values and the fact that the "democracy issue" has greatly prolonged the timetable for reunification give Taipei political influence in both Washington and Tokyo.

- China's constant threats of force actually empower Taipei in its relationship with Washington, and cause the United States to plan for the worst.

- Taiwan is a litmus test of U.S. credibility as an ally, a condition that in turn creates a perception on the island that U.S. military backing is unconditional.

Policy Implications

- Taipei's high-risk diplomatic approach carries with it the very real possibility of miscalculation, which could easily lead to great power conflict.

- The United States would benefit from exploring with Beijing ways in which to demilitarize the issue of Taiwan independence so that the threat of great power conflict over Taiwan is greatly moderated.

- Tensions may eventually lessen substantially if Beijing can be encouraged to substitute political deterrence for military deterrence.

- In order to ensure that the U.S. position in the region would survive a Taipei-provoked conflict should the United States choose not to become directly involved, Washington can undertake extensive talks with Japan designed to ensure that Japan does not lose confidence in Washington.

Organization of the Essay

The first four sections of the essay respectively explore the four factors of the complex U.S.-Taiwan-Japan-China relationship outlined above:

Geostrategic Issues and Considerations
Democracy in Taiwan: The Influence of
    Democratic Values
China's Policy of Threatening the Use of Force
The Symbolic Importance of Taiwan to
    U.S. Credibility

A conclusion summarizes the report and offers policy implications.

The year 2005 has turned out to be a more difficult period for Sino-U.S. relations than many observers anticipated. A series of trade issues, in particular the growing trade deficit and concerns over the lack of Chinese enforcement of WTO intellectual property obligations, have combined with both concerns regarding China's currency being overvalued and growing geo-strategic anxiety over China's rise and its military modernization to shift the policy spotlight away from Taiwan as a potential "troublemaker" and place it squarely on Beijing.

This is quite a change from the winter of 2004–05 when Beijing's policy focus changed from considerations related to when reunification with Taiwan ought to take place, to a policy of halting moves toward independence by the government in Taipei. Much to the gratification of the White House, Beijing has gone along with the U.S. policy of no unilateral changes to the cross-Strait status quo. Meanwhile, Taiwan's President Chen Shui-bian has become more restrained in his ambitions to redefine Taiwan's constitutional structure in a way that presages *de jure* independence for Taiwan. As a result, an equilibrium exists (albeit an uneasy one), and the atmosphere of near crisis prevalent not quite a year ago has abated.

Looking back, one of the fascinating aspects of the existing relationship between Taiwan, the People's Republic of China (PRC), Japan, and the United States is the degree to which the Chen Shui-bian administration in Taipei has managed to seize the political initiative and put the three great powers of Northeast Asia in a reactive mode. Unfortunately, the way by which a small nation of only 23 million people has been able to accomplish this feat of diplomatic jujitsu is by stoking the coals of Taiwanese nationalism on the island to a point just short of crisis with the PRC. Washington and Tokyo have not been amused by the willingness of Taipei to play diplomatic "chicken" with Beijing because the stakes of a miscalculation by either side are so high for all concerned. The purpose of this paper is to explore this situation and consider alternatives that could reduce the possibility of Taiwanese "provocations" eliciting great power responses.

The main argument is that Taiwan's leverage is derived from four interrelated factors, which are examined respectively in the first four sections of the paper:

- Strategic considerations stemming from Taiwan's geographic position in Northeast Asia lead Tokyo and Washington to prefer the status quo, while leading China to strive for reunification. The increasing power of the People's Liberation Army (PLA), however, is making both Japan and the United States nervous regarding China's ability to coerce a change in the status quo in the near future.

- Shared democratic values and the fact that the "democracy issue" has greatly prolonged the timetable for reunification give Taipei political influence in both Washington and Tokyo.

- China's constant threats of force actually empower Taipei in its relationship with Washington, and cause the United States to plan for the worst.

- Taiwan is a litmus test of U.S. credibility as an ally, a condition that in turn creates a perception on the island that U.S. military backing can be relied upon unconditionally. The United States should work to ensure that the U.S. position in the region, and the value of the United States to Asian nations as the balancer against China, would survive a Taipei-provoked conflict should the United States choose not to become directly involved. Washington can strive to achieve this by undertaking extensive consultations with Japan designed to ensure that Tokyo does not lose confidence in Washington and that the U.S.-Japan alliance remains strong.

While Taipei has been effective in drawing the United States into a de facto military alliance, and has caused Beijing to shift its Taiwan policy from reunification to halting independence (which is another way of supporting the status quo), Taipei's high-risk strategy carries with it the very real possibility of miscalculation.

Because miscalculation could lead to great power conflict, it is important to try to demilitarize the Taiwan issue. A conclusion thus offers a summary of recommendations necessary to achieve such a demilitarization. As one scenario, tensions may eventually lessen substantially if Beijing begins to substitute political deterrence for military deterrence. In addition, the United States and Japan should seek ways to mitigate the

possible impact on U.S. credibility if Washington decided not to intervene militarily should Taiwan recklessly and foolishly precipitate a crisis with China.

Geostrategic Issues and Considerations

Of the four factors, geography is the only element of strategy that does not change. Geography, to a very large degree, determines strategic interests and dictates the strategic choices in most national policies.

Taiwan's Strategic Importance to the PRC

When East Asia is considered in its totality—i.e., both continental and maritime domains, it is clear that China dominates the continent. This has been the case ever since Mao Zedong grove the U.S.-backed Nationalist Chinese allies off the continent in 1949 and U.S. forces were fought to a standstill on the Korean peninsula from 1950 to 1953. During the United States' last land war in Asia, the Vietnam War, the Johnson administration refused to countenance a number of seemingly sensible military actions against North Vietnam lest such moves draw the PRC directly into the war. Moreover, Vietnamese and Russian military capabilities have declined precipitously in the past two decades, and while the Indian army has made great strides since the 1962 Sino-Indian border skirmish, extreme Himalayan terrain ensures a secure buffer against a major invasion in either direction. On the continent, China is militarily supreme.

A very different situation exists, however, on the PRC's maritime frontier. Here, the United States and its island and archipelagic allies—including Japan and Taiwan—predominate. This has been an area of strategic vulnerability ever since China first encountered the West (including Westernized Japan) in the nineteenth century, and remains so today. Since defeating its only rival for primacy, Japan, in World War II, the United States has been the dominant military power in littoral Asia.

From Beijing's vantage point, the combination of the Ryukyu chain and Taiwan effectively act as a picket fence around the East China Sea, potentially constraining either access to the eastern seaboard of central and northern China (including Shanghai) or egress for PRC maritime traffic to the Pacific Ocean. James Lilley, former U.S. ambassador to China, accurately noted that Taiwan "is the cork in China's bottle." Taiwan falling into the PRC's hands would "end what China feels to be a blockade on its ability to control its surrounding seas."[1]

Taiwan Is Strategically Important to Tokyo

Tokyo has long been aware that the location of Taiwan has made the island strategically important to Japan. It was the Imperial Japanese Navy that persuaded the Japanese government to insist on the annexation of Taiwan in 1895; Japanese naval strategists believed that in order to become a "Western" industrialized society, Meiji Japan would require maritime trade to bring raw materials to Japan and to transport Japanese goods to countries around the world. As early as 1879, when Tokyo asserted sovereignty over the Ryukyu kingdom by unilaterally annexing this island chain,[2] Japanese strategists recognized the importance of having control over the islands spread along the major sea lanes between Japan and Southeast Asia.[3]

One hundred and ten years has not changed this geostrategic reality. As a major trading and energy-importing nation, Tokyo still realizes that Japan's economic viability is dependent on the maritime trade routes from the Middle East and Southeast Asia that pass through waters proximate to Taiwan. Because a hostile power in possession of Taiwan could easily disrupt maritime traffic bound for Japan, Taiwan is strategically significant to Japan.

Japan's vulnerability to economic isolation is not simply a conceptual problem for Tokyo. The U.S. submarine campaign in World War II, which succeeded in economically isolating Japan, is a historical reminder of the importance of preventing a disruption to maritime commerce. Hisahiko Okazaki has been explicit in spelling out the strategic implications of the PRC annexation of Taiwan: such a development would not only compromise the sea lanes upon which Japan's Middle Eastern oil imports travel (e.g., the Bashi Channel east of Taiwan), but also give China improved leverage in its relationship with Southeast Asia, which could have an indirect impact on Japan's significant economic interests in that region.[4]

Taiwan's Value for U.S. Hedging Strategy

Official U.S. policy has no explicit geostrategic caveats regarding reunification so long as any such unification is peacefully achieved with the consent of the people of Taiwan. There is no question, however, that as long as the long-term impact on regional stability occasioned by China's rise remains unclear, perpetuation of the status quo makes geostrategic sense. The history of World War II is a reminder to the United States that Taiwan's geographic position in East Asia is important. Japanese air power launched from bases in Taiwan destroyed General Douglas MacArthur's air force at Luzon in December 1941, and greatly facilitated the Japanese conquest of the Philippines.[5] Thus, PLA naval and air bases on the east coast of Taiwan would permit China to project power more easily throughout littoral East Asia, and provide the PRC with the ability to interrupt seaborne commerce destined for Northeast Asia. With Taiwan and its Pratas island group in PRC hands—along with the Paracels seized from Vietnam in 1974 and many of the Spratly islands, China would have territorial sea and economic exclusion zone claims to large chunks of the South China Sea.

Impact of China's Rise on Cross-Strait Stability

The difficult reality for Taiwan is that it is always going to be only one hundred miles from China, is always going to be one-fiftieth the size of China in terms of population, and is always going to be hugely disadvantaged in terms of the size of military establishments, long-term military potential, and the resources available for defense. Finally, as an island nation with few natural resources, Taiwan is always going to be dependent on maritime imports.

Taiwan has not been swallowed up over the past half-century largely because the Taiwan Strait presents a natural barrier to the power of the PLA, and because other great naval powers have helped to keep Chinese air and naval power on the west side of the strait. The Japanese were so much more militarily advanced than China in the 1894–95 Sino-Japanese War that they could promise to march on Beijing if their demands—including the annexation of Taiwan—were not met. Fifty-five years later it was the United States that was strong enough to underwrite Taiwan's security and permit the Republic of China (ROC) to survive.

During much of the Cold War, when China's military potential was either focused on the threat from the Soviet Union or was consumed by domestic unrest (such as the "Cultural Revolution") the defense establishment remained wedded to a doctrine of "People's War." The United States was thus able to fulfill its defense obligation with the U.S. forces then stationed in East Asia, which were principally responsible for the defense of Japan or Korea Taiwan did not require a large separate increment of "dedicated" U.S. military power. In this sense the defense of Taiwan was an "economy of force" commitment—a situation that soon will no longer be true due to steady improvements in the PLA. Soon, the cross-Strait balance will no longer grossly favor the combined capabilities of the United States and Taiwan.

The PLA's single-minded focus on Taiwan in recent years has, however, given the PLA the military capabilities necessary to reach Taiwan in a way that was not possible in earlier decades. The Chinese military is beginning to match Taiwan's qualitatively superior capabilities with equally, or nearly as advanced, Russian systems. As the December 2004 PRC defense white paper makes clear, the PLA is investing more in naval and air forces for the express purpose of establishing air and sea control over the seaward approaches to the PRC.[6] If not balanced by increased U.S and Taiwanese capabilities, the PLA's modernization will inevitably change the defense equation for both Taiwan and the United States.

Summary

In sum, Taiwan's geographic position creates geostrategic interests on the part of the United States and Japan that are different from those of the mainland. Washington and Tokyo's interests favor perpetuation of the status quo so long as the nature of a "risen China" remains an open question and the PRC's military modernization has the potential to destabilize the region. Neither the United States nor Japan is likely to press Taiwan on the issue of reunification. Tokyo and Washington will be content so long as Taipei does not go beyond the status quo and seek permanent separation of Taiwan and the mainland.

Democracy in Taiwan: The Influence of Democratic Values

In 1986 President Chiang Ching-kuo decided to gradually roll-back Kuomintang (KMT) authoritarian rule in Taiwan. Once in place, these political reforms resulted in a fairly rapid dismantlement of the institutions of repression. By 1996 Taiwan could boast of having a very lively democratic system. The 2000 elections actually resulted in a change in ruling party, and Chen Shui-bian—who had been jailed for democratic activism decades earlier—became president.

Democratic Values and the United States

This democratization process has had a major impact on the relationship with the United States by broadening Taiwan's political support to both major U.S. political parties. As Richard Bush writes: "Previously, American liberals had criticized the KMT for its repressive rule. Now the island was a poster child for American values, made all the more prominent by the fact that political repression was still the order of the day across the Taiwan Strait."[7]

Democracy and Reunification

The advent of democracy in Taiwan has also made it much more politically difficult for Washington to push Taipei into a unification dialogue in order to bring an end to Washington's 50-year security obligation. One of the most significant consequences of democracy took place in 1991, when Taiwan President Lee Teng-hui approved a set of Guidelines for National Reunification. In retrospect, this change put the island on a very different political trajectory in that Taipei dropped the pretense that the ROC represented the only legitimate government of China. As long as the PRC and the ROC each claimed to represent the true Chinese state and each aimed to reunify the country under its own political model, there was no dispute regarding concepts of "one China." Each side asserted it would end the Chinese civil war by "recovering" the territory occupied by the other.

Instead, Taipei's new guidelines accepted the PRC as the legitimate government of the part of China that Beijing controlled. This move effectively nullified the underlying premise of the 1972 Shanghai Communiqué that "Chinese on either side of the Taiwan Strait maintain there is but one China and that it is a part of China." As Harry Harding has stated, "Taiwan basically abandoned the vision of one country, one legitimate government that had been pursued by Chiang Kai-shek, Chiang Ching-kuo, and for that matter Mao Zedong and Deng Xiaoping."[8] The 1991 Guidelines for National Reunification softened the political blow of backing away from the old formulation of "one China" by stating that the ROC still envisioned a "one country, one system" future but only when the PRC had become "democratic, free, and equitably prosperous"—just like Taiwan.

The notion of reunification only when the mainland becomes democratic is implicit—but not explicit—U.S. policy as well. The U.S. policy of supporting no unilateral changes to the status quo was articulated in the oval office by President Bush in the presence of PRC Premier Wen Jiabao. This policy in effect means that the people of Taiwan have a veto over any reunification scheme with which they do not agree. Polls in Taiwan have repeatedly indicated that the citizens of Taiwan are not interested in reuniting with a mainland that is controlled by the Chinese Communist Party (CCP). Ironically, while applauding this presidential statement as a warning to Chen Shui-bian, Beijing was also endorsing a policy that does not promise any near-term resolution of this issue. That Beijing would be pleased over preservation of the status quo is testimony to how much Chen Shui-bian has managed to change the terms of the cross-Strait debate.

While the status quo may satisfy Washington over the long term and Beijing in the near term, the leadership in Taiwan remains distinctly unsatisfied. The status quo does not meet the growing desire of Taiwan's polity for greater international recognition of its democratic success. President Chen Shui-bian captured this desire in a 2004 speech on Taiwan's National Day: "There is no reason that the 23 million people of Taiwan should continue to be 'politically isolated' and remain as international nomads without due acknowledgement. Taiwan must stand tall on the international stage, with parity and dignity."[9]

The Bush Administration

In the early years of the first term of George W. Bush, the administration made conscious efforts to show U.S. sympathy regarding Taiwan's anomalous situation—the island is a full-blown democracy recognized by only a handful of insignificant countries, and excluded from virtually all international institutions that require "statehood" as a criterion for membership. By the middle of 2003 the Bush administration was characterized as " . . . pursuing a policy toward Taiwan that was more heavily weighted toward Taiwan than at any time since U.S. normalization of relations with the PRC."[10]

What this meant in practice was a decision to allow Chen Shui-bian to make an extended transit stop in the United States, including visits with two dozen members of Congress and attending public functions and meetings with local elected officials. Taiwan's Vice President Annette Lu, an outspoken independence advocate, was also permitted the same transit privileges. In a remarkable departure from previous practice, Taiwan's defense minister was authorized to visit the United States to attend a conference in Florida organized explicitly so he and his sizable entourage would be able to meet with an array of various defense contractors as well as with the Deputy Secretary of Defense Paul Wolfowitz and other officials from the Department of Defense (DoD). The administration also approved a Taiwan arms sales package that included submarines, something no previous administration was willing to authorize.[11]

Although having made an unprecedented good faith effort to both positively acknowledge Taiwan's democracy and give the island more "international space," the Bush administration's enthusiasm for the Chen administration began to wane in late summer of 2003. President Chen announced that he was planning to resolve some of the island's most difficult policy debates through the process of national referenda. This immediately provoked concern in Beijing because the CCP leadership is convinced that the referenda process is a slippery slope that will inevitably lead to a national referendum on independence—something Beijing absolutely opposes, seeing it as a concrete step toward *de jure* independence. A referendum could legitimize a declaration of independence as an act that reflects the will of the people of Taiwan.[12]

Because Beijing was concerned, Washington—deeply embroiled as it was in Afghanistan and Iraq—was also concerned. The Bush administration feared that Chen Shui-bian had embarked on a course that would eventually undermine stability across the Taiwan Strait. The last thing Washington wanted was another crisis on its hands. Washington was especially concerned because Chen was persisting in this course despite signals sent from the highest levels in the U.S. government that Taiwan should not go forward with a plan that could lead to a crisis. Chen's attitude regarding Washington's warnings was that he would not bow to pressure from Washington. "Taiwan is not a province of one country nor is it a state of another . . . I don't think a democratic country can oppose our democratic ideals."[13] From Washington's perspective, Chen was ignoring U.S. interests, a development which was especially irksome given how far the Bush administration had gone to expand the range of U.S.-Taiwan relations.

Chen's statement captures perfectly how the issue of shared democratic values empowers Taiwan when it deals with Washington. By seizing the moral high ground, Chen made it difficult for Washington to be too publicly critical of the direction in which Chen appeared to be heading, namely making changes to Taiwan's constitution. Private and diplomatic interventions fell on deaf ears. By brushing aside Washington's worries over provoking a crisis with Beijing, Chen Shui-bian was apparently willing to ignore President Bush's concerns over Taiwan's actions provoking a conflict with China. Assistant Secretary of State for East Asian and Pacific Affairs James Kelly stated in Capitol Hill testimony: "Because the possibility for the United States to become involved in a cross strait conflict is very real, the President knows that American lives are potentially at risk."[14]

Ten months after the March 2004 election in Taiwan, Chen himself suffered a political setback. In the December 2004 parliamentary elections, the people of Taiwan did not grant President Chen and his pan-Green coalition the majority in the Legislative Yuan that Chen was seeking. The election results were a relief to many China and Taiwan experts in the United States, both in and out of government, because the results seemed to demonstrate that the people of Taiwan were willing to restrain President Chen and his pan-Green alliance from going too far and risking conflict with the PRC.

These same experts remain worried, however, that continued assertive steps by Taipei, even if considered incremental, to seek a more independent status would pose a potentially explosive and unpredictable series of challenges to stability. Such a development could in turn lead to an escalation of tensions and possible conflict between the PRC and the United States that neither side desires.[15]

On January 22, 2005 a new element may have been introduced into the democratic values equation. President Bush's inaugural address may have reenergized Taipei's democratic value leverage by making clear that the goal of U.S. foreign policy is to spread democracy. This statement was surely greeted with smiles in Taipei because such an articulation comports nicely with Taipei's two-year-old initiative to promote an Asia-Pacific Democracy Alliance. In commenting on the implications of the inaugural address, Robert Kagan notes that: "In Asia, too, we may be on the threshold of a strategic reevaluation that places democratic allies, not China, at the core of American strategy."[16]

Democratic Values and Japan

Japan is very conscious of PRC sensitivities regarding Taiwan. Japan's official policy is found in a joint Sino-Japan communiqu "the Government of the People's Republic of China reiterates that Taiwan is the unalienable part of the territory of the People's Republic of China. The government of Japan fully understands and respects this stand . . ."[17] At the same time, Japan has also made an effort to maintain strong informal ties with Taipei.

Taiwan, for its part, has assiduously cultivated better ties with Japan, both to enhance the island's security and to try and gain greater international space. President Chen has attempted to build upon the foundation of historic and cultural connections between Japan and Taiwan, and—replicating the relationship with Washington—make democratic political values the predominate factor of the relationship.

Starting in the mid-1990s, Taiwan President Lee Teng-hui became an object of intense scrutiny by the Japanese mass media because of his charisma and intense admiration of Japan. Lee is from the generation of Taiwanese who remember Japanese colonial rule fondly. He himself was a graduate of a prestigious Japanese university, served in the Japanese military during World War II,[18] and speaks fluent Japanese. Historical and cultural ties have easily blended with democratic values to create a generally sympathetic Japanese political attitude toward Taiwan. Shared democratic values make it easier for pro-Taiwan Japanese politicians to offer overt support of Taiwan even at times when official Japanese policy may be more favorably disposed toward Beijing.

Prime Minister Koizumi came up through the ranks of Japan's Liberal Democratic Party (LDP) as a member of the Mori faction, a group with a reputation for being pro-Taiwan. Unsurprisingly, in late 2002 Japan changed its policy guidelines regarding travel to Taiwan by government officials in order to permit division chiefs and even higher-ranking officials to visit the island on a case-by-case basis. Throughout 2003 Taipei and Tokyo took a series of relatively minor steps designed to improve political relations. These efforts culminated in a private visit in December 2003 by former Prime Minister Yoshiro Mori to Taipei, where he met with President Chen.[19]

Despite closer political relationships, Tokyo shares Washington's alarm regarding Chen's insistence on taking steps toward constitutional revision that will be certain to aggravate Beijing. Japan is conscious of the fact that any conflict in the Taiwan Strait that involves the United States will require that U.S. forces utilize facilities in Okinawa and perhaps elsewhere in the southern Ryukyus. Though Taiwan was not specifically mentioned in the 1997 U.S.-Japan Guidelines for Defense Cooperation, which mentioned the vague term of "area around Japan," the above scenario would directly involve Japan.

Tokyo has been willing of late to make much more explicit its concerns regarding conflict over Taiwan. In the February 19, 2005 joint U.S.-Japanese statement on shared strategic goals following the "2+2" meeting (secretaries of state and defense meeting with their Japanese counterparts), Washington and Tokyo made clear that they had discussed the Taiwan issue. The official statement called for a peaceful resolution of issues concerning the Taiwan Strait and for China to become more militarily transparent. The fact that Taiwan was explicitly mentioned was noteworthy and suggests that Tokyo is becoming much more concerned over China's ability to use military muscle to coerce Taiwan.[20]

Like Washington, there is a strong values-based aspect of Tokyo's relationship with Taiwan. Economic linkages also remain strong, of course, but the values-based relationship has a connection to Japan's past that is unique. While China continues to berate Japan over the "history question," Taiwan both values and publicly embraces its historic relationship with Tokyo. Taiwan represents the only "success story" to emerge from Japan's imperialistic history during the first half of the twentieth century. Japanese can consider their colonial activities in Taiwan with pride, or at least not shame.[21]

The particular combination of geographic proximity, a positive historic memory, and shared democratic values all contribute to Taipei's ability to influence Japanese public opinion. Over the years this ability has led Japan to adopt a more congenial Taiwan policy.

China's Policy of Threatening the Use of Force

While Taiwan's dynamic democracy and quest for international space will continue to feature in the geopolitical landscape, this dynamism need not inevitably lead to war. The reality is that Beijing is the only party that constantly threatens the use of force—in effect keeping its finger on the trigger of conflict. The PRC claims to desire a peaceful resolution; according to China, Beijing has only emphasized forcible alternatives because Taipei would otherwise choose independence. By implication, this suggests that Beijing would back away from forcible alternatives if Taipei would refrain from initiatives that make Beijing worry about *de jure* independence. This section will examine the validity of this pretext.

How Taiwan "Benefits" from Saber Rattling

The Chen administration would prefer to change the status quo peacefully, ideally with the blessing of Beijing or even unilaterally without the risk of war. Taiwan's ruling government is inhibited from doing so because Beijing will not agree to a peaceful separation. Since 1991 the political leaders of Taiwan have been able to operate just below the PRC's use-of-force threshold, have

gradually cultivated a distinct Taiwanese identity, and have diminished public sentiment on the island for eventual political reunification with the mainland. Unfortunately, this dangerous political strategy keeps the Taiwan Strait crisis pot at a near boil, and is slowly alienating Washington and keeping Beijing in a near constant state of agitation.

This strategy has, however, had some success. Because of Taipei's incremental approach toward creating a separate Taiwanese political identity, Beijing's policy has changed focus from promoting reunification to simply preventing Taiwanese independence. Taipei's short-term success may in fact signal a pyrrhic victory, however, since these gains have provided focus and a sense of urgency for PRC military modernization and, as a result, is increasing the prospect of cross-Strait conflict.

While Taipei's efforts agitate Washington, Taipei derives its greatest leverage through manipulating Beijing and causing the CCP leadership to feel a need to constantly rattle sabers. With every rattle, U.S. officials fear that Beijing's use of force is more, rather than less, likely. As the perceived threat to Taiwan grows, Washington becomes even more involved in planning for Taiwan's defense. As a result, Washington has taken a number of steps, including: agreeing to sell previously prohibited sophisticated weapons to Taiwan, reestablishing previously prohibited military contacts with the ROC military, actively examining how China might attack Taiwan, and actively considering what courses of action the United States should pursue in the event of a Chinese attack. In the security realm, Taipei and Washington have become markedly more cooperative over the past five years.

PRC Military Modernization

The PRC is being very systematic in its approach to military modernization.[22] David Finkelstein has written: "Years from now we will look back at the 1990s, especially the period from 1995 to 2000 as the point when the PLA dedicated itself in earnest to becoming a more professional military organization and a more operationally competent organization."[23] The Chinese military is putting in place a series of regulations that are remarkable in scope and ambition.[24] Wide-ranging reforms focus on the examination of new operational concepts, the modernization of the PLA's weapons, integration of state-of-the-art technologies, rethinking command and control relationships, personnel recruitment and retention, professional military education, and improving logistics. The PLA is at last beginning to reap the benefits of China's economic development and resulting growing wealth. The PLA's ballistic missile force provides China with a military capability for which there are still no proven defenses; Beijing today has the ability to punish Taiwan immediately should the island declare independence.[25]

An Alternative to the Use of Force

The combination of growing military capabilities on one side of the Taiwan Strait and an energetic, highly nationalist democracy on the other side creates a powerful incentive for Beijing to employ its new capabilities. To discourage the use of force, either Chen Shui-bian must stop inciting the PRC or Beijing must consider alternative approaches.

In terms of the latter, one approach would be to make better use of diplomacy. China's rising economic power has actually led to tremendous growth in Beijing's global political and diplomatic influence. The PRC can now exert great leverage by granting or withholding business opportunities, and by negotiating between many potential suppliers for the purchase of high-end first-world manufactured goods. Perhaps the most dramatic example of political leverage derived from economic clout was the proposed lifting of the economic sanctions on the sale of military equipment to China that was imposed by the European Union (EU) following the Tiananmen incident in 1989. Sustained diplomatic effort by the United States over the past twelve months to persuade the EU to refrain from rolling back the sanctions actually seemed to be failing—until Beijing persisted in passing anti-secession legislation authorizing the use of force, the EU was on the verge of revoking the sanctions. True, Beijing's apparent misstep has made Washington's concerns more credible to Europeans. Both Germany and France still argue, however, that lifting the sanctions is a necessary symbolic step in recognizing China's status as a rising power. Moreover, as China has pointed out, the sanctions are an impediment to greater economic cooperation.[26]

The PRC's increasing global influence thus now provides Beijing with a credible substitute for its "use-of-force" policy as a means to deter Taiwan independence.[27] Beijing could use its diplomatic influence to gain a commitment from nations around the world to announce official statements of non-recognition in the event that Taiwan declared independence, thereby making threats of force from the PRC unnecessary. If Taiwan declared independence and was not recognized, and in the process lost even its unofficial representation in major capitals around the world, the island's international situation would be much worse than it is today. The PRC's growing military, instead of being actively brandished, would instead be a latent reality. Beijing would thus be pursuing a policy reminiscent of Theodore Roosevelt's maxim, "speak softly, but carry a big stick."

At least conceptually, such a course of action would reduce the leverage that Chen Shui-bian and his pan-Green coalition currently wields. The impact that such a change in policy would have on public opinion in Taiwan is difficult to assess; certainly such a change in PRC tactics would help shift the debate in Taiwan from the current focus on independence as an end in itself to a consideration of how Taiwan could sustain such independence if unrecognized by the international community. Such a development would force politicians to confront the reality that Taiwan is not likely to ever become a *de jure* independent state without the explicit acquiescence of Beijing, something that no one thinks will be forthcoming. Finally, by backing away from overt threats to use force, China would also reduce the likelihood of becoming embroiled in a conflict with the United States and Japan over Taiwan.

The Symbolic Importance of Taiwan to U.S. Credibility

For well over a century, the United States has proclaimed itself a Pacific power. Even though the United States is not Asian in a geographic sense, U.S. commitment to the region is an enduring one for the sake of both Asia and the United States. As Colin Powell stated in June 2003: the U.S. is "a Pacific Power" and "we will not yield our strategic position in Asia."[28]

A fundamental interest for Washington today is the preservation of regional stability, which in turn requires forward-deployed U.S. forces in the region. As noted in the 2001 *Quadrennial Defense Review Report*, the United States remains committed to a presence in East Asia that is strong enough to "deter forward without massive reinforcement" in order to maintain stability; stability, in turn, is the *sine qua non* for economic development, which then creates prosperity.[29] This fundamental strategic goal can only be accomplished through the United States' bilateral alliance system. Alliances are the bedrock of the U.S. strategic position in Asia because access to bases and facilities, especially those in Japan and Korea, allows the United States to maintain large numbers of U.S. forces permanently in the region.

When the basing agreement between the Philippines and the United States was abrogated in 1992, however, the United States lost access to crucial air hubs on the periphery of Asia. This loss has made U.S. defense commitments to maritime Southeast Asia, as well as to Taiwan, much more difficult to sustain. Without these Philippine airfields, U.S. ability to introduce hundreds of land-based aircraft into the region is constrained; with the exception of Japan, the United States lacks facilities within "untanked" range of the Taiwan Straits from which to operate. The loss of these airbases in the Philippines provides a cautionary example of how domestic politics in nations hosting U.S. forces can undercut U.S. strategic interests and defense commitments. When the reliability of U.S. commitment is called into question, or when the perceived need for a U.S. presence is not compelling enough to overcome the drawbacks of a U.S. presence, democratic allies might request the departure of U.S. forces from that country.

Is Taiwan a Litmus Test?

The point of the preceding discussion is to provide a context for considering how Taiwan may be viewed by Asian governments as a litmus test for U.S. reliability as a stabilizing presence. The United States demands much of its Japanese and Korean alliance partners—including financial support, some degree of extraterritoriality for U.S. military personnel stationed in allied nations, inconveniences inflicted upon local populations caused by U.S. training activities, and de facto U.S. sovereignty over base facilities.

Would such allies be willing to accept the "costs" of U.S. bases if the United States was perceived as either unreliable or unwilling to come to the aid of an ally that was threatened or attacked by China? Would U.S. credibility and reliability as an ally be called into question if Beijing could successfully force Taipei to reunify, or even force Taipei—against the popular will of the people of Taiwan—to begin discussions leading to reunification? Governments in Tokyo and Seoul, and certainly elsewhere in the region, might conclude that relying upon the United States to balance China and guarantee national security in the case of an assertive China is a very high-risk, low pay-off strategy. After all, sentiment in Japan and South Korea might reason that China is always going to be a close neighbor, whereas the Pacific Ocean separates the United States from Asia. If the United States was unable or unwilling to defend Taiwan—a de facto ally much praised for its democratic success, why put up with all the problems and costs associated with a U.S. presence?

Asian nations do have other alternatives. One is to consider how best to live peacefully alongside China without a U.S. military presence in the region. Beijing has been promoting the idea that bilateral military alliances are relics of the Cold War. Perhaps Beijing is correct. Maybe the 50-year-old alliance-based security architecture that Washington still espouses has outlived its usefulness. Perhaps the way forward for Asia is what China sees as a new concept of security, one based on collectivism, non-intervention, and dialogue. China disavows attempts to exclude the United States from the economic life of Asia, and instead claims to be simply calling into question Washington's assertion that a U.S. military presence in Asia provides stability.

Credibility—Vietnam Then and Taiwan Now

Predictions of the dire implications for U.S. interests over any loss of U.S. credibility are not new. Arguments for staying the course in Vietnam in the 1960s were often based on the preservation of credibility. Following the strategic defeat in Vietnam, however, there was no noticeably negative impact on either the U.S. position in Asia or on U.S. credibility in general. If Washington's credibility survived Vietnam, why would it not also survive the loss of Taiwan? Is Taiwan really that much of a litmus test, especially if rash action on Taipei's part was widely perceived as having precipitated a PRC use of force?

Both conflicts began as an ideologically driven civil war over whether communism would be the political system that unified the country. In the Taiwan scenario, China has since replaced political ideology with sovereignty as the rationale for reunification—the so-called "one country, two systems" policy. Taipei and Washington, on the other hand, still consider political ideology as central. One must bear in mind, however, that the PRC does not claim sovereignty over other nations of Asia. Perhaps then a failure in the face of the sovereignty dispute over Taiwan would, like Vietnam, not result in a loss of credibility. This might be especially true since all of the countries of Asia have signed on to the "one China" principle, effectively siding with Beijing in the dispute.

In contrasting Vietnam and Taiwan for insights into the issue of credibility, the more salient consideration is likely to revolve around the differences in influence and power between North Vietnam in the 1970s and China today. North Vietnam was never perceived as a military threat to all of East Asia.[30] China, on the other hand, poses a potential threat to the interests of U.S. allies

who host U.S. bases, particularly Japan. It is Japan that hosts the most important bases for the forward deployment of U.S. power, and if those bases were to be shut down (as in the Philippines), the United States' entire strategic approach to East Asia would have to be rethought. Because Japanese bases make a substantial forward presence possible (and such a presence is how the United States preserves stability), the most important aspect of the credibility issue is its impact on the U.S.-Japan alliance.

Given Japan's strategic concerns over Taiwan falling into the PRC's hands, Tokyo would likely be deeply conflicted should Taiwan provoke China to use force and should the United States choose to stand aside. On the one hand, U.S. involvement would require the use of Japanese bases, which would directly involve Japan in the conflict. On the other hand, if the United States does not respond, would Japanese confidence in its ally be affected? In this case, Washington would have to communicate clearly to Japan that any U.S. failure to go to war with the PRC as a result of Taiwanese miscalculation and rashness is unrelated to Washingon's treaty obligation to defend Japan, including in the case of any Chinese aggression against Japan. Tokyo might also insist that Washington become unequivocal in its willingness to support Japanese claims to the disputed islands and other areas claimed by both Tokyo and Beijing.

Washington and Tokyo have recently decided to put in place a regular process for addressing this issue as an aspect of what they term "common strategic objectives." This is a good venue for discussions related to the full range of Taiwan conflict scenarios.[31] At one level uniformed officers could explore alternative scenarios, including the full spectrum of possible options ranging from a PRC "bolt-out-of-the-blue" attack to a Taiwan-precipitated crisis. Concurrently, at the policy level of government the strategic and policy implications associated with the range of alternatives needs to be explored, perhaps in a series of so-called "seminar scenario exercises." Given both the political sensitivities in Japan and Beijing's likely adverse reaction, these are the sorts of issues that must be explored behind a veil of secrecy.

Credibility and the U.S.-ROK Alliance

The issue of U.S. credibility with allies other than Japan must also be considered. In the case of South Korea, so long as North Korea remains a military threat and the U.S. continues to be committed militarily to the defense of South Korea, the U.S.-ROK alliance would probably survive if the United States opted not to fight in a Taipei-provoked crisis with Beijing. Seoul, like Tokyo, would probably be pulled in two different directions. South Korea would be grateful for not having to choose between China and the United States regarding the use of U.S. bases in Korea, but would have to deal with anxiety concerning the value of the U.S. commitment to the ROK in the event of a crisis on the Korean Peninsula. The current plans to greatly reduce the U.S. Army presence in the ROK do have the potential to cast doubt on U.S. reliability should the United States choose to stand aside in a crisis instigated by Taipei. So long as U.S. ground forces are deployed along the demilitarized zone—a place where they would be involved almost immediately in combat with any invading North Korean army—there is little doubt concerning U.S. willingness to become involved. Indeed, as long as South Korea believes it must deter North Korea, Seoul has no other choice but to rely on the U.S. alliance in order to make deterrence credible.

Credibility from Taiwan's Perspective

Perhaps the most difficult aspect of the credibility issue concerns the perception in Taipei. Taiwan authorities seem to have convinced themselves that, regardless of the circumstances, they can count on U.S. intervention should China attack. On a number of occasions during visits to Taipei, I have been told that the United States would not dare to stand aside due to worries of a loss of credibility—even if Taiwan had provoked the crisis. The importance of U.S. regional credibility would weigh too heavily.

Whether or not such impressions are correct, the illusion of unconditional U.S. backing frees Taipei from the precautionary measures of thinking through the consequences of provoking the PRC. This may be why Deputy Secretary of State Richard Armitage, in a television interview, responded to the question, "Will we defend Taiwan from China if they attack?" with the following comment:

> We have the requirement with the Taiwan Relations Act to keep sufficient forces in the Pacific to be able to deter an attack, [but] we are not required to defend. These are questions that reside with the U.S. Congress, who has to declare an act of war.[32]

Although contradicting the 2001 statement of the Bush administration that the United States would defend Taiwan at any cost, Armitage's reply was intended to introduce a degree of uncertainty in the minds of ROC leaders in Taipei, and to regain a degree of ambiguity in U.S. strategic intentions. This last statement still leaves the issue of U.S. credibility hanging. Would Washington believe the defense of Taiwan necessary in order to preserve U.S. standing and influence in East Asia? So long as the U.S.-Japan alliance remains firm and U.S. forces maintain access to bases in Japan, issues surrounding U.S. credibility in the face of a rising China will not likely undermine the U.S. position in East Asia.

Conclusion

This paper has examined the interrelated factors contributing to Taipei's ability to manipulate the cross-Strait political dialogue. This co-optation has placed the United States, China, and Japan in positions where they must respond to Taipei. Japan and the United States would likely be more than happy with an indefinite perpetuation of the current status quo, as long as economic exchanges between Taiwan and the mainland continue to improve. China, until recently, has not been satisfied with the status quo. A mere four years ago Beijing was so impatient with the lack of progress toward reunification that it was threatening to pre-emptively attack Taiwan. That impatience has since disappeared (at least publicly), to be replaced by a policy geared toward halting Taiwan independence—which is merely another way of supporting the current status quo.

Of the four factors examined in this paper, the first was the geostrategic relationship of the four parties. Neither Taiwan, the United States, or Japan have any interest in changing the current political situation through reunification. Taipei is disinterested because the island does not want to be absorbed into China. The United States and Japan are disinterested because they are strategically satisfied with the status quo so long as the PRC's future impact on power relationships in East Asia remains uncertain.

None of the three parties involved should want to change the second factor, the shared democratic values between Taiwan, Japan, and the United States. Democracy on Taiwan demonstrates not only that Chinese people can thrive in a democratic political environment, but also that the Chinese do value personal freedoms associated with democracy as much as any other people on earth.

The success of democracy in Taiwan has changed everything in the cross-Strait relationship. Taiwan is even more secure now that political change on the island has tipped the political balance in the United States in favor of support for an "embattled" democracy. Yet, paradoxically, democratization has also increased Taiwan's peril, as the DPP and pan-Green coalition continue to associate democracy and *de jure* independence in a way that threatens Beijing with the specter of permanent separation. Shared democratic values can, however, only go so far; they do not bestow upon Taipei the privilege of ignoring the national security interests of democratic partners.

The PRC's threat to use force is the third and most important factor addressed by this paper. Beijing must certainly realize by now that while the threat of force is enough to scare the Taiwanese away from a declaration of independence, it is not enough to make the island desire reunification. In fact, the threat of force actually contributes to a perpetuation of the status quo. Over the long term, the threat of force is a losing proposition. It militarizes the situation and makes the prospect of great power conflict over Taiwan a very real possibility. The PRC's growing global influence provides Beijing with a credible substitute for a militant policy as a way to deter Taiwan independence. By backing away from overt pledges of using force, China would also reduce the threat of conflict with both the United States and Japan over Taiwan. While not being able to resolve the issue of reunification, a diplomatic approach would go a long way toward demilitarizing the issue.

Finally, the issue of U.S. credibility in the face of a PRC attack on Taiwan is one that demands more thought. This author was among those who applauded President Bush's introduction of strategic clarity into the Taiwan situation in 2001 with his "do whatever it took" statement because it was a direct way to address Beijing's pre-emptive policy, otherwise known as the "third if," (i.e., China would attack if Taiwan refused to get serious about reunification). What the Bush administration did not immediately do, however, was to make sure that Taipei did not interpret this as a blank check. It is in Washington's interests that Taiwan be in doubt over whether the United States would underwrite the island's security regardless of how provocatively Taipei acted toward Beijing.

This paper has sought to examine the issue of credibility more closely to determine if such a conclusion is accurate. Would U.S. interests be at risk if Washington did not intervene in the event that Taiwan provokes a conflict? In my analysis, the key is Japan. The United States should work to ensure that the U.S. position in the region and its value to Asian nations as the balancer against China would survive any lack of response to a Taipei-provoked conflict. Washington can strive to achieve this by undertaking extensive consultations with Japan that are designed to ensure that Tokyo does not lose confidence in Washington and that the U.S.-Japan alliance remains strong. Bilateral U.S.-Japanese discussions on the issue should take place before any such scenario occurs.

On balance, the fact that Taipei has been able to manipulate the PRC, the United States, and (to a lesser extent) Japan, is not a desirable situation for any of the three major powers involved. By subtly changing the status quo so that all three major powers are now committed to preserving it, Taipei may have actually introduced some stability into the situation. Much remains to be done, however, in order to ensure that Taipei's strategy does not further change the status quo in a way that would precipitate a war. Japan has an important role to play by making clear that it will not support an independent Taiwan against the wishes of Beijing; the PRC has the leading role to play by seizing the opportunity to move away from threats of force. Washington needs to ensure that Taipei understands that the United States will not underwrite foolish or reckless behavior that jeopardizes U.S. national interests.

Notes

1. Ambassador James Lilley, quoted in Nancy Bernkopf Tucker, "If Taiwan Chooses Unification, Should the United States Care?" *Washington Quarterly 25,* no. 3 (Summer 2002), 22.

2. The island chain includes Okinawa and stretches southward all the way to Taiwan.

3. The Ryukyu kingdom had been a Chinese tributary since 1372 and concurrently a district of the Southern Japanese Satsuma domain since 1609. When negotiations between Tokyo and Peking to resolve the status proved fruitless. Japan unilaterally annexed them. See S.C.M. Paine. *The Sino-Japanese War of 1894–1895: Perceptions, Power and Primacy* (New York: Cambridge University Press, 2003), 90–91.

4. Hisahiko Okazaki, "The Strategic Value of Taiwan" (paper prepared for U.S.-Japan-Taiwan Trilateral Strategic Dialogue, Tokyo, March 2, 2003) http://www.glocomnet.or.jp/okazaki-inst. While Okazaki's interpretation may be a bit overdrawn, many Japanese do share his view.

5. H.P. Willmott, *Empires in the Balance: Japanese and Allied Pacific Strategies to April 1942* (Annapolis, MD: U.S. Naval Institute Press, 1982), 146–48. Willmott provides an excellent assessment of the impact of Japanese airpower flying from Formosa at the start of World War II.

6. State Council Information Office, *China's National Defense in 2004,* Beijing, December 2006, 6.

7. Richard C. Bush, "The United States and Taiwan" (paper presented at the International Conference on the United Nations and Taiwan, New Century Institute, September 2003), 6.

8. Harry Harding, "'One China' or 'One Option': The Contending Formulas for Relations across the Taiwan Strait," (lecture, Asian Affairs Committee of the Association of the Bar of New York, November 1, 2000), reprinted in the *National Committee for U.S.-China Relations Newsletter*, March 2001.

9. For a printed version of Chen's speech, see "President Chen's National Day Address," *Taiwan Update* 5, no. 11 (October 29, 2004), 5 http://www.tecro.org/taipei_update/pdf-issues/102904.pdf.

10. "Taiwan: Recent Developments and U.S. Policy Choices," *CRS Issue Brief for Congress* (updated July 16, 2003), CRS–12.

11. Worth remembering is that, due to successful PRC economic and diplomatic pressure, no country except the United States is willing to sell arms to Taiwan.

12. The author most recently discussed the slippery slope metaphor with a delegation from a variety of Chinese think tanks in May 2004 during an extended meeting focused on the Taiwan issue. This has long been a Chinese concern and has been reinforced of late by the series of incremental steps taken by Lee Teng-hui and Chen Shui-bian toward *de jure* independence.

13. John Pomfret, "Taiwanese Leader Condemns Beijing's 'One China' Policy; Chen Dismisses Fear in U.S. of Rising Tension," *The Washington Post*, October 7, 2003, A18.

14. Assistant Secretary of State for East Asian and Pacific Affairs James Kelly, testimony to the House International Relations Committee, April 21, 2004 http://hongkong.usconsulate.gov/uscn/state/2004/042101.htm. One of the many important points made by Kelly in his testimony was that "there are limitations with respect to what the United States will support as Taiwan considers possible changes to its constitution."

15. On December 5, 2004 the Foreign Service Institute and CNA sponsored a seminar exercise on cross-Strait issues, during which this point was emphasized by U.S. experts.

16. Robert Kagan, "A Higher Realism," *Washington Post*, January 23, 2005, B7.

17. Quoted in Lam Peng-er and Ja Ian Chong, "Japan-Taiwan Relations: Between Affinity and Reality," *Asian Affairs. An American Review* 30, no. 4 (Winter 2004): 249. This article contains an excellent discussion of all facets pertaining to the Taiwan-Japan relationship.

18. Ibid., 256–59. Some 200,000 Taiwanese fought in the Imperial Japanese Army, suffering an estimated 30,000 dead.

19. David Fouse, "Japan-Taiwan Relations: A Case of Tempered Optimism," *A Special Assessment: Asia's Bilateral Relations* (Honolulu: Asia-Pacific Center for Security Studies, October 2004), 4–6.

20. U.S. Department of State, "Joint Statement of the U.S.-Japan Security Consultative Committee," February 19, 2005 http://www.state.gov/r/pa/prs/ps/2005/42490.htm.

21. David M. Finkelstein has written that, "During the half century the people of Taiwan lived a regimented and often repressive existence as second-class citizens within the Japanese colonial empire. At the same time, however, the same spirit and resolve which Meiji modernizers exhibited at home was applied in their first colonial possession. Japan quickly transformed an underdeveloped and all but neglected frontier area on the fringe of the Ch'ing empire into a relatively modern, economically developed, and self sufficient island whose standard of living in Asia was second only to the Japanese themselves." David M. Finkelstein, *Washington's Taiwan Dilemma, 1949–1950: From Abandonment to Salvation* (Fairfax, VA: George Mason University Press, 1993), 46–47.

22. For a good summation of current developments in Chinese military modernization, see U.S. Department of Defense, "FY-04 Report on PRC Military Power," May 29, 2004. For analysis by non-DOD experts, see James R. Lilley and David Shambaugh, eds., *China's Military Faces the Future* (Armonk, NY: American Enterprise Institute and M.E. Sharpe, 1999); Larry Wortzel, ed., *The Chinese Armed Forces in the 21st Century* (Carlisle, PA: Strategic Studies Institute, December 1999); Andrew Scobell and Larry Wortzel, eds., China's *Growing Military Power: Perspectives on Security, Ballistic Missiles and*

Conventional Capabilities (Carlisle, PA: Strategic Studies Institute, September 2002); and David Shambaugh, *Modernizing China's Military: Progress, Problems, and Prospects* (Berkeley, CA: University of California Press, 2002).

23. David Finkelstein (presentation to the Council on Foreign Relations Task Force on Chinese Military Modernization, September 24, 2002).

24. To illustrate this point, Appendix II of the 2002 Defense White Paper includes a four-page list of the new laws and regulations promulgated since 2000 alone.

25. The Patriot PAC–3 missile defense system has been fielded and shows potential, but has yet to prove itself against a large number of incoming missiles. The Taiwan of today is not in much better shape than England was against German V-2 ballistic missiles during World War II. The best thing for Taiwan to do is traditional "entrenchment and bomb-proofing."

26. Frank Umbach, statement, December 2004, to the Symposia on Transatlantic Perspectives on Economic and Security Relations with China, U.S. Economic and Security Review Commission, 108th Congress, U.S. Government Printing Office, 83–85   http://www.uscc.gov. See also Daniel Dombey and Guy Dinsmore, "EU and U.S. Seek to Defuse China Tensions," *Financial Times*, January 31, 2005   http://news.ft.com/cms/s/b617aa84-73b4-11d9-b705-00000e2511c8.html.

27. As noted above, China has already been able to deter arms sales to Taiwan from every country other than the United States.

28. U.S. Secretary of State Colin Powell, "Remarks at Asia Society Annual Dinner," June 10, 2002 http://www.asiasociety.org/speeches/powell.html.

29. U.S. Department of Defense, *Quadrennial Defense Review Report*, September 30, 2000, 4.

30. North Vietnam may have been viewed as a threat to Southeast Asia perhaps, but certainly not to Northeast Asia, where U.S. allies have resided.

31. "Joint Statement of the U.S.-Japan Security Consultative Committee."

32. Deputy Secretary of State Richard Armitage, interview by Charlie Rose, PBS, December 20, 2004.

MICHAEL MCDEVITT (Rear Admiral, retired) is Vice President and Director of the Center for Naval Analyses at the CNA Corporation. These views are his own and do not represent the views of the CNA Corporation. He can be reached at <mcdevitm@cna.org>.

Keywords: Taiwan; China; United States; Japan; Foreign Relations

Taiwan Examines Its Policies of Diplomacy

I-CHUNG LAI

Taiwan's diplomatic plight in recent years has been troubling for many concerned with the island's political survival. Unable to compete with China's growing political and economic influence, in the last three years alone Taiwan has lost six of its thirty diplomatic allies—Chad, Grenada, Dominica, Senegal, Liberia and Vanuatu—with another critical ally—the Vatican—rumored to be contemplating a transfer of recognition as well (*Taipei Times*, April 5, 2005). While such challenges are hardly a novelty in Taiwan's struggle for recognition on the international arena, it is one that Taipei has found itself losing, particularly in recent years. With few options remaining and its back to the wall in its fight for international statehood, Taiwan has recognized the necessity of reexamining its policies toward diplomatic relationships.

Mounting Challenges . . .

Wielding both tremendous political and economic influence, China's modus operandi in persuading Taiwan's existing allies to switch diplomatic recognition has consisted of both sticks—as in the cases of both Macedonia and Chad—and carrots—economic incentives that Taiwan has been hard-pressed to counter [1]. Concerned that Taiwan is competing in an already lost race for diplomatic recognition, a number of domestic observers have engaged in debates over Taiwan's longstanding policy of financial assistance in return for diplomatic recognition. Some have criticized the wisdom behind the government's strategy of what they view as unconditional assistance to countries with seemingly little political and strategic importance [2]. These countries, they argue, not only possess little political and economic capital—even collectively—but also demonstrate questionable loyalty, answering to the calls of the highest bidder. Others have questioned whether Taiwan should engage in the struggle for international diplomatic recognition at all. Given its limited resources, Taiwan is simply unable to win the "bidding competition" for diplomatic recognition vis-à-vis China. Taiwan's generous financial assistance to its allies has come under considerable international criticism as well. Most recently, New Zealand Foreign Minister Winston Peters condemned Taiwan's participation in "checkbook diplomacy" as a destabilizing force in the Pacific that has resulted in the delay of political reforms and the prolonging of the social upheaval on the Solomon Islands (*Taipei Times*, August 18).

. . . Result in a Pragmatic Strategy

In response to these concerns, in the last six years, Taipei has significantly changed its practices of providing international assistance to countries with formal diplomatic relations with Taiwan. Rather than providing direct monetary assistance, much as it had done in the past, aid now appears in the form of international assistance programs, which are evaluated according to the joint needs of both the recipients as well as Taiwan. These international assistance programs cover issues as broad as the digital divide, agricultural and fishery technology and medical assistance. When evaluating the merits of each individual program, the Taiwanese government now takes into consideration the extent to which the programs allow for Taiwan's added participation in the region as well as the extent of economic benefits derived by both countries. Furthermore, all major assistance programs are now highly transparent and are administered through the non-governmental organization, the International Cooperation and Development Fund (ICDF), which is under constant congressional oversight.

In addition to the implementation of international assistance programs, Taiwan has also utilized multilateral institutions as an additional instrument to secure its existing diplomatic relations. The most recent example of such is the "Taiwan-Pacific Allies Summit," the first of which was held on September 5 in Palau

(*Taipei Times*, September 6). Drawing upon its experiences with its Central American allies, Taiwan merged its existing bilateral relations with Palau, Tuvalu, the Marshall Islands and the Solomon Islands to produce the new multilateral body. While the long-term sustainability as well as the effectiveness of such an institution remains to be seen, such an effort is likely to shift Taiwan's efforts away from sustaining formal bilateral relations and refocus them on developing a role in regional cooperation.

"New Thinking" on Diplomatic Relations

Recognizing that it has been on the losing end of China's diplomatic offensive, a number of policymakers and academics have called for a reevaluation of not only Taiwan's strategy toward maintaining current and obtaining additional diplomatic allies, but also its underlying policy for seeking international allies. Following China's decision to sever diplomatic relations with Taiwan and resume relations with China, Taiwan's Democratic Progressive Party (DPP) Chairman Yu Shyi-kun notably declared that Taiwan's international status should not be measured by the number of Taiwan's diplomatic allies [3]. Rather, Taiwan's status is a decision that should be made only by the Taiwanese people themselves. Given that the previous goals of Taiwan's international assistance programs were to sustain Taiwan's diplomatic relations with existing allies and to prevent China's encroachment, a shift in Taiwan's policies would result in an entirely different program. Rather than devoting the bulk of its assistance toward its existing diplomatic allies, Taiwan would choose the targets for its aid programs—focused on the establishment of broader social, economic and political relations—based upon Taiwan's strategic interests [4]. Taiwan would not be relegated to participating in the "bidding game" against China's diplomatic offensive and instead, could focus on longer-term objectives.

Yet some, including this author, have pointed out that in order for such a policy to be truly actionable, questions regarding the potential loss of all diplomatic allies and consequently, the pragmatic and concrete benefits that have been afforded to Taiwan through its diplomatic relations would have to be answered. Strictly speaking, from the perspective of international law, the ending of a formal relationship would not denote the loss of Taiwan's statehood, though its status as a state with international legitimacy would be severely weakened with no formal recognition as support. Moreover, the loss of diplomatic allies would also eliminate the critical channels that Taipei currently relies upon to voice its concerns in international organizations that it has been denied membership, particularly the United Nations. Without such channels, Taiwan's already muffled voice may become altogether inaudible.

There is no question that Taipei must reconsider its existing policies toward the cultivation and preservation of its diplomatic allies. Its current strategy of utilizing international assistance programs as its primary instrument of foreign policy is simply unsustainable, especially given China's considerably deeper coffers and its mounting political power. What has yet to be determined, however, is a cohesive policy that effectively promotes Taiwan's statehood and interests on the international arena while taking into account its limited resources.

Notes

1. In the case of Macedonia, in 1999, China vetoed the continuation of the UN peacekeeping operation in Macedonia in order to force Skopje to sever its diplomatic relations with Taipei. According to press reports, China employed similar means to convince Chad to switch diplomatic recognition (AFP, August 8).
2. Comments made to this author in various conversations.
3. Statements made while speaking with the press on August 6.
4. The "Co-prosperity Project with Allies Countries in Central and South America" project, managed by the Council for Economic Planning and Development (CEPD), is a project to deepen the comprehensive economic, social and cultural relationship between Taiwan and the Central and South American countries. The contents of the project can be viewed at http://goca.cepd.gov.tw/.

Taiwan's Economy: Missing a Needed "Link" to China and the World

TERRY COOKE

A maxim of globalization holds that all economics are global, all politics local. From the vantage point of early autumn 2006, this formula captures both the persistence of ongoing cross-Strait economic activity as well as the current stasis of political relations between Beijing and Taipei. Yet economics is never entirely independent of politics, no less across the Strait of Taiwan than elsewhere in the world. Instead of separate vectors—the economic and the political—heading in different directions and at different speeds, we have a composite view of halting and fitful progress, a trajectory which tends to show one jarring step backward for every two cautious steps forward.

To mark the current point in the trajectory of cross-Strait economic integration (and to understand how we arrived here), five signposts of the evolving relationship are particularly noteworthy:

(1) Taiwan's Economy Continues a Steady, Albeit Less Breathtaking, Ascent

Taiwan's economy ducked the Asian Financial Crisis but not the bursting of the dot.com bubble. With an economy heavily dependent on linkages to the global information technology supply chain, the March 2000 "Tech Wreck" forced Taiwan's economy into a lower-growth gear. Despite that, and the ensuing slow-down in the world economy, Taiwan's performance in recent years has been fully appropriate for a mature economy with a per capita income in 2005 of close to US$15,000 [1].

In 2006, the fundamentals of Taiwan's economy appear sound. The growth rate for the year is projected to exceed 4.25%. Unemployment is stable at around the 4% level [2]. Taiwan continues to expand its foreign exchange reserves among the world's top tier, behind China and Japan. Foreign Direct Investment (FDI)—although well short of the "Golden Year" levels of the 1990s—is picking up thanks to strength in LCDs, mobile devices and other sectors.

(2) Taiwan's Economy Transforms, with Increasing Dependence on the Mainland

The most clear-cut feature of Taiwan's economic transformation during the past six years has been its growing economic dependence on, and integration with, the mainland. Three key indicators have been the following:

Ranking of Taiwan's Export Markets: From January 2000 through March 2002, Taiwan's exports to China and Hong Kong were in rough parity with its exports to its traditional top trading partner, the United States. Over the two-year period from March 2002 to March 2004, however, the U.S. Department of Commerce noted that Taiwan's exports to China and Hong Kong roughly doubled to the level of $5.0 billion per month, while exports to the United States remained stagnant at under the $2.5 billion per month level.

Asymmetrical Trade Dependence: By 2003, Taiwan had allowed China to become far more important to Taiwan's economy (absorbing 23% of Taiwan's total exports) than Taiwan was to China's economy (absorbing only 2.4% of China's total exports).

True Share of Taiwan's FDI Stake in China: While most official sources place Taiwan's "reported share" of FDI into China in the 7–8% range, the "estimated true share" of Taiwan's FDI contribution has emerged closer to the 20–22.5% range when adjustment is made for "round-tripped" money and for investment via British Virgin Islands (BVI) and Cayman structures. This level of FDI participation falls just short of Hong Kong (25–27.5%) and is significantly ahead of the United States (9.0%), Japan (8.0%) and Europe (5.5%) [3].

(3) "Three Links," Cross-Strait Policy, and the Mainland Affairs Council Lose Steam

Since mid-2006, the Chen Administration has slipped dramatically in its efforts to have cross-Strait policies keep pace with the strengthening domestic economy and, particularly, with Taiwan's increased integration with the mainland economy. Previously, throughout 2005 and early 2006, two factors had been working broadly in favor of a reinvigorated cross-Strait policy: (1) high-profile and economically-oriented visits to the mainland by opposition leaders James Soong of the People's First Party (PFP) and, more successfully, Lien Chan of the (Kuomintang) KMT; and (2) growing "popular support for direct cross-Strait passenger-flight links" (70% favorable) and for "an open policy on tourism from China" (62% favorable) [4]. In recent months, though, a rising chorus of corruption allegations against Chen's administration and family members, repeated attempts to organize a presidential recall vote by the opposition Pan-Blue parties and persistent street protests organized by Chen's erstwhile ally, Shih Ming-teh, have all combined to force the Chen Administration onto the defensive. With less than a 20% approval rating, Chen is now largely dependent upon his "deep-green" base and has become highly susceptible to pressure from Lee Teng-hui's Taiwan Solidarity Union (TSU) party, which ardently opposes closer economic interaction with the mainland. As a result, no breakthrough beyond the limited charter activity has occurred with the crucial "missing link" of direct cross-Strait passenger-flights. More generally, as the Chen Administration battles for its own survival and its ability to serve out the remainder of its term, much of the previous momentum for implementing a forward-looking agenda to reposition Taiwan's economy vis-à-vis that of China's and a globalizing world has been lost.

Even minor components of a more forward-looking agenda, which were enacted earlier, are now being implemented in counterproductive ways. Companies that registered with the government for purposes of cross-Strait investment have become the focus of audits and increased scrutiny. Instead of making it easier for multinational enterprises (MNE) to hold regional meetings in Taiwan by raising the number of Chinese nationals allowed to participate, the red tape of the visa procedures has prompted leading MNEs to openly question whether it is worth the effort to bring their Greater China and Asia meetings to Taiwan.

This situation can be contrasted with the still cautious, but more confident approach to cross-Strait affairs pursued during Chen Shui-bian's first term of office from 2000 to 2004. Then, as now, the policy watchword formulated for the purpose of managing cross-Strait relations was "active opening, effective management" (jiji kaifang, youxiao guanli). As pursued by Tsai Ing-wen, then-director of the Mainland Affairs Council and the originator of this policy, this formula was not in danger of ringing hollow in either aspect. On the political ascendancy, Chen was then trying to find new political balance-points in sensitive areas of cross-Strait relations ranging from managing the rapid expansion of the Taiwan Semiconductor Manufacturing Company (TSMC), United Microelectronics Corporation (UMC) and the island's foundry chip industry to meeting Washington's concerns in export control policy. While muscular in its exercise of an effective veto in Cabinet votes on cross-Strait policy, the Mainland Affairs Council was attuned to the challenges that Taiwan faced in adjusting its economy to the demands of a rapidly globalizing economy. It appeared able to engage in the "effective management" of cross-Strait links to the extent that it sought proactively to create a new "opening." This "opening" was predicated on striking a balance between newly emergent forces of domestic politics and the demands of globalization for the freer movement of people, goods, capital and ideas.

(4) Taiwan Struggles to Avoid Bilateral and Regional Marginalization

Following its accession to the multilateral World Trade Organization (WTO) on January 1, 2002, Taiwan began looking more actively for additional avenues to end its effective isolation in the area of bilateral trade agreements. Initially, this was largely a reflection in the economic sphere of active resistance to China's efforts to diplomatically isolate Taiwan wherever possible. This took on more concrete relevance, however, as bilateral trade agreements—led by China—began to proliferate, picking up the slack from the faltering of the five-year Doha Round of WTO talks.

In mid-2006, Taiwan has real reason to be concerned about its lack of participation in bilateral trade agreements. It is the only Asian economy of any size not to be a signatory to a significant agreement with a bilateral trading partner in the region.

On a global scale, the major exception to Taiwan's position in economic diplomacy has been the resumption of Taiwan's economic dialogue with the United States through the U.S.-Taiwan Trade and Investment Framework Agreement (TIFA) talks. Initially established in September 1994 as a high-level forum for consultation on a broad range of trade, investment and economic issues, the TIFA talks were subsequently suspended in October 1998. Suspension was due principally to U.S. dissatisfaction with Taiwan's slow progress in protecting a broad range of intellectual property rights, as well as with a mixed (and changing) bag of more sector-specific concerns, including agricultural licensing and import requirements; pharmaceutical testing, labeling and certification; telecommunications market barriers; and financial service constraints. Despite the boost provided by Taiwan's WTO accession in 2001, the TIFA forum remained stalled until Deputy U.S. Trade Representative Karan Bhatia's visit to Taipei in late May of this year.

While these talks did not, and were not expected to, clear the docket of outstanding issues between the countries, Taiwan did hope to use the successful resumption of TIFA talks as the springboard toward rapid consideration of a U.S.-Taiwan Free Trade Agreement (FTA). In a practical sense, this is all but impossible under President Bush's current Trade Promotion Authority (TPA). At most, the resumption of TIFA talks means that a necessary box has now been checked to potentially allow for a more deliberate evaluation of the merits of a U.S.-Taiwan FTA, subject to renewed TPA legislation [5].

(5) Taiwan's Business Community Votes with their Feet

A final perspective worth examining is the response of Taiwan's business community (taishang) to the current lack of progress in cross-Strait ties. While the government encourages the business sector to devote additional attention and capital to established markets in the West and to the emerging market of India, Taiwan's businesses remain focused on the opportunities on the mainland. Yet because of restrictions that Taipei has placed on the share of business that a Taiwan-based company is permitted to conduct in the mainland (the so-called "40%" rule), many companies are now moving to list separately in Hong Kong as a way to circumvent this restriction. By raising capital in Hong Kong to support separate business operations in Hong Kong and the mainland, Taiwanese companies are essentially voting with their feet in favor of the long-term prospects of the mainland economy and against the economic policies of the Taiwanese government.

From any perspective, this development does not portend well for Taiwan's future trajectory of globalization. The trendline is perhaps apparent in the shift of Taiwan's competitiveness relative to that of both Hong Kong and China. A comparison of the World Economic Forum's national competitiveness rankings over the past five years reveals that in 2001, Taiwan's economy was ranked 7th in the world with Hong Kong 13th and China 39th; in 2006, Hong Kong had risen to 11th, while Taiwan had slipped to a tie with a surging China at 13th.

Conclusion

In the heat of their partisan battles, Taiwan's politicians are again losing sight of a simple truth that both Taiwan's business community and China's political leadership in Beijing have fixed firmly in their sights. In today's world, the strength of a national economy is only as strong as that economy's ability to adapt to a changing world. That adaptation requires decisive moves to open up economies to the freer movement of people, goods, capital and ideas across national borders. China continues to do just that and the world continues to respond. With its geographic proximity and economic complementariness, Taiwan could be positioned advantageously at the crest of this global wave, successfully riding China's emergence as a regional super-economy.

Instead, Taiwan seems to be falling back into a defensive and blinkered position. Rather than forging an approach that shows confidence in win/win outcomes, politicians are again acting in ways to effectively constrict cross-Strait economic commercial interaction. Part of this is simply the result of distraction stemming from Taiwan's current political crisis. Yet politicians have also increasingly played to the economic insecurities of their constituents. Neither factor, however, works in Taiwan's long-term economic interests. The litmus test of a sound economic policy in Taiwan should be the clear understanding that better economic links to China mean better economic links to the world. While this view is now being lost from the sight of a badly weakened Chen Administration, China and the global economy continue to move forward.

Notes

1. The OECD recognized Taiwan as joining the ranks of the world's advanced economies in December 2001. Taiwan's per capita income of $15,000 is estimated as $27,600 on a PPP basis, according to the CIA's World Factbook.
2. 2006 Taiwan White Paper in Taiwan Business Topics, May 2006, p. WP6 (American Chamber of Commerce in Taipei).
3. "Greater China in Global Crossroads," a presentation by Dr. Komal S. Sri-Kumar, Managing Director & Chief Global Strategist, Trust Company of the West at Annual Shareholders' Meeting of the Asia Vest Partners, TCW/YFY Ltd, Los Angeles, April 2004.
4. 2006 Taiwan White Paper in Taiwan Business Topics.
5. For more detailed analysis, see the author's "Taiwan's FTA Bid: Process and Prospects from the Global IT Supply Chain Perspective," *The Shifting Paradigm in U.S., China, and Taiwan Relations,* edited by Peter C.Y. Chow (Edward Elgar Publishing Ltd., forthcoming).

A Big Awakening for Chinese Rivals
Hong Kong and Shanghi Look Afar

Kai-Yin Lo

Hong Kong over the past decade, China's premier business centers, Hong Kong and Shanghai, have engaged in a friendly rivalry, touting their relative strengths in hopes of attracting investment. Now they are waking up to the theories of a growing number of experts that cities must nurture their "creative capital" in order to entice capital of a more conventional sort.

Both are now taking a cue from experts in urban regeneration like John Howkins and Richard Florida, who argue that cities succeed by establishing themselves as fun places to live that attract the creative classes—writers, musicians, publishers, architects—and provide an environment for this elite to change society.

The cities' efforts are paying off with the return of people like the Hong Kong-born architect Edwin Chan, a co-planner of the Guggenheim Museum in Bilbao, Spain, and now a partner in the Los Angeles-based architectural firm of his boss, Frank Gehry. Chan fled his home city at an early age to pursue a career in the arts abroad. So did the composer Bright Sheng, a Shanghai native who is Leonard Bernstein Professor of Music at the University of Michigan in Ann Arbor and who received the MacArthur Foundation Fellowship in music in 2001.

When he left China, Chan complained that Hong Kong was "not nurturing." Sheng found Shanghai "suffocating." Skip forward 20 or 30 years and both men are regular commuters, lured by China's buzz and the exploding opportunities now on offer.

Hong Kong and Shanghai are taking as reference points cities like London, where long-term planning starting in the Thatcher era succeeded in revitalizing the city, resulting in a surge in property prices, multinational investment, tourist income and a flowering of the arts.

As the Hong Kong-Shanghai competition goes beyond business to enter new spheres, from the arts and design to sports, lifestyle, entertainment, tourism and the convention business, each city is taking steps to manipulate its image for greater emphasis on creativity.

Shanghai's determination to enter the world league of cities is reflected in the breakneck pace of building, as well as the high priority given by the city's leaders to "cultural enterprises," backed by national leaders in Beijing who cherish their Shanghai affiliations. Since the early 1990s, the Shanghai government has invested $230 million in cultural complexes in the city center, more than any other Chinese city, although Beijing is quickly catching up.

Shanghai, which will hold the World Expo in 2010, is using this as a target date for reaching world-class status. The World Expo plans were on the agenda in October at a conference called by Mayor Han Zheng, with an international advisory committee that enlisted world business leaders, and the mayors of Paris and Seoul, to provide suggestions on how Shanghai might boost its international competitiveness.

By comparison, Hong Kong may seem a bit tired, despite its famous skyscrapers, efficient infrastructure and legacy of British institutions.

The difference between the two represents a difference in stage of life, with Hong Kong taking a more relaxed approach to events that Shanghai is experiencing for the first time.

Hong Kong leaders envision a spectacular 40-hectare, or 100-acre, cultural center in the West Kowloon district that will increase the city's appeal, but they have run into snags of a type that Shanghai has yet to encounter: Citizens' groups have questioned not only the finances of the plan, but whether the development, no matter how iconic, will provide a basis for organic and sustainable growth in arts and culture.

The competition is at its sharpest when it comes to positioning for business. Shanghai is the logical choice for multinationals that need to keep a close watch on the vast Chinese consumer market they desire. Hong Kong, a traders' city, is friendly to exporters, small and medium-size enterprises and financial services.

Hong Kong remains significantly more attractive than Shanghai as an operational base because of its mature business culture, its bilingualism in English and Chinese, its efficiency and its rule of law, which includes vigilance over intellectual property rights, especially protection against rampant Chinese counterfeits.

Somewhat belatedly, the Hong Kong government has recognized the power of the creative industries to energize its economy and to add value to the advanced manufacturing industries in the adjacent Pearl River Delta on the mainland, where Hong Kong business controls 70 percent of the work force. This recognition has resulted in a $32 million innovation and design fund for helping small creative industries and a renewed pledge for support from the city chief executive, Tung Chee-hwa, in his policy address last week.

Under way is an aggressive program to establish Hong Kong as the hub of design in the region. Lifestyle Asia, an annual event organized by the forward-looking Hong Kong Design Center and the Hong Kong Trade Development Council, has become Asia's foremost design conference. Last autumn, three major design and branding conferences took place, attracting a stellar list of speakers, from the architects Tadao Ando and Frank Gehry to the designer Philippe Starck, the Guggenheim Museum's Thomas Krens, the innovation strategist Larry Keeley, and the luxury brand supremos Bernard Arnault of LVMH and Santo Versace.

The conventional wisdom about Shanghai is that it dazzles with its speedy development of "hardware," from commercial buildings to cultural and entertainment venues, while Hong Kong is strong on institutional and legal "software." The truth is more complex, and requires a look at the cities' cultural background.

Historically, both cities achieved prominence through their foreign connections, Shanghai as a treaty port, Hong Kong Island as a British imperial possession, together with its leased territory on the adjacent mainland. Still, both absorbed and assimilated the dominant regional cultures of their Chinese hinterlands.

In Shanghai's case, that meant drawing upon one of the pre-eminent centers of China's literary culture in the Song and Ming dynasties (the 10th to 17th centuries), the so-called Jiangnan region centered in nearby Suzhou and Hangzhou. These cities were renowned for their creativity, taste and individuality, in contrast to the formal style associated with government-dominated Beijing. "Suzhou style" was reinterpreted as Shanghai style as that city prospered. By the 1930s, together with Berlin and Chicago, Shanghai attracted global attention with its mix of sophisticated opulence and the demi-monde.

Both Shanghai and Hong Kong are indelibly associated with their colonial pasts. However, after 56 years of Communist rule, Shanghai is currently reveling in its economic growth and newness. Colonial residues remain in the stately edifices on the Bund, the city's famous waterfront, and the hybrid Chinese-

European residences still standing in the old French concession, largely retained for their tourist value.

In contrast, Hong Kong has kept many virtues of its British colonial masters, if little of their architecture. Its legal institutions, individual liberties, deep-rooted ethical standards, vigilance against corruption and efficient civil service are the cornerstone of its business, political and civic culture.

Visiting the city recently, Bruno Marquet, executive director of the Pompidou Center in Paris, paid Hong Kong a backhanded compliment by describing it as "Chinese, but not very Chinese." This perception reflects Hong Kong's attractiveness to Westerners, but does not adequately measure the connection between Hong Kong's culture and its hinterland, historically looked down upon by northerners as provincial.

Hong Kong remains an extreme example of southern China's linguistic, ethnic and cultural diversity. If Shanghai's strength is the strategic vision of its leadership and the renewal of the colorful culture of its heyday from the 1920s to 1940s, Hong Kong is spurred by a kind of creative combustion and resourcefulness.

An emblem is the late James Wong Jim, an icon of Cantopop music, whose lyrics were the defining expression of Hong Kong's golden era of popular culture in the late 1970s and 1980s. His composition "Under the Lion Rock," the title song of a television series, speaks to the sentiments of many in Hong Kong, who came by chance or as refugees after the Communist revolution in 1949, and thrived despite adversity.

In a seminar at the University of Hong Kong last year, Wong said: "We were not consciously creating anything. Hong Kong culture is just ordinary living." His definition encompasses the mix of commercial instincts, hard work and entrepreneurship that translates into a Hong Kong lifestyle based on business success, materialism, flexibility and an international outlook.

The recent clamor in Hong Kong for a greater political say signifies the maturing civic consciousness of the city's populace, who are determined to defend their liberties, rights and way of life. The Basic Law, the 1997 charter by which China governs Hong Kong, stipulates that this lifestyle—and the capitalist system that makes it possible—will remain for 50 years.

Shanghai, menawhile, held a Hong Kong Culture Week for the first time last autumn. The theme of an exhibition at the Grand Theater was Hong Kong's colorful lifestyle, which Shanghai, and indeed the rest of China, are striving to emulate.

Over time, differences between Shanghai and Hong Kong are likely to persist, although in some respects the cities may come closer together. They may not be rivals in the true sense but, like other major brands, they thrive on competition with each other.

KAI-YIN LO is a designer, consultant and writer based in Hong Kong.

Hong Kong: "One Country, Two Systems" in Troubled Waters

"Chinese central government officials are reluctant to allow political reform in Hong Kong to proceed too rapidly or to be driven primarily by public demonstrations and aggressive pro-democracy activists."

CRAIG N. CANNING

China's unique "one country, two systems" experiment with Hong Kong began its seventh year on July 1, 2003. That day also saw an estimated 500,000 Hong Kong citizens take to the streets in a massive public demonstration opposing antisubversion legislation sponsored by Hong Kong's government.

The July 1 demonstration precipitated a series of significant developments: the government's temporary withdrawal of the antisubversion legislation, the resignations of two top Hong Kong officials, new initiatives for political reform spearheaded by pro-democracy advocates, and verbal attacks in the local and mainland media characterizing democrats and other reformers as unpatriotic. In April 2004, Beijing issued historic new interpretations of Hong Kong's constitution that effectively closed the door on efforts to hold direct elections for the territory's next chief executive in 2007 and the Legislative Council in 2008.

Some political reform activists pronounced the central government's actions the death knell for one country, two systems, while pro-Beijing leaders and government officials in Hong Kong as well as central government representatives minimized their impact. Despite these widely disparate interpretations, it is clear that public protests and political activism in Hong Kong over the past year and a half reached new heights. Clearly, the activism also produced concerns that prompted central government leaders to seize the initiative in defining their authority in the struggle over the timetable for democratic reform in Hong Kong. In doing so, China's leaders did not end the one country, two systems experiment, but they did open an important new chapter in it.

"A High Degree of Autonomy"

"One country, two systems" originated in the early 1980s with Deng Xiaoping, the principal architect of China's post-Mao re-forms, who introduced the concept during Sino-British negotiations for Hong Kong's return to Chinese sovereignty after 156 years of British colonial rule. Deng's proposal was designed to bridge the gap separating China's socialist system from the system of governance that had evolved in Hong Kong under the British. In theory, the one country, two systems framework sought to preserve and protect Hong Kong's distinctive political, social, and economic system—its rule of law, self-governance, and freedoms of assembly, speech and religion—for 50 years after the territory's reversion to Chinese sovereignty. The details of the one country, two systems model were ironed out in the late 1980s and enshrined in the final version of the Basic Law, Hong Kong's mini-constitution, in 1990.

The Basic Law codifies the relationship between the People's Republic of China and the Hong Kong Special Administrative Region, the official name for Hong Kong upon its reunification with China. It promises the territory a "high degree of autonomy" while specifying the fundamental rights and duties of Hong Kong residents and stipulating the structure and functions of the executive, legislative, and judicial branches of government. It gives Beijing responsibility for Hong Kong's defense and foreign policy, but allows for independent participation by the Hong Kong government or international organizations in a wide range of fields, including trade (membership in the World Trade Organization, for example), finance, communications, culture, and sports. The ultimate authority for interpreting and amending the Basic Law is vested in the Chinese central government, specifically the Standing Committee of the National People's Congress.

Hong Kong government under the Basic Law is designed to limit popular participation in politics and to concentrate decision-making authority in the hands of a chief executive, his hand-picked advisers, and a cabinet whose members head

Hong Kong's civil service bureaucracy. The chief executive is selected by an 800-person Election Committee and then formally appointed by Beijing. The Basic Law also calls for a 60-member Legislative Council. Popularly elected representatives from geographical districts within Hong Kong will occupy 30 seats after a September 2004 election—an increase from 20 seats in 1997 and 24 seats in 2000. The other 30 seats are chosen by "functional constituencies" representing major trade and occupational sectors in Hong Kong such as business, finance, labor, law, and education.

Article 68 of the Basic Law states that the "ultimate aim" is to achieve direct popular election of all Legislative Council representatives sometime in the future but only "in accordance with the principle of gradual and orderly progress." In sum, negotiated autonomy came with an expectation that Hong Kong would be governed, at least for its first decade, by a powerful executive branch, a relatively weak legislature, an independent judiciary (appointed by the chief executive but on the recommendation of an independent commission), and limited popular participation. That participation can be changed only after elections in 2007 and 2008 with two-thirds majority support in the legislature, the chief executive's agreement, and Beijing's ultimate approval.

The chief executive is of crucial importance to the one country, two systems experiment. Conservative businessman Tung Chee-hwa, son of shipping magnate C. Y. Tung, took office on July 1, 1997. Born in Shanghai in 1937, Tung moved to Hong Kong with his family 10 years later. He attended university in England, worked for General Electric in the United States, and eventually assumed control of the family business in Hong Kong on his father's death in 1982. Known for his integrity and commitment to China and its heritage, Tung Chee-hwa seemed the ideal person to serve as Hong Kong's first chief executive. He was also Beijing's top choice.

Despite his qualifications, Tung Chee-hwa has had mixed success in his role as Hong Kong's top official. A series of events beyond Tung's control—especially the 1997 Asian financial crisis—combined with the blunders and missteps of a fledgling politician have kept his public opinion-poll ratings consistently low, except during the first months of his tenure. He was reelected to another five-year term by the Election Committee in February 2002 and reappointed by Beijing the next month.

Perhaps the most serious challenge to one country, two systems during Tung's first term was the "right of abode" controversy. The problem arose when permanent residency seekers mounted a legal challenge to the Hong Kong government after it introduced a new ordinance in July 1997 tightening regulations for proving "right of abode" status. The new rules required proof that at least one parent was a Chinese citizen holding permanent residency in Hong Kong at the time of the claimant's birth. After Hong Kong's Court of Final Appeal upheld the claimants' legal challenges to the new ordinance in January 1999, the Hong Kong government asked the Standing Committee of the National People's Congress to review the case.

The Standing Committee's review produced a new interpretation of immigration provisions in the Basic Law that supported the Hong Kong government's position. But the Standing Committee's decision in turn generated a massive new legal challenge that again ended up before the Court of Final Appeal in Hong Kong. In January 2002 the Court of Final Appeal ruled against the claimants and for the Hong Kong government, acknowledging the ultimate authority of the Standing Committee of the National People's Congress to re-interpret Basic Law provisions. The court, in effect, reversed its own 1999 decision.

The Security-Legislation Tempest

A greater test of the one country, two systems model came just a few months into Tung's second term. In September 2002, the Hong Kong government released a public "consultation paper" outlining the main provisions of antisedition and antisubversion legislation it planned to introduce in the Legislative Council. Having carefully avoided this potentially divisive issue during Tung's first term, government leaders explained that the legislation was needed to revise or eliminate outmoded laws left over from the British colonial administration. The principal motive, however, was the obligation under Article 23 of the Basic Law, as Beijing authorities occasionally pointed out, that Hong Kong "enact laws on its own to prohibit any act of treason, secession, sedition, subversion against the Central People's Government, or theft of state secrets, to prohibit foreign political organizations or bodies from conducting political activities in the Region, and to prohibit political organizations . . . of the Region from establishing ties with foreign political organizations." In brief, Beijing wanted Article 23 security legislation passed as soon as the Hong Kong government deemed it feasible in order to prevent Hong Kong from becoming a base, as it had been at times during the revolutionary tumult of the early twentieth century, for Chinese or foreign groups actively opposing or seeking to overthrow the Chinese government.

The government's consultation paper drew immediate attention from Hong Kong citizens. A central concern was a provision in the proposed legislation granting the government authority to ban for national security reasons organizations in Hong Kong that were illegal in mainland China—groups such as Falun Gong, the spiritual organization branded an "evil cult" and suppressed in China since 1999 but still active in Hong Kong. Would the proposed legislation undermine Hong Kong's autonomy by extending mainland China's laws into Hong Kong despite fundamental differences between the two legal systems? Moreover, what legal rights would targeted groups or individuals in Hong Kong possess after implementation of Article 23 anti-subversion legislation? Could Hong Kong journalists who criticized the Chinese Communist Party or Chinese central government face charges of sedition, thereby undermining the territory's freedom of the press?

Beijing authorities have long hoped that the one country, two systems formula would eventually enable not only Hong Kong's but also Taiwan's reunification with mainland China.

These and other questions generated controversy and revealed sharp divisions in Hong Kong society over the following months. Large demonstrations both for and against the proposal were held. In early 2003 the Hong Kong government announced that it would formally introduce the bill in the Legislative Council in the spring, and a vote was eventually set for July 9, 2003.

In March an unanticipated health crisis arose as some Hong Kong residents became ill with the mysterious, highly contagious, and potentially lethal form of atypical pneumonia called Severe Acute Respiratory Syndrome (SARS), and this crisis added to the controversy and anti-government criticism over Article 23. Although the World Health Organization (WHO) pronounced the disease under control in June, a total of 1,755 Hong Kong citizens had been stricken, of whom 299 died. According to WHO statistics, SARS infected 8,098 people worldwide between November 2002 and September 2003, killing 774. The vast majority of victims, more than 7,000, resided in mainland China and Hong Kong.

SARS' toll in Hong Kong extended far beyond the personal tragedies of individual illnesses and deaths. The territory's economy, still struggling from a series of downturns in previous years, took an even harder hit because of SARS. The deflation plaguing the economy continued, and economists began to revise downward by as much as 2 percentage points their projections for Hong Kong's GDP growth in 2003. The government became the target of widespread criticism for failing to quickly recognize the seriousness of SARS as well as for its tardiness in taking preventive measures to combat the disease.

Tung's government forged ahead with its plan to pass a security bill, apparently unaware that Article 23 legislation was rapidly becoming a lightning rod for public anxiety, merging broad dissatisfaction with the economy, SARS fears, sagging confidence in government leadership, and worries about the future of Hong Kong's freedoms under one country, two systems. In the spring of 2003 the government introduced the security bill to the Legislative Council, which held three public consultation sessions while its Bills Committee scrutinized the legislation's provisions in preparation for a vote on July 9. But squabbles, finger-pointing, and walkouts detracted from the consultation and legislative-review processes. Although the government modified a few aspects of the bill, its efforts failed to mollify the legislation's opponents. As July 1, 2003, and the sixth anniversary of Hong Kong's reversion to Chinese sovereignty approached, leaders of the Civil Human Rights Front—a loose coalition of 45 nonprofit groups—and other opponents of the security bill formulated plans for a major public demonstration against Article 23 legislation.

July 1, 2003

From the Hong Kong government's perspective, July 1, 2003, should have been a grand occasion. Wen Jiabao, the popular Chinese prime minister appointed in March by the National People's Congress, was scheduled to pay his first visit to Hong Kong. He planned to participate in ceremonies marking the sixth anniversary of Hong Kong's reversion, witness the signing of an important new free trade agreement between China and Hong Kong, and consult with Tung Chee-hwa and other government leaders.

On June 29, the first day of his three-day visit, Wen joined Chief Executive Tung in observing the signing ceremony of the Closer Economic Partnership Arrangement (CEPA), the free trade agreement negotiated over the previous 18 months. By lifting tariffs on many Hong Kong goods exported to China, reducing restrictions on mainland tourists, allowing mainland Chinese to purchase property in Hong Kong, and constructing a new bridge linking Hong Kong with the Pearl River Delta, CEPA was expected to provide a much-needed boost to the city's economic recovery efforts after it took effect on January 1, 2004.

At the conclusion of the CEPA signing ceremony, Tung, looking ahead to the anniversary celebrations on July 1, reportedly reassured Wen about the public demonstration planned for that day, commenting that no more than 50,000 to 60,000 people were expected to participate. Instead, an estimated 500,000 Hong Kong residents took to the streets on a hot summer afternoon to stage a peaceful and orderly protest. This was not only the largest public demonstration in Hong Kong since reversion in 1997, but also the largest on Chinese soil since May and June 1989, when a million Chinese participated in pro-democracy demonstrations in Tiananmen Square and about a million Hong Kong citizens marched spontaneously to condemn Beijing immediately after the bloody June 4 crackdown on the pro-democracy movement.

Despite the enormous public protest, Tung continued his campaign to advance the security legislation, offering to remove the provision giving the executive branch authority to ban Hong Kong organizations outlawed by the Chinese central government but remaining insistent on a July 9 vote. Opponents of the bill were outraged and called for Tung's resignation. Tung eventually deferred the vote after James Tien, chairman of the pro-Beijing Liberal Party and a member of Tung's Executive Council, resigned from the council on July 6, following a quick trip to Beijing. The loss of Tien's support and presumably the votes of many in his party had dimmed prospects for the bill's passage.

Tung's decision to postpone a Legislative Council vote on the security bill did not end the furor. Pro-democracy reform activists and opponents of the legislation now called not only for Tung's resignation but also for constitutional changes allowing the direct election of the next chief executive in 2007 as well as the direct popular election of Hong Kong's fourth Legislative Council in 2008.

On July 16, 2003, Tung sacked two members of his cabinet: Secretary for Security Regina Ip, the government's main champion of Article 23 legislation; and Finance Secretary Antony Leung, who had attracted public criticism for purchasing a luxury automobile a few weeks before introducing a new auto tax policy, thus dodging the tax. Tung held a press conference the following day, promising to do a better job as chief executive, but he did not apologize for the security legislation uproar. Two days later Tung flew to Beijing for high-level meetings with the central government's top leaders—including new President and Party General Secretary Hu Jintao, Prime Minister Wen Jiabao, and Vice President Zeng Qinghong, a close associate of former President and Party Secretary Jiang Zemin, one of Tung's key supporters. The Beijing trip and its media coverage made clear that, despite his difficulties at home, Tung retained support in Beijing and would not resign in the face of massive protests.

In early August 2003, Tung appointed Henry Tang as the new financial secretary. Ambrose Lee was designated secretary for security. Shortly after his appointment, Lee in mid-August announced his intention to launch a fresh round of public consultations on the security bill, thereby signaling the government's determination to persevere with Article 23 legislation. Predictably, the bill's opponents objected again. Facing strong pressure from opponents of the bill and from his own supporters, Tung finally withdrew the legislation on September 5, 2003.

The Reformers' Moment

What appeared to the pro-democracy camp as a string of victories since July 1 fueled further efforts to achieve political reform. Political activists began to focus their attention on the 2004 Legislative Council elections. Their strategy was straightforward: if the Democratic Party and other pro-democracy parties could capture all 30 seats open to direct popular election in 2004—riding the wave of anti-security legislation and pro-constitutional reform sentiment—and if they could also cultivate support from a few legislators in the 30-seat functional-constituency section of the Legislative Council, pro-democracy lawmakers would command a majority in the legislature and might be able to push through constitutional reform measures. And if Chief Executive Tung could then be persuaded to back such reforms, Beijing would face an unpalatable choice of either approving the reforms or defying both the executive and legislative branches of the Hong Kong government as well as popular opinion.

Despite the many "ifs" in this strategy, two developments in the second half of 2003 provided some evidence that it might be feasible. First, the number of registered voters increased sharply by 150,000 in July, following the protest demonstration. Second, many Democratic Party and other pro-democracy candidates won election in Hong Kong's district council races on November 23, 2003, while members of a pro-government party and other candidates associated with the government's security bill suffered defeat. The significance of these developments was not lost on attentive observers in Beijing.

Central government leaders could not ignore the implications of the massive public protest of July 1, 2003.

Chinese central government leaders revealed their worries in several ways in late 2003 and early 2004. On December 3, President Hu Jintao signaled Tung in a meeting in Beijing that he was concerned about recent political developments in Hong Kong. Hu's statement was underscored the next day when

China's official New China News Agency published a treatise by four well-known legal scholars that laid out several principles for Hong Kong's political development. The bottom line in their argument was that Hong Kong lacked the right under the Basic Law to implement political reform on its own; the Chinese central government would make the final decisions. These and other subtle actions by Beijing made the central government's message clear: whatever steps Hong Kong might take toward political reform would require close consultation, careful review, and ultimate approval by the Chinese central government.

The Standing Committee Responds

Despite these signals from Beijing, demands for political reform focusing on future elections persisted into 2004. As the Hong Kong government continued to face calls for political reform, Beijing took firm action. On April 6, 2004, the Standing Committee of the National People's Congress issued an interpretation of the Basic Law stating that the Hong Kong chief executive must obtain approval from the Standing Committee before introducing any electoral reform bills to the Legislative Council. In effect, the Standing Committee asserted its right to approve not only the final product at the end of the reform process but its initiation as well. The Standing Committee also ruled that Hong Kong's Legislative Council lacked the right to introduce electoral reform legislation on its own, thereby reserving that privilege for the executive branch.

On April 26, just three weeks later, the Standing Committee issued another set of rulings in response to a Hong Kong government request for guidance in regard to the 2007 and 2008 elections. The Standing Committee explicitly forbade the direct election of the chief executive or the Legislative Council because it would contravene the voting rights and procedures spelled out in the Basic Law. The rulings also upheld procedures stipulated in the Basic Law allowing bills from the executive branch to pass more easily than those introduced by the legislative branch. And finally, the Standing Committee refused to approve an increase in the number of Legislative Council seats open to direct popular election in 2008, stating that the precisely balanced ratio with constituency appointments—currently 30/30—must remain fixed.

Anticipating that these decisions would produce political fallout, the central government dispatched several officials to Hong Kong to explain the Basic Law interpretations in person. As expected, public protest demonstrations took place in Hong Kong in April 2004. But the largest of these, according to estimates of protest organizers, attracted about 15,000 individuals—a figure well below those for other public demonstrations since July 1, 2003. In early May 2004, Democratic Party member Martin Lee, one of the best known pro-democracy advocates in Hong Kong, attempted to introduce an amendment in the Legislative Council charging the Standing Committee with "an abuse of power" under the Basic Law. However, the Hong Kong government quickly advised the Legislative Council that such a motion was "out of order." Council President Rita Fan agreed, and Lee's amendment was blocked.

Notwithstanding the demonstrations and other efforts by pro-democracy advocates, the Standing Committee rulings of April 2004 and the actions of Chinese central government officials and pro-Beijing leaders in Hong Kong made clear that in the near term little if any hope remained for political reform—including direct elections in 2007 and 2008—beyond the increase in directly elected Legislative Council seats already written into the Basic Law.

A May 2004 public opinion poll revealed that support for universal suffrage in the 2007 and 2008 elections had dropped sharply—from more than 80 percent of those polled in July 2003 favoring universal suffrage for both the Legislative Council and chief executive elections down to 66 percent in May 2004 for the legislative balloting and 55 percent for the election of the chief executive. Among the factors helping to explain these changing poll results were long-awaited indications in early 2004 of an improving economy, as well as Hong Kong residents' growing recognition that ultimate authority for constitutional change rests with the Chinese central government and that the reform timetable would not be dictated by street protests and legislative activism.

Despite these indications that Hong Kong citizens had registered Beijing's message, another large public protest occurred on July 1, 2004. Approximately 350,000 people joined a peaceful demonstration against the Standing Committee's recent rulings and in support of democratic reforms in Hong Kong. Although Beijing had declared its preeminent authority over the territory's political reform, the July 2004 protest illustrated that Hong Kong citizens are still willing to openly express their discontent.

Beijing Takes Off the Gloves

Why did worried leaders of the Chinese central government adopt a more aggressive and interventionist stance toward Hong Kong in the first half of 2004? While the answers lie primarily in problems that the leadership perceived in Hong Kong itself, Beijing's actions were also prompted in varying degrees by China's leadership transition, the country's rapid economic growth and its potentially destabilizing consequences, developments in Beijing's relations with Taiwan and the United States, and China's evolving role in the international community and global economy.

Central government leaders could not ignore the implications of the massive public protest of July 1, 2003. Even more alarming to Beijing was the subsequent initiative by pro-democracy activists to accelerate the pace of political reform in a drive to achieve universal suffrage in the elections of 2007 and 2008.

In this context the leadership of Chief Executive Tung posed several dilemmas for Beijing. First, Tung's sustained unpopularity helped fuel the discontent manifesting itself in public demonstrations and political reform initiatives. In addition, Tung's political ineptitude reduced his administration's ability to cope with "people power" and other political reform challenges in Hong Kong, virtually compelling central government authorities to become more directly involved but also inviting

accusations that Beijing was infringing on the "high degree of autonomy" promised Hong Kong in the Basic Law. Yet to remove Tung from office before the end of his second term would reflect poorly on the central government's leaders who had endorsed him twice. It also could encourage more "people power" and legislative activism, and besmirch the one country, two systems experiment in its early years.

Retaining and supporting Tung, as Beijing officials opted to do in July 2003, meant that they would have to grapple more directly with the political reform initiatives emerging in Hong Kong. Consequently, Hu Jintao, Wen Jiabao, and other high-ranking central government leaders sought to influence the situation in Hong Kong in late 2003 and early 2004. They did so through their comments to Hong Kong government officials and their public statements urging the people of Hong Kong to concentrate on economic development and to consider the overall national interest. It was also in this context that the Standing Committee in Beijing issued its interpretations of the Basic Law in April 2004 foreclosing the possibility of direct elections in 2007 and 2008.

Central government decisions may also have been influenced by recent leadership changes in China. Some analysts suggest that Beijing's hard line on political reform in Hong Kong reflects political maneuvering within the Communist Party associated with the transition from third- to fourth-generation leaders. They argue that the continued influence of former President and Party Secretary Jiang Zemin, currently chairman of the Party's Central Military Commission, and his allies is mainly responsible for Beijing's hard-line decisions. But there is no consensus on this assessment. Other experts suggest Hu has already begun to neutralize Jiang's influence.

A more compelling argument points to China's sustained high-level economic growth, which is generating not only rapid social and economic change but also wide-ranging problems such as high unemployment and underemployment, sharp regional disparities, mass labor migration, insufficient health care and health insurance, rapidly widening economic extremes, and a growing gap in living standards between urban and rural China. Any single one or combination of these problems could swiftly trigger substantial popular opposition to the Party or government in China. Consequently, Chinese central government officials are reluctant to allow political reform in Hong Kong to proceed too rapidly or to be driven primarily by public demonstrations and aggressive pro-democracy activists. Little wonder that Prime Minister Wen and other top leaders frequently remind Hong Kong of the value of—and the symbiotic relationship they see between—"prosperity and stability."

The Taiwan Factor

Two aspects of the "Taiwan factor" must also be considered. First, Beijing authorities have long hoped that the one country, two systems formula would eventually enable not only Hong Kong's but also Taiwan's reunification with mainland China. Taiwan's leadership, it should be noted, has invariably criticized one country, two systems and any hint of Beijing's intrusion into Hong Kong's autonomy, stressing that the Hong Kong model is inappropriate for Taiwan. The recent struggle over political reform in Hong Kong has only strengthened Taiwan's hand in this argument.

Second, from Beijing's perspective the democratization movement in Taiwan has precipitated a variety of unwelcome developments since the Nationalist-dominated government first legalized opposition parties in 1986. In addition, democratization in Taiwan has coincided with a steadily growing sense of Taiwanese identity—one political manifestation of which is the pursuit of independence and international acceptance of Taiwan as a sovereign nation separate from China.

In Hong Kong's case, independence is not an issue. The practical impossibility of achieving an independent Hong Kong, given the territory's extreme dependence on mainland China for everything from its water supply to its economic wellbeing, is recognized and accepted on both sides of the border. What the "Taiwan factor" contributes to central government leaders' attitudes toward Hong Kong is recognition of the inherent volatility and unpredictability of the democratic process, a lesson recently reinforced for them by the narrow and acrimonious reelection of Taiwan President Chen Shuibian in March 2004.

Sino-American relations also have been a factor in the Chinese leaders' calculations. The improved bilateral relationship since 9–11, along with China's growing importance to the United States in its efforts to resolve the dispute over North Korea's nuclear weapons program and to stimulate growth of the American economy, has reduced the likelihood that the Bush administration would mount a serious challenge to Beijing over its Hong Kong policies.

China's entry into the World Trade Organization in November 2001, its deepening engagement with the global economy, and its growing involvement and stature in the international community are also influencing Hong Kong-mainland relations. Hong Kong no longer appears indispensable to Beijing for China's trade and economic development. Today many observers believe the situation has reversed itself: Hong Kong's economic fortunes seem highly dependent on China and on Beijing's policies. The effect has been to increase Beijing's and reduce the reformers' political leverage.

The Fate of "One Country, Two Systems"

Does all of this mean that one country, two systems is dead? Far from it. Both Beijing and Hong Kong have much to gain from seeing this unique experiment through to a successful conclusion. The Basic Law is a "living document"—its provisions provide the framework for life and governance in the Hong Kong Special Administrative Region, but they must be revisited and reinterpreted as conditions and circumstances change.

The recent interpretations of the Basic Law by the Standing Committee of the National People's Congress underscore Beijing's determination to ensure that political reform in Hong Kong takes place gradually and that it not be dictated by street protests or what Beijing may perceive as opportunistic political activism. Since the Standing Committee's rulings in April 2004, some voices in Hong Kong government, media, and other circles have begun calling for less confrontational "new approaches" involving improved dialogue and a process of quiet, measured steps. These steps may hold the promise of achieving future political reforms on a mutually acceptable timetable.

The central government's recent decisions appear to tie Hong Kong firmly to Beijing's interpretations of the Basic Law regarding political reform. But if the struggles between Hong Kong and Beijing amount to a new chapter in one country, two systems, it seems far from the final chapter. The nature of Hong Kong's self-governance and of its general relationship to mainland China is yet to be determined.

CRAIG N. CANNING is an associate professor of history at the College of William and Mary.

Glossary of Terms and Abbreviations

Ancestor Worship Ancient religious practices still followed in Taiwan, Hong Kong, and the People's Republic of China. Ancestor worship is based on the belief that the living can communicate with the dead and that the dead spirits to whom sacrifices are ritually made can bring about a better life for the living.

Brain Drain A migration of professional people (such as scientists, professors, and physicians) from one country to another, usually in search of higher salaries or better living conditions.

Buddhism A religion of East and Central Asia founded on the teachings of Siddhartha Gautama (the Buddha). Its followers believe that suffering is inherent in life and that one can be liberated from it by mental and moral self-purification.

Capitalist A person who has capital invested in business, or someone who favors an economic system characterized by private or corporate ownership of capital goods.

Chinese Communist Party (CCP) Founded in 1921 by a small Marxist study group, its members initially worked with the Kuomintang (KMT) under Chiang Kai-shek to unify China and, later, to fight off Japanese invaders. Despite Chiang's repeated efforts to destroy the CCP, it eventually ousted the KMT and took control of the Chinese mainland in 1949.

Cold War A conflict between the communist and anti-communist (democratic-capitalists) blocs, without direct military conflict.

Communism In theory, a system in which most goods are collectively owned and equally distributed. In practice, a system of governance in which a single authoritarian party controls the political, legal, educational, and economic systems in an effort to establish a more egalitarian society.

Confucianism Often referred to as a religion, actually a system of ethics for governing human relationships and for ruling. It was established during the fifth century B.C. by the Chinese philosopher Confucius.

Cultural Revolution Formally, the Great Proletarian Cultural Revolution. In an attempt to rid China of its repressive bureaucracy and to restore a revolutionary spirit to the Chinese people, Mao Zedong (Tse-tung) called on the youth of China to "challenge authority" and "make revolution" by rooting out the "reactionary" elements in Chinese society. The Cultural Revolution lasted from 1966 until 1969, but the term is often used to refer to the 10 year period from 1966 to 1976. It seriously undermined the Chinese people's faith in the Chinese Communist Party's ability to rule and led to major setbacks in the economy.

De-Maoification The rooting-out of the philosophies and programs of Mao Zedong in Chinese society.

Democratic Centralism The participation of the people in discussions of policy at lower levels. Their ideas are to be passed up to the central leadership; but once the central leadership makes a decision, it is to be implemented by the people.

ExCo The Executive Council of Hong Kong, consisting of top civil servants and civilian appointees chosen to represent the community. Except in times of emergency, the governor must consult with the ExCo before initiating any program.

Feudal In Chinese Communist parlance, a patriarchal bureaucratic system in which bureaucrats administer policy on the basis of personal relationships.

Four Cardinal Principles The Chinese Communists' term for their commitment to socialism, the leadership of the Chinese Communist Party, the dictatorship of the proletariat, and the ideologies of Karl Marx, Vladimir Lenin, and Mao Zedong.

Four Modernizations A program of reforms begun in 1978 in China that sought to modernize agriculture, industry, science and technology, and defense by the year 2000.

Gang of Four The label applied to the four "radicals" or "leftists" who dominated first the cultural and then the political events during the Cultural Revolution. The four members of the Gang were Jiang Qing, Mao's wife; Zhang Chunqiao, former deputy secretary of the Shanghai municipal committee and head of its propaganda department; Yao Wenyuan, former editor-in-chief of the *Shanghai Liberation Daily*; and Wang Hongwen, a worker in a textile factory in Shanghai.

Great Leap Forward Mao Zedong's alternative to the Soviet model of development, this was a plan calling for the establishment of communes and for an increase in industrial production in both the cities and the communes. The increased production was to come largely from greater human effort rather than from more investment or improved technology. This policy, begun in 1958, was abandoned by 1959.

Great Proletarian Cultural Revolution *See* Cultural Revolution.

Gross Domestic Product (GDP) A measure of the total flow of goods and services produced by the economy of a country over a certain period of time, normally a year. GDP equals gross national product (GNP) minus the income of the country's residents earned on investments abroad.

Guerrilla A member of a small force of "irregular" soldiers. Generally, guerrilla forces are used against numerically and technologically superior enemies in jungles or mountainous terrain.

Han Of "pure" Chinese extraction. Refers to the dominant ethnic group in the P.R.C.

Ideograph A character of Chinese writing. Originally, each ideograph represented a picture and/or a sound of a word.

Islam The religious faith founded by Muhammad in the sixth and seventh centuries A.D. Its followers believe that Allah is the sole deity and that Muhammad is his prophet.

Kuomintang (KMT) The Chinese Nationalist Party, founded by Sun Yat-Sen in 1912. *See also* Nationalists.

LegCo Hong Kong's Legislative Council, which reviews policies proposed by the governor and formulates legislation.

Long March The 1934–1935 retreat of the Chinese Communist Party, in which hundreds of thousands died while journeying to the plains of Yan'an in northern China in order to escape annihilation by the Kuomintang.

Glossary of Terms and Abbreviations

Mainlanders Those Chinese in Taiwan who emigrated from the Chinese mainland during the flight of the Nationalist Party in 1949.

Mandarin A northern Chinese dialect chosen by the Chinese Communist Party to be the official language of China.

Mao Thought In the post-1949 period, originally described as "the thoughts of Mao Zedong." Mao's "thoughts" were considered important because he took the theory of Marxism-Leninism and applied it to the concrete conditions existing in China. But since Mao's death in 1976 and the subsequent reevaluation of his policies, Mao Thought is no longer conceived of as the thoughts of Mao alone but as the "collective wisdom" of the party leadership.

May Fourth Period A period of intellectual ferment in China, which officially began on May 4, 1919, and concerned the Versailles Peace Conference. On that day, the Chinese protested what was considered an unfair secret settlement regarding German-held territory in China. The result was what was termed a "new cultural movement," which lasted into the mid-1920s.

Nationalists The Kuomintang (KMT). The ruling party of the Republic of China, but its army was defeated by 1949. Was the only political party in Taiwan until the 1990s.

Newly Industrialized Country (NIC) A term used to refer to those developing countries that have enjoyed rapid economic growth. Most commonly applied to the East Asian economies of South Korea, Taiwan, Hong Kong, and Singapore.

Offshore Islands The small islands in the Formosa Strait that are just a few miles off the Chinese mainland but are controlled by Taiwan, nearly 90 miles away.

Opium A bitter, addictive drug made from the dried juice of the opium poppy.

Opium War The 1839–1842 conflict between Britain and China, sparked by the British import of opium into China. After the British victory, Europeans were allowed into China and trading posts were established on the mainland. The Treaty of Nanking, which ended the Opium War, also gave Britain its first control over part of Hong Kong.

People's Procuracy The investigative branch of China's legal system. It determines whether an accused person is guilty and should be brought to trial.

People's Republic of China (P.R.C.) Established in 1949 by the Chinese Communists under the leadership of Mao Zedong after defeating Chiang Kai-shek and his Nationalist supporters.

Pinyin A newer system of spelling Chinese words and names, using the Latin alphabet of 26 letters, created by the Chinese Communist leadership.

Proletariat The industrial working class, which for Marx was the political force that would overthrow capitalism and lead the way in the building of socialism.

Republic of China (R.O.C.) The government established as a result of the 1911 Revolution. It was ousted by the Chinese Communist Party in 1949, when its leaders fled to Taiwan.

Second Convention of Peking The 1898 agreement leasing the New Territories of Hong Kong to the British until 1997.

Severe Acute Respiratory Syndrome (SARS) A grave respiratory illness that emerged in 2003 as an epidemic in Hong Kong and part of mainland China.

Shanghai Communique A joint statement of the Chinese and American viewpoints on a range of issues in which each has an interest. It was signed during U.S. President Richard Nixon's historic visit to China in 1971.

Socialism A transitional period between the fall of capitalism and the establishment of "true" communism. Socialism is characterized by the public ownership of the major means of production. Some private economic activity and private property are still allowed, but increased attention is given to a more equal distribution of wealth and income.

Special Administrative Region (SAR) A political subdivision of the People's Republic of China that is used to describe Hong Kong's status following Chinese sovereignty in 1997. The SAR has much greater political, economic, and cultural autonomy from the central government in Beijing than do the provinces of the P.R.C.

Special Economic Zone (SEZ) An area within China that has been allowed a great deal of freedom to experiment with different economic policies, especially efforts to attract foreign investment. Shenzhen, near Hong Kong, is the largest of China's Special Economic Zones.

Taiwanese Independence Movement An organization of native Taiwanese who wanted to declare Taiwan an independent state. Had to organize outside of Taiwan, as its leaders were persecuted in Taiwan by the KMT. Only with the recognition of the legitimacy of competing political parties in the 1990s could they adopt the goal of an independent Taiwan.

Taoism A Chinese mystical philosophy founded in the sixth century B.C. Its followers renounce the secular world and lead lives characterized by unassertiveness and simplicity.

United Nations (UN) An international organization established on June 26, 1945, through official approval of the charter by delegates of 50 nations at a conference in San Francisco. The charter went into effect on October 24, 1945.

Yuan Literally, "branch"; the different departments of the government of Taiwan, including the Executive, Legislative, Judicial, Control, and Examination Yuans.

Bibliography

PEOPLE'S REPUBLIC OF CHINA

PERIODICALS AND NEWSPAPERS

The following periodicals and newspapers are excellent sources for coverage of Chinese affairs:

Asiaweek
Asian Survey
China Business Review
China Daily
The China Journal
The China Quarterly
The Economist
Far Eastern Economic Review
Journal of Asian Studies
Journal of Contemporary China
Modern China
Pacific Affairs
South China Morning Post

GENERAL AND BIOGRAPHIES

Jasper Becker, *The Chinese* (New York: Free Press, 2000).
Insightful portraits of peasants, entrepreneurs, corrupt businessmen and party members, smugglers, and ethnic minorities by a resident journalist. Reveals much about the effect of the government's policies on the lives of ordinary people.

Ma Bo, *Blood Red Sunset* (New York: Viking, 1995).
Perhaps the most compelling autobiographical account by a Red Guard during the Cultural Revolution. Responding to Mao Zedong's call to youth to "make revolution," the author captures the intense emotions of exhilaration, fear, despair, and loneliness. Takes place in the wilds of Inner Mongolia.

Jung Chang, *Wild Swans: Three Daughters of China* (New York: Simon and Schuster, 1992).
A superb autobiographical/biographical account that illuminates what China was like for one family for three generations.

Kwang-chih Chang, *The Archeology of China*, 4th ed. (New Haven, CT: Yale University Press, 1986).
_____, *Shang Civilization* (New Haven, CT: Yale University Press, 1980).
Two works by an eminent archaeologist on the origins of Chinese civilization.

Nien Cheng, *Life and Death in Shanghai* (New York: Grove Press, 1987).
A gripping autobiographical account of a woman persecuted during the Cultural Revolution because of her earlier connections with a Western company, her elitist attitudes, and her luxurious lifestyle in a period when the Chinese people thought the rich had been dispossessed.

B. Michael Frolic, *Mao's People: Sixteen Portraits of Life in Revolutionary China* (Cambridge, MA: Harvard University Press, 1980).
A must read. Through composite biographies of 16 different types of people in China, the author offers a humorous but penetrating view of "unofficial" Chinese society and politics. Biographical sketches reflect political life during the Maoist era, but the book has enduring value for understanding China.

Peter Hessler, *River Town: Two Years on the Yangtze* (New York: HarperCollins, 2001).
Insights into Chinese culture by a Peace Corps volunteer who lived in a Yangtze River city from 1996 to 1998. The author gains considerable insights into the life of Fuling, a city that partly flooded when the Three Gorges Dam was completed.

Yarong Jiang and David Ashley, *Mao's Children and the New China* (New York: Routledge, 2000).
More than 20 ex-Red Guards who participated in the Cultural Revolution were interviewed in Shanghai in the mid-1990s. They reminisce about their lives then, revealing much about life in Shanghai during a critical period in China's political history.

Zhisui Li, *The Private Life of Chairman Mao* (New York: Random House, 1994).
A credible biography of the Chinese Communist Party's leader Mao Zedong, written by his physician, from the mid-1950s to his death in 1976. Fascinating details about Mao's daily life and his relationship to those around him.

Heng Liang and Judith Shapiro, *Son of the Revolution* (New York: Vintage, 1984).
A gripping first-person account of the Cultural Revolution by a Red Guard. Offers insights into the madness that gripped China during the period from 1966 to 1976.

Anchee Min, *Becoming Madame Mao* (Boston: Houghton Mifflin, 2000).
This novel vividly portrays Mao's wife, Jiang Qing, tracing her life from early childhood through her failed career as an actress, her courtship with Mao Zedong in the caves of Yenan, and her ultimate demise as a member of the notorious Gang of Four. A real page-turner.

Chihua Wen, *The Red Mirror: Children of China's Cultural Revolution* (Boulder, CO: Westview Press, 1995).
A former editor and reporter presents the heartrending stories of a dozen individuals who were children when the Cultural Revolution started. It shows how rapidly changing policies of the period shattered the lives of its participants and left them cynical adults 20 years later.

James and Ann Tyson, *Chinese Awakenings: Life Stories From the Unofficial China* (Boulder, CO: Westview Press, 1995).
Lively verbal portraits of Chinese people from diverse backgrounds (for example, "Muddy Legs: The Peasant Migrant"; "Turning Iron to Gold: The Entrepreneur"; "Bad Element: The Shanghai Cosmopolite").

HISTORY, LANGUAGE, AND PHILOSOPHY

Johan Bjorksten, *Learn to Write Chinese Characters* (New Haven, CT: Yale University Press, 1994).
A delightful introductory book about writing Chinese characters, with many anecdotes about calligraphy.

William Theodore De Bary, ed., *Sources of Chinese Tradition*, Vols. I and II (New York: Columbia University Press, 1960).
A compilation of the major writings (translated) of key Chinese figures from Confucius through Mao Zedong. Gives readers an excellent understanding of intellectual roots of development of Chinese history.

William Theodore De Bary and Weiming Tu, eds. *Confucianism and Human Rights* (New York: Columbia University Press, 1998).
Articles debate whether the writings of Confucius and Mencius (a Confucian scholar) are relevant to today's human rights doctrine (as defined by the United Nations).

John DeFrancis, *Visible Speech: The Diverse Oneness of Writing Systems* (Honolulu, HI: University of Hawaii Press, 1989).
Discusses the evolution of the Chinese written language and compares it with other languages that use "visible" speech.

Patricia Buckley Ebrey, *The Cambridge Illustrated History of China* (New York: Cambridge University Press, 1996).
A beautifully illustrated book on Chinese history from the Neolithic Period to the People's Republic of China. Includes photos of artifacts (such as bronze vessels) and art (from Buddhist art to modern Chinese paintings), which enrich the historical presentation.

John King Fairbank and Merle Goldman, *China: A New History,* 2nd Enlarged Edition (Cambridge, MA: Harvard University Press, 2006).
Examines forces in China's history that define it as a coherent culture from its earliest recorded history to the present. Examines why the ancient and sophisticated China had fallen behind other areas by the nineteenth century. The Chinese Communist Revolution and its aftermath are reviewed.

William Hinton, *Fanshen: A Documentary of Revolution in a Chinese Village* (New York: Random House, 1968).
A gripping story based on the author's eyewitness account of the process of land reform carried out by the CCP in the north China village of Long Bow, 1947 to 1949.

Edgar Snow, *Red Star Over China* (New York: Grove Press, 1973).
This classic, which first appeared in 1938, is a journalist's account of the months he spent with the Communists' Red Army in Yan'an in 1936, in the midst of the Chinese Civil War. It is a thrilling story about the Chinese Revolution in action and includes Mao's own story (as told to Snow) of his early life and his decision to become a Communist.

Jonathan D. Spence, *The Search for Modern China, 2nd edition* (New York: W. W. Norton & Co., 2000).
A lively and comprehensive history of China from the seventeenth century through the 1990s. Looks at the cyclical patterns of collapse and regeneration, revolution and consolidation, and growth and decay.

Song Mei Lee-Wong, *Politeness and Face in Chinese Culture* (New York: Peter Lang, 2000).
Part of a series on cross-cultural communication, this book discusses how politeness is portrayed in speech and how it relates to a central concept in Chinese culture: "face" and "losing face."

POLITICS, ECONOMICS, SOCIETY, AND CULTURE

Julia F. Andrews, *Painters and Politics in the People's Republic of China, 1949–1979* (Berkeley, CA: University of California Press, 1994).
A fascinating presentation of the relationship between politics and art from the beginning of the Communist period until the eve of major liberalization in 1979.

N. Susan D. Blum and Lionel. M. Jensen, eds., *China Off Center: Mapping the Margins of the Central Kingdom* (Honolulu, HI: University of Hawaii Press, 2002).
Arguing that there are many "Chinas," these articles offer new insights into the complexity and diversity of China. Interpretative essays on topics such as linguistic diversity, regionalism, homosexuality, gender and work, popular music, magic and science. Ethnographic reports on minorities.

Susan Brownell and Jeffrey Wasserstrom, eds., *Chinese Femininities and Chinese Masculinities: A Reader* (Berkeley, CA: University of California Press, 2002).
A reader that investigates various issues through the lens of feminist and gender theory.

Thomas Buoye, Kirk Denton, Bruce Dickson, Barry Naughton, and Martin K. Whyte, *China: Adapting the Past, Confronting the Future* (Ann Arbor, MI: The University of Michigan Center for Chinese Studies, 2002).
Articles on China's geography and pre-1949 history, including environmental history, Confucianism, and the Boxer Uprising. It also examines the last few decades, including homosexuality, the Internet, and culture; several short stories.

Guidi Chen and Chuntao Wu, *Will the Boat Sink the Water? The Life of China's Peasants* (New York: Public Affairs, Perseus Books, 2006).
An award-winning book of reportage. While most of the world focuses on China's rapid economic growth, these reporters present stories about the poor peasants in China's vast countryside. Theme challenges mainstream view that China's peasantry was the primary beneficiary of the Chinese Communist revolution, and argues that even under a Chinese-style market economy, the peasantry continues to suffer.

Deirdre Chetham, *Before the Deluge: The Vanishing World of the Yangtze's Three Gorges* (New York: Palgrave MacMillan, 2002).
A portrait of life along the Yangtze River just before it was flooded to fill up the Three Gorges Dam. Examines the policies that led to the dam, the criticisms of was, and the hopes and fears of what this dam might generate other than electricity.

Paul Close, David Askew and Xu Xin, *The Beijing Olympiad: The Political Economy of a Sporting Mega-Event* (New York: Routledge), 2007.
Looks at the motivations for Beijing to host the Olympics in 2008, and the opportunities and dangers for China embedded in this event. Chapters on the relationship of the individual, nationalism, and capitalism to the Olympics, as well as on how the Olympics can serve as a "coming out party" for an ambitious state.

Elisabeth Croll, *China's New Consumers: Social Development and Domestic Demand* (New York: Routledge), 2006.
Examines the expansion of the domestic market for Chinese-made goods, but challenges the conventional wisdom that there is an insatiable demand for goods among Chinese consumers. Looks at new expectations and social aspirations because of the consumer revolution, the livelihoods and lifestyles of various categories of Chinese consumers, and the government's policy of encouraging internal consumption. Includes chapters on consumption patterns of the rural poor, children, youth, and the elderly.

Deborah S. Davis, ed., *The Consumer Revolution in Urban China* (Berkeley, CA: University of California, 2000).
Articles cover the impact of China's consumer revolution on urban housing, purchases of toys, clothes, and leisure activities for children, and bridal consumerism.

Michael S. Duke, ed., *World of Modern Chinese Fiction: Short Stories & Novellas From the People's Republic, Taiwan & Hong Kong* (Armonk, NY: M. E. Sharpe, Inc., 1991).
A collection of short stories written by Chinese authors from China, Taiwan, and Hong Kong during the 1980s. The 25 stories are grouped by subject matter and narrative style.

Elizabeth Economy, *The River Runs Black: The Environmental Challenge to China's Future* (Ithaca: Cornell University Press), 2004.

The central government's inability to cope with the growing environmental crisis has led to serious social, economic, and health issues, as well as a steadily rising involvement of citizens in non-governmental organizations. Such civic participation may lead to greater democratization and the development of civil society.

Barbara Entwisle and Gail E. Henderson, eds., *Re-drawing Boundaries: Work, Households, and Gender in China* (Berkeley, CA: University of California Press, 2000).

Looks at how gender inequality affects types of work, wages, and economic success. Examines issues of work and gender in China's cities and countryside and among the "floating" population.

Merle Goldman and Elizabeth. J. Perry, eds., *Changing Meanings of Citizenship in Modern China* (Cambridge, MA: Harvard University Press, 2002).

Studies of citizenship in China over the last century. Focuses on the debate over the relationship of the individual to the state, the nation, the community, and culture.

Ellen Hertz, *The Trading Crowd: An Ethnography of the Shanghai Stock Market* (Cambridge, England: University of Cambridge Press, 1998).

An anthropologist examines the explosion of "stock fever" since the stock market opened in Shanghai in 1992. Looks at the dominant role of the state in controlling the market, resulting in a stock market quite different from those in the West.

Alan Hunter and Kim-kwong Chan, *Protestantism in Contemporary China* (New York: Cambridge University Press, 1993).

Examines historical and political conditions that have affected the development of Protestantism in China.

William R. Jankowiak, *Sex, Death, and Hierarchy in a Chinese City* (New York: Columbia University Press, 1993).

Written by an anthropologist with a discerning eye, this is one of the most fascinating accounts of daily life in China. Particularly strong on rituals of death, romantic life, and the on-site mediation of disputes by strangers (e.g., with bicycle accidents).

Maria Jaschok and Suzanne Miers, eds., *Women and Chinese Patriarchy: Submission, Servitude and Escape* (New York: Zen Books, 1994).

Examines Chinese women's roles, the sale of children, prostitution, Chinese patriarchy, Christianity, and feminism, as well as social remedies and avenues of escape for women. Based on interviews with Chinese women who grew up in China, Hong Kong, Singapore, and San Francisco.

Yarong Jiang and David Ashley, *Mao's children and the New China* (New York: Routledge, 2000).

More than 20 ex-Red Guards who participated in the Cultural Revolution were interviewed in Shanghai in the mid-1990s. They reminisce about their lives then, revealing much about life in Shanghai during the critical period in China's political history.

Ian Johnson, *Wild Grass: Three Stories of Change in Modern China* (New York: Pantheon Books, 2004).

The author portrays three ordinary citizens who, by testing the limits of reform, may cause China to become a more open country.

Lane Kelley and Yadong Luo, *China 2000: Emerging Business Issues* (Thousand Oaks, CA: Sage Publications, 1998).

Looks to the emerging business issues for Chinese domestic firms and foreign firms.

Conghua Li, *China: The Consumer Revolution* (New York: Wiley, 1998).

An impressive account of China's rapidly growing consumer society. Looks at the forces that are shaping consumption, China's cultural attitudes toward consumerism, consumer preferences of various age groups, and the rapid polarization of consumer purchasing power.

Jianhong Liu, Lening Zhang, and Steven F. Messner, eds., *Crime and Social Control in a Changing China* (Westport, CT: Greenwood Press, 2001).

Focuses on crime in the context of a rapidly modernizing China. Shows the deeply rooted cultural context for Chinese attitudes toward crime, criminals, and penology that might well interfere with reform.

Stanley B. Lubman, *Bird in a Cage: Legal Reform After Mao* (Stanford, CA: Stanford University Press, 1999).

Traces the victories and frustrations of legal reform since 1979, but is based on a thorough examination of the pre-reform judicial system.

Michael B. McElroy, Christopher P. Nielsen, and Peter Lydon, eds., *Energizing China: Reconciling Environmental Protection and Economic Growth* (Cambridge, MA: Harvard University Press, 1998).

Research reports address the dilemmas, successes, and problems in China's efforts to reconcile environmental protection with economic development. Addresses issues such as energy and emissions, the environment and public health, the domestic context for making policy on energy, and the international dimensions of China's environmental policy.

Joanna McMillan, *Sex, Science and Morality in China* (New York: Routledge), 2006.

Looks at the supposed "opening up" of the sexual world in China and discovers a world still defined by a deep conservatism, a propensity to judge sexual practices based on old-style morality, as well as intolerance of difference. Describes such topics as the coverage of sexual anatomy and sexual function by marriage manuals, transsexuals, homosexuals, masturbation, Viagra, sexual dysfunction, sex shops, prostitution, and many other related topics as presented by China's sexologists and the media.

Gina Marchetti, *From Tian'an Men to Times Square: Transnational China and the Chinese Disaspora on Global Screens, 1989–1997* (Philadelphia: Temple University Press), 2006.

The portrayal of China in the media and in film since the crackdown on demonstrators in 1989. Interviews with Chinese and non-Chinese film makers provide basis for analysis of how global capitalism and other political and social forces have affected the aesthetics of film and presentation of China and the Chinese throughout the world's Chinese communities.

Katherine Morton, *International Aid and China's Environment: Taming the Yellow Dragon* (New York: Routledge), 2005.

Case studies on the three major donor approaches to giving environmental aid to China: helping to build the environmental infrastructure (Japan), introducing market measures and incentives (World Bank), and increasing stakeholder participation in order to improve decision-making (UNDP). Contrasts these with the Chinese emphasis on regulatory control. Examines impact of these three approaches to strengthening sustainable environmental capacity in China.

Andrew J. Nathan and Perry Link, eds., and Liang Zhang, compiler, *The Tiananmen Papers: The Chinese Leadership's Decision to Use Force Against Their Own People—In Their Own Words* (New York: Public Affairs, 2001).

Widely believed to be authentic documents that reveal what was said among China's top leaders behind closed doors during the Tiananmen crisis in 1989. These leaked documents lay out the thinking of China's leaders about the students and workers occupying Tiananmen Square for almost six weeks—and how they eventually decided to use force.

Kevin J. O'Brien and Lianjiang Li, *Rightful Resistance in Rural China* (New York: Cambridge University Press, 2006).
Examines question of how weak, unorganized groups go about resisting state control and articulating their demands. The focus is on resistance in rural China that relies on the use of officially-sanctioned policies, values, laws, and rhetoric to challenge political and economic elites who have abused their power, not implemented policies, or failed to live up to their professed ideals. Looks at how rightful resisters gain legitimacy by using approved channels and not resorting to illegal or criminal activity.

Suzanne Ogden, *Inklings of Democracy in China* (Cambridge, MA: Harvard University Asia Center and Harvard University Press, 2002).
Asks whether liberal democracy is possible or even appropriate in China, given its history, culture, and institutions. Looks at a broad array of indicators. Argues for fair and consistent standards for evaluating freedom and democracy in China and for comparing it with other states.

Suzanne Ogden, Kathleen Hartford, Lawrence Sullivan, and David Zweig, eds., *China's Search for Democracy: The Student and Mass Movement of 1989* (Armonk, NY: M. E. Sharpe, 1992).
A collection of wall posters, handbills, and speeches of the prodemocracy movement of 1989. These documents capture the passionate feelings of the student, intellectual, and worker participants.

Elizabeth J. Perry and Mark Selden, eds., *Chinese Society: Change, Conflict and Resistance,* 2nd edition (New York: Routledge, 2003).
A collection of articles on the resistance generated by economic reforms since 1979. Topics include suicide as resistance, resistance to the one-child campaign, and religious and ethnic resistance.

Paul G. Pickowicz and Yingjin Zhang, eds., *From Underground to Independent: Alternative Film Culture in Contemporary China* (Lanham, Md.: Rowman & Littlefield), 2006.
Examines the evolution beginning in the early 1990s from underground to quasi-independent film making in China: film making that is independent from the state-controlled system of film production, distribution, and showing, and which depends on private (including foreign) funding. Includes articles on diverse topics, such as independently-made documentaries, and film clubs in Beijing.

James Seymour and Richard Anderson, *New Ghosts, Old Ghosts: Prisons and Labor Reform Camps in China* (Armonk, NY: M. E. Sharpe, 1998).
A look inside labor camps in China's northwestern provinces, including details about prison conditions and management, the nature of the prison population, excesses perpetrated in prisons, and fate of released prisoners.

David Shambaugh and Richard H. Yang, *China's Military in Transition* (Oxford: Clarendon Press, 1997).
Collection of articles on China's military covers such topics as party–military relations, troop reduction, the financing of defense, military doctrine, training, and nuclear force modernization.

Susan L. Shirk, *China, Fragile Super Power* (New York: Oxford University Press, 2007).

China portrayed as very pragmatic in both its foreign and domestic policies because of a leadership motivated by fear of its own citizens. Chinese Communist Party leaders seen as insecure and afraid of losing power in spite of economic success and development.

Stockholm Environment Institute and United Nations Development Program (UNDP) China, *China Human Development Report 2002: Making Green Development a Choice* (New York: Oxford University Press, 2002).
Examines the key issues for sustainable development in China. Also looks at the government's response and the creation of environmental associations to address the issues.

United Nations Development Program, *China: Human Development Report* (New York: UNDP China Country Office, Annual report).
Provides measurements of the effect of China's economic development on human capabilities to lead a decent life. Areas examined include health care, education, housing, treatment and status of women, and the environment.

Jianying Zha, *China Pop: How Soap Operas, Tabloids, and Bestsellers Are Transforming a Culture* (New York: W. W. Norton, 1995).
Examines the impact of television, film, weekend tabloids, and best-selling novels on today's culture. Some of the material is based on remarkably revealing interviews with China's leading film directors, singers, novelists, artists, and cultural moguls.

Yuezhi Zhao, *Media, Market, and Democracy in China: Between the Party Line and the Bottom Line* (Urbana, IL: University of Illinois Press, 1998).
Raises the basic question of whether the expected value of a "free press" will be realized in China if the party-controlled press is replaced by private entrepreneurs, and a state-managed press is required to make a profit.

TIBET AND MINORITY POLICIES

Robert Barnett, *Lhasa: Streets with Memories* (New York: Columbia University Press, 2006).
Examines the interplay of forces from Tibetan history and culture, Chinese control, and modernization to create the streets and life of Tibet's capital today.

Melvyn C. Goldstein, *The Snow Lion and the Dragon: China, Tibet, and the Dalai Lama* (Berkeley, CA: University of California Press, 1997).
The best book on issues surrounding a "free" Tibet and the role of the Dalai Lama. Objective presentation of both Tibetan and Chinese viewpoints.

Melvyn C. Goldstein and Matthew T. Kapstein, eds., *Buddhism in Contemporary Tibet: Religious Revival and Cultural Identity* (Hong Kong: Hong Kong University Press, 1997).
An excellent, nonpolemical collection of articles by cultural anthropologists on Buddhism in Tibet today. Studies of revival of monastic life and new Buddhist practices in the last 20 years are included.

Hette Halskov Hansen, *Lessons in Being Chinese: Minority Education and Ethnic Identity in Southwest China* (Seattle, WA: University of Washington Press, 1999).
Examines Chinese efforts to achieve cultural and political integration through education of a minority population in Chinese cultural values and communist ideology.

Donald S. Lopez, *Prisoners of Shangri-la: Tibetan Buddhism and the West* (Chicago, IL: University of Chicago Press, 1998).

Explodes myths about Tibetan Buddhism created by the West. Shows how these myths have led to distortions that do not serve well the cause of greater autonomy for Tibet.

Orville Schell, *Virtual Tibet: Search for Shangri-la from the Himalayas to Hollywood* (New York: Henry Holt and Co., 2000).
Examines the journals of those hoping to find a spiritual kingdom in Tibet. Notes the perilous journeys undertaken for the last 200 years in pursuit of this quest, and the disappointment of almost all in what they found.

FOREIGN POLICY: CHINA AND THE INTERNATIONAL SYSTEM

Gerald Chan, *China's Compliance in Global Affairs: Trade, Arms Control, Environmental Protection, Human Rights* (Hackensack, NJ: World Scientific Publishing Co., 2006).
Assesses China's compliance with international rules and norms in the four areas of the title. Asks whether China has acted "responsibly" from the perspective of US-China relations. First looks at how China sees its "responsibility" to the world community, given its own history, culture, ethics, and level of economic development. Case studies of compliance with WTO rules, with the norms and regulations of the arms control and disarmament regime, with newly formed international environmental norms, and with Western notions of human rights, which are at odds with China's primary definition of human rights.

Jian Chen and Shujie Yao, eds. *Globalization, Competition and Growth in China* (New York: Routledge, 2006).
Chapters look at reforms in the financial sector, foreign direct investment, globalization, and China's strategies for development. Considerable technical analysis as well.

Alastair Iain Johnston and Robert S. Ross, eds., *Engaging China: The Management of an Emerging Power* (New York: Routledge, 1999).
A collection of articles on how various governments, including Korea, Singapore, Indonesia, Japan, Taiwan, the United States, and Malaysia, have tried to "engage" an increasingly powerful China.

Samuel S. Kim, ed., *China and the World, Chinese Foreign Policy Faces the New Millennium (4th edition)* (Boulder, CO: Westview Press, 2001).
Examines theory and practice of Chinese foreign policy with the United States, Russia, Japan, Europe, and the developing world as China enters the new millennium. Looks at such issues as the use of force, China's growing interdependence with other countries, human rights, the environment, and China's relationship with multilateral economic institutions.

Richard Madsen, *China and the American Dream: A Moral Inquiry* (Berkeley, CA: University of California Press, 1995).
Looks at the emotional and unpredictable relationship that the United States has had with China from the nineteenth century to the present.

James Mann, *About Face: A History of America's Curious Relationship With China, From Nixon to Clinton* (New York: Alfred A. Knopf, 1999).
A journalist's account of the history of U.S.–China relations from Nixon to Clinton. Through examination of newly uncovered government documents and interviews, gives account of development of the relationship, with all its problems and promises.

Ramon H. Myers, Michel C. Oksenberg, and David Shambaugh, eds., *Making China Policy: Lessons From the Bush and Clinton Administrations* (New York: Rowman and Littlefield, 2002).
Examines the policy of the United States toward China during the George Bush and Bill Clinton administrations (1989–2000). Includes an account of China's perception and response to America's China policies.

Michael D. Swaine and Zhang Tuosheng, eds., *Managing Sino-American Crises: Case Studies and Analysis* (Washington D.C.: Carnegie Endowment for International Peace, 2006).
Looks at the pattern of management during crises between the U.S. and China. Case studies of wars in Korea, Vietnam, and conflicts over Taiwan, as well as incidents such as the U.S. bombing of the Chinese Embassy in Belgrade and the U.S.-China aircraft collision.

Ian Taylor, *China and Africa: Engagement and Compromise* (New York: Routledge, 2006).
China's policies toward African states reflect its stated foreign policy imperative of opposing the spread of "hegemonism" while trying to find a place for the expansion of its own economic interests. Need for China to fulfill aspirations as a great power complicated by an international system that has been hostile to its ambitions, in part by shutting China out from access to natural resources in many places. Chapters on the history of China's relationship with Africa, and its present relationship with specific African countries.

David Zweig, *Internationalizing China: Domestic Interests and Global Linkages* (Ithaca, NY: Cornell University Press, 2002).
Case studies on issues that connect domestic interests to China's foreign policy and international linkages, and the diminished role of bureaucrats in regulating the internationalization of China.

HONG KONG

PERIODICALS AND NEWSPAPERS
Hong Kong Commercial Daily
Hong Kong News Online
Hong Kong Standard
South China Morning Post

POLITICS, ECONOMICS, SOCIETY, AND CULTURE

Robert Ash, Peter Ferdinand, Brian Hook, and Robin Porter, *Hong Kong in Transition: One Country, Two Systems* (New York: Routledge Curzon, 2003).
Investigates changes since the 1997 handover in Hong Kong's business environment, including the role of public opinion and government intervention, and the evolving political culture.

Ming K. Chan and Alvin Y. So, eds., *Crisis and Transformation in China's Hong Kong* (Armonk, NY: M. E. Sharpe, 2002).
Examines political and social changes in Hong Kong since it was returned to China's sovereignty in 1997.

Robert Cottrell, *The End of Hong Kong: The Secret Diplomacy of Imperial Retreat* (London: John Murray, 1993).
Exposes the secret diplomacy that led to the signing of the "Joint Declaration on Question of Hong Kong" in 1984, the agreement that ended 150 years of British colonial rule over Hong Kong. Thesis is that Britain was reluctant to introduce

democracy into Hong Kong before this point because it thought it would ruin Hong Kong's economy and lead to social and political instability.

Michael J. Enright, Edith E. Scott, and David Dodwell, *The Hong Kong Advantage* (Oxford: Oxford University Press, 1997).

Examines the special relationship between the growth of Hong Kong's and mainland China's economies, such topics as the role of the overseas Chinese community in Hong Kong and the competition Hong Kong faces from Taipei, Singapore, Seoul, and Sydney as well as from such up-and-coming Chinese cities as Shanghai.

Wai-man Lam, *Understanding the Political Culture of Hong Kong: The Paradox of Activism and Depoliticization* (Armonk, N.Y.: M. E. Sharpe), 2004.

Through case studies of protest, Lam challenges the view of a politically apathetic Hong Kong populace. Looks at role of ideology, nationalism, gender, civil rights, and economic justice as motivating political participation in Hong Kong.

C. K. Lau, *Hong Kong's Colonial Legacy: A Hong Kong Chinese's View of the British Heritage* (Hong Kong: Chinese University Press, 1997).

Engaging overview of the British roots of today's Hong Kong. Special attention is given to such problems as the "identity" of Hong Kong people as British or Chinese, the problems in speaking English, English common law in a Chinese setting, and the strictly controlled but rowdy Hong Kong "free press."

Jan Morris, *Hong Kong: Epilogue to an Empire* (New York: Vintage, 1997).

Witty and detailed first-hand portrait of Hong Kong by one of its long-term residents. Gives the reader the sense of actually being on the scene in a vibrant Hong Kong.

Christopher Patten, *East and West: China, Power, and the Future of Asia* (New York: Random House), 1998.

The controversial last governor of Hong Kong gives a lively insider's view of the British colony in the last 5 years before it was returned to China's sovereignty. Focuses on China's refusal to radically change Hong Kong's political processes on the eve of the British exit. Argues against the idea that "Asian values" are opposed to democratic governance, and suggests that "Western values" have already been realized in Hong Kong.

Mark Roberti, *The Fall of Hong Kong: China's Triumph and Britain's Betrayal* (New York: John Wiley & Sons, Inc., 1994).

A fast-paced, drama-filled account of the decisions Britain and China made about Hong Kong's fate beginning in the early 1980s. Based on interviews with 150 key players in the secret negotiations between China and Great Britain.

Ming Sing, *Hong Kong's Tortuous Democratization: A Comparative Analysis* (New York: Routledge Curzon), 2004.

An examination of the governance in Hong Kong since the 1940s, and the constraints to democratization. Looks beyond the limits imposed by Beijing to other forces, including lack of public support and weak pro-democracy forces, to explain why democracy has not yet emerged.

Alvin Y. So, *Hong Kong's Embattled Democracy: A Societal Analysis* (Baltimore: Johns Hopkins University Press, 1999).
Traces Hong Kong's development of democracy.

Steven Tsang, *A Modern History of Hong Kong* (New York: I.B.Tauris), 2004.

History of British colonial rule from before the Opium Wars. Examines problems in creating the rule of law and an inde-

pendent judiciary in Hong Kong, and the impact of trade with China on Hong Kong's society and economy.

Frank Welsh, *A Borrowed Place: The History of Hong Kong* (New York: Kodansha International, 1996).

Best book on Hong Kong's history from the time of the British East India Company in the eighteenth century through the Opium Wars of the nineteenth century to the present.

TAIWAN

PERIODICALS AND NEWSPAPERS
Taipei Journal
Taipei Review

POLITICS, ECONOMICS, SOCIETY, AND CULTURE

Bonnie Adrian, *Framing the Bride: Globalizing Beauty and Romance in Taiwan's Bridal Industry* (Berkeley, CA: University of California Press), 2003.

A fascinating ethnographic study of Taipei's bridal photography as a narrative on contemporary marriages, intergenerational tensions, how the local culture industry and brides use global images of romance and beauty, and the enduring importance of family and gender.

Muthiah Alagappa, ed., *Taiwan's Presidential Politics: Democratization and Cross-Strait Relations in the Twenty-first Century* (Armonk, NY: M. E. Sharpe, 2001).

Focuses on Taiwan's presidential elections in March 2000 and the impact of those elections one year later on the democratic transition from a one-party-dominant system to a multiparty system. Also examines the degree to which Taiwan under the leadership of Chen Shui-bian was able to consolidate democracy.

Robert Ash and J. Megan Greene, eds., *Taiwan in the 21st Century: Aspects and Limitations of a Development Model* (New York: Routledge, 2007).

Examines what is unique, or at least special to Taiwan's economic and political development that makes taking Taiwan as a model for China or other Asian countries questionable. Also notes those aspects of Taiwan's development model that might be replicable.

Christian Aspalter, *Understanding Modern Taiwan: Essays in Economics, Politics, and Social Policy* (Burlington, VT: Ashgate, 2001).

A collection of articles on Taiwan's "economic miracle" and such topics as Taiwan's "identity," democratization, policies on building nuclear-power plants and the growing antinuclear movement, labor and social-welfare policies, and the role of political parties in developing a welfare state.

Melissa J. Brown, *Is Taiwan Chinese? The Impact of Culture, Power, and Migration on Changing Identities* (Berkeley: University of California Press, 2004).

Author explores the meaning of identity in Taiwan. From 1945–1991, Taiwan's government claimed that Taiwanese were ethnically and nationally Chinese. Since 1991, the government has, in a political effort to claim national and cultural distance from the mainland, moved to a position asserting that their identity has been shaped by a mix of aboriginal ancestry and culture, Japanese cultural influence, and Han Chinese cultural influence and ancestry. Examines cultural markers of identity, such as folk religion, footbinding and ancestor worship as well as how identities change.

Richard C. Bush, *At Cross Purposes: U.S.-Taiwan Relations* (Armonk, N.Y.: M. E. Sharpe, 2004).

The former head of the American Institute in Taiwan (1997–2002) examines why President Roosevelt decided that Taiwan ought to be returned to China after World War II, the U.S. position on the Kuomintang's repressive government rule, the nature of the U.S. "2-China" policy from 1950 to 1972, and the basis for U.S. military and political relations with Taiwan.

Fen-ling Chen, *Working Women and State Policies in Taiwan: A Study in Political Economy* (New York: Palgrave, 2000).

A study of the impact of social welfare and state policies on the relationships between men and women since 1960. "Gender ideology" has changed and, with it, women's views of the workplace and their role in society. Examines related issues of childcare, wages, the women's movement, and women in policy-making system.

Ko-lin Chin, *Heijin: Organized Crime, Business, and Politics in Taiwan* (Armonk, N.Y.: M. E. Sharpe), 2003.

An examination of the connection between Taiwan's underworld (*hei*—black) and business/money (*jin*—gold) to politics that has accompanied Taiwan's efforts to democratize since emerging from martial law after 1987. Looks at ways in which black-gold politics have undercut democratization through vote buying, political violence, bid rigging, insider trading, and violence.

Bernard D. Cole, *Taiwan's Security: History and Prospects* (New York: Routledge, 2006).

An objective, well-written, and interesting account of Taiwan's complex security issues by a faculty member at the National War College. Full of valuable insights concerning the strategic issues of Taiwan's defense that only someone with military training and academic research capabilities can offer. The perfect starting point for understanding the strategic standoff that continues in the triangular relationship among the U.S., the P.R.C., and Taiwan.

Bruce J. Dickson and Chien-min Chao, eds., *Assessing the Lee Teng-hui Legacy in Taiwan's Politics: Democratic Consolidation and External Relations* (Armonk, NY: M. E. Sharpe, 2002).

Focuses on the impact of Lee Teng-hui presidency (1996–2000) on democratic consolidation, the role (and demise) of the Nationalist Party and the rise of the Democratic Progressive Party, and the economy. Also examines President Lee's impact on security issues.

A-Chin Hsiau, *Contemporary Taiwanese Cultural Nationalism* (New York: Routledge, 2000).

Traces the development of Taiwanese cultural nationalism. Includes the impact of Japanese colonialism, post–World War II literary development, and the spawning of a national literature and national culture.

Chen Jie, *Foreign Policy of the New Taiwan: Pragmatic Diplomacy in Southeast Asia* (Northampton, MA: Edward Elgar, 2002).

Outstanding book on Taiwan's foreign policy (1949–2000). Shows patterns in Taiwan's diplomacy and provides basis for theories and insights about Taiwan's policies, frustrations, sensitivities, and motivations in international affairs. Also covers Taiwan's policy toward the millions of "overseas Chinese."

David K. Jordan, *Gods, Ghosts, and Ancestors: The Folk Religion of a Taiwanese Village* (Berkeley, CA: University of California Press, 1972).

A fascinating analysis of folk religion in Taiwan by an anthropologist, based on field study. Essential work for understanding how folk religion affects the everyday life of people in Taiwan.

Robert M. Marsh, *The Great Transformation: Social Change in Taipei, Taiwan, Since the 1960s* (Armonk, NY: M. E. Sharpe, 1996).

An investigation of how Taiwan's society has changed since the 1960s when its economic transformation began.

Shelley Rigger, *Taiwan's Rising Rationalism: Generations, Politics, and "Taiwanese Nationalism,"* Policy Studies 26. (Washington D.C.: East-West Center Washington, 2006).

Challenges conventional assumptions that identifying as a Taiwanese equates to a pro-independence stance or to opposition to improved ties with the China Mainland. Looks at generational differences in attitudes among Taiwanese.

Murray A. Rubinstein, ed., *Taiwan: A New History (expanded edition)* (Armonk, NY: M. E. Sharpe, 2007).

A collection of articles on a wide range of topics, from aborigines and the historical development of Taiwan during the Ming Dynasty, to topics in Taiwan's more recent history. These include such topics as Taiwanese new literature, identity and social change in Taiwanese religion, socioeconomic modernization, and aboriginal self-government.

Scott Simon, *Sweet and Sour: Life-Worlds of Taipei Women Entrepreneurs* (Lanham, Maryland: Rowman & Littlefield Publishers), 2003.

Examines the contradictions and tensions that characterize the lives of Taiwan's female entrepreneurs, who spear-headed Taiwan's economic "miracle." Presents portraits of these women, including street vendors, a hairdresser, a café owner, a fashion designer, and more. Sheds light on urban life and on impact of patriarchal culture on male-female relations.

John Q. Tian, *Government, Business, and the Politics of Interdependence and Conflict across the Taiwan Strait* (New York: Palgrave MacMillan, 2006).

Examines the complexities of the Taiwan-China mainland relationship generated by the many situations in which both sides must compromise in order to advance their interests. Looks at the specifics of cross-strait trade and investment, how industrial organization and the financial system affect economic interactions, and how local governments in Mainland China attract Taiwanese investors.

Index